Through

Christoper Lee is a writer a... ... ...
recent series for BBC Radio is ... ...
vious publications include *Nice...... Two Centuries
in Prose and Poetry* (1986, rev. edn. 1998) and the *Official
History of Sussex County Cricket Club* (1989).

Also available from Oxford Paperbacks

The Impossible Art of Golf: An Anthology of Golf Writing
Edited by Alec Morrison

The Oxford Book of Letters
Edited by Frank Kermode and Anita Kermode

The Oxford Book of London
Edited by Paul Bailey

To Michael

with love from Jacqueline

Christmas 1997.

Through the Covers

AN ANTHOLOGY OF CRICKET WRITING

Edited by

Christopher Lee

Oxford   New York

OXFORD UNIVERSITY PRESS

1997

Oxford University Press, Great Clarendon Street, Oxford OX2 6DP

Oxford New York

Athens Auckland Bangkok Bogota Bombay Buenos Aires
Calcutta Cape Town Dar es Salaam Delhi Florence Hong Kong
Istanbul Karachi Kuala Lumpur Madras Madrid Melbourne
Mexico City Nairobi Paris Singapore Taipei Tokyo Toronto
and associated companies in
Berlin Ibadan

Oxford is a trade mark of Oxford University Press

First published by Oxford University Press 1996
First issued as an Oxford University Press paperback 1997

British Library Cataloguing in Publication Data

Data available

Library of Congress Cataloging in Publication Data
Through the covers : an anthology of cricket-writing / edited by
Christopher Lee.
Includes indexes.
1. Cricket—Literary collections.   2. English literature.
3. Cricket.   I. Lee, Christopher.
PR1111.C67T40   1996   820.8'0355—dc21   96–38106
ISBN 0–19–288010–1

1 3 5 7 9 10 8 6 4 2

Printed in Great Britain
on acid-free paper by
Biddles Ltd.
Guildford and King's Lynn

Contents

Contents

Introduction

Once upon a time, cricket was *the* English game: that, was once upon a time. Today it is the game of the English-speaking peoples, a legacy of empire, because cricket, as a *national* sport, is played only in the Commonwealth. Only in English do umpires call 'Over', batsmen bid 'Come one', and bowlers appeal. Even 'owzat!' is peculiar to the language, for we must remember, an Englishman's crease is his castle.

Just as Englishness expresses an illusion, so cricket is synonymous with a code of fine conduct which echoes times past or, more realistically, perceptions of long-gone ethics. Of course, this is another illusion. We grow up with a notion that some bad behaviour is 'not cricket' or that a dear departed soul had a 'good innings'. Yet the perpetrator of misconduct probably scoffs at the admonition and it cannot be known if the dead take comfort at having had a good knock. After all, few batsmen like getting out.

There is little doubt that the fine ideals of cricket remain dear to its followers and its stewards, especially when modern society often displays little care for these things. Equally, the history of the game is full of cant, dishonesty, and doubtful conduct. There are examples in Victorian times of games being rigged and players taking bribes, of doubtful gamesmanship, and of captains determined to win at all costs. But the iconoclast need not dwell for long on these matters. There are few undiscovered secrets in cricket's history, few reputations remaining to be fouled.

As a pastime, cricket existed long before the British Empire; indeed some say the earliest sighting was in the fourteenth century illustrated manuscript, 'The Romance of Alexander'.[1] Here we see six figures—nuns and monks. To the right, four stand with cupped hands as if waiting to catch the ball. To the left, a nun holds the ball while a monk grasps a large, curved stick. From this, Joseph Strutt suggests that a form of cricket was played during these times.[2] Perhaps. It would be churlish to suggest that the clerics' cupped hands be shaped for prayer and not for slip catches.

Whatever the truth (and cricket is a game of truth) a stick and a ball

---

[1] About 1340.
[2] *Sports and Pastimes of the People of England*, London, 1801.

in crude or sophisticated forms have been the implements of pastimes for centuries and it would seem that cricket evolved from a game played with a crooked stick. We find references to the game in the well-scanned court records of sixteenth century Guildford and further south in Sussex a reference to church windows being broken by a cricket ball (on a Sunday) and 'a little childe had like to have her braynes beaten out with a cricket bat'.[3] By the eighteenth century, cricket was so well established that the pastime was now a game and the darling of the gamblers, tricksters, and wastrels. Hundreds of guineas were commonly laid and thousands of guineas often risked by the landed gentry. Before the century was out, the MCC was formed and the Laws (not rules, but laws) published.

With the game came songs, verse, prose, and often disapproval.

I have heard of cricket matches, which I own, however, to be so strange and incredible that if I had not received them from eye-witnesses I could never have yielded to them any belief. . . . Cricket is certainly a very innocent and wholesome exercise, yet it may be abused if either great or little people make it their business. It is grossly abused when it is made the subject of public advertisements, to draw together great crowds of people who ought all of them to be somewhere else. Noblemen, gentlemen, and clergymen have certainly a right to divert themselves in what manner they think fit—nor do I dispute their privilege of making butchers, cobblers, or tinkers their companions, provided they are gratified to keep their company; but I very much doubt whether they have any right to invite thousands of people to be spectators of their agility at the expense of their duty and honesty. The time of people of fashion may be indeed of very little value, but in a trading country the time of the meanest man ought to be of some worth to himself and the community . . . it draws numbers of people from their employments to the ruins of their families. It brings together crowds of apprentices and servants whose time is not their own. It propagates a spirit of idleness at a juncture when, in the utmost industry, our debts, our taxes, and decay of trade will scarce allow us to get bread. It is a most notorious breach of laws, as it gives the most open encouragement to gaming, the advertisements most impudently reciting that great sums are laid, so that some people are so little ashamed of breaking the laws that they had hand in making, that they give public notice of it.[4]

Anyone who has wondered how so many people get time off to watch modern test matches, may read with amusement this tract from more than two hundred years ago. Also, let those who feel the mod-

[3] Bill of Presentment of parishioners to the Bishop of Chichester, c.1622.
[4] *Gentleman's Magazine*, 1743.

ern game is full of commercialism take heart that very little is new under the cricketing sun.

What perhaps sets cricket aside from most sports (apart from boxing) is the passion and poetry of the verse and prose that has come about at every level of the game. The deeds of the village blacksmith have been recounted with as much delight as those of its Leviathans, most of whom have emerged from calm, rural backgrounds rather than turbulent seas. Why this should be is not clear although the fact that cricket has been a constant in villages, counties, and countries for close on two hundred years must have some bearing.

Undoubtedly, cricket has attracted the articulate and, sometimes, the literate. Neville Cardus, E. W. Swanton, Lord Byron, A. A. Milne, P. G. Wodehouse, Edmund Blunden, Alan Ross, C. L. R. James, Frank Keating, G. D. Martineau, Siegfried Sassoon—now there's an eleven. And the Robertson-Glasgows, Friths, Macdonells, Ashley-Coopers, de Selincourts, and so many more as well.

But what to put in an anthology? Perhaps the question should be: what to leave out? The richness of verse and prose does not rest on some opinion of literary value. Few, for example, would claim that reflection on the Walker family in *The Walkers of Southgate* would force its way into any collection of fine writing. It is here because it illustrates a style of writing and a mood of reverence of the times in which it was written. So too do the extracts from *Chats on the Cricket Field* by W. A. Bettesworth. Where else would we find the thoughts of Prince Christian Victor who liked playing Service cricket and recognized that there was 'the honour of one's regiment to keep up'. Richard Daft's descriptions of cricket are well known, but here we have his observations of a groundsman and, quite delightfully, the notion of fat cricketers.

Even when the selection of a writer and subject seem to be obvious, I have tried to include material that is often overlooked. So, instead of descriptions of Ranji's magical batting, we have his early life and how he came to play in England. Equally, the pieces on W. G. Grace concentrate on his early life and character rather than on the often-told stories of his finest hundred, or his gamesmanship.

This anthology has attempted to bring to the casual reader of cricket, as well as to the enthusiast, something of the game's history in such a way that even brief entries from, say, *Cricket Scores*, *Notes*, *etc.* set out the humour, social development, and contrasts of the sport—when it is less than sporting. For cricket's sense of history is everywhere in its writings. The high and the mighty, the low and the lesser, talk of honour and often in a jargon and sentiment that cross social lines and age barriers. In John Finnemore's *Teddy Lester—Captain of Cricket* we have every schoolboy's idea of public-school cricket in an age gone by. But the way of speaking, the adult's tactical approach could easily have been found in a country dressing room of the 1920s and 1930s.

There is not a great deal of good cricket fiction. The cricket novel has never stretched the writer's curiosity. De Selincourt is an obvious exception, but often we find cricket as a chapter rather than a whole volume. That may be as it should be. We should not take the game so seriously. Or should we? The poets have. Cricket poetry has often been in praise of the game and its players. Yet even poets have rarely attempted, or bothered, to pen disturbing political thoughts about cricket. We seldom find a verse that would mirror C. L. R. James's clear ideas of politics and race.

It was tempting to have a poetry section. Instead I have let poems find their own place because they compete on equal terms with prose in any cricket anthology. Indeed, it would have been wonderful to have had more space for poetry; in many ways cricket is a game of rhyme, and stanza, and beautifully crafted moments that, although inspirational for the gifted few, must conform to tight rules which oddly, prose need not.

Cricket is a game where deftness, guile, artistry, curiosity, and wonderful imagination are displayed at the wicket and far into the outfield. It is a game of contrasts and, sometimes, no second chance. When a batsman is out, then that is it. He, or she, must go. Even a Bradman must retrace his steps to the pavilion at Lord's, out for a duck, when all wanted to see his hundred. It is a game when the most obscure may be brought on to bowl, take the wickets and then, having had one glorious afternoon, disappear for the rest of an undistinguished career. And it is a game when old large-knuckled men may sit in the last of the sun and watch and dream of days gone by. For cricket is a game of memories.

Through the Covers

The Season Opens

EDMUND BLUNDEN

'A Tower we must have, and a clock in the tower,
Looking over the tombs, the tithebarn, the bower;
The inn and the mill, the forge and the hall,
And the Loamy sweet level that loves bat and ball.'

So a grey tower we have, and the centuried trees
Have arisen to share what its belfry-light sees,
The apple-plats richest in spring-song of all,
Kitchen-gardens and the field where they take bat and ball.

The stream with its moments of dance in the sun
Where the willows allow, runs and ever will run
At the cleft of the orchard, along the soft fall
Of the pasture where tourneys become bat and ball.

And now where the confident cuckoo takes flight
Over buttercups kindled in millions last night,
A labourer leans on the stackyard's low wall
With the hens bothering round him, and dreams bat and ball;

Till the meadow is quick with the masters who were,
And he hears his own shouts when he first trotted there;
Long ago; all gone home now; but here they come all!
Surely these are the same, who now bring bat and ball?

Cricket Country, 1945

※

The Lure of Cricket

E. V. LUCAS

How to explain the fascination that cricket exerts? It is not simple. That
it should attract the proficients is understandable, although they are
liable to continual mischances and mortifications such as no other game
presents; but the curious thing is that it attracts the incompetents as

well; those who never make a run, and cannot bowl, and yet, doomed
only to dreary waiting in the pavilion and to fatiguing fielding, turn
up punctually on every occasion, hoping for the best, and even (such
is the human heart's buoyancy) expecting it. There is no other game
at which the confirmed duffer is so persistent and so undepressed. It
is for the experts, victims of misfortune, that depression waits; it is they
who chew the cud of bitterness.

The phrase about 'the glorious uncertainty of cricket' applies to the
individual as much as to the fortunes of the struggle. For there is no
second chance: the batsman who is out first ball must retire to the
pavilion and brood on his ill-luck until it is time to field and forget
it—when, as likely as not, he will miss a catch and enter purgatory
again. The lawn-tennis player, no matter how badly he is playing, com-
pletes the set; the footballer, no matter how inept, kicks again; the polo
player and the hockey player, though covered with shame, are assured
of their full afternoon's sport. But it may easily be the best batsman's
fate to have nothing to do but watch more fortunate batsmen receiving easier bowling than he did. This constant risk of making no runs
would, you would think, deflect boys and men from the game. But
no. The cricketing temperament, always slightly sardonic, accepts it.
The uncertainty spells also glory.

There is also, still further to nourish this sardonic tendency, the
weather. No game depends more upon friendly atmospheric conditions,
and no game therefore is so frequently spoiled. One wonders sometimes if England may not have had a totally different climate when
cricket was chosen as its national summer game; for one reads little of
rain in the accounts of early matches. Were we to choose again should
we again select cricket? The answer, I am sure, is yes, so undefeatable
is our optimism; but surely there are more clouds than there used to
be?

The conditions of the game are unique and fascinating. No other
game lasts so long: Test matches are often played to a finish; first-class
matches are spread over three days of changing fortunes which every
ball may affect; the village match occupies four or five hours, equally
packed with drama. If it is exciting to watch the ups and downs of
these struggles, where the proverbial glorious uncertainty of the game is
ever present, think what it must be to be one of the two-and-twenty
participants. And under propitious skies how benign are the circumstances of the struggle! The sun shines, the turf is warm and scented.
But perhaps, when all is said, the secret of the spell of cricket lies in

the possibilities of every ball. The bat awaiting the ball is indeed an implement of destiny, but the ball which the bat awaits is more fateful. In its flight through the air, after it has left the bowler's hand and before it reaches the batsman, the spectator can live a lifetime.

The mechanics of cricket are, I imagine, now fixed. There will be no new strokes; no new varieties of bowling; all that the lawgivers of the MCC will have to do in the future is to deal with minor details and the politics and finance of the game: the control of Test teams, the county championship and so forth. But these are trifles. Let us do honour to the giants, let us go to see them when we ourselves are past playing and even when we are young and emulous; but gate-money cricket remains spectacular and apart. Cricket is not the county ground, although that may be the Heaven on which every boy's eyes are fixed; cricket is the backyard, the garden, the playground, the school-field, the club and college ground, and, above all, the village green.

'Oh,' wrote an old enthusiast to me during the period of strife at Adelaide early in this year (not of Grace) 1933; 'Oh, all this psychology! I like better the local match on a small ground where all the better balls were hit into the hayfield and lost. In despair a pudding was produced and a hefty butcher smote it so violently that he knocked the cover clean off it. The cover was caught by the wicket-keeper, but the core was missed by point. And the deuce and all arose. Was he out or not? I say he wasn't, putting the case before the cover. But never mind—that's cricket, and it's the reason why the game will always be loved in spite of journalists and prizes to readers. There's something about cricket that defeats snobs and conquers the press-gang. It's a lovely game, is now and ever will be.'

Should every county ground be closed and never another shilling of gate-money leave our pockets, cricket would still be in England's lifeblood, drawing its undismayable devotees from every section of the nation: the cricket that has such a hold on the young that they take their bats to bed with them, and on the old that they cannot see half a dozen urchins in the street, with only a lamp-post for stumps, without pausing for a minute or two to watch; the cricket that stirs up such a turmoil of hopes and fears in our breasts that to consult the barometer can be almost an anguish.

English Leaves, 1933

✻

A Game for All Classes

G. M. TREVELYAN

In Stuart times cricket had grown up obscurely and locally, in Hampshire and Kent, as a game of the common people. The original method of scoring, by 'notches' on a stick, argues illiteracy. But in the early eighteenth century cricket enlarged both its geographic and its social boundaries. In 1743 it was observed that 'noblemen, gentlemen and clergy', were 'making butchers, cobblers or tinkers their companions' in the game. Three years later, when Kent scored III notches against All England's 110, Lord John Sackville was a member of the winning team of which the gardener at Knole was captain. Village cricket spread fast through the land. In those days, before it became scientific, cricket was the best game in the world to watch, with its rapid sequence of amusing incidents, each ball a potential crisis! Squire, farmer, blacksmith and labourer, with their women and children come to see the fun, were at ease together and happy all the summer afternoon. If the French *noblesse* had been capable of playing cricket with their peasants, their châteaux would never have been burnt.

English Social History, 1944

*

Country Cricket

F. GALE

I can remember the first cricket match I ever saw as well as if it happened yesterday; and moreover I can give the names and description of many of the players.

The *locus in quo* was the meadow opposite the Green Lion at Rainham, in Kent, which is situated halfway between London and Dover. The cricket field is now built over. It adjoined the vicarage garden, in which a stand was erected for my brother and myself, and from which we, as little boys, saw the first game of cricket we ever witnessed, in the summer of 1830, as we had come into Kent from a Wiltshire village where cricket was not known.

Our grand stand was immediately behind the wicket. Farmer Miles, a fine-set-up man, was the best bowler, and he bowled under-arm, rather a quick medium pace, and pitched a good length and bowled very straight, his balls curling in from the leg; for be it remembered that but two years had elapsed since it was allowable to turn the hand, knuckles uppermost, in delivery. I was seven years old at the time, and was perfectly fascinated at the sight; and as the gardener, an old crick-eter, stood by me all day and explained the game, before the sun had set I had mastered most of the main points in it. One thing I am cer-tain of, which is that there was an on-break from Farmer Miles' bowl-ing; for I watched the balls pitch and curl.

The dress of the cricketers was white duck trousers and flannel jackets, and some wore tall black hats and some large straw hats. A few old fogies, veterans who played, had a silk pocket-handkerchief tied round the left knee so that they could drop down on it without soil-ing their white trousers; for in the rough out-fielding when the balls jumped about anyhow old-fashioned fieldsmen would drop on one knee, so that if the ball went through their hands by a false bound their body was in the way. Josiah Taylor, the brazier, was long-stop, and played in black leather slippers with one spike in the heel which he claimed as his own invention, as cricket-shoes were little known. The umpire was Ost, the barber, who appeared in a long blue frock-coat like Logic's, the Oxonian, in 'Tom and Jerry', and who volunteered 'hout' to a fieldsman who stopped a bump-ball; and when remonstrated with by men of both sides remarked, 'Surely first "bounce" is "hout" at cricket and trap.' This occasioned a change of umpire. There were two very hard hitters, Charles Smart, a tall young fellow, son of a rich farmer, and 'Billy Wakley', a very stout tall young farmer; there were many hits to the long-field off and on, which were well held; and Charles Watson, a promising lad of about sixteen, the butcher's son, who played for the first time in a man's match, immortalised himself by making a long catch close to the vicarage hedge. The batting most-ly consisted of hard-hitting, and the catching was good. The booth was made up of rick-cloths strained over a standing skeleton woodwork frame; and on the right of it was a round table with six or eight arm-chairs placed on either side; a large brass square tobacco-box out of which those who sat round the privileged table could help themselves by putting a halfpenny into a slit which caused the box to open (on the same principle as the chocolate and sweet-stuff automatic pillars seen now at railway stations), kept company with a stack of clay-pipes.

The arm-chairs were for the accommodation of the principal farmers and magnates of the parish who subscribed to the matches and who sat in state and smoked their pipes—as cigars were little known—and drank their grog out of rummers—large glasses which stood on one gouty leg each and held a shilling's worth of brandy and water; and for the accommodation of the smokers, the ostler, who always appeared in his Sunday best costume, which consisted of a 'Sam Weller' waistcoat with black calico sleeves, brown drab breeches, and top-boots, provided a stable horn lanthorn, the candle in which he lit with the aid of the flint and steel tinder box, and brimstone matches; for lucifers were not yet invented.

Another honour belonged to the knights of the round table: as the cricket ground was bounded on the southern side by the high road, and as coaches were passing all day, the drivers never forgot the 'Coachman's Salute' with whip and elbow and nod of the head as they drove by, and this was always returned by a cheery wave of the hand from the cricket ground. The patriarchs of the village had a form to themselves on the left hand of the booth; and old Billy Coppin, the half-pay naval purser, who had a snug little house on the bank of the roadside, sat outside his door waving his pipe and crying out, 'Make sail, my lads, make sail,' whenever a good hit was made.

When the match was over, one of the villagers, an ill-tempered thatcher, who was always ready for a set-to, picked a quarrel with someone from a neighbouring parish, and they adjourned to a quiet corner close to our grand stand behind the booth, pulled off their shirts and had a pretty stiff rough and tumble fight, which I described, in my innocence, at supper when I went in, and thereby got the gardener into a scrape for allowing me to see it. A very serious relative told me that she was 'cock sure' of the future fate of the two men who fought, quoting cases out of Dr Watts's hymns. Let us hope that some of the Doctor's tips have proved wrong.

Cricket, 1893

*

The Early History of Cricket

S. M. TOYNE

'If the French *noblesse* had been capable of playing cricket with their peasants, their châteaux would never have been burnt,' Trevelyan wrote in his *English Social History*. He was alluding to cricket in the eighteenth century, when for one day in the week, Sunday as often as not, social differences were forgotten. Villagers, their wives and children, watched together and applauded their favourite team and players, while sporting bets were placed. A team without its singer or its fiddler was almost unheard of; in fact, the bet, the song and the tankard were as necessary for an enjoyable day's cricket as the bat, the ball and the wicket. The gay scene thus evoked might be dismissed as an imaginative dream, no more real than an eighteenth-century description of the Golden Age, were it not borne out by historical evidence.

As early as 1700 may be found this notice of a two-day match to be played on Clapham Common in March: 'These are to inform gentlemen, or others who delight in cricket playing, that a match at cricket of ten gentlemen on each side will be played for £10 a head each game (five being designed) and £20 the odd one.' Other matches were played for a crown a head, but after the game had become fashionable in the 1740s, betting rose to fantastic sums of £1,000 or more. Of one match it has been stated that side bets among spectators and players totalled £20,000. In the early part of the nineteenth century, the game itself was in danger of ruin, since it had become the chief medium for national gambling. Bookmakers attended the matches, odds were called as the fortunes of the game fluctuated, and side bets on the scores of individual players led to bribery and cheating. One noted player took £100 to lose a match. It was not until the MCC had been recognized as the ruling authority that reforms were effected, and only at the beginning of the Victorian era was the game wholly purged from this canker.

Even the Hambledon Club (1750–92) was said to have usually staked £500 on each match. The glories of this club have been immortalized in the lively narrative of John Nyren. From his account of a match in 1772, we can estimate the hold that cricket had over the hearts of the people. It might seem a fanciful story, did we not know that he was a player and his father, proprietor of 'The Bat and Ball', captain of the side:

There was a high feasting held on Broad-Halfpenny during the solemnity of one of our grand matches. Oh! it was a heart-stirring sight to witness the multitude forming a complete and dense circle round that noble green. Half the county would be present and all their hearts with us—Little Hambledon pitted against All England, was a proud thought for the Hampshire men. Defeat was glory in such a struggle—Victory indeed made us 'a little lower than the angels'. How those fine brawn-faced fellows would drink to our success! . . . Punch, not your modern cat-lap milk punch . . . but good unsophisticated John Bull stuff—stark—punch that would make a cat speak! . . . whenever a Hambledon man made a good hit worth four or five runs, you would hear the deep mouths of the whole multitude baying away in pure Hampshire 'Go hard—Go hard—Tick and turn' . . . but I cannot call to recollection an instance of their stopping a ball that had been hit out among them by one of our opponents. Like true English men, they would give an enemy fair play.

That was cricket, indeed, yet less than sixty years later Miss Mitford, an ardent supporter of the game, paints a very different picture, showing the evil effects of the gambling craze and of increasing social cleavage:

I anticipated great pleasure from so grand an exhibition. What a mistake! There they were—a set of ugly old men, whitehaired and baldheaded (for half of Lord's were engaged in the game, players and gentlemen). Mr Ward and Lord Frederick the veterans of the green, dressed in light white jackets with neckcloth primly tied round their throats, fine japanned shoes, silk stockings and gloves, instead of our fine village lads with their unbuttoned collars, their loose waistcoats and the large shirt sleeves, which give an air so picturesque to their glowing bounding youthfulness, there they stood railed in by themselves silent, solemn, slow-playing for money, making a business of the thing, grave as judges, taciturn as chess players, a sort of dance without music, instead of the glee, the fun, the shouts, the laughter, the glorious confusion of the country game, but everything is spoilt when money puts its stupid nose in . . . so be it always when men make the noble game of cricket an affair of betting and hedgings and maybe cheatings!

Such, in George IV's reign, was the blight hanging over cricket. Miss Mitford might have added that the mania for making money out of cricket had led to lawsuits, free fights and fatal accidents. On October 31st, 1776, 'A terrible affair happened at Tilbury Fort', when Kent were due to play Essex. Essex asserted that Kent had brought in a 'foreign' player, whereupon 'a battle ensued and, the Kentish men being likely to be worsted, one of them ran to the guardhouse and getting a gun from one of the invalids fired and killed one of the opposite party'. Both sides got guns from four soldiers, then 'fell to it, doing a lot of mischief. An old invalid was run through the body with a bayonet and a sergeant was shot dead!' So wrote the *London Chronicle*, and this was only one of many recorded rows. Yet by the end of the century cricket had spread widely throughout England and Wales. Buckley[1] records 43 counties and 508 places where it was being played, and this excludes 'other places' unnamed. But if it is in the eighteenth century that cricket began to achieve universal popularity, it was nevertheless certainly played in Queen Elizabeth's reign.

'John Derrick a gentl,' according to a document in the Guildford Records, swore on oath in 1596, 'being ffyfty and nyne yeeres or there-abouts . . . that hee being a scholler in the ffree schoole of Guldeford, hee and diverse of his fellowes did runne and play there at Creckett and other plaies . . .'. He was giving evidence in a case brought to pre-vent the enclosure of some waste land, used by sawyers as well as school-boys. The first use of the word cricket is in Florio's *World of Words*. In this he renders 'sjittare' or 'sqvillare' as 'to make a noise like a cricket, to play cricket-a-wicket: to make merry'. There is no reason to doubt that Giovanni Florio, son of an Italian Protestant, who had taken refuge in England, did not mean the game of cricket. He was a highly edu-cated man, tutor in the house of Cecil, and showed intimate know-ledge of English games in his *Garden of Recreation* (1591).

On the false assumption that cricket was one of those 'unlawful games', classed with 'bull and bear baiting interludes', it has been freely stated that James I's 'Declaration of Sports' in 1618 was directed, among other things, against cricket. But cricket is not named in this document. The very first mention of a ground reserved specifically for cricket, and rated as such, is at Smithfield in 1661; it was owned by the innkeeper of 'The Ram'. This offers sound evidence that cricket was not an 'un-lawful game'. Moreover, when cricket is first mentioned in connexion with bull-and-bear baiting and cock-fighting, it is on record that the people of Sheffield and Leeds encouraged it as an alternative sport. 'The Burgesses of a Parish Church (Leeds) paid 14 shillings and 6 pence to professional cricketers' precisely for that purpose.

Though King James's Declaration of Sports deprecated the playing of any game, until after Divine Service, it nevertheless stated that 'the King's pleasure was that the Bishops and all other inferior churchmen

[1] G. B. Buckley, *Fresh Light on pre-Victorian Cricket, 1709–1837.*

shall be careful to instruct the ignorant . . . and reform them that are misled in their religion . . .' and encourage them in their Sports. The Declaration tells us that it is applying to the whole kingdom 'the directions given in Lancashire' on King James's return from a progress to Scotland in 1617. A crusade against games had been started by the Puritans in that county, which then, as at the beginning of the Civil War, contained a high percentage both of Puritans and of Roman Catholics. Until 'to our great regret' this crusade began, popish recusants were 'being converted to our great contentment'; but 'this amendment' ceased because 'their priests will persuade them that no honest mirth or recreation is lawful or tolerable in our religion.' King James saw the light. If there were no games, there would be no converts to Anglicanism. The extreme Puritans were doing him a disservice when they brought cricketers before the Ecclesiastical Courts, whenever these courts showed Puritanical leanings. In spite of the warning in the Declaration, cases were still brought forward, not without success, and this Puritan attitude to cricket had a profound bearing on its history.

Much of the evidence for the early history of cricket, and for the English people's attitude to it, is to be found in the records of these Ecclesiastical Courts. Two typical cases may be cited in which cricketers were brought up for trial side by side with other laity, who were charged with 'swearing, drunkenness or fornication'. Of the first case at Boxgrave (near Goodwood) in 1622, the verdict of the Archdeacon's Court on the five men playing cricket on the Lord's Day is not given. The second case in 1640, just before the outbreak of the Civil War, when the Declaration was still operative, is in the nature of a trial of strength between the divergent views of Royalists and Parliamentarians on games. The scene was laid at Maidstone, which the Rector, Thomas Wilson, described some ten years later as 'formerly a very profane town in as much as I have seen . . . crickets and many other sports openly and publicly indulged in on the Lord's Day'. The charges preferred against the unfortunate cricketers were cunningly laid in the Canterbury Archdeacon's Court: (1) they were breaking the Lord's Day, (2) they smashed a window, (3) if a child had been passing on the common, the ball might have beaten its brains out! They were sentenced only on counts 1 and 2.

How popular cricket had become before the Civil War cannot be gauged with any certainty, but it must have been widely known, or Sir William Dugdale would not have mentioned it in his diatribe against Oliver Cromwell. He branded the great Independent as a 'roysterer' who had spent 'a dissolute youth' playing at 'cricket and football'. Whatever truth there may be in this, it is a fact that soon after the execution of Charles I the Commonwealth set about discouraging amusements of all kinds; their view of cricket seems to have been the same as of other games—'undesirable on all days, but damned on the Lord's Day'. Between 1649 and the Restoration cricket was, nevertheless, occasionally played on week days, and Wykehamists continued to play 'at Hills', it being stated that Bishop Ken as 'a junior' in 1650 'on his fifth or sixth day is found for the first time attempting to wield a bat'.

As soon as the bells had pealed in welcome for the home-coming of Charles II, the games of the people were enthusiastically resumed. The commons south of the Thames became the regular battlegrounds of cricketers. A club was started at St Albans, with the 4th Earl of Salisbury as one of its earliest Presidents. Taverners began to see that a cricket pitch could be an added source of income, and during the next century a tavern was frequently considered to be the natural companion of a ground. Sometimes, as in the case of the White Conduit Field and the Artillery Grounds, the innkeeper was 'the master of the field' and responsible for its upkeep. Since the journals and 'intelligencers' published in those days did not give news of sport, we have scant records of the game before 1700. Teonge, a naval chaplain, tells of games near Aleppo in 1675, when the Governor came to watch the 'kricket' from 'a grand pavilion'. But, for the most part, references to the game take the form of cautionary tales upon the evils of Sabbath-breaking; admonitions against letting 'this manly exercise . . . interfere with the duties of a man's life', and other moralizings upon 'the fashion of playing cricket this summer' (*A World Bewitched*, 1699). In a broadsheet, *The Devil and his Peers* (1711), a charge is brought against the Duke of Marlborough and Charles Townshend, that they staged a boys' match in Windsor Forest and gave bribes to the players in order to secure votes for their party. This, if true, was by no means the only case of cricket's being used for political purposes. Frederick, Prince of Wales, and his Court, until his death in 1751, exploited the sport for their own ends, thereby gaining considerable popularity with the crowds that flocked to the 'grand matches' played for ever-increasing stakes. In London and the Home Counties, during George II's reign, cricket matches were so many, and so widely advertised, that no events attracted so great a concourse of people, especially when patronised by Royalty. We have a record in 1735 of 'a memorable match', staged at Kennington Common, where great crowds saw the Prince of Wales lead a team of players from London and Surrey 'from a pavilion specially erected' to do battle against Kent captained by Lord George Sackville. By a coincidence, the activities of the Prince's cricketing clique have come down to us because the old system of scoring on 'notched' sticks was now replaced by sheets recording the names of players and their individual scores.

One 'grand match', played in 1744, may be cited in example of the interest aroused by the game; even the contemporary newspapers allowed space not only to report the scores, but even to mention the onlookers. These included the Duke of Cumberland, then recovering from the wound he had received at Dettingen and who may be regarded as the founder of Army cricket, the Prince of Wales, the Sackvilles, Admiral Vernon and probably Lord Sandwich. To the last a poem is dedicated written in pseudo-Homeric style, telling of the glories of the encounter. An entertaining light is thrown on Sandwich's attitude to cricket by his remark to the Admiralty in the following year, upon his appointment as First Lord; 'I'll be at your Board', he told them, 'when at leisure from cricket'! This was at a moment when Britain was engaged in the formidable war of the Austrian Succession.

The Sackvilles—the Duke of Dorset and his brothers—were at this time practically the feudal Lords of cricket; one was the constant companion of the Prince, the other a member of the Duke of Cumberland's staff. And Admiral Vernon's presence at this match must have been a great draw. He was one of the most popular commanders of the age and had himself learnt his cricket at Westminster School, where the excellence of the scholars' games attracted 'many elegant persons', and others too, to witness their matches. Tradition has it that the first game of cricket to be played in Jamaica was in 1741–2 during Vernon's West Indian command.

Cricket enthusiasts may praise patrons such as these for their encouragement of cricket, but it must be laid to their charge that by their extravagant stakes they set a deplorable fashion in gambling. A Sackville, captaining the Old Etonians *v.* All England, once staked 1,500 guineas and side bets ran to £25,000. Could the integrity of a poor man—a groom, a gardener, a part-time professional—withstand the temptation of a bribe to 'queer the pitch'? Especially since we have on record that the employment of servants and the granting of tenancies by great lords and landed gentlemen often depended on cricket ability. One reason why cricket survived the dangers of corruption is that in many a village, and especially in the north of England, it was played simply for enjoyment and for no other reason. Often these games had local rules of their own, and differed considerably from cricket as we know it today.

In the extreme north, for instance, the farmers and country people of the North Riding of Yorkshire and South Durham had been playing their own form of cricket from time immemorial. Their milk stools—'Criccies'—laid on their sides, formed their wickets; curiously enough, they were of the same dimensions as the original wickets sketched in Lillywhite's *Scores and Biographies* (1847), which were in use before the London Club published the first rules in 1744, thereby regularizing the precise measurements of upright wickets. This northern region developed a game which had 'a profound influence on the lives of those lonely, but hardy people of the broad acres'; even today, some would be prepared to maintain that cricket in its most elementary form was first played in these parts. Certainly, these northerners cared little for rules drawn up in the south, for as late as 1798 a local Derby between Yarm and Stockton was played 'on agreed rules', and the imported umpires were congratulated on carrying out their duties 'like true gentlemen'. The whole of this district still abounds in small clubs dating from early times.

The MCC honoured the centenary of the Norton-on-Tees Club in 1921 by sending a side containing some well-known players, such as Hendren and Durston, and in the evening on the village green a lively resurrection was witnessed of the old scenes immortalized by Nyren—the dancing, the fiddlers, the blazing flares—and the ale. This outpost—and possibly birthplace—of cricket was socially and commercially completely cut off from the centres of 'big' cricket in Sheffield, Leeds, York and Hull, which in their turn were for some fifty years or more isolated from the south.

It is not surprising, therefore, that the story of cricket in the North and South displays marked contrasts. Rivalries between town and town and village and village were common to both, but in the North, there were no wealthy patrons, and no extravagant stakes; cricket sprang from the people and remained a people's game, especially in its stronghold—industrial Sheffield. For as the tempo of the Industrial Revolution increased, and people flowed in from the country to the towns, cricket became an urban as well as a village game. Sheffield, a centre for smelting iron from Norman if not Roman times, had expanded very rapidly under the impetus received from the introduction of cast steel and the incorporation of the Cutler's Company in 1740. As the city grew, so did enthusiasm for cricket. Teams from different firms and factories competed against each other, and the supporters of the men of Sheffield travelled every year in great numbers to watch the principal match of the season against Nottingham.

These matches were played in deadly earnest and more than once led to blows. A dour Sheffielder named Osguthorpe stayed in 'for several hours' till the score crawled to 50 for eight wickets. The Sherwood Foresters (spectators apparently) so hampered him, that the match was abandoned. The men of Sheffield retaliated on the return match by putting in the visitors, 'tired out with their journey', to bat 'at 6 p.m. on a pitch' so sodden and slippery 'they could neither strike nor run'. Having dismissed their opponents for fourteen, the cunning Yorkshiremen, according to the *Derby Mercury* in 1772, had coal slack spread on the pitch and, by this brilliant piece of tactics, gained an easy victory; they may well claim to be the originators of the use of sawdust! The tale of these encounters, which lasted from 1771 to 1860, alleviates to some small extent the grim stories of the 'satanic mills' and the appalling conditions of the industrial revolution. Some employers must have been more enlightened than is popularly supposed, else how did these workmen manage to get so much time off from their labours?

The York club, one of the oldest existing clubs in the country, boasted two recognized grounds, as did Sheffield, and we have copies of the articles of association in 1784, with the minutes of a meeting. Austerity and discipline were enforced on the members, who were bidden to assemble at 4 a.m. on Heworth Moor and were fined if not ready to play as the Minster clock chimed five! The better ground was on the Knavesmire, scene of the Gimcrack Stakes and Ebor handicap. Since the First World War, the western end of the great race-course has been laid out for cricket, and in the evenings and on Saturday afternoons half a dozen games are to be seen in progress, as they were two hundred years ago. Of great antiquity is the rivalry between York and Hull and to this day it is the match of the year; to this day, also, a fine is imposed on teams or players if not present at the appointed time.

From York, cricket spread slowly northwards through Richmond, Bedale and Thirsk, till a link was formed with the keen cricketers of the Stockton area. The huge stakes of the South had no place in these matches, although a modest crown would in the natural course of events be laid to back an opinion. The big match at Nottingham was originally for 42 guineas or £25, and in the early part of the nineteenth century the stakes increased to £500, but this is an exception. To the credit of cricket, it may be noted that when the increasing use of machinery caused temporary unemployment, ten shillings a man was paid to those 'not in employ' in one match. The unemployed still managed to play, and a party of Luddites once caused some consternation when they turned up in force and drew nearer and nearer to the wicket. All was well, however, since the Luddites were merely prompted by curiosity to view some star players from London who had travelled north!

By the end of the century, cricket had become a national game, played in every town or village. The improvement in the roads made communications easier and teams travelled farther afield, till eventually North was linked with South. Differences in rules had to be ironed out, and the formation of the Mary-le-Bone Club in 1787–8 by the 'influential gentlemen' of London, including the Dukes of York, Dorset and Richmond, provided the answer to the question of who should be the ruling body.

The story of 'Lord's' and the MCC has been frequently told, and it is enough here to say that one of its greatest achievements was to impose 'the rule of law' upon the game. There has been 'no written constitution' to support the MCC's world-wide authority, but cricketers had begun to regard it as an impartial judge even before it moved its headquarters to the present ground in 1812 and all conundrums were thenceforth sent to its committee for solution.

The playfellows of John Derrick on the waste land near Guildford would never have dreamed that 250 years afterwards their crude game with bat and ball could have developed into a national institution, nor could anyone even a century later have prophesied its influence on the social life of England. In the South it inspired ballad and song, and the saga of the Hambledon Club which, reverently preserved and adorned by E. V. Lucas, is a national possession. In the North it contributed to the solidarity of the working classes, though players from other social strata were always welcome and often became prominent members of the clubs. The political interlude was short-lived, and at no time has the game been the preserve or perquisite of any one party or class. Appreciation of the enemy's point of view, a sense of fair play, ability to endure set-backs—these are among the virtues called for by the game, and if they are also typically English virtues, cricket may be said in many ways to be highly representative of the national character.

History Today, June 1955

*

Chant Royal of Cricket

H. S. VERE HODGE

When earth awakes as from some dreadful night
　　And doffs her melancholy mourning state,
When May buds burst in blossom and requite
　　Our weary eyes for Winter's tedious wait,
Then the pale bard takes down his dusty lyre
And strikes the thing with more than usual fire.
Myself, compacted of an earthier clay,
I oil my bats and greasy homage pay
　　To Cricket, who, with emblems of his court,
Stumps, pads, bails, gloves, begins his summer sway.
　　Cricket in sooth is Sovran King of Sport.

As yet no shadows blur the magic light,
　　The glamour that surrounds the opening date
Illusions yet undashed my soul excite
　　And of success in luring whispers prate.
I see myself in form: my thoughts aspire
To reach the giddy summit of desire.
Lovers and such may sing a roundelay,
What'er that be, to greet returning May;
　　For me, not much—the season's all too short;
I hear the mower hum and scent the fray.
　　Cricket in sooth is Sovran King of Sport.

A picture stands before my dazzled sight,
　　Wherein the hero, ruthlessly elate,
Defies all bowlers' concentrated spite.
　　That hero is myself, I need not state.
'Tis sweet to see the captain's growing ire
And his relief when I at last retire;
'Tis sweet to run pavilionwards and say,
'Yes, somehow I was seeing them today'—
　　Thus modesty demands that I retort
To murmured compliments upon my play.
　　Cricket in sooth is Sovran King of Sport.

The truth's resemblance is, I own, but slight
    To these proud visions which my soul inflate.
This is the sort of thing: In abject fright
    I totter down the steps and through the gate;
Somehow I reach the pitch and bleat, 'Umpire,
Is that one leg?' What boots it to enquire?
The impatient bowler takes one grim survey,
Speeds to the crease and whirls—a lightning ray?
    No, a fast yorker. Bang! the stumps cavort.
Chastened, but not surprised, I go my way.
    Cricket in sooth is Sovran King of Sport.

Lord of the Game, for whom these lines I write,
    Fulfil my present hope, watch o'er my fate;
Defend me from the swerver's puzzling flight;
    Let me not be run out, at any rate.
As one who's been for years a constant trier,
Reward me with an average slightly higher;
Let it be double figures. This I pray,
Humblest of boons, before my hair grows grey
    And Time's flight bids me in the last resort
Try golf, or otherwise your cause betray.
    Cricket in sooth is Sovran King of Sport.

King, what though Age's summons I obey,
Resigned to dull rheumatics and decay,
    Still on one text my hearers I'll exhort,
As long as hearers within range will stay:
    'Cricket in sooth is Sovran King of Sport'.

*

Cricket Scores, 1731–1767

H. T. WAGHORN

Sept. 1731. A great cricket-match was played on Moulsey Hurst, near Hampton Court, between the Kingston men and the county of Surrey for 25 guineas a-side, which was won by the latter. Some thousands of persons of both sexes were present on this occasion.

July 1733. A great cricket-match was played at Moulsey Hurst, in Surrey, between eleven Surrey men and eleven of Middlesex, which were very hard matched. The Surrey men beat by only 3 notches; at which were present the Prince of Wales, accompanied by several persons of distinction, and his Royal Highness was pleased to order a guinea to be given to each man for their great dexterity, &c.

Just as his Royal Highness was returning from that cricket-match into the Court, a hare was put up amongst the tents in the camp on the Green, which being pursued by several soldiers, &c., she took the water; and several Horse Grenadiers being also in pursuit in their jack-boots, jumped in after her, and caught her before she had swam quite into the middle of the Thames; who all laying claim, a water battle ensued before they could bring their booty on shore, which afforded his Highness and the nobility much diversion.

July 1733. A match of cricket was made between his Royal Highness the Prince of Wales and —— Stede, of the county of Kent, Esq.; his Royal Highness being to choose eleven men out of the twenty-two that played that day on Moulsey Hurst, which Mr —— Stede is to match, for a plate of £30, to play at the said place on Wednesday next.

July 1733.[1] The above cricket-match, for a silver cup given by his Royal Highness the Prince of Wales, was played for on Moulsey Hurst, near Hampton Court, by eleven men on a side; eleven on one side were picked by Mr —— Stede of Kent, and the other eleven were picked out of the twenty-two that played at the same place.

Aug. 1758. There was a grand match at cricket on Kennington Common between Faulkner, Harris, and three more of the London Club against five picked men of Camberwell, Stretham, and Clapham. The county in their innings got 16, and the Londoners got 11; but the second they won the game, with three wickets to go down. There were considerable odds laid against the Londoners at going off.

April 1761. A great match at single-hand cricket was played on Epsom Downs, for 100 guineas, between the famous Baker of Ewell and a young fellow by the name of Die-Game,[2] of Headly. The Baker went

---

[1] First match for a silver cup.

[2] *Sept.* 15, 1761. One Bry, a famous cricket-player, known by the name of Die-Game, was apprehended at East Sheen near Richmond, charged with horse-stealing, and committed to take his trial at the next Assizes for county Surrey. This Bry or Die-Game was tried and capitally convicted at the Kingston-upon-Thames Assizes, county Surrey, on Saturday, April 10, 1762. On the following Monday he received a reprieve by the judge.

in first and got 65 notches, on which the bets ran high against Die-Game, but he beat his antagonist after a contest of upwards of four hours. A large sum of money was won and lost on this match.

July 1761. On Tuesday last a great cricket-match was played at Wesburn Green, near Beaconsfield, in Bucks, between eleven married[1] and the same number of single men of that county for £100, which was won by the former.

June 1762. Last Monday, June 21, was played a cricket-match, which has been so long depending, between the gentlemen of Guildford and the gentlemen of Chertsey, on Marrow Downs, when the former brought 99 and the latter 101. There was several hundred pounds depending.

July 1762. On Monday the great cricket-match between Kent and Surrey for 100 guineas, and on which some thousands depend, began to be played near Carshalton, but was not decided, a dispute arising about one of the players being catched out when Surrey was 50 ahead the first innings. From words they came to blows, which occasioned several broken heads, as likewise a challenge between two persons of distinction. The confusion was so great that the bets were withdrawn.

Aug. 1762. A cricket-match for a considerable sum was played in the Artillery Ground, eleven a-side, London against Kent, which was won by the former, who had seven hands to come in.

Same date. A cricket-match was played on Laleham Common between Chertsey, in Surrey, and the gentlemen of London and Middlesex, which was won by the latter, who had five to go in when they beat them.

Sept. 1762.[2] One day last week the following remarkable match at cricket was played in Tothill-fields, Westminster, between two butchers belonging to St James's Market. The wickets were placed on each side of a large piece of water 24 yards over, close to the side of it, and the men played naked in the water, when after upwards of an hour's diversion one of them gave up the wager to his antagonist.

Tuesday last, Sept. 7, 1762. A great cricket-match was played on Molsey Hurst between the gents of London & Middlesex and Surrey, which was won by the former. Large sums of money were depending on the match.

Aug. 1763. Tuesday, the grand cricket-match between the gentlemen of Middlesex and Surrey, which began on Monday last in the Artillery

[1] The first married and single match.
[2] A remarkable single match, played naked in the water.

Ground, was finally determined, when the former won by a great majority.

On Monday, Sept. 12, 1764, a great cricket-match, that has been so long depending, between the gentlemen of Hambledon,[1] in Hants, called Squire Lamb's Club, and the gentlemen of Chertsey, was played at Laleham Borough. Chertsey went in first and got 48 notches; Hambledon got 76. Second innings, Chertsey headed [added] 87; John Edmonds and Thomas Baldwin turned the game by getting upwards of 40 notches. Time expired, and they postponed it till next morning, when Chertsey went in and got 12 notches; Hambledon went in, three were out for 4 notches; the next five won the game. Chertsey had three men much hurt, and Hambledon had two, Mr Steward having a finger broke and his knee sprained. On this match great sums of money were depending.

During the cricket-match a gentleman of fortune at Weybridge was taken up by a warrant for a bastard child, which caused a great deal of diversion. The gentleman drew his sword on the occasion, and afterwards presented a pistol, and went off in triumph.

Monday, Aug. 9, 1765. In the afternoon a cricket-match was played in the Artillery Ground by the gentlemen of Surrey and Dartford for 100 guineas a-side, in the presence of near 12,000 spectators, which was left undetermined,—the mob (many of whom had laid large bets), imagining foul play, several of whom were dangerously wounded and bruised; but the match being renewed on Tuesday, it was won by Surrey.

Sept. 1765.[2] A few days since a cricket-match was played at Upham, Hants, by eleven married against eleven maiden women, for a large plum-cake, a barrel of ale, and regale of tea, which was won by the latter. After the diversion the company met and drank tea; they spent the evening together, and concluded it with a ball.

On Monday, Sept. 23, 1765, a cricket-match was played at Marybone-fields[3] between eleven gentlemen of Westminster and eleven gentlemen of Marybone parish, which was won by the latter, with two hands to spare to go in at the last innings. The match was for a silver cup, valued at 10 guineas, given by Mr Lowe, proprietor of Marybone Gardens.

---

[1] This appears to be the formation of the Hambledon Club, previously called Squire Lamb's Club.
[2] This is the first married and single ladies' match.
[3] First on Marybone Grounds.

Oct. 1767. A few days ago a great match at cricket was played near Croydon, for 200 guineas, by a farmer with a gold-laced hat and ten others with silver-laced hats, against eleven gentlemen of the Hambledon Club, which was won by the latter by a majority of 262 notches. It was remarkable that the Hambledon Club got two new hands from Hampshire, who kept in three hours and a half and got 192 notches, the greatest thing ever known.

Cricket Scores, Notes, &c., 1899

*

A Selection of Cricket Notices
Fresh Light on 18th Century Cricket

G. B. BUCKLEY

1718

On Monday the first inst. was played a famous game of Cricket in the White Conduit Fields at Islington by eleven London gamesters against eleven Kentish gamesters, who call themselves the Punch Club Society, for half a guinea a man. After a trial of their skill, which lasted about four hours, the Kentish men, whether it was for want of their celestial liquor (punch) to cheer up their exhausted spirits, I cannot determine; but be that as it will, they thought they should be worsted and there-fore to the surprise of a numerous crowd of spectators, three of their men made an elopement, and got off the ground without going in, and made the best of their [way] home, hoping thereby to save their money; but we hear the London gamesters are resolved not to be bubbled in that manner, and are therefore determined to commence a suit at law against them to oblige them to pay their money. (*Saturday Post*, 6 Sept.)

The Rochester Punch Club Society are very much surprised that men who call themselves the London Gamesters should risk the little repu-tation they have upon a forgery, since it would have been a much greater wonder to the numerous crowd of spectators if the Rochester men had not beat all those bragging hectors, but no gamesters, than that three of their men should not be able to bear the violence of the rains, which fell so heavy it was impossible to continue the game. To

convince them that the Rochester men do not think they had the worst
of the match, they are willing to meet eleven of the best of them, whenever they please, at Dartford in Kent, where they will play them for a
guinea a head; but they think proper to give them this advice, that if
they cannot choose better men than they did the last encounter, it will
be but throwing away their money and they had much better stay at
home. If in spite of this caution they dare venture, the Rochester men
don't doubt but sprightly Punch will easily overcome foggy Ale. (*Saturday
Post*, 20 Sept.)

As the result of a law-suit in which the Kent men were stated to have
been the plaintiffs, the match was played out the following year, and
was won by London.

1726

A letter from an anonymous correspondent at Whittle [Writtle] in Essex
to the following effect:

A Justice of the Peace in the neighbourhood was obsessed with the
idea that such games as Cricket, etc., were only pretences to collect a
crowd of disaffected people in order to raise a rebellion; and he therefore went on Saturday, September 10th with a constable, and caused
the Proclamation to be read in form to disperse the few well meaning
neighbours who were innocently at that play.

The late Lord Chief Justice, Sir John Pratt, had made a rule ordering a Cricket match to be played on Dartford Heath. Was it lawful to
play Cricket in Kent, but not in Essex? (*Mist's Weekly Journal*, 24 Sept.)

1787

On Mon., Aug. 6, began to be played at Hinckley the great Cricket
match between Leicester and Coventry which ended on Tues. in favour
of Leicester 45 notches ahead.

COVENTRY

John Payton	run out	0	b. Graham	7
John Cartridge	run out	3	c. Shergold	17
John Crump	b. Wilkinson	2	c. Dufty	1
James Crump	b. Wilkinson	1	b. Graham	1
Chas. Hoggins	b. Wilkinson	2	b. Wilkinson	6
W. Elliot	b. Wilkinson	0	b. Graham	5
John Collins	b. Graham	6	b. Wilkinson	8

Thos. Harris	c. Dufty	4	beat down his stumps	4
R. Sparrow	b. Graham	o	not out	1
James Payton	run out	o	b. Wilkinson	21
J. Crutchloe	not out	o	b. Graham	4
Bye balls		5		2
		23		77

LEICESTER

Wm. Barsby	b. Crump	6	run out	25
Wm. Clarke	b. Crump	o	c. John Payton	25
M. Graham	b. Sparrow	1	c. Crump	4
G. Davis	b. Crump	1	c. Jas. Payton	13
John Shergold	run out	2	run out	8
C. Wilkinson	b. Sparrow	1	c. Crump	2
T. Fielding	c. Crump	1	b. Crump	2
E. Higginson	b. Sparrow	o	b. Sparrow	6
John Mitchell	c. Payton	o	b. Crump	4
Wm. Bates	not out	o	b. Crump	0
J. Dufty	b. Crump	o	not out	31
Bye balls		1		12
		13		132

This match being made for 100 guineas, and each party in full practice, great expectations of a high treat were formed by the lovers of this manly diversion. The laurel was also contended for by two distinct counties, and prior to the commencement of the play each party entertained the highest opinion of each others character, as players and gentlemen.

Coventry went in about 10 o'clock, when we never remember to have seen greater instances of attention and agility; especially in the two Leicester bowlers, Mr M. Graham & Mr C. Wilkinson; the latter, who is but a youth in the Olympic School, gained as much fame as will contemporize his name with the Small's and Lumpey's of the day.

The first innings Coventry scored only 23 which rather elated the Leicester youths with hopes of an easy conquest, but on taking their innings, so much skill was displayed by the Coventry players that Leicester scored but 13 notches.

Leicester went in in their second innings and gained 132 notches.

Coventry went in in the afternoon, and at half past 7 (which was the hour agreed) the wickets were struck, with 3 men out on the Coventry side and 69 notches to win.

Tuesday morning 10 o'clock the wickets were again pitched; and we never remember to have seen an innings played with greater coolness or attention to the game: and the Leicester balls appeared to an incredible concourse of people to be directed with uncommon judgment, yet the Coventry batsmen stood their ground till one o'clock when victory declared for Leicester. *Leicester Journal*, 11 Aug.

Re above, 'great animosities, we are sorry to say, seem to have arisen between the parties.

'The Leicester youths having left the field of honour and retired to the *Bull Inn* to regale themselves after the fatigues of the day, to their utter astonishment a large body of colliers made their appearance in the market place, using every gesture that was hostile and alarming. The inhabitants of Hinckley became exceedingly alarmed and were obliged to have recourse to blows for their own defence. About 4 o'clock there seemed but one alternative: the Hinckley shopkeepers having shut their windows, a scene of bloodshed ensued scarcely to be credited in a country so entirely distinguished for acts of humanity.

'At length the colliers were worsted, and several left upon the field of action to all appearance in the most dangerous situations; the remainder were driven to the boundaries of their county. At present we have not heard of any lives being lost, though the weapons used in the contest were the most dangerous and alarming.' *Aris's Birmingham Gazette*, 13 Aug.

Fresh Light on 18th Century Cricket

*

Old Clarke

E. V. LUCAS

Lillywhite's Cricket Scores and Biographies vol. iii

'William Clarke's first match at Lord's, he being now thirty-seven years of age, thus appearing on this celebrated spot very late in life indeed for one who was afterwards so successful. His next match at Lord's did not take place till 1843, and, what is more extraordinary, he was never chosen for the Players in their match against the Gentlemen till 1846, at which period he had reached the mature age of forty-seven, and had already participated in the game for thirty seasons! He began cricket very young, his name being found in the Nottingham Eleven in 1816, but it was long before his merit was discovered at "Head Quarters". His bowling, which was slow under-hand, was wonderfully accurate in length and precision of pitch, cruelly deceptive, with a twist from the leg to the off, and getting up remarkably well. He obtained many wickets by the impatience of his adversaries, running in and trying to hit balls away for runs which could easily have been played down had the batsman stayed his ground. His general knowledge of the game and his skill in managing the field was also wonderful. He seemed to find out the defects of his adversaries' batting almost as soon as they had received a few balls, and he would arrange his field accordingly, generally with success. His only fault in management was that he would continue to bowl too long, being very unwilling to be changed, "always expecting to get a wicket with his next over". As a batsman he made some good scores in excellent style, hitting freely and well, though his average will not be found high, but he was often "not out". In 1846 he was engaged as a practice bowler by the Marylebone Club at Lord's (which, indeed, was the means of bringing him into notice), and remained there a few seasons. In 1846 also he originated the "All England matches."

'Altogether, Clarke participated in the game, from first to last, for forty-one seasons—which has been done by few if any cricketers in matches of note. His career, therefore, may be considered as one of the most wonderful on record, for (as before stated) he did not come *much* into notice in the great matches till he was about forty-seven years of age, long before which time many a good cricketer has abandoned the game, as being too old. Clarke also greatly excelled in the game of fives, and met with a severe accident when between twenty and thirty years of age while so engaged, the ball striking him in the right eye, causing him to lose the sight of it. This was, of course, a great disadvantage to him during his cricketing career.

'He also had a good knowledge of betting on races, &c., and was a crafty and fox-headed cricketer altogether. Clarke was originally by trade a bricklayer, but afterwards a licensed victualler, and for some years was landlord of the Bell Inn at Nottingham, opening in 1838 the famous Trent Bridge Ground, and retiring from business in 1847. He was born at Nottingham, December 24, 1798. Height 5 ft. 9 in., and weight

13 st. 11 lbs. Latterly, however, he lived in London, where he died, at Priory Lodge, Wandsworth Road, August 25, 1856, aged 57. He is buried in Norwood Cemetery . . . At the end of the year 1852 Clarke fell down (while playing) and broke his arm. It was thought he would not have been able to appear any more, but he continued to do so till the last year of his life.'

The Quarterly *for October,* 1884

'About 1836, W. Clarke, perhaps the most famous slow bowler of the century, appeared at Lord's (making his *début*, oddly enough, when he was 37 years of age), and for many years held a most commanding position from the skill with which he used to defeat even the best batsmen. He carried, we think, further than any bowler before him, the theory of bowling not merely to hit the wicket but to get his opponent out. He used to study each man's play, find out his weak points, and cruelly press his knowledge. "We shall have a '*h*accident', sir, soon, I know we shall!" was his favourite expression when a batsman had apparently mastered him—and accident we are bound to state there usually was. "How do you get out Mr A.?" he was once asked. "Nothing easier," he replied. "I bowl him three balls to make him proud of his forward play, and then with the fourth I pitch shorter twist and catch him at the slip."

'If Clarke had a fault, it was the somewhat English one of never knowing when he was defeated. He was always sanguine of a wicket next over. Lord Frederick Beauclerk had the same failing, if failing it be. "I knew I should get you!" he once said to Mr Ward. "Yes, but I have scored eighty," was the reply. It has been the same with other celebrated bowlers. "Do you not think we had better have a change?" was once said to one of the best slow round-arm amateur bowlers of the last decade, by a somewhat weary cover-point. "Yes, I think we had—I will *go on at the other end*." '

The Hambledon Men, 1907

*

Mr Mynn

WILLIAM CAFFYN

Mr Mynn was without doubt the most popular cricketer of his day. When I played with him towards the end of his career he was always the centre of attraction on every cricket field, and the spectators would crowd about him when he walked round the ground, like flies round a honey-pot. His immense popularity threw even the superior abilities of Pilch and Parr into the shade. He was beloved by all sorts and conditions of men, and he in return seemed to think kindly of every one. He had an affectionate regard for his old fellow-players who had fought shoulder to shoulder with him through his brilliant career, and there are many players who were just becoming known to him in his latter days who could bear witness to the kindness and encouragement he showed to them. As a bowler he was very fast, with a most stately delivery, bowling level with his shoulder. As a batsman he was a fine powerful hitter. He played a driving game, setting himself for this and not cutting much. Against fast bowling he was magnificent, and against slow of an inferior quality he was a great punisher. Against the best slow bowling of the day he did not show to so much advantage. He had not that *variety* of play which enables a batsman to deal with this sort of bowling to the best advantage. His pluck and gameness were something wonderful, and were shown in every department of the game.

He had an iron constitution which nothing seemed to upset. He liked good living, and seemed especially to enjoy his supper. I have often seen him eat a hearty supper of cold pork and retire to bed almost directly afterwards!

A curious custom of his was taking a tankard of light bitter beer to bed with him during the night. 'My boy,' he once said to me when he saw me taking a cup of tea, 'beef and beer are the things to play cricket on!'

71 Not Out

*

The Beginnings of International Cricket

H. S. ALTHAM AND E. W. SWANTON

The Visit to the States, 1859

In the year 1859 cricket entered upon its last, or oceanic, stage, for at the end of the English season twelve professional cricketers crossed the Atlantic to play a short series of matches in Canada and the United States. This tour was afterwards described in detail by Fred Lillywhite, who took part in it as official scorer and Press agent, and those who are interested in conditions of travel and hotel life in North America half a century ago will find much to interest and amuse them in his little book, in addition to a full description of the cricket.

A much shorter and most readable account is to be found in a chapter of that capital book *71 Not Out* by William Caffyn, who was himself a member of the team.

This considerable venture was due to the enterprise of, on the one hand, the old Eton and Cambridge cricketer, W. P. Pickering, and the Montreal Cricket Club, the leading cricket body in America, and, on the other, Mr Edmund Wilder, President of the Cricketers' Fund (which subsequently developed into the Cricketers' Fund Friendly Society), Fred Lillywhite, and, among the actual players, George Parr and John Wisden. Negotiations between the parties concerned had been opened three years before, and eventually during the Canterbury Week the final arrangements were concluded. On the guarantee of the Montreal Club, each of the twelve players was to receive £50, in addition to the whole of their expenses. They were to play five matches, at Montreal, New York, Philadelphia, Rochester, and Hamilton, the two middle games being against Twenty-two of the USA, the first and the last against Twenty-two of Lower and Upper Canada respectively, whilst the Rochester game was against a Combined Twenty-two.

The team, if not absolutely representative, was nevertheless very strong: it consisted of wellnigh the pick of the All England and United Elevens, six from each, and its territorial composition is not a bad index of the relative county strengths of that period. From Notts came Parr, Grundy, and Jackson; from Sussex, Wisden and John Lillywhite; from Cambridge, their two famous 'cracks', Hayward and Carpenter, with

Ducky Diver; while Surrey contributed no less than four—Stephenson, Julius Cæsar, Lockyer, and Caffyn.

The twelve set sail from Liverpool on September 7th, and after a baddish passage of fifteen days, cast anchor in the St Lawrence beneath the Heights of Abraham, which Wolfe had won for the Empire a hundred years, almost to the day, before them. The opening match at Montreal was well patronized, especially by the fair sex. The Canadians were very keen, but found the England bowling too much for them, especially George Parr's lobs, which obtained 16 wickets: they were beaten by 8 wickets. A complimentary dinner at the St Lawrence Hotel, then the best and biggest in Canada, wound up a successful first chapter, and the tourists set out on their journey to New York. Fred Lillywhite is not a little querulous over this stage in their travels, and especially over the treatment meted out to his precious scoring-booth on wheels; but we rather gather from Caffyn's account that he was a bit of a grouser, and finally called down on his head the wrath of old George Parr, who consigned him and booth alike to a considerably warmer climate. At Hoboken, New York, the interest evinced in the English team was at least as great as it had been in Canada. Over 2,000 people visited the ground on the Sunday before the game started, and more than 25,000 are said to have watched the game. The ground was bad, and the play of the US Twenty-two very inferior, England winning by an innings and 64 runs. Caffyn, in the second innings, took 16 wickets for 25 runs!

The next stage was to Philadelphia, a city which, though Quaker in origin, was nevertheless the centre of all athletic enthusiasm in the Continent, and at least a thousand ladies graced the ladies' stand. Unfortunately the weather was by this time (October 10th) beginning to break up, and only a couple of wagon-loads of sawdust contrived to make play possible at all on the sodden ground! The tourists won by 7 wickets, but were able to be very complimentary to the Twenty-two on the standard of their play and to Hammond, an old Kent cricketer, who was their professional, on the results of his teaching. A week later the last of the officially arranged matches was begun at Hamilton. In spite of the rain and the growing cold, there was no lack of attendance and enthusiasm, especially for Tom Lockyer's wicket-keeping. The Surrey man played up to his audience, returning John Jackson's balls so quickly to the bowler that some of the less experienced of the spectators could not be convinced that the ball had ever been delivered at all! Once more England triumphed—this time by 10 wickets. A final match, extra to the original programme, was played at Rochester against a Combined Twenty-two. This was interrupted on the second day by a heavy fall of snow, and only finished under conditions which made the tourists field in great-coats, mufflers, and gloves! The chronicler feelingly observes that 'the most agreeable innings on such a day could only be obtained indoors with a hot dinner before you and a bottle of old port to follow'. This match, too, the tourists won by an innings, so that when on their return passage down the St Lawrence they passed the good ship *Nova Scotia* in which they had voyaged from England, they could proudly display for its information a large board with the chalked-up legend, 'Won All Matches'. After experiencing even rougher weather than on their way out, the Twelve reached Liverpool on November 11th. On page 140 of Caffyn's *71 Not Out* there is an excellent photograph of the team taken on board the *Nova Scotia* immediately before they sailed. The same authority records that they made something like £90 a head out of their two months' trip.

First Tours in Australia

Two years later, in 1861, another team left England, this time for Australia. The promoters of this tour were Messrs. Spiers and Pond, who in the summer of that year sent over a certain Mr Mallam to make the arrangements. It was at a dinner in Birmingham, after the North and South match, that the leading professionals were first definitely approached. The terms, £150 a head, with all expenses, did not commend themselves to George Parr and the northern players, and for the moment it looked as if the scheme would fall through. Mr Mallam then approached Mr Burrup, the enthusiastic secretary of the Surrey CCC, and through his good offices succeeded in persuading H. H. Stephenson and six other members of that famous side to form the nucleus of a team. To these were added five others, including Tom Hearne and the two Yorkshiremen, Iddison and E. Stephenson. H. Stephenson's selection to captain the side caused a good deal of ill-feeling among the northerners; why it is not easy to understand, considering that they had refused to undertake the trip themselves.

The team left Liverpool on October 18th and landed at Melbourne on Christmas Eve, when they were met by over 10,000 people and driven in a coach-and-four to an official reception. So great was the popular enthusiasm over the visit that for their first day's practice they were driven off some miles to a secret destination in the bush, in order that they might have some peace from the attentions of their admirers.

The opening match at Melbourne against Eighteen of Victoria saw a crowd of over 15,000 on the ground when, to the strains of the National Anthem, the Englishmen took the field. Each wore a very light helmet-shaped hat, and a sash and hat ribbon of a distinctive hue corresponding to a colour set down on the score-card against each man's name. The heat was terrific, but thanks to the batting of Caffyn and Griffith, England made 305, and ran out winners by an innings and 96 runs. In all twelve matches were played, including one at Hobart against Twenty-two of Tasmania. Six were won, four drawn, and two were lost. Of these latter, one was against Twenty-two of Castlemaine, the other, at Sydney, against a combined Twenty-two of NSW and Victoria.

The tour, all told, was a great success. Caffyn and Griffith had splendid records with both bat and ball, and Stephenson scored great success as an orator. The Englishmen were immensely impressed with the Melbourne ground, which in its water supply, pavilion, grand-stand capable of holding 6,000 people, and banked seats for the general public, represented, even at this early date, a standard unapproached by anything we could show at home.

Messrs. Spiers and Pond are said to have cleared £11,000 over their enterprise.

At the end of the tour one of the English team remained behind, having accepted a permanent post as cricket coach to the leading club in Sydney. This was Charles Lawrence, the Surrey player, a good all-round cricketer and renowned among his contemporaries as a judge of the game.

In the winter of 1863–1864 a second team, this time under Parr's captaincy, visited the country and, like its predecessor, enjoyed a great success. The side was, with the exception of E. M. Grace, exclusively professional. All the matches played were against odds, but just before the finish the Twenty-two of NSW came very near to spoiling the Englishmen's unbeaten record by running them to a margin of 1 wicket, amid a scene of intense excitement. At the end of the tour William Caffyn was engaged as coach by the Melbourne Club, and thus entered upon that period of seven years' devoted work in that town and at Sydney to which the Australians in this early period of their cricket education owed so much. In his *71 Not Out* Caffyn writes most interestingly about his experiences as a coach, and pays the warmest tribute to the energy and enthusiasm with which the southern cricketers worked at the game, noticing especially their ceaseless attention to and pride in fielding.

Nine years passed before, in the winter of 1873, W.G. took out the third English team on what was for him virtually his honeymoon tour. The side included four other amateurs, of whom the captain's younger brother, Fred, was one. Once more all the matches were against odds, and only three matches out of the fifteen played were lost; but there seems unfortunately to have been a good deal of friction on more than one occasion. Nevertheless it was a further stimulus to the Colonial interest in the game, and the appearance of the Champion created immeasurable excitement. A foolish story had got about that W.G. had backed himself in £500 to £50 that he would never be bowled in Australia, so that when H. F. Boyle hit his leg-stump in the opening match against Victoria the enthusiasm and the 'Cooee's' beggared description. Though in the last and most important match of the tour his eleven defeated a combined Fifteen of NSW and Victoria, W.G.'s parting words to Boyle at the farewell dinner were indeed prophetic: 'If you ever come to England, and your bowlers are as good there as they are here, you will make a name for yourselves.' Four more years were to pass and the name would be made, indeed!

The Australians in England, 1878

The sponsors of the first Australian tour in England were James Lillywhite, who acted as their match-making agent, and, on the part of the tourists, J. Conway, of Melbourne, who officiated as manager throughout the tour. The captain of the team was David Gregory, one of the remarkable family of seven brothers, five of whom played for NSW, and uncle of both Sydney Gregory, who has played more innings in Test Matches than any other cricketer, and of J.M., the great all-rounder of the 1921 team.

The programme arranged for them was a long one, thirty-seven matches in all, of which twenty were against odds, and it says much for the health and stamina of the tourists that, with only twelve regular players at their disposal, they were hardly ever obliged to call upon outside or occasional assistance. At this time South Australia was still in its cricket infancy, so that of the twelve, six hailed from NSW, five, including Midwinter, who joined the side in England, from Victoria, while one man, G. H. Bailey, came from Tasmania. After a preliminary tour in New Zealand, the Australians reached Liverpool on May

14th. They suffered a rude shock in the specimen of an English summer that awaited them, and must have felt that sweaters were more desirable than the silk shirts with which their bags were stored. The opening match at Nottingham found their batsmen helpless under the novel conditions against Shaw and Morley, and they had to admit defeat by over an innings.

It was on May 27th that English cricket suffered the shock of its life. When, on a showery morning after a heavy night's rain, and with 'casual water' standing in puddles on the ground, the first Australian Eleven drove in their brake on to Lord's ground, they passed practically unrecognized by the 500 or so spectators that had by then mustered; twelve hours later England was ringing with the news that the flower of its cricket had been beaten in a single day, and crowds came flocking to the Tavistock Hotel in Covent Garden to look on the men who had thus flung open a new era in the history of the game. It was just after noon when W.G. and Hornby opened the MCC innings to the bowling of Allan and Boyle. Allan's first ball was hit to the leg boundary by W.G., but the next had him easily caught at square-leg. That fine Cambridge cricketer, C. Booth, was bowled by Boyle in the next over. Hornby and Ridley then added 22 runs, and it was nearly twenty minutes to one when Gregory took off Allan and gave the ball to Spofforth. In ten overs (four balls each) the innings was over, and the greatest bowler of all time had made his name.

In rather over half an hour's batting before lunch the Australians lost the wickets of their crack batsmen, Charles Bannerman, Horan and Alec Bannerman, for 17 runs, Alfred Shaw having in that time bowled 13 overs for 1 run! After lunch 5 more wickets fell for an additional 6 runs, but the last 2 wickets added 18, leaving the Australians with a lead of 8. Shaw's complete analysis worked out at 33 overs, 25 maidens, 10 runs, 5 wickets; whilst at the other end his compatriot, Morley, had taken 5 for 31.

The news of the sensational cricket had brought London swarming up to Lord's, and when at 4 p.m. Grace and Hornby opened the Club's second innings to Spofforth and Boyle, more than 5,000 people, in a state of intense expectancy, filled the ring. If there had been sensations enough already, they were nothing to what was to follow. Off Spofforth's first ball W.G. was missed at the wicket, but the second beat and bowled him, while the third did the same for A. J. Webbe. Not to be outdone, Boyle clean bowled Booth and Ridley in his first over, and with Hornby badly hurt by the 'Demon' in the next, five of the best batsmen were gone for a single run. Wild and Flowers then manfully added 16 runs; but though Hornby, with W.G. to run for him, reappeared amid a storm of cheers, nothing could stem the tide, and shortly after five o'clock the last wicket fell with the total at 19.

Wanting but 12 runs to win, the Australians lost Bannerman for 1, beaten by a fast break-back from Shaw, but at twenty minutes to six Horan made the winning hit. The scene at the finish beggared description, and the winners could not have been more heartily cheered had Sydney or Melbourne been the scene of their victory.

Punch, sensitive as ever to history in the making, greeted it with the following lines:

> The Australians came down like a wolf on the fold,
> The Marylebone cracks for a trifle were bowled;
> Our Grace before dinner was very soon done,
> And Grace after dinner did not get a run.

The defeat of the MCC was a nine-days' wonder, and made the reputation of the Australians at a single stroke, and their subsequent record more than justified the prophets who, watching their initial practices at Nottingham, had foretold that they 'would beat more than would beat them'.

How came it, then, that with such slender resources in batting the Australians more than held their own under the strange conditions of their first tour? To some extent they were aided by the weather, which was uniformly bad all through the season: on the dead and difficult wickets the cross-bat vigorously applied frequently brought in as good a harvest of runs as its more decorous and academic brother. But the root of their success lay, beyond all question, in their bowling, and it is no exaggeration to say that this was a real revelation to English cricketers. In Spofforth, Boyle, Garrett, and Allan they had a quartet superior to any that could be found in England. Allan was never in full health during the tour, and failed to produce the form which had won for him in his own country the title of 'the bowler of a century', but he had days when the amount of work he got upon his left-hand slow medium impressed the best English batsmen. What strikes me as most curious is that no contemporary account that I have found says anything about his swerving, yet Spofforth himself says that Allan had the greatest swerve he had ever seen, and secured his swerve by bending his knees and bowling the ball from 23 yards, thus giving it an upward curve and room for the air friction to operate. Garrett was fast medium and of a more or less familiar type, in that he relied on length and, to some extent, on the off-theory; but, when the wicket helped him, he could spin the ball back sharply and had a disconcerting knack of making it get up quick as well. Boyle had length, flight, and leg-spin; his length was immaculate, he was always on the stumps, and his record of 62 wickets for 10 apiece in eleven a-side matches speaks for itself.

And, lastly, there was the 'Demon'. It was on that fatal day at Lord's that Spofforth was first so dubbed, and when we conjure up a picture of him as he bowled in the first innings, the reason is not hard to find. A tall, rather slim figure, but lissom, wiry and full of vitality; a very high action, an atmosphere of undisguised hostility, and a subtle and unresting brain behind it all. There was never a more thoughtful bowler than the 'Demon'; it is said that he would often lie awake at night turning over and over in his mind the best methods of attacking the great batsmen opposed to him. When first he came to England he was a definitely fast bowler, with an extra fast ball, frequently a yorker, up his sleeve; like many of his fellows, he was quick to observe and profit by all that he saw in England, and by 1882 he had moderated his speed to fast medium, but perfected the art of disguising his change of pace. On a fast, true wicket he had not the strength or stamina of a Richardson, or quite the electric quality of Lockwood at his best, but given the slightest help from the pitch, he was, beyond all doubt, what the Champion proclaimed him—the greatest bowler in the world. Like the famous Yorkshire bowler, George Freeman, Spofforth never overdid his great power of spin: he always aimed at doing just enough to beat the bat and hit the wicket; but probably his greatest asset was his consummate gift for concealing a change of pace, in which it is possible that Lohmann alone of English bowlers approached him.

Now in 1878, when the Australians first came over, English bowling lay to a great extent under the spell of Alfred Shaw. The preceding decade had witnessed a revolution in method, the great and widespread improvement in grounds, together with the rapid development of aggressive batting, for which W.G.'s example was no doubt largely responsible, had in a very few years almost driven the race of fast bowlers off the cricket field. Their place had been taken by a generation of slow and slow-medium bowlers, who took Shaw as their model, and relied on a perfect length, often at some distance wide of the off-stump. It was the Australians who showed us what could be done by two new factors in attack—the off-break, bowled at a fast pace and in frontal attack on the wicket, and a readjustment of the field. In those days mid-on and square-leg were commonly regarded as places where the comparative 'rabbit' could be tucked most safely away, and it was a revelation when on the sticky wickets of 1878 Boyle proceeded to take up his position at silly mid-on, often no more than 6 or 7 yards from the bat, and catch men out off defensive strokes to the off-breaks of Spofforth and Garrett. Boyle is the original prototype of the modern 'suicide squad' and his enterprise marks a decisive step in the process which, in the last 20 years, has orientated the field completely afresh.

In fielding, the Australians of 1878, while earning the outspoken praise of their contemporaries, were not considered superior to the best that we could show, except in throwing, in which, from their first appearance, they were recognized as reaching a standard to which we could not aspire.

At an interval of nearly sixty years it can do no harm if we record the single fact that the whole-hearted enthusiasm of our visitors sometimes involved impatience and resentment at the umpires' decisions when unfavourable to themselves. Umpiring has been something of a difficulty in Australia throughout its cricket history, and the first touring eleven were apt at times to impute to English umpires motives as questionable as those from which they had themselves perforce suffered in their own country. This tendency led to a most unfortunate incident in a match at Philadelphia during their homeward journey, and culminated in the once notorious, if now forgotten, scene on the Sydney ground during the tour of Lord Harris's Eleven in the winter of 1878–1879.

Lord Harris in Australia

The team which Lord Harris took to Australia in 1878–1879 was originally to have been under the captaincy of I. D. Walker, and to have consisted entirely of amateurs. A family bereavement ultimately prevented any of the Walkers from taking part, and several other gentlemen who had undertaken to go were later obliged to cry off. Lord Harris, therefore, upon whom the captaincy had devolved, was forced to strengthen his attack by including the two Yorkshire professionals, Emmett and Ulyett. The latter, although he took 65 wickets for 11 apiece, was hardly as successful as had been hoped, but Tom Emmett got through a prodigious amount of work, and came out with the splendid record of 137 wickets at a cost of just over $8\frac{1}{2}$ each. The only other bowler of any repute was A. P. Lucas. In batting, with the captain, Lucas, Hornby, Webbe, Penn, and the two Yorkshiremen, the side was strong and constantly scored heavily, but nothing could make up for the shortage of bowling, and not for the last time were Englishmen to find that the best of fieldsmen at home were only too liable to drop catches in the strange atmosphere of the Antipodes. Moreover, they had no first-class wicket-keeper. The programme consisted of only thirteen matches, but it is significant that of the five eleven a-side games three were lost, one each to Victoria and NSW, and the other to the Australian Eleven of 1878. In the latter match the chief agent in our downfall by 10 wickets was Spofforth, who took 13 wickets for 110 runs; but the Englishmen were almost equally impressed with Evans of NSW, at this time reputed to be the best all-rounder in Australia, but never successful later on in reproducing his best form in England.

A History of Cricket, 1926

*

Cricket of Fifty Years Since

REVD JAMES PYCROFT

As to cricket fifty years since, the ground on Cowley Marsh had only recently been made by Mr Walker, of Magdalen, and was called the Magdalen ground, in distinction from Bullingdon, which for many years had been the only University cricket ground. On Bullingdon, Brasenose College had a ground distinct from that of the Bullingdon Club. Both of these grounds were more for feasting and Tilting (for there was a Tilting club) than for cricket, the Magdalen ground alone deserving notice for real practice and play.

At this time, professionals either at the public schools or at the Universities, were almost unknown. Cowley used to supply some useful bowlers, but all underhand. Such rustics as Hoskings, Blucher and Peter (short for Pieria Bancolari) were well-known names. Very fast and straight underhand bowling, my experience leads me to say, is better to give a beginner correct form and good defence in practice, than round-arm bowling. I have known such players, with very little practice against the round bowling, give their opponents a great deal of trouble.

At this time, Broadbridge and Lillywhite, who were the first round bowlers—as good, if not better than any since—were at their best. 'I bowl the best ball of any man in England', said Lillywhite; 'and Mr Harenc the next.' Mr Stenning, of Brighton, told me he once saw Broadbridge and Lillywhite bowl sixty-four balls without a run to Pilch and Wenman. Wenman, though of a different style, was almost as good as Pilch; and as to Pilch, Hillyer—the best bowler next to Lillywhite—said he was more afraid of being hit by Pilch when past his best, than by George Parr in his prime, and we have no professional now better, if as good, as George Parr.

I think I may say there were about six players in my time at Oxford who would be in the Eleven now. My standard of comparison is this: the late Vice-Chancellor Giffard scored one hundred and five in one innings at Lord's against Harenc, Sir F. Bathurst, and other bowlers of the MCC when the ground was by no means easy. The Rev. F. B. Wright, and Payne, both Wykehamists, scored sixty each against Broadbridge and Lillywhite in an MCC match, though they had not played against them before. Wordsworth, Popham (the late Francis Popham, of Littlecote), Price, Harenc, Fagg (who played for Kent under the name of Frederics), and Buller were just as likely to have done as much. My own average was double that of Giffard's in my last year, and Daubeney and one other scored as much as Giffard; so I say we had six, though not all in the Eleven at the same time, not to be denied now.

This match at Oxford against the MCC with Broadbridge, Lillywhite and Wenman at the wicket, I well remember. Wright (the Rev. F. B.), father of Mr Wright of the Oxford eleven of 1865, and of Rossal School, and now of Eastbourne, had the same fame as a hard hitter as Mr Thornton has now, and, if not quite his equal in this respect, better as an all-round player. He went in second innings rather late—thirty being wanted to win—the field set far out for his hitting. Still he hit one for five runs just over the head of little Peter, who was fielding for Mr Aislabie; he was stepping in and swiping to save the game, as his part-ner's last bat was worth little. Wright was caught from a dropping ball from that most artful of all bowlers, Broadbridge, and the match was lost by thirteen runs.

I said afterwards, 'Peter, if you had been a foot taller you would have caught that ball.' 'No, I shouldn't, sir,' was the reply; 'I was fielding for Mr Aislabie (a Falstaff of twenty stone), and he couldn't have caught nothing; then why should I? No, sir, I wouldn't catch Mr Wright out to please the Marylebone gentlemen nor nobody.'

At this time the Wykehamists were the best players of the day. They showed the best style of batting, and were particularly famous for field-ing. Their rush in to meet the ball, their clean scoop up and quick return, were remarkable. At Winchester they used to qualify by prac-tising till they could throw over a certain building in the neighbour-hood, which required a first-rate throw. 'The Wykehamists against the rest of the University' was for several years an annual match, and once the Wykehamists played, and won, a match—'The Wykehamists against the two Universities', at Lord's. One Eleven of the school against Eton and Harrow was long mentioned as the finest field ever seen—the same as was said nearly fifty years after of Mr Game's Oxford Eleven.

The school matches for 1825 were originally Eton and Harrow. There was much betting in those days. When Winchester at first agreed to play, little was known of them. But when Price was seen bowling down a single stump repeatedly at Lord's the day before the match, the odds altered at once, and men were in a hurry to hedge.

At this time the only schools for cricket were truly schools—the pub-lic schools. For there, a good style of play became traditional, and few could learn it elsewhere. There were few professionals, save at Lord's to teach the art, but there Caldecourt was a first-rate teacher. He and old Sparkes were about this time engaged at Cambridge, so the Oxford ground knew few but public schoolmen—a limited number of course. Nets for practice were unknown: gloves and pads were only made to order and under special directions. I used to wear a pad on one ankle, and a few padded finger-stalls on one hand; one or two only of my friends had some such inventions of their own. So we could not guard our wickets, as now, against twisting balls with our legs—we were obliged to keep them out of the way. When in 1836 I saw Wenman wicket-keeping with a common leather glove on one hand it seemed strange, though Wenman's hands had not the work of players now. He rarely kept wicket in two matches the same week. When Lord Frederic Beauclerc first saw leggings he never imagined they would be allowed in a match—'so unfair to the bowler'. This want of leggings necessi-tated the 'draw' between legs and wicket, a very useful hit still, and only unsafe because men know not how to make it. This also will account no little for the long scores of the present day, not to forget there were no bounds, all hits were run out.

And, lastly, instead of, as at present, a place in the Eleven defying all reading for the summer term, we had seven men either classmen or prizemen in the Eleven of 1836—the first of the annual matches against Cambridge. The following men, all known to fame, were in the Eleven in my time: Vice-Chancellor Giffard, Bishops Ryle and Wordsworth; Dr Lee, Provost of Winchester; Canon Rawlinson and Charles Duke Yonge, Professor of History at Belfast, a well-known author.

It was a little later that professional assistance became common, though earlier in 1830 I remember Sparkes with the Lansdowne and Bayley with the Kingscote clubs. A man as eminent as Fuller Pilch, though not of the MCC, would have a series of engagements to keep him in full practice in county matches, such as Hampshire, Kent, Sussex and Surrey, for these were the strongest counties, but not many professionals had regular practice; few of the county players had constant practice, or rather to be called paid men than professionals. The counties were reduced to select men, who played more on their reputation than on their assured efficiency on any given day. The batting of the professionals was not likely to be strong, because, as Cobbett said to me, 'We have no practice but in bowling; our batting must come of itself, except with Pilch and one or two others.' This disadvantage, and not inferiority of play, will also account for the smaller scores of those days.

At this time (1832–6) little, if any, but the (then) new round-arm bowling was to be seen in the best matches, and not much of the old remained at Oxford, though Mr Kirwan, with a kind of undetected jerk as fast as Freeman, if not faster, defied almost all comers at Cambridge; Brown, of Brighton, faster still than Kirwan, was playing at that time, his bruised hip and side after every match proving plainly, as he told my friend Cooke, that the umpires should have pronounced his bowling a jerk.

Whoever looks over the old score books will see 'wides' scored from even the best bowlers. As to amateur bowlers, the wides were common indeed in the early days of round bowling. The rule then required an arm nearly horizontal, and this was an action clearly contrary to the nature of the muscles. A little higher you had full command. Caldecourt said that with this little elevation of the hand, 'if Lillywhite were not watched, as by country umpires, who thought what Lilly did must be right, he bowled a hundred times better than any man ever did bowl; it was cruel to see how he would rattle about either the knuckles or stumps'. So with this cramped style of low bowling little accuracy could be expected but from a man who bowled almost daily, as for his livelihood. This rule of low delivery, however, was so frequently broken that the rule was altered about twenty years since, and a high hand was allowed, and now, so natural is the action, any man can learn to bowl straight. Wides are hardly expected, and wides never were expected and did not score in the days of the old underhand bowling till the ever memorable single-wicket match, when, Osbaldeston being ill, Lambert alone played and beat Lord F. Beauclerc and Hammond. For then Lambert bowled wides right and left to his Lordship, and made him lose his temper, and then got his wicket. Then a wide was first made to forfeit one. Nowadays men speak of underhand bowling as 'slows'. Much of the old bowling might be so called, but Osbaldeston, Brown, Harvey Fellows, Kirwan, and above all, Marcon, were faster than any round bowler I have ever seen.

To refer to Marcon, for swift underhand bowling, Henry Grace related to me that in one match he saw a young farmer come in with his bat over his shoulder, saying, 'Fast as he is, I'll have a crack at him.' The first ball that came took his bat clean out of his hand and right through the wicket! So, the old delivery in reality admitted of the greater speed. Still, most of the old bowlers were slow. Budd, Beldham, Lord F. Beauclerc, and Lambert are the names most frequently seen in the old scores, and they were about the pace of Clarke. Clarke spoke of Lambert as a better bowler than himself, as also, he said, was Warsop, of Nottingham. Clarke, aged forty-eight, came forward about 1850, having long lain fallow, as superseded by Lillywhite and his school: and let those who think such a style, at least when brought to perfection, would in these days be hit out of the field, reflect that Pilch, Felix, G. Parr, Mynn, Caffin, and Joe Guy had all tried stepping in and free hitting, and were all obliged to treat Clarke's bowling with great care and respect. The Gentlemen had small chance against the Players in Clarke's day.

At Oxford we used to play an annual match with the town, including the Cowley ground bowlers. Once, when good bowling was unsuccessful, they put in Tailor Humphreys to bowl twisting sneaks, and the wickets fell faster than before Hoskings, one of the best of fast bowlers at that time. The old fast bowling required a very straight bat. In 1848–9, when I captained the North of Devon side against the South and the Teignbridge club, men worth a hundred an innings in good country matches, we played the old fast bowling against the round, and in two matches we ripped them up for about twenty-five in each innings— four innings for a hundred runs! But our bowling was really good. My friend Cawston once took three middle stumps in one over! Of course this kind of bowling requires a very accurate pitch. Mr Budd, one of the slows, like Clarke, I have seen pitch as true as possible almost every ball through a long innings. Clarke had naturally, from a crooked arm, once fractured, almost too much break on his balls, and he therefore always chose at Lord's the pavilion end for his balls to break against the hill. With the slope in his favour his break became too great.

With slows a deal of spin for break and for an abrupt rise was necessary. Budd once bowled me out by a ball that rose over my shoulder and still fell on the wicket. Slows are still tried in good matches, sometimes very successfully, as with Humphrey, for Sussex, but save Clarke and Budd, who from the first practised nothing else, I have never seen any as accurate as they should be. Clarke for four years was never beaten off, and strange to say he succeeded, though too old to field his own bowling well. This is indispensable for a slow bowler, 'as also is it,' said Clarke, 'to be able to send in unexpectedly a good fast ball, to defend yourself when men take liberties with you'. In my own play I have always thought I had an advantage in being well drilled with underhand bowling first. It necessitates a perfectly straight bat. Few man play quite straight—men remark it at once when a man does play quite straight—a good proof that such play is rather the exception than the rule.

Canon Rawlinson, then at Trinity College, was one of our eleven— a fair long-stop and a most heartbreaking bat. He would block by the hour: his runs must come of themselves. His play reminded me of a man who asked Pilch, 'Shall I be out (a vulgar error) if I don't move my bat?' 'No, sir, but you'll be out if you do.' Many a shooter have I seen bowled which found Rawlinson's bat still unmoved in the block-hole. Still, by the course of time and the mere chances of the game, he was credited, in an MCC match, with twenty-five runs against Bayley and Cobbett, two of the best bowlers of the day. I was once in a match with him, 'The Wykehamists against the University', and when I had scored thirty he had scored five; but since if he had the first ball of an over he usually had all the four; he had three times as many balls as I had and ought to have scored not five, but about a hundred. Charles Wordsworth, of Christchurch, before-named as good at everything, was a brilliant bat—a very free hitter. No University eleven, before or since, could ever have left him out, though in one eleven in Mr Mitchell's time, every man was known to be capable of fifty runs in a first-rate match. On the Magdalen ground we used to practise with six wickets along the upper side, facing, at a distance of about fifty yards, six along the lower side. Here we had twelve men batting, and twelve men between the rows bowling—no small number for hours daily in danger's way: I wonder they could escape serious blows. Men used to be very careless, but I never saw any accident of much consequence, though a great many narrow escapes. A ball, hit fifty yards, once touched my hair.

As to accidents, I asked old Beldham, who played from the end of the last century, and also Caldecourt, who saw more play than any man from the time Beldham left off, and neither had ever seen any serious accident—none, at least, by which a man sustained material and lasting injury. The most painful I ever saw was that of a son of Sir George Burrowes, who between the innings of a match at Lord's, was struck on the face from a very fast ball from a catapult which was being tried. Burrowes was about the place where a long-stop would have stood, and the ball bounded up from hard ground. Still, though the doctor feared the sight was gone, two years after he said that he was not much the worse. I can also speak favourably from my own long experience; so accidents must have been very few.

Summers, a good player in the Nottingham eleven, died four days after a blow on the head while batting at Lord's—but he did enough, by a journey to Nottingham, to render fatal any case of concussion. Many a man has been hit much harder than poor Summers, for he had no external mark of injury, though the shock broke a little vessel. This I heard from Alfred Shaw, who kindly watched over him from first to last, but could not persuade him to lie by and obey the doctor.

Now it is pertinent to the present question to chronicle the fact that it was not the speed of bowling, but the fly-about uncertainty of it, that gave rise to padding. Mr Budd's cricket dress, representing the fashion of his day, was nankeen knee-breeches and silk stockings, a second pair of stockings being doubled down to form a neat roll, to guard the ankle bone. We never saw him wear a glove of any kind, though we have seen him opposed to Mr Kirwan's bowling. He had also played through the days, not only of Browne of Brighton, and W. Osbaldeston—faster than Jackson's—of whom it may be said that they were not encountered very often; but Howard bowled commonly in Mr Budd's day, and Mr Brande bowled very frequently too, and both of these players bowled at a rattling pace, and yet they were ordinarily encountered without pads of any kind.

During our Oxford career, from 1833-36, Price (a name long remembered at Winchester), and a noted Cowley man, old Hoskings, were players who certainly could vindicate underhand bowling from the modern term of 'slows', yet there were not half-a-dozen pads of any kind to be seen in the tent. The first greave was claimed as an original and knowing invention, by Henry Daubeney (*fuit!*), remembered by not a few at the present day, one of the freest of the Wykehamists—then the best hitters and fieldsmen of all the public schools. By this device Daubeney used to stand up to leg balls far more boldly than he otherwise could have done, and as to the power with which he hit them, he hit Mr Lowth for a fair seven, near Stonehenge, on ground that in no way favoured the hit.

At that time (1836) Price was the last remaining representative of the old school of bowling, and from that time pads began to grow in size, shape, and variety; not, we say, because we feared the pace, but simply because no one knew where to look out for what was called round-bowling, but which always was as high or higher than the shoulder.

Oxford Memories, vol. ii, 1886

❊

A Voyage across the Atlantic

FRED LILLYWHITE

The Start

from the Docks was made at half past two o'clock, on Wednesday, the 7th, per tug, to the ship anchored in the Mersey. The owners had contracted to convey the English party to and fro. Passengers arrived on board just before three o'clock. The tug conveyed a vast number of cricketers and supporters of the game in Liverpool, who gave three hearty English cheers for the success of their countrymen.

At 4.15 the anchor was weighed, the sailors timing their labours to a popular and nautical ditty, the words of which were about as follows:

> Here's success to the old black-jack
> Whisky, jolly;
> And may we all get plenty of that
> Whisky, boys—ho—jolly.

The melody came to a premature close, and the good ship was then fairly on her way to Quebec. We soon arrived at the acknowledged starting point from England, where the firing of a gun announced the same. Passed the Isle of Man at 10.45, seventy-five miles distant from Liverpool, and all retired to rest; the only one who had selected a spot for his future accommodation, in case it might be required, was John Lillywhite, and this was immediately behind the wheel. The morning of

Thursday, September 8

was lovely. Most of the cricketers were on deck at six o'clock. The sea was calm with a fresh and favourable breeze; we were off the Irish coast, going at the rate of eleven knots an hour. At twelve o'clock a.m. we were distant from Liverpool 220 miles. At this period a heavy sea sprung up, with a head wind, which reduced our 'going' from eleven to five knots an hour. Stephenson, Caffyn, John Lillywhite, and Jackson were not quite so comfortable as when on land, and were frequently evincing their arithmetical propensities, by casting up their accounts, the balancing of which they found to be a most troublesome and unpleasant operation.

Our places having been secured, both for berths and meals, those who were well now began to 'look up' the officers of the ship, and we very soon found that we had a jolly lot to deal with, which increased our confidence, and made us, at once, *sailors*. Our first conversation with Captain Borland raised him high in our estimation as a good hearted, thoroughly courageous, experienced and weather-beaten sailor. His expressions gave us reason to think that he would make every one present comfortable, if possible. Some of the cricketers, however, *thought* that unless he could prevent the ship from rolling about, his attempts to secure our comfort would not be attended with very great success. We received many indulgences, and much valuable information from Mr McDonald, the first mate, whose eye was sure to be where any-thing might be going wrong, and the seamanlike manner in which he gave his commands, procured for him the ready obedience and respect of all the sailors. Then we had the excellent attention of the purser, Mr Jenkins, who apparently could not do too much to oblige us. The chief engineer also is a gentleman of great eminence in his profession, so that we felt no doubt about our safe arrival at Quebec. The kindness and attention of Mr Jones, the second mate, was also particularly noticed by the English cricketers; in fact, the whole of the officers and crew, down to the captain's boy, Jack, were as pleasant a ship's company as one could possibly wish to sail with. We had now ascertained the exact time for meals, and, with the exception of those whose stomachs would not allow them to 'devour', all attended to the sound of the bell. Breakfast at half past eight, at which there was no lack of *rolls*, lunch at twelve, dinner at four, tea at seven, and supper from nine to eleven. It was about four, p.m., this day, Thursday, that the shores of Ireland were fast lessening in the distance; the sky was no longer blue, and the waves began to get *very* 'bumpy', so much so, as Wisden remarked, 'as to require the immediate use of the roller', upon which some one said, 'there were always plenty of rollers on the sea shore'. Among those at this period who were particularly noticed to be labouring under disagreeable heaviness were John Lillywhite, at the wheel, Caffyn, Stephenson and Jackson in their bunks. At 4.30, p.m., we had the last look at land through the captain's glass, and then ascertained that we should have 1600 miles more to accomplish ere we should again have the pleasure of a similar sight. The captain here ordered more sail up, as the 'wind was drawing aft a little'. There was not anything like the number of passengers at dinner, as on the previous day, when in the Mersey, no doubt from the fact that they could not relish food under the circumstances. Among the English party, who took possession of the seats allotted to them, were Hayward, Carpenter, Parr, Wisden, Lockyer, Cæsar, Grundy, and Fred. Lillywhite, and most of these did not remain long, as the ship began to roll fearfully. Later in the evening the breeze freshened almost into a gale, and the quicksilver in the barometer fell rapidly. Upon casting one's eye round the deck, the usual places were filled by those to whom a sea voyage was anything but one of pleasure, and these appeared exceedingly desirous of putting foot on land again. Upon turning round you would find two or three passengers on their backs, an excellent position, when the ship takes a severe roll. Caffyn and Stephenson here attempted the task of going below, when an alarming pitch at the moment caused them both to be precipitated to the bottom of the steps, and nothing more was seen of them for two days and a half. At this moment, too, Lockyer, who had up to this period been perfectly well, very good naturedly enquired of Grundy, 'how he liked the motion', to which question, he could get no answer, but a sigh, his heart and stomach being too full for utterance, except in one peculiar way. A rubber at whist, among those who were well, finished the night, and most were at rest at half-past nine o'clock.

Friday, September 9

Shortly after five o'clock, a.m., all sails were hauled in, the boatswain's whistle being heard all over the ship. The equinoctial gales had evidently set in, of which the breakfast seats, at half-past eight o'clock, gave ample proof. 'Oh! a mere cat's-paw', says the chief officer. 'Oh! thankee', replied Lockyer, exerting, among others, his very utmost to keep on his legs. The gale increased, and we were in the midst of a hurricane. Some half of the passengers did not leave their berths, and the head-aches were numerous and violent—one passenger especially, a Frenchman, who had No. 81, a berth above Fred. Lillywhite, did not leave it for sixty-five hours. In the depth of his distress the poor fellow kept shouting 'stewhart', although that functionary's hands were too full to attend to him immediately. Owing to the novelty of the situation, the groaning of some, the splash and thump of the waves against the sides of the ship, the howling of the wind, the flapping of the sails, and the incessant tramp of feet upon deck, sleep was quite out of the question; so there lay the unfortunate foreigner, with nothing to keep breath in his body, but warm water and sugar, a very poor sweetener in his cup of bitter annoyances. After his sixty-five hours rest, he attempted to land himself on the floor of the berth, endeavouring, first, to get a footing on the side of his fellow passenger's bunk, but, in so doing, the brass railings, on which he entirely depended for his safe landing gave way, and he was prostrated on the spot he had so industriously endeavoured to make; he was, consequently, rolled about and bruised, until the 'stewhart', which word he could only just utter, could make his appearance. Parr and Wisden were immediately opposite, and having heard the poor fellow's groaning, and the laughing of his partner, which could not be restrained, were witnesses of the sight that presented itself. Owing to the fearful pitching of the ship, Fred. Lillywhite could render no other assistance than to 'wake up' the steward, who 'Monsieur', was now totally unable to call for. The 'moving tale' had to be related regularly shortly before lunch, the poor Frenchman, with the warm water and sugar, being anxiously enquired after by other passengers, as well as by the Cricketers. One more circumstance occurred; after so lengthened a confinement below upon so poor and watery a diet, he, of course, became exceedingly weak, and could scarcely utter a syllable, and not being anxious to again trust to the brass rod, he obtained through his partner the presence of the steward; whereupon he was requested to bring 'the scales'; this being asked in such a feeble voice, coupled with the singularity of the term, that worthy had some difficulty in understanding him, and it was sometime ere the poor gentleman could clearly explain what he required. It turned out to be a ladder, that he might descend without the assistance of his deceitful

friend, the brass rod. Having safely landed, and still assisted by the
steward, he uttered the words, in a very low and plaintive voice, that
'it was von dam nuisance, and he vould not again shail on the vater!'
He was in fearful agony, and could not for the world manage to get
his legs into his pantaloons without assistance. This at length was accomplished by the steward, and the Frenchman managed to crawl a few
yards from his berth.

Among the Cricketers who could not get up at any time during the
day, were John Lillywhite, Caffyn, Jackson, and H. H. Stephenson,
and they were consequently visited, and the renowned fast bowler
wished much for a 'back door to Ollerton', his residence in Notts.
Caffyn 'would not venture to leave England again, under any circumstances; if he did, he would forfeit £100; and could not understand
however he was induced to ride over such waves, and see no land. Let
me once get back to Reigate, (his residence), and no more water, in
order to play Cricket Matches.' John Lillywhite was very ill, but quiet
in his berth, not being at all talkative; others were also bad, including
Grundy, Lockyer, and Diver, who were seldom seen. Julius Cæsar did
not fancy himself so much in the capacity of a sailor as that of a cricketer. Parr, Wisden, Hayward, Carpenter, and Fred. Lillywhite were 'as
being on shore'. The latter was invariably on deck, from midnight till
eight bells announced four o'clock, a.m.; when, after partaking of a cup
of coffee, either with the first or second mate, he retired to his berth
until lunch time. The sea this night was breaking on the deck most
fearfully, and for the first time one was reminded, 'of a life on the ocean
wave'. Diver played his part in his usual steady manner, but was not
quite 'at home', expecting, and, in fact, rather wishing to be 'bowled
out'. Stephenson was 'all abroad', but, nevertheless, often paid a visit
to 'his bunk'. Wisden was a thorough sailor, enjoying both meals and
his pipe of tobacco; he thought, when at his meals, that 'the waves
allowed too much for the break', and Parr thought their five ton
Leamington roller, and 'Charley', with their high priced mare,[1] might
take off the 'ridge and ferroll', and stop the 'bumping'. Singing was
attempted this, (Friday), evening, but owing to the condition of the
passengers, most of whom were suffering from sickness, the concert
was a failure. The chirping cricketers could neither lift up their heads
nor their voices, except in the most plaintive strain. All the worthy captain's persuasion could not get a ditty, either from Grundy, Caffyn, or

[1] 'Charley' is their Leamington man—the high priced mare cost 50 (s.)

Carpenter, who possessed the largest amount of vocal talent among the cricketers.

Saturday, September 10th

was a fine morning, and many faces were visible that had not been seen since Thursday. Met this morning, one of the 'renowned party', at half past eleven, a.m., who, for some unknown cause, had not been seen at the dinner table since Wednesday. We walked arm and arm by way of mutual support, for the ship was pitching most provokingly. In reply to my question, he said, 'he had not been at all poorly the evening before, but only went below for the purpose of arranging the contents of his "chest".' 'Ah, you mean "stomach",' said I. He then remarked, that he thought I looked white, (my appearance resembling Lockyer's colour in July,) but I expressed my fear that he was going to be ill again; to which he replied, 'do you think so?' and immediately re-tired to his berth, probably to complete the arrangements of the *chest* aforesaid.

We were this morning doing only six and a half knots, and up to this date Parr, Carpenter, Wisden, Cæsar, and Fred. Lillywhite were always seated at the dinner table; others nowhere to be found, only those who still occupied their unenviable seats on deck. Between one and two o'clock the gale abated, and some little time after the wind was more favourable, and the log found us going at nine knots an hour, having done altogether 560 miles. During the day, all, with the exception of Stephenson, seemed pretty well recovered, so much so as to venture upon smoking. The captain, ever ready to serve or entertain us, introduced a game called 'shuffle-board', in which the captain, the engineer, the purser, &c., played with us. The carpenter of the ship chalked the deck.

The game is played thus:—At the distance of eight or nine yards the players slide along the deck a piece of solid wood, about the size of a quoit, and those who get 100 up first wins. Many exciting games were played, to the temporary advantage of the officers of the ship, who, from their experience and knowledge of the 'roll of the vessel', had many points in their favour. Matches were made for champagne,— Moet's best, six shillings per bottle. Several games were very exciting, and often caused a large attendance of passengers of both sexes to wit-ness the contests. The purser and engineer were the two best players. This, Saturday afternoon, rain came on, which drove the players to the 'smoking' saloon, kindly placed at our disposal by the captain's orders, with his servant boy, 'Young Irish Jack', to attend upon us. Whist and loo constituted the amusements of the evening. The *Nova Scotian* Harmonic Society was afterwards effectively established. The smoking saloon was the hatchway, snugly arranged for the purpose; Mr W. Nicholson, an elderly and a very witty gentleman, from Sheffield, was unanimously voted as president, and which office he filled with the greatest efficiency. The time of meeting was to be half-past seven o'clock each evening, weather and stomachs permitting; a jolly Saturday evening at sea was spent. We drank in the most enthusiastic manner to the health of 'wives and sweethearts', and success to the noble ship. A vice-president having been appointed for the meeting on Monday evening, the party retired at eleven o'clock to their respective berths. Distance done during the last twenty-four hours, as per announcement of the log that day, was 160 miles. Much speculation took place each day during luncheon, about 'setting the log'; sweeps were got up, and the officers' opinions on the subject were anxiously sought by the 'cricketing novices', whose knowledge as to 'how the ship was going', was very limited. On

Sunday, September 11

arrangements had been made for church service, to be performed by the Hon. —— Rose, the Solicitor-General of Montreal. A fearful gale however again arose, which precluded the attendance of the passengers. The wind was favourable for Quebec, but it blew a hurricane and rained the whole of the day; when the ship pitched the screw was out of water, and the passengers were scattered about the deck, resembling, as Lockyer thought, very much 'a floorer at skittles'; this occurred so frequently during the day, that the 'nines' would have been quite common. At half past twelve o'clock the log announced that day 235 miles, notwithstanding the fearful rolling and pitching of the noble ship. During tea an exciting scene occurred. Caffyn in attempting to imbibe the fragrant beverage, had the cup shaken from his hand, and it was soon smashed below, falling over the banisters, with numerous others, among the berths. The head of an elderly gentleman came into such violent contact with a panel as to split it open, not the panel, but the head, he at the same time good humouredly remarking, that his friends would have some reason for saying that he was a little cracked. A passenger on entering the cabin-door seized hold of the first mate's chair, which was fixed; however, by his weight the chair gave way, and in endeavouring to save himself, he made fast very quickly, owing to a severe roll of the ship, to the captain's chair, placed in a similar position as the chief officer's; this piece of furniture also giving way, the two were dashed against the side of the ship, one being dangerously wounded, and the other very severely bruised. Lurch No. 1 carried away an immense quantity of cups and saucers; No. 2, caused the violent collision between the two gentlemen above alluded to; No. 3, cleared off knives, forks, and spoons; No. 4, plates, dishes, &c.; No. 5, pitched some pickled onions, which Jackson was trying to convey to his mouth into his lap; No. 6, caused a cup of tea, in the waiter's hand, to be deposited in Fred. Lillywhite's lap, having previously destroyed the arrangement of his locks.

Monday, September 12

was a lovely morning, all quite recovered, and did not want to be 'at home'; in fact, they repudiated the idea of being ill, or having been so. A very grand morning for shuffle-board; the matches made were numerous and interesting; Lockyer proved a victim; about 190 passengers mustered to witness the contests. Shortly after twelve the rain again coming on, put a stop to the play, and the 'talent' retired to the smoking saloon, where whist and loo predominated until the time arrived for the meeting of the Harmonic Society, which was a numerous one. A convivial evening was spent, after a very excellent spread of four courses had been done justice to. The repast was admirably served by the chief steward and his attentive assistants.

Mr Nicholson, the president, Diver, Grundy, and Carpenter were the principal contributors to harmony. The captain honoured the company with his attendance, and the above vocalists were rapturously applauded, so much so that the question of an extra gallery, and charge for admission was mooted by the managers. At the conclusion of the concert, each evening, the captain's health was drank with such evident enthusiasm, as to leave no doubt as to the soundness of the lungs of those present. A similar compliment the officers of the staff had never before witnessed on the briny ocean nor perhaps ever will again. The log to-day shewed 200 miles, having a head wind. On

Tuesday, September 13

the members had sufficiently recovered to call the roll at 9.15. The great Roman commander, Julius Cæsar, ordered all to muster, and discharged them for the day. An important shuffle-board match was to be played, and several pounds, as well as bottles of champagne depended upon the result. The contest was between the captain of the ship and Fred. Lillywhite, against Lockyer and John Lillywhite; a most exciting game ensued; the purser was sworn in as marker, and the whole of the passengers, including cabin and steerage, were present. The game proceeded, one heading the other, until the marker announced ninety-nine for White, (Captain and F. L.,) and ninety-five for Black. The latter had the last throw, and of course the odds were in their favour, they having the option of displacing their opponent's pieces, which were on the figures. The White side getting a three, caused their score to be 102, but Lockyer for Black removed Fred. Lillywhite's piece from the figure 3, and put his, (Lockyer's), partner's in its place, his own piece of wood going on the 'to on'. Here a dispute arose among the contending parties, as to whether White was not entitled to the game, having *first* obtained the required number of 100; Black, however, contended that their 'ten on', was obtained by the three he had made by that throw, but, there being no laws, and the circumstance never having happened before, to the recollection of any of the officers, it was agreed that the four should throw again, which resulted in Lockyer and John Lillywhite winning by one only. Shortly after this contest a heavy fog set in, with rain; in this melancholy condition the fog whistle was sounded every two minutes for the whole day and night. All at dinner to-day; concert at night. The log shewed that a distance of 192 miles had been accomplished in twenty-four hours.

Wednesday, September 14

The fog was much worse, and the whistle still exercising its disagreeable office, to the annoyance of the passengers. The wind was still dead against us, with a heavy sea. Saw an enormous number of porpoises; 'some tarnation good sport, I guess, there would be with a gun', said a Yankee captain, who was also a 'tarnation enquirer', being most inquisitive to know everything about the 'doings' of the English party, so that he might invest his dollars.

The doctor having been taken ill, the unfortunate Frenchman had now to go to him for advice. Distance now done was 1,400 miles. All remarkably well, and most of them were at whist during the afternoon. Log to-day 213 miles. A fearful gale again set in, and lasted through the next day.

Thursday, September 15

'Dreadful!' says Caffyn. 'Well, plenty of wind about', says Lockyer, but, 'not much land', replies John Lillywhite. Hayward, Parr, and others began to enquire of the captain, very seriously, whether it was really dangerous. During this afternoon Parr had unfortunately to encounter a kettle of boiling water in the smoking-saloon, which Cæsar, owing to a roll of the ship, had accidentally upset, he himself measuring his length on the floor of the cabin, among the glasses of grog, &c. This day will long be remembered by all the Cricketers. The gale commenced about seven o'clock in the morning. The waves were mountains high, and one passenger who had crossed the Atlantic sixty times, said he had never experienced it so rough. Again cups and saucers, basins, glasses, knives, spoons, &c., were equally distributed about the saloon, and passengers, were often under the disagreeable necessity of knocking each other down. Two sails were carried away to-day, and it was expected that a number of sailors engaged aloft would also follow. At 11.30, p.m. when all the passengers had retired, the engines were found to be damaged, and they were of course stopped; this fact, whether in our berths or out, would soon become known and felt by all; we accordingly made no progress whatever, having a head wind. It was not long before a great many passengers were anxiously making enquiries as to the amount of injury, but no one could get further information than, 'Oh! merely to try whether she will answer to her sails'; the trial, however, lasted three hours. Up to twelve o'clock this day we had done, during the twenty-four hours, 250 miles, altogether 1,650. We had no concert this evening, being totally unable either to sit, stand, walk, or do anything but to bring one's self to an anchor on deck, and stand the drenching. Some managed by dint of perseverance to remain in the smoking saloon, but the agonising expression of their faces would have been a fortune to Leech. At bed time numerous accidents occurred among the passengers; one young gentleman especially had the misfortune to break the bridge of his nose, by falling from the top to the bottom of the cabin stairs. The Captain was busily engaged among his men, giving strict orders.

Friday Morning, September 16

There was no improvement in the weather, and nearly the whole of us remained in our berths, for we were so very frequently disturbed in our rest, during the whole of the night, that we were scarcely disposed to turn out during the day. Towards evening the gale abated; we had only been doing three knots an hour. We saw during the day an immense quantity of porpoises, which, by their apparently unwieldy gambols, caused great amusement. At twelve the log shewed, from the last return, that we had only progressed eighty miles, making altogether, 1730; the afternoon was very cold, and was spent at whist. We now began to entertain the expectation of shortly sighting land. Concert in the evening, and all as jolly as sand-boys. Our worthy, respected, and talented president of the *Nova Scotian* Harmonic Society was in high glee on the occasion of our meeting, and having explained the cause of his absence, which appeared to be totally unavoidable, he immediately took his seat, and harmony was the prevailing feature, 'the Jew in the Corner' was the favourite. About eleven o'clock, p.m., that night, some two or three who remained on deck, had the pleasure, for the first time in their lives, of seeing some icebergs. Notwithstanding that these stupendous fabrics were beautiful objects for contemplation by day, they were particularly awkward customers to come in contact with at night. Though the chief officer himself stood at the bow, with his quick eye watching ahead, twice we came too close to them to be at all pleasant. The northern lights were splendid. On

Saturday, September 17

many of the passengers were awoke early in the morning, by the novel and startling cry of 'icebergs a-head! icebergs on the larboard bow!' and, 'icebergs on the beam!' and all ran hastily to the deck, and there discovered that they were in the midst of large numbers of them. We had an opportunity of forming an estimate of their size, for a large ship was sailing past one of the latter, and her main-top-gallant-mast only reached one-third the height of the berg. In calculating its total altitude, we did not forget to take into consideration the fact of there being at least eight feet of ice below water, for every foot above; some navigators go so far as to say there are eleven.

Concert this evening, which lasted until eleven o'clock, when, all but the sleepless ones retired, more particularly as land was expected to be seen in the early hours of the morn of

Sunday, September 18th

we were in a fog, but it having at length cleared away, the welcome cry of 'land, ho!' sent a thrill to all hearts. We borrowed the chief officer's glass, and saw in the distance the bleak, bluff, inhospitable-looking coast of Newfoundland, with its cliffs, and snow-covered mountains; this was our first glimpse of land for ten days, and we gazed upon it with rapture. Soon after we doubled Cape Race, and, by and by, the revolving light upon Cape Ray became visible. By seven o'clock in the morning we were off a lovely little island, and could see the green trees waving upon the heights. In another six or seven hours the captain ascertained that he had taken a wrong course, (owing to the fog and the compasses) going up the 'White bay', instead of the Gulf of St Lawrence. By this we lost fourteen hours, about 140 miles. It was, however, a lovely trip, water like a pond; there were rugged rocks on each side of us, water-falls, and a quantity of bears and wolves. We had arrived within about two miles of the end of the bay, before our error was discovered, we then made a turn round, and enjoyed very much the Sunday afternoon's excursion. All the passengers were in strong force this afternoon, both ladies and gentlemen, and the dinner-table had its full complement—the Cricketers especially doing ample justice to the contents of the table, knowing that all rough usage on the part of the sea was at an end, and that having once got the right course, and sighted Belle Isle, we should have 700 miles of river and splendid views, among which were conspicuous the White huts of the French settlers.

Monday, September 19

At three o'clock this morning we sighted the light-house of Belle Isle, and on we steamed at eleven knots an hour. At 6.30 we saluted the worthies who officiate in that lovely department. Plenty of icebergs. Passed the *North Britain*, bound for Liverpool, at five, p.m., another of the company's steamers, distance from us about 100 yards. Three hearty cheers were given from both ships as we passed, and on the side of the *North Britain* was written in chalk, '*Persia* not arrived'. This steamer left Liverpool on September 3rd, four days before us, so that she encountered a severe voyage. Early in the evening the Captain remarked, 'they are making pretty merry there in the smoking saloon, Whose voice is that, Tom?' 'The Jew in the corner', replied Lockyer; they have again voted him to the chair. Then Carpenter struck up with—

> There's a sweet little cherub that sits up aloft,
> To keep watch for the life of poor Jack.

which ditty was speedily followed by Grundy's performance of his celebrated 'Dolly Dobbs', by which time Captain Borland, and the engineer, were among the company, as well as several aristocratic passengers, who were anxious to spend some time with the English party, ere they separated at Quebec. The chorus of Grundy's song, was as follows, and is his own composition.

Wigel wagel, shigel shagel,
  Rigel ragel dom;
Rumpty doodle, tadel fudel,
  Didel, dadel dom.

A specimen of rhyming seldom met with on board a ship, and which here, as elsewhere, received an unusual amount of approbation. This evening was a very merry one, and the song, jest, and merry glee were kept going till past twelve o'clock.

Tuesday, September 20

Passed Anticosti island, which is half the size of England. The day was spent at shuffle-board and whist. The huts of the settlers were now far more numerous. Very dull day. Some Americans were talking of their revolvers to-day, and 'guessed' at many things.

Wednesday, September 21

The pilot landed at Father point, 11.20, a.m., we were then about 150 miles from Quebec. Fishing smacks of all descriptions were continually passing. Of the scenery up the river to Quebec, one cannot well have the assurance to attempt a description; pen cannot describe it; the brush cannot paint it; the poet and the artist must throw both away in despair; we never beheld anything so beautiful. The pure sky above us, the magnificent St Lawrence beneath and beyond, the loveliness of the shores, strewn with many a picturesque village, and exquisite little church; together with the bold, dark outline of the stately mountains on either side of us, formed a glorious picture that could be gazed on at once with wonder and delight.

Shortly before one o'clock on the morning of—

Thursday, September 22

we heard a hoarse, sullen, rumbling sound, like the roar of distant artillery, which broke the stillness of the morning; the heavy anchor had plunged into the blue depths beneath us, and the voyage was ended.

The English Cricketers' Trip, 1860

❖

Cricketers of my Time

JOHN NYREN

They who are acquainted with some of the remote and unfrequented villages of England, where the primitive manners, customs, and games of our ancestors survive in the perfection of rude and unadulterated simplicity, must have remarked the lads playing at a game which is the same in its outline and principle features as the consummate piece of perfection that at this day is the glory of Lord's, and the pride of English athletæ—I mean the one in which a single stick is appointed for a wicket, ditto for a bat, and the same repeated, of about three inches in length, for a ball. If this be not the original of the game of cricket, it is a plebeian imitation of it.

My purpose, however, is not to search into the antiquities of cricketing, but to record my recollections of some of the most eminent professors of my favourite pastime who have figured on the public arena since the year 1776, when I might be about twelve years of age. From that period till within a few seasons past, I have constantly been 'at the receipt of custom' when any rousing match has been toward; and being now a veteran, and laid up in ordinary, I may be allowed the vanity of the quotation, 'Quorum magna pars fui.'[1]

I was born at Hambledon, in Hampshire—the *Attica* of the scientific art I am celebrating. No eleven in England could compare with the Hambledon, which met on the first Tuesday in May on Broad-Halfpenny. So renowned a set were the men of Hambeldon, that the whole country round would flock to see one of their trial matches. 'Great men', indeed, 'have been among us—better, none'; and in the course of my recollections I shall have occasion to instance so many within the knowledge of persons now living, as will, I doubt not, warrant me in giving the palm to my native place.

The two principal bowlers on my early days were THOMAS BRETT and RICHARD NYREN, of Hambledon; the *corps de reserve,* or change-

---

[1] I learned a little Latin when I was a boy of a worthy old Jesuit, but I was a better hand at the fiddle; and many a time have I taught the gipseys a tune during their annual visits to our village, thereby purchasing the security of our poultry-yard. When the hand of the destroyer was stretched forth over the neighbouring roosts, our little Goshen was always passed by.

bowlers, were BARBER and HOGSFLESH. Brett was, beyond all comparison, the fastest as well as straightest bowler that was ever known: he was neither a thrower nor a jerker, but a legitimate downright *bowler*, delivering his ball fairly, high, and very quickly, quite as strongly as the jerkers, and with the force of a point blank shot. He was a well-grown, dark-looking man, remarkably strong, and with rather a short arm. As a batter, he was comparatively an inferior player—a slashing hitter, but he had little guard of his wicket, and his judgement of the game was held in no great estimation. Brett, whose occupation was that of a farmer, bore the universal character of a strictly honourable man in all his transactions, whether in business or in amusement.

Richard Nyren was left-handed. He had a high delivery, always to the length, and his balls were provokingly deceitful. He was the chosen General of all the matches, ordering and directing the whole. In such esteem did the brotherhood hold his experience and judgement, that he was uniformly consulted on all questions of law or precedent; and I never knew an exception to be taken against his opinion, or his decision to be reversed. I never saw a finer specimen of the thoroughbred old English yeoman than Richard Nyren. He was a good face-to-face, unflinching, uncompromising, independent man. He placed a full and just value upon the station he held in society, and he maintained it without insolence or assumption. He could differ with a superior, without trenching upon his dignity, or losing his own. I have known him maintain an opinion with great firmness against the Duke of Dorset and Sir Horace Mann; and when, in consequence of his being proved to be in the right, the latter has afterwards crossed the ground and shaken him heartily by the hand. Nyren had immense advantage over Brett; for independently of his general knowledge of the game, he was practically a better cricketer, being a safe batsman and an excellent hitter. Although a very stout man (standing about five feet nine) he was uncommonly active. He owed all the skill and judgement he possessed to an old uncle, Richard Newland, of Slindon, in Sussex, under whom he was brought up—a man so famous in his time, that when a song was written in honour of the Sussex cricketers, Richard Newland was especially and honourably signalised. No one man ever dared to play him. When Richard Nyren left Hambledon, the club broke up, and never resumed from that day. The head and right arm were gone.

Barber and Hogsflesh were both good hands; they had a high delivery, and a generally good length; not very strong, however, at least for those days of playing, when the bowling was all fast. These four were our tip-top men, and I think such another stud was not to be matched in the whole kingdom, either before or since. They were choice fellows, staunch and thorough-going. No thought of treachery ever seemed to have entered their heads. The modern politics of trickery and 'crossing' were (so far as my own experience and judgement of their actions extended) as yet 'a sealed book' to the Hambledonians; what they did, they did for the love of honour and victory; and when one (who shall be nameless) sold the birthright of his good name for a mess of pottage, he paid dearly for his bargain. It cost him the trouble of being a knave—(no trifle!); the esteem of his old friends, and, what was worst of all, the respect of him who could have been his *best* friend— himself.

Upon coming to the old batters of our club, the name of JOHN SMALL, the elder, shines among them in all the lustre of a star of the first magnitude. His merits have already been recorded in a separate publication, which every zealous brother of the pastime has probably read. I need, therefore, only subscribe my testimony to his uncommon talent, shortly summing up his chief excellences. He was the best short runner of his day, and indeed I believe him to have been the first who turned the short hits to account. His decision was as prompt as his eye was accurate in calculating a short run. Add to the value of his accomplishment as a batter, he was an admirable fieldsman, always playing middle wicket; and so correct was his judgement of the game, that old Nyren would appeal to him when a point of law was being debated. Small was a remarkably well-made and well-knit man, of honest expression, and as active as a hare.

He was a good fiddler, and taught himself the double bass. The Duke of Dorset having been informed of his musical talent, sent him as a present a handsome violin, and paid the carriage. Small, like a true and simple-hearted Englishman, returned the compliment, by sending his Grace two bats and balls, also *paying the carriage*. We may be sure that on both hands the presents were choice of their kind. Upon one occasion he turned his Orphean accomplishment to good account. Having to cross two or three fields on his way to a musical party, a vicious bull made at him; when our hero, with the characteristic coolness and presence of mind of a good cricketer, began playing upon his bass, to the admiration and perfect satisfaction of the mischievous beast.

About this time, 1778, I became a sort of farmer's pony to my native club of Hambledon, and I never had cause to repent the work I was put to; I gained by it that various knowledge of the game which I leave in the hands of those who knew me in my 'high and palmy state' to speak to and appreciate. This trifling preliminary being settled, the name and figure of TOM SUETER first comes across me—a Hambledon man, and of the club. What a handful of steel-hearted soldiers are in an important pass, such was Tom in keeping the wicket. Nothing went by him; and for coolness and nerve in this trying and responsible post, I never saw his equal. As a proof of his quickness and skill, I have numberless times seen him stump a man out with Brett's tremendous bowling. Add to this valuable accomplishment, he was one of the manliest and most graceful of hitters. Few would cut a ball harder at the point of the bat, and he was, moreover, an excellent short runner. He had an eye like an eagle—rapid and comprehensive. He was the first who departed from the custom of the old players before him, who deemed it a heresy to leave the crease for the ball; he would get in at it, and hit it straight off and straight on; and, egad! it went as if it had been fired. As by the rules of our club, at the trial-matches no man was allowed to get more than thirty runs, he generally gained his number earlier than any of them. I have seldom seen a handsomer man than Tom Sueter, who measured about five feet ten. As if, too, Dame Nature wished to show at his birth a specimen of her prodigality, she gave him so amiable a disposition, that he was the pet of all the neighbourhood: so honourable a heart, that his word was never questioned by the gentlemen who associated with him: and a voice, which for sweetness, power, and purity of tone (a tenor), would, with proper cultivation, have made him a handsome fortune. With what rapture have I hung upon his notes when he has given us a hunting song in the club-room after the day's practice was over!

GEORGE LEER, of Hambledon, who always answered to the title among us of 'Little George', was our best long-stop. So firm and steady was he, that I have known him stand through a whole match against Brett's bowling, and not lose more than two runs. The ball seemed to go into him, and he was as sure of it as if he had been a sand-bank. His activity was so great, and, besides, he had so good a judgement in running to cover the ball, that he would stop many that were hit in the slip, and this, be it remembered, from the swiftest bowling ever known. The portion of ground that man would cover was quite extraordinary. He was a good batsman, and a tolerably sure guard of his wicket; he averaged from fifteen to twenty runs, but I never remember his having a long innings. What he did not bring to the stock by his bat, however, he amply made up with his perfect fielding. Leer was a short man, of a fair complexion, well-looking, and of a pleasing aspect. He had a sweet counter-tenor voice. Many a treat have I had in hearing him and Sueter join in a glee at the 'Bat and Ball' on Broad-Halfpenny:

> 'I have been there, and still would go;
> 'Twas like a little heaven below!'

EDWARD ABURROW, a native of Hambledon, was one of our best long fields. He always went by the name of Curry; why, I cannot remember, neither is it of the utmost importance to enquire. He was well calculated for the post he always occupied, being a sure and strong thrower, and able to cover a great space of the field. He was a steady and safe batter, averaging the same number of runs as Leer. We reckoned him a tolerably good change for bowling. Aburrow was a strong and well-made man, standing about five feet nine; he had a plain, honest-looking face, and was beloved by all his acquaintance.

BUCK, whose real name was PETER STEWART, is the next Hambledon man that occurs to my recollection. He, too, played long field, and was a steady man at his post; his batting, too, reached the same pitch of excellence; he could cut the balls very hard at the point of the bat—nothing like Sueter, however—very few could have equalled *him*. Buck was a dark-looking man, a shoemaker by trade, in height about five feet eight, rather slimly built, and very active. He had an ambition to be thought a humorist. The following anecdote may serve both as a specimen of his talent, and of the unfastidious taste of the men of Hambledon. When a match was to be played at a distance, the whole eleven, with the umpire and scorer, were conveyed in one caravan, built for their accommodation. Upon one occasion, the vehicle having been overturned, and the whole cargo unshipped, Buck remained at his post, and refused to come out, desiring that they would right the vessel with him in it; for that 'one good turn deserved another'. This repartee was admired for a week.

The tenth knight of our round table (of which old Richard Nyren was the King Arthur), was a man we always called 'The Little Farmer'; his name was LAMBORN. He was a bowler—right-handed, and he had the most extraordinary delivery I ever saw. The ball was delivered quite low, and with a twist; not like that of the generality of right-handed bowlers, but just the reverse way: that is, if bowling to a right-handed hitter, his ball would twist from the off-stump into the leg. He was the first I remember who introduced this deceitful and teasing style of delivering the ball. When all England played the Hambledon Club, the Little Farmer was appointed one of our bowlers; and, egad! this new trick of his so bothered the Kent and Surrey men, that they tumbled out one after another, as if they had been picked off by a rifle corps. For a long time they could not tell what to make of that cursed twist of his. This, however, was the only virtue he possessed, as a cricketer. He was no batter, and had no judgement of the game. The perfection he had attained in this one department, and his otherwise general deficiency, are at once accounted for by the circumstance, that when he was tending his father's sheep, he would set up a hurdle or two, and bowl away for hours together. Our General, old Nyren, after a great deal of trouble (for the Farmer's comprehension did not equal the speed of lightning), got him to pitch the ball a little to the off-side of the wicket, when it would twist full in upon the stumps. Before he had got into this knack, he was once bowling against the Duke of Dorset, and, delivering his ball straight to the wicket, it curled in, and missed the Duke's leg-stump by a hair's-breadth. The plain-spoken little bumpkin, in his eagerness and delight, and forgetting the style in which we were always accustomed to impress our aristocratical play-mates with our acknowledgement of their rank and station, bawled out —'Ah! it was *tedious* near you, Sir!' The familiarity of his tone, and the genuine Hampshire dialect in which it was spoken, set the whole ground laughing. I have never seen but one *bowler* who delivered his balls in the same way as our Little Farmer; with the *jerkers* the practice is not uncommon. He was a very civil and inoffensive young fellow, and remained in the club perhaps two or three seasons.

With TOM TAYLOR the old *eleven* was completed. There were of course, several changes of other players, but these were the established picked set—the *élite*. Tom was an admirable field—certainly one of the very finest I ever saw. His station was between the point of the bat and the middle wicket, to save the two runs; but Tom had a lucky knack of gathering in to the wicket, for Tom had a licence from our old General; so that, if the ball was hit to him, he had so quick a way of meeting it, and with such a rapid return (for no sooner was it in his hand, than with the quickness of thought it was returned to the top of the wicket), that I have seen many put out by this manœuvre in a single run, and when the hit might be safely calculated upon for a prosperous one. He had an excellent general knowledge of the game; but of fielding, in particular, he was perfect both in judgement and practice. Tom was also a most brilliant hitter, but his great fault lay in not sufficiently guarding his wicket: he was too fond of cutting, at the point of the bat, balls that were delivered straight; although therefore, he would frequently get many runs, yet from this habit, he could not be securely depended on; and, indeed, it was commonly the cause of his being out. I have known Lord Frederick Beauclerck (certainly the finest batter of his day) throw away the chance of a capital innings by the same incaution—that of cutting at *straight* balls, and he has been bowled out in consequence. Taylor was a short, well-made man, strong, and as watchful and active as a cat; but in no other instance will the comparison hold good, for he was without guile, and was an attached friend.

The Young Cricketer's Tutor, 1833

❊

Cricket

THE REVD MR REYNELL COTTON, OF WINCHESTER

Assist, all ye Muses, and join to rehearse
An old English sport, never praised yet in verse:
'Tis Cricket I sing, of illustrious fame,
No nation e'er boasted so noble a game.
    Derry down, &c.

Great Pindar has bragg'd of his heroes of old—
Some were swift in the race, some in battles were bold;
The brows of the victor with olives were crown'd:
Hark! they shout, and Olympia returns the glad sound!
    Derry down, &c.

What boasting of Castor and Pollux's brother—
The one famed for riding, for boxing the other;
Compared with our heroes, they'll not shine at all—
What were Castor and Pollux to Nyren and Small?
    Derry down, &c.

Here's guarding and catching, and throwing and tossing,
And bowling and striking, and running and crossing;

Each mate must excel in some principal part—
The Pentathlum of Greece could not show so much art.
    Derry down, &c.

The parties are met, and array'd all in white—
Famed Elis ne'er boasted so pleasing a sight;
Each nymph looks askew at his favourite swain,
And views him, half stript, both with pleasure and pain.
    Derry down, &c.

The wickets are pitched now, and measured the ground;
Then they form a large ring, and stand gazing around—
Since Ajax fought Hector, in sight of all Troy,
No contest was seen with such fear and such joy.
    Derry down, &c.

Ye bowlers, take heed, to my precepts attend:
On you the whole fate of the game must depend;
Spare your vigour at first, now exert all your strength,
But measure each step, and be sure pitch a length.
    Derry down, &c.

Ye fieldsmen, look sharp, lest your pains ye beguile
Move close like an army, in rank and in file;
When the ball is returned, back it sure, for I trow,
Whole states have been ruined by one overthrow.
    Derry down, &c.

Ye strikers, observe when the foe shall draw nigh;
Mark the bowler, advancing with vigilant eye;
Your skill all depends upon distance and sight,
Stand firm to your scratch, let your bat be upright.
    Derry down, &c.

And now the game's o'er, IO victory! rings,
Echo doubles her chorus, and Fame spread her wings;
Let's now hail our champions all steady and true,
Such as Homer ne'er sung of, nor Pindar e'er knew.
    Derry down, &c.

Buck, Curry, and Hogsflesh, and Barber and Brett,
Whose swiftness in bowling was ne'er equalled yet;
I had almost forgot, they deserve a large bumper;
Little George, the long-stop, and Tom Sueter, the stumper.
    Derry down, &c.

Then why should we fear either Sackville or Mann,
Or rapine at the loss both of Boynton and Lann?—
With such troops as those we'll be lords of the game,
Spite of Minshull and Miller, and Lumpy and Frame.
    Derry down, &c.

Then fill up your glass, he's the best that drinks most.
Here's the Hambledon Club!—who refuses the toast?
Let's join in the praise of the bat and the wicket,
And sing in full chorus the patrons of cricket.
    Derry down, &c.

And when the game's o'er, and our fate shall draw nigh
(For the heroes of cricket, like others, must die),
Our bats we'll resign, neither troubled nor vex'd,
And give up our wickets to those that come next.
    Derry down, &c.

Privately printed, 1790

*

Amateurs and Professionals
1873–1962

CHRISTOPHER BROOKES

At first sight, it may seem slightly odd that the distinction between
'amateurs' and 'professionals' should have assumed such importance at
exactly the time that cricket was supposed to be taking on the mantle
of the 'national' game. But on closer examination it soon becomes clear

that this was not a coincidence. The separation of amateurs and professionals was closely linked to the emergence of county cricket as a major spectator attraction. For many at Lord's and elsewhere, the presence of a largely working-class audience and a growing number of working-class players conjured up a prospect too unpleasant to contemplate. To prevent a return to the situation which had existed during the heyday of the professional XIs, a way had to be found of limiting the impact of this new working-class presence. The answer was to create a pair of roles, one of which reaffirmed the rights and privileges of the gentleman while the other defined the duties and obligations of the artisan. Provided this were done, cricket could become 'popular' without reneging on its élitist traditions.

In its most extreme form, the separation of amateur and professional cricketers created two distinct worlds. Amateurs had their own dressing-rooms, ate apart and even entered the field of play by a separate gate. Their initials were placed before their names on the scorecard, while the professionals' came after. As well as playing, professionals were obliged to bowl to club members at the nets and to undertake a number of menial tasks around the ground. For example, before each match they helped roll the wicket and put out the boundary ropes or boards. On the field, particularly from the turn of the century, it was the same story. The individuality and flair of the amateur lent matches their spectacular appeal, while the application and consistency of the professional sustained their competitiveness. For the true amateur, cricket could never be more than an exciting and entertaining diversion, though this did not mean that he played any less hard. For the professional, however, it was his life. Every innings and every over were part of a career upon which his hopes and ambitions depended. Because of these pressures, professionals were held to be unsuited to the responsibilities of captaincy. At least, this has been the orthodox interpretation of Lord Hawke's famous plea, 'Pray God, that a professional should never captain England.'

Another way of looking at the traditional preference for amateur captains is to consider the background to the rise of the amateur–professional distinction. From 1900 onwards, most county cricketers were professionals and the majority of these came from a working-class background. This was also the period when labour (and Labour) first began to challenge the traditional authority of land and capital. Relationships between the working classes and the rest of society often reached the level of overt hostility. In industry, agriculture and even leisure, benevolent paternalism and the type of control it implied gave way to more rigid and often formal sanctions on the nature and frequency of inter-class relationships. In this atmosphere, the professional cricketer was affected more than any other sportsman. The triumphs of the touring XIs of the 1850s and 1860s were painfully fresh in the memories of those who had never appreciated that type of cricket, even less the popularity it had achieved. Players like Clarke, Parr, Jackson and Daft had become schoolboy heroes; it was unthinkable that the county professional should be allowed to steal the limelight to the same extent. To prevent a recurrence of this situation, the relationship between amateurs and professionals in first-class cricket had to be reconsidered. Prince Ranjitsinhji, one of the greatest players of the day, pointed the way to a more appropriate definition of the professional's role in an article he wrote in celebration of Queen Victoria's Diamond Jubilee.

A professional in former times was entirely the servant of his club, and in a servant's position. In the exhibition elevens, he became a free member of a club with equal rights with other members, and also in a way a public character, supported by and responsible to the public. These two aspects of a professional's position are worth remarking on with reference to this position of modern professionals playing for counties. A modern professional who represents his county is partly a servant of a club, partly a servant of the public, and partly a skilled labourer selling his skills in the best market. He may or may not have a local interest in the club he represents: that is another aspect of his case.

As Ranji suggests, the redefinition of the professional's role in first-class cricket had to embrace a return to something akin to the master–servant role of the eighteenth century, whilst at the same time paying lip-service to the demands of a free labour market and democracy. Once the desirability of a return to the pre-1846 *status quo* had been established, it was but a short step to argue that it was the amateur who, as captain, was best equipped to look after the interests of the game itself. Looked at in this light, any other justifications for amateur captains amount to self-fulfilling prophecies.

The ideals and values on which county cricket was founded bore the stamp of what has been described as the 'games-dominated tory-imperialism' of the late-Victorian ruling classes. Service in some far-off outpost of the Empire demanded self-discipline and obedience above all else. Cricket, contemporaries believed, encouraged the same qualities. The Hon. R. Grimston summed up the whole argument when he wrote,

I claim for our cricket ground and football field a share, and a very considerable share too, in the formation of the character of the English gentleman. Our games require patience, good-temper and perseverance, good pluck, and above all implicit obedience. It is no bad training for the battle of life for a boy to be skinned at football, or even given out wrongly at cricket, and to be able to take the affliction quietly and with good-temper, and in a gentlemanly spirit.

Nowhere has the relationship between cricket and qualities of character needed to succeed in the 'battle of life' been better expressed than Sir Henry Newbolt's oft-quoted poem, 'Vitae Lampada':

> There's a breathless hush in the Close tonight—
> Ten to make and the match to win—
> A bumping pitch and a blinding light,
> An hour to play and the last man in.
> And it's not for the sake of a ribboned coat,
> Or the selfish hope of a season's fame,
> But the Captain's hand on his shoulder smote—
> 'Play up! Play up! and play the game!'
>
> The sand of the desert is sodden red—
> Red with the wreck of a square that broke,
> The Gatling's jammed and the Colonel dead,
> And the regiment blind with dust and smoke.
> The river of death has brimmed his banks
> And England's far, and Honour a name,
> But the voice of a schoolboy rallies the ranks:
> 'Play up! play up! and play the game!'
>
> This is the word that year by year
> While in her place the School is set,
> Every one of her sons must hear,
> And none that hears it dare forget.
> This they all with joyful mind
> Bear through life with a torch in flame,
> And falling fling to the host behind—
> 'Play up! play up! and play the game!'

When Kent won the Championship in 1906, a contributor to the *National Review* went so far as to claim that it was 'Because they were imbued that that co-operative and sporting enthusiasm, that superb playing for the side and not for the self, that sacrifice of the individual for the team's sake . . . there is something Imperial both in the form of the Kent team and in the popular recognition thereof.'

In an age less secular than ours, it was perhaps inevitable that someone would trace a relationship between success on the cricket field and entry to the most sought-after élite of all:

Put your whole soul into the game, and make it your very life. Hit clean and hard at every loose ball. 'Steal a run' whenever you safely can, for the least bit of work that helps anyone nearer to God is blessed work, and gladdens the Captain's heart. Be alert and ready, and you will keep up your end. Lay on hard, and you will run up a grand score. And when 'time' is called you will 'bring out your bat', your conscience will say 'Well done', and those you have cheered and helped will say, 'A good man! Thank God for such an innings!' Aye, and when on the resurrection morning you come out of the pavilion, leaving your playing clothes behind you, and robed like your glorious Captain-King, you and all the hosts of God will see and understand your score as you cannot now, and your joy will be full as you hear the Captain, 'the innumerable company of angels' and the whole redeemed Church of God greet you with the words, 'WELL PLAYED, SIR!'

During the early years of county cricket, it was the ability to live up to the highest moral and ethical standards which justified the automatic selection of an amateur as captain. By the end of the last century, however, this rationale had begun to change. Qualities of personality were gradually replaced by an emphasis on social stature. Thus one famous journalist of the day argued that 'County sides are best led by a man socially superior to the professionals.' One might have supposed that such a blatant assertion of class differences would have offended those who retained a belief in the inherently democratic properties of cricket. But the 'amateurs for captain' lobby easily dispelled any doubts on this score:

Cricket will always be a gloriously democratic game, but in county cricket, the captain should always have some standing . . . the Leicestershire committee have selected as their captain, Sir Arthur Hazelrigg, who has never participated in a first-class match in his life, and was not even in his school XI, nor yet in a university trial.

For much of the last quarter of the nineteenth century, the argument over who should captain county teams continued alongside another, equally vitriolic, debate over the merits of county cricket itself. Its opponents were particularly active about the turn of the century. In 1902, for example, an anonymous author in *The World's Work* wrote, 'It will be an evil day for cricket when changes are made which are based upon the assumption that cricket depends more on gate-money than on the support of country gentlemen, more on its first-class fixtures than on the games at our country houses.' The debates began to overlap as soon as questions were asked about whether or not county cricket should continue to be run as a business. Critics of this trend claimed that financial pressures were undermining the moral and ethical basis of the game. Mr C. E. Green, a county cricketer himself and later President of the MCC, was one of the many who felt that 'County cricket has become too much of a business, and too much of a money-making concern. There is, I am afraid, very little real sport in it now as a game, and the feeling of *esprit de corps* which ought to exist in conjunction with real county cricket is fast disappearing.'

One aspect of county cricket worried Mr Green and his colleagues more than any other. By admitting the interests of a paying audience, they felt that it would not be long before the counties would be obliged to increase the numbers of matches they played and to field their best team as often as possible. At this point, much of the spontaneity of the game would be lost and, more seriously, many amateurs, finding that the game was occupying too much of their time, would be forced to withdraw completely. As it was, the true amateur, 'men like Lord Hawke, who have the taste and the means to go on playing first-class cricket strictly and purely as amateurs' were rapidly becoming a rare breed. In many cases, the amateur's only recourse was to accept some form of payment for his services. Though this broke all the rules of amateurism, by 1900 at least four different ways of justifying these payments had been devised. The first of these, the payment of hotel and travelling expenses, was 'a custom that is perfectly recognised, and perhaps in no way lowers the status of those who receive this help'; the second involved receiving expenses in excess of those actually incurred; the third receiving compensation for losses incurred by the player's 'business' in his absence, and the fourth receiving a regular salary as payment for services which he did not perform and never thought of performing—for example, as an 'assistant secretary'. 'The fault', as contemporaries saw it,

lies with the custom, the system approved by the custom . . . and it is a system that is an almost necessary result of the immense, the all-embracing demands on a man's time that first-class cricket makes . . . A man cannot make a decent pretence of attending to a business or a profession and yet play first-class cricket, excepting only in the case of professions like school-mastering and the law, with their long vacations, which nevertheless only give a man the necessary freedom at the latter end of the season.

Even more trenchant opposition came from those who saw in the attention given to county cricket 'a disease characteristic of all sections of society', a threat to England's economic growth and, above all, to her national security. So much emphasis on cricket at school instilled a false idea of the relative values of work and play. The result, many feared, would be a generation ill-fitted to hold their own with others whose education had been conducted on 'sounder' lines. Certainly games had a value—'when played in the right spirit, they are an admirable training for the more serious battles of life. They impress upon boys the necessity for patience, resourcefulness, and unselfishness as no other form of education could.' The danger was that in enjoying sport, boys tended to forget about work. And if the energies of the rich could be dissipated so easily, what was to stop the same malaise afflicting the rest of society? 'When the upper-classes thus magnify the importance of games it is not surprising that the lower class follow suit. It is obviously impossible for the great majority themselves to play games, but they can pay to look on—they cannot go to race-meetings, but they can bet in the streets.'

These, then, were the main criticisms being levelled at county cricket at the beginning of the present century. In view of the dangers inherent in this type of mass entertainment, it is not surprising to find that the professional cricketer, the paid seducer of the masses, soon came under heavy fire. In the opinion of another anonymous writer, this time in the *Saturday Review*,

They [the professionals] are for the most part a very well conducted and responsible body of men, and many of them would do credit to any station of life in which they were placed, but it must be remembered that cricket brings them into association with men of the best manners, and above all of unimpeachable character, whose traditions of the game, brought from school and college, make unfairness or even sharp practice as impossible to them as cheating at cards. It is from these men that cricket takes its tone in this country, and that tone is sustained by their determination to have no pecuniary reward of any sort in the matches in which they play.

To the bigots, and to those who were genuinely worried about the consequences of county cricket, a revival of country-house cricket seemed a much better idea. After all, it 'was truly amateur, people who wanted to play to win regardless of other aspects, would not find themselves again invited, nor again would fine exponents, but not so fine characters.'

For a while it looked as though their wishes might be granted. In Edwardian England, the organization of country-house cricket matches was as elaborate and as widespread as county games. One who played in many of these matches, Mr C. K. Francis, described how,

We used to stay in various country houses for about a week, playing two or three matches sometimes against very good teams. The cricket weeks at Preston Hall, Croxteth, Lees Court, Scarborough, Hothfield, Compton Verney, Wilton, Rood Ashton, Patshill, Northernwood, Escrick, Southgate, Vice Regal Lodge are only a few that I can remember out of the many.

But like so much of Edwardian England, country-house cricket never really recovered from the Great War. The problem was not so much changing tastes as a lack of players and spectators; in many cases, entire teams had died in the Flanders' mud. There were many who, like Alec Waugh, saw in the post-war world a rejection of everything they had valued and believed in.

It is sad to think how quickly that world has passed, and how effectively the machinery of our industrial system has already taken cricket for itself. Nyren's game is no longer entertained for a few. It is has become a part of the national life, and probably, if the Bolsheviks get their way with her, it will be nationalised with the cinema and the theatre and Association Football.

While country-house cricket was enjoying an Indian summer, county cricket was slowly consolidating its position as a popular, profit-making business. By the outbreak of war the virtues of the Championship were accepted by all but a few unrepentant diehards. Thanks largely to the efforts of no lesser figure than the captain of England, Lord Hawke, even professionals were now viewed with only the mildest suspicion. Rich and poor alike were now convinced of the value of the entertainment provided by the combination of amateurs and professionals in county cricket. When Ranji was asked 'What excuse is there for the existence in the community of a class that does nothing for the general welfare?', his answer summed up the new feeling:

Now I should be the last to say that a man of ability should give all his time to cricket. That would be quite absurd. But I do not think that the life of one who devotes himself to cricket is either altogether wasted or quite useless to his fellow-men, for the simple reason that cricket provides a very large number of people with cheap, wholesome and desirable entertainment.

The type of cricket envisaged by Ranji was far removed from the elegance and privacy of the country-house. It was more than a game, rather 'a huge institution, highly organised and demanding the entire time of those actively engaged in it'. Its home was a special arena, the county ground, its rationale was profit, and its motif spectacle. 'The county clubs were no longer glorified local clubs, but in addition business concerns. They provided popular amusement and good cricket: in fact they became what they are now—local in name and partly local in reality, but also run upon exhibition or, as I called it, spectacular lines.'

The factor that finally clinched the professional's place in county cricket was expediency. Only professionals had the time to acquire the skills and the consistency of application expected by first-class cricket's audiences, and only they were in a position to play as often as required:

The development of cricket has taught them [the audience] what the game can offer when played skilfully, and they would cease to come if matches were poor or if they sank to the average standard that can be attained by men who only played cricket occasionally and as a recreation. There are players who can come into first-class cricket from other pursuits, and make centuries. But players like Mr W. H. Patterson and Mr D. C. Steel are very rare indeed . . . I cannot see how cricket as a great institution for providing popular amusement, could, as things are now, exist without a class of people who devote themselves to it.

The indispensability of professionals, however, was not seen as a reason for granting them any special privileges. Even their most ardent supporter would not have claimed other than that they were good workers, reliable and honest, and as such worthy of preservation. In the words of another president of the MCC, Lord Harris,

A more discerning body of men it would be difficult to find. Their work, especially among those who do not rise to the top of the ladder, is very hard; they are always expected to be keen . . . It would be a distinct loss if such a body of men were to be withdrawn from our cricket fields . . . Therefore, let us by all means encourage them to persevere in their profession, so they may do their part towards the welfare of the community.

Others were less easily convinced. There was nothing intrinsically wrong in having professionals in a team: the danger was that they would carry the typically 'professional' approach to the game too far.

The skill with which Shrewsbury uses his legs upon a treacherous wicket is nothing short of miraculous. His comrade-at-arms, William Gunn, can also play the game very ably: so can Mr Stoddart and Mr Jackson—a fact not generally known. The difference between the play of the two amateurs and the two professionals is that the latter makes use of the method when it is not necessary to use it, whereas Stoddart and Jackson only do so where there is no other course open save wild slogging. It is not the use of the method, but the abuse of it, that can with fairness be criticised.

Off the field, the professional was treated rather in the same way as white emigrants to one of the colonies. Simplicity and honesty were the most sought-after qualities.

As the Championship became an established feature of the English summer, county cricket gradually acquired a set of values which incorporated a distinctive vision of the cricketer. According to this vision, professionals played cricket not for the money nor for the glory, but because they loved it. And, as Virgil once observed, 'Omnia vincit Amor'.

There is little doubt that most professionals were quite willing to accept this image of themselves. If it wasn't true, it was nevertheless comforting. For one thing, it helped to dispel any doubts about the wisdom of following such an unusual career or the adequacy of the rewards it promised. Not that many professionals at the turn of the century would have had second thoughts about either. From the young professional's point of view, the earnings of players like Hirst and Rhodes must have seemed more than attractive, and the gulf between potential earnings and the wages they actually received on joining a county —one pound a week, without a winter retainer—was bridged by their 'love of the game'. In his autobiography, Sir Jack Hobbs recalled how it was these considerations that persuaded him to try his hand at county cricket. After leaving the York Street Boys School in Cambridge, for which the fees were four-pence a week, he described how,

I began to feel deeply that there was a career in front of me. Apart from the glamour, the earnings of professionals in those days (*c*.1900) seemed to my mind very big. I had been told that they were getting five pounds a match. It seemed big money. But even the earnings paled in my imagination compared with the glory of playing for a county—say, for instance, for Surrey, the county of my hero Tom Hayward . . . Cricket had become with me an all-absorbing passion. It was my supreme ambition. It stuck out a mile in my mind before anything else. My father's occasional remarks about county players fired my hopes. Love of the game must have been bred in my blood.

Hobbs's recollections, full of youthful enthusiasm and ambition, contrast sharply with the sober reflections of another professional test cricketer, Fred Root of Worcestershire.

It is popularly supposed that there is quite a lot of money in first-class cricket. If there is, I have not found it. It is the worst paid of all professional games.

With Worcestershire, the recompense for 1,500 overs a year, which yield an average crop of over 150 wickets a season, and 47 innings producing between 800 and 1,000 runs for twenty weeks' cricket, brought in under £300. During the period of depression it was suggested that the Worcestershire professionals should agree to a ten per cent reduction, and other clubs were circularised as to the amount of wages paid to their professionals. I was informed that at least four other counties paid less than Worcestershire, and several other counties paid the same rate. Out of this, hotel accounts for away matches, taxi fares, flannels, and cricket equipment have to be paid by the professional.

Root's opinion of the cricket career was undoubtedly influenced by the fact that, in his case, it involved a lot of hard graft and paid less well than he had anticipated. Even allowing for a slight element of bias, his account leaves one in little doubt that, between the wars, the average professional must have found it hard to make ends meet. Under these circumstances, many players must have considered the prospect of a benefit with an urgency born of despair. Yet Root goes on to quote examples of professionals actually turning down the offer of a benefit. One player, in what was to be his last year with Worcestershire, turned down the chance of a second benefit with the words, 'No, thank you, I can't afford it.' The truth of the matter, as Root went on to explain, was that risks involved in taking a benefit often outweighed the profits that might be expected.

A beneficiary has to bear the whole of the expenses of both the home and away fixture of his club for the match he decides upon. He is not given an absolutely free choice of the fixture, the most profitable generally being denied him. Wages for players, umpires, gatemen, policemen, scorers, and so on, have to be paid, as well as the travelling expenses. It is not always possible to insure against the vagaries of the weather.

The belief that, on retiring, a professional cricketer seldom found any difficulty in getting a good job was by the end of the nineteenth century firmly entrenched as part of the game's mystique. For many players, the prediction turned out to be true: for the county secretaries who were responsible for employing the budding professionals, it was always convenient. What had started as little more than a hopeful promise gradually acquired the mantle of inevitability.

A first-class cricketer, whose character is good, can rely with certainty upon obtaining on his retirement from county cricket a suitable and well-paid berth, which he will be capable of filling for many years. Frequently, too, their fame and popularity help cricketers to find good businesses upon their retirement, when usually they have a certain amount of money, gained from their benefit match, to invest.

In general, the professional's own view of his prospects in county cricket and on retirement was noticeably more restrained than those of his employer. Sir Jack Hobbs, for instance, was under no illusion about the difficulties that a professional was likely to face: 'There is no royal road to success in cricket. It is a rough, hard road, and only a few can win through.' His advice to young players contained a sobering reminder of the unpredictability of cricket:

Seek first a position in some business so that there may be something to fall back on in the case of failure at cricket or dislike of it . . . Cricket is too precarious. It is all right, if you can rise to the top and get the plums. Otherwise, it is a bare living for a few years, with nothing at the end; one saves a few pounds in the summer and spends them in the winter.

Many people today might find it difficult to accept that Hobbs's forebodings were not just a trifle exaggerated. His contemporaries, however, knew only too well how realistic they were. Consider what Fred Root had to say on this score:

Many of the cricket heroes of the past are getting what consolation they can out of their memories—and an unskilled job at a pittance of a wage. During their innings they played life's game according to the rules of the circles in which, by unavoidable circumstances, they were compelled to enter. But dress suits are superseded by, in some cases, the corduroy of the pauper: and the presents and souvenirs have disappeared into the clutches of rich uncles owning shops denoted by the sign of the three brass-balls.

It is an interesting comment on the professional's position in county cricket that so few publicly expressed their grievances during their playing days. By and large criticism was confined to Proust-like reflections in autobiographies, and even in this context it was often left to the reader to draw his own conclusions. Tom Dollery, a professional who captained Warwickshire shortly after the Second World War, was content for the most part just to describe the conditions under which professionals worked, but the implication cannot be missed:

At Edgbaston before the war the professionals were crowded into one small room and the amateurs—sometimes only one amateur—had the use of a dressing room twice the size. While accommodation was being wasted like that, the members of the professional staff who were not actually in the team for the match had to change in any nook they could find before they went out to bowl.

The distinction between amateurs and professionals remained a feature of first-class cricket until 1962. Over the years many players, amateurs and professionals, had resented the separation that it fostered, though few had said so openly. On one famous occasion, Patsy Hendren contrived to ridicule the whole arrangement by refusing an invitation from the ten amateur members of an MCC team and walking alone through the professional's gate on to the pitch at Lord's. By 1950 many of the most abrasive aspects of the distinction had disappeared—at Lord's for instance, all players have lunched together since shortly after the end of the Great War—and by the time they were formally dropped 'amateurs' and 'professionals' belonged to history.

But when all is said and done, the most amazing feature of the distinction between amateurs and professionals was its durability. Greated in a world of privilege and privacy, it survived the shattering effects of two world wars, the invention of the telephone, radio and television and the introduction of universal franchise and trade unionism. Nothing, it seemed, could upset the equilibrium of social relationships in first-class cricket. Nothing, that is, except the economic circumstances that finally led to the disappearance of the amateur.

English Cricket, 1978

❋

What Came of Wearing a Forester Ribbon

W. E. W. COLLINS

Report of the rather vexatious incident which occurred to a lady, upon the occasion of a visit to Rome in Carnival time.

The following morning we were at Civita Vecchia. I was now informed that upon landing we entered the States of the Church, and all our luggage would have to pass through the Custom-house. As we had no servant with us, our English friends kindly suggested that our boxes should go with theirs under the charge of their Italian servant, who would look after them at the Custom-house and meet us at the station. Poor Rozelli, he little knew what he was undertaking. You must remember it was just after the time when Garibaldi had been fighting so hard for Italy, and the Pope had found his temporal dominions considerably reduced. There was consequently a very bitter feeling throughout the States of the Church against all Italians who were not the subjects of his Holiness, and no sooner did any one set their foot in his dominions than they became liable to the closest watching, and imprisonment for the slightest offence of a political nature. We were at the station, and had taken our tickets for Rome, when the elder of our two English friends came to me in a state of great agitation, and asked me almost fiercely what I was doing with the Italian tricolour in my box?

I was utterly at a loss to comprehend his meaning, and said I knew nothing about any Italian tricolour, and was quite sure I had no such thing. 'Yes,' he said, 'you have some kind of a loose white dress in your box, such as is worn at the Carnival, and it has Garibaldi's ribbon all over it.'

I thought for a moment. 'Can it be my dressing-gown?' I said, a light beginning to dawn upon me; 'that is trimmed with a red, white, and green ribbon, but that has nothing to do with Garibaldi; it is nothing in the world but the ribbon of the Free Foresters' Cricket Club: I had it made to wear at a cricket match, and thinking it a pity to throw it away had it transferred to my white dressing-gown. You surely cannot mean to say that this has given offence?'

'Given offence!' he replied; 'we may think ourselves very lucky we are not now all under arrest: my man Rozelli has been nearly frantic, for he of course knew nothing about it, and the very first thing that came to view when your box was opened was this "rebel" ribbon. Of course the authorities inquired what was the meaning of it, and all poor Rozelli could do was to shake his head and say, "I am innocent." He has been taken to the Consul about it now, and I have no idea how it will all end.'

At this moment Rozelli appeared, and looking reproachfully at me, began a long story in which he told us how we had narrowly escaped imprisonment, but that being English had saved us. The ribbon had been torn off the dressing-gown by the Custom-house officials and kept there; and a little jacket which they could not strip, the ribbon being rather tightly sewn on, they had also kept.

The man Rozelli, it seemed, was a Roman by birth, and had years ago been in the service of the celebrated Lola Montez. He was well known to the police, and was closely watched the whole time his master remained in Rome. For ourselves, as soon as we got over the annoyance, we thought it a great joke, but I do not think Rozelli ever understood it. I believe we were all more or less watched by the police during our stay in Rome. It was the Carnival week, and I had an opportunity of seeing the long white wrappers that were worn to keep off the *confetti*, and for one of which my poor innocent dressing-gown had been taken, it being supposed by the Custom-house officers that I was taking it to Rome to wear at the Carnival to create a demonstration in favour of Garibaldi. Little did the Free Foresters dream when they fixed upon their colours what a foolish adventure they would cause! I was told I could have my ribbon given back to me at Civita Vecchia on leaving, but when after a week of sightseeing and gaiety we retraced our steps, I said to James, 'No, we will not ask for it; let us give them the trouble of taking care of it *for ever*.' And so I suppose the Free Foresters' ribbon still remains in the Custom-house.

Annals of the Free Foresters, 1895

*

The Song of Tilly Lally

WILLIAM BLAKE

O, I say, you Joe,
Throw us the ball!
I've a good mind to go
And leave you all.
I never saw such a bowler
To bowl the ball in a tansy
And clean it with my hankercher
Without saying a word.

That Bill's a foolish fellow;
He has given me a black eye.
He does not know how to handle a bat
Any more than a dog or a cat;
He has knock'd down the wicket,
And broke the stumps,
And runs without shoes to save his pumps.

Songs from an Island in the Moon, c.1784

*

Wicket Keepers

G. D. MARTINEAU

'Have me to bowl, Box to keep wicket, and Pilch to bat—and then you'll see cricket!' So runs old William Lillywhite's famous definition of the game at its highest moment; and this recognition of the wicket-keeper's place in the eternal duel may be regarded as significant of the march of events. It is also a fitting tribute to Thomas Box, who has been classed as a pioneer of wicket-keeping.

This little man from Ardingly, in the old forest country of Sussex, with his broad face and side-whiskers, represents a distinct advance towards the modern specialist wicket-keeper. He was really the first of his kind, since he would not have won a regular place in a first-class side for anything but his wicket-keeping.

When he appeared for Sussex in 1828, at the age of nineteen, the three round-arm 'Tests' with England had been played, and the first bowling revolution had arrived at its parliamentary stage. In that year, the legislators cautiously allowed the bowler to raise his hand elbow-high, and the early pictures of Box doubtless belong to the period following this amendment. He stands against a background of trees, river, and downland, as unprotected as Ned Wenman, and in much the same attitude, except that his hands are some inches above the bails. At a later phase we see him standing upright (but in a moment of repose), with something of a middle-aged 'spread', yet still possessing a good crop of hair and side-whiskers, in the act of pulling on a pair of stout gloves, his legs encased in knee-length pads. A neat little windmill, topping a distant down beyond long-leg, assures us that the scene is still Sussex.

There are similarly divergent descriptions of Box's methods, and it may be assumed that he developed them in the light of experience and according to the changes in bowling, particularly after 1835. To begin with, then, Box stood nearly upright, set himself to look after the straight and off balls, and left the leg deliveries to long-stop. There were famous long-stops in those days, and for some time afterwards. The little Wykehamist, Charles Ridding (1825–1905), long-stopped brilliantly against the fastest bowling for some years before he entered the

Church. Jemmy Dean, when not bowling, filled this place as well as any man in England. The chief Sussex bowlers of Box's early days— Lillywhite, who 'rose well to the bails', Broadbridge, and Dean—were not fast, and the mighty George Brown was past his dog-destroying best; but presently there came the midget Johnny Wisden, with his vast break-back (he made his boyhood's home with Tom Box on his father's early death), and when Box kept for the Players, he had to take Sam Redgate's shooters as well as the teasing twists of Hillyer.

He was looked upon as the Players' regular wicket-keeper between 1834 and 1853, being generally preferred to Wenman—and when William Clarke made his first appearance in the match in 1846, he had an opportunity of appreciating Box's value behind the stumps, which led subsequently to his inclusion in Clarke's famous All England XI.

In the well-known picture of 1847, the team's wicket-keeper is William Dorrinton (1809–1848), a tailor from Town Malling, whose batting was an additional asset; but he had very little chance, with Wenman as well as Box to be considered, and his appearances in representative matches usually meant that the other two were incapacitated.

Tom Box, moreover, had begun to improve his batting, developed a smart late cut, was often good for twenty or thirty, and had made 79 for Sussex against the bowling of Alfred Mynn when he was assisting the MCC and Ground. Box once had the misfortune to run out William Clarke, who, wrathfully deciding that he 'would not go in within ten of the fool', opened the next innings himself and put his wicket-keeper in just above the byes.

It was during his travels with the All England XI that Box fell a victim to the sometimes cruel buffoonery of George Parr's elder brother, Sam, who was an incorrigible practical joker.

It was well known that Tom Box's hair was one of his little vanities, and on this occasion he allowed himself to be persuaded to place himself in the hands of a local barber for a trim. Sam Parr had already been to the shop and informed the man that he was in charge of a gentleman suffering from a disease of the brain, whose hair should be cut as short as possible in the hot weather.

He accompanied Box to the shop, and kept him diverted with conversation, so that, despite frequent cautions against taking too much off, the barber, urging his client to keep calm, gave him something like an old-fashioned regimental hair-cut.

The author of the jest slipped away towards the end of the proceedings, and, when Tom Box beheld the disaster in a mirror, he raged so alarmingly that the barber, perceiving that he was now alone with a man reported to be mentally unstable, fled for his life.

Though he appeared so regularly against the Gentlemen and toured up and down with Clarke's All England team, playing in as many as 43 matches in 1851, Box's most faithful service was given to Sussex, and, for 24 consecutive seasons (1832–1855), he did not miss one of the county's engagements, ending the latter summer with a bag of 58 victims—catches and stumpings equally divided. His last appearance for the county was in the following season.

In his later years, it was remarked that he had abandoned the uprightness of the older wicket-keepers and was developing something more like the stooping attitude of the 'moderns'. His keeping seems to have been of the unspectacular and workmanlike order; he took lessons from Jenner in style and elegance of movement, without aspiring to Jenner's mobility. Denison said that he was 'as much superior to any other wicket-keeper as was Mr Jenner in the years preceding his advent'.

As an expert in the keeping of cricket grounds, Tom Box, while still an active player, was manager of Ireland's Gardens, Brighton, originally the ground laid out by George IV when Prince of Wales. A smart-looking little man, with florid complexion, light hair, and whiskers, he was a well-known figure in the town, where he kept both cricket grounds and hotels. After the lease of Ireland's Gardens had expired in 1847, he became proprietor of the new Brunswick Ground, close to the sea at Hove, which he kept so well that, on its acquisition by the builders in 1872, the excellent turf was removed to the present County Ground.

Old Tom Box had left Brighton for London before this and taken over the King's Head, at the top of Bear Street, Leicester Square, which rapidly became the resort of cricketers. He ended his days in Cadogan Square, on the ground opened in 1872 by the brothers Prince, whose ignorance of cricket must indeed have been shocking to the old wicket-keeper after a lifetime devoted to the game.

The Valiant Stumper, 1957

*

The Catch

ALFRED COCHRANE

Stupendous scores he never made,
But perished ever with despatch:
No bowling genius he displayed,
But once, in a forgotten match,
   He made a catch.

No doubt a timely stroke of luck
Assisted him to do the trick;
He was at cover, and it stuck:
It travelled fairly low and quick—
   The kind that stick.

His friends the proud achievement classed
As fortune's most eccentric whim,
And ere a week or two had passed
The memory of the catch grew dim
   To all but him.

To all but him, for he relates,
With varying ornament and phrase,
The story to the man who waits
Unwilling in Pavilion ways,
   On rainy days.

The catch has grown in splendour now—
He had a dozen yards to run;
It won the match, as all allow,
And in his eyes there blazed the sun,
   And how it spun.

Life of old memories is compact,
And happy he for whom with speed
Blossoms a gorgeous tree, where fact

Has planted, in his hour of need,
  A mustard seed.

Collected Verse, 1903

*

Missed!

P. G. WODEHOUSE

The sun in the heavens was beaming;
The breeze bore an odour of hay,
My flannels were spotless and gleaming,
My heart was unclouded and gay;
The ladies, all gaily apparelled,
Sat round looking on at the match,
In the tree-tops the dicky-birds carolled,
All was peace till I bungled that catch.

My attention the magic of summer
Had lured from the game—which was wrong;
The bee (that inveterate hummer)
Was droning its favourite song.
I was tenderly dreaming of Clara
(On her not a girl is a patch);
When, ah horror! there soared through the air a
Decidedly possible catch.

I heard in a stupor the bowler
Emit a self-satisfied 'Ah!'
The small boys who sat on the roller
Set up an expectant 'Hurrah!'
The batsman with grief from the wicket
Himself had begun to detach—
And I uttered a groan and turned sick—It
Was over. I'd buttered the catch.

Oh ne'er, if I live to a million,
Shall I feel such a terrible pang.

From the seats in the far-off pavilion
A loud yell of ecstasy rang.
By the handful my hair (which is auburn)
I tore with a wrench from my thatch,
And my heart was seared deep with a raw burn
At the thought that I'd foozled that catch.

Ah, the bowler's low querulous mutter,
Point's loud, unforgettable scoff!
Oh, give me my driver and putter!
Henceforward my game shall be golf.
If I'm asked to play cricket hereafter,
I am wholly determined to scratch.
Life's void of all pleasure and laughter;
I bungled the easiest catch.

Pearson's Magazine, 1908

✳

Cricket as a Sport

DR W. G. GRACE

Any article on Cricket as a Sport would not be complete without touching upon the advantages and disadvantages of the game. I may begin my remarks by saying that it is always a pleasure for me to emphasise the good qualities of any sport I love or follow, and that it is particularly so in the case of Cricket, with which I have been so closely associated for so many years;—a sport which has so few drawbacks in proportion to its advantages. It is not the first time by a great many that I have thought over the merits of Cricket and other sports, weighing carefully all that could be advanced in favour of them, and I hope I shall be pardoned for saying that somehow or another I could come to no other conclusion than that Cricket, while universally admitted to be our national game, is also the King of games, in that it holds its sway over its followers from boyhood to old age. Boyhood, manhood, and old age are the three stages we set up in human life, and it is the peculiar influence Cricket has on them that to my mind gives Cricket as a Sport a position above all others.

Let us take the first stage, that of boyhood. A boy may play many games that he will benefit from physically, but I question whether he can play any one that has the same educating influence physically and mentally as Cricket. 'Train up a child in the way he should go', is one of the oldest of our sayings applying to the moral education of a boy. How rarely do we find the moral education of a boy as fully considered as the physical in any branch of sport? There are games innumerable in which the physical element is almost the only one that has proper attention. Some of them, indeed, have a weakening rather than a strengthening influence morally. The boy begins the game without knowing what is said in favour of it or against it. Physical enjoyment and development are the only points aimed at, and for lack of a judicious teacher he unconsciously develops selfishness and conceit. It may be in a game such as Lawn Tennis where luck has little or no foothold, and science is sure to tell. The boy is fighting for his own hand, and if his skill be slightly greater than his opponent's, the result is a certainty for him. A boy half fifteen better in play than another at Lawn Tennis can be relied upon to win nine times out of ten, and the boy knows it. There is not the glorious uncertainty about it that there is in Cricket, and, as I have said, for lack of a judicious teacher, the boy is apt to develop selfishness and conceit.

Cricket is its own teacher, whether the boy be batting, bowling, or fielding, but more especially in batting. The boy cannot depend on scoring largely two days, or two matches, in succession, and as likely as not sees the hero of the hour to be one of whose capabilities he was inclined to think poorly. His success with the ball is almost as uncertain—to-day, he can do great things; to-morrow, he can do but little. In the field it is nearly the same. Usually most brilliant, he unaccountably mis-fields a ball or drops a catch which converts a possible victory into defeat for his side.

There is no better lesson to be learnt in any form of sport or work, for it is the lesson that leads to modesty, and charity of speech and thought of others. Self is forgotten, when success does not attend the boy's effort, and his only wish is that another will do what he hoped to do, and bring victory to his side. Ill-luck may dog his footsteps for weeks at a time, but he has learned another lesson which will be invaluable to him for all time in the more serious affairs of life, that of patience. And the charm of the whole thing is that he has learned all of those lessons from the game itself. Growth of mind, growth of heart, and growth of body go together, and after a year or two's experience we have the modest, manly and self-reliant cheerful type of boy we like to associate with English boyhood. He goes into the battle of life with an equipment which will enable him to fight successfully under most conditions, for he has the wherewithal that is a passport to all sorts and conditions of men. He has played with all sorts and conditions of boys (for Cricket is not a sport that is confined to high or low, rich or poor), and he has learned to respect his comrades whatever their social position may be, for they, too, have developed the qualities that command respect and win confidence.

I know of no game in which a father can so safely leave his boy to himself as the game of Cricket, for his all-round education goes on of itself year after year; but I know a few that very quickly develop priggishness, conceit, and self-sufficiency. Cricket is a healthy, invigorating sport, for is it not as a rule played in sunny weather and on a green field? The element of danger is of the slightest, and we rarely hear of a serious accident to a player, either in practice or in a match. The accidents that have occurred have been mostly at practice, and very often caused by the careless crowding of spectators. Years ago in practice, low short nets were very much in use, and it was nothing short of a wonder that accidents were not more numerous; to-day, long high nets are in use on most good grounds, and the possibility of an accident is very small.

An additional inducement to the playing of the game is the absence of gambling amongst the players. Professionalism as a rule means gambling in all kinds of sport; but Cricket, though it has a greater number of professional players to-day than any time in its history, is above suspicion in that respect, and is worthy of the support of every right thinking person. There is no great difficulty in the way of playing it on the score of expense, such as applies to some other games and sports. The poorest boy has every encouragement to pursue it, for Clubs are in existence everywhere in town and country that include all classes. Village Cricket, though seemingly overshadowed by County and more important Cricket, has still its old charm; and the healthy rivalry which made the game so dear to myself thirty years ago is just as strong to-day in every village in almost every county in England. So far what I have said is in favour of the game: to my mind there is little to be said against it, in fact the only drawback I can discover is the time it takes up, which is certainly more than at any other out-door game.

Compared with the exercise to be obtained in other games I grant that the indifferent player is somewhat unhappily situated at Cricket, but it must not be forgotten that he has his thrills of excitement also, and that a small score to him is of as much moment as a large score to the proficient player. Then, there comes the large score occasionally; an achievement which is never forgotten, and creates the hope of others to follow. Hope springs eternal in the batsman's breast; the poor, despised batsman rises to the occasion now and then, and whether it be in Village Cricket, County Cricket or International Cricket, he may achieve something that is a pleasant memory for the rest of his life. His superior nerve perhaps enables him to do something that superior skill alone cannot do, and on a day of small scores his double figure is worth a century. That is a point I have not yet touched upon, the power of nerve that can be cultivated to a certain extent, without which nothing great can be accomplished in any sport. There are few Cricketers, however great their skill, who can walk to the wicket without a tremor at a critical stage of a match, but the history of former achievements flash before them and by sheer strength of will they keep it under.

The other day I came across the following words by an enthusiastic Golf player; — 'Of all the games which the idleness of man has invented, none requires such absolute concentration of sense and mind, and such steady nerve as Golf. Equability of nerve and pulse is much more essential in it than in the comparatively clumsy game of Cricket.' I have said somewhere else that 'wherein lies the charm of Golf I know not', for my practical experience of it has been limited, but for any player, however eminent, to take upon him to make such a statement means that he can know little of the nerve required for a great match at Cricket. I can only assume that the writer has never gone through the stages of nervousness which are common to all Cricketers, possibly he has never played the game. Nerve, I have no doubt, is required in playing Golf as well as other games, but as the Golf player is as a rule fighting for his own hand, the nerve required cannot be so great as that of the batsman who has to think more of his side than himself at a critical moment.

When we come to the manhood stage, Cricket, as a sport, loses none of its charm. Experience and judgment have ripened, and all the fine points of the game are more noticed. Mental power has grown and the weakness and strength of an opponent have to be divined before anything great can be done. The old habit of playing by rule has to be abandoned, and the varying conditions of light and weather have all to be carefully considered. The mental enjoyment is now as great as the physical, and every ball bowled, and every ball played, is full of meaning. Defeat is more keenly felt, just as victory is more enjoyed. We are now at the stage when friendships are made which last for life. Sport is the friendship-maker, and as Cricket is spreading yearly, players have no difficulty in making friends wherever they go. No better passport of introduction can any young man have than his skill and enthusiasm for the game.

If we but think for a moment of the spread of the game in Australia, India, Ceylon, and America, what I have just said will appeal to every cricketer. He has only to go to any one of them with his cricketing abilities to receive a hearty welcome, and a helping hand in other matters. Or take the case of a clergyman or a member of the medical profession in the country. What better means can there be devised for bringing either into close and friendly contact with the villagers than playing the game. Not only does he receive the respect due to his position, but he also obtains a sympathy that is beneficial professionally, and an insight into their ways and habits that without playing the game could not be obtained in a lifetime. Cricket is the sport to create kindly feeling, and all the little weaknesses and eccentricities which are more or less peculiar to us all are forgotten.

When we come to Old Age, there is perhaps another story to tell as far as playing the game is concerned, although I cannot help thinking a great many give it up long before there is occasion to. But after all, when old age comes creeping on, there is still the part of spectator and critic to be played. The next best thing to playing the game is seeing our boys play it. Perhaps we do not all have boys, or the duties of life may have scattered them over the face of the earth; but we have all the imperishable delight implanted in our hearts of watching a close and exciting contest. Twenty years ago on some of the most important grounds in England the spectators could be counted by hundreds. But what a change has taken place! Given a good match and a sunny day and you will see that the crowd has increased to thousands. Most of them have played the game at some time or another with more or less proficiency, and if you were to ask them whether the old love for the game had died down with the increase of years, they would tell you, on the contrary, that it had grown, and that the measure of delight watching the game was almost as great as that experienced in playing it. In their boyhood and manhood they had cultivated and acquired something more than the proficiency to play the game. They had cultivated and acquired a love for a green field, a sunny day, and an exciting contest that still gives them delight, and will continue to do so as

long as eyes can see and heart throb to the strong fellow-feeling which
pervades all true sportsmen.

The Cricket Annual, 1892

∗

Two Points of View

WILLIAM DEWAR (EDITOR)

Oxford

CAPTAIN — L. C. H. PALAIRET, ORIEL COLLEGE
TREASURER — H. M. BURGE, UNIVERSITY COLLEGE
SECRETARY — W. H. BRAIN, ORIEL COLLEGE

Notwithstanding that no fewer than seven old Blues were at their
command, the Oxford authorities were hardly satisfied with the strength
of the eleven, and naturally turned to the Freshmen's matches, in anticipation of finding some material with which to strengthen it. Among
these, however, as events subsequently proved, there was little that was
calculated to inspire confidence. Still in one case it must be confessed
that the University judgment has been shown to be singularly at fault,
and while at Oxford R. W. Rice was adjudged as painfully slow and
possessed of scarcely a good stroke, his play for Gloucestershire has
proved him to be a batsman much above the average. The trial matches
served in great measure to confirm the reputation brought up from
Repton and Rossall by C. B. Fry and F. A. Phillips, and practically
secured for them a position in the eleven, while some of the Seniors
improved so greatly upon the previous season's form that four of them,
R. T. Jones, V. T. Hill, J. B. Wood, and T. S. B. Wilson were also
included, displacing two old Blues in H. D. Watson and A. J. Boger.
So far the form of the Dark Blues was more promising than in 1891,
but the exhibition made against the Gentlemen of England was not
very reassuring. Any hopes held out by the narrow victory over Lancashire
were promptly extinguished by the overwhelming defeat at the instance
of Surrey, followed by one little less severe from the MCC. In the later
matches, however, Oxford showed to better advantage, and in the last
of them, at Lord's, actually foreshadowed, on a minor scale, the great
performance which distinguished the inter-University match a few days
later. Still it must be admitted that when they entered the field against

Cambridge they were generally voted the weaker side. Luck, too, seemed against them at the start, two of the best batsmen being dismissed before a run was scored, and notwithstanding a capital exhibition of cricket while C. B. Fry and M. R. Jardine were together, up to the fall of the fifth wicket there was little ground for a change of opinion as to the ultimate result. But a surprise was in store when V. T. Hill joined Jardine. The latter, who had been batting very steadily, still played most careful, correct, and watchful cricket, while the latter, a left-handed batsman, hit out with a fearless resolution that went a long way to demoralise the Cambridge fielding. In an hour and forty minutes the pair put on 178 runs, of which Hill's share was 114, and if he had a slice of luck, as almost any player of his style must have to get so great a score, it must still be allowed that it was a wonderful display. Jardine's innings was even more meritorious, and was indeed the principal factor in Oxford's victory, and the greatest praise that can be given him is to state that his score of 140 was absolutely without a fault. While it would scarcely be correct to say that Jardine had given no previous indication of so great ability, inasmuch as he came up from Fettes College, near Edinburgh, with quite a phenomenal reputation, he certainly had done nothing at Oxford to confirm it, and on that account his fine performance was almost as surprising as it was gratifying. In the second innings, after Cambridge had done a good deal to regain the ground lost in their first venture, L. C. H. Palairet, assisted by C. B. Fry, G. F. H. Berkeley, and again by Jardine, followed up the advantage gained earlier in the game, and finally secured a splendid and somewhat unexpected victory for Oxford by five wickets. It is only in accordance with his subsequent play for Somerset to find the Oxford Captain at the head of the batting averages, although only beating Jardine by the smallest of fractions, and the pair have put a wide gap between themselves and V. T. Hill, who comes third. In the bowling G. F. H. Berkeley, without doing anything surprising, realised the expectations formed that he would prove the best bowler on the side, while T. S. B. Wilson's fast deliveries also met with a fair degree of success.

Cambridge

PRESIDENT — THE PROVOST OF KING'S COLLEGE
TREASURER — THE MASTER OF PETERHOUSE
ASSISTANT TREASURER — MR J. DOUGLAS,
SELWYN COLLEGE
SECRETARY — MR P. H. LATHAM, PEMBROKE COLLEGE
CAPTAIN — MR F. S. JACKSON, TRINITY COLLEGE
DEPUTY CAPTAIN (DURING MR JACKSON'S ABSENCE IN
INDIA) — MR C. M. WELLS, TRINITY COLLEGE

With so much of the previous year's talent at their disposal, and that of so good a quality, the Cambridge eleven of 1892 bade fair to be a very strong one. No fewer than seven old Blues were available; and there were besides, in the Seniors, several others who were good enough to have got into the team in any ordinary year. Of course, the loss of two such players as S. M. J. Woods and G. MacGregor was a serious one; and it would be difficult to replace them in any eleven, but C. P. Foley, and W. I. Rowell had done so very little, and the fresh talent promised so well, that there were not wanting those who prophesied that the side would be quite as strong all round as before, and certainly more consistent. The result of the season's play has not borne out these anticipations, for, notwithstanding that the eleven are much above the average of University teams, they have exhibited the same inconsistency in play as in 1891, and have sometimes displayed all-round form which made them equal to almost any side that could be brought against them, and at others failing to a degree that would not have been creditable in a second-class eleven. The trial matches again resulted in a difficulty about completing the team, so evenly balanced were the claims of several of the players, but ultimately the vacant places were given to two Seniors, L. H. Gay and H. R. Bromley-Davenport, the former being indispensable behind the wickets now that MacGregor's services were lost, and to a couple of Freshmen in J. Douglas, of Dulwich, and P. H. Latham, of Malvern. Cambridge opened the season remarkably well by beating a strong eleven got together by A. J. Webbe, who undertook the task usually performed by C. I. Thornton. Highly creditable as was the performance, it will be noted that it was marked by the same inconsistency which characterised Cambridge's play to the end of the season and after having all the worst of the opening, owing to some very unequal cricket in the first innings, which caused them to have to follow on, their second venture exhibited batting of such a high all-round order that in the end they won by 97 runs. Up to the time of their meeting Oxford at Lord's, they had made a slightly better record than their rivals, but this unevenness in their play had not gained them many friends, and while they still remained favourites, opinion was not so decidedly on their side as it had been some weeks earlier. Losing the toss in the great match at Lord's, they practically lost the game by bad fielding on the first afternoon. Three times V. T. Hill was let off in the long field, and had the earlier of these chances been taken, the match might have had quite a different termination. Then little excuse can be offered for the feeble batting and errors of judgment in the first innings. F. S. Jackson, C. W. Wells, and A. J. L. Hill all lost their wickets through attempting very badly judged runs, and this appeared to have so depressing an effect that the last four wickets fell for only a small addition to the score. Following on in a minority of 205, Cambridge, up to a certain point, gave the finest exhibition of batting they had shown during the season, every one of the side who went in on the Friday showing excellent form. Still, when five wickets had fallen, they wanted 26 to save the innings' defeat and Oxford seemed sure of an easy victory. It was then commenced the partnership of P. H. Latham and E. C. Streatfeild, who, while they were together, put on no fewer than 155 runs, the former batting with marked caution and judgment, and the latter hitting all round the wicket with great power. After both were out on the Saturday forenoon, the side quickly collapsed, no one being able to play J. B. Wood's lobs, and the last three wickets fell to that bowler for 23 runs, Oxford finally winning by five wickets. A comparison of the averages will quite bear out the opinion that Cambridge were the better side of the two Universities, notwithstanding their failure in the match with Oxford. It is true no one comes out with figures so good as those of L. C. H. Palairet and M. R. Jardine, but the strength of the batting is more equally distributed, and in the bowling nothing that was done on the side of the Dark Blues can compare with the work accomplished by F. S. Jackson, the Cambridge Captain.

The Cricket Annual, 1892

*

The Blues at Lord's

SIEGFRIED SASSOON

Near-neighboured by a blandly boisterous Dean
Who 'hasn't missed the match since '92',
Proposing to perpetuate the scene
I concentrate my eyesight on the cricket.
The game proceeds, as it is bound to do
Till tea-time or the fall of the next wicket.

Agreeable sunshine fosters greensward greener
Than College lawns in June. Tradition-true,
The stalwart teams, capped with contrasted blue,
Exert their skill; adorning the arena
With modest, manly, muscular demeanour,—
Reviving memories in ex-athletes who
Are superannuated from agility—
And (while the five-ounce fetish they pursue)
Admired by gloved and virginal gentility.

My intellectual feet approach this function
With tolerance and Public-School compunction;
Aware that, whichsoever side bats best,
Their partisans are equally well-dressed.
For, though the Government has gone vermilion
And, as a whole, is weak in Greek and Latin,
The fogies harboured by the august Pavilion
Sit strangely similar to those who sat in
The edifice when first the Dean went pious,—
For possible preferment sacrificed
His hedonistic and patrician bias,
And offered his complacency to Christ.

Meanwhile some Cantab slogs a fast half-volley
Against the ropes. 'Good shot, sir! O good shot!'
Ejaculates the Dean in accents jolly . . .
Will Oxford win? Perhaps. Perhaps they'll not.

Can Cambridge lose? Who knows? One fact seems sure;
That, while the Church approves, Lord's will endure.

Satirical Poems, 1926

∗

Lord's, 1928

C. A. ALINGTON

Lord's—Lord's on Wednesday evening!
Cambridge fieldsmen crowding round,
Oxford's hardly a chance of saving it—
Hardly a chance, but still you found
   Elderly cricketers gnawing their sticks,
   Blameless Bishops, forgetful of Jix,
   Publicly praying at half-past six,
And prayers and curses arise from the Mound
   On that head of carrots (or possibly gold)
   On that watchful eye on each ball that's bowled—
And a deadly silence around the ground.

Lord's—Lord's on Friday evening!
Two men out and an hour to play—
Lose another, and that's the end of it,
Why not call it a harrowing day?
   Harrow's lips are at last on the cup,
   Harrow's tail unmistakably up,
   And Eton! Eton can only pray
For a captain's heart in a captain's breast,
   And some decent batting among the rest,
   And sit and shiver and hope for the best—
If those two fellows can only stay!

Stay they did—can we ever forget it?—
Till those who had bidden us all despair
Lit their pipes with a new assurance,
Toyed instead with the word 'declare':

Harrow's glorious hours begin,
Harrow's batsmen hurrying in,
One and all with the will to win,
Cheers and counter-cheers rend the air!
Harrow's down with her colours flying
Great in doing and great in dying,
Eton's home with a head to spare!

Eton Faces, 1933

*

The Universities

WILLIAM DEWAR

With the fifty-eighth match between Oxford and Cambridge, the University season of 1892 came to an end, for one can hardly regard the match with Dublin University as forming part of it, and the result of the great contest exemplifies the axiom that it is the unexpected that happens, in cricket as in other matters. Before the season was well under way, and with only the knowledge of the material that was available by each, Cambridge were unhesitatingly pronounced by the critics as the better side, and the question was less which eleven would win, as by how much Oxford would be defeated. The subsequent games played by both sides did something to modify the confidence of this opinion, but nevertheless it remained unchanged, for Cambridge not only won one more match than the rival University, but her victories were on the whole more pronounced and her defeats less decisive than those of Oxford. The hopes of the Dark Blues lay rather in the fact that the play had revealed the possession by Oxford of two or three players who were capable, at any time, of turning the scale in a game, and one of these, L. C. H. Palairet, quite justified on other fields, as well as for his University, the high opinion formed of his cricket. It was quite in accordance, however, with the proverbial uncertainty of the game that none of those to whom the critics directed attention took the leading part in what will long remain one of the most remarkable of the inter-University contests. Quite unexpectedly a long and prolific stand was made in the first innings for Oxford by M. R. Jardine and V. T. Hill, which practically put the question of their defeat outside the region of calculation, and notwithstanding that Cambridge in a great measure justified their reputation by the splendid effort they made on the afternoon of the second day, after following their innings, the failure of the last few batsmen gave Oxford an opportunity which they were quick to improve. Palairet followed up what Jardine and Hill had begun, and Cambridge were finally defeated by five wickets. There are one or two points about the match which are specially deserving of notice. The Cambridge second innings of 388, for instance, just ties with the highest total previously recorded for an innings, that made by Cambridge in 1872, and while Jardine's 140 falls three below the best individual score, hit by K. J. Key in 1886, he still creates a record for the highest aggregate, his 179 in the two innings being greater than anything previously accomplished in the inter-University matches. The total number of runs scored in the match, 1,100, is also in itself a record, and it is the first time, too, that three separate hundreds have been made during its progress. Again, the mention of 1886 recalls the almost precisely similar performance of that year to the great feature in the present game, when the memorable stand made by K. J. Key and W. Rashleigh turned the tide of fortune, and enabled Oxford to win by 133 runs. Of the fifty-eight matches played, Cambridge have now won twenty-nine, Oxford twenty-six, and three have been left unfinished.

The Cricket Annual, 1893

*

The Season of 1892

WILLIAM DEWAR

For the first time in the history of the game, each of the leading counties has played all the others with an acknowledged claim to be included in the first class, and whether influenced by this fact or not, there can be no question that the salient feature of the Season of 1892 has been the greatly increased interest taken in county cricket. Not many years ago, and before the counties themselves were willing to formally admit the press classification, the visit of an Australian team was considered as an almost indispensable necessity to an interesting season. Now matters have altogether altered for the better, and while our Antipodean cousins will be heartily welcomed whenever they come, the lesson of the past season has taught us that the cricket of the year, even without them, can be sufficiently full of excitement to gratify the most exacting. The hearty manner in which the counties have entered into the championship contest has stimulated the public interest in their doings to a wonderful degree, and it is needless to say that the course of Notts was followed with the keenest attention up to their memorable meeting with Somerset in August, nor will it soon be forgotten how, with the honours of the Championship fairly in their grasp, they suffered a couple of unexpected defeats, and allowed Surrey to retain possession of the title. It is not well for the game, and for the public interest in it, that any one county should prove invincible year after year, and for that reason, if for no other, it might have been well that some county other than Surrey should have been at the top of the list. But there can be no question that incidents such as those which caused the retrogression of Notts, whereby it is shown that the greatest apparent certainty may be upset, do much to add to the attractiveness of cricket and enable it to retain its hold upon the public attention.

Notwithstanding the generally bleak character of the summer, the wickets as a rule have been drier than in 1891, with a consequent increase in the average rate of run-getting. This is seen in the much greater aggregates many of the players were able to compile, no fewer than nine batsmen amassing totals of over 1,000 runs as against four in the previous year. Of these, six were amateurs, H. T. Hewett, A. E. Stoddart, L. C. H. Palairet, W. W. Read, W. G. Grace, and S. W. Scott, and the remaining three professionals, Shrewsbury, Gunn, and Abel. Of the amateurs, two, W. G. Grace and W. W. Read, were veterans of such long standing that many looked upon the previous season's figures as indicating a decadence of their powers, and there was the more gratification, therefore, to find them batting with all their old resolution and power. But the greatest surprise was created by the refreshing vigour of another veteran's cricket, and nothing in Stanley Scott's past career had led any one to anticipate so fine a display of strong batting as he gave on almost every occasion he went in on a dry wicket. He has the credit also of having played the highest innings of the year in first-class cricket, hitting up two hundred and twenty-four for Middlesex at Lord's in the first of the two matches with Gloucestershire. A. E. Stoddart is of a younger school, but his reputation was already made as one of the most brilliant hitters of the day, so that while he improved upon his figures in 1891, he was only tending to confirm the position already conceded to him. Quite different was it with the remaining two. H. T.

Hewett, the Somerset captain, like many other left-handed batsmen, was known to play what is called unorthodox cricket, and, upon bad wickets especially, had the courage to go in for hitting as the most likely game to pay. But the terrific punishment meted out by him to all bowlers alike, and upon almost all sorts of wickets, came somewhat as a revelation, and not only enabled him to make the highest aggregate of the year, but established his reputation as the best left-handed batsman of recent years, and his performance, in the opinion of many, is superior to any thing ever done by either J. Cranston or F. M. Lucas. Should the Australians visit England next year, as arranged, and bring with them their two famous left-handed batsmen, Bruce and Moses, it is to be hoped that Hewett will still retain the form that has distinguished him in the past season, and thus afford an opportunity for a comparison. His fellow-countryman, L. C. H. Palairet, the Oxford captain, who has done so much to advance Somerset to her present position, is the youngest of the amateurs who have run into four figures, and he thoroughly deserves the distinction he has gained by his consistently good play. Although in the inter-University match he only played a secondary part to M. R. Jardine and V. T. Hill, he nevertheless, by his fine batting in the second innings, contributed in no small degree to the winning of that game by Oxford, and he claims the higher distinction of having assisted H. T. Hewett to create a new record for the first wicket, the pair putting together no fewer than three hundred and forty-six runs on the Taunton ground against Yorkshire before they were parted. The previous record, made by W. G. Grace and B. B. Cooper, for the Gentlemen of the South *v.* the Players of the South, at the Oval in 1869, had stood for twenty-three years, and was beaten by sixty-three runs. In one sense the Oxford captain forms an admirable foil to W. G. Grace, the pair being the youngest and the oldest of the great batsmen of the year, and when it is borne in mind that the Gloucester veteran was the acknowledged champion several years before Palairet was born, it will serve to emphasise very strongly the extraordinary ability of the greatest cricketer the game has ever seen.

Of the professionals who have scored over a thousand runs, Notts supplies two in Shrewsbury and Gunn, and Surrey the other in Abel, all three being among the only four who claimed a similar distinction last year. The great Notts batsman, indeed, comes out at the head of all the averages for the year, but the season had run through nearly half its course before he was seen at his best, and it was only after his great score of two hundred and twelve at Lord's against Middlesex that he played with all his accustomed ability, and frequently with more freedom than one usually associates with his play. Unlike the amateurs, there were no fresh reputations of any importance made among the professionals, almost every one who has attained distinction being already well known to fame. Lockwood, by his uniform success, made good his claim to be considered the best bowler of the year, if not, indeed, the best all-round man on a side, but probably the most marked advance made by any player has been by Wainwright, who, both in batting and in bowling, has greatly enhanced his reputation. He found a place this year for the first time in a representative match, playing for the Players against the Gentlemen both at Lord's and the Oval, and completely justified his selection. The season has furnished three instances of conspicuous failure, and singularly enough all three of them are among the bowlers, Sharpe, Martin, and J. J. Ferris falling very much below their previous standard. Various theories have been advanced for Sharpe's want of success, the one finding most acceptance being that a winter's cricket abroad is more detrimental to the following summer's form than is generally believed, but those who are disposed to dispute the truth of this contention may point to W. G. Grace and W. W. Read, whose visits, the one to Australia and the other to South Africa, appear to have reinvigorated their Cricket to a wonderful degree.

One of the most marked features resulting from the formal recognition by the Counties themselves of the Championship competition has been the desire to bring each match engaged in to a definite conclusion if possible. How much will be risked upon occasion to secure this was seen upon the Headingley Ground at Leeds, when the Surrey Captain closed his innings and put Yorkshire in,—on a difficult wicket, it is true,—to get one hundred and forty-six to win, and with just two hours and five minutes to make the runs in. Yet when an hour and five minutes had elapsed the Surrey Captain must have been in an uncomfortable frame of mind, for in the previous half hour Wainwright and Tunnicliffe had raised the Yorkshire score from twenty-one to seventy-six, and were batting so confidently that if they kept together there seemed a prospect of the runs being hit up in the time. They did not do so, and, as every one now knows, Surrey won with just three minutes to spare. This is only one instance out of many showing how useful, and how beneficial in its influence upon the game, has been the closure rule passed in 1889. But that it has not done all that is required is evident, for the Notts and Gloucester match at Cheltenham again brought to the front the vexed question which the rule was expected to settle. In that match, when Notts had put on two hundred and eighty-seven for the loss of four wickets during the first day's play, and the game was delayed till half-past one on the second day, it seemed to be expected that the later batsmen on the side would throw their wickets away in order to put Gloucester in as soon as possible. This they did not do, and after the match some strong comments were made about their playing for their averages instead of sacrificing their innings in the hope of winning the game. The incident, however, has served to show that Rule 54 has not accomplished all that it was necessary should be done. It is not Cricket for a man to deliberately knock his own wicket down, and if it is desirable in the interests of a side that some of the batsmen should not do their best, then the rules should provide means by which they may be allowed to do nothing. This they partly do now. The power given to a captain to close his innings on the last day of a match has done much to stimulate public interest in the County contests by decreasing the probability of their being drawn, and it must surely commend itself to reason that what is legitimate and advantageous on the last day should be equally permissible at any period during the game.

Reference has already been made to the creation of a new record for the score at the fall of the first wicket, and it would scarcely be just to close this notice of the season without some reference to another performance, almost as remarkable in its way. W. G. Grace has proved himself a batsman of such exceptional excellence that one is not surprised to find achievements recorded of him which have no parallel in what has been done by other players, and among such feats is the making of two separate hundreds in a first-class match. This Mr Grace has done on three occasions, namely—at Canterbury, in 1858, for South *v.* North of the Thames, one hundred and thirty and one hundred and two not out; at Clifton, in 1887, for Gloucester *v.* Kent, one hundred and one and one hundred and three not out; and at Clifton again, in 1888, for Gloucester *v.* Yorkshire, one hundred and forty-eight and one hundred and fifty-three; but up to the present year he has been alone in its accomplishment. Henceforward, however, another name will be associated with his in the performance of this exceptional feat, as G. Brann succeeded in making one hundred and five and one hundred and one in the two innings of Sussex against Kent, at Brighton, on August 23rd and 24th. The rarity of the achievement will always secure for it no small amount of distinction; but if anything in the present case could invest it with more than ordinary interest, it will be found in the fact that a feat so extraordinary should alone have been done by a batsman for the county which finished absolutely last of all in the first-class list.

The Cricket Annual, 1892

＊

In Certamen Pilae / The Cricket Match

WILLIAM GOLDWIN

translated by Harold Perry

In Certamen Pilae	*The Cricket Match*
Vere novo, cum temperies liquidissima coeli	'Tis early Spring, the lucid air and smiling Skies make all things fair:
Arridet, suadetque virentis gratia terrae	green Nature bids our feet, with speed,
Veloces agitare pedes super aequora Campi;	disport them on the level mead.
Lecta cohors juvenum, baculis armata repandis	I see a chosen company, with curving bats armed gallantly,
Quos habiles ludo Manus ingeniosa polivit,	(smoothed by deft hands for use) —and lo!
In Campum descendit ovans; sua gloria cuique.	with shouts into the field they go. each boasts his own peculiar grace,
Hic Magis aptus humum celeri transmittere planta,	*this* skims the ground, supreme in pace,
Et vigilante oculo variis discursibus omnes	hawk-eyed the moment's need to spy
Ire redire vias; longe torquere per auras	and to and fro unerring fly.
Doctior ille pilam, atque adversos rumpere ventos;	*that* best can hurl the ball afar and bursts the wind's opposing bar;
Tertius arte valet quo non praestantior alter	*that other* fears no rival's skill, when, o'er the even turf, his will
Per sola plana *Orbem* dextrae libramine justo	sends forth a poisèd sphere, too fleet to reck the batsman's answering beat.

Fundere, qui rapido cursu
    praeverteret ictum.

Adventum excipiunt *Manus*
    Adversaria laetis
Alloquiis nectuntque moras,—
    mox jurgia miscent
Civilesque iras, quod vult
    imponere ludo
Quisque suas leges. *Nestor*,
    cui cana senectus
Conciliat cultum turbae
    veniamque loquendi,
Se densae immiscens plebi vice
    fungitur aequi
Judicis, et quanquam positis
    campestribus armis
Jamdudum indulsit senio, non
    immemor artis
Proponit justas leges, et
    temperat iras.

the friendly foe's loud-voiced array
greets their approach, then comes
    delay,
then quarrels rife, while all exclaim
and all would lord it o'er the
    game.
now some grey veteran intercedes,
and wins their love, the while he
    pleads:
a Daniel come to judgment, he
to all around speaks equity.
though now his arms be laid
    aside,
and marred by years his early
    pride,
yet rich is he in cricket lore,
and proves that they need strive
    no more.

Deinde locum signant, qua se
    diffundit in aequor
Plana superficies; Hinc illinc
    partibus aeque
Oppositis bifido Surgentes
    vertice furcae
Erectas modicum quas distinet
    intervallum
Infiguntur humo; Tum virgula
    ponitur alba,
Virgula, qua dubii certaminis
    alea pendet,
Et bene defendi poscit:
    Coriaceus Orbis
Vi ruit infesta, quem si fortuna
    Maligna
Dirigit in rectum, subversaque
    Machina fulcris

the Lists are set where, (happy
    chance!)
the meadow yields a smooth
    expanse;
opposed, on either hand, appear
twin rods that forkèd heads
    uprear,
with ends set firmly in the green,
(nor wide the middle space
    between),
and next a milk-white Bail is laid
from fork to fork, whereby is
    swayed
the dubious issue of the fight,
and all must guard it with their
    might.
the Leathern Orb speeds forth like
    fate,

Abripitur, cedas positis inglorius
    armis.
Stant Moderatores bini
    stationibus aptis
Fustibus innixi, quos certo
    attingere pulsu
Lex jubet, aut operam cursus
    perdemus inanem.

and should its destined line be
    straight
and raze the bail's support, defeat
ensues and sorrowful retreat.
each at his wicket, near at hand,
propped on his staff, the Umpires
    stand,
the runner's bat must touch their
    pale,
or else the run will nought avail.

Parte alia, visus qua libera
    copia detur,
Parvo in colle sedent duo
    pectora fida, parata
Cultellis numerum crescentem
    incidere ligno.

on a low mound, whence clear
    the view,
repose a trusty pair and true:
their simple task, with ready
    blade,
notches to cut, as runs are made.

Tum Cortatores digitis capita
    aequa recensent
Ordine dispositi: Medias it
    nummus in auras
Arbiter et primas partes decernit
    agendas
Aut his, aut aliis. Nondum
    discrimine coepto
Stant in procinctu juvenes; dum
    cautior ille,
Mittere cui data cura pilam,
    rursusque remissam
Effugio prohibere, Manu
    alterutraque tenaci
Excipere attactam, praescripta ad
    Munia jussit.
En! Quali studio sese disponit!
    Ut acres
Excubias agitat circum diffusa
    juventus
Expectans ludi Monitum,
    trepidantiaque haurit

the Players now ranged out at
    length,
two sides are picked, of equal
    strength.
a Coin goes up, now, Fortune,
    say,
who first shall bat, or we, or they!
ere yet the brave encounter start,
each youth stands ready for his
    part,
yet graver cares must him befall,
whose office is to bowl the ball,
then stop its sharp return and
    hold
it fast, by either hand controlled
while others to their work he
    sends,
how busy he to gain his ends!
around him spreads the brisk
    array,
and waits the word that heralds
    'Play'.

Corda pavor pulsans, famaeque
    arrecta cupido.

Et jam dulce paratur opus:
    Par nobile primum
Heröum certamen init, duo
    fulmina ludi;
Inde, dato signo, pila lubrica
    viribus acta
Carcere prona fugit, volitansque
    per aequora summa
Radit iter rapidum: sese *Hostis*
    poplite flexo
Inclinat, cita currentis vestigia
    lustrans
Si modo subsultet, tum certum
    assurgit in ictum
Bracha vi torquens celeri,
    longeque propellit
Clangentem sphaeram. Superas
    volat illa per auras
Continuo stridore ruens, atque
    aethera findit.

At coelo observans Catus
    Explorator in alto
Insidias parat, erectis palmisque
    cadentem
Excipit exultans, dextraque
    retorquet ovanti.
Hinc laetus sequitur clamor,
    dolor obruit illos
Moerentes tacite casum infelicis
    Amici;
Grande malum! Ast uno avulso
    non deficit alter.
Aemulus hic laudum furiisque
    ultricibus actus
Ingreditur scenam, et damnum
    reparare minatur:

the Issue's joined, two chiefs of
    name
go forth, both heroes of the
    game.
the word is given, and, urged
    with might,
speeds the greased ball in level
    flight,
and o'er the grassy surface sweeps;
with bended knee the batsman
    keeps
a forward stance, to watch its way
and mark it rise, then *sans* delay,
his arms descend with lightning
    fall,
to smite amain the ringing ball;
and, ringing on, sublime it flies
and disappears into the Skies.

meanwhile some wary Scout
    afield
brings craft to make the victor
    yield,
views the descent with upward
    eyes,
till his stretched hands secure the
    prize;
then gaily throws it up once
    more,
cheered by his friends' exultant
    roar.
but silent bows the foeman's head,
in anguish for a comrade sped.
woe worth the day! yet, eager
    still,

Successum Dea dira negat: vix
   terque quaterque
Cursum *Orbis* peragit, vix dum
   tria sensit ab hoste
Verbera, praecipiti cum protenus
   impete missa
Virgam sede levem rapit,
   eluditque Minantem
Ille indignanti vultu sua tela
   reponit
Atque Deos atque astra vocans
   crudelia, donec
Succurrens partes implêrit
   proximus haeres,
Qui jam languentem causae
   socialis honorem
Instaurare velit; sod et hic
   quoque numino laevo
Orditur lusum; nam dum
   cursusque recursusque
Alternos iterat, Vestigia lubrica
   ponens
Labitur infelix, pronus
   metamque sub ipsam
Procumbit; tremefacta gemit sub
   pondere tellus
Ingenti, risuque exultat rustica
   turba.
Quemque manent sua fata, trahit
   suus exitus omnes.
Ah! Nimium properans; Seu fors,
   sive artis egestas
Nisibus invidit; retro sublapsa
   refertur
Spes omnis juvenum vultuque et
   corde relanguent.

another comes the breach to fill.
fired with high hopes, his noble
   heat
essays to overwhelm defeat.
yet Fortune frowns, the bowler's
   force
four times accomplishes the course.
and thrice the batsman plays his
   part.
then, headlong flung with
   desperate art.
the ball prevents the bat, and
   sheers
the light bail rudely from its piers.
the Victim, reddening with
   dismay,
shoulders his bat and walks away,
mourning his luck and low estate,
until the coming of his mate.
he, to a sinking banner true,
renews a fray he soon shall rue.
anon, between the wickets pent,
on runs this way and that intent,
he slips, he falls, unhappy soul!
upon the threshold of his goal,
flat on the earth, with sounding
   thwack,
while jeers aloud the rustic pack.
to each his innings: and its end,
that comes too soon our case to
   mend;
for, be it *Fate*, or lack of Skill,
our efforts are but failures still;
back flows the current of success,
as downcast looks and moods
   confess.

Adversum auspiciis
  melioribus agmen arenam
Intrant, perpetuisque fatigant
  ictibus Orbem;
Fervet opus; manat toto de
  corpore sudor;
Mox ubi ludendi processerit
  ordo tenore
Felici, litemque unus discriminat
  ictus,
Impete pulsa pila in coeli
  sublimia templa
Provehitur rapiente Noto,
  lusumque coronat;
Concertata diu Victoria
  concrepat alis,
Et complet clamore polum
  fremituque secundo.

'neath happier stars, the aspiring
  foe
distress the ball with blow on
  blow:
hot is the pace, each brow
  bedewed,
with linkèd triumphs oft renewed
waxes the strife, but one notch
  more,
and mastery will crown the score.
'tis done! the stricken sphere
  ascends
heavenward, on airs the South
  Wind lends:
and, ended now the long debate,
Dame Victory claps her wings,
  elate,
and makes the Sky with cheers
  articulate.

Musae Juveniles, 1706
trans. *Etoniana*, 1922

*

Border Cricket

ANDREW LANG

A Border player, in his declining age, may be allowed to make a few remarks on the game as it used to be played in 'pleasant Teviotdale', and generally from Berwick all along the Tweed. The first time I ever saw ball and bat must have been about 1850. The gardener's boy and his friends were playing with home-made bats, made out of firwood with the bark on, and with a gutta-percha ball. The game instantly fascinated me, and when I once understood why the players ran after making a hit, the essential difficulties of comprehension were overcome. Already the border towns, Hawick, Kelso, Selkirk, Galashiels, had their elevens. To a small boy the spectacle of the various red and blue caps

and shirts was very delightful. The grounds were, as a rule, very rough
and bad. Generally the play was on *haughs*, level pieces of town-land
beside the rivers. Then the manufacturers would encroach on the cricket-
field, and build a mill on it, and cricket would have to seek new settle-
ments. This was not the case at Hawick where the Duke of Buccleuch
gave the town a capital ground which is kept in very good order.

In these early days, when one was only a small spectator, ay, and in
later days too, the great difficulty of cricket was that excellent thing in
itself, too much patriotism. Almost the whole population of a town
would come to the ground and take such a keen interest in the fortunes of their side, that the other side, if it won, was in some danger
of rough handling. Probably no one was ever much hurt; indeed, the
squabbles were rather a sham fight than otherwise; but still, bad feeling was caused by umpires' decisions. Then relations would be broken
off between the clubs of different towns, and sometimes this tedious
hostility endured for years. The causes were the excess of local feeling,
and perhaps the too great patriotism of umpires. 'Not out,' one of
them said, when a member of the Oxford eleven, playing for his town-
club, was most emphatically infringing some rule. 'I can *not* give Maister
Tom out first ball,' the umpire added, and his case was common enough.
Professional umpires, if they could be got, might be expected to prove
more satisfactory than excited amateurs who forgot to look after no
balls, or to count the number of balls in an over. But even professionals, if they were attached to the club or school, were not always
the embodiment of justice.

The most exciting match, I think, in which I ever took part was for
Loretto against another school. In those days we were very weak indeed.
When our last man went in, second innings, we were still four runs
behind our opponent's first score. This last man was extremely short-
sighted, and the game seemed over. But his partner, a very steady player,
kept the bowling, and put on some thirty-eight more. We put our
adversaries in to get this, and had lowered eight wickets for twenty
eight. I was bowling, and appealed to the umpire of our opponents
for a palpable catch at wicket. 'Not out!' Next ball the batsman was
caught at long-stop, and a fielder triumphantly shouted, 'Well, how's
that?'

'Not out,' replied the professional again, and we lost the match by
two wickets.

If this had happened on the Border there would have been trouble,
and perhaps the two clubs would not have met again for years. I have

no doubt that a more equable feeling has come in among those clubs which retained a good deal of the sentiments of rival clans. The Borderers played too much as if we were still in the days of Scotts and Carrs, and as if it were still our purpose

> To tame the Unicorn's pride,
> Exalt the Crescent and the Star.

Sir Walter Scott encouraged this ardour at football when he caused to be unfurled, for the first time since 1633, the ancient banner of Buccleuch, with its broidered motto 'Bellendaine'. The dalesmen, the people from the waters of Yarrow, Ettrick, and Teviot, played against the souters of Selkirk, all across country, the goals being Ettrick and Yarrow. The townsmen scored the first goal, when the Galashiels folk came in as allies of the shepherds, and helped them to win a goal. 'Then began a murder grim and great', and Scott himself was mobbed in the evening. But he knew how to turn wrath into laughter.

''Tis sixty years since', and more, but this perfervid ardour, while it makes Border cricket very exciting, is perhaps even now a trifle too warm. The great idea, perhaps, in all country cricket is not so much to have a pleasant day's sport, win or lose, but to win merely. Men play for victory, as Dr Johnson talked, rather than for cricket. This has its advantages; it conduces to earnestness. But it does not invariably promote the friendliness of a friendly game.

Border cricket is very pleasant, because it is played in such a pleasant country. You see the angler going to Tweedside, or Teviot, and pausing to watch the game as he strolls by the cricket-ground. The hills lie all around, these old, unmoved, unchangeable spectators of man's tragedy and sport. The broken towers of Melrose or Jedburgh or Kelso look down on you. They used to 'look down', as well they might, on very bad wickets. Thanks to this circumstance, the present writer, for the first and only time in his existence, once did the 'hat trick' at Jedburgh, and took three wickets with three consecutive balls. Now the grounds are better, and the scores longer, but not too long. You seldom hear of 300 in one innings on the Border.

In my time the bowling was roundhand, and pretty straight and to a length, as a general rule. Perhaps, or rather certainly, the proudest day of my existence was when I was at home for the holidays, and was chosen to play, and bowl, for the town eleven against Hawick. I have the score still, and it appears that I made havoc among Elliots, Leydens, and Drydens. But they were too strong for our Scotts, Johnstons, and

Douglasses: it is a pleasure to write the old names of the Border clans in connection with cricket. The batting was not nearly so good then as it is now; professional instruction was almost unknown. Men blocked timidly, and we had only one great hitter, Mr John Douglas; but how gallantly he lifted the soaring ball by the banks of Ettrick! At that time we had a kind of family team, composed of brothers and other boys, so small that we called ourselves *Les Enfants Perdus*. The name was appropriate enough. I think we only once won a match, and that victory was achieved over Melrose. But we kept the game going on and played in all weathers, and on any kind of wickets. Very small children would occasionally toddle up and bowl when the elder members of the family were knocked off. Finally, as they grew in stature, the team developed into 'The Eccentric Flamingoes', then the only wandering Border club. We wore black and red curiously disposed, and had a good many Oxford members. The Flamingoes, coming down from Oxford, full of pride, had once a dreadful day on the Edinburgh Academy Ground. We were playing the School, which made a portentous score, and I particularly remember that Mr T. R. Marshall, probably the best Scotch bat who ever played, and then a boy, hit two sixes and a five off three consecutive balls. It is a very great pity that this Border bat is so seldom seen at Lord's; his average for MCC in 1886 was 85. The Flamingoes lasted for some years, and played all Teviotdale and Tweedside.

In those days we heard little of Dumfries and Galloway cricket, into which Steels, Tylecotes, and Studds have lately infused much life. In recent years, Lord Dalkeith, Lord George Scott, and Mr Maxwell Scott, of Abbotsford, have contributed very much to the growth of Border cricket. Money has never been very plentiful north of Tweed, and when scarcely any but artisans played, the clubs could not afford good grounds, or much professional instruction. In these respects there has been improvement. Perhaps the boys' cricket was not sufficiently watched and encouraged. Veterans used to linger on the stage with a mythical halo round them of their great deeds in the Sixties. Perhaps the rising generation is now more quickly promoted, and better coached than of old. I feel a hesitation in offering any criticism because I had only one quality of a cricketer, enthusiasm, combined for a year or two with some twist from leg. But, if I never was anything of an expert, my heart hath always been with those old happy scenes and happy days of struggling cricket.

Cricket, 1893

*

Edwardian Cricket

DAVID FRITH

Of all the phases in cricket's history none has the seductive charm of the late-Victorian and Edwardian period. The glorious designation 'Golden Age' might almost as easily be conferred upon other times: the 'Middle Ages' of 'Felix, Wenman, Hillyer, Fuller Pilch, and Alfred Mynn', or part of the between-wars period, when Hammond, Bradman, and Headley were on display, or even recent years, when skill and flair have probably been spread more thickly over the cricket-fields of all Test-playing countries than ever before—granted that at least another thirty years must pass before the 1970s are lit by the soft, romantic shafts of museum lighting.

The remoteness of the pre-First World War epoch and the recognition that, assuredly though it was to end some way or other, it *did* end abruptly and indescribably tragically—for these reasons, the players of that time (and not only the household names) are hallowed in cricket lore. They did, after all, reflect the moods of the life around them. It was a time of complacency, security and opulent pride for Britain and her splendid Empire, and the ascent of wide-girthed 'Teddy' to the throne heralded warm, succulent breezes of gaiety which dislodged and dispersed inhibitions. Notwithstanding the high rates of infant mortality, drunkenness, poverty and prostitution, and a life expectancy for men of only 46, many shared the conviction of Cecil Rhodes that the British were the world's first race, and the more of the world they inhabited the better it would be for humanity; this absorption would also ensure the end of all wars. Perhaps the man had a point.

Class distinctions held firm, in cricket as in real life, though it has long been a prime claim for English cricket that it has brought all breeds of men together in a pavilion. This it may have done, creating an additional mystique, but it could never bring about any real fusion of species. The county club professional, glad to lodge with his fellows in one-star or even starless hotels, addressed the amateur as 'Mister' or 'Sir' and answered to his Christian name or nickname if he were favoured, but more likely to his surname, though without resentment. The amateur—the 'gentleman'—came usually from public school, the yield from which, C. B. Fry once wrote, apart from being 'the most valuable product of education in Europe', had 'an apologetic gaucherie, a kind of communal symbolism in refutation of any possible accusation of "side"'. He had a position in the family business, the church, one of the other professions, or, as an Australian newspaper stated of one of the English amateurs in the 1890s, 'he does nothing for a living'. The county amateurs occupied separate and usually more comfortable dressing-rooms, and took the field through a separate gate. Wilfred Rhodes, late in his long life, compared this with the apartheid of South Africa—again, without resentment.

The dissolution of clear divisions, in sport as in wider life, has been hastened by two world wars and a succession of economic and political upheavals. The workers were then still some way short of governing their own affairs, just as professional cricketers found no cause, inclination or opportunity to govern the game themselves (until the 1970s). That is not to say that all was serenity. W. G. Grace's remuneration, which made a mockery of his amateur status, provoked sharp if not widespread criticism, and in 1896 he persuaded the Surrey secretary to issue a statement on the matter before confirming his willingness to lead England in the Test match against Australia. The importance of W.G.'s presence can be imagined. At the same time, Andrew Stoddart, one of the world's great batsmen, withdrew from the England team partly because of a heavy cold and partly because of an attack by the *Morning Leader* upon him for allegedly making money out of the game when he was supposed to be a man of independent means.

Yet the sounds of these two crises have been lost in the echoing thunder of 'The Strike'. Five of the professionals—Abel, Hayward, Lohmann, Richardson (all of Surrey), and Gunn—wrote to the Surrey secretary demanding a match fee of £20 each, double the normal amount. Lohmann and Gunn would not be moved, but the other three relented in the face of an unconciliatory committee, and joined in the glory of match and series victory.

In this year there had already been a disturbance of a different kind, though not unfamiliar to modern sports-followers. Ranjitsinhji, the noble Rajput, heir to the throne of Nawanagar, was considered by MCC to be ineligible to play for England, and had to wait until the second Test for his debut. The Lancashire authorities had no compunction in selecting him,[1] and he rewarded them with a magical 62 and 154 not out, finishing with a trickle of blood curling down from

[1]. In those days the Test Ground's Committee selected the side.

an earlobe, the price of a rare missed hook against the Australian express bowler Ernie Jones (the same incorrigible colonial who sent a ball swishing through W.G.'s beard).

There were other irregular goings-on. In 1890, Stoddart felt it was more important to assist Middlesex against Kent at Tonbridge than England against Australia at Lord's. He was again chosen for the second Test match, at The Oval, but preferred to play in the county match at Bradford. When Lord Hawke got wind of this he stopped two of his professionals, George Ulyett and Bobby Peel, from playing in the Test. Whatever justice there was in this may be deduced from the scoreline: Mr A. E. Stoddart c. Ulyett b. Peel 7 c. Jackson b. Peel 0. At least Stoddart played under his own name. It was not uncommon for certain amateurs to play under false names, which can hardly have helped the cricket-writers in the compiling of averages—numerical columns that, incidentally, had yet to be transformed into pagan deities, for the worship of the masses.

The seventh Lord Hawke was born in 1860, a descendant of Admiral Lord Hawke, hero of the Battle of Quiberon in 1759. Like his ancestor, he had a deep sense of consideration for his men. Yet history has treated him unkindly. He is thought of as a symbol of unapproachability, of repression, and of privilege. Autocratic as well as aristocratic he may have been, but he was a leader, and the undisciplined group of cricketers that were Yorkshire became a team under Hawke (the White Rose county won nine Championships in the twenty seasons to 1912): a team of professionals with a new set of standards as well as security unknown by their predecessors. His Lordship concerned himself with such revolutionary ideas as winter payment, talent money, and the safeguarding of benefit proceeds for a cricketer's old age. He demanded loyalty in return—and a proper code of conduct from predominantly uncultured men. So that when Peel drowned his sobriety once too often, urinating on the pitch, he was sent from the ground and from Yorkshire's payroll forever. One wonders what television news editors of today would have made of that.

The demarcation between amateur and professional cricketer was officially ended, perhaps somewhat late, on November 26, 1962, when, financially at least, all cricketers became players and equal—subsequently give or take an overseas star signing. At a stroke, the 156 years of Gentlemen *v.* Players matches were sealed off and mummified. Since 1806, the best of the paid players had played the pick of the unpaid in meaningful contests which had matched fervour with delight. With the years, 'shamateurism' had become quite widespread, and so yet another anachronism was killed off. The most apt and perhaps predictable graffiti one could find today on the old walls of Lord's, The Oval, Headingley or Old Trafford would be Egalitarianism Rules, OK?

The golden years either side of 1900 were, of course, the years of Grace. He came on to the scene as a teenager in 1864, utterly transformed the game in the 'seventies and 'eighties, boomed back to irresistible form in 1895, a bearded giant of 47, and partook of Test cricket as late as 1899, when, still an exceptional figure at the crease but a handicap in the field, he 'plotted' his own omission by asking fellow-selector C. B. Fry, as he arrived later than the others for their meeting at the Sports Club, whether he thought Archie MacLaren ought to play in the next Test match. 'Yes, I do,' said Fry. 'That settles it,' chimed W.G.—the 'it' being his exclusion. He was within a month of his 51st birthday, and could have been said to have had a good run; but his withdrawal left a void not dissimilar in scale to the Avon Gorge. He may not have gone on every tour of Australia (few amateurs found the time), but he *was* cricket. More than that: he was a pillar of English life.

W. G. Grace's influence was to last long after his final appearance in first-class cricket, at The Oval in 1908, and his death in 1915 shook the nation almost as much as Churchill's fifty years later. For decades Dr William Gilbert Grace had been perhaps the most famous man in England, rivalling Gladstone and the Prince of Wales. His beard, his bulk, and his batsmanship ensured this. He took the art to new heights, driving even the most fearsome of bowlers to the boundary and to distraction, reducing them to bowling almost out of the reach of his barn-door bat. He combined forward-play with back-play, struck perilous shooters into the far distances, revealed abnormal reserves of stamina, overawed players and spectators, overwhelmed opponents physically and psychologically, and sometimes over-bowled himself. He made 54,896 runs and 126 centuries in first-class cricket, figures that have been overtaken, against expectation, even if his pre-eminence has not. He remains the most famous cricketer of them all, and he elevated the game in public esteem.

Fry once compared him to Henry the Eighth, who, like W.G., was a legend and premier athlete in England long before becoming over-weighted with flesh and sundry complications. No-one can calculate the exact depth of W.G.'s influence, though E. G. V. Christian was one of many who attempted to frame The Champion's supremacy in this verse, which he attributed to his cousin:

> The bat is, as the sonnet is, but small;
> Yet with it batsmen, a stouthearted band,
> Waged ceaseless, changing conflict with the ball.
> Till Grace arose; and in his mighty hand
> The thing became a sceptre, which be wields
> Unchallenged yet, Lord of the Playing Fields.

There were others, of course. Most of them were batsmen, for then, as now, bowlers were the drudges. It was an age of so-called classical batsmanship inasmuch as style, fostered at the public schools, was upheld practically as an end in itself. Nor would it have been too difficult to excel at the drive off the front foot when bowling was consistently directed at the off stump and the length was honourably full. Indeed, short balls and legside deliveries almost mandatorily brought forth an apology from the bowler. One evening at Hove, Ranjitsinhji proclaimed the pride of that generation of batsmen when he loudly deplored a mark made on his flimsy leg-guards by the ball, though the pioneers of the pull, the sweep, and the unabashed 'cow shot', such as Walter Read and the two senior Graces, were less fussy, as was Gilbert Jessop, the greatest of improvisators and one of the strongest and most dramatic of hitters, all crouching five-foot-seven of him.

With the coming of swerve bowling and the googly (sneered at by some as nothing more than a gimmick and an unsportsmanlike ploy) the game lost some more of its innocence: the flowing forward-play was stunted, batsmen worked more within their creases, and such magnificent back-foot players as Jack Hobbs of England, Charles Macartney of Australia, and Herby Taylor of South Africa emerged. The princely ranks of MacLaren, Palairet, Jackson, Stoddart, Ranji, Fry, Spooner, Trumper, all picturesque dispatchers of the ball to the sightscreen—where one existed—were absorbed by the years, like a lost legion, with few heirs.

While cricket's evolution did not halt with the Great War, the game in 1914, while different in attitude, was not much removed *technically* from the cricket of today. The six-ball over, a new ball after 200 runs, six runs for hits out of the playing area, the declaration, a wider bowling crease, the follow-on—all these areas of conduct were established. Boards of Control had been set up in England in 1898 and Australia in 1905, and the Imperial (later democratically broadened to International)

Cricket Conference came into being in the summer of 1909. Compared with today's broad conglomerate of full and associate member countries, the original ICC was cosily select, consisting of MCC, Australia, and South Africa. Not even Philadelphia, then a force in the game, was granted admission.

English tours abroad were now firmly under the control of MCC, the sometimes haphazard exploits of privately-promoted Test tours left behind in the nineteenth century. The touring cricketers from England were ambassadors, showing the flag in the colonies, providing a fond link for the settlers from the Old Country and a sight of some curiosity for the native-born. In turn, Australian and South African cricketers were expected to be rough-hewn, and they often were. They were additionally expected to lose, and often did. And sometimes they won, and it did nothing to weaken the bonds of the farflung Empire. Indeed, the ethics of cricket, as exemplified in Newbolt's oft-quoted and oft-parodied *Vitaï Lampada*, were inextricably bound up in the most dramatic of all struggles. With the Gattling jammed and the Colonel dead and the regiment blind with dust and smoke, 'the voice of a schoolboy rallies the ranks: "Play up! play up! and play the game!"' The verse would have been an inspiration on the bumping pitches and in the blinding light of Omdurman and Ladysmith and Mafeking.

It was at Mafeking that the dashing Yorkshire amateur Frank Milligan was mortally wounded during Plumer's attempt to relieve Baden-Powell's garrison. Brought down from his horse by Boer rifle-fire, he had to be left by his fellow skirmishers, who could do nothing to save him. In his personal effects was a Yorkshire fixture-card for the 1900 season. 'He could not guess', stated the report sorrowfully, 'that he had played his last match.'

Cricketers streamed out to the conflict. Major R. M. Poore, only a few months after scoring 1499 runs at an average of 107 for Hampshire, went to the USA to buy mules for the Government, then set out for the scattered front. Jack Ferris, who with Charlie Turner had formed one of Australia's most successful bowling partnerships ever before joining Gloucestershire, went to war with Colonel Byng's South Australian Light Horse, and died from fever. Prince Christian Victor, a grandson of Queen Victoria, and fine wicketkeeper-batsman at Wellington and Oxford, died in Pretoria from enteric fever a few weeks before Ferris, leaving the monarch sleepless and averse to food in her grief. Not only the young were claimed. George Strachan, the old Surrey and Gloucestershire player, was another fever victim at 51, while in charge of a concentration camp in the Transvaal. As plaintive as any was the fate of Commander Egerton, whose legs were blown off by a shell. 'That ends my cricket!' he is said to have cried. It ended his life.

On the more felicitous side, South African batsman Jimmy Sinclair was so large that the quartermaster of Little's Scouts could not manage to find a patrol jacket to fit him in the whole of Sterkstroom or Naauwpoort.

The struggle went on, but cricket kept its head down. It was to take a global war a dozen or so years later to cause bats and balls to be laid aside, with W.G. himself, in a letter to the Press, urging all sportsmen to take up arms.

During the last few of Victoria's 63 years on the throne crowds continued to flock not only to the Test matches but to County Championship games, patronising them in numbers such as no modern midweek spectator—*rara avis* that he is—would readily credit. The Oxford–Cambridge annual match, too, drew big attendances, as did the Gentlemen–Players. Even the Eton *v.* Harrow at Lord's, then still a vogue occasion, was viewed by deep ranks of gentlemen in grey toppers and morning coats, with their elegant, corseted ladies, ankles covered, parasols on high.

From international to school match, there was but one way to see them on the move—and the same applied to the rarely-seen Queen— and that was *in the flesh*. The conveniently communicative yet dehumanising electronic age was some way off, even if Marconi in 1901 was picking up the first Transatlantic wireless signal, transmitted from Cornwall to Newfoundland, and even if Lumière and Paul were busy with their brief and jerky moving pictures.

How were the hypnotic and beneficent effects of cricket evaluated during those years of hansom cabs and gaslight, of negligible income tax and flimsy wages, when no women and only 58 per cent of men in Britain had a vote? J. M. Barrie, creator of Peter Pan, speaking at an Authors' Club dinner in honour of P. F. Warner,[1] England's triumphant captain in Australia in 1903–04, said he had read the news of the victory while walking along Piccadilly 'with hansoms and four-wheelers passing over me constantly'. But he scarcely felt them!

Barrie said he thought that the man who invented cricket 'did a

---

[1] A third choice as captain, incidentally. The series was won without the services of F. S. Jackson and C. B. Fry, who were forced to decline the leadership. A. C. MacLaren had already declined Australia's invitation to take out another team.

bigger thing than the man who wrote *Hamlet*'. The same William Shakespeare was utilised by *Punch* after Warwickshire's memorable first Championship in 1911. In F. H. Townsend's cartoon, the Immortal Bard says to the successful young captain, Frank Foster: 'Warwick, thou art worthy!' (*Henry VI*). It was a popular win, for until Kent's first Championship in 1906 no county outside the Big Six—Surrey, Nottinghamshire, Middlesex, Yorkshire, Gloucestershire, and Lancashire —had won the title in 42 years of reckoning. Today almost any of the seventeen counties has fair prospects of taking the title.

A clue to the attraction of cricket came during the tour of Australia by Stoddart's team in 1894–95, when the five Test matches generated an excitement seldom equalled before or since. It was even reputed that the little silver-haired Queen herself, not renowned as a cricket enthusiast, eagerly perused the cabled reports dispatched from the distant colony by the pioneering *Pall Mall Gazette*. Three years later, when Australia thrashed the visiting Englishmen four Tests to one, it was seriously suggested that Harry Trott and his team of Victorians, South Australians, and New South Welshmen had done more for the movement towards the country's Federation than all the posturing, agitating politicians put together.

Conan Doyle doted on the game, and was a useful player; perhaps as many as 300 of his characters had names suggested by those of cricketers with whom he was familiar. The creator of Sherlock Holmes took only one wicket in first-class cricket; but it was worth at least a dozen others; it was W. G. Grace's, and Doyle wrote a 19-stanza 'epic' verse to commemorate his triumph. Then there was his brother-in-law, E. W. Hornung, who launched the cricketing burglar Raffles upon an unsuspecting public. Even he, though, fell sad in 1915:

> No Lord's this year; no silken lawn on which
> A dignified and dainty throng meanders.
> The Schools take guard upon a fierier pitch
> Somewhere in Flanders.

Siegfried Sassoon, Ernest Raymond, A. A. Milne, E. V. Lucas—they and many others in the literary field nurtured longings for the sunlit field that expressed themselves in their work. And then there was Wodehouse. P.G.W. had opened the bowling for Dulwich College at the turn of the century with Neville Knox, who was to return some devastating performances for Surrey and the Gentlemen before his shins gave way. Until disenchantment set in years later, Wodehouse derived much joy—and considerable revenue—from engaging 'Mike Jackson' in a stream of cricketing escapades. It is quite well-known, too, that Jeeves, one of the two most famous butlers of all time, was named after a Warwickshire all-rounder, who perished in the Great War.

Nostalgia comes and goes. The most celebrated of laments known to cricket was written by the wretched Lancastrian Francis Thompson, some years after Wilfrid Meynell had retrieved him from his pestilent drug-ridden twilight world on the Thames Embankment. Sitting at Lord's, he thinks of the Red Rose team of 1878:

> I look through my tears on a soundless-clapping host
> As the run-stealers flicker to and fro,
> To and fro:—
> O my Hornby and my Barlow long ago!

Hornby was a dasher, on the rugby as well as the cricket field; but it was a source of wonder that anybody should have pined for Dick Barlow, who specialised in such monstrosities as five runs in two-and-a-half hours (twice in county matches) and 90 in almost six hours (in a Test against Australia, evoking some satirical verse in *Punch*). Yet upon reflection, this is probably exactly the kind of patience tied to pain that appealed to Thompson's tortured mind.

Rather surprisingly, we find E. V. Lucas sufficiently disgruntled in 1906 to write that 'not only has cricket lost many of its old simplicities, it has lost its characters too. In the late process of levelling up, or levelling down, individuality has suffered.' That has a modern ring about it. So does a paragraph in the *Daily Graphic* in July, 1907: 'The medical profession tell us that nervous symptoms are strongly marked in the diseases of the present day, and that deaths from nervous breakdown are rapidly increasing. Perhaps the reason for this may be found in the nervous tension of this age. Weaklings resort to strong drugs to fight off debility and disease, and deceive themselves with so-called nerve tonics and cure-alls.' In *Wisden* the mighty Surrey and England fast bowler Tom Richardson, emphatically never a weakling, was endorsing the virtues of Dr Williams' Pink Pills, which had relieved his rheumatic joints: 'When I retired from county cricket,' testified the Titan turned publican, 'my nervous system was impaired. I began to get upset over trivial matters. My appetite fell off, and my memory often failed me. But the most worrying trouble was insomnia.'

Civilisation, or more precisely industrialisation, was advancing too rapidly even then. The motor car was driving the horse off the high-way at such a rate that machines simulating the trot, canter and gallop were marketed to stimulate the liver and quicken the circulation.

Andrew Lang's *Ballade of Dead Cricketers*, an elegy to the great play-ers of Hambledon, can have done little to swell ground attendances in his own time. It needed someone to put a perspective upon it, as it always does, and C. B. Fry, in earnest vein, wrote, in his 1939 auto-biography: 'I have a notion that the cricket of the 'nineties and early nineteen-hundreds was more amusing to watch, but I am not at all sure that the game of today is not more difficult to play. The fast bowl-ing, however, were it here, would make a difference.' E. E. Bowen, of Harrow fame, summed it up in lighter lines:

> There were wonderful giants of old, you know,
> There were wonderful giants of old;
> They grew more mightily, all of a row,
> Than ever was heard or told;
> All of them stood their six-feet-four,
> And they threw to a hundred yards or more,
> And never were lame or stiff or sore;
> And we, compared to the days of yore,
> Are cast in a pigmy mould.

Beyond argument there was an abundance of cricket glory in those years, but, viewed from the 1970s, it was less a remote and isolated period than a halfway house. A match to assert this was that between England and Australia at Trent Bridge in May, 1905. In England's large second innings Warwick Armstrong resorted to negative bowling wide of leg stump to a packed legside field during the Jackson–Rhodes part-nership, tactics that wrongly have come to be regarded as peculiarly modern, and which brought heaps of criticism down upon Armstrong, though it was not missed by all observers that the batsmen ignored the bait despite England's position of strength. Then, on the third and last afternoon, Australia were struggling to avoid defeat. Victor Trumper's back injury prevented him from batting, and as wickets continued to fall, a remarkable incident occurred, something which positively could not have been seen as typical in the fanatical competitiveness of sport in the 1970s. Australian batsman Charlie McLeod ran to the pavilion to ask his captain if he should appeal against the light, which was grow-ing poorer by the minute. The umpires would almost certainly have agreed to suspend play, but Joe Darling ruled out any appeal. Australia had been out-played, and harboured no desire to escape in this way.

In considering the captain's sense of chivalry, that of McLeod, who need not have consulted him, deserves approval.

County cricket's following was ardent, at a peak. Surrey were the only county to match Yorkshire, and won the Championship in 1887, 1888, 1889 (shared), 1890, 1891, 1892, 1894, 1895, 1899, and 1914, never to win it again until the 1950s, when they made up for lost time. Grubby Kennington Oval echoed to Cockney cheers through the years of 'Obbs, 'Ayward, 'Ayes, 'Olland, 'Enderson, 'Itch, not forgetting 'Habel'. The amateurs came and went, but the feeling was pronounced: this was the working-men's ground of the South—with Leyton catering for the East Enders.

They might have been Ovalites or Essex-followers whose exchange was quoted in a 1900 edition of *Cricket*: Scene—top of a bus, Sunday morning. Gentleman in shirtsleeves, looking at newspaper: 'This yer Fry and old Bosun-quett 'ave been and done it *this* time, any way.' Gentleman in very cheap flannel suit: 'What might they 'ave done?' 'Why the've both bin and made an 'undred in each innings.' 'Well, I don't see nothing in that. Old W.G., he done it three times, and so did young Fawrster.' 'I didn't say as they 'adn't, but they never done it both at the same time, did they?' 'No, can't say as they did. It *do* make a difference, of course.'

The notable pride verging on insularity associated with Kent was even then strengthening, aided by the county's first-ever Championship in 1906, which was hotly pursued by others in 1909, 1910, and 1913. *Cricket* in December 1912 was critical: 'I do think sometimes that the Kent cricket crowd is just a little *too* much wrapped up in Kent's doings. "Seen an evening paper?" I asked a Kentish partisan at the end of one of those grey days. "Yes. Nothing done at Dover," he answered. "What of the Test match?" "Oh, Frank Woolley's going strong—5 for 29." What was the Australian total? That he did not know! What had happened on other grounds? He really hadn't noticed! And he was not the only one of his kind whom I met.'

Not that they were much less committed up North, where factory chimneys coincidentally but invariably belched extra smoke when the visiting batsmen were trying to get a sight of the ball. At Bramall Lane, Sheffield, where the grinders constituted as tough and demanding an audience as any, a fieldsman risked smutty trousers if he reclined on the turf during a break in play.

Country-house cricket was enjoying its heyday, played by carefully-chosen teams on the private grounds of some of the more sporting

landlords of England, mostly in the South. There the gentlemen of
such clubs as I Zingari, Free Foresters, the Grasshoppers, and Eton
Ramblers played their cricket, exercised impeccable table manners (if
they desired a return invitation), and danced the evening away. Through
a colourful splash of blazers and hat-ribbons, the umpires—butlers,
gamekeepers or gardeners of His Lordship—would commence proceedings, which comprised an exhibition of all that was attractive and
honourable in the summer pastime. Country-house cricket as it was
then staged became next to extinct after the Great War, a poignant loss
for those survivors who had been part of it.

Club cricket had gone its informal way for many seasons, and it took
the War to bring about some organised administration in the South.
The Club Cricket Conference was founded in 1915 in an endeavour to
keep clubs together. The headlong rush into competitive league cricket
on Saturdays which came just over half a century later would have
horrified the majority of club cricketers of Victoria's and Edward's time.

Not that club cricket was 'soft'. County amateurs played regularly
with local clubs, and usually put personal performance before patronising gesture. Precedents had been set in the 1880s with quadruple-
centuries by J. S. Carrick and A. E. Stoddart—both at least partly immune
from criticism by the absence of a law permitting declarations—and
with the second-wicket stand of 605 by A. H. Trevor and G. F. Vernon
in the Orleans Club's innings of 920 at Rickling Green. There was no
lack of sincerity about these feats.

A conversation overheard in the spring of 1900[1] further dispels suggestions that club cricket, if loosely organised, was soft: Scene—An
office in the City, Monday morning. 'Hallo Jack, what's up?' 'Beastly
stiff. Played in a match on Saturday.' 'How did you bowl?' 'I began
with three wides, and the batsman said that it was dashed rot to send
such a fool against a good team. The next ball hit him hard on the
funny bone and nearly made him howl; as it went on and took his
wicket he was pretty sick. Then I hit another man on the chin and
bowled *him*, and he said it was a beastly shame to try a fast bowler on
such a wicket.' 'Did you go off?' 'Yes, about twenty minutes afterwards. But they were all out then!'

Enthusiasm was never enough, however, and when Dr L. O. S.
Poidevin, an Australian who played cricket for Lancashire and Davis
Cup tennis for Australasia, expressed the belief in 1910 that 'club
cricket in this country is too magnificently disorganised to ever do itself

---

[1] From *Cricket: A Weekly Record of the Game.*

justice or reach anything above hopeless mediocrity in standard of play'
he was pinpointing a shortcoming that to this day has had some bearing upon England's fortunes in international cricket. Club cricket in
Australia and South Africa was already well established as a supply-line
to the first-class ranks.

Where disciplines *were* introduced at the sub-senior levels in England
by the Victorians was in the leagues of the North and Midlands. In
1888 the Birmingham League was formed, in 1890 the Lancashire League,
and by the end of the century countless clubs in Yorkshire, Durham,
Northumberland, Cheshire, and Staffordshire had title honours to play—
and play hard—for, with mayors of boroughs accepting club presiden-
cies and more benevolent mill-owners taking an active interest. It was
almost entirely amateur—the time of famous professionals on lucrative
contracts lay in the years after 1918—but it was keen. . . .

Just as, in its own way, village cricket was keen. The vicars and
'squires' and blacksmiths of today somehow have a less authentic aura
about them than the characters who lunge, trip and laugh their way
through the pages of Sassoon, Macdonell, and de Selincourt. Then, as
now, the oddly-attired men and youths who cavorted on rude fields in
approximate accordance with the Laws of Cricket were considered the
very soul of the game, though an England Test XI has hardly ever contained a player with such rustic beginnings. That, many a villager would
claim defiantly, is something of which to be proud.

Village cricketers, metropolitan club cricketers, county cricketers,
cricketers from all corners of the Empire: they fell by the hundred and
thousand in the filthy mud at Ypres, at Loos, at Arras, at the Somme,
at Neuve Chapelle, at Mons, at Gallipoli. The 1915 *Wisden Cricketers'
Almanack* listed 44 war casualties, the 1916 edition 285, 1917 almost
500 (plus a reprieve for Cambridge and Gloucestershire cricketer Rev.
A. H. C. Fargus, who, it was discovered, had missed his train, leaving
the *Monmouth* to sail to its Pacific doom without him). The 1918 *Wisden*
told of over 400 war deaths, plus 84 from previous years, and the 1919
Almanack listed 330, with another 46 lately advised from 1917, including Australian fast bowler Albert 'Tibby' Cotter, aged 33, who enlisted
with the Australian Light Horse and was slain at Beersheba when he
raised his classical brow above the trench, doubting the scene reflected
in his army issue periscope. Another casualty of some sporting significance
was Norman Callaway, whose solitary innings for New South Wales,
in February 1915, amounted to 207 runs in as many minutes. What
cricket-field glories might have awaited a batsman of such demon-
strable potential?

Most of the slaughtered were young and had played for this or that public school, and sometimes for a University and county. Clifton College alone lost more than 500 of her sons in the conflict, one of whom was 23-year-old Lieut. G. W. E. Whitehead, of the Royal Flying Corps, attached to the Royal Air Force. He was killed less than a month before the war ended. Captain of the College eleven in 1913 and 1914, he had already made a score of 259 not out against Liverpool, and if any individual tribute could be said to speak for the tragic depletion of British manhood, 'An Old Cliftonian's' might:

George Whitehead was a perfect flower of the public schools. He was not limited to athletics only, great though he was in this respect. Intellectually he was far above the average, and was as happy with a good book as when he was scoring centuries. His ideals were singularly high and though gentle and broad-minded, he always stood uncompromisingly for all that was clean. So modest was he, that strangers sometimes failed to realise his worth.

Well might J. C. Squire, another of the cricket-loving poets of the time, have written: 'My God,' said God, 'I've got my work cut out.'

The Golden Age of Cricket, 1978

*

Ranji

ROLAND WILD

1889–1893: Sensation at Cambridge

It was an adventurous journey that he was making to England. Indians received a frigid welcome to the life of an English University, and conditions were very different from those of to-day. Ranjitsinhji had no bitterness in his heart at the loss of his kingdom, and his college principal had been accurate in attributing to him the virtues of manliness and courage.

It was perhaps intuition and foresight which made Chester Macnaghten decide to take care of him in London, and it was not surprising that he found his way to the Oval with his pupil during that summer. Surrey were playing the Australians, and Ranjitsinhji gained his first impression of the spell of cricket over an English crowd. In the lunch interval, they went round to the pavilion, and Chester Macnaghten introduced his pupil to some of the giants of the game. He shook hands with

Percy McDonnell and with C. T. B. and G. H. S. Trott, and was duly awed by such close contact with the illustrious. In later years this meeting was to give rise to an obstinate legend, for it was believed that he had actually taken lessons from these masters of cricket.

But such encouragement was not readily extended to him, and few people were disposed to listen to the eulogies of the head-master of an Indian school who claimed to have discovered a brilliant natural cricketer in the slim youth in his charge.

In point of fact, Ranjitsinhji was then more attracted by tennis. He was a natural player of style, and his quick eye gave him an advantage over men of greater experience. But watching cricket, accompanied by all the pomp and ceremony of a first-class engagement, a query came into his mind—was there not, he wondered, some quality of heroism in this cricket game that was lacking in lawn-tennis?

Six months he stayed in London with Chester Macnaghten, and in 1889 it was arranged for him to go to Cambridge to live in the house of the Chaplain of Trinity College. The Reverend Louis Borissow was his new guardian, and it was a typical English household that he now joined, with young people to meet and numerous children to provide an uproar. It was a new experience both for the Borissow family and for 'K. S. Ranjitsinhji' as he was now called. There began, in the Borissows' house in Chaucer Road, a friendship that was to last for many years—long after the bearded tutor's duties were over. There was discovered, to the general surprise, a fund of humour in the Rajput youth that seemed almost inappropriate, and in that atmosphere he was light-hearted and ready for any practical joke, slowly overcoming his shyness and modesty.

Arrangements were made for him to play games at St Faith's School on the Trumpington Road. Mr R. S. Goodchild, the head-master, noticed immediately his natural cricket skill, and prophesied a great future for him. In later years Mr Goodchild was able to make an interesting comparison between Ranjitsinhji and Duleepsinhji, for both played their first English cricket at St Faith's. Duleepsinhji, says Mr Goodchild, came to him with more experience, having been coached by his uncle, whereas Ranjitsinhji relied almost entirely upon a natural ability. Ranjitsinhji was frequently bowled by boys at school—Duleepsinhji was invincible.

Academic brilliance was not so apparent in these early days, and there were occasions when Mr Borissow regretted that his pupil's enthusiasm for sport and hobbies was not available for his studies. Mr Borissow, indeed, called him lazy and irresponsible, and prophesied that he would never pass Little-Go.

'Will you bet on it?' surprisingly asked his pupil.

'Certainly,' declared Mr Borissow.

Ranjitsinhji won the bet in 1892.

During his first summer vacation he went to Bournemouth with Tom Hayward, the famous Surrey cricketer, for whom he had a great admiration. Hayward was to bowl to him, but proof of the diversity of his sporting interests at that time is shown by his participation in a tennis tournament in which he actually beat the famous Ernest Renshaw. Not yet would he give up his other sports in favour of cricket, and it is perhaps fortunate for the cricket world that he did not choose to be an all-rounder. He began to play football, both Association and Rugby, and rackets, and he spent many hours at the billiards tables. At all of these games he showed the same natural ability, and it was later considered that with a little practice he could have represented Cambridge at Association football, rackets, tennis, and billiards as well as cricket. But an accident to his knee prevented him from playing any more football, and in any case it was obvious that his natural inclinations were in the cricket field. The chief object of his admiration was Arthur Shrewsbury, one of whose bats he secured.

In 1890 he played cricket for the Cassandra Club and for FitzWilliam Hall, and time after time slashed a hundred runs up on the board with abandon and ferocity. He had no style to speak of and relied entirely upon his natural 'eye'. Recalling these days many years later, he said naïvely: 'I found a great difference between the English style and my own.' It was his own style that went to the wall.

But he certainly scored a great many runs, and his name began to be mentioned by a knowledgeable sporting journalist as a natural bat. But this prophet's remarks were ridiculed as extravagant, and received little attention. Cricket, after all, was the English game. . . .

He played most frequently on Parker's Piece, and it was here, on the vast ground where many matches were played simultaneously, that he performed a feat of endurance that not surprisingly has gone down to history. His side had gone in early in the day and Ranjitsinhji had knocked up 132 before noon. After lunch he walked over to watch another match, and finding one team a man short, offered to bat for them. In a short time he had made a century and carried his bat. Returning to his original match, he found his side still batting, whereupon he joined yet another game and made 120 runs. Such was cricket on Parker's Piece, but Ranjitsinhji in later years frequently recalled that day when he had made three separate centuries, and claimed another world's record.

Mr Goodchild took him to Fenner's, but the authorities remarked with some acidity that Parker's Piece cricket was one thing, Fenner's another. But with this introduction he was able to practise at the nets, and he now received invaluable tuition from first-class professional bowlers, including Dan Hayward, Sharp, Richardson, Lockwood, and Watts. It was here that he was first seen by F. S. Jackson, the Captain of Cambridge (now Sir Stanley Jackson). Mr Jackson noticed him taking on relays of bowlers almost throughout the day and asked him why he must tire himself out. Ranjitsinhji's reply was instructive: 'I must practise endurance,' he said. 'I find it difficult to go on after thirty minutes.'

Mr Jackson was unimpressed, and his opinion remained unaltered when, a few days later, he saw Ranjitsinhji knocking the bowling about in a match on Parker's Piece.

Sir Stanley recalls a walk across Parker's Piece one day when he stopped to watch a match because of the enormous crowd. Asking the reason, he found that Ranjitsinhji was batting. In the few minutes that he remained the Cambridge Captain saw what he describes as 'dangerous cricket, with many unorthodox strokes, Ranjitsinhji nearly going down on his knees to pull a ball to leg'.

But even if Parker's Piece cricket was not considered very serious, the young Rajput's scoring had to attract attention. Two other feats caught the public imagination. Playing for the Cassandra Club against the old Perseans, he made 206 not out, and on another occasion he actually ran 12 runs off one hit. There seemed indeed to be little wrong with his powers of endurance, and he was now being acclaimed as a real 'discovery' by Mr Newton Digby, the cricket writer. It was known that he was going up to Trinity, and Mr Digby boldly claimed for him a place in the Trinity XI, but the reward for this prophet's accuracy was to be told that he had 'Ranjitsinhji on the brain', and indeed it was almost shocking to suggest that a University College should be helped by an Indian.

Sometimes the professionals despaired of his style, for not yet had he corrected his many faults, chief of which was a habit of running away from the ball when he thought he was going to be hit on the body. His right leg moved well away from the wicket and he exposed his stumps time after time. Dan Hayward was unable to persuade him to keep his foot on the ground and play a defensive stroke. But Ranjitsinhji disliked above all things to play for defence only, and the professional's ultimate cure was to peg down his right foot to the turf.

And thus was cricket history made. Thus was born the greatest scoring stroke ever known. For Ranjitsinhji, with his right foot perforce immovable, still refused to be on the defensive. To the amazement of the bowlers he twisted his body, flicked his wrists, and smashed the ball round to leg. They sent him good-length balls and he treated them in the same manner. They declared that it was risky, unconventional, and in fact 'not cricket'. His reply was to score fours off them.

He called the stroke the 'leg glance' and would freely admit that it was evolved through the necessity for defending himself. Many years later he gave different accounts of his invention, amongst which was the following: 'I was scared of a high ball one day, and let go of the handle with my right hand to protect my head. With my left hand I held up the bat. The ball hit the bat and went for a four.'

'Where were you looking?' he was asked.

'Towards the slips,' replied Ranjitsinhji, 'but I had my eyes shut!'

Meanwhile the young Rajput was gaining confidence in the domestic atmosphere of the Borissow household, and soon became a favourite, revealing the good nature which had always been part of his character. He was devoted to the children, and when the nurse went out for the afternoon he deputised for her with entire success and popularity in the nursery. The first time Mrs Borissow visited the upstairs regions to see how her children were reacting to an Indian guardian, she found the room strangely quiet, the only sound being Ranjitsinhji's voice. He was reading the Bible and elaborating from his own considerable knowledge. He was already deeply religious, and while at Cambridge wrote a prayer that was used in many British schools at the wish of the King. 'O Powers that be', he wrote, 'make me to observe and keep the rules of the game. Help me not to cry for the moon. Help me neither to offer nor to welcome cheap praise. Give me always to be a good comrade. Help me to win, if I may win, but—and this, O Powers, especially—if I may not win, make me a good loser.'[1]

One of his hobbies was photography, and he converted an attic in the house into what he called the Box-room Studio, and for a year or two the Borissow family and their friends were frequently presented

---

[1] The prayer formed the basis of six favourite maxims of His Majesty, and is now displayed in the study at Buckingham Palace.

with portraits of themselves, signed at the bottom with quite a professional touch: 'K. S. R., The Box-room Studio'.

In 1892 Ranjitsinhji surprised his tutor by passing into Trinity. He looked round for rooms in Cambridge, chose the most expensive, and decided to rent two floors, usually intended for two tenants. The rooms are now part of the Dorothy Café in Sidney Street, but were then situated over a baker's shop, one Mr George Barnes being both baker and landlord. The furniture followed the usual undergraduate idea of comfort; but he spent large sums on carpets, table cloths, and curtains, and promptly fell in love with the dark and overcrowded rooms. The furniture was to remain in his possession all his life as a reminder of those, the happiest days he ever spent; and years after, when his frequent returns to Cambridge were occasions of civic importance, he would often steal away with a friend to the Dorothy Café and sit happily in the crowded tea-room, recalling the exact position of his favourite armchair.

His bed was under the window in another room, and he added to the congestion in the sitting-room by the addition of a ping-pong table for the amusement of his friends. The two upstairs rooms he kept empty of furniture.

It was at this stage that he was joined by Popsey, that widely-travelled parrot which became famous as his constant companion. Popsey's age, even in 1892, was not a subject for discussion, but she was still with him when he died, although her pristine beauty had been marred by the loss of the majority of her feathers. Popsey suffered a drastic change in her habits when she was brought out of the racy atmosphere of a public-house, and a strict censorship had to be exercised over her language. Ranjitsinhji chastised her with a lead pencil when her remarks bore evidence of her Bohemian upbringing, or when she bit with ferocity at his fingers. But in later life, up to the age of approximately 100, she was blameless in deportment and speech, and if a parrot can be said to be passionately attached to anybody, Popsey was devoted to Ranjitsinhji throughout the forty years of their companionship.

In March of that year he was to be seen at the nets, sometimes being hard at practice from eleven o'clock in the morning till four in the afternoon. Frequently he was ridiculed for his insistence on obtaining the best bowlers, but the results of his self-confidence were seen in his consistent progress, although it was a long time before his many faults were eradicated. He defied all the rules of style and yet connected bat and ball with really devastating effect. And the leg glance continued to excite hostile criticism. Indeed, when he first exhibited this feat of legerdemain at Lord's, elderly critics shook their heads and deplored the entry of the juggler's art into a dignified game. But the fours continued to go down in the scoring book, to the consternation of writers who referred to the glance as 'a patent stroke of Ranji's own invention'. Other great cricketers attempted to imitate it, and to emulate that suave flow of his wrists to leg, but there has been nobody to execute the movement with such accuracy and grace.

But Ranjitsinhji himself would never agree that his cricket was due to natural genius. He attributed his success more to painstaking practice, and cited a picturesque parallel one day when Paderewski described to him the early endeavours of the world's greatest pianist.

Paderewski, with whom Ranjitsinhji made close friends during a session of the League of Nations, recalled how he had been advised to give up his ambitions to play the piano. His professors told him he would never be able to play, but the great Polish pianist had a secret. He had already composed a few pieces of music, which he found to his astonishment that nobody else could execute. So he ignored the advice of his teachers and plodded on day and night with the conviction that he had music in his soul. The span of his hands was such that he could attempt with ease movements which were impossible to others.

Ranjitsinhji listened attentively: 'It was the same with my cricket', he said. 'I had a natural eye, but I had a lot of trouble before I was anything of a bat.'

And he was already a great theorist. He would argue for hours on technical points of the game, and those who took the trouble to make a friend of him—and there were very few in 1892—found that he was studying the technique of the game even while he seemed to achieve his results by pure jugglery and quickness of eye.

Recognition of his merits was inevitable, although there were many who thought that University sport would come to an end when an Indian played for a College XI. Ranjitsinhji was picked for Trinity, and although at first he was ignored by other members of the team, and sometimes sat alone and friendless in the pavilion, his modesty and his real love of the game soon convinced his fellows that here was a young man who was not, after all, very different from any other cricketer with a white skin. It seems incredible to-day to recall that only forty years ago this spirit was general in England, but in point of fact Ranjitsinji was the first Indian to be accepted on terms of friendship and equality by undergraduates at Oxford and Cambridge.

His path was the track of the pioneer. There were no Indian boys at the public schools, and being an unknown quantity to the undergraduate, he was not included in the free-and-easy companionship of University life. There were times when he longed for friends to share his enthusiasm. But cricket changed his life at Cambridge, and when he justified all his self-confidence by finishing second in the batting averages for the season, he found a place established for him in popularity for which he had always been eager. He was delighted on the first occasion that an undergraduate visited his rooms, and from that moment passed muster on his merits when judged by English standards. He was recognised as a fervent sportsman with a skill difficult to reconcile with his appearance of frailty, and there were already suggestions that he might be tried for the University XI.

But this was talk of an almost revolutionary nature. It was one thing for an Indian to play for his College, but if he were a member of the University team, he might one day expect to play at Lord's, the impregnable stronghold of the English game. The imagination quailed before such a prospect.

Sir Stanley Jackson gives to-day an illuminating illustration of the feeling prevalent in 1892. Sir Stanley records that Ranjitsinhji might have been good enough for his Blue during his first year at Trinity, but that he himself, as Cambridge Captain, never so much as considered his inclusion in the 'Varsity Team. It was indeed only through a fortunate accident that Sir Stanley created history by conferring the greatest 'Varsity cricket honour on an Indian. During that winter Lord Hawke took a team of amateurs to tour India, and familiarity with Indians in their own country gave the Cambridge captain a new viewpoint. On his return in 1893 he was able to see the matter in a different light, and the prejudices of 'stay at homes' were ignored, but Sir Stanley willingly admits that but for that cricketing tour in the East, Cambridge University might have let slip the chance of playing one of the greatest cricketers who ever wore pale blue.

Revelling in his new-found popularity, Ranjitsinhji probably had little time for consideration of his future and his destiny. There was no news from India, and although sometimes he talked to friends about the loss of his rightful heritage, he found them more disposed to discuss the leg glance and the weather prospects. His allowance arrived with regularity and for some time totalled £800 a year. He learnt that the usurper, Jaswantsinhji, now called Jassaji, and aged eleven, was at the Rajkumar College and that he was not shining at any of the sports in which Ranjitsinhji himself had excelled.

He had not yet begun to regret the circumstances which had led to his disinheritance, and for a time at any rate he took every pleasure as it came, content enough to have around him the new friends whom he had gained by his skill on the cricket field. The little dark sitting-room over the baker's shop in Sidney Street was crowded every evening, and Ranjitsinhji's soft and beautiful voice could be heard arguing late into the night on the theory and practice of the game. His hansom cab awaited him outside, and he felt a glow of pride whenever he hailed it to visit another undergraduate party. They played poker in his rooms, and Ranjitsinhji was the most frequent winner, having an uncanny gift that could be likened to a sixth sense. Gaining confidence as friendship ripened, he would play practical jokes on his guests, and when they complained of the whisky, he took immense trouble to please them by putting the same whisky into other bottles, laughing delightedly at their solemn assurances that a vast improvement had been effected.

There was a piano for his friends, making the available space still less adequate, and after the nightly supper parties, Sidney Street re-echoed with the voices of 'hearties', robust though tuneless.

He was not always secure from the attention of the Proctors, although he was usually capable of outwitting them when they came to demand forfeit for minor offences. Many times, after a long chase in pursuit of a fast-running Indian undergraduate criminally lacking a gown, the bull-dogs would arrive at the Sidney Street rooms to find an elegant figure stretched in front of the fire, having obviously been there for hours, for Ranjitsinhji seemed to have the gift (invaluable to an undergraduate) of being able to run swiftly and continuously without showing guilty signs of heavy breathing. And it was with Oriental impassivity that he demonstrated how absorbed he had been in his studies.

He gave many presents to his friends, and often enough he would return from a visit upstairs with a tiny ivory model, pressing it into the hand of a visitor as he left. Newton Digby, the journalist, was often in the party, and to him he gave a superlative pipe in a vain attempt to stop him smoking cigarettes. He himself smoked little and drank less, and it was noticed that very often his dinner would be a sand-wich. He looked thin and frail, but there were steel muscles in his slen-der arms, and the secret of those lightning flashes of the bat was a perfect co-ordination of eye and muscle.

With the change in his social life it was inevitable that the annual grant, regularly sent to him by the State, would be severely strained. Ranjitsinhji had not been born in the purple at the Court of Jamnagar. His earliest experiences of life had been in the quiet village in the Plains, in the carefully- and economically-run household of his father, who was dependent upon the acres that he had inherited in appanage as a cadet of the State. Neither had he lived at the Court after his adoption, owing to the danger always present. Thus he had no experience of that brilliant and lavish hospitality for which the Rajput rulers of Jamnagar had long been famous. Nevertheless, he had inherited the traditions of his House, and there was prominent in his mind a feeling that it was incumbent upon him to entertain in the most lavish and extravagant manner possible.

He spent little on himself, but it seemed to be essential for him to show generosity to his friends, and it was this unselfish fault which resulted, in the course of a few years at Cambridge, in Ranjitsinhji's income being completely insignificant when compared with his expenditure. It was not self-indulgence nor a desire to display his riches that drove him into debt, but a natural and apparently pressing need to please his friends before giving any consideration to pounds, shillings, and pence. There were also included in the reckoning some magnificent but uneconomic gestures on his own account. He was the possessor, for instance, of the first motor-car ever seen in Cambridge, and Mr Goodchild still recalls one alarming afternoon when he looked out from St Faith's School to find the roads blocked and a vast concourse of people gathered in admiration round a spluttering and self-willed automobile, with Ranjitsinhji in partial control.

But whatever the causes, there were melancholy figures to prove that during the next few years he lived superbly in excess of his income. He was always visiting the Cambridge jeweller's shop, buying expensive watches and running up a bill which he could not hope to meet for many years. His negotiations with the best Cambridge tailor were on a similar scale, for he fitted himself out with dozens of suits for every occasion regardless of the cost. His generosity to friends was, however, undoubtedly the chief cause of his sad financial situation, which he treated with a gaiety and casualness that showed something of the spirit of his aristocratic ancestors when they were arranging some elaborate Court function. He presented gold cigarette cases to acquaintances, signet rings to the professionals who coached him, and precious ivories to casual visitors.

The result was the expected one. He could not pay his way, and the justifiable impatience of tradesmen nearly resulted in his being made a bankrupt. It says much for his honest attitude in this situation that it was his chief creditor who eventually succeeded in persuading others to hold their hand.

Ranjitsinhji's method of placating importunate creditors relied more on persuasiveness than logic. When his tailor, who was a personal friend, challenged him conversationally with the remark: 'But can you *pay*, sir?' he replied: 'Of course I can't, but you will get your money one day.'

And sure enough the kindly tradesmen who had for years held their hand were paid in full—plus 5 per cent.—when Ranjitsinhji was able to settle all his debts. Many of them also received special commands to meet him in London, and to take new orders from the customer who had once owed them a small fortune.

It was with a kind of joyous fatalism that he ran into debt, never troubling even to be fitted for his clothes, but telegraphing to the tailor to try the clothes on himself, as he was of similar build. He had a kindly thought for everyone, and would go out of his way to extend a helping hand to others in trouble. A certain sports-shop proprietor, disappointed at a local council election, found that his whole stock of cricket bats had been signed with the name that had already become famous to hero-worshipping small boys, and the run on his shop for these treasures did something to compensate him for a political set-back.

Ranjitsinhji was very popular in the Cambridge Liberal Club, which he used to visit almost every evening to play billiards. His politics were a highly coloured form of Radicalism, and he took part in several debates on more or less serious subjects, once making a witty speech on the subject: 'Should Cromwell have been executed instead of Charles I?'

The Sidney Street rooms were open to all, and among the company taking their departure in the early morning after a prolonged poker party there would be the jeweller, the tailor, the sports-shop proprietor, and the photographer, Mr Harry Stearne—all creditors who were on excellent terms with the young Rajput on the strength of their common interest in sport.

He fished with them and shot with them, for the gun and the rod were now becoming almost as popular with him as the bat. Life was very full and very exciting. It would have been a miracle if, with his temperament, he had become unduly worried over his debts.

1893–1896: 'Immense, Audacious, Unstoppable'

So a new idol came to cricket. Before the end of 1893 Ranjitsinhji was established with other god-like names in the annals of the greatest English game—with Grace and Fry and Archie MacLaren. At the same time signal honour was done to him by English cricket crowds, for at long last they learnt his name (or something like it) and no longer stumbled over its unfamiliar syllables or 'compromised', as the Cambridge undergraduates had done, by calling him 'Smith'.

His name now became 'Ranji', with a familiarity that meant affection. It was a kind of pass-word in cricket, a synonym for dashing, sparkling, and daring batting. The name clung to him long after honours fell thick upon him, and to the day of his death he was better known by these two syllables, that had first echoed round the stands of an English cricket ground, than by his titles that belonged to proud Rajput history.

(Indeed, at the crowning moment of his life, when at last he had achieved his ambition and was launching his princely career on the Gadi of Nawanagar, he did not smile when fellow-Princes acclaimed him with the traditional ceremony of their Order. But an Englishman in the glittering company raised his champagne glass and gave him a toast. 'To Ranji!' he whispered, and suddenly the new ruler's face lit up with smiles at the memories that the name recalled.)

The majority of the public did not know his real name, nor did it care. In later years the fact that he was a Maharaja was ignored. It was enough that he was the Ranji who had saved England on the cricket field. The London *Star* printed a leading article about the new name and reported that their compositors had addressed a memorial to the editor requesting that a simpler name be found for one who was so often in print.

Punch also took advantage of his name and printed many allusions to 'Run-get-Sinhji'. And a Cockney cricket spectator, almost delirious with excitement, is said to have been so overcome with admiration that he delivered in stentorian tones from the stand an appeal to one 'Ramsgate Jimmy'.

Perhaps more than anything else, these facetious comments revealed how sensational a step it was for an Indian to gain national sporting honours forty years ago. Yet another illuminating incident occurred when Ranjitsinhji was touring with a Cambridge team and the opponents asked: 'Does the dark fellow speak English?' They were told that he knew a word or two of the language. That evening 'the dark fellow' rose after dinner and made a witty speech. For a number of cricketers it was the worst moment of their lives.

It was not until he played for Cambridge against the Australians that he was selected to be in the team against Oxford, and when he did appear at Lord's in the 'Varsity match, so much fuss was made of him that he was quite bewildered. But already many counties were competing for his favours, and in that year he definitely refused the request of Surrey to join them. He played for the Gentlemen *v.* Players, and twice more against the Australians—for the South of England and for the Past and Present of Oxford and Cambridge. During the 'Varsity's match against Yorkshire he gave a striking demonstration of the magic of his movements. 'Long John' Tunnicliffe drove a ball with all his strength to where Ranji was standing in the deep. As the batsmen were running, the wicket-keeper called out: 'Where is it?' F. S. Jackson shouted: 'Run after it, Smith, what are you standing there for!'

But Ranji produced the ball out of his pocket, having caught it though it had been invisible to everybody else.

By the end of the season his was already a name to conjure with. He was twentieth in first-class batting averages, and third in the Cambridge averages. He was a close friend of the Cambridge captain, ever afterwards known as 'Jacker', and in later years the friendship continued when Sir Stanley Jackson was Governor of Bengal, and Ranji was the Jam Saheb of Nawanagar. He called Jackson 'my first captain' and found in him a man who could take an interest in his hopes of acceding to the Gadi. They talked cricket together, and the Cambridge captain declared that he had found a method of getting him out. 'I should bowl at your left elbow', said Jackson, 'and place as many men as possible to leg.'

This, in a word, was 'leg theory', or 'body-line bowling', and Ranji's comment at the time is important in view of recent events.

'Yes, you would get me out, Jacker,' he said. 'But it would not be cricket.'

Ranjitsinhji, 1934

*

Early Recollections

W. G. GRACE

My earliest recollections of any cricket match are connected with a visit which William Clarke's All England team paid to Bristol in 1854. Clarke's combination used to travel about the country, playing matches against eighteen or twenty-two players of different districts. In this way a great deal was done to stimulate interest in cricket, as a visit from the All

England team was a red-letter day wherever they went. My father organised this match, and captained the local twenty-two. The game took place in a field behind the Full Moon Hotel, Stokes Croft, Bristol, and I remember driving in to see the ground which my father's gardener and several other men were preparing. It was originally a ridge and furrow field, and had been specially re-laid in the previous autumn. The pitch was first rate, but the rest of the ground was rough and uneven. I was with my mother, who sat in her pony-carriage all day. I don't remember much about the cricket, but I recollect that some of the England team played in top hats. My mother was very enthusiastic, and watched every ball. She preserved cuttings of the newspaper reports of this and most other matches, and took great care of the score books. I have several of her scrap-books, with the cuttings pasted in, and very useful I find them, because in those days 'Wisden's Annual' was not in existence, and no proper record was kept. I see from the score-book that my eldest brother, Henry, and my Uncle Pocock played besides my father.

The All England brought down a first-class team, consisting of A. Clark; Bickley, who was a grand bowler; S. Parr; Caffyn, the great Surrey man; George Parr, the famous Nottingham cricketer; Julius Cæsar, of Surrey fame, and one of the very best all-round cricketers of his day; George Anderson, the genial Yorkshireman, one of the finest hitters of his time; Box, the celebrated wicket-keeper; J. B. Marshall, who was a great supporter of cricket; Edgar Willsher, of Kent; and W. Clarke, the slow underhand bowler—most of whose names are still famous in the annals of cricket. It is doubtful whether nine men out of the eleven could have been excelled, and as was only to be expected, the West Gloucestershire twenty-two were beaten—by 149 runs.

I cannot recall any more cricket until the next year, when almost the same team came down and played a second match on the same ground. This year my brother, E.M., played. W. Clarke, who acted as secretary and manager of the All England Eleven, was present, but did not play, as his eyes were troubling him. What makes me remember his presence was that after the match he came up to E.M. and gave him a bat, because he had long-stopped so well upon the rough ground. E.M., who was only fourteen at the time, came specially from school at Long Ashton to play in the match, and everybody congratulated him. It was a great thing then to have a bat given you by one of the All England players, and E.M. put it up in front of the pony-carriage with great pride. I see from the score-sheet that E.M. was given out leg before wicket. I wonder if he was satisfied with the decision? In the first innings my brother Henry was top scorer with 13, and in the second my father with 16. Uncle Pocock made 15. There were no other double figures reached by the West Gloucestermen, who made 48 in the first innings and 78 in the second. The fielding ground was very rough, but the wicket was good, as may be seen by the scores of the All England. Julius Cæsar made 33 and 78 off his own bat. Of course, the All England team won again—this time by a hundred and sixty-five.

The next thing I remember was a cricket week in 1858 and 1859 at Badminton, the Duke of Beaufort's residence. The celebrated I Zingari team was invited down and played three matches—*v*. Cirencester, Kingscote Club, and Gentlemen of Gloucester. In 1858 the Hon. Spencer Ponsonby (now the Hon. Spencer Ponsonby-Fane) was playing for the I Zingari, and so was Mr J. L. Baldwin, the founder of the club. Next year Mr Harvey Fellows, the famous fast bowler, was one of the team, and Mr R. A. Fitzgerald, with whom I went to Canada in 1872.

We drove over, and I remember that the Duke entertained us very hospitably. I also recollect that the Duke was at that time training five couple of hounds for a match (which, however, never came off) of 'horses against hounds'. The hounds were to run against three horses carrying eight stone seven over the Beacon Course of four miles at Newmarket.

I learned the rudiments of cricket when quite a child. As small boys we played about the garden in a rough and ready way, and used to make the nurses bowl to us. In 1850 my father had moved from Downend House to the 'Chestnuts', which was a great improvement, because it had two orchards, and the grounds were larger. My father laid out a cricket pitch in one of the orchards, which E.M., who was already a keen cricketer, improved by his own efforts. My father, my brother Henry, and my uncle Pocock practised at every spare moment, and we youngsters fielded for them from the time we could run about. Then they would give us a few balls, so I soon learned how to handle a bat. Uncle Pocock took special pains with me, and helped me a great deal, by insisting on my playing with an upright bat, even as a child. I soon got so fond of the game that I took every opportunity of playing, and when I couldn't play proper cricket, I used to chalk a wicket on a wall and get a stable-boy and one or two youngsters from the village to join me. So I got some sort of practice—sometimes with a broom-handle instead of a bat. We played all the year round, and at all hours of the day. I consider that a great deal of my quickness of eye is due to the fact that the boys with whom I played bowled a very large proportion of fast underhand 'daisy cutters', which used to jump about in a most erratic way, and needed a lot of watching. I also played fives, a game which is good practice for the eye during the winter months.

When I was at boarding-school cricket was encouraged by the masters, and I used to play as often as possible. Then I began playing for the West Gloucestershire Club, in which my father was the leading spirit. Of course, I used to go in last, and if I got a run or two I thought I was very lucky. As early as 1857 I played three or four innings for the West Gloucestershire Club. I was then only a boy of nine, and I couldn't be expected to do very much against the elevens we played, which were composed of grown-up men. As I grew older I played oftener, and in 1859 had eleven innings, which realised twelve runs.

The year 1860 marks an epoch in my cricket career. On the 19th and 20th of July (I was then in my twelfth year), I was selected to play for West Gloucestershire against Clifton, which was a keen rival of my father's club, and one of the crack teams in our neighbourhood, as it is to-day. I mention that particular match, because it was the occasion of the first score I remember making. I went in eighth (my brother E.M., who at this time was in rare form, had already made 150, and my Uncle Pocock 44) and added 35 before stumps were drawn. My father and mother were delighted, and both were very proud next day when I carried my score on to 51. I do not think my greatest efforts have ever given me more pleasure than that first big innings. In that year I had four innings, and made 82 runs. My average came down a good deal in 1861, when I played ten innings, and made only 46 runs, but it looked up a little the next season with five innings and 53 runs. But it was not until 1863 that I began to score with any consistency. That year was really the beginning of my serious cricket, for then I played in most of the West Gloucestershire matches. In 19 innings I made 350 runs, not against schoolboys, but against the best gentlemen cricketers of that time, many of them 'Varsity men, and capital players.

One of the most extraordinary matches I ever played in took place about this time. The story has been told before, but I think it will bear re-telling. My eldest brother Henry, who was in practice as a doctor at Kingswood Hill, was captain of a small club at Hanham, and frequently asked me to go over and play in matches against neighbouring village clubs. Over these matches a good deal of feeling usually sprang up, and not a little jealousy existed between the clubs. Victory was a great thing on the one hand, and defeat often a source of much annoyance on the other. My brother arranged a match between Hanham and Bitton, a village about a mile away. The Bitton team, knowing that we had a good eleven, secured some strangers, including one or two of the best men from Bristol, to help them. My brother E.M. put his cricket bag in the carriage, and came with us, pretending that we might be one short. When we arrived at the ground the captain of the Bitton eleven was delighted at E.M.'s appearance, and said, 'Teddy, I am glad you've come. I think we shall give them a beating to-day.' Without letting us know, E.M. had promised to play for the other side.

It was a wet day, and the wicket was very soft, but we commenced the match, and our side got the worst of it, E.M. taking most of the wickets. When the Bitton men went in a second time they wanted only ten runs to win the match. As E.M. went out to take his place at the wicket an old friend said, 'I haven't seen a good hit today.' E.M. laughingly replied, 'All right, I'll show you one. I'll win the match with one hit.' He tried to carry out his promise, and was bowled first ball by a shooter. We were glad to get E.M. out so cheaply, but never thought we had the remotest chance of winning the match. However, we began to feel very jubilant when three or four more wickets fell one after another without a single run being made. Some of the Bristol men had changed their clothes, thinking they would not have to bat. We chaffingly called out, 'You had better get ready. You'll be wanted yet.' Sure enough they were but they only walked to the wickets to walk back again. Only one man scored at all. He made three, and just when he looked like winning the match for them an excited partner ran him out. As the result of the match was now hanging in the balance the excitement became tremendous, especially as the Bitton men scored three off a bye. Ultimately, we got the whole eleven out for six, and so won the match by three runs. It was one of the closest finishes I ever saw.

'W.G.' Cricketing Reminiscences, 1899

*

W.G.

BERNARD DARWIN

'W.G.', said an old friend of his, 'was just a great big schoolboy in everything he did.' It would be difficult in a single sentence to come nearer to the clue to his character. He had all the schoolboy's love for elementary and boisterous jokes: his distaste for learning; his desperate and undisguised keenness; his guilelessness and his guile; his occasional pettishness and pettiness; his endless power of recovering his good spirits. To them may be added two qualities not as a rule to be found in schoolboys; a wonderful modesty and lack of vanity; an invariable kindness to those younger than himself, 'except', as one of his most devoted friends has observed, 'that he tried to chisel them out l.b.w.'

If one had to choose a single epithet to describe him, it would, I think, be simple. 'I am not a psychologist,' he says in one of his books, and his estimate was doubtless accurate. He did not think very deeply or very subtly about anybody or anything; perhaps not even about cricket, although his knowledge of it was intuitively profound, his judgment of a cricketer unique. Of all the stories about him none is better known than his answer to a question as to how a particular stroke should be made: 'You put the bat against the ball.' It may be read in one of two slightly different senses, and in either it seems to reveal something of his character. Take it as a serious attempt to explain the whole secret of a stroke, an earnest endeavour to help the learner, and in that sense it shows his essential simplicity. Again it may be taken as a reflection on those who want to be too clever and abstruse, and I imagine that W.G. did not want people to be clever. He was too modest to have the contemptuous arrogance of the unlearned towards learning; that belongs to the lout, and he had no trace of it, but for his own part he liked best the other simple folk like himself. His interests were all of the open air. If people wanted to read books, no doubt they got pleasure from it, but it was a pleasure that he could not really understand. Wisden, yes, perhaps, to confirm a memory or refute an argument, or in winter as an earnest of the summer to come; but in a general way books were bad for cricket. 'How can you expect to make runs', he said to one of the Gloucestershire side, 'when you are always reading?'; and added, almost gratuitously, 'You don't catch me that way.' I have searched in vain for anyone who ever saw him take the risk, except in the case of a newspaper or a medical book in which he wanted to look up a point.

W.G. was not an intellectual man, and even as regards his own subject his was not an analytical brain, but by instinct or genius—call it what you will—he could form a judgement of a cricketer to which all others bowed. One who played much with him has given me two instances to which many more might, of course, be added. A schoolboy who had made innumerable runs for his school, and was generally regarded as an extraordinary cricketer, played in his first first-class match with W.G., and made a respectable score. Everybody crowded round the oracle to hear the verdict, and expected a favourable one.

'He'll never make a first-class cricketer'—that was all, and it turned out to be entirely true. Here is a converse example. When Mr Jessop first appeared for Gloucestershire, those who now realise that they ought to have known better were struck only by the more rough-hewn and bucolic aspects of his batting. 'What have you got here, old man?' they asked W.G. rather disparagingly. 'Ah, you wait and see what I've got here,' he answered with a touch of truculence, and went on to say that in a year or so this would be the finest hitter that had ever been seen. That this verdict also turned out true is hardly worth the saying.

Moreover, if W.G. did not possess what is generally called cleverness, he had, within certain precise limits, a remarkable acuteness. He might not think deeply, but on his own subjects he could think quickly. 'A man must get up very early in the morning', said the Game Chicken, 'to get the best of John Gully,' and many a cricketer might well have said it of W.G. He had that sort of quickness of apprehension that may, without disrespect, perhaps be called cunning, and is often to be found, a little surprisingly, in those who seem at first sight simple-minded and almost rustic. He had plenty of shrewdness too in judging the qualities of men, so far as they interested him and came within his sphere. He might occasionally do ill-judged things in the excitement of the moment, but at the bottom of everything there was a good hard kernel of common sense.

We are told that when W.G. first appeared in first-class cricket he was shy, and we can picture him a tall, gawky, uneasy boy. He had not been to a public school; he came from a small country doctor's family; he had met few people except in his own country neighbourhood, and he suddenly found himself among those who had had a different sort of up-bringing. It is no wonder that he was silent and uncomfortable; but fame and popularity are wonderful softeners of that agony of shyness, and, if he perhaps kept a little of it deep down inside him, there was no external trace of it. He was perfectly natural with all whom he met, and if he liked them he was soon friendly and hearty with them. He was helped by a wonderful unselfconsciousness. He seemed to take himself for granted, at once a supreme player of his game, and, off the field, as an ordinary person, and did not bother his head about what impression he made. He was far better known by sight than any man in England. Long after his cricketing days were over, he had only to pass through a village street in a motor-car for windows to be thrown up and fingers to be pointed, but he seemed, and really was, as nearly as possible unaware of it, unless perhaps his admirer was a small child, to whom he liked to wave his hand. This unselfconsciousness pervaded his whole existence. He had come, as has been said, from a home comparatively countrified and uncultivated; he kept, to some extent at least, its manners and its way of speech all his life. He mixed constantly with those who were, in a snobbish sense, his superiors and had other ways and other manners, and I do not believe that he ever gave such things a thought. He recognised different standards in the houses he stayed at, to the extent that there were some to which he ought to take his 'dancing-pumps', and that was all. He liked friendliness and cheerfulness wherever he met it; he was ready to give it himself, and never thought of anything else that could be demanded of him.

I do not know if I am right, but he gave me the impression that the one thing that would not go down with him was any elaborateness of manner, any too formal politeness. I remember a little scene on a golf course. I was playing with him in a foursome, and someone unintentionally drove into us from behind. W.G., always jealous of his rights in any game, resented it, but the driver of the ball apologised with extreme politeness, and surely all would now be over. But it was not; the more careful the apologies the less did W.G. let the poor man alone, until he made the rest of the foursome feel very uncomfortable. I thought then, and I think now, that if the offender had come up, and said cheerfully, 'Doctor, I'm awfully sorry,' and had even clapped him on the back, all would have been well, but he was of the sort that cannot for the life of them clap people on the back, and nothing could atone.

It has been said that W.G. liked simple jokes, and if they were familiar ones of the 'old grouse in the gun-room type' so much the better. He liked jokes to do with conviviality, for he was a convivial soul. Essentially temperate in his everyday private life, he enjoyed good things on anything in the nature of an occasion; he had, as I fancy, a kind of Dickensian relish for good cheer, not merely the actual enjoyment of it but also the enjoyment of thinking and talking about it, and he combined with this, of course, a much greater practical capacity than Dickens ever had. A whole bottle of champagne was a mere nothing to him; having consumed it he would go down on all fours, and balance the bottle on the top of his head and rise to his feet again. Nothing could disturb that magnificent constitution, and those who hoped by a long and late sitting to shorten his innings next day often found themselves disappointed. His regular habit while cricketing was to drink one large whisky and soda, with a touch of angostura bitters, at lunch, and another when the day's play ended; this allowance he never varied or exceeded till the evening came, and, despite his huge frame, though he never dieted, he ate sparingly. His one attempt at a weight-reducing regimen was the drinking of cider. As he believed in a moderate amount of good drink, so he disbelieved strongly in tobacco. He had been brought up in a non-smoking family (though his brother Alfred became a backslider), and stuck to its tenets religiously all his life. It was an aphorism of his that 'you can get rid of drink, but you can never get rid of smoke'. He constantly proclaimed it as his own private belief, but he never made any attempt to put his team on any allowance of tobacco.

Mr A. J. Webbe tells me that he remembers at his mother's house in Eaton Square, W.G. marching round the drawing-room after dinner, bearing the coal-scuttle on his head as a helmet, with the poker carried as a sword. It is an agreeable picture, and we may feel sure that W.G. was ready to go on marching just a little longer than anyone else, for his energy was as inexhaustible as his humour was childlike; he must be playing at something—billiards or cards, dancing or coal-scuttles, anything but sitting down. The simplicity of his humour often took, naturally enough, a practical direction; in one corner of his mind there probably lurked all his life amiable thoughts of booby traps and apple-pie beds, and he was even known in an exuberant moment on a golfing expedition to hurl rocks at a boat like another Polyphemus.

He carried his practical joking into the realms of cricket, as when, according to a well-known story, he caused the batsman to look up at the sky to see some imaginary birds, with the result that the poor innocent was blinded by the sun and promptly bowled. With this we come to one of the most difficult questions about W.G.: did he at all, and, if so, how far, overstep the line which, in a game, divides fair play from sharp practice? There is one preliminary thing to say, namely that there is no absolute standard in these matters, and that standards differ with times and societies. The sportsmen of the early nineteenth century did, naturally and unblushingly, things that would be considered very unsportsmanlike nowadays. In those days everything was a 'match': each party must look after himself; it was play or pay, and the devil take the hindermost. Anybody who reads the autobiography of the Squire, George Osbaldeston, will get an insight into the sporting morals of that day. 'A noble fellow, always straight', said Mr Budd of the Squire: but he deliberately pulled a horse in order to get the better of those who in his estimation had over-reached him, and, generally speaking, it was one of his guiding principles in all sports not to let the cat out of the bag. He never did what he thought a dishonourable thing, but he had a different standard of honour from our own. I believe that in W.G. was found something of a survival of this older tradition. He had his own notions of what was right and permissible, and I am convinced that he would never willingly have done anything contrary to them; the difficulty arose when other people did not think something permissible and he did. He would never have dreamed of purposely getting in the way of a fieldsman who might otherwise have caught him, but to shout cheerfully to that fieldsman, 'Miss it', was—at any rate in a certain class of cricket—not merely within the law, but rather a good joke.

The law was the law, though in his intense keenness he could not wholly rid himself of the idea that it was sometimes unjustly enforced against him; what the law allowed was allowable. It was always worth appealing; if the umpire thought a man was out l.b.w., it did not matter what the bowler thought. 'You weren't out, you know', he was sometimes heard to say to a retiring batsman against whom he had appealed, and thought no shame to do so: everything was open and above board; if the umpire decided you were out—and he sometimes decided wrong—that was all about it. He wanted desperately to get the other side out, and any fair way of doing so was justifiable; he never stooped to what he thought was a mean way. No man knew the law better, and it could seldom be said against him that he was wrong, but rather that he was too desperately right.

In the matter of enforcing rules—and on this particular occasion W.G. was clearly in the right—the manner of his bringing up ought always to be remembered. His early cricket had been played with a father and three elder brothers who were going to stand no nonsense from the younger ones. The boy was taught to behave himself, and this meant, amongst other things, to stick to the rules. It was natural enough that when he grew older he expected other players to behave themselves too. It may be said that he did not sufficiently distinguish between big points and small ones, but the answer is that, where cricket was concerned, there was for W.G. no such thing as a small point. It might seem trivial to more easy-going or more flexibly minded persons; never to him; and if things were not, as he thought, just right, he came out bluntly and impetuously with his opinion.

His elder brothers had not had any excessive consideration for his

young feelings, and it may be that, on the field of play, he had not a
great deal of consideration for other people's. No doubt W.G. at point
could be a little trying to the highly strung batsman. 'These Graces
chatter so', said Sir Timothy O'Brien, who did not suffer things
gladly, and with W.G. and E.M. both fielding close to the wicket, and
neither having any too tender a regard for the batsman, perfect concentration of mind was difficult to attain. He appealed freely himself
when he was bowling, and, subject to discipline, he approved of other
members of his side appealing too. 'Why didn't you appeal, Fred?' he
snapped at the bowler after the over. 'Well, sir,' said Roberts, 'I looked
towards you at the time.' A young Gloucestershire amateur, not the
bowler, once got a formidable Australian stonewaller given out, and
there was some little unpleasantness. He asked W.G. if he had been
right to appeal. 'Right,' was the answer; 'I should think you were right.
Why, if you hadn't, we might never have got him out.' One small story
on this point may be allowed, because it is so agreeably typical of all
the parties concerned. F. S. Jackson, as it is still natural to call him,
was playing for Yorkshire against Gloucestershire in his first season of
county cricket. E.M. stood a minimum of yards away at point, W.G.
almost equally near on the leg-side, and they 'chattered' across their
victim in their best manner. Lord Hawke, the Yorkshire captain, made
some excuse to come on the field, and said to the young batsman, 'Are
these two old beggars trying to bustle you?' 'I don't know,' was the
answer, 'but anyhow they can't.'

W. G. Grace, 1978

*

A Reminiscence of Cricket

ARTHUR CONAN DOYLE

Once in my heyday of cricket,
    Oh day I shall ever recall!
I captured that glorious wicket,
    The greatest, the grandest of all.

Before me he stands like a vision,
    Bearded and burly and brown,

A smile of good-humoured derision
  As he waits for the first to come down.

A statue from Thebes or from Cnossus,
  A Hercules shrouded in white,
Assyrian bull-like Colossus,
  He stands in his might.

With the beard of a Goth or a Vandal,
  His bat hanging ready and free,
His great hairy hands on the handle,
  And his menacing eyes upon me.

And I—I had tricks for the rabbits,
  The feeble of mind or of eye,
I could see all the duffer's bad habits
  And guess where his ruin might lie.

The capture of such might elate one,
  But it seemed like some horrible jest
That I should serve tosh to the great one,
  Who had broken the hearts of the best.

Well, here goes! Good Lord, what a rotter!
  Such a sitter as never was dreamt;
It was clay in the hands of the potter,
  But he tapped it with quiet contempt.

The second was better—a leetle;
  It was low, but was nearly long-hop;
As the housemaid comes down on the beetle
  So down came the bat with a chop.

He was sizing me up with some wonder,
  My broken-kneed action and ways;
I could see the grim menace from under
  The striped peak that shaded his gaze.

The third was a gift or it looked it—
  A foot off the wicket or so;

His huge figure swooped as he hooked it,
   His great body swung to the blow.

Still when my dreams are night-marish,
   I picture that terrible smite,
It was meant for a neighbouring parish,
   Or any old place out of sight.

But—yes, there's a but to the story—
   The blade swished a trifle too low;
Oh wonder, and vision of glory!
   It was up like a shaft from a bow.

Up, up, like the towering game-bird,
   Up, up, to a speck in the blue,
And then coming down like the same bird,
   Dead straight on the line that it flew.

Good Lord, was it mine! Such a soarer
   Would call for a safe pair of hands;
None safer than Derbyshire Storer,
   And there, face uplifted, he stands.

Wicket-keep Storer, the knowing,
   Wary and steady of nerve,
Watching it falling and growing
   Marking the pace and the curve.

I stood with my two eyes fixed on it,
   Paralysed, helpless, inert;
There was 'plunk' as the gloves shut upon it,
   And he cuddled it up to his shirt.

Out—beyond question or wrangle!
   Homeward he lurched to his lunch!
His bat was tucked up at an angle,
   His great shoulders curved to a hunch.

Walking he rumbled and grumbled,
   Scolding himself and not me;

One glove was off, and he fumbled,
  Twisting the other hand free.

Did I give Storer the credit
  The thanks he so splendidly earned?
It was mere empty talk if I said it,
  For Grace was already returned.

Collected Poems, 1922

✻

On Umpires and their Verdicts

W. E. W. COLLINS

Once again the village umpire. For, turning over in my mind the events of the days when I was young, I arrive at the conclusion that the old village umpire's ideas of the game were as crooked as his morality. On what principle was he commonly selected? I seem to fancy that superior knowledge of the laws of cricket was seldom taken seriously into the reckoning. Doubtless in those rare villages where the worship of the goddess Astræa—if that was the name of the patroness of fair-play— still survived, a man under authority, and therefore of supposed or implied respectability, might be called to stand,—the parson of the parish for choice, or if not the parson, the churchwarden, or the parish clerk, or the Sunday-school master. In my own primeval village the same man combined in his own person the two last-named offices, and I can distinctly remember that he was the recognised village umpire. For the parson, my own father, was generally to be found captaining the side, and was quite the canniest bowler in the district. A real good bowler of the old school, underhand, of course, medium of pace, a slight twist from the leg, and with bewildering accuracy of pitch. Our churchwardens, substantial farmers both, and that in more than one sense of the word, had other and more important fish to fry, and so were not available. For Saturday, our usual cricket day, was also market day in the county town. So, in default of higher dignitaries, the clerk, a cobbler by trade, was the man for the post.

That pair, too, I take it, were parish clerks and Sunday-school masters rolled up into one, whom, as a tiny boy at school, I watched on a Whit-Monday officiating in a match played between Radley and some neighbouring village. My impression is that a stony-hearted matron— I was seldom without a cold in those days—must have laid an embargo on my playing on that Whit-Monday in the minimus game on the school-ground. For to pose as spectator when I might be playing myself never at any time commended itself to my fancy. I would rather play for Sharnbrook *v.* Barnbrook than watch an international match from the pavilion at Lord's. My companion for the occasion was no less a 'swell' than the captain of our so-called second eleven—as a matter of fact it was the first eleven of the Junior Club,—a fine athlete, but a poor scholar. For though several years my senior, he was in my own form, and I commonly had the honour of writing his verses for him. It was he who, being a person of varied information on other points than prosody, had got wind of the affair, and being temporarily incapacitated by reason of a vaccinated arm, he had made up his mind to go and see the fun, and was pleased not only to invite my company but to get for us both the required permission to go 'out of bounds'. Out of bounds we went accordingly, and arrived at our destination, not more than a quarter of a mile from the school-ground, even as the stumps were being pitched. The wicket, a mown patch in the middle of some pasture land, suggested the idea that the groundsman had prepared it by the simple process of inviting all the sore-backed donkeys in the neighbourhood to come and roll upon it; and some of the donkeys had apparently omitted to take off their shoes. There was the old familiar booth, with long table garnished by quart pots. There were the selected champions, easily distinguishable from the vulgar herd by the circumstance that the whole twenty-two of them were already stripped for the fray, guiltless indeed of flannels,—as indeed were the whole of our minimus game,—but in their shirt-sleeves, and sporting all sorts and colours of fancy caps. One gentleman, who affected a sort of oriental smoking-cap with a tassel hanging down behind, especially commanded our admiration. There, too, were the rival umpires, also by their dress easily distinguishable. *Prætextati?* Well, no! It was hardly my idea of holiday attire, even though it was worn on Whit-Monday. With tall hats, white ties, and black coats, the umpires rather recalled the idea of an Eton master or a well-to-do undertaker, except for the fact that each was carrying in his hand a long white wand, of which the more ordinary use—for I never on any other occasion saw the implement handled on a week-day—was for the rapping of the heads of unruly or sleepy boys in church on Sunday. At first we thought that these were carried by way of adding dignity to the office, but presently were persuaded that they were brought with an eye to business and for the better edification of recalcitrant batsmen. When the fieldsmen began to straggle out we managed to secure an excellent position for seeing on the top of two convenient ant-hills, of which there were many in that country. Our point of vantage had the drawback, to be sure, of being about where cover-point might have preferred to stand. But the ring was not too closely kept, the other thirty or forty spectators squatting or standing in groups pretty well where they liked, and the off-side fieldsmen were few and far between. It may be that the position of the field in cricket of that type is, or used to be, regulated by the position of the liquor tent. For John Hodge on Whit-Monday is apt to be a thirsty soul. Having chosen our seats, then, we sat down and waited for developments, and with the very first ball of the match came a very startling development. The batsman, having demanded 'block', hammered out a mighty grave in the pitch, assumed a defiant attitude, and had a lusty but unsuccessful mow at the first ball. This, rather to our surprise, was round-arm, not very fast, but tolerably straight,—at that date, let me say, wides were quite fashionable. The ball rose straight up off the pitch, and as the batsman stooped for the mow, hit him fairly and squarely in the eye. This, I regret to say, to our intense delight. For when were small schoolboys anything but brutal? The batsman flung down his bat and clapped both hands to his eye. There was no appeal. But the umpire, in exactly the same voice as I could imagine him leading the responses in church, first enunciated 'Hout!' and then volunteered the further information 'Leg afront!' My companion fell backwards off his seat, and fairly shouted with laughter. For a moment the batsman, still with both hands to his eye, appeared inclined to dispute the decision. But when the umpire, advancing majestically down the pitch, both by word of mouth and gesture with the wand showed himself ready to have recourse to compulsion, the injured innocent thought better of it, and retired to the tent, leaving his bat— probably one of the only pair on the side—behind him.

How good a weapon, by the way, was now and again one of those 'club' bats! A result, no doubt, of constant hammering. I offered a sergeant down at Woolwich ten years ago thirty shillings for the bat with which I had seen him make some gorgeous drives in a match on privates' ground.

'If it was mine, sir, you should have it and welcome,' was the civil answer, 'but it belongs to the club, and I should have to ask the secretary.' And the secretary declined to part with it at any price.

Alas! that I saw no more of that game. My companion's form of showing his appreciation of the performance—for he continued his inane cackling—evidently did not commend itself to the rustic mind, and the school was not always on very good terms with the village. So when we saw the two umpires, after a brief consultation, advancing in our direction, we thought it prudent to decamp.

Here let me remark that another old schoolfellow, who apparently was also present on the occasion, and whose memory is probably as dependable as my own, having read my account of the scene in 'Maga' wrote to me and suggested the following emendation:—

'Ho, I'm hout, am I?' exclaimed the batsman, and with that he hurled his bat at the umpire's head.

My correspondent, however, chivalrously adds that in the course of constant narration he may possibly have thus embellished the story 'off his own bat'. Is it not true of many a good story that it 'vires acquirit eundo'?

Occasionally, too, without doubt, the choice of the umpire was influenced by considerations of a man's fighting-weight and capacity. An instance of this kind came very near home to me in the first 'out' match I played for a village near Rugby.

'I was thinking, sir,' said our secretary, the village baker, 'as we'd do well to ask Mr "Ho"'——the gentleman's name really began with a vowel—'to stand for us in our match agin B——.'

As all that I knew about Mr 'Ho' was that he had a very red nose, and was reputed to be bibulous, I was rather inclined to demur to the proposition.

'But does he know anything at all about the game?'.

'Well, I ain't a-going to say as he's quite what you'd call not a Lillywhite's guide, like. But he's uncommon 'andy with his fists, is Mr "Ho", and we most in general counts on meeting some roughish customers at B——.'

I at once withdrew my objection, but for some reason or another Mr 'Ho' could not be prevailed upon to stand, and we had to go without him. Fortunately, perhaps, we were comfortably beaten, and so the affair did not resolve itself into a match of fisticuffs. Even so, the baker remained firm in his conviction that had we been lucky enough to secure Mr 'Ho's' assistance the match might have ended in our favour.

Or again, a man with a reputation for having a Benjamin's portion of mother-wit, or the gift of singing a good song, might be the favoured candidate for the post, The bard, from the Homeric age even until now, has ever been a welcome guest in village as well as courtly

circles. And a glib tongue and ready wit—be they seasoned with never
so much vulgarity—have been found to carry great weight when a rustic audience is agape to listen. Certainly an intensely vulgar carpenter
was an important factor of success in two football matches which I
played for a certain village nigh upon thirty years ago. He was not a
player, nor yet an umpire, but he used to prowl about the touch-line,
and indulge in such truly awful reflections upon the personal appearance, performances, and general morality of the opposition side, that
two of them were constantly employed in hunting him round the
ground, while the game went on without them. As the obstreperous
carpenter was fleet of foot, and the sympathies of our gallery of brick-
makers pre-enlisted in his favour, he managed to elude the punishment
he so richly deserved, and was wise enough to make himself scarce
before the end of the match. After I heard him insult, in the most out-
rageous manner, a fine player and most excellent fellow on the other
side, I drew the line, and refused to play again if he was admitted to
the ground. But the villagers elected to retain the services of the carpenter, the more valuable auxiliary.

That a genial disposition and what may be termed all-round respectability still rank higher in the estimation of the rustic cricketer as qualifications
for the important post of umpire, than a too intimate acquaintance
with the niceties of the game, may be inferred from the following story.

A singularly good-natured but very short-sighted friend of mine was
invited by the captain of a village team to officiate as umpire in a
rustic match.

'But', pleaded the gentleman, speaking what I fear was the veritable
truth, 'I know so very little about the rules, and, besides, I am very
short-sighted.'

'Oh, sir, that don't matter not a rap,' was the encouraging answer.
'Him as is going to stand at t'other end ain't got but one eye, and he
don't know nothing at all.'

But to leave the matter of selection, and hark back to partiality. I
played once in a match near Daventry, where it was the clearest case
of pull devil pull baker that I ever saw in my life. The 'baker' was on
our side, and by virtue of his superior talent, or better luck in receiving more appeals, we won the match. But I am bound to say that the
other party was bad to beat. It is well to be modest on occasion, and
I will admit that my own contribution to the success of my side was
worse than insignificant. The other side went in first, and I happened
to be keeping wicket. One particular decision given by the 'devil' was

intensely aggravating to the bowler and myself at the time, though we could afford to laugh at it afterwards. The last ball of an over, a straight and fast yorker or indeed full pitch, landed on the batsman's foot, which was actually in the block-hole.

'How's that?' simultaneously from bowler and wicket-keeper.

'Hover'.

'But I appealed for l.b.w.', explained the bowler.

'You says "how's that?" and I says "hover", and hover it is.'

Nothing more could be extracted from the umpire, and two at least of our side were inclined to chuck up the match there and then. But point, a wise man, and one who knew the ropes, came and whispered in my ear—

'Never mind, it's all right. Our man is worse!'

And when I glanced at the stout party who was moving up from the short-leg position, I caught his eye, and was not a little comforted. Comforted for the time only; later on I was equally disgusted with him and with myself. Bad as the wicket was, I had every chance given me of making a record score that day. For the bowling was by no means straight, and the feat of getting out at one end without being clean bowled resolved itself into an impossibility. What I actually did was to score exactly five runs in four completed innings. Forewarned that no mercy would be shown to me if I either left my ground or allowed the ball to hit my leg or to pass the wicket on the off side when the 'devil' would have the decision, I amused myself by gently stopping every ball sent down from one end by a very short-pitched and simple slow bowler. Where the 'baker' had his say, I was run out, caught at the wicket, and badly l.b.w. before I retired clean bowled. Even then our umpire was not by any means satisfied. This he showed by giving vent to sundry inarticulate sounds, palpably intended to attract my attention, and by making a series of grimaces as I walked away. Just as I was leaving the ground in the evening he came up and volunteered to carry my bag to the cart.

'What sort of a game was that, mister, to walk away without giving a chap a chance? You might have lost the match by it. Why didn't you appeal, they chucking up the ball and all?'

This was Greek to me at the time, but in the following week came enlightenment, and I learned for the first time the fact that here and there were to be met with at that date 'Rules of the Ground' as distinct from the MCC authorised version of the laws of cricket. For I fell into conversation with a parson, who, like many other men of my acquaintance, was in full possession of a grievance. It appeared that he had been coaching his choir boys in cricket, and was not a little proud of their prowess. But playing their first match away from home they had been beaten.

'And I want your opinion,' he concluded, in a querulous voice, of the type that drives me distracted when I hear it from a pulpit, 'for I don't think myself that it was quite fair.'

'What was not fair?'

'Why, you see, my boys were only beaten by nine runs, and they had to get quite twenty of the other side's wickets down, and twelve or thirteen were clean bowled.'

'But how many were playing on a side? The whole choir?'

'Only eleven.'

'Two innings, then?'

'Oh no; but it's a rule of the ground that we were playing on, that if any of the field either throws up the ball, or says "out" before the umpire has spoken, it doesn't count "out", and—and my poor boys had never played that way before.'

Poor parson! And was that what was in the 'baker's' mind?

Curiously enough, many years later I knew in the flesh a thoroughly honest boy-cricketer, who must have imbibed from some unknown source a very similar idea of the game. Watching a match between two preparatory schools, I saw a simple catch held at cover-point.

'Poor old Jack!' I murmured.

But then? There was a momentary hesitation, and the bowler, to whom the ball had been returned, stared expectantly at the batsman. And the batsman stared into space. Finally the latter prepared to receive the next ball. And the bowler, after another brief period of hesitation, went on bowling.

'Great Scot!' I exclaimed to a man who was sitting next to me, 'surely that was out!'

'Never saw a clearer case in my life!'

'Could it have been an optical delusion? Could it have——?'

'No; look at the umpires,' he interrupted me. The umpires were masters of the rival schools, and each had set his heart on victory. We could see that the man by short-leg was shaking with laughter, and the other looking—thinking, too—daggers. Jack so far profited by his escape that he made nineteen more runs—his side eventually won the match by fifteen—before he was bowled off his pad. Even then he seemed inclined to stop, and the wicket-keeper had to appeal.

We intercepted the retiring batsman on his way to the pavilion, and I tackled him at once.

'I say, Jack, weren't you caught at cover-point?'

'Well, I thought so,' he admitted.

'But don't you generally go when you're caught at cover-point? He isn't a boundary, exactly.'

'I thought you ought never to go out till the umpire has given you out. And nobody asked him.'

'A very good rule, too, Jack,' struck in my companion. 'Just you stick to it, and you'll do!' And then, dragging me away, he added: 'Jack is very honest, but not over bright, and if you tell him to go out when he thinks he is out, you will find him marching off and saying he is l.b.w. some day.'

The bowler, of course, when put on his defence, gave the ordinary answer of the modern preparatory schoolboy—

'Why didn't you appeal, you little donkey?'

'Please, sir, I didn't know I had to.'

Right for once! But has not that stereotyped form of reply been called upon to play its part in reference to every duty and function of preparatory school life—except, perhaps, to the eating of sweet stuff?

Here is a story, bequeathed to me as a legacy by one who was a good friend, whether on the cricket-field or off it. . . . I little dreamed at the time that I was to see his face again no more.

On this occasion, away from home on a holiday, he was taking a bicycle-ride with a view to seeing something of a country new to him. He had started after breakfast, and, riding along leisurely, presently came to a field in which there were evident preparations for a cricket-match. There were flags on the ground, red posters on the gate, and an old fellow was standing by the pitch which he had apparently just marked out. S—— dismounted, and leaving his machine inside the gate, strolled on to the ground and had a look at the wicket.

'Hulloa!' to the old man, 'your crease is much too broad.' For he had noticed at once that the popping crease was at least twice the usual width.

'You says as my crease is too broad, do yer? Well, I says it ain't, so there!'

As the old gentleman seemed inclined to be crusty, and the width of the crease was of no particular consequence to S——, he elected to hold his tongue.

Pleased, apparently, to have silenced criticism, the old fellow presently went on to impart instruction.

'You said as my crease was too broad, didn't yer!'

S—— nodded.

'P'raps you can tell I this, then. Who do it belong to? Whose prop-utty bee's un?'

'I'm sure I don't know.'

'Then I tell 'ee. See here now.' And with that the speaker planted a tolerably large boot lengthways in the middle of the crease, so that he was literally standing *on* the crease, with no part of his foot either inside or outside. 'It's mine!' very emphatically. 'I be umpire, and if I've a mind to say "Hin!" I says "Hin!" and if I've a mind to say "Hout!" I says "Hout!"'

Leaves from an Old Country Cricketer's Diary, 1908

*

Umpire Lee

LORD DUNSANY

Once as I read through wastes of prose,
    And wearied of the labour,
These words tremendously arose
    Like sudden flash of sabre,
'When umpire Lee
Was hit on the knee
    By a very fast ball from Faber'.

'Twas but a humble cricket match
    And but a daily's pages,
And yet it somehow seemed to catch
    A splendour from the ages
When poetry
Was apt to be
    The diction of the sages.

There stood these scintillating lines
    Mere common prose their neighbour,

To cheer us as a light that shines,
   Or sound of pipe and tabor,
'When umpire Lee
Was hit on the knee
   By a very fast ball from Faber'.

Privately printed (after a match report in the *Sunday Times* of the
Eton *v*. Winchester match of 1935)

*

The Old Trent Bridge Ground-Keeper:
Tom Foster and William Mee

RICHARD DAFT

The visitor to the old Trent Bridge Ground at Nottingham can
scarcely fail to have noticed when a county match is played there a
little old man with white hair and whiskers, limping about between
the innings superintending the rolling and sweeping of the wickets.
This individual is well known to all the frequenters of Trent Bridge as
'Billy Walker', the custodian of the ground. To his more intimate
friends he is known as 'Fiddler', of which nickname more anon.

Walker is a native of Radcliffe-on-Trent, as were his father and grand-
father (and great-grandfather for anything I know) before him. The
present Trent Bridge groundsman was brought up to the trade of a
gardener, and a very excellent one he became in after life, filling the
office of head gardener to several gentlemen in Nottinghamshire,
Lancashire, and elsewhere. All the Walkers are musical. The father of
the subject of my sketch was a great man with the violin. He not only
played on that instrument, but made one which is still, I believe, in
his son's possession. The maker of it wrote out the names of all his
sons and daughters with the dates of their birth on a piece of parchment, and fastened it inside the violin previous to fixing on the back.
Owing to his great fondness for the violin, Mr Walker, senior, received
the name of 'Fiddler', which in due time descended to his son, the present Trent Bridge groundsman, and has now been conferred on *his* son,
who assists his father on the ground. In his younger days the guardian
of the Trent Bridge was well known in Nottinghamshire as a skittles
player. At this game he was the lion of his native village and of the

surrounding district. Many have been the innocent strangers who have suffered signal defeat at this old English pastime at the hands of Mr William Walker.

On one occasion William and some friends went to a small town in a distant part of the county at which the annual fair or 'wake' was being held. While refreshing themselves in the bar of one of the inns of this place, the conversation turning to the subject of skittles, one of Mr Walker's friends declared he would back him to play anyone in the town for a sovereign. One of the natives no sooner heard this challenge than he crossed over to a corner of the room where a friend was sitting and told him in a mysterious voice to 'go and fetch "Nobble 'Em",' and presently the gentleman who bore this name, and was the champion skittles player of the town, appeared on the scene, and a match between him and Mr Walker was soon concluded. A most exciting game followed, which ended in the defeat of 'Nobble 'Em', the local champion, who, however, played one of his very best games, and so delighted were Walker's friends at his victory that they carried him shoulder high to the nearest public house and there entertained him to his heart's content.

Once only at skittles was William taken in. There was years ago a man named Blatherwick, a resident of Nottingham, who was undoubtedly the best player in the county. Once Walker and a Mr F——, a keen sportsman, were together in a distant village, and having business to transact in different parts of the place, each went his way, agreeing to meet at a certain spot later in the day. Mr F——'s business led him to a public house where there was a skittle-alley, in which, on the present occasion, a lively match was being played between two very fair players. Their play, however, did not meet with the approbation of Mr F——, who declared that he had a friend in the village whom he was ready to back for any amount against the best man on the premises.

'I'll back this man here to play him for a fiver,' said one of the players eagerly, as he pointed to a quiet-looking man who had been a spectator of the match which had just been concluded, and who, from the remarks he had made on the game, Mr F—— was quite convinced knew nothing of the science of skittles. However, the stranger after a good deal of persuasion allowed himself to be backed for a five pound note, and the match was no sooner made than Mr F—— went off in high spirits to fetch his friend Walker, who, when he made his appearance, quickly recognized in the quiet gentleman who was to be his opponent the renowned Mr Blatherwick, of Nottingham!

'They've done you this time, sir,' William remarked to Mr F——.

However, there was no getting out of the match, and though William was defeated he was very far from being disgraced for he ran his opponent very closely throughout the game. After his appointment to the charge of the Trent Bridge Ground, Walker effected a great change in the wickets on that enclosure. Years ago the wickets would not wear at Trent Bridge, but thanks to an application in winter of a special kind of marl or clayey soil, which Walker has procured at different times from a certain part of Nottinghamshire, the wickets at Trent Bridge became second to none.

This preparation of his Walker always designated as 'hair oil'. Some years ago he was invited to inspect the Old Trafford cricket ground at Manchester, and, having strongly recommended an application of the Nottinghamshire 'hair oil', several truck loads were afterwards despatched to Old Trafford. William returned from Manchester, speaking in the highest terms of the Lancashire executive, and of 'the princely manner in which they had treated him' during his visit.

William's manner of speaking of his wickets is rather amusing. He always talks of the wicket as if it were himself; consequently his conversation when on this subject is apt to be very puzzling to strangers. 'I'm better this match than ever I was. They'll never be able to wear me out; I shall be just as good on the third day as I shall be on the first.' Again, 'So-and-so can never get any runs except when he bats on me.'

A Cricketer's Yarns, 1892

*

Some Stout Cricketers

RICHARD DAFT

Stoutness is generally considered as a sure preventative to a man's playing cricket. During my time I have seen many a man have to give up the game owing to his getting too stout, but then again I have known instances where men thus heavily handicapped have put to shame many slim young players, by the extraordinary agility they have shown in the cricket field.

When thinking of stout cricketers, the mighty form of the great

Alfred Mynn naturally presents itself to my mind's eye. Mynn, however, until quite the extreme end of his career never lost his activity. He was always in good condition and had the advantage of having his weight equally distributed all over him as it were. He was 'massive' rather than stout, and always carried himself as erect as a dart. For so large a man, too, he was exceedingly light in his movements. Sir Henry Bromley,[1] one of the greatest supporters Notts cricket ever had and a player himself of no mean order, had in the cricket field both in his appearance and movements a great resemblance to the old 'Lion of Kent'. Old Tom Bignall, who rendered such excellent service for Notts in years gone by, was very stout during the last years of his career, stouter then than he is now I believe. Tom, however, carried his weight well for a considerable time. Eventually it was his fielding that was affected sooner than his batting.

Old Joe Rowbotham of Yorkshire, too, was a 'heavy weight', as was also his fellow county player, Roger Iddison. For a stout cricketer, however, my old friend Mr A. Shuker, who at one time represented Derbyshire, was by far and away the most active man I ever saw in my life. Mr Shuker was below medium height, and must have weighed fully sixteen stone. But I have seen few ten stone men who were as active in the field as he. He was an exceptionally brilliant fielder, could get down to the ball with extraordinary quickness, and was also a very good fast bowler and a really splendid bat. He scored very heavily in local matches for a great many years, and if he had been able to devote more time to County cricket could not have failed to have made a prominent name in it. He was also a very good football player, generally playing full back, and was a very fine kick. He was equally good too at the games of lawn tennis and fives. When I think of the way Mr Shuker used to play in these games, and then see the way some men of his weight of my acquaintance move about, the contrast is rather startling.

I remember once playing against an enormously stout gentleman, who, when he came in to bat, evidently felt very nervous about one of our bowlers, a very fast one, who was opposed to him. The fat gentleman seemed to think that when standing at guard it was safest to

[1] Sir Henry Bromley, fourth Bart., was the first President the Nottinghamshire County CC ever had, and he occupied the position from 1869 until December, 1879. When playing cricket he generally wore knickerbockers instead of the more orthodox trousers. At Southwell in 1864 he scored 47 for Gentlemen of Nottinghamshire *v.* Gentlemen of Yorkshire.

stand as wide of the wicket as possible; indeed he carried out this idea so far that to the fielders and spectators he seemed to be standing almost as near to short leg as he was to his own wicket, and when he lifted his bat up it left the three stumps vacant for the fast bowler to knock down. This, after two or three balls had whizzed past the wicket in dangerous proximity to the corpulent batsman's body, he succeeded in doing. The wicket was 'spreadeagled', and I never saw a man so pleased at getting bowled out as the batsman was on this occasion.

One cricketer of note was so heavy that it is reported that a four post bed gave way under him at an hotel where he slept, causing such an awful crash that the people in the adjoining rooms thought the house was falling down. Old Hickling, who for many years kept the Trent Bridge Inn and Ground after old Clarke's time, was an immensely fat man. He accompanied the team which Sir Robert Clifton took to Paris in May, 1864, as umpire, and greatly astonished the Frenchmen by his corpulence and size. They always spoke of him as 'de John Bull' and could not but believe that he was padded all over, and used to walk round him like a farmer inspecting cattle at a show. Hickling during his Parisian visit was, I have been told, much disgusted with the French living, and his being utterly unacquainted with the language made him still more irritable. He missed the large joints of beef and mutton which he was accustomed to see on his own table at home. 'Come over to England, confound you!' he is said to have exclaimed to an unfortunate waiter on one occasion, 'and *we'll* show you how to live—and how to die, too,' he concluded, thinking probably of Waterloo.

Another colossal cricketer was Mr Thomas Butler, the brother-in-law of George Parr. He, however, was more of the Alfred Mynn type. He was quite as tall and almost as heavy as Alfred. Like most big men, he was exceedingly kind-mannered and good tempered. He was very keen on boxing, and used to be very fond of sparring at his own shadow on the wall. A friend would often assist him in this eccentric performance by playing the violin. He would generally begin to play very slowly, and Mr Butler would 'feint' and manœuvre cautiously with his shadow for a time, then the tune would go quicker, and the fighting began, quicker and quicker went the fiddle, and quicker and quicker Mr Butler would hit, dodge and guard. So excited did he used to get towards the end of the performance that I believe on some occasions he thought he had a real antagonist to deal with.

A Cricketer's Yarns, 1892

*

The Deserted Parks

'Solitudinem faciunt: Parcum appelant'

LEWIS CARROLL

Amidst thy bowers the tyrant's hand is seen,
The rude pavilions sadden all thy green;
One selfish pastime grasps the whole domain,
And half a faction swallows up the plain;
Adown thy glades, all sacrificed to cricket,
The hollow-sounding bat now guards the wicket;
Sunk are thy mounds in shapeless level all,
Lest aught impede the swiftly rolling ball;
And trembling, shrinking from the fatal blow,
Far, far away thy hapless children go.

 The man of wealth and pride
Takes up a space that many poor supplied;
Space for the game, and all its instruments,
Space for pavilions and for scorers' tents;
The ball, that raps his shins in padding cased,
Has wore the verdure to an arid waste;
His Park, where these exclusive sports are seen,
Indignant spurns the rustic from the green;
While through the plain, consigned to silence all,
In barren splendour flits the russet ball.

Notes by an Oxford Chiel, 1867

❊

Prince Christian Victor

W. A. BETTESWORTH

Cricket, August 6th, 1896

If it had not been that, while he was in residence at Magdalen College,
Oxford, Prince Christian Victor was contemporary with Mr H. Philipson,
one of the very best wicket-keepers of the day, he would undoubtedly
have received his 'blue'. Not only was the Prince a wicket-keeper of

the highest promise, but he was also a batsman who would soon have become first-class if he had been able to play regularly in good cricket. He was captain of the Wellington College eleven[1] and of the Royal Military College eleven at Sandhurst, where he went after leaving Oxford; and if circumstances had permitted, he might easily have become a great cricketer. But his duties as an officer called him away to India, and, moreover, he had to give up wicket-keeping, so that he was obliged to content himself with playing Army and club cricket, in which he met with very great success. He scored a large number of hundreds, his highest innings being 230 in a house match at Wellington. It will be remembered that he accompanied the Expedition to Ashanti in 1895, and, although it was not his fortune to see any fighting, he showed by his coolness and presence of mind that he was an officer who might be relied on in times of danger. Indeed, he was several times on active service in India, was mentioned in despatches, and received the frontier medal and two clasps. Cricketers have not forgotten, and are not likely to forget, that the Prince afterwards served with distinction through the greater part of the Boer war, and then died in the service of his country and his King.[2]

Prince Christian Victor did not greatly care for football, but, nevertheless, he was one of the famous TMF's—Terrible Magdalen Forwards, as they were christened by Mr Percy Simpson, the Rugby Blue, himself their leader, and a close friend of the Prince's at School and College—and, as he was very strongly built, he was able to render good service to his side.

It was in 1890 that he went with his regiment to India, where he made many runs, and managed the Murree CC, up in the hills, near Rawal Pindi. 'Our cricket ground at Murree', he said, 'was on the top of a hill, and when a hit to the boundary was made, the ball used to go several hundred feet down the "Khud" as it is called; so, in order not to stop the game, each umpire had an extra ball in his pocket, and as soon as one was hit away, we went on with another, while a coolie

---

[1] Prince Christian Victor was in the Wellington Eleven of 1883 and two following years, being captain in his last year. He was the eldest son of Princess Helena Augusta Victoria (third daughter of Queen Victoria) and HRH Prince Christian of Schleswig Holstein, KG, and therefore nephew of our late King, Edward the Seventh.

[2] He fell a victim to enteric fever on October 29th, 1900, and, in accordance with his desire, was buried in Pretoria, in the heart of the country he helped to win for England. He was born on April 14th, 1867, and was thus only thirty-three years of age at the time of his death.

fetched the one that we had been playing with. Our cricket there was some of the pleasantest I have ever played. Poor Farmer, who afterwards died in Egypt, up the Nile, was one of our side, and a very good player he was too.'

In his first year in India, in 1893, the Prince had an average of 68, while he four times made over a hundred. His best innings was 205.[1] 'At that time,' he said, 'it was generally thought that nobody had ever scored 200 in India, and so, as soon as I had made just over this number, I got out purposely, in order to win the match. I was not tired, and could have gone on very easily. Afterwards, we found out that larger innings had previously been played in India, which was disappointing. I believe, however, that the scores have been beaten since then. In 1892 I did not play at all, for I was at a place where there was no cricket. In 1894 I came home.'

'When you began to play again in England, did you find, like most other cricketers who have been in India, that you had apparently lost your game?'

'Yes. I could not understand it at all—I never seemed able to do right, and, as far as I remember, I only once made more than 70. The light seemed different—in India it is so very bright. But last year (1895) I was all right again, and made a great many runs, chiefly for my club, the Green Jackets, at Winchester, and also at Dover. I haven't made a duck since about the middle of 1894, though I must have played 50 or 60 innings.'

'You did not get a chance of playing cricket while you were in Ashanti?'

'We were going to get up a match at Coomassie, but after much talk about it, we came to the conclusion that we might as well abandon any idea of playing, chiefly because we had no bats, and, what was of still more importance, no ball.'

'Had you played much before you went to Wellington?'

'I began when I was quite a child. At Cumberland Lodge, Windsor, we had a footman named Rayworth who used to bowl to my brother and me, and he taught us the rudiments of the game.[2] My brother is

[1] Made for the King's Royal Rifles *v*. Devonshire Regiment at Rawal Pindi.
[2] It may be of interest to point out that this is not the only association of Royalty and cricket at Cumberland Lodge, for King George the Fourth, when riding in the Great Park, at Windsor, once came across a large party of his domestics playing the game near the Lodge. At the unexpected approach of the King the servants began to scamper in all directions, but His Majesty, much

about eighteen months younger than I. When we were a little older we formed a boys' eleven, and played matches once a week in the neighbourhood. In 1878 I went to a private school near Bracknell, where I was in the eleven. When I was nearly fourteen years of age, and could play fairly well for a little boy, I went to Wellington; and during the holidays that year—it was 1881—we had many boys' matches, playing several times at Wokingham against a team chosen by Mr Murdock, the member for Reading.[1] Sometimes we also played for his team. I remember that Richards, who has often played for Hampshire, and A. P. Douglas (brother of the Cambridge Blue), who is in the Artillery, used to play with us.'

'How long was it before you were in the Wellington eleven?'

'I had been at the College two years, and was originally played as a bowler—I was what a boy calls a fast bowler, and at that time I really did not bowl badly. At my private school I bowled very decently for a little boy, but I slipped the cartilage in my knee and was never able to do so well afterwards. In my first year in the Wellington eleven we had a decidedly good team, of which M. H. Milner, well-known in racing circles, was captain. A. C. M. Croome was also in the team. I don't remember what my average was that year, but in the following year it was about twenty-three or twenty-four; I rarely bowled—in fact I hardly bowled at all, and was played for my batting and fielding. We had not a good eleven.'

'When did you become captain of the Wellington Eleven?'

'In 1885. We had a very good player indeed in E. W. Markham, and he and I practically made all the runs. He had an average of 42, and I think mine was about 32. In that year I became a member of I Zingari, for whom I have played off and on since then. In 1887 I went up to Scarborough and played for I Zingari against the Gentlemen of England, making 35 in the first innings; in the second I was bowled first ball by Stoddart.'

In 1896, the Prince only played about a dozen times, but he was nearly always very successful. 'I like Regimental cricket very much indeed', he said, 'for it is always so keen, and there is, moreover, the

amused, sent one of the gentlemen in attendance to desire them to continue their game, and never to let his approach interrupt their sports. The King then continued his ride in another direction, observing to his attendants that cricket was a noble game, and that when he used to play cricket he enjoyed it as much as anyone.

[1] Mr Charles Townshend Murdock (Conservative), who died in July, 1898.

honour of one's Regiment to keep up. I am afraid that the private soldiers are more enthusiastic over football . . .'.

Chats on the Cricket Field, 1910

*

In the Services

BRIGADIER W. E. CLARK

'Oh, these soldiers! Play on till 9 o'clock if they can! They all field, most of 'em can bat a bit, but not one of 'em can bowl at all!!!' This caustic but perhaps not too inept summary of cricket in the three Services was blurted out one evening at Lord's by a professional just as two military sides, struggling in bad light and heavy drizzle, started on the extra half-hour in a desperate attempt to make a finish.

Service cricket played, as so frequently it must be, on grounds and under conditions both possible and impossible, often immediately after a long spell of work begun in the small hours of the morning or even earlier, is ever full of hope if sometimes short of skill. At times, however, circumstances will disconcert the stoutest optimist. A burly stoker once, who had petitioned for first ball in a battle on a rough-and-ready wicket on Dartmoor, stopped the first two from a bowler—faster and more erratic even than the wicket—with his ribs, just missed the next one with his head, and turned the fourth ball off his chin sharply to cover-point. He ran. His partner, a good player, scurried home and protested vigorously at the run. He was put in his place with: 'That's all right. I don't care a damn who bats at that end, but it ain't going to be me any more.'

While officers have always followed the call of their boyhood's game, for the past 80 years or more there has always been in ships or units, especially those recruited from England, a sufficiency of the lower grades ready to fill a side against challengers on any ground, oversea or even hostile, if need be. This generally has meant one-day cricket, beyond which, owing to his constant and uncertain movement, the bluejacket has seldom aspired. But in the land forces, where better conditions for cricket have obtained, in Victorian days fine players were found among the men who had learnt their cricket in the ranks and proved successful professionals later in life with county sides. In recent times, however, it has been rare for lads of high cricket possibility to enlist. Boys of such type probably get greater chances than they did formerly of showing skill when young, and so they get marked down and snapped up by the county scouts. Throughout all three Services, too, it must be recognized that the lately born but intense attraction of Association football has usurped loyalty formerly accorded to the older game, which admittedly takes up so much more time and presents so many more difficulties where pitches are concerned.

It may be of interest now to trace briefly the story of Service cricket down to modern times. There is record of Captain the Hon. Charles Lennox, later fourth Duke of Richmond, a fine player of his time, having joined the 35th Foot at Edinburgh in 1790 and helped to introduce the game to Scotland. He also in 1792 was elected president of the garrison cricket club in Dublin. So it is evident that military cricket was afoot in those days. During the first three decades of the MCC's existence, about which period history of the game is somewhat nebulous, the Navy certainly, and the Army in the main, were busy with affairs too insistent to afford much scope for cricket. The Navy during these decades, and for many years later, continued to have little opportunity for enjoying the game which, apart from the big events, was confined to matches between teams gathered from communities, in certain counties only, resident within short distance of one another.

After settling with Napoleon, detachments of the Army, when stationed in cricket playing districts, no doubt took part in occasional contests against sides from neighbouring towns and villages. At times, too, if quartered in sufficient strength, the soldiers ventured after bigger quarry. In the MCC's first recorded military fixture the Royal Artillery, with help from a distinguished amateur not belonging to the Regiment, beat the Club at Lord's on June 8, 1818, in a 12-a-side match by nine wickets. A return meeting at Woolwich a week later, with the Gunners getting the same help, resulted in a tie, the assistant, it is said, having hit a 9. Most certainly the occasion would be suitably celebrated in the mess, which at that period, together with the regimental band, was rising to fame for social entertainment.

These home-and-home games continued for years. Another annual encounter of early origin was started in the next year between the Gunners again and West Kent, who had their ground then, as now, at Chislehurst. Eton are recorded as having played the 1st Life Guards in 1836. So it is clear that military cricket, where travel by horse, either ridden or driven, permitted, was fully active during the first half-century of the MCC's life. The first 30 years of Queen Victoria's reign saw more important changes and advances than any other period of cricket history. Universities and the big public schools started regular annual fixtures. The railway began to assert its usefulness and enabled cricketers to extend their battlefields afar. Grounds were opened in many places hitherto unknown to the clash of bat and ball. Wandering groundless clubs, headed in 1845 by I Zingari, came into being in large numbers, of which the fittest survive to carry on their mission of bringing better cricket and good manners wherever they be entertained. Country houses and messes enlarged their hospitality and cricket tents to a far wider circle of friends than had been possible before.

The period started as one of great eating. The gifted reporter of All Muggleton *v.* Dingley Dell depicts his puppets giving higher thought to dinner than their cricket. In a book of 1851 the Perpetual President of I Z. inveighed against gluttony at midday dinner, forerunner of our luncheon, during the progress of a game. He instanced a schoolboy bowler who after the said meal was reduced to a succession of wides and no-balls as a result of his having 'devoured an entire duck with condiments'. At the end of this period, just after 75 years of MCC's life, two happenings occurred. In 1863 a boy of 15 made 32 runs against the best professional bowling in England at his first appearance. In 1864 overarm bowling was made lawful. And so came modern cricket.

From now on records of Service cricket gradually have grown voluminous. The oldest inhabitants can still give first-hand evidence of early things. Cricket in the Services has improved in the sense that more games are played; far less extravagance takes place in eating and drinking; there are many more good players, though it is doubtful if the highest class Service performers are any better than those of the past generation; grounds are better kept and their equipment is better. But, alas! it all costs more. However, while purses stand it, what could be more pleasant than to meet friendly foes among the Sappers at Chatham, or the Marines at Eastney? St Cross, with its sloping ground, and Burton Court, with its narrowness, have attractions of their own for visitors as well as kindly hosts. Turning to reminiscence, the young officer skipper in the company cup match no doubt still sees slippery-soled Sergeant Smith juggling with a chance from the best bat on the other side, knowing full well what the next moment will bring forth. The private soldier who was heard to tell a comrade that important cricket was the order of the day for the morrow, 'The Command are playing the First Zingarees', probably has his quip ready for to-day. It is doubtful, however, whether, as occurred immediately after the Great War, a young officer, a good cricketer—naval, be it said, in defence of his military brother—on being asked whether he would like to be made a Free Forester, said that he was sorry to decline but that he really could not afford to join any more dance clubs, got another chance.

It is worth while noting that, in good modern cricket, while each bowler has his individual tricks, batsmen have subtle distinctions by classes according to their provenance. The experience of playing with first-class opponents enjoyed by undergraduates at Oxford and Cambridge has always given the young men hailing from these places an advantage denied to ex-cadets of the Army, whose coaching at the military educational establishments has been, and is, on a scale of insignificance. Consequently, apart from an occasional genius, the young officer has every reason for gratitude towards the great wandering clubs for any improvement in his play after leaving school. A few years at the start of his service spent in a station blessed with second-class cricket has often rendered him fit to compete on level terms with the average University cricketer no longer in practice to first-class professional bowling. If he starts his career overseas, on the other hand, he is less lucky. At some places plenty of cricket is obtainable, but abroad good cricketers are few, and wickets generally are not good enough to raise the standard of a youngster's play. The sailor's plight is more difficult than that of the soldier. Being sent to sea as a midshipman gives him but little chance. It is true that for the past 50 years or more naval cricket has, like the Army's, profited by entertaining good sides at home ports. But officers are seldom in shore billets, and then usually for short and uncertain periods. This drawback has naturally lessened the production of high-class naval batsmen, through no inherent failing in individuals. The result of these conditions is that the military batsman has usually a light-hearted touch about the make-up of his technique which is absent where a player has had early schooling against first-class counties. The naval player, as a rule, is more impetuous still, and sometimes lacks self-confidence in batting, but woe betide the opponent who underrates his fielding. In that the sailor is nearly always quick among the quick.

The airman has not landed long enough on the cricket ground for any generalized appraisement. The officer, as in the case of the older Services, is caught young for Cranwell, and likewise lacks good cricket training. No doubt, however, since capable mature players of its own making are now holding the reins of cricket in the Royal Air Force, which is following the lines of the other Services in the conduct of the game, the teams of that arm, if not yet, will shortly be equally doughty warriors in the second-class cricket world.

Thanks to inability of players to take part in first-class cricket while still serving, there have been but few great ones in the Services in modern cricket, though there is a fair sprinkling of names to be found in the pages of Wisden. Officers, on odd occasions at home, or while on long leave from abroad, have often played for counties, and several after retirement have captained county sides. Of those the most renowned name which comes first to mind is E. G. Wynyard, whom duty twice forced to decline tours in Australia with English sides. A. J. Turner played for the Gentlemen at the Oval in the summer of his twentieth birthday, and was invited in 1899, the next year, to play for the same side at both Lord's and the Oval, but was prevented by duty from doing so. He would probably have earned still greater fame but for a forearm wound received in South Africa which considerably handicapped his batting afterwards. A. C. Johnston was reaching high position just before the Great War, wherein he was badly crippled. G. G. Napier and C. H. Abercrombie, had they survived the War, might well have gone far, if, indeed, the former be not held to have done so already while an undergraduate. R. M. Poore and D. C. Robinson are others who have shone in first-class company. At the present time there are players of all three Services who get asked to play in first-class cricket when duty spares them, and one or two of these are tapping at the door of greatness in the game.

Mention of disasters which befell some of the Service players of great promise recalls a pathetic incident which illustrates the unsuspected friendship which the game inspires. One morning in October, 1914, someone visiting the officers' pavilion at Aldershot happened on the dear old groundman, who, with a copy of *The Times* of the day in his hand, sobbed bitterly as he told kindly stories of 'his' cricketers who had already fallen, the while he sorted out their bags from those of other players still keeping up their end in Flanders Field.

The MCC 1787–1937, 1937

Cricket at Harrow

LORD BYRON

High, through those elms, with hoary branches crown'd,
Fair Ida's bower adorns the landscape round;
There Science, from her favour'd seat, surveys
The vale where rural Nature claims her praise;
To her awhile resigns her youthful train,
Who move in joy, and dance along the plain;
In scatt'd groups each favour'd haunt pursue:
Repeat old pastimes, and discover new;
Flush'd with his rays, beneath the noontide sun,
In rival bands, between the wickets run,
Drive o'er the sward the ball with active force,
Or chase with nimble feet its rapid course.

Alonzo! best and dearest of my friends. . . .
. . . when confinement's lingering hour was done,
Our sport, our studies, and our souls were one:
Together we impell'd the flying ball;
Together waited in our tutor's hall;
Together join'd in cricket's manly toil.

Hours of Idleness, 1807

*

Lord Harris

W. A. BETTESWORTH

The Cricket Field, May 11th, 1895

From the time that he was in the Oxford University Eleven until, after
holding office in Lord Salisbury's Government as Under Secretary for
India, and again as Under Secretary for War, he was appointed Governor
of the Bombay Presidency, there was no more popular cricketer in
England than Lord Harris. Returning to England in March, 1895, he
was a few weeks later elected President of the MCC, to the great

satisfaction of every cricketer, from the schoolboy to the county player. As a batsman he had few superiors, and as a field he was about the most dangerous man in England to try to bustle or to tempt with a catch. His abilities as a captain were speedily recognised, and when he directed the fortunes of the Kent Eleven he showed what may be done by a man who has all the moves of the game at his finger ends, for, with a team that was usually weak in bowling, he accomplished results which astonished his opponents. It is possible that there may be captains who, in their inmost hearts, may cherish a thought that they have occasionally out-manœuvred him, but if so they are likely to hold their peace, lest some of his manœuvres should be recalled to their mind.

In India Lord Harris played in a few matches for Government House, and never failed to make his hundred once a year. At first the native Press attacked him violently for playing cricket, and up to quite the fourth year some of the more violent vernacular papers alleged that he did nothing else, but in the end it was the general opinion that by taking part in the game he had done a vast amount of good. He had convinced the upper classes among the natives that there was nothing derogatory in playing cricket, and consequently they were more inclined to help the young men of their own race in their efforts to extend the game. It is hardly too much to say that if Lord Harris had never been Governor of the Bombay Presidency, cricketers would never have heard of Ranjitsinhji, much less have had the opportunity of watching his wonderful batting.

Before Lord Harris left India the Parsees expressed themselves as very grateful for what he had done in improving their relations socially with Europeans. In answer to a question he said, 'All races play—Hindoos, Parsees, and Mohammedans, but the Bombay Parsee Eleven is the best native eleven, and is equal to the best Bombay Presidency European eleven. The scene on the Bombay cricket-ground at one of the big matches is very striking, with the magnificent buildings in the background, and the 10,000 to 20,000 spectators, chiefly natives in their picturesque dress, completely absorbed in the English game.'

'How would the Parsees compare with English teams?'

'It is difficult to speak with accuracy, but I think they would probably beat most county gentlemen's elevens, and I should say that they would be about equal to a county gentlemen's eleven if it included one or two professionals. They are very good fields, but naturally no better than men of other races. Young men with good eyes, who can stoop quickly, cannot help fielding well. The Parsees have a decided aptitude for bowling, considering what a small community they represent, and one of them, Writer, is quite first-class. He is as nearly like George Wootton as can be, both in pace and delivery, but is not quite so good. As bats, natives have not the patience and stubbornness which are required in first-class players. Two curious incidents occurred in the two matches in 1894 between the Parsees and the Presidency. In the first match at Bombay the Parsees declared their innings at an end, and the Englishmen had an hour to play out time. When the bell rang they had one wicket to fall and no chance of getting the runs. The English captain went on with his innings, and allowed the Parsees to get the last wicket and win. At Poona in the return match the positions were exactly reversed. The Parsees at "time" had one wicket to fall, and their captain continued the game, and allowed the Englishmen to win.' . . .

'In one of the matches, in which we made a large score, I went in last. I played a ball very hard on to the ground, and it went first bound into mid-off's hands. The umpire, without waiting for anybody to appeal, waved his umbrella over his head, and shouted, "Out! out! out!" Of course, I went out, and the innings closed, but even his own side remonstrated with the umpire. Subsequently he went up to his fellow umpire, and deplored his bad luck in making a mistake in such a match, because, he said, "I've never made a mistake when umpiring before." "Then," said the other umpire, "you ought to be put in a glass case."'

'There is another important question about which your opinion will be welcomed, the question of "buying" professionals, as it is termed.'

'If "buying" is the right word to use, I should say that there has always been a tendency to buy professionals, and it seems to me that it would be impossible to prevent a man from seeking an opening for his abilities as a cricketer in some county other than his own. And if he can obtain employment in winter at the place where he is engaged in the summer, it is not unnatural that he should grasp the opportunity. What I do think is unsportsmanlike is to offer a professional already playing for his county better terms in order to induce him to leave it. It is very difficult to draw a line between openly advertising for outside men, and doing what I did in the case of the Hearnes. They had come to live at Catford before I had anything to do with the eleven. By birth, they were qualified for Middlesex. Old George Hearne, their father, asked me to play young George in the Kent Colts' match. I said, "Yes, but there must be an agreement that if I bring him out he is to stick to the county." There is no documentary evidence of the engagement—simply an understanding which was honourably adhered to on both sides. Just in the same way Herbert and Walter Hearne were Buckinghamshire men, who were invited to come to Kent when they were quite young, on the chance of their turning out to be good. I draw the line between taking an untried man and tempting away one who has already made a sufficient reputation to be chosen for his county.'

'You do not blame the professional?'

'It seems to me that he is entitled to exchange his proficiency for the best engagement he can make wherever the offer may come from. Possibly he may be influenced by county feeling to a greater or less extent, but that is a matter of individual sentiment which one cannot assess beforehand. If it is non-existent, I do not blame him for making better terms outside his county than he can inside. But I do blame the county which tempts away a professional who is already playing for another county.'

Chats on the Cricket Field, 1910

*

Mr Charles Absolon

W. A. BETTESWORTH

The Cricket Field, September 8th, 1894

In the year 1831 Mr Absolon played his first match.[1] Sixty or seventy years afterwards he was possibly just a little past his prime, but, as many a heartbroken batsman would admit, his lob bowling had by no means lost its deceptive qualities.[2] Young players who never had the felicity of meeting him were apt to refer to him as 'an old fossil', but when their time came to step up to the wicket with the intention of adding him to their collection, they were apt to find that he was no fossil at

[1] For Wallingford against the Oxford Union Club on Cowley Marsh, Oxford. In the following year he played an innings of 127 for Wallingford *v.* Berwick (Oxon.). Among his opponents in the 1831 match was Mr W. Bacon, who survived until October 5th, 1899.

[2] In 1892 he took 200 wickets and in the next year 209. Between 1871 and 1893 he did the hat-trick 59 times, and in 1897, at the age of 80, took over a hundred wickets in the season. He had been a total abstainer since 1857 and never smoked.

all, but a very lively though somewhat bulky insect which bored holes in their wickets. Mr Absolon annually took at least 200 wickets, and a very easy multiplication sum will show that altogether he had a record of which any man might well be proud.[1] Among many wonderful performances he once took all the twenty wickets in the two innings for Wood Green against United Willesden, and, no doubt, like Alexander, he sighed that on that day there were no more worlds to conquer.[2] The services that he rendered to the game were great, and not the least of them was his persistent endeavour, which met with a large measure of success, to get employers to give a half-holiday on Saturdays to their assistants. His first victory of this kind was gained for the club for which he played regularly at the time—Nicholson's Distillery—and the proprietors of Price's candle manufactory soon followed the lead. With the example of two such large firms to point to, Mr Absolon was soon able to obtain the assent of hundreds of other firms to his scheme.

For many years his doings as a cricketer were annually chronicled in *Bell's Life*, and towards the end of his career dozens of newspapers recorded his deeds at the end of each season. Until a few years before his death he could still go through an amount of work in the cricket field which would have made an invalid of many a younger man. 'In one week in 1894' he said, 'I played in three matches, travelling over 200 miles, and was down for a fourth which was scratched. To finish off the week I had a day's partridge-shooting on the Saturday on Lord Salisbury's estate, and by the time I reached home again I was about tired out.'

'Do you find it more difficult to bowl now (1894) than you did ten years ago?'

'Not a bit. You see the action is very easy, and I don't get tired by running, because I don't run at all. Of course, I can't follow up the ball now. I always stand slip in the field, and can still put out my arms as quickly as ever to reach the ball. If I had to run my own runs when

---

[1] In 1868 he took 441; in 1870, 453; in 1871, 433; in 1872, 519; in 1873, 420; and in 1874, 500. Between 1868 and 1893, when he was 76 years of age, he took 7,339 wickets and scored 24,189 runs. At the age of 72 he made 1,052 runs in a season. Unfortunately, particulars of all his early, and, therefore, probably his best, performances have not been preserved. (The book which contained them was lent to a 'friend' and never returned.)

[2] This was at the age of 55, when playing for Wood Green *v.* United Willesden, at Wood Green, in July, 1872. He bowled down ten wickets, six were caught off him, two hit wicket off his bowling, and he caught two off other men's bowling.

I am batting I couldn't go in at all, but nobody ever raises any objection to my having someone to run for me.'

'You must have a remarkably strong constitution.'

'When I was a boy I used to be very thin, and looked delicate. My father thought that the cause of this was that I was over-exerting myself by playing cricket whenever I got the slightest chance, and he sent for Dr Marshall, who used to attend the family, and told him that I looked so "hatchet jawed" that he was seriously alarmed for my health. Dr Marshall examined me very carefully, and then said: "I'll tell you what it is. I think he's got the strongest constitution of any youngster I ever saw—in fact, it is strong enough to stand any amount of cricket." So I rejoiced, and was allowed to give my constitution a fair chance. But I have always taken care of myself. For thirty-seven years I have been a teetotaller (1894), and it is fifty-five years since I tasted spirits. I never could smoke, nor could my father. Thirty years ago, Bob Thoms said that when I was too old to play, nothing would please me better than to be presented with a perambulator in which I might be taken to see matches.'

'Have you studied other people's lob bowling much?'

'Well, I don't think you could say that I have really studied it much, but I always like to see it. I can't help thinking that a mistake is being made in letting it drop out of first-class cricket so entirely. Perhaps I don't understand the merits of modern bowling as much as I ought to, but, at any rate, I don't think cricket is as well worth watching as it was in the days of underhand. You go to a match nowadays and see some tremendously fast bowler. Presently a ball goes to the boundary, and you look up at the scoring board to see whether the runs are being counted as byes or as a hit. If you find it is not a bye you clap your hands, and say, "Well hit, sir". But there is not one spectator in ten who can see whether a ball which goes behind the wicket off a fast bowler is hit or not.'

'Who was the most promising young cricketer you ever had occasion to play with?'

'Why, Mr W. G. Grace, of course. He had played for me several times during his holidays when he was a boy, until at last people wouldn't stand him. They said that they liked to see him bat, but they would prefer to see him bat against somebody else. So I had to leave him out of my teams. But there came a time when I asked him again to play for me. The Stratford Club had brought a very strong team against me, including several county players, and as my two best bowlers, whose wives and families were at Margate, had to leave early to catch a train, I got beaten. One of the county men laughed at me because of this, and I said to him, "All right; you can make up your mind that when I come down to Stratford for the return, I'll give you such a hiding that you won't forget it. You can bring as many county men as you like." So I told "W.G." what had happened, and he promised to play for me. Then Bill Mortlock said he would like to go; and Pooley, who was then playing for Middlesex, said that he mustn't be left out. J. C. Gregory, the Surrey captain, came, and so did W. Wade, the Blackheath bowler, and a few others who knew a little about the game. There were small boxes round the ground which were used as dressing-rooms, and I told W.G. to go at once into one of them, and not to come out until we were ready to begin if I won the toss, for I was afraid that some-body would know him and would object to his playing. Well, I *did* win the toss, and he soon began to make himself at home. By-and-bye an old gentleman came on the ground, and said to some of the Stratford spectators, "Well, my boys, how are you getting on?" They replied that the first two men wouldn't get out. So he took his opera-glasses and surveyed the scene of play. Presently he said, "Why, good heavens! they've got Grace! I say, old 'un [that was me, you know], whom have you got there?" I said quite pleasantly, "That one—oh! that's Grace." And then they let me have it, I can tell you. But it was too late for them to raise objections, and we kept them fielding all day while we made about 400 runs. W.G. made about a hundred. That was the last time he ever played for me.'

'Have you ever got Mr Grace out since he began to be famous?'

'Oh, yes. I was playing in 1875 for a Twenty-two against the United All England Eleven. The match was over in two days. For the third day it was arranged that an eleven, of which I was one, should play a single-wicket match against Mr Grace, Charlwood, and W. R. Gilbert. They won the toss, and nearly everybody on the ground was ready to bet that we should not get them out in the day. You could have got a barrowful of money on the match—I wish I had done it. Our captain gave me the ball and said to me, "Go on, old man; place your field." I said, "What *me*? Well, of course I'll have a go if you like"; though I can tell you I was pretty bashful about it, for there were 3,000 people on the ground. However, as it happened, I got all three wickets in nineteen balls for 6 runs."

'In one match that I played [in Oxfordshire] a man kept on sticking his leg right in front of the wicket. Several times I asked the umpire his opinion on the matter, but he always said "Not out". At last I couldn't stand it any longer, and fairly shouted, "How's that?" He very deliberately walked up to the wicket and pointed his finger at the batsman. Then he said: "Now, look 'ere, Tom, I warns you this time. If you does it again I'm blowed if I don't give you out. So there!"'

[Mr Charles Absolon was born at Wallingford, in Berkshire, on May 30th, 1817, and died at Finsbury Park on January 4th, 1908.]

Chats on the Cricket Field, 1910

✳

The Rev. Canon M'Cormick

A. W. PULLIN ('OLD EBOR')

Ireland has not produced many first-class cricketers—probably for the reason that the opportunities for their development are restricted. Among the small band known to cricketing fame, the Rev. Canon M'Cormick ranks an easy first. 'Joe' M'Cormick—the familiarity of the cricket-field needs no apology though reproduced in print—was not actually born in Ireland, but his Hibernian descent is obvious, and as a matter of fact his cricket associations with the Green Isle were as close as his name suggests.

On going up to Cambridge Mr M'Cormick soon became so popular that had a letter been addressed to 'Joe, Cambridge', it would have reached its proper destination without delay. He never received any real instruction in cricket until he got there; yet he became so rapidly proficient that he was awarded his Blue in 1854, and in 1856 was captain of the Light Blues, who then beat their Oxford rivals by 3 wickets. He grimly recalls an incident that occurred in the year when he was captain of the Cambridge Eleven.

'I strolled on to a cricket-ground at Liverpool, where some gentlemen were practising. I asked if I might be allowed to bowl, and immediately hit the wicket. "You can't do that again, sir," said the batsmen. But I did. The other gentlemen in turn went in, and each was soon bowled. Then one of them said, "Might I ask, sir, who you are?" I replied, "M'Cormick." "What, the Cambridge captain? Ah, that accounts for it."

'While at Cambridge', says Mr M'Cormick, 'I was one day playing on Parker's Piece, and Percival Frost, the celebrated mathematician, was in with me. I hit a very fast bowler hard to leg and ran 9 for it. It took three men to throw the ball up. Visiting Cambridge only a few months before Frost's death, he said at a dinner-party, "I remember one of your hits, when you nearly killed me with running!" That was the hit for 9.'

It is appropriate here to explain that Canon M'Cormick has a splendid physique. He stands 6 feet 3 inches, and in his athletic days weighed 13 stone 4 lb. As a bowler he was medium pace, and broke chiefly from leg, though he could do the break from the off also.

'I learnt my bowling', says he, 'principally from old Buttress, who was really the father of break-bowling. He had a very easy and deceptive delivery, and just when a man was flattering himself that he had his measure, he would, without perceptible change of action, send him down an entirely different ball and bowl him.

'Old Buttress, I am sorry to say, was rather too fond of his glass, otherwise there is no doubt nobody would have surpassed him in his success as a bowler. One incident of his career is well worth recalling. The United All-England Eleven had been beaten by the All-England team on several occasions, and being anxious to change the order of events, they engaged the services of Buttress. In order that he might be thoroughly fit, they took charge of him and kept him away from drink for several days, and got him to practise carefully. The result was that the Eleven were soon out. His success so delighted him that he forthwith proceeded to make merry. The next day he could not bowl a bit! On another occasion Buttress accomplished the extraordinary feat of bowling the All-England Eleven out in a Twenty-two match for 12 runs!'

In Mr M'Cormick's college days the great battle was on the friendly cricket-green between Town and Gown. 'It was a match', he says, 'which always excited great interest, the Town at that time being very strong. The famous Robert Carpenter made his first appearance in cricket for the Town in one of these matches, and very successful it was. I was captain of the 'Varsity Eleven, and it was determined to play the match on Parker's Piece. The town came in crowds, and the University managed to win a most exciting match by 2 wickets, I being the top scorer with 52.'

It is difficult to say whether the Canon was considered better with the bat than with the ball. Tom Hayward thought he had more command over the ball than any other bowler of his day. His great height,

6 feet 3 inches, gave him a long reach; and he was a very hard hitter all round the wicket. As a fielder he stood very close in, and was as alert as he was daring. In a Zingari match at Carlow, when 'Bob' Marsham was bowling, the batsmen said it was no cricket, because Mr M'Cormick stood so close up at third man and caught them off the bat as they blocked the ball in the old-fashioned way! Just an instance or two of this smartness in the field. In playing for I Zingari, a professional cut the first ball with all his might to third man, where M'Cormick held it with his right hand. The batsman appealed to the umpire as to whether he was out! One of the fieldsmen observed, 'Ha! one of Joe's rat-traps.'

The highest hit Mr M'Cormick ever saw was in a match MCC *v.* Cambridge, when Marylebone went in to get 93 to win. At the turning-point of the match John Lillywhite let out with all his force and hit the ball sky high to middle-wicket. M'Cormick, who was bowling, shouted to middle-wicket to get out of the way, and brought off the catch, which won the match. An onlooking friend was asked, 'Were you not anxious about that catch?' to which the reply was made, 'No; I knew the ball would never go through Joe's big hands.'

There is no touch of egotism in the narration of these incidents. Canon M'Cormick thinks a great deal more of the performances of others than he does of his own. 'The finest catch I remember', says he, 'was one made my Mr V. E. Walker, in Gentlemen and Players, from a hit by Caffyn straight back at him, which was never above two inches from the ground, and which Mr Walker took with one hand. Mr I. D. Walker was very clever in getting to the ball, but he never was equal to V.E. either as a fielder or bowler. Mat Kempson was a perfect short-slip, while at point and third man E. M. Grace never had a superior.'

Drawing on his rich stock of reminiscences, Canon M'Cormick recalls a couple of incidents which testify to old Clarke's wonderful judgment as a bowler. Says he: 'The late Earl of Bessborough, then the Hon. Fred. Ponsonby, told me that he once visited Clarke at Nottingham, and they talked about Felix running out and hitting Clarke. The latter said, "Mr Ponsonby, come into the back-yard." They went. Clarke had a set of wickets pitched, and he said, "Now, Mr Ponsonby, when Mr Felix runs out at me I think I will have him. Just watch this." He then hit the top of the stumps with a full-pitch ball several times in succession. A little later Felix and Clarke faced each other at Lord's, and Felix ran out to hit him. Thereupon Clarke sent in a fast full-pitcher and bowled him.'

Reference to a conversation with the Earl of Bessborough has just been made. It reminds Canon M'Cormick of his last match in Ireland, only a year or two before the death of the noble Earl. 'I played for his eleven against the officers of Clonmell, and did the hat trick. I was fifty-three years of age at the time. Lord Bessborough afterwards told his friends at Lord's that "Joe M'Cormick did the hat trick in my match the other day, and after each wicket he turned round to me, as I was umpiring, and said, 'Well, I think that is about as rotten a ball as I ever bowled'." Sometimes "rotten" balls get wickets, as in this instance. Lord Bessborough also once paid me the high compliment at Lord's of saying I was one of the best judges of cricket in the country, but it is not an opinion I should venture upon myself. The same has been said of many others, but particularly of my old friend Mr R. A. H. Mitchell.

'These Irish matches in the old days were great fun. The Revd A. R. Ward, who was fully 20 stone weight when he was in the Eleven at Cambridge, was too heavy to turn round to leg-balls. In one of them, as he was playing one a man called out, "Mick, did ye see him? Sure, he cocked his leg."'

There was some prejudice against a clergyman taking part in cricket in the days after Mr M'Cormick was ordained, and for that reason he sometimes played under the assumed name of 'J. Bingley', or 'J. Cambridge'. One of his greatest feats as a bowler was performed after he was ordained. Playing on a good wicket against the Messrs Walkers' team at Southgate, for England, he took 9 wickets for 34 runs in the first innings, and 7 for 33 in the second, and was not changed after once being put on. Speaking now of the prejudice against cricket, the worthy Canon, with a long experience behind him, considers it unreasonable, but adds the following weighty words:—

'I cannot understand a man, unless he is a professional, devoting his whole life to cricket. There are so many more serious things that he can do, that it should not be his only object in life to play cricket. Far be it from me to preach against cricket, for no one loves or has loved it better than I. So long as a man does not give too much time to it, be he clergyman or layman, by all means let him play cricket. But he must have some more serious object in life besides. The remark applies equally to athletics. There is too great a tendency to make heroes of men who please the popular fancy.'

Talks with Old English Cricketers, 1900

✳

The Rev. E. S. Carter

A. W. PULLIN ('OLD EBOR')

The contents of a man's private scrap-book necessarily give an insight into his tastes and character. The writer has been privileged to read at will the scrap-book of the Rev. E. S. Carter. He found in it one pasted extract that revealed at a glance the old Oxford cricketer's ideas of the relationship that should exist between the Church and the doctrine of muscular Christianity. The extract is a quotation from an address delivered by a certain member of Church Congress, when the Parliament of the Church held its sittings at Croydon, a quarter of a century ago. The subject was the religion of public amusement. Its exponent scornfully satirised the pious jellyfishes of the pulpit. He exhorted them to 'unstarch their ephods of prudery', and to show concern, 'not merely as men but as clergymen, in the existence of harmless healthy amusements, the want of which is a most fertile source of sin and crime'. As an example of how this might be done, the speaker asked the country parson not to refuse his place as an active member of the parish eleven, 'for so shall he find that the fine hit to leg, which opened the mouths of the rustic spectators on the Saturday, will leave them a little open on the Sunday morning; and that he whom the parson has taught to twist will be the more ready to listen to his dissuasives from tortuous conduct'.

The Rev. E. S. Carter is no pious jellyfish of the pulpit. You have but to seek an acquaintance with his career in the world of cricket to know that the healthy doctrine of muscular Christianity has had in him an earnest disciple and a capable exponent. If you are privileged to have an afternoon's talk with him in his study, you will find him a delightful *raconteur*, brimming over with anecdote and mirth; and you will quickly come to the conclusion that his ephod of prudery has long since been unstarched.

Edmund Sardinson Carter was born on February 3, 1845, at Malton, and followed the footsteps of his father when he entered the Church. Those who have a weakness for trying their luck at a wishing-stone will be interested in his boyish experience, which was certainly very curious. This is what he says:—

'When fourteen years of age I became a King's Scholar at Durham, and when my course was nearly run there I paid a visit to the Finkle

Abbey wishing-stone, and I wished three things, all most unlikely, as I then thought, to occur. The first was that I might go to Oxford; the second, that I might play in the Oxford Eleven; and the third, that I might row in the Oxford Boat. They were all realised, the first two within eighteen months. I won a scholarship which took me to Oxford in 1864; in 1866 and 1867 I played in the University Eleven; and in 1867 and 1868 rowed in the Oxford Boat. Only about eight other gentlemen have gained these double blues, of whom the Rev. Canon M'Cormick and the Rev. J. Aitken are still living.

'I was prevented from playing with the 'Varsity Eleven a third year owing to an attack of pleurisy, which compelled me to take a voyage in a sailing-ship to Australia.

'The trip did me immense good, for whereas I only weighed 10 stone 10 lb. when I went aboard, on reaching Melbourne I pulled the scale at 13 stone 4 lb. As luck would have it, the first man I saw in Australia at the end of the Sandridge Pier was G. P. Robertson, who played with me in the Oxford Eleven the year before. He was living in Melbourne, so at once got me down to the ground and enrolled me as a member of the Melbourne CC, with the result that I was chosen to play against the Aboriginals and in the Inter-Colonial match, Victoria *v.* New South Wales at Sydney.'

On returning to England the young student and cricketer took Orders, and was appointed to the curacy of Christ Church, Ealing. Five years after he was appointed Vicar Choral at York Minster and Curate at St Martin-cum-Gregory, to the rectorship of which he subsequently succeeded. In 1882 he was installed Vicar of St Michael-le-Belfrey, York, a cure which he holds to-day.

Mr Carter's stories are even better than his cricket. 'Mr A. N. Hornby used to bring an Eleven, including Crossland, to play the Yorkshire Gentlemen. When I went in first against Crossland, Mr Hornby said, "Now, Crossland, the gentleman that has come in is a clergyman. Don't use any hard language—you'll shock his feelings." Well, Crossland bowled away as quiet as a lamb, until I got 45 or 46, when he bowled me with a snorting shooter that knocked my wicket to pieces. Crossland could then keep quiet no longer, for he blurted out, "I downed his old pulpit for him that time".'

'Here is another good parson's story. We were playing at Oulton (a village near Pontefract), and there were four or five parsons in the team. A. J. Irving and Smith-Dorrien went in first, and I think got about 40 or 50 each. Then went in Hamilton, an old Cambridge man, who got about 40, and after him H. M. Sims, who hit the first four balls he received out of the field (it was a narrow boundary). The bowler then relieved his feelings by the remark, "Nah, then, is there ony more o' theease meenisters to come in? I didn't come 'ere, tha knows, to laake at knur and spell."

'Mention of the Rev. H. M. Sims reminds me that he once played for Yorkshire at Sheffield, and turned out in his beautiful new Cambridge blue jacket to field at cover-point. As if by a concerted signal, the cry went up all round the ground, "Tak thi jacket off!" He took no notice. By-and-by a ball went to him, and he misfielded it and it went to the boundary. Then came the cry louder than before, "*Nah*, will ta tak thi jacket off!" I have often been struck with the ready wit and keen appreciation of cricket crowds, especially those at Sheffield. The only time I played against the Australians there I was fielding alternately at cover-point and square-leg. I was standing near the scoring-box at deep square-leg, and twenty minutes passed before the ball came to me. It came along with a beautiful hop, and I promptly returned it, whereupon a voice in the crowd shouted, "Here endeth the first lesson." And with a series of laughs and ripples, "Here endeth the first lesson" went all round the enclosure.

'It may be as well to mention, *apropos* of this exclamation of the Sheffield crowd, that I was *not* the young curate of whom the story is told that after exceptional success in some big match on a Saturday, announced at the close of the First Lesson in church on the following day, "Here endeth the first innings."

'I played ten or eleven years ago for a Clerical Eleven of England against Lord Lewisham's Eleven, at Lewisham. A lady, who with her daughter went to see the match, was stated to have said, "I do hope that I shall see the clergymen bat." On arriving on the ground the daughter said, "Oh, mamma, how lucky! The clergymen are in." "How do you know, dear?" asked the mother. "Oh, don't you see they have got their surplices on." Of course the clergymen in question were the umpires in their white coats.

'An amusing story was told me about Tom Emmett, which, if true, shows how his wit did not desert him even under most uninspiring circumstances. He was on his way to Australia with the team taken out by Lord Harris. Tom was a bad sailor; Lord Harris was a good one. During the crossing of the Bay of Biscay poor Tom was prostrate with *mal de mer*; but one fine morning when they had rounded Cape St Vincent and got into comparatively smooth water, Tom crawled timidly up the companion-ladder, and halted with his face just high enough to see over the ship's side, to observe his lordship enjoying a cigarette on deck. His lordship opened the conversation, "Glad to see you out, Tom; but you don't look very well." "No, my lord," replied Tom, "I don't feel very bright." Then, having a look overboard he exclaimed with a sigh, "I don't think they've had the heavy roller on, my lord."

'I was playing once with George Freeman in a match in which there was a deaf umpire. Freeman appealed for "leg before wicket", but the umpire simply put his hand to his ear, and said, "Beg pardon?" George asked again, "How's that?" "What for?" re-queried the umpire. "Leg before wicket, of course", said George. "Oh, not out, of course", replied the umpire: "I only once in my life gave one of my own side out leg before wicket. What time is dinner? That's t' main thing wi' umpires."

'Umpires are, as a rule, credited with very good appetites on match days. Certainly I have known some who would have made poor "fasters". I played once in a match for the Ealing CC *v.* Wimbledon. Rain interfered considerably with the play, and consequently there was more time expended over luncheon than would otherwise have been the case. One of the umpires "did himself" very well, and on a remark being made to this effect, he said, "I've not done half so well as I did at Esher the other day." "What did you do at Esher?" "Why, I began with a bit of roast-beef; then I had a bit of boiled beef; then I had a bit of lamb; then I had a bit of duck; then a friend of mine recommended the veal-and-ham pie, so I had a bit of that; but I liked the boiled beef best, so I went back to that and *made my dinner off it.*"

'Talking about umpiring stories reminds me of an old gentleman who, when I was a boy, umpired for a famous cricketing village in the North Riding for which I played several years. His umpiring attire included blue stockings and fustian breeches. He had a son who used to bowl, and who is still living. Before the match commenced he would remark, "Noo, lad, which end is thi going to bool fro'?" "I shall bowl from this end." "Then at this end I stands." By-and-by the old gent would say, "Oh dear, lad, thi's getting on badly." That acted like a signal, for "How's that?" was soon heard, and out the batsman had to go.

'Umpires are, as a rule, anxious to give fair and unbiased decisions. There have been instances in which they could not resist the temptation to give "the benefit of the doubt" to "their own side". On one occasion, in my own experience, an expected umpire did not turn up, and a man on the ground was engaged to take his place. Just as the play was going to begin, he said, "Just let me understand, which side am I umpiring for?"

'On another occasion, I took a parish team to play in a match on the Castle Howard Park ground. We were leading by about 50 runs when the last man of the opposing side came in. I had taken 2 wickets with "lobs" in my previous over, and it was about three minutes from time to draw stumps when I was preparing to deliver the last over, confident that I could get the last wicket. Suddenly the umpire—not ours—pulled his watch out and said, "There's not time for this over to be concluded. I shan't allow it to be commenced." And with that he took the bails and left the ground, leaving us not victors, but only with the match "drawn in our favour".

'When I came to York Minster as vicar-choral nearly a quarter of a century ago, I was given to understand that the Dean, Dr Duncombe, didn't like my playing cricket. But one Sunday morning an accident happened which rather reconciled him to my playing. The collections in those days were made with bags which had three wooden handles, convenient for passing from hand to hand, but very inconvenient for arranging on the alms-dish, especially when it came to the last three or four. On this occasion the choir-boys, who did the collecting, had placed the bags on the plate more carelessly than usual, with the result that as I was handing it up to the Dean the top bag fell off. Instinctively I made a grab at it, holding the dish, which was very heavy, in my left hand, and I caught it before it reached the ground, and replaced it safely on the plate, and gave it to the Dean. Some members of the congregation, who saw the incident, audibly tittered; but I know that I broke out into a cold sweat at the thought of what would have happened if, while catching the falling bag, I had sloped the dish holding all the rest. After the service the Dean said with a smile, "Well, Mr Carter, I see there *are* some advantages in being able to play cricket."'

Talks with Old English Cricketers, 1900

✳

Cricket and the Church

F. S. ASHLEY-COOPER

There was a time, it may surprise many to know, when it was considered derogatory for a clergyman to participate in the game. Even during the past eighty years some excellent players have been obliged almost
to abandon match playing on account of their Bishops not regarding
it with a favouring eye. One such was the Rev. E. T. Drake, who retired
from first-class cricket on taking Holy Orders, the Gentlemen in consequence losing one of their best men when opposing the Players, whilst
another was the late Rev. John Morley Lee, a very good all-round cricketer, who played an innings of 110 at Canterbury in 1848, and who was
a most rapid runner between wickets, especially when in with Mr
R. T. King. Some excellent players, however, contrived, by playing
under an assumed name, to appear occasionally in great matches without angering their Bishop: thus, the Rev. J. Dolphin became J. Copford,
and Canon M'Cormick—known to the many-headed as 'Joe'—J. Bingley
or J. Cambridge. One can readily understand the Bishop of London
forbidding one of his clergy to take part in a great match advertised as
being played for £1,000 a side, as was the case with the Rev. J. Dolphin
in 1831. In 1744 a commentator on the game wrote: 'The robust *cricketer* plays in his shirt. The Rev. Mr W——d, particularly, appears
almost naked.' Then, and for long afterwards, it was the rule, and not
the exception, for matches to be played for large stakes and for heavy
wagers to be decided by the result. In these circumstances it was
only natural that the Bishops should not approve of the game, and
that Miss Mitford should deliver herself of a denunciation of 'making
the noble game of cricket an affair of bettings and hedgings, and
maybe of cheatings.'

It is gratifying to know that many eminent Churchmen were partial
to the game in their youth. Good Bishop Ken, a friend of Izaak Walton
(the Father of Angling), was born in 1637 and educated at Winchester,
and, whilst there, 'is found attempting to wield a cricket bat'. At least
so says the Rev. W. Lisle Bowles, as quoted in Timbs's *School Days of
Eminent Men*. Thomas Ken was a boy at Winchester in 1656, and his
name is still to be seen cut out on stone in the College cloisters with
that date annexed to it. He attended Charles II on his death-bed, and

it was to him the king apologized for being 'such an unconscionable long time in dying'. He is now best known as the author of our favourite morning and evening hymns. Christopher Wordsworth, afterwards Bishop of Lincoln, was captain of Winchester, and his brother, Charles Wordsworth, in later years Bishop of St Andrews, was for five years in the Harrow Eleven. In 1825, when Harrow and Winchester met for the first time, the brothers were the rival captains. Not only were there two future Bishops in the elevens, but Henry Edward Manning, afterwards the famous Cardinal, played for Harrow, and Christopher Wordsworth often recalled with interest in later years that he 'caught out Manning'. At Oxford Manning was for a time a private pupil of Charles Wordsworth, who on one occasion sent him a cricket bat with a poetical epistle. Wordsworth received in reply a similar epistle in twelve stanzas from Manning, of which the following is a specimen:

> The bat that you were kind enough to send,
> Seems (for as yet I have not tried it) good;
> And if there's anything on earth can mend
> My wretched play, it is that piece of wood.

The future Bishop, on reading the verses, is said to have remarked with demure sarcasm that they 'fore-shadow a mind capable of making strong statements on insufficient evidence'.

The Cardinal at all times referred to his cricket at Harrow with the greatest pleasure, and throughout his life took an interest in the game. He is reported to have asked one of his priests, 'Would you like to enter heaven with a chalice in one hand and a cricket bat in the other?' which recalls an impromptu epigram by an Irish versifier:

> When all the nations throng the judgment hill,
> Where Peter, with his great keys, guards the wicket,
> England, in lazy flannels lounging, will
> Question the Fisherman: 'Did you play cricket?'

The late Mr George W. E. Russell has told how, on July 15, 1888, being the first day of the Eton and Harrow match at Lord's, a few old Harrovians of different generations met at a Harrow dinner. The Cardinal, who had just turned eighty, was invited. He declined to dine on the ground that he never dined out, but he would on no account forgo the opportunity of meeting the members of his old school, and he recalled with pride that he had been for two years in the Harrow Eleven. He appeared as soon as dinner was over, gallantly faced the cloud of cigar smoke, was in his very best vein of anecdote and reminiscence, and stayed till the party broke up. A few years before his death he expressed a wish that an account of his career should appear in *Scores and Biographies*, and one was accordingly inserted.

It is, by the way, of interest to recall that the Sixth Form game of 1823-4 at Harrow comprised among its players a future Cardinal (Manning), an Archbishop (R. C. Trench), three Bishops (Perry, Charles Wordsworth and Oxenden), and a Dean (Merivale).

The Rev. J. C. Ryle, who appeared for Eton against Harrow and Winchester in 1833 and 1834, and for Oxford against Cambridge in 1836 and 1838, was afterwards Bishop of Liverpool, and wrote innumerable pamphlets. John Coleridge Patteson, of Eton and Oxford, was murdered in 1871 by the savages of Nukapu, near the island of St Cruz, being then Bishop of Melanesia—a title held later by the old Kent cricketer, Cecil Wilson. All students of the game, too, will remember how C. T. Studd, one of the best of amateur players, suddenly abandoned participating in great matches in order to become a missionary in China. He believed that he would not be obliged to master the intricate Chinese language, but that he would miraculously receive the gift of that tongue. Although so far removed from his native land, he occasionally played, but always in Chinese dress and pigtail, as he had adopted the native costume in accordance with the rules of the mission of which he was a member.

Who is there would be so bold as to state that such men as Ken, Charles Wordsworth, Manning, Christopher Wordsworth, Ryle, Henry Lascelles Jenner (a former Bishop of Dunedin), Patteson, Studd and Wilson have not derived a considerable measure of their success in life from indulging when young in cricket, which is capable of endowing players with many fine qualities, of which unselfishness is one of the most marked? At the present time many of the clergy are numbered amongst the most enthusiastic supporters of the game. In Bow Church, on April 13, 1915, the Bishop of Lincoln said: 'Thank God for our English games! They have taught us how to be good-tempered in defeat, generous in victory; they have taught us how to "play the game".' Elevens composed entirely of Church of England ministers often take the field; it is, in fact, well known that such a team has more than once been drawn entirely from the clergy attached to St Mary's, Southsea.

That cricket is a game from which great benefits, both moral and physical, can be derived is evident to everybody who has more than a passing acquaintance with the pastime. In this respect a story is told of a miner who, after being on most unfriendly terms with his Vicar for many years, one day asked him to visit him, as he had met with a severe accident. After several visits the clergyman had the curiosity to inquire the motive which had dispelled his antipathy. 'Oh', said the miner, 'that hit o' yourn to square-leg for six a fortnight ago converted me.' The force of the remark can be understood when it is added that at the time the hit was made the miner had placed himself on the leg side within a few feet of the ecclesiastic. Remembering the above incident, one can sympathize with the Rector who said that what the parish wanted was not a theologian, but a fast bowler with a break from the off. A hit for six, or a good bowling feat, may at times effect as much good as an Archbishop's sermon.

Probably the best cricketing clergyman there has ever been was Lord Frederick Beauclerk, the greatest all-round player in the world just over a hundred years ago, and for twenty-two years Vicar of Redbourne. Lord Frederick was of a very choleric nature, and, if things did not go altogether to his liking, would express himself in far from pacific terms. Living in times far different from the present, he did not think it derogatory to arrange money matches, both at cricket and running. He once served Mr E. H. Budd so shabby a trick that the latter, good fellow though he was, could not help stating that 'Lord Frederick's behaviour was most unbecoming in a man in Holy Orders'. In 1818, as is generally known, the famous 'Squire' Osbaldeston, in a sudden fit of rage caused by being defeated at single wicket, erased his name from the list of members of the MCC, and in so doing obliterated the only two other names beginning with 'O'. In later years Osbaldeston regretted his hasty act, and asked his friend Budd to wait on Lord Frederick and Mr William Ward, two leading members of the Club, in order to see whether he could not induce them to place his name again on the books. Ward was agreeable, but Lord Frederick, who had a spite against the Squire, would not countenance such a thing—'The insult was too great . . . etc., etc.' Budd told Osbaldeston the result of his visit in the presence of a clergyman, a mutual friend, who remarked, *à propos* of Lord Frederick's attitude: 'I should not have thought his Lordship capable of so mean an act—and he a DD too!' Osbaldeston's terse and enigmatical reply was simply, 'DD can stand for many things besides Doctor of Divinity.'

Lord Frederick made no secret of the fact that he reckoned to make six hundred guineas a year out of the game. He was, too, a hunting parson of the old school, and his parishioners, knowing his great interest in sport, were probably not surprised when his clerk, Moody, announced one Sunday morning, before giving out the hymn, that 'The Vicar is going on Friday to the throwing-off of the Leicestershire hounds, and cannot return home until the following Monday. Therefore next Sunday there will not be any service in this church.' This recalls the fact that about forty years ago a worthy Canon, then nearer ninety than eighty in age, used to tell the following story relating to his younger days. 'One Sunday morning', he would say, 'upon being asked by the clerk in the vestry how I was, I replied that I felt very upset, for my cricket bat, which I had used at Eton, had been lost or stolen, and in a thoughtless moment added that I wouldn't have lost it for five pounds. As soon as the service commenced I forget all about the matter, but it was suddenly recalled to me by hearing the silly fellow begin to give out the Church notices by announcing: "Parson says as 'ow some bloke 'as stole 'is cricket bat. He wants it back, and will pay five pounds for it." On my return home I mentioned the incident to my wife, who said at once that she had put the bat in an oak chest, thinking I should not require it again that year. The publicity made me very uncomfortable at the time, but I can afford to laugh at the incident now, after an interval of fifty years.'

The Rev. T. A. Anson was in his day a wonderful wicket-keeper, who earned immortality in the match at Lord's between Gentlemen and Players, in 1843, by stumping G. Butler off one of Alfred Mynn's tremendous shooters, using the left hand only; C. G. Lane, whom Richard Daft described as one of the best amateur batsmen he had ever seen, was a prominent member of the famous Surrey team of the sixties; E. Elmhirst, who was always being told by his candid friends that if he could preach as well as he could play cricket he would one day become an Archbishop, was a brilliant wicket-keeper; William Ridding, who also excelled behind the wicket, appeared with success for Winchester, Oxford and the Gentlemen, and in the match against the Players, in 1849, stumped Joe Guy off one of Harvey Fellows's terrific deliveries; E. H. Pickering, a celebrated old Etonian, was once called upon so suddenly to bat in a Gentlemen *v.* Players match at Lord's that he was obliged to go to the wicket in clerical garb; H. B. Biron, the first man to score as many as two hundred runs in an innings in Sussex, and a pupil of Fuller Pilch, was for many years a valuable member of the Kent Eleven, both with bat and ball; and R. T. King, a great boxing enthusiast, was the most famous of points. The foregoing are the names of but a very few of the many clergymen who have achieved success on the cricket field; the list could be considerably extended were there any necessity to do so. Canon M'Cormick, to whom reference has already been made, held a curious record for one in Holy Orders, for he could state that he once gained the verdict over Nat Langham, the only man who ever beat Tom Sayers. He was frequently told in chaff, in consequence, that he had missed his vocation, and that instead of being a clergyman he should have adopted 'the Ring' as a profession. Amongst cricket historians the Rev. James Pycroft occupies an honoured place; whilst the Rev. Robert Stratten Holmes, the author of the greater part of the official chronicle of Yorkshire cricket, is the possessor of one of the best cricket libraries in the world.

Whether cricket should or should not be indulged in on Sundays is a subject on which various opinions have been expressed. In past times, when the population of the country was far less than it is now, when each village was a small world in itself and had little intercourse with the towns even of its own county, and before the railways had spread an iron network in every direction, Sunday cricket was not only frequently played on the village greens, but was commended by people whose opinion was entitled to respect and whose influence was great. The famous Dr Parr, with his pipe and jug, used to sit on the green at Hatton, in Warwickshire, on Sunday afternoons, watching his parish lads play at cricket, the absentees from church not being allowed to take part. The public-houses were deserted, and it is recorded that there was no better-conducted parish than the Doctor's. (It was Parr, the friend of Johnson and Sheridan, who, when his first wife killed his favourite cat, retaliated by cutting the throat of her parrot.)

In *Our Village* Miss Mitford, who loved the game, gives a charming description of Sunday afternoon practice, every word of which, even at this distance of time, tempts one to quotation. In *The Life of Charles Kingsley*, too, edited by his wife, mention is made of the fact that the Sunday afternoons in his parish, Eversley, Hampshire, used to be devoted to cricket by the young men of the neighbourhood. The 'muscular Christian's' remarks to his own son respecting the fact was to the effect that the players, chiefly agricultural labourers, had no time in the week for the pursuit of the king of games. About forty years ago Canon Benham, in the course of some very interesting notes on early cricket, referred in the following words to Sunday cricket being played in his native village: 'There was always play on Sunday evenings. The young men used to take their bats and stumps to church and deposit them in the belfry till afternoon service was over, after which the adjournment to the field took place. I know a good many decent people who will say, "And a very good thing too." Well, this I think I may fairly say: They were dressed in their best, and very natty and respectable they looked in their white frocks and beaver hats, with their sweethearts to look on. It was a gala evening when the weather was warm and bright, and they were on their good behaviour, and I do not remember any riotous conduct or drunkenness arising out of it all, any more than I have seen in the Champs Élysées on a Sunday evening; but I am decidedly in favour of the English quiet Sunday all the same.' In the next village the old parson used to stand in his field, which adjoined the cricket meadow, and look on with interest, pipe in mouth. Many of my readers probably have heard the story of that most genial—if somewhat eccentric—Archdeacon down in the West, now a hale and lively old man of eighty-five or thereabouts, who went away for a Sunday, having entrusted his parish to a neighbour. When he came back, his friend reported: 'Capital congregation and very well-behaved, but I am very sorry to tell you that after church they all went off to cricket.' 'Of course they did', was the reply, 'and if I had been here I should have gone with them.'

How different was this dear old Archdeacon from the Vicar of Maidstone in the reign of Charles the First! In *The Life and Death of Tho. Wilson*, Minister of Maidstone, published anonymously[1] in 1672, occurs the following passage (p. 40): 'Maidstone was formerly a very profane town, inasmuch as I have seen Morrice-dancing, Cudgel playing, Stool-ball, Crickets, and many other sports openly and publickly on the Lord's Day.' Thomas Wilson, who was born in 1601 and died in or about 1653, refused to publish the *Book of Sports on the Lord's Day* in his church on Sundays when commanded to do so. It must be remembered, however, that not until very long afterwards was cricket generally considered a fit game for gentlemen. In *Annals of the West Kent Cricket Club* Mr Philip Norman records that the Rev. John Lockwood, a very enthusiastic player a hundred years ago, held some Church preferment at Coulsdon or in its immediate neighbourhood, and eventually gave up cricket because members of his congregation were always asking him in the churchyard on Sunday if he would play in a match on the Monday, which he thought lowered his dignity as a clergyman.

On several occasions proceedings have been taken against persons for participating in the game on Sundays. As far back as November 20,

---

[1] The author was Mr George Swinnocke.

1817, several persons 'who had long resisted the threats and entreaties of the inhabitants of Old Buckenham', were convicted before a magistrate at Larlingford (Norfolk) and fined for playing cricket on Sunday, October 2nd, on Old Buckenham Green.

Of more interest, however, is the following, recorded on the last page but one in a volume of Accounts of the Churchwarden and Overseers for the parish of Eltham, 1625–55:

This year 1654	An account of all such moneys as hath been receyved for misdemenrs of whom & howe disposed of		
Cricket players on y^c Lords Day	Rec^d of Francis Clayford	2^s
	of Edw. Layton	2^s
	of John Poole	2^s
	of Will Foxe	2^s
	of Will Starbrock	2^s
	Widd Roodes sonne	2^s

And what curious experiences some country clergymen can relate of their village cricket! One of the most amusing concerns the Vicar who went in when six wickets were down for about a dozen runs and carried out his bat for sixty, winning the game for his side almost single-handed. On his way to the tent, with honours thick upon him, he was greeted by the following remark from a parishioner, a day labourer, who was almost dancing for joy at the victory: 'Lor', Parson, what a man ye be! Ye saved us all last Sunday, and now ye've come an' saved us on a Saturday!'

It is not usual to hear the game referred to from the pulpit, but a visitor to a certain church near London about twenty years ago[1] noticed one peculiarity during the service which struck him as being remarkable. The clerk preceded the hymn immediately before the sermon with two announcements, as follows: 'The members of the cricket club connected with this congregation will meet for the transaction of business to-morrow evening at seven o'clock. The usual prayer meeting on Friday at seven-thirty.' The clerk who blended Christianity and cricket so delightfully was indeed a sportsman quite of F.G.'s creed. As recently as 1893 a clergyman announced from the pulpit of his church, in Hampshire: 'On Saturday next we play the return cricket match with T—— (a neighbouring village). I shall umpire on that occasion, when I trust that our united endeavours will meet with success.' His

---

[1] This written in 1927.

expression was certainly an ambiguous one, recalling to mind the fact that it takes a strong eleven to play a side with a twelfth man.

It would be instructive to know in how many of the old parish registers cricket is mentioned. There is a well-known reference to the game in the Chailey (Sussex) parish register of 1737—'John Boots, killed at Newick by running against another man on crossing the wicket. Buried May 14'—but in how many other such books is the game alluded to? Sermons on the game have occasionally been heard. As far back as 1837, on the eve of a match between Kent and Sussex, the Vicar of West Malling denounced from the pulpit as sinners all those who attended to witness the play, whether they betted or not. In 1883 the Rev. Mr Mercer, of Ballarat, preached a cricket sermon, taking his text from Ephesians v, 13; whilst a few years ago the Rev. W. Carlile, of London, discoursed on 'MacLaren's Centuries', 'Surrey's New Bowler', 'C. B. Fry', and 'Warner or MacLaren?' In March 1903, at Christ Church, Crowborough, Sussex, the Rev. G. Hugh Jones preached a sermon entitled 'L.b.w.: a Parable of the Cricket Field', taking his text from St Matthew xiii, 34. Amongst the famous players who have had reference to the game made on their tombstones may be mentioned William Lillywhite, Cobbett, Mr John Willes ('He was a patron of all manly sports and the first to introduce round-arm bowling in cricket'), Fuller Pilch, Mr Alfred Mynn, Richard Daft, John Summers, Tom Humphrey, Harry Jupp, George Lohmann, Arthur Shrewsbury, Alfred Shaw, Mr A. N. Hornby and Barlow. In Holy Trinity Church, Marylebone, is a stained-glass window to the memory of an Harrovian, Second Lieutenant L. S. G. Jones, of the Monmouthshire Regiment, who died of wounds in June 1917, aged nineteen. The School crest and buildings are prominent in the design, which also includes three figures each about three feet in length. The one in the centre is allegorical—of a soldier holding a broken sword. The others portray a young Harrovian, the one on the left wearing a wide Harrow straw hat and reading a book, and that on the right in flannels and blazer with a cricket ball in his right hand and a cricket bat in his left. Possibly the memorial is unique: certainly it is very beautiful.

Canon Benham used to relate an interesting tale concerning the late Archdeacon Harrison. 'That very pleasant old man had a nephew who was reckoned the "lion-hitter" of Kent, and he had indoctrinated his uncle with a love of cricket; and I found my bedroom walls covered with cricket scores. It is said that during the Canterbury Cricket Week the worthy Archdeacon's pony-chaise stood waiting at the door. The news would come down to the Archdeacon in his study busy with the

Fathers, "Mr Charles just a-goin' in, Sir," and down went the pen, and away went the Archdeacon in time to see the nephew's performance.' Such enthusiasts deserve to reach a ripe age, like Canon Beadon, who died in 1879 at the patriarchal age of 101 years and six months. The Canon had managed the Bullingdon Club, at Oxford, with Stephen Lushington, afterwards the famous judge. He and his father held the living of North Stoneham for more than 118 years.

A few years ago an experience was related concerning a schoolboy captain who was a very great believer in the efficacy of prayer. He did not go to such lengths as a French Princess of the Revolution period who, even if she dropped a ball of wool, would fall on her knees and pray that she might be able to reach far enough to recover it without being obliged to ring for a servant to move a small article of furniture beneath which it had rolled; but on the night before the match against the Town—the chief fixture of the season—he prayed earnestly that victory might be his. And his request was granted, much to the surprise of his opponents, the majority of whom were duly impressed by his explanation. Strange to say, after the return game had ended in a tie, the Town captain stated that he also had invoked Divine aid, and that, in the circumstances, the result was the only one possible. The School leader readily accepted the statement, but his young followers made no secret of the fact that they considered their opponent had not been 'playing the game' in benefiting from their captain's idea, which they appeared to regard as copyright.

Mr J. M. Framjee Patel, in *Stray Thoughts on Indian Cricket*, has shown that appeals by cricketers for supernatural aid are not confined to Englishmen. Some Parsi players told him that, when they were in a corner and badly wanted to draw a match, they prayed and invoked the help of the elements, and that a thunderstorm came to their rescur, stopping play and causing the match to be drawn. If such a practice became at all common in this country, the MCC would doubtless find it necessary to issue an official recommendation worded somewhat as follows:

In the best interests of the game cricketers are earnestly requested to rely solely on their skill to ensure success, and in no circumstances to appeal for supernatural aid. This is not intended to apply to those clergy of the Church of England who may be directed by their Bishop, for the general welfare, to pray for rain.

Cricket Highways and Byways, 1927

❊

The Church Cricketant

NORMAN GALE

I bowled three sanctified souls
　　With three consecutive balls!
What do I care if Blondin trod
　　Over Niagara falls?
What do I care for the loon in the Pit
　　Or the gilded Earl in the Stalls?
I bowled three curates once
　　With three consecutive balls!

I caused three Protestant 'ducks'
　　With three consecutive balls!
Poets may rave of lily girls
　　Dancing in marble halls!
What do I care for a bevy of yachts
　　Or a dozen or so of yawls?
I bowled three curates once
　　With three consecutive balls!

I bowled three cricketing priests
　　With three consecutive balls!
What if a critic pounds a book
　　What if an author squalls?
What do I care if sciatica comes,
　　Elephantiasis calls?
I bowled three curates once
　　With three consecutive balls!

Cricket Songs, 1894

*

Holy Bowlers

FRANK KEATING

The bat is in its scabbard, the sponsors' tents dismantled, and the taut umbrellas furled. The Ashes have been won and lost. This week, the County Championship finishes. At the time of writing, the final of the *Church Times* Cup has just been settled. It is always played in September on the historic Walker Ground at Southgate in London. This summer (that of 1985), the Diocese of Chichester's XI devoutly, if soggily, won their way through to the final. They met the Diocese of Liverpool, the holders, who have had a crack XI for some years now (which may or may not have something to do with the fact that their Bishop is the former opening batsman for Sussex and England, the Rt Rev. David Sheppard). Nevertheless, surprisingly, Liverpool were beaten by Chichester (who batted first) by 51 runs—Chichester 167 for 8; Liverpool 116 for 10.

The Church and cricket boast ancient bonds, from the villages to the first-class game. In international arenas, there has never been doubt about which side He is on. The Lord giveth runs and taketh away wickets. When Sir Pelham Warner was manager of the 'Bodyline' tour to Australia in 1932, he asked a Bishop on the liner going over whether it was permissible to pray for victory in the forthcoming series. The Bishop asked to sleep on the query, presumably sought Divine guidance on his bunk through the night, and gave his ruling at breakfast—'Anything that conduces to the glory of England was a meet and fitting subject for prayer.' England, of course, won the series.

I am surprised, reflecting on the number of dog-collars that have jauntily hung from nails in pavilion dressing-rooms through two centuries, that the *Church Times* Cup competition is not an older one. It was begun in 1950. The runners-up prize, by the way, is traditionally donated by Charles Farris & Co., the well-known ecclesiastical furnishers. What can that be? A lectern? A chalice even? Or perhaps, a gallon of sweet Cyprus communion sherry?

You have to be ordained to nudge the selectors for *Church Times* matches. You can only play for the Diocese you serve. Once, there was a whiff of skulduggery in the sacristy. A note in the definitive history, *The World of Cricket*, mentions 'an attempt to flout the competition's qualification rule, but since it was dealt with firmly there has been no repetition'. I fancy that short entry might have been contributed by Canon Hugh Pickles who, as Vicar of Blewbury in the Oxford Diocese, was a founding father of the tournament. 'The Rev.' remains one of the most loved characters of Cotswold cricket and its fringes. Spies reported him at Cheltenham in midsummer when Gloucestershire were chasing the Championship, circling the boundary edge in meditation, dreaming dreams of Graveney's graces, his ever faithful companion, 'Justice', at his heels. Twenty years ago, Canon Hugh petitioned his then Bishop of Oxford for permission to go to Jamaica. His Lordship, more than surprised, thought it an application from one of his priests to transfer to the missionary fields. This was serious. Pickles to the Palace. He explained that Graveney's Worcestershire team, having won the previous year's Championship, were to tour Jamaica for a fortnight and he would like to accompany them. The Bishop, relieved, let him go—even though the tour was in Lent.

For years I played against 'The Rev.' when, each August, he would bring his bat—was it for the Berkshire Gents, or the South Oxford Amateurs?—to those blissful cricket weeks at Douai's wide green park pitch, sheltered then by friendly elms, high above Woolhampton in the Berkshire Hills. Pickles was not at all a bad bat. But it was eerie bowling at him—for he modelled his style, unashamedly and exactly, on his hero, Tom Graveney. His style, that is: the technique and the results were somewhat different. As Graveney was my own boyhood hero it was, as we were able to say in those days, 'rather queer' that this precise impersonator at the other end was unable to read my arm ball, to spot my half-volleys, or even my slower one for c-&-b's. From a distance in the outfield, if you squinted your eyes, it really was Tom out there—until the ball was bowled.

They were both tall, angular men. Both had nutbrown arms under loosely-rolled sleeves. And rather beaky, autocratic noses, though with the adjoining laugh-lines always ready and willing. If Tom changed his batmaker, so would the cleric. Or style of glove. Pickles would wear his flannels exactly as Tom did, loose and ample at the rear, unlike the 'sexy' tightness favoured today by such as Lamb and Gatting and Richards. When Pickles walked to the wicket, short-stepping, light-treaded, keen, it was Tom to a T. He would take guard with the same perfunctory vim as the *nonpareil*, survey the field just as foxily and certain—point of bat handle resting lightly on his hip. Then, exactly four precise tugs at the long peak of his cap, as he settled over his bat; two more tugs for assurance as the bowler began his approach. Then, again, just four, almost imperceptible, taps of his bat where the crease met the little toe of his right foot. Graveney to perfection. So too as the arm came over, perfect stillness. As the ball left the hand, a high, swirling backlift, and . . . there, mime artist became artisan, for the Rev. Pickles would play the Graveney cover drive to *everything* he was confronted with.

It made him pretty easy to bowl at. *Rev Pickles . . . b Keating* was inked in quite often. It gave me a buzz, too. Always good to nab a great. And Graveney was certainly that.

Hugh Pickles once wrote a loving and stylish memoir on Worcestershire cricket which Heinemann published as part of its *County Champions* series of essays. Worcester long had a tradition of giving a first-class game to Scotland, one of whose very best cricketers was the Rev. J. H. Aitchison, who set out his stall at the wicket like a Presbyterian Boycott and of whom Keith Miller remarked, 'I'm glad his Holiness is not a Pom Englisher, else we could be here all day for years.' One time, Worcester's legendary leg-spinner with the crab-like shuffle to the wicket, Roley Jenkins, kept beating the Rev. Aitchison's prodding bat, clocking him on the pads, but never getting any satisfaction from the umpire even with his googly. Finally, and exasperated, Roley followed through to the batsman's end. 'Vicar,' he said, 'I hear you're a parson?' 'That's right, I am,' said Aitchison. Retorted Roley, 'Well, if I had your ruddy luck, I'd be Archbishop of Canterbury!'

Roley had trouble with the cloth. A few years later, against Sussex, he had the same sort of spell against Bish-to-be, the Rev. Sheppard. This time Roley let go a choice selection of old pro's expletives at the end of an over and rolled off, still cursing, to spend the rest of the afternoon in the outfield. As he batted on, the outburst gave Sheppard the theme for his Sunday sermon the next morning—'Faith is like facing Roley Jenkins: no hesitation—if you decide to go forward, go forward all the way.'

As you would expect, the Bishop of Liverpool has been the subject of many of the summery circuit's best yarns. On his 'sabbatical' tour to Australia under Dexter in 1962–63, he kept spilling catches (although, in his prime, he was a superlatively safe fieldsman). 'If t'ball balloons towards thee again, Reverend,' Fred Trueman is alleged to have advised, 'joost put y'bloody 'ands together as if y'were prayin.' On that tour, Sheppard baptised a baby in Melbourne Cathedral. 'Please don't drop this one', said the worried mother as she handed over her first-born.

By the end of his batting career, Sheppard gave as good as he got.

One day at Bristol, Gloucester's roly-poly off-spinner, Bomber Wells, kept squirting the thing through the cleric's guard, but never hitting the wicket. 'Been on your prayer mat all night, Vicar?' enquired Bomber at the end of an over. 'In a way, I suppose,' said the Rev. David, adding, 'but don't you pray at night, Brian?' 'No,' said the aggrieved Bomber, 'my faith is in 90 per cent skill and ten per cent luck.' 'Well,' replied Sheppard, 'my sort of prayer is in profit today, wouldn't you say?'

The Church and the stately game have long been entwined. On the eve of his ordination, the Rev. Henry Venn gave away his bat, saying never again would he gladly hear the cry, 'Well struck, parson!' In 1856, the Rev. W. Fellows struck the then, first recorded, world record hit from bat to bounce of 175 yards. The Rev. Vernon Royle, great-grandfathers reckon, was as sharp a cover-point for Lancashire as Cyril Washbrook or Clive Lloyd.

The late and still much missed Ian Peebles, who was a better writer, companion, and softly humorous raconteur than he was even a demon leg-break bowler for England (and Scotland, come to that), contributed a beautiful piece in the *Guardian* just before his death half a dozen years ago. He played in the 1930s when coloured-cap clerics often made up the county cricketing cadre.

Ian himself was a son of the manse. His father was a West of Scotland Anglican and cricket nut, who took Ian to Glasgow when he was 10 years old in 1919 to see Scotland routed after the Australian Imperial Forces XI had made 745 for 6 dec. When young Peebles came south and, after Oxford, played for Middlesex, he knew the form. He recalls a Homeric battle at Lord's between the Rev. Tom Killick—one of the country's leading amateur bats of the period—and Hampshire's bowler, the Rev. Steele. Finally Steele knocked his fellow priest's castle over, after a splendid 53, and as tailender Peebles passed Killick on the way to the wicket he asked him what Steele bowled. Replied the Rev.— 'Good ol' Church of England: just straight up and down and no nonsense.'

There was a lot of it about in those inter-war years. Canon Gillingham was a force in moral standards as well as the Essex batting order. Once, in the dressing-room at Leyton, the Canon rebuked that old pro with the pungently purple tongue, Charlie McGahey, for swearing. 'Now, now, Charlie, that does not sound like a gentleman to me.' At that precise moment the Rev. was peeling off his trousers. 'If it comes to that,' replied McGahey, observing this revelation of virile masculinity, 'you don't look much like a lady to me, sir.'

The Rev. J. H. Parsons, of Warwickshire, had a simpler method. He carried about a swearbox with him, fining the professionals threepence for every blasphemy—6d if addressed to an umpire. Parsons must have been a heck of a fellow. Somebody should write a book on him. His father was a chef at Brasenose College, then a Birmingham pub-keeper. Parsons himself was apprenticed as a car-tester in Coventry, became a hero at Gallipoli, was commissioned in the field, won the MC in the last British cavalry charge at Huj, and led a North-West Frontier garrison . . . then came home to Edgbaston to cause havoc round the Championship with his straight driving. He did not believe in the cut or glide. He was ordained in 1929 after being talked into the idea by the Archdeacon of Coventry between innings at Edgbaston one Saturday. Thereafter, following the tea interval on Saturdays, he was excused slip fielding and allowed to ruminate in the deep to prepare his sermons. He ended up Canon at Truro Cathedral.

In recent years, the Rev. A. R. Wingfield-Digby was long a fixture in Oxford University sides and might well have swung for a county side had his first vocation been cricketing. Peter Roebuck, the Somerset opening bat and author, tells how the Combined Universities' XI beat Yorkshire in the 1976 B & H first round at Barnsley. It has, it seems, taken Yorkshire a decade to recover: 'A grave voice announces, "From the river end, A. R. Wingfield-Digby." This is more the sort of thing the crowd expected, and it draws ironic cheers. A fine double-barrelled name—should see some leather fly. They settle into their seats, content . . . "Wingers-Diggers" plays up to it, of course. We're only thankful he's not wearing a cravat and striped cap . . . His bowling looks innocu-ous, indeed palpably innocuous, but as the ball floats down it contains sufficient cunning to trap the unwary. Digby does have one advantage over lesser mortals: as a man of the cloth he can summon formid-able powers to his assistance. Our Reverend trundles up to bowl his loosener. A shade short (atheists call 'em long hops), it causes Leadbeater to essay a hook to the midwicket boundary. He succeeds only in edg-ing it on to his stumps. Well, there you are, you see.'

Just two balls later, the England player, Old, having been sent in to knock the theology student to kingdom-come, is plumb lb to the Reverend Andrew. Ah, the power of prayer and a God-fearing ump.

Anyhow, the *Church Times*. This advertisement appeared in their columns on June 30, 1967:— '*Old-fashioned vicar (Tractarian) seeks col-league. Left-hand fast bowler preferred. Good golf handicap an asset but not essential. Fine church with good musical tradition. Parish residential and farming*. Box HV 521.' I just wonder if Canon Pickles inserted that? Well, he is always rather gloomy when the Diocese of Oxford fail to make the final of the Cup. And how useful such a curate would be in the nets—well, even Graveney was sometimes just slightly fallible against Davidson-type left-handed fast bowling.

Gents and Players, 1987

*

A Controversial Trio

DAVID FOOT

Charlie Parker, Cec Parkin and Jack MacBryan played their best cricket in the 1920s. It was an evocative epoch. The Australians whacked us as we recovered from the First World War. Our Test selectors had aberrations. There were Hobbs, Sutcliffe and Woolley—and Hammond on the way. Some counties still seemed to parade more kaleidoscopic fancy caps than resolute shots but that only reflected the social tableau of the times.

The amateurs and the pros continued to go their separate ways as they walked off the field. It was simply a microcosm of the British class structure and found a tacit acceptance by the majority of the professionals—though not by Parker, a farm worker's son who had been reading about the Russian Revolution, and not entirely by MacBryan, an amateur who professed to have more regard for the game's paid craftsmen.

Charlie Parker played for Gloucestershire, and only Wilfred Rhodes and Tich Freeman took more wickets. He bowled his left-arm spinners at nearly medium pace. I shall dwell on his marvellous bowling but not to the exclusion of his improvised skills in the art of pugilism and physical altercations even with Sir Pelham Warner. He played only once for England and we shall try to discover why.

Cec Parkin was the Lancashire bowler it was impossible to define. He was a sort of off-spinner, yet such a label is defamatory to him. He started as a quickish bowler and ended at what was good medium pace for someone who turned the ball so much. To the despair of wicket-keepers he was inclined to experiment incessantly, often with six different deliveries in an over. He could spin the ball from leg and was renowned for his comically slow googlie. Indeed he *was* a comic, cricket's 'bag of tricks', whose jaunty antics and handsome grin on that strong face masked an abrasive nature and the misery that was to follow. He was an Old Trafford hero. We'll look at the elation that went with it—and the poignant suddenness of his decline.

Jack MacBryan was, until his death in 1983, our oldest surviving Test cricketer. He, like Parker, played only once for his country. He was a fine opening bat for Somerset. The style was classic and, during the summers he headed his county's batting averages, he was perhaps the most perfectly correct exponent in the country. He was an amateur who spoke his mind. Mostly he spoke out about other amateurs. It wasn't the best way to gain Test recognition.

More and more in my research, I discovered how much my three cricketers had in common.

They hardly knew each other. But they found themselves on occasions playing with or against each other in representative matches. They were generous in mutual praise. 'Parker's a wonderful bowler—I don't know what Gloucestershire would have done without him', wrote Parkin. 'MacBryan? He's one of us in attitude,' Parker, the pro, used to say.

It wasn't just the others' cricket that they admired. They knew they were similar birds, although one had a flat North Country voice, another caressed rural vowels and a third carried the well-modulated tones of upmarket comfort. They were contrary and perverse. They hated cant and pussy-footing. They were never, whatever the company, inhibited about dispensing invective. And, they were all self-destructive.

Jimmy White, an expansive North Country financier with a minimal knowledge of cricket, was the man behind Rochdale, when Parkin played in the league. Cec warmed to self-made men because they didn't really give a toss for protocol. White once went along to watch Parkin playing for the Players against the Gents. During the afternoon, his raucous voice boomed out across Lord's: 'Hey, which are the Gentlemen here?'

There were polite coughs and indignant looks. Parkin chuckled to himself—and approved. So would Parker and MacBryan, for complicated psychological reasons.

The three of them could be bad tempered. But that is altogether too superficial and sweeping. It's of more value to explore the paradox. Charlie was loved by the fellow professionals at Bristol, Gloucester and Cheltenham, even by one wicket-keeper, the late Vic Hopkins who was plucked straight from village cricket at Dumbleton and plunged to distraction as he attempted to comprehend the devious turns, ruthless rambles and short cuts of Charlie's deliveries.

Parkin could upset Arthur Gilligan in a Test match and then have the persuasive charm necessary to enlist the former England captain as the writer of an affectionate foreword to one of his books. He was one of the most magnetic professionals of his day. Spectators, not only those of Lancashire, came specifically to watch him. They giggled at his visual jokes and the bewildering variety of his bowling. He didn't seem to scowl when he was punished. They saw the broad smile: they only read, or heard rumour about, the other side to his nature.

MacBryan was supposedly rude, snobbish and ungenerous of spirit. There is evidence, however much he chose to obscure it in that affectedly gruff and cynical manner of his, that he could be kind and compassionate. His father ran a private home for the mentally sick and Jack was a frustrated psychiatrist himself. As a sixteen-year-old schoolboy he spent hours with a woman patient who had tried to kill a baby. 'I developed a considerable liking for her, in her plight.'

Long after his own marriage had ended, he sustained a long and loving friendship with a much younger woman who, like that patient, also had a serious mental condition. I was told: 'His concern for her was exceedingly tender.'

Journalistic instinct drew me to all three cricketers. I have long wanted to write about Charlie Parker. I grew up on stories about him and suspected that a third of them were true. It seems to me they all were. Now was the chance to set out his achievements as a spin bowler—and to discover for myself what really did happen in a hotel lift after one of the county's annual dinners.

I went to Blackburn to talk to Reg Parkin, himself a former county cricketer with Lancashire, about his father. I came to know Jack MacBryan well in the last years of his variegated life. The more I delved, the more my 'trio' became intrinsically linked in my mind. All were absorbing characters; all were dogged by controversy of the kind they almost chose to embrace.

Controversy has always been part of cricket. It titillates and enlivens the human fabric. Much of it is unseemly but we are inclined to relish it in retrospect. Journalists get blamed for emblazoning it in black type across the back pages. The hypocrites tut-tut only after reading every word.

Parker belonged to Gloucestershire, from where 'W.G.' left abruptly after the most acrimonious of committee meetings and the innuendos. Long after, Tom Graveney also packed his bags and walked out. If it was a petulant exit, it appeared to me at the time that he had every reason to make it.

Parkin's Lancashire had a long history and a short fuse. There were tetchy exchanges with Yorkshire and Middlesex just before and after the turn of the century. Archie MacLaren, once in a paddy, threatened to go off and join Hampshire. Walter Brearley always implied he was on the point of departure. And I haven't started to write of S. F. Barnes's prohibitive contractual negotiations.

When it comes to MacBryan's Somerset, the controversies tower as high as the Blackdown Hills. Didn't the county once restart a fixture against the Australians, on their first visit to Taunton, after play had been called off for the day? The Aussies rapidly curtailed a boozy picnic on the Quantocks and returned to the county ground by horse and trap. And, oh yes, there was the Taunton match against Sussex when the war-wounded last man hobbled out in a lounge suit and just failed to make it in time. And . . . well, what's new about cricket controversy?

My three cricketers are dead and they played the game during decades which I don't personally remember. They can't dispute actions and attitudes which I attribute to them. How much am I entitled to weave my imagination around the factual evidence?

From my days as a sixteen-year-old junior reporter, callow and naïve, when I summoned up enough sagacity not to change my shorthand notes to assist a brash Sunday paper in a libel action it faced, I have retained an obsessive interest in truth and the justifiable interpretation of it.

Alan 'Jock' Dent wrote of the famous dramatic critic James Agate as the Ego diarist: 'He wasn't exactly a liar. But in his writing he was inclined to soar into something which he defined and defended as "the higher truth". It consists in embroidery upon, or elaboration of what actually happened or was said.'

Ryszard Kapuscinski, one of Poland's finest journalists, said the other day in the course of a long interview in the *Observer*: 'What do you understand by a fact? Coal production figures are a fact. But mood is also a fact, and so is human expectation.'

Neville Cardus, a wordsmith without malice, adopted a somewhat cavalier regard for facts. He knew well enough what his revered employer C. P. Scott had to say about them being sacred. He was too good a *Manchester Guardian* journalist, of course, to get a symphony conductor's name wrong or to miss the accurate details of a hat-trick at Old Trafford. But he couldn't resist telling us just why the musicians were in such a headlong rush to reach the end of the score, or what the successful bowler had had for breakfast.

In his beloved Lancashire dressing room, gnarled old pros would discover what the engagingly verbose Cardus had written about one of them. He'd decorate his prose with splendid, descriptive quotes from the players themselves. 'But I never even spoke to him,' they'd protest, basking at the same time in such a flattering piece of fiction.

Late in his life, the loquacious Sir Neville would readily discuss his evocative journalistic liberties with other cricket writers. 'But, my dear chap, it's the SPIRIT of the thing that counts. Often when I quoted a player in my report, he may not literally have said those things.' Then the pause and the smile. 'But he'd have liked to . . .'

I shall no doubt be accused of inventing one or two of the more dramatic incidents involving Parker, for instance. The truth is that I went to great pains to authenticate them. I was also cautious, over matters of mood, in my imaginings.

Cecil Parkin's career was ruined by what went in the newspapers under his name. 'Whenever I open my mouth, I'm in trouble,' he said, without too much sign of changing his ways or mellowing his comments. Cheques from Fleet Street have proved irresistible to many cricketers over the past sixty or so years. One imagines Percy Fender was well recompensed for the reports he sent back during the 1920–21 tour of Australia. The journalistic excursion upset the cricket authorities and some of the players. Very soon, Test players were debarred from this source of income.

Plum Warner was one of several incensed by Parkin's indiscreet dalliance with newspapers. Nothing less than the most abject apology would do in the case of Gilligan, he said with finger-wagging admonition. He wrote that if the imprudent Parkin wasn't careful, he'd be regarded as 'the first cricketing Bolshevist'. What, ahead of Charlie Parker, down in Bristol?

Cardus, never averse to a mildly obscure allusion, called Cecil 'the Jack Ketch of cricket'. He was the executioner of the Duke of Monmouth after Sedgemoor, I eventually discovered. The records imply he needed five chops at the head. A historian friend, with a murky academic sense of humour to complement a penchant for the summer game, suggested that Jack Ketch obviously had a tendency to play down the wrong line. It was something Cec, Charlie and Jack often chose to do in life.

For someone who seemed to thrive on contentious behaviour and be ready to discuss it in print, Cec could be selective. I found little in his own writing about one unpleasant scene in 1920 when he was playing for Rochdale.

During a match in the early season he was so incensed by several decisions given against him by the umpires that he stormed off the pitch. The game was held up until his pique subsided and he was persuaded by his captain to start playing again. It led to his suspension by the Central Lancashire League.

There was an embarrassing impasse as he refused to apologize. Rochdale, no doubt swayed by his considerable ability as a league cricketer and as the best crowd-puller they had ever known, supported Parkin. Eventually, in an atmosphere of huffy compromise, honour was satisfied.

Honour was never satisfied in the case of Charlie Parker. 'Those buggers in high places made sure I'd only play once for my country.' If anyone ever collates cricket's most famous quotations, there will have to be a place for Parker's: 'Mr Bloody Warner will go to bed when I've finished with him.'

The best and kindest sports editor I ever worked under was George Baker, of the *Bristol Evening World*, who started as a lift boy when Rothermere moved into the West Country in 1929. Two years later he was walking out to open the innings in an evening fixture against Bedminster, one of Bristol's oldest established clubs. 'I was astonished to find that Charlie was one of the umpires. He was my great hero and I was utterly overawed.'

After several overs the bronze-faced umpire patted George on the shoulder. As the fielders changed over, Charlie gently took the bat from sixteen-year-old George and went through the forward defensive shot. He did it without ostentation. The unsolicited advice, given with infinite consideration in a twenty-over evening beer match, made a lasting impression on the young batsman.

Some years later, when Parker had finished playing and was doing some coaching in Bristol, George Baker was talking to his hero again. 'What's the greatest asset of all for a bowler, Charlie?'

The answer came back without hesitation. 'Direction . . . any bowler can learn to spin a ball. But knowing exactly where it's going to pitch is so much more important.'

Cricket grounds between the wars were, despite the hard times—heightened it seemed in Bristol by those stark orphanages—full of characters in the crowd. At Ashley Down there was an old man with a fiddle. He meandered in and out of the spectators with a tune and a song which he artlessly composed himself for every occasion. Out in the middle, Parker, poker faced and cap over one eye, was knocking over castles.

'Give us a song about Charlie.'

> Now this Charlie Parker's
> A regular old tartar . . .

The metre was suspect and the lyrics undistinguished. But the instant ditty wafted out from the mid-wicket boundary to the bowler's end. The cloth-capped crowd laughed. If Charlie heard, his expression didn't give him away. George Baker, by now a copy-boy, hurried back to the office to write a story about an old man and his fiddle.

Nothing is more revealing, I have often found, than the conversational shorthand of cricketing contemporaries. 'Charlie? Oh yes, quick tempered, I'm afraid,' said Bob Wyatt. 'Jack MacBryan? Ah yes, a man of prejudices,' said Gubby Allen.

Wyatt returned to the Somerset amateur. 'He was very upset, you know, when he didn't go to Australia.' J. C. W. MacBryan, as I discovered in my meetings with him, had no doubts at all about the reason for his rejection. When Wyatt started playing county cricket, rightly proud of his bowling, it happened that Mac was one of his first victims. He made his debut at the beginning of May 1923 against Worcestershire and took a solitary wicket. Then, against Somerset at Taunton at the end of the month, he took three more—MacBryan, Dar Lyon and Charlie Winter, an amateur from Repton.

The memory prompted an observation from both J.C.W. and R.E.S. 'Well I had already scored 62,' the Somerset man recalled. Wyatt said: 'My captain, Freddie Calthorpe noted my successes as a bowler and told me I couldn't do both. That was nonsense, of course. I was dropped down the batting order. I got my first hundred at No. 9.'

Background material for psychological studies—of the kind I like to think my three elongated profiles are—isn't gleaned in the main from record books. It comes from snippets of fascinating and unlikely information. Who'd have thought the fiery Parker would have a comprehensive knowledge of the Bible and could recite long sections verbatim? Who'd have thought Parkin liked to leave his pub on a Sunday and go up into the pulpit of a local church, of almost any denomination, 'to speak of sport and God'.

Their attitudes to money provided another eloquent facet to the trio's complex characters. Jack MacBryan liked a bottle of good claret, hosted a party with financial bravado and really had no spare cash to speak of. Charlie Parker was always borrowing from his team mates. Cecil Parkin was called mercenary on occasions and that angered him.

He was a hard negotiator when it came to wages as a league player. He knew his worth and let people know. When he played a Test match in Sydney, he heard that a visiting MP from Lancashire was offering a tenner to any England player who scored a hundred.

'What chance have I got if I go in last?' he asked the philanthropic Member.

'All right then, Cecil. For you a fiver if you get 25.'

There was no hope of an England win as he walked to the wicket. His mind was on the two bowlers, Ted McDonald and Arthur Mailey, and a fiver to augment his appearance money. He told the bowlers. 'What about it, then—there's nothing at stake.'

Mailey was seldom ungenerous in spirit. Perhaps McDonald was already thinking of becoming a citizen of Lancashire. Parkin made 35 and the MP was waiting for him as he came off the field, wallet in hand.

He wasn't a man to miss a financial trick but, as son Reg said, he had a big family to bring up. There was rancour from him because a number of leading Lancashire supporters decided not to support his benefit fund. 'Ee, you're too keen on the brass, Ciss,' someone once told him.

Parkin resented any suggestion that he was mean. He retorted, with some justification, that he made 'great sacrifices in time and money', travelling miles around the country speaking at dinners and cricket functions. Few village clubs, however small, asked him in vain. Never, he claimed, did he ask for any kind of fee.

Unlike MacBryan and Parker, he laughed a lot. He did when he saw George Gunn coming down the wicket to Ted McDonald of all people. He did whenever Jack Russell pulled a tin of cough sweets out of his pocket to dissuade Cecil from appealing. (Why is it that Essex has traditionally produced so much fun?) He did, unabashed, when Somerset's Guy Earle hit him farther out of the ground at Old Trafford than anyone else, before or since.

'I went up to him next morning and told him he owed me 4s 6d.' The handsome ex-skipper of Harrow wanted to know why. 'Because I needed a taxi to get the ball back!'

Parkin was well aware of Earle's unsubtle reputation. He regretted that he wasn't in the Lancashire side which went to Taunton in 1926. That was when Earle, as if doing his brutal best to exorcise the nightmarish memory of the famous Eton–Harrow match he let slip, smashed a straight drive through the window of the elevated Dickensian press box.

It was a demoralizing, not to say hazardous, occasion for the Fourth Estate. In the same match Ernest Tyldesley did the same on the way to his seventh hundred in consecutive fixtures. I trust neither was given a glowing write-up. As one adept in trench warfare and evasive action at Taunton, coping with the insensitively directed fusillade of aggression from muscular warriors like Botham and Richards, I know when to be sparing in my prose.

I hope you will detect the whiff of pure humour in my story of three absorbing cricketers. There was Charlie with his classical music, Jack with his embroidery and Cecil with his conjuring tricks.

Yet could there ever have been a more unholy trinity?

Cricket's Unholy Trinity, 1985

*

Andrew Ducat, an Obituary

ANONYMOUS

The sudden death at Lord's, on July 23, 1942, of Andrew Ducat, Surrey batsman of high talent and effective execution, England international Association footballer, captain of a cup-winning Aston Villa team, and in recent years cricket coach at Eton, came as a shock to countless friends and admirers. A man of delightful disposition, quiet and unassuming, he endeared himself to all who met him and as a reporter of games, after giving up activity in the field, he revealed his character in unbiased, accurate descriptions of matches and criticisms of the high-class players who were his successors. The last time I saw Ducat he sat a few feet from me in the Press box at Lord's. He passed a pleasant remark as he joined his fellow writers and we watched the cricket, intent on the players in the field. Next thing I heard of him, a few days afterwards, was his final and fatal appearance at the crease, where we had seen other cricketers play the game with all the energy of keen sportsmen such as always identified his own efforts.

That Ducat should collapse and die, bat in hand, was the last thing anyone would have expected of such a well-set-up, vigorous, healthy-looking and careful-living man. Evidence of those in the field proved clearly that he expired directly after playing a stroke and as he prepared to receive another ball, for he was dead when carried to the pavilion. The medical report gave the cause of death—failure of a heart that showed signs of definite weakness.

The loss of Ducat in this way may be attributed to the War, but for which there would not have been the Home Guard for him to join. His Surrey Unit were playing their Sussex brothers-in-arms, and Ducat was not out at lunch-time. On resuming, he raised his score from 12 to 29 before the catastrophe occurred.

The Wisden Book of Cricketers' Lives, 1986

✻

Wicket Maiden

VERNON SCANNELL

It is a game for gentle men;
Entirely wrong that man's spare rib
Should learn the mysteries of spin.

Women should not be allowed
To study subtleties of flight;
They should bowl underarm and wide.

Or, better still, not bowl at all,
Sit elegant in summer chairs,
Flatter the quiet with pale applause.

It shouldn't happen, yet it did:
She bowled a wicked heartbreak—one,
That's all. God help the next man in.

The Cricketer's Companion, 1960

✻

An Instinctive Cricketer

CYRIL ALINGTON

Edward Lyttelton's cricket was of a piece with the rest of him. Although in mature years—and this too was characteristic—he was prolific of theories about the game, and even wrote a manual of instruction, it is impossible to believe that his cricket was not ninety per cent instinctive. Those bold incisive cuts, that neat but severe driving, those swinging leg-hits were far more redolent of the carefree aggressiveness of gifted youth than of the thoughtful elaborations which accompany, and to some degree spoil, the development of all games. He himself believed very strongly that modern cricket was a travesty of the gay, adventurous pastime of his youth, and showed the courage of his convictions by resigning his membership of MCC a good many years ago. But that this was, fundamentally, no desertion of the game he had loved was shown by the frequency with which at the end of his life old memories came crowding into his mind, and the feel of a walking-stick in his hand would often spirit him away to Fenner's or Lord's of the seventies, and almost unconsciously he would show how Alfred Shaw was driven out of the ground, or Spofforth cut to the boundary. And when in recent years that white-haired figure, in full canonicals, made its entry into church or chapel, who in the congregation would have suspected that behind the rapt uplifted gaze, wayward fancies often flitted through his mind. Once, late in life, he was trying to convince a sceptical companion that he was no longer interested in the game. As the short-lived argument proceeded, he flashed out, 'Well, it's certainly a rum thing, but I never go into a Church without visualizing the spin of the ball up the nave.'[1]

Much of E.L.'s cricket after he left Cambridge was played on Free Forester tours, where no doubt the music which was such a prominent feature of them was an added attraction—E.L. was one of the regular

---

[1] A young man being interviewed for a possible appointment on the cricket field at Haileybury thus records his first introduction to E.L.: 'I remember being much struck by the easy and natural way he passed instantaneously from the subject of the Holy Spirit's work in the young to the excellence of a sudden brilliant stroke by one of the batsmen. It was something quite new in my experience of schoolmasters, and gave me my first impression of the soul of E.L.; his heart was in both worlds.'

basses in the famous glee quartette. His career in first-class cricket was confined to five years, 1878–82, to very few matches at that, even by old standards, and his fame rests upon his captaincy of the most successful of all University elevens, his century in the same year (1878) against the Australians, which by general consent was the most brilliant innings of the season, a dashing 79 against Emmett and Freeman, and 44 and 66 for the Gentlemen at Lords. The descriptions of these innings all mention the speed of his scoring, which often seems to have reached a standard which an acknowledged hitter would find it hard to beat, and it is clear that he was a most aggressive and punishing player.

The last innings he ever played must have been in Upper Club in 1913, for the masters against a powerful Eton eleven. The boys were determined that the beloved, but no doubt quite *passé*, old player should score a run or two, and the fast bowler sent down a couple of slow balls, both of which were crisply hit for four. Then they set to work in earnest and bowled their hardest, but lo! the thing went on. No one who saw that brilliant little innings will forget the perfect balance and economy of effort with which ball after ball was despatched through the covers and past third man, and when it came to an end, and he moved for ever from the cricket-field where his earliest triumphs had been won, the delighted cheering that accompanied him had in it not only congratulation but also an astonished realization that the fine art of batsmanship was not entirely a modern discovery, nor ancient reputations merely amiable exaggeration.

Edward Lyttelton, 1943

❋

The Band at Play

RALPH WOTHERSPOON

In Festivals or Cricket Weeks
Muffled or intermittent squeaks
Denote the presence of a band,
But what I fail to understand
Is why half-hearted use is made
Of local instrumental aid.

If you have music, I submit
That you should make the most of it.
The band might play the batsman in,
That stirring march from 'Lohengrin'
Would fill the bill; now how about
A tune to play the batsman out?
No difficulty here at all,
Handel's C Major 'March in Saul'.
'The Rosary', 'Lest we forget',
'Funeral March of Marionette',
'Good-bye for Ever' (this to be
A second innings threnody) . . .
Such melodies as these I think,
(Culled and arranged by Herman Finck),
As incidental to the action
Should merit general satisfaction.

The Cricketer, 1940

✳

The Golden Age of Digby and Charles

ANTHONY MEREDITH

The sun poured down on The Oval as over 20,000 people made their way there. The traditional Bank Holiday fixture of Surrey *v*. Nottinghamshire was a very big attraction. Fifty police constables, hired specially for the occasion by the Surrey Committee, were casting an avuncular eye over their exuberant charges, blissfully unconcerned about being so heavily outnumbered.

Batting at no. 6 for Surrey on this auspicious summer morning was Digby Jephson, 27 years old and just established in the county team after some phenomenal performances in club cricket. He was a hard-hitting batsman as well as a subtle bowler of underarm lobs. The Ovalites, suspicious at first of this unfashionable mode of bowling, had just begun to take him to their hearts. An extra buzz of anticipation now travelled round the ground whenever he was given the ball. There was much amusement at his bowling action whereby, with a few crab-like steps, body bent double and with knuckles scraping the turf, the ball was sent on its spinning flight. Quick runs or quick wickets would usually result, for Digby's lobs seemed to elicit a belligerent response from the most pacific of batsmen. As the ball was struck, raucous encouragement and laughter would echo round the ring. And if a wicket fell—to a catch on the leg-side boundary or the stumping of a stranded charger—the cheerful abuse would transfer from perspiring bowler to retreating batsman. Digby Jephson was rapidly becoming one of The Oval's great ornaments and pleasures.

Digby was also a journalist, a stockbroker and a poet. He took his poetry very seriously. Tradition relates that he would come in from batting, unbuckle his pads and retire to some solitary spot, to scribble down the poetic inspiration of the moment. Most of his poems were about cricket. He wrote one about The Oval on an August Bank Holiday. The first verses describe the pre-match excitement:

> 'Tis August Bank Holiday, 10 a.m.,
>   And the turnstiles every one
> Are galloping round with incessant click
> To the hurrying feet that come fast and thick,
> The thousands who struggle—they must be quick
>   If they wish to see every run!
>
> And the motley throng that goes surging by
>   Is a sight to gladden the day,
> For on every face is there hope serene,
> Their work is behind them, their pleasure's keen;
> This one day at least in the year, I ween,
>   Will strengthen them on their way.
>
> There are soldiers, sailors, and postmen there,
>   There are clerks from their high-backed stools,
> There are tinkers, tailors, and booing brats,
> And swells of the city in silken hats,
> And men from the clubs in immaculate spats,
>   But they all of them know the rules.
>
> And all of them push till at last they squeeze
>   Through the members' or turnstile gate,
> Swells of the city and men of the clubs
> Separate now from the folk of the pubs,
> A moment when *wealth* against *labour* rubs—
>   In pavilion and ring they wait.

The pavilion which he mentions had only just been built. It was one of a number of splendid new structures around the country, buildings which also helped to emphasize the great divide of spectators into 'wealth' and 'labour'. Lord's had led the way with a new pavilion in red brick and terracotta, its grandeur in keeping with cricket's growing importance within the life of the nation. Surrey had asked the architect of Old Trafford's new pavilion to design one 'second to none in the country in its internal arrangements'. Two buildings, pavilion and tavern, had accordingly arisen the previous winter at The Oval, costing the very large sum of £38,000.

The comfort which the new pavilion offered the Surrey members— and there were some 4000 of them—contrasted sharply with what was available to the general public, paying sixpence to come through the turnstiles. Such was the attraction of Surrey cricket to the spectator that, if there was no room on the grass, he would cheerfully spend a whole day standing on the terraces. Jephson's poem continues:

> The great green circle of play is curtailed
>   By some stakes and a piece of twine,
> And the people lie on the sun-scorched sward,
> Like an ocean surf held back by a cord,
> The ground is as soft as a three-inch board,
>   But they stretch there line upon line.
>
> The asphalt terraces, tier upon tier,
>   Rise packed with their load of sardines,
> The straw-hatted thousands who wait the play,
> Who have come to stand for the livelong day,
> And swelter and sweat in the same old way;
>   Though some try to lie down by the screens.
>
> And now of a sudden a hush is felt.
>   Then a murmur goes swiftly round
> The Ring, as the players in spotless white
> Emerge at last to prepare for the fight
> By a knock at the nets in the blazing light
>   On a cast-iron August ground.

The matches proceeded in leisurely fashion in the Golden Age. A 12 o'clock start, the usual time, might easily be delayed if a player had been held up *en route* to the ground. There was, however, some entertainment for the crowd before the match began, because it was unthinkable to start a day's play without net practice, which was watched avidly.

The description of the players in 'spotless white' may be misleading to a generation brought up on washing detergent advertisements. Pads tended to be cleaned now and then rather than every day. Socks were often black. Boots, though no longer totally brown, were sometimes two-toned, white and brown. And around many an ample waist in those golden days of plenty were belts or ties in varying hues. A light-blue one sufficed for Digby—he had won a Blue for three years at Cambridge—as he emerged down the central steps of the new pavilion, chatting to Frank Crawford, one of the two other amateurs in the side.

The crowd could readily recognize Digby Jephson by his unusual rolling gait; he had had the misfortune to be born with one leg shorter than the other. He was of medium height and had distinctive features. His dark hair was centrally parted, his full moustache drooped slightly at the edges, and a high brow and Roman nose lent him a scholarly look. It was a handsome, animated face. His friend, Frank Crawford, a tall, powerfully built 19-year-old, was one of Surrey's best hopes for the future, expected to develop into a famous hitter. They crossed the grass together, boon companions, while at the nets, already mustered, were some of the professionals. Bobby Abel, diminutive hero of the Ovalites, was already batting, indulging in much more ambitious shots than he was likely to show when he got to the middle:

> The 'Guv'nor' is there, he is always there,
>   First to come and the last to go;
> And he slogs away like an Albert Trott,
> Till all the bowlers are tied in a knot;
> The critics remark 'What an eye he's got!
>   He ain't always so blooming slow!'
>
> And Lockwood is there, and Tom Hayward too,
>   With Tom Richardson close behind,
> And all of them pile up four after four,
> They raise in the nets a colossal score,
> They'd like to make these in the match, or more,
>   And contented they'd be in their mind!
>
> A quarter to twelve and the bell is rung,
>   And the nets disappear apace,
> The ground is cleared and the players retreat;
> The five-ton roller retires from its beat,
> Drawn by Apted's men, who sweat in the heat;
>   There is pride in Sam's genial face.
>
> And then down the steps both captains come,
>   Anxious in mind and slim,
> They spin on the grass and the toss is won,

And Surrey should bat till the setting sun
Glides 'into the West' when his work is done,
Like the youth from the city dim.

'Anxious in mind' both captains probably were, but 'slim' both of them were not! In particular, Sir Kingsmill Key of Surrey had one of the biggest paunches in county cricket, a fact not unremarked upon by the Ovalites. But Surrey did indeed bat on till nearly the set of the sun, Digby scoring a bright 54 in their total of well over 300. They had time to capture one Notts wicket before the close of play, sending the Bank Holiday crowd home in happy vein. The next day came Digby's chance to bowl. In his first spell he clean bowled John Gunn, a member of the famous bat-making family, and in his second he finished off the Notts tail, taking 3 for 32 in his 12 five-ball overs.

The crowed watched with approval as Notts followed on. An innings victory looked likely, but Notts had two magnificent professional batsmen. One of them, Arthur Shrewsbury, fell cheaply, but William Gunn, uncle of John Gunn, occupied the crease for over eight hours in scoring 236 not out and he saved the match. Digby bowled 23 overs of lobs and was treated with the greatest respect, but failed to take a wicket. Time and again he tempted Gunn, who stood 6 feet 4 inches and had an enormous reach, but he was unable to encourage a lapse of concentration. Perhaps it was this innings of Gunn's which encouraged a young lady to write admiringly that year: 'There is something strong and trustworthy about Gunn. He resembles an apparently immovable rock, as he stands before his wicket, his broad white hat half hiding the keen, kind face.'

Meanwhile, on the same August Bank Holiday, another large crowd was enjoying another sun-blessed match. Leicestershire were playing Essex at Leicester. Both counties were newcomers to first-class cricket, but Essex had already developed into one of the best teams in the country, in just four seasons.

It was no surprise to any but the most partisan of home supporters when Essex made a weak Leicester attack suffer in the Bank Holiday sunshine. Their leading professional batsman, 'Bob' Carpenter, made a hundred, their famous batting 'twins', Perrin and McGahey, each scored fifties and Charles Kortright, batting at no. 7, struck the ball mightily in the late afternoon. By the close Essex were well beyond 400 and on the next day Kortright completed his hundred, 112 out of 515.

The Bank Holiday crowd had probably hoped to see him bowl rather than bat, for in 1898 his name was on everybody's lips as England's leading amateur fast bowler. Less than two weeks before, Kortright had played a memorable part in W. G. Grace's Jubilee match, the fixture between the Gentlemen and Players at Lord's which had been arranged to coincide with the Doctor's fiftieth birthday. Kortright was now considered faster than England's other fast bowlers, Richardson, Lockwood and Mold. He was also wilder and less predictable. There was much eager speculation as to what he might do to the Australians on their coming tour the following year. Many spectators, therefore, came back the day after the Bank Holiday to see Charles Kortright bowl.

He was a wonderful sight to watch. A long, menacing run, elbows pummelling the air like pistons, strides ever lengthening. Then a flurry of delivery in a strange, baulking action. Finally, a fiery follow-through, right down the wicket, with athletic fielding if needed. The whole procedure was accompanied by the most aggressive of facial expressions. He did not indulge in these deliberately to intimidate the batsman. But a bat at 22 yards was simply like the proverbial red rag to him and, at its sight, a bull-like hatred flared up within him. 'He runs at you, just as if he were jumping a gate,' muttered one batsman expressively.

There was aggression too in Kortright's face when in repose. Smiles did not come easily. The broad chin suggested pugnacity. And there was a startling lack of hair! It was receding early, thinning on top, and this year, for the first time since boyhood, he was without his moustache. Nearly all his Essex team-mates favoured the still-fashionable moustache. There was a stark severity about Charles Kortright.

If the crowd had come to see the Demon bowling at his best, it was not disappointed. Leicester were bowled out twice, to an innings defeat, and Kortright bowled 45 torrid overs, taking 8 wickets. Three dismissals were by courtesy of wicket-keeper Tom Russell, who somehow managed to cling on to searing snicks. The other five wickets were clean bowled. This was Kortright's usual method of removing a batsman, beating him by sheer pace.

The spectators at Leicester, watching the Demon in full cry, were witnessing cricket at its most exciting. The Ovalites too were similarly privileged, as the Lobster plied his art to their delight. The Golden Age of Charles and Digby may therefore seem to have been an idyllic period in cricket's history. So it was, for some participants. But the extent of the idyll depended on one's social and financial position; the same dichotomy between 'wealth' and 'labour' existed for the players as for the Ovalites in Digby Jephson's poem. For the wealthy, amateur cricket offered a stimulating diversion, a most attractive alternative to the humdrum business of the real world outside 'the great green circle of play'. For the amateur of limited means and the poorly paid professional, cricket was no hobby but rather an uncertain means of livelihood of precariously short duration.

It is significant that, from those four county teams playing out their Bank Holiday matches in 1898, one member of each side ended his days in tragedy. 'Timber' Woodcock, Leicestershire's fast bowler, poisoned himself; at 44 he was penniless and out of work. Fred Bull, the Essex slow bowler and assistant secretary, killed himself for similar reasons. Arthur Shrewsbury of Notts, for many years one of England's leading professional batsmen, succumbed to the strain of his own eminence and, at 47, believing himself seriously ill, shot himself. Tom Richardson, one of the most talented fast bowlers ever to play for England, met so mysterious a fate that suicide must remain a distinct possibility. At 41, he was both penniless and ill. The night that he died on a French mountainside, he had crept out of his hotel in slippers and collarless shirt, eluding the watchfulness of his friends. Earlier, he had written the saddest of testimonies (for, of all things, a nerve-tonic advertisement): 'When I retired from cricket, my nervous system was impaired. I began to get upset over trivial matters. My appetite fell off and my memory often failed me. But the most worrying trouble was insomnia.' The deaths of Woodcock, Bull, Shrewsbury and Richardson are not isolated examples. Many other players of the Golden Age lived ill-starred lives. For many of its participants, therefore, the Golden Age of cricket was far from perfect.

The cricket itself, was *that* at least golden? Certainly it was full of drama and rich in personalities. Its chief protagonists, men like Grace, C. B. Fry and Ranjitsinhji, now enshrined in their own legends, have transcended the passage of time. As often as not, the leading players were difficult personalities, possessing, like Homeric heroes, over-large egos and an exaggerated sense of the honour due to them. Indeed crises on and off the field loomed so large throughout the period that one must seriously question whether cricket's Golden Age has not been misnamed. For it mirrors with strange exactitude the constant anxieties that beset the modern game. On that August day in 1898, however, not many of cricket's problems were uppermost in the spectator's minds as they revelled in the sunshine, while the Demon and Lobster contributed richly to their holiday entertainment.

The Demon and the Lobster, 1987

✳

The Seven Brothers

W. A. BETTESWORTH

The five eldest of 'the noble scions of the Southgate Family', as the brothers were once described in a local newspaper, began their education at Stanmore, where they played cricket on the common on a fairly good wicket. Although the teaching of cricket at preparatory schools had not in those days become almost a science in itself, the boys were by no means allowed to spend their hours of leisure in picking up the rudiments of the game as best they might. Fortunately for them and for all cricketers who were to come after them they had a master named Mr A. Woodmass, irreverently known as 'Old Woody', who was extremely fond of cricket. He took great pains with the young Walkers, and taught them much that was useful.

Of his early schooldays at Stanmore Mr V. E. Walker says: 'Old Woody used to bowl slowish underhand, which possibly was the cause of our taking to it. As a batsman he was somewhat of a "stick". We had a "cricket waggon", which was built on four low wheels. This was loaded with our cricketing paraphernalia, including a tent, and we used to push and pull it to the cricket ground, sometimes also making use of a very large kite to lighten our labours. On the breaking up of the school during my residence there the waggon and cricket box were given to my family, as my father had considerably helped towards the whole outfit. This curious old box, with divisions for bats etc., as well as the waggon, is still in my possession. The kite had, I fancy, about come to the end of its life, and broke up with the school.'

The three eldest brothers went to Cambridge University after leaving school, and R.D. went to Oxford. It was intended that I.D. should go to Cambridge, but when it was practically certain that he would go into residence his mother died and his plans were altered.

Like so many other famous players, the members of the family who were at Harrow and Oxford or Cambridge failed to distinguish themselves very greatly in the matches against Eton, and in the University match. The two brothers, John and Fred, who were at Cambridge, made 86 between them against Oxford in thirteen completed innings; they took one wicket, made five catches, and stumped two batsmen. At the same time it must be remembered that they were both wicket-keepers of unusual ability. The only time that one of them did anything of note in batting was in 1852, when Mr Fred scored 13 and 36. At Oxford the only representative of the family was R.D. He scored 84 in ten innings, exactly half the runs being made in his very first innings. In addition to this he took nine wickets, meeting with nothing like his usual success, and caught three batsmen. Altogether the record of the family at the University is 170 runs for twenty-three completed innings—an average of 7; ten wickets, eight catches, and two men stumped. If their fame rested on this they would be deserving of commiseration.

In the Eton *v.* Harrow match four of the brothers played at various times from 1850 to 1863, inclusive. In 1851 A.H., then the only representative, was prevented by illness from playing; from 1855 to 1858 the family was not represented, as V.E. had left, while R.D. and I.D. were too young to be in the eleven. The record of the family is not much more brilliant here than in the University matches. The four brothers between them scored 157 runs in sixteen innings, and were three times not out. They took thirty-one wickets and made six catches. The highest score was the 29 in 1854 of V.E., who in the previous year had made two 'duck's eggs' in the Eton match.

Against Winchester the record is a little better, chiefly because A.H. scored 74 and 17 in the match of 1852. In five more innings he and V.E. between them made only 19: a total of 110 for seven completed innings. They took seventeen wickets and made four catches. Neither R.D. nor I.D. played against Winchester, for the matches were discontinued before their time.

In an amusing poem written by Mr E. E. Bowen in 1883, entitled 'Giants', the doings of the Family at Harrow are referred to as follows:

> There were splendid cricketers, then, you know,
>   There were splendid cricketers then;
> The littlest drove for a mile or so,
>   And the tallest drove for ten;
> With Lang to bowl and Hankey to play,
> Webbe and Walker to score and stay,—
> And two that I know but may not say—
> But we are a pitiful race of clay,
>   And never will score again.
>   For all of we,
>   Whoever we be,
> Come short of the giants of old, you see.

> E. E. BOWEN, 1883

Few things in the history of the cricket of the brothers are more remarkable than the way in which they almost invariably failed in their first appearances, and almost invariably atoned immediately afterwards for their bad start. As a rule they failed absolutely, making a 'duck's egg' with a regularity which must have given them much amusement as time went on, and a new comer had to take his turn, with the family tradition facing him in all its baldness.

One of the chief reasons why all the brothers were so successful as cricketers was that they each had a profound knowledge of the game in all its branches. Because of this knowledge they were all good captains, for they knew how to take instant advantage of the mistakes made by their opponents. The way in which, when they were batting, they carefully watched the placing of the field was very noticeable, and if an opposing captain misplaced his field he was likely to suffer severely for his want of judgment. When three or four of the brothers were on the same side they formed a remarkable combination. To quote a criticism by Mr Fred Gale in *Lillywhite* of 1880, 'The "Walker combination", when V.E. was bowling and fielding his own bowling at short mid-on and mid-off, with I.D. and R.D. like two terriers watching a rat-hole, in the field, was nearly if not quite as fatal as the three Graces very often; and I fancy, on the authority of older and wiser men than myself, there is no instance within the memory of living cricketers when the strategy of the game was better displayed than when three Graces or three Walkers were on the out side.'

The Walkers of Southgate, 1900

❧

Mr John Walker

W. A. BETTESWORTH

Six feet two inches in height, and broad in proportion, Mr John Walker was easily recognised when he was on the cricket field; indeed, old cricketers say that his figure was as conspicuous in the field as is that of Dr Grace at the present time. For several years he was considered to be as good a batsman as anyone in England, while, as a field, he was unsurpassed. Born on September 15th, 1826, at Southgate, he was thirty-eight years of age when he first met Mr W. G. Grace, the great batsman who was to put the deeds of all his predecessors and contemporaries so completely in the shade. In *Cricket* Dr Grace has recorded his first impressions of the batting of the eldest of the Southgate brothers, and has stated how pleased he was to see the South Wales bowling hit about by him. Not less was he pleased when Mr Walker gave him a word or two of praise for his good batting in the second innings. This 'word or two of praise' was characteristic of Mr John, and indeed of all the family. There are dozens of amateurs and professionals still living who remember how they were encouraged by a few words from Mr John, often spoken when the *débutant* was fearing that he had made a failure, and that he was not cut out to play in important matches. Whether Dr Grace took a leaf out of Mr John's book or not, it is certain that he also has over and over again gladdened the heart of a beginner by a timely word of advice, or sympathy, or congratulation.

Mr John Walker could not fail to be popular, for, in addition to natural *bonhomie*, which is described as being irresistible, he was such a staunch supporter of the game that every cricketer wished him well. It is hardly possible to take up a newspaper of his time without finding a reference in it to his 'generous patronage'. And this was not a mere figure of speech by any means; for his purse-strings were always open either to further some good object in connection with the game, to reward a deserving professional, or to help him when he needed assistance. Need it be stated that there were amateurs also who could have said much about his generosity? His kindliness of heart was proverbial, and even isolated cases of the deepest ingratitude did not discourage his faith in human nature. In all his brothers he had willing helpers in these good works, and when he died at his house at Southgate on August 14th, 1885, and was succeeded by his brother Fred, no professional suffered. When he was taken to his last resting-place, the churchyard and the church were filled with such a vast assemblage as to cause astonishment even to those who well knew how greatly he was loved and honoured. Cricketers of every shade of society were there, from the highest to the lowest, while the whole village mourned.

It was not alone by deeds of kindliness that he did so much good for the game. He encouraged first-class play by spending large sums on remaking the cricket ground at Southgate, and in arranging matches there against the great teams of the day. His was a strictly private club, and he had more than enough personal friends to have filled his team for any number of matches in the year. But he kept his eyes open, and when he saw or heard of a promising young player, who had not much chance of appearing in good cricket, he speedily gave him an invitation to play for Southgate. To appear in his team very soon became an honour eagerly sought after, and any rising young cricketer would have given his ears to have received an invitation from Mr John to form one of the Southgate Sixteen against the United All England Eleven. One qualification in the young cricketer who aspired to play at Southgate was absolutely essential: he must be a good field. On this point there were no half measures with Mr Walker, nor, for the matter of that, with any of his brothers.

In addition to giving the best of cricket on the Southgate ground, Mr Walker never rested until he had placed the Middlesex County Club on a sound basis. Practically there was no club at all until he took the matter up; but when he once set out upon a task there was no turning back. The difficulties to be overcome were enormous. It was next to impossible to obtain a ground, and, as a matter of fact, a permanent ground never was obtained, owing to the ever-advancing builder, until the Marylebone Club offered a home to the county at Lord's in the time of Mr I. D. Walker. But by steadily working, in season and out of season, Mr John at last not only succeeded in making the county club a reality, but (which was infinitely more remarkable) managed to work its members almost to a pitch of enthusiasm. For a time, after the county cricket club had seemed to be on the high road to success and permanency, it began to be thought that all Mr John's efforts had been in vain, for although a temporary home for the club was found near the Cattle Market in Copenhagen Fields, the builders invaded it. But by this time other members of the family were beginning to take Mr John's place in the cricket field, and gradually he retired from first-class cricket, owing to ill-health.

As a cricketer he played the game with the utmost strictness from the time that the first ball was bowled until stumps were drawn. There was nothing that he hated more than 'tomfoolery' in the field. To 'play the game' was his great idea, and when he was captain of a side he took good care that everybody played it. He was undeniably a first-rate captain, without being absolutely a great one. Somewhat of a martinet in the field, he liked to see every man on his side working his very hardest, and few men would have been bold enough to venture to rouse his anger by foolishness or careless fielding. From his place behind the wicket he surveyed his forces, and manoeuvred them like a general from an eminence, very seldom making anything in the nature of a mistake.

As a batsman he made the utmost use of his height and strength, and played with a straight bat. He was a very fine hitter indeed, more particularly on the off side, and, chiefly because of his great reach, he was exceptionally good against fast bowling, easily smothering balls which would have presented great difficulties to most other men. His greatest innings was without doubt his 98 against the Players in 1862, when to make a score of even 30 or 40 was thought a great perform- ance against the combined strength of so many famous bowlers. Mr Walker was then 36 years of age, he was engaged in business, and could not take regular exercise. Every hit had to be run out, and it is not remarkable that men who saw the match are agreed that, if boundary hits had been in vogue, his score would have been very largely increased; they may, however, have altered their opinion since the experiments at Lord's in 1900. The innings was all the more wonderful because, when it was begun, the Gentlemen seemed to be hopelessly out of the run- ning, as usual. Whether Mr Walker would have ever made huge scores of two and three hundred if it had been his fortune to play on the hard and enamelled wickets of modern times is open to doubt, for he would not, under any imaginable circumstances, have been a man to keep his average always before his eyes. Like all his brothers he played cricket because he loved the game, without a thought about what would be said about his average in future days.

If he had never been worth a run he would have been worth play- ing in any eleven for his wicket-keeping and fielding alone. There was absolutely no place in the field which he could not fill as ably as any other cricketer of the day, and he was one of the safest catches ever seen. It was not often that he bowled in great matches, because he could be more useful as wicket-keeper, but on occasions, generally when his side was in a difficulty, he worked great destruction with his lobs or slow round-arm bowling. If he had not been a first-class wicket- keeper he would have been a first-class bowler. He was every inch a cricketer and every inch a man. For many years he was on the Committee of the MCC and the Surrey Club, and was Vice-President of the Middlesex County Club from its formation in 1864 until his death. With his brothers he frequently played in Club and Ground matches for Surrey.

In his early days he was one of the supporters of the old Clapton Club,[1] being assisted in his efforts to promote the club's success by Mr W. Nicholson, who himself was a famous wicket-keeper and batsman.

[1] The Clapton Club was formed in 1832 and re-formed in 1854.

For three years, 1847, '48, and '49, Mr Walker was in the Cambridge eleven as a wicket-keeper, being captain in 1848. He was chosen to play in the Oxford match of 1846, which took place on the Magdalen ground at Oxford, but was unavoidably detained in London.

Mr Walker was the originator of a remark which, having become historical, is often attributed to other famous cricketers. All the humorous journals have from time to time illustrated the saying with variations. He once went up to Lord's, after he had retired from first-class cricket, but to his surprise no match was in progress, while the ground was deserted. 'What does this mean?' he asked. 'A glorious summer day and no cricket! It's as bad as a Sunday without *Bell's Life*.'

It frequently happened that when cricketers who could shoot (whether amateurs or professionals did not matter in the least, if they were good fellows) were playing at Southgate, they were given a day's shooting by Mr John after the match was over. On one occasion old John Lillywhite had a day's shooting in Kent with some of the members of the family, including Mr John, but he was not very successful. On the way to the railway station in the dusk of the evening, he espied a belated 'cock rooster' sitting alone on a gatepost. 'I think I can hit *him*', said old John, and, taking steady aim at a distance of a few yards, he brought down his quarry. Greatly elated at his success, he was all the more ready for an elaborate joke which he had planned. 'He had managed to get hold of a live rabbit in the course of the day', says George Hearne (old George), 'and put it in a hamper without fastening the lid. Arrived at Charing Cross station he gave the hamper in charge of a porter with the strictest injunctions to take the greatest possible care of it, as it contained something of much value. The porter seized the hamper. In putting it down he naturally took hold of the top part, with the result that the lid came wide open, and out jumped the rabbit. Old John Lillywhite pretended to be in a state of frantic despair at the loss of this valuable animal, which went so fast that the spectators could not exactly see what it was, and for a quarter of an hour the station was in an uproar. Mr John Walker laughed till he nearly cried—and so did we all, but in the end we had to tear John Lillywhite away, for the rabbit was never heard of again.'

The Walkers of Southgate, 1900

✳

The Names

THOMAS MOULT

There's music in the names I used to know,
And magic when I heard them, long ago.
'Is Tyldesley batting?' Ah, the wonder still!
. . . The school clock crawled, but cricket-thoughts would fill
The last slow lesson-hour deliciously.
(Drone on, O teacher: you can't trouble me.)
'Kent will be out by now.' . . . (Well, if you choose
To keep us here while cricket's in the air,
You must expect our minds to wander loose
Along the roads to Leicester, Lord's and Leeds,
Old Trafford and the Oval, and the Taunton meads. . . .)

And then, at last, we'd raid the laneway where
A man might pass, perchance, with latest news.
Grey-grown and grave, yet he would smile to hear
Our thirsty questions as we crowded near.
Greedily from the quenching page we'd drink—
How its white sun-glare made our young eyes wink!
'Yes, Tyldesley's batting still. He's ninety-four.
Marlow and Mold play well. Notts win once more.
Glo'ster (with Grace) have lost to Somerset—
Easy: ten wickets: Woods and Palairet. . . .'

So worked the magic in that summer lane.
The stranger beamed. Maybe he felt again
As I feel now to tell the linked names
Jewelling the loveliest of our English games.
Abel and Albert Trott, Lilley, Lillywhite,
Hirst, Hearne, and Tunnicliffe—they catch the light—
Lord Hawke and Hornby, Jessop, A. O. Jones—
Surely the glow they held was the high sun's!

Or did a young boy's worship think it so,
And is it but his heart that's aching now?

Willow Patterns, 1969

*

Memories of a First Test Match

JACK HOBBS

A young batsman is walking with his captain to the wicket. They are opening the innings for England at Melbourne. In the vanished past, under the blazing southern skies.

Thousands of clapping hands hail them—the handclaps of an excited throng who have poured into the town and packed round the arena from all parts of the country. Some are backwoodsmen who live a thousand miles away . . . sheep-farmers, planters, merchants, stockriders . . . Men of the great cities also—rich men, poor men, tinkers, tailors, soldiers, sailors . . . All sorts and conditions, typical of a whole continent cricket-mad, clapping the rival side as sportsmen always do, but mad for Australian victory.

I see the earnestness on that young cricketer's sun-tanned face. I understand the expression in his eyes. Indeed, I know better than anyone how anxious and determined he is to make good with the bat he carries, because that young man is myself as I used to be, and the Test match the first in which I ever played.

How vividly it all comes back! The years fall away from me: more than twenty years of endeavour in the best and most lovable of games. I was twenty-five when I first batted for England, and had only played a brief while in any sort of big cricket. It was towards the end of my third summer with Surrey that the newspapers spoke of me as a likely member of the next MCC team for Australia.

'Hobbs might with advantage be taken to Australia this winter', said one well-known sports-writer, and I got such a thrill when I read his recommendation that I have kept the cutting in my scrap-book ever since! 'He has the proper temperament for cricket, and is always seen at his best upon the very fast wickets which have usually to be encountered in the Antipodes.'

It began to dawn upon me then that I had a chance of being chosen, although I resolutely kept myself from counting too much on it because of the possible disappointment.

But as the English cricket season of 1907 drew to an end and it became known that Reginald Spooner, C. B. Fry, and P. F. Warner were doubtful whether they could make the trip, and that George Hirst, J. T. Tyldesley, Dick Lilley and Tom Hayward had decided to stand

down—because, I believe, the terms offered them were unsatisfactory—
I felt my chance was coming.

And so it was. On August the eighteenth a letter reached me from
Lord's, signed by 'F. E. Lacey, Sec., MCC.' As I scanned it my eyes
caught stray phrases: 'England team . . . Australia in September . . . I
have been instructed to invite you . . .' I hardly needed to read anything else in that magical message.

My dream had come true—and how quickly! Until that summer the
height of my ambition had been to play for a county—Surrey was the
county I always thought of. As a youth I naturally exchanged views
with my pals about the future we would like to have with bat and ball,
but none of us ever dared to think of playing for England. I knew only
eleven or twelve were wanted at a time, and it never seemed within
my power to become one of them. Only when I got fairly going for
Surrey and the critics put my name forward as a candidate for the next
tour 'down under', did I begin to dream of the possibility.

And there I was, in the winter of 1907–8, a full-fledged All-England
player!

The match was the second Test of the series, though; not the first.
I had not struck form at the start of our Australian campaign, and like
Ernie Hayes, also of Surrey, and another slow starter, I was left out of
the opening game at Sydney. It was as twelfth man that I looked on,
as helpless as any spectator, while England were being beaten. They
put up a fine show, especially George Gunn with 119 and 74, but they
lost by two wickets, Australia having pulled the game round splendidly
after being 89 behind with only three men to bat.

It had been a toss-up whether Ernie Hayes or I would play in the
second of the Test series, and I was chosen. The Australians won the
toss and batted first, so that I was given a whole day—New Year's Day,
as it happened—in which to find my feet before I went in.

'So you are playing this time, Jack', said the great Australian, Clem
Hill, as I took out my bat for a practice-knock in front of the pavilion
before play started.

'Yes, I am going to have a shot', I answered.

'Hearty congratulations, then, and good luck', came the kind wish:
and it heartened me, for I had not been having the best of fortune on
the tour.

Also, at the back of my mind I harboured an uneasy suspicion that
A. O. Jones, our captain, did not feel particularly enthusiastic about
me. Jones was not the captain, however, with whom I opened the
England batting. He had fallen ill, and F. L. Fane acted in his place.

In that first innings I scored 83. I was determined to do my very best, so I took not the slightest risk, and batted for three hours. I remember thinking about my wife and my friends at home, thousands and thousands of miles away, and wondering what they would be saying when they heard how I had gone on.

How very far off they had seemed, but how very near I felt to them at the end of that successful debut! I visualised the placards of newspapers at home, proclaiming how we were going on. I pictured my pals looking down the scores to see how many I had made—for I had formed some good London friendships in addition to those I retained at Cambridge. I could almost hear their voices, chiming out: 'Well done, Jack!' Separating them from me until that blissful moment there had been so many things—the huge crowds which gave the England team a send-off at St Pancras station and Tilbury docks, the wide blue seas, the five weeks' voyage in the *Ophir*, Naples, Vesuvius, the Red Sea, Colombo . . . and half the vast sun-scorched continent of Australia.

I had been very homesick on the voyage out. Joe Hardstaff, the old Nottinghamshire player, whom the Australians were soon calling 'Hot Stuff', had also a wife at home, and we each had a youngster a few months old. Naturally we chummed up and sympathised with one another, although the six months which were to pass before we saw England again seemed a lifetime! . . . A strange coincidence, is it not, that Hardstaff was to be one of the umpires at the Oval in 1930, twenty-three years later, when I made my Test farewell!

That first Test match of mine is a vivid memory to me for another reason than that I made a decent score. It had the most thrilling finish I have ever known in International cricket.

To Australia's score of 266 we replied with 382, of which Kenneth Hutchings made a glorious 126—Hutchings, the handsome dark amateur of Kent, whom one recalls for his fielding almost as much as his batting. He had a throw-in from long-field which, although it travelled at a tremendous pace, was not aimed by drawing his arm back in the customary way, but by a flick of the wrist.

Hutchings, like Colin Blythe, another member of our touring party, was killed in the War. He was a most delightful companion, always ready to take his part in our life off the field of play. I can hear him now, at a concert on the boat, joining in the 'Indian Love Lyrics' with George Gunn, and earning as loud applause as J. N. Crawford had done the same evening when he sang 'The Trumpeter'.

Commencing their second knock at Melbourne 116 behind, the Australians lived up to their grand fighting reputation by wiping off the arrears with only one wicket down, and then they went on to score 297.

When I took my place in the field I could not have hoped for a finer 'close-up' view of some of their giant batsmen in action—Victor Trumper, who made 63, and 'Monty' Noble, who made 64, both of them heroes of mine ever since I was in my 'teens: Clem Hill, who made only 3; Warwick Armstrong, top scorer with 77, and Charlie Macartney, who might have shaken hands with me as a newcomer, for it was his first season in Test cricket as well as mine. In that particular innings he made 55.

Of course I had played earlier against some of these never-to-be-forgotten Australians, though not until now as an All-Englander. Trumper and Hill, for example. Trumper had caught me out at the Oval when the Cornstalks, touring England in 1905, defeated my own county, while in the same season Clem Hill ran me out at 93 with a magnificent throw from the deep-field which probably robbed me of my century.

His fame as a batsman was at its height even so early as that. I was deeply impressed by Trumper's technique in two ways: his wrist-work, and his audacity. Charlie Macartney was to equal him in audacity later on, but 'Vic' was always more graceful with it.

Trumper was a big personality as well as a cricketing genius. Everybody felt his charm, and even the Sydney schoolboys knew of his generosity, for he had a sports outfitters' business, and somebody told me that if a youthful customer found the price of a bat too much for him, why, 'Vic' hadn't the heart to let him go out of the shop without it! This explains, perhaps, why Trumper never made a fortune out of business.

Most of us have got an enemy somewhere, but he hadn't. I never heard a word spoken or even hinted against him. Cricket lost Victor Trumper during the war-years, but the news of his death in 1915 did not come as the shock it might have been. He was never a strong-looking man; ill-health overtook him and he just faded away.

Now let us get back to the actual cricket.

On the sixth day England, in their fourth innings, wanted 282 to win. We all batted hard, although I only made 28 and George Gunn got a 'duck'. Everybody except poor George scored double figures, and yet in spite of this we were still 73 behind when our eighth wicket fell, and it seemed as if defeat was again to be ours.

But then came one of the transformations for which cricket was, is, and always will be, famous. Humphries and Barnes stayed at the wicket until we wanted 39. We hardly dared hope that these runs would be got by Barnes and Fielder, who were both in the side for their bowling. And yet . . . had not Hazlitt and Cotter knocked off the 56 that Australia wanted in the first Test, and were not Hazlitt and Cotter in the side for *their* bowling? Anyway Barnes and Fielder stuck it gallantly; the total crept up and up, until the score-board read 281 for 9. This brought the score dead level, and our two bowler-batsmen were still together!

'Don't you move!' So, to one another, whispered the rest of us as we looked out from the dressing-room. The tension had become almost overwhelming: and there we stood, crowding, half-dressed at the windows with socks or shoes in our hands, not daring to stir a muscle lest the two batsmen out in the field were put off their game! Cricketers are very superstitious in some ways. If things are going all right there is great anxiety that everybody should sit tight and keep their places. If they don't . . . ! Among us in the dressing-room I remember noticing Hayes, as excited as any, although he was not playing. Incidentally, Ernie never got a place in this series at all.

Sid Barnes faced the bowling. He had a death-or-glory expression on that keen face of his. He and Fielder were so excited that they decided to run wherever the ball went. Barnes hit it towards cover—only a few yards, but they ran for all they were worth.

If Jerry Hazlitt, the fieldsman, had thrown straight there might have been a different finish to tell about: but Hazlitt too was excited, and he threw the ball wildly, so wide of the stumps and the stumper that three Australians tried one after another to stop it and failed as it flew to the boundary!

When that winning run was completed Fielder ran on and on for sheer joy and didn't slow down until he was half way to the pavilion.

Playing for England! 1931

✳

To John Berry Hobbs
on his Seventieth Birthday

16 December 1952

JOHN ARLOTT

There falls across this one December day
The light, remembered from those suns of June,
That you reflected, in the summer play
Of perfect strokes across the afternoon.

No yeoman ever walked his household land
More sure of step or more secure of lease
Than you, accustomed and unhurried, trod
Your small, yet mighty, manor of the crease.

The game the Wealden rustics handed down
Through growing skill became, in you, a part
Of sense, and ripened to a style that showed
Their country sport matured to balanced art.

There was a wisdom so informed your bat
To understanding of the bowler's trade
That each resource of strength or skill he used
Seemed but the context of the stroke you played.

The Master: records prove the title good:
Yet figures fail you, for they cannot say
How many men whose names you never knew
Are proud to tell their sons they saw you play.

They share the sunlight of your summer day
Of thirty years; and they, with you, recall
How, through those well-wrought centuries, your hand
Reshaped the history of bat and ball.

John Arlott's Book of Cricketers, 1979

✳

Garfield Sobers

JOHN ARLOTT

For a few months of 1969, out of sheer weariness, Garfield Sobers ceased to produce the figures of the finest cricketer of modern times. Like all such lapses, his failure prompted little men to berate the great. His lack of success is unquestionable, but it no more detracts from the historic fact of his eminence than some indifferent verses make Coleridge less than a great poet. The only remarkable fact about Sobers's bad spell was that it did not occur sooner under the heaviest sustained strain any cricketer has ever known.

No one who has watched him for any appreciable period can doubt that he is the finest all-rounder in the world. Merely to see him come out on the field, his long, hungry stride a strangely tigerish blend of the relaxed and the purposeful, is to recognize a great athlete. Most would agree, too, that he is the most giftedly versatile player the game has ever known. At Test level he has scored more runs than all but five men, all batsmen, pure and simple, in the entire history of the game; only eight bowlers have taken more wickets and three players have made more catches. No one approaches his triple record.

Figures, however, tell only part of the story: they cannot show that he is an excitingly brilliant player yet, also, essentially effective. In six different ways—as batsman, fast-medium bowler, finger-spinner, wrist-spinner, close fieldsman and captain—he has taken up cricket matches and remoulded them to his own design. No aspect of his cricket has been more amazing than his capacity for combining quality and quantity of effort; it is as if a single creature had both the class of a Derby-winner and the stamina of a mule. He is the only man ever to have performed the 'impossible' double of 1000 runs and 50 wickets in an Australian season—and he did it twice.

There can never have been such an all-round performance as his in the 1966 West Indies–England series. In the first Test he scored 161, bowled 49 overs for three wickets and West Indies won: at Lord's, where he and Holford, by their long, unfinished sixth-wicket stand made a draw against all probability, he had innings of 46 and 163 not out and one wicket in 43 overs: at Trent Bridge, the second West Indian win, 3 and 94, five wickets in 80 overs: at Leeds, in the match which

decided the rubber, he made 174 and bowled 39 overs for eight
wickets. When, at The Oval, it seemed as if the side suddenly relaxed
after winning the series, he scored 81 and 0 and, in England's only
innings, took three wickets. His overall figures for the series: 722 runs,
average 103, 20 wickets at 27.25 off 269.4 overs. He made ten catches,
and captained the side skilfully and perceptively.

So it was not surprising that, when England went to the West Indies
in 1967–68, he decided, after the first three Tests had been drawn, to
back himself to bring off another win by his own efforts. At Port-of-
Spain he made the declaration which brought down on him the con-
demnation of all those who bemoan lack of enterprise in the modern
cricketer. Everyone remembers that England won the match by seven
wickets and took the rubber with it. Not so many recall the efforts of
Sobers to draw the series in the final match. He scored 152 and 95 not
out, bowled 68 overs for six wickets and pressed England so hard that
they held on for a draw with only one wicket standing. He came straight
from those matches to England to take up the captaincy of Nottinghamshire. They had been fifteenth in the Championship table of 1967;
in Sobers's first season they were fourth—their highest for 36 years:
Sobers was first in the batting averages, second in the bowling, took
more catches than anyone else except the wicket-keeper—and hit six
sixes from a six-ball over.

The Cricketer, 1970

*

Sobers

E. W. SWANTON

Forty years ago on Thursday a slim, loose-limbed youth of 17 made his
way to the crease in the electric atmosphere of Sabina Park, Jamaica,
to play his first innings for the West Indies.

The score, unbelievably, was 110 for seven. They were all out for 139:
Gary Sobers at No 9 made 14 undefeated. In England's innings of 414
he took four wickets for 75 with slow left-arm spin. When the West
Indies batted again the youngster made 26 and though he had been
chosen chiefly as a bowler, talent of a high order was plain to see.
(England, thanks to Trevor Bailey's inspired bowling on the first day,

won by nine wickets, so halving the rubber—a recollection to cherish in 1994).

Such was the first of Sobers's 93 Test matches wherein he built up a monument of achievement secure in its pre-eminence: 8,032 runs at an average of 57.78, including 26 hundreds; 235 wickets at 34 each; 110 catches: this despite the fact that of all great cricketers none was more indifferent than he to figures and records.

For just 20 years he decorated the Test scene in his inimitable way, an all-rounder of unparalleled versatility, completely unselfish, and with an unquenchable urge, whether batting, bowling in any of his three styles, or fielding, to attack—and, in so doing, of course, to entertain. He was always conscious of the game's obligation to give pleasure, yet was the reverse of a show-off. He allowed his cricket to speak for him. And speak it did, all over the world.

And now in his native island of Barbados, grand affairs are afoot to mark Sobers's emergence on to the Test scene back in 1954. His old comrade-in-arms, Senator Wesley Hall, is the mainspring of the Sir Garfield Sobers 40th anniversary celebrations. These will reach their climax on the rest day of the Barbados Test in a dinner for 800. The celebration proceeds will be paid into a Trust Fund to ensure his financial security. The truth is he was prodigal by nature, almost spendthrift in his prime when any reward was meagre as compared with all the ample emoluments open to a top cricketer today.

How right and proper all this is. For Barbados could not have had a better ambassador than its most famous living son. Where so many modern heroes have shown feet of clay, Sobers has never swerved from the principles of sportsmanship and fair play in which he was brought up, and which became second nature to him. He has always been a modest winner and a cheerful loser, an ideal model for young and old.

In his *Sir Gary*, one of the best of all cricket biographies, Trevor Bailey traces his subject from earliest beginnings, brought up frugally among a family of six by a saint of a mother in a small one-storey wooden house. Gary was only five when in January 1942 his seaman father went down with all hands in a ship bringing supplies to Barbados.

There was no lack of neighbourhood father-figures to encourage his passion for cricket, but it was a white one, Wilfred Farmer, then captain of the police team, later to be Commissioner for Police in Barbados, who spotted him in a softball game, and, impressed by the lad as well as by his cricket, recruited him into the police band. The police played in the BCA League from which the Barbados team was chosen: at the age of 16 he was picked to play for his country against the touring Indians. He took seven wickets in 89 overs of slow left-arm spin for a match return of seven for 142. Installed in the island team with the three Ws, Worrell, Weekes and Walcott, his call to the Jamaica Test followed a year later.

When, many years afterwards Sobers, staying with Bailey in Essex at the time, heard that Farmer was in hospital he took the next train to London to see him. Characteristic though this was, I would mention here that he has always been remarkably unconscious of colour, making friends among men and women regardless of their skin. He was equally at home among his family and contemporaries in Barbados or in his five-year captaincy of Notts or when his all-round virtuosity was bringing the Sheffield Shield to South Australia.

He has been lucky in the close friendships which have always been necessary to his carefree, gregarious nature. Until his death, Sir Frank Worrell (who recommended that Gary succeed him in the West Indies captaincy) kept a very close eye, especially after the death of Gary's boon companion, Collie Smith. Gary was driving on a journey from Lancashire to a charity match: he was unhurt in the crash, Collie was killed.

In 1969 he married a charming Australian, Prue Kirby, and they had two sons. She was a stable factor in his life for the best part of 20 years.

There has never been a cricketer who apart from outstanding quality as batsman and fielder could offer three bowling methods according to what the situation demanded. He soon added wrist-spin to his orthodox style and in the Central Lancashire League with Radcliffe, then began to bowl over the wicket at speed with the new ball. The late in-swing, coupled with the ball that drifted away, made him and Alan Davidson of Australia for some years as dangerous opening bowlers as any in the game.

Sobers's activity in the field, however valuable, was nevertheless secondary to Sobers at the wicket. His 365, the highest Test score, against a weakened Pakistan attack, was notable for stamina and concentration but not typical in that his other big innings against the best bowling were shaped more specifically to the needs of the side.

He rates with particular pleasure the 163 not out with which he and his young cousin David Holford (105 not out) pulled the Lord's Test of 1966 out of the fire. The point always remembered about that record partnership of 274 for the sixth wicket, is that he gave confidence to his inexperienced partner by allowing him a full share of the bowling.

When the South African tours to England and Australia were cancelled in 1970 and 1971, Sobers captained powerful Rest of the World sides in some of the best cricket seen in both countries. His heartfelt opening address at Lord's to a mixed side of five West Indians, five South Africans, two Pakistanis, an Australian and an Indian revealed a diplomatic awareness that bound his team in a spirit they found unforgettable. Gary was in his element in all respects and at Melbourne some months later played an innings of 254 which Sir Donald Bradman described as 'probably the best ever seen in Australia'. The Don later wrote: 'With his long grip of the bat, high backlift and free swing, I think, by and large, Gary Sobers consistently hits the ball harder than anyone can remember.' So spake the oracle.

Equally crucial to the picture, of course, was the most rigid of straight bats in defence. The only possible chink in the armour, as I saw it, was a reluctance to move either foot very much when he first came in. I usually wanted to see a spinner confronting him early on.

Among pictures in the mind was a stroke off Jeff Jones of Glamorgan in a Bridgetown Test. Jones achieved a fast bouncer to which Gary jumped and with both feet off the ground cut to the square boundary like a rocket. At Dover for Notts against Kent, having taken 11 wickets in the two innings, he batted in appalling light, to win the match against time.

Sobers scored the fastest 100 of the season in 77 minutes without a false stroke; it was dark when he finished and the fielders had been lucky to escape without injury.

There were two phases to his Test captaincy, the first highly successful, the second not so, and it was a relief when he was succeeded by Rohan Kanhai. He inspired by his example and was a shrewd tactician, but by the 1970s after nearly 20 years of almost continuous all-round cricket winter and summer, he had lost his zest for the job.

Sir Garfield Sobers was not only the most captivating and glamourous of cricketers. In Bailey's words 'he has, quite simply, been the greatest of all time, the most complete all-rounder ever'. That is my judgment without reservation.

Daily Telegraph, 26 March 1994

✳

The Cricketer Assessed

IAN PEEBLES

The word genius has a slightly suspect ring when applied to physical prowess, possibly because it is so frequently and loosely used. On the other hand it is not easy to find another which describes that extra quality which brings certain athletes to a pitch of perfection beyond ordinary human excellence. Such performers occur but rarely, and are recognisable by reputation and record long after they have ceased to be active. In the case of cricket, and particularly of batsmanship, they number at most about half a dozen over a century, that being roughly the period for which the game has existed in its modern form.

Four names immediately arise as being pre-eminent beyond dispute, Grace, Trumper, Hobbs and Bradman. Two others, Ranjitsinhji and Macartney, are contenders as great players of unique individuality in each case, but neither would have the unanimous support for 'canon-isation' accorded the first four. If cricket had been played entirely on the off-side Wally Hammond would be a certain inclusion, but O'Reilly demonstrated that he was vulnerable in certain quarters. There then follows a certain number of superb players many of whom would find some sponsors for election to this élite, but be opposed by strong rival factions.

It is a bold but tenable claim that Denis Compton at his best could take his place with these immortals. His claim is based on his superior-ity over all contemporary rivals, his mastery in every technical aspect of batsmanship, the absence of any point of weakness, and his ability to sustain a sequence of fine strokes over a long period without error. The qualities were endorsed by his domination of the finest bowlers in the world of his day.

In so far as the complicated technique of batting is natural, Denis Compton was a very natural unaffected player. There were no thrilling postures, as when Archie MacLaren picked up the bat. There was no flashing follow through. But there was a most pleasing impression of smooth power. It always seemed to me that deep 'plonk' from the very middle of the wood marked a Compton innings as unmistakably as the boom of a Cunarder Queen's fog-horn.

He was a natural batsman also in that he was not much given to abstruse theorising. That is not to say that he is not without ideas about the game. He has many, but they are good down to earth practical views. One interesting result of good sound sense was that in playing to the off from the front foot he left a very noticeable gap between bat and pad which aroused the suspicions of the purist. But this he did deliberately in order to give himself more freedom of swing and greater power. These advantages he sensibly argued easily out-weighed the added margin of safety afforded by the pad for, if he miscued, he could well be out in a number of ways. It is to be remembered that Bradman was criticised for the same unorthodoxy but that, in both cases, the objection was academic in that they almost invariably met the ball with the middle of the bat. The real answer is, of course, that with the natural powers given both these players they could afford to do things calculated to bring certain disaster to lesser performers.

In after years he remarked that the only other theory he could remember evolving was that if he stood just clear of the leg stump he was safely positioned for his famous sweep, of which he was particularly fond. Thus, although he always took guard on the leg stump, he would move slightly back from his mark.

In considering his strokes one could well start with the sweep for it was largely the key to the *mood* of all his play. As he played it, this was a characteristic and unique stroke. Of all the strokes the sweep is the most problematical and, in its mortality rate, the most baffling stroke in the entire range of batsmanship. It is deceptive in its apparent simplicity and tempting, if successful, in its profitability. In essence it consists of advancing the front foot just inside the line of the overpitched ball and swinging a flat bat with a scything natural movement across the flight of the ball. This uncomplicated, apparently foolproof gambit has been the downfall of countless good, and even great players. Frequently one has seen the ball punched solidly to the square-leg boundary. Far more frequently one has seen it nicked up off the top edge and caught near or far, according to the pace of the bowler. As often it has flopped gently off the striker's gloves to in-field or wicket-keeper. Least satisfactory of all a figure, kneeling on one knee as though about to be dubbed, has received the thoroughly disgruntling accolade of the umpire's up-raised finger, which is to say l.b.w., front leg.

The Compton sweep was unique in that it brought its author a great many runs with almost complete safety. As this would imply, it was rather different in technique from the usual full blooded swing. In playing it the striker would put his front foot *well* inside the line of the ball, and so was able to hit it much finer than the normally square direction taken by this stroke. The swing of the bat was comparatively slow and deliberate, the ball being patted away in the direction of fine leg. Although struck very late it was a firm *hit* from the face of the bat, not a deflection. There was a playful quality about this manœuvre which, with an impish late cut at a similar angle to the off, lent a welcome urchinlike leavening to the most majestic Compton innings. With the ever present possibility of panic and uproar between the runners, this lent to the most tense situation an aura of good humour which would occasionally break into broad comedy.

He loved to hook and excelled in this stroke as in every other. As he played the shot it was perhaps less spectacular than as applied by Hendren or Bradman, but no less effective. With the confidence of superb sight and reflexes he would station himself right in the line of the fastest bouncer. He seldom missed but, if he did, he was liable to be hit on the head, as occurred at Manchester when he made a fractional error against Lindwall. From the firm 'gun platform' of well set feet he would ply the bat with the power of his heavy shoulders and arms in a smooth horizontal swing. Prudent leg-side fielders seeing the preliminary moves would start taking evasive action, but there was one recorded exception. That truly astonishing close fielder Alan Davidson, aptly nicknamed 'The Claw', stood a few yards distant at short leg in the Oval Test Match of 1956. When Denis, having made 94, middled a long hop from Archer the fielder instead of falling flat on his face thrust out a prehensile right hand and caught this bullet with the air of a man picking an apple off a tree. It seemed to the astonished striker that he appeared to be murmuring a polite word of thanks.

All the other strokes came easily and naturally and, as in the case of Bradman, Hobbs and the other truly great players there was no chink of weakness in any area. Such being so Denis had no particular preference, or dislike, for any type of bowling. He took a great joy in combating the wiles of the spinners whom he would attack boldly, rushing out on the charge at every opportunity. The fact that he was a very good spinner himself added zest to the contest. He played the finest fast bowlers of the era, Lindwall, Miller, Adcock, Heine, Statham and Trueman, with relish, and courage, physical and moral, but with due respect, considering Lindwall to be consistently the best. They, in their turn, attacked him fiercely but without rancour, knowing that they could do so without restraint as he could cope with any threat they offered to person or property.

Of all the immortals, with whom I have bracketed him, in temperament he was closest to Trumper in his cheerful, open-handed attitude to the game of cricket. In modern times much is made of the so-called 'killer instinct' which is presumably the streak of ruthlessness enabling a man to crush and rout a beaten opponent. If, as is occasionally argued, this is an essential ingredient of the true champion it would debar both these cricketers from this category. Both brought devastation to many scenes by brilliance and domination, but neither was ever unchivalrous, nor took any pleasure in the humiliation of a tired or weakened opposition. They both played with such an uncalculating *joie de vivre* that even the hardest hit could scarce forbear to cheer. They also never lacked for consideration and generosity.

There is an illustrative tale which I have always considered the essence of this spirit. Soon after the war Denis played one of his major innings in a county championship match. He was attacked throughout the day by one of the several veteran fast bowlers who had returned in the late middle age of a cricketer to get their teams restarted. This particular veteran took a fair pasting but remained unflagging of spirit when asked to bowl an evening spell. By then he had little left but spirit, and there was surprise and applause when his first over to Denis was a maiden. But the non-striker knew better and, meeting in mid-wicket he asked Denis why he had suddenly let up. At this the striker betrayed a certain embarrassment. 'Oh well,' he said, 'I thought the old boy looked just about all in.' It is possible that on balance the British have a sentimental preference for chivalry as against the 'killer instinct'.

He had definite tastes in the matter of bats but, as one might expect, was unfussy. Provided it had a short handle and was very light, around two pounds two ounces, with a measure of resilience it would do. The preference for extreme lightness is interesting in view of the impression of great weight and solidity one had when it was applied to the ball. This, of course, came from physical power and exquisite timing, and it was for the last reason that he was not exceptionally destructive of bats despite the amount of hard work they had to achieve. It was typical of his practical view of the job that when asked, as he often was, how he held the bat his only reliable method of enlightening the inquirer, and himself, on this point was to get hold of a bat. The grip was, in fact, orthodox, with the top hand less to the front than in the case of most English batsmen. The overall impression was of great strength and flexibility, the two powerful hands commanding the entire length of the short handle.

There is one count upon which purists might question the admission of Compton to the small esoteric band of Immortals. The four players I have named were all good runners between the wickets. I have made no attempt to conceal the fact that Denis was not. 'W.G.' paced his eighteen stone shrewdly and it was because of this, whatever the myths about brow-beaten umpires, that he was very seldom run out. Victor Trumper was a most carefree batsman but a good judge of time and distance. His only foible seems to have been a love of snatching a single off the first ball bowled to him. (For this information I am indebted, as for much else, to Aubrey Faulkner who recalled Reggie Duff being run out by a South African cover who, with local knowledge, came in ten yards for the first ball of a Test Match. In passing Aubrey said Trumper would have been run out off the second by exactly the same stratagem had not an elated cover this time failed to pick the ball up.) Jack Hobbs was a beautiful runner and, with Herbert Sutcliffe, as good a combination as ever was. Don Bradman was an equally superb runner, fast, alert, exact.

Not even those who suffered muscular injury or nervous spasms from association with Denis at the wicket would describe his running as a hissing and a byword—the transgressor's intentions were so palpably amiable and well intended. Rather the general attitude was one of indulgent wariness amongst his own side, and expectation on the part of the opposition. The situation was most aptly expressed by his one-time captain, John Warr, who said that a call from Denis ought never to be regarded as more than an opening bid.

In any case, to my mind this slight frailty between the wickets would be no bar to his place at the top, for we are concerned with the pure quality of batsmanship, not the harvesting of its profits.

Denis Compton, 1971

*

The Master

NORMAN GALE

Overhead a sky of speedwell,
    Pampered yards of green below;
Girls to flutter each Brightonian
    Substitute for Romeo;

Tents with beer for barleycorners
   Husky at the luncheon hour;
All of these are proof that Cricket's
   Bursting fiercely into flower.

Hove is where I breathe contented
   Now that lilac in array
Publishes the white and purple
   Masterpieces due to May.
Here I puff a cloud and wonder
   What decrees of darkling Fate
Govern heroes soon to tackle
   Every subterfuge of Tate.

Sinfield neck-and-crop to Langridge,
   Nothing but a leg-bye scored!
Enters now the dreaded Hammond,
   Gloucester County's overlord.
Deeper, Cover Point! and deeper,
   You that guard the boundaries there!
When she comes you won't have even
   Half a tick of time to spare!

Thud! She's made a fat civilian
   Scuttle to preserve the bone
Threatened by a bomb of leather
   Wensley could but leave alone.
Thud! She's squandered twenty schoolboys
   Rolling in a general laugh.
How the antic figures caper
   Furious on the Telegraph!

This is almost youth recovered!
   Keen I quiver in my chair,
Even sensing those electric
   Crackles common to the hair.
This is England for the English,
   Now that Hammond, come in May,
Drives his flock of Fours, presenting
   Ringside hearts with holiday!

Close of Play, 1936

D. R. Jardine

R. C. ROBERTSON-GLASGOW

It was no joke for a bowler when D. R. Jardine came in at number five for Surrey on a perfect Oval wicket—Hobbs, Sandham, Ducat, Shepherd, Jardine. He used to say: 'The position is peculiar. Either you hustle to a sticky wicket with your pads crooked, or else you go in when there are already so many runs on the board that it doesn't matter whether you make nothing or a hundred!'

Jardine stopped playing first-class cricket at the age of thirty-three; that is, in his prime. He had never played regularly. By then he had been twice to Australia. Twice running he had headed the batting averages. He had captained England abroad and at home, and had played a classic century against the fierceness of Constantine and Martindale at Old Trafford in 1933. But when summer 1934 came round, and the Australians were here again, he was in the Press Box. Rightly or wrongly, he had differed with the Marylebone oligarchy; and he was lost to English cricket when he was much needed. I remember a spectator at Leeds, where Bradman batted on and on, calling up to the Press Box: 'We want you out there, Jardine.' And, upon my word, we did. For the captain was gone, Larwood was injured and out of it. English cricket was at its lowest ebb since the disasters of 1920 and 1921.

Few great batsmen can have matured so early. At the age of fourteen he looked like a County batsman in miniature, and I am sure that at seventeen he could have walked from the Winchester eleven into a Test side and done reasonably well. Among amateurs of his time he was the supreme example of orthodoxy, but what placed him above the others was the strength of his back-play, which equalled that of the best professionals. His skill was to a great degree inherited, his father, M. R. Jardine, having made a century for Oxford v. Cambridge and played many fine innings for Middlesex. To this was added natural intelligence and coaching of the very finest order, first at Horris Hill, where he enjoyed the influence and precept of the famous Evans family, then at Winchester, where his skill was polished by such notable cricketers as E. Rockley Wilson and H. S. Altham.

His own model and hero was C. B. Fry; and in many ways Jardine resembled him; in the method of his back-stroke—the right leg well

over, the left away from the stumps, the stance boldly upright; in concentration, and in the powerful will to improve; and in a certain combativeness of character, which not only made him a most stubborn
fighter in a crisis but led him into first place in one of cricket's most
perplexing controversies.

But the time to see Jardine batting was in a care-free net on a summer evening in the Oxford Parks; and many of these we had together.
Here he would show every stroke in the game, all played with grace
and power, and with an abandon which he hardly ever allowed himself in a set match. And that was the one weakness in all this strength,
that the stringency of an occasion was reflected in a corresponding
restriction of his art, which was in itself so effortless and fluent. Something
of iron in his temperament would not let him play free and full in the
greater matches. It is said that the best innings he played in Australia
was one of 140, in 1928, against New South Wales. Bradman has told
me that it was one of the finest displays of stroke-play that he has ever
seen. But, in general, as the task grew greater, the strokes grew fewer.
He remained a terrific problem for the bowler to solve; but my point
is that he had it in him to kill a bowler, yet was so often content to
wage a long battle on fairly level terms.

As a captain I should rank him very high. He was thorough and
observant. His preparations and his study of individual methods were
exhaustive. None knew more exactly what he meant to do nor could
express his thoughts more pointedly if some plan misfired. He took far
more pains than many knew to weigh the abilities and inclinations of
his own team. He had the true Scottish dislike of waste in material or
words; but his cursing, at its best, was Elizabethan in scope and variety. His wit could be both deep and broad, as when, after batting for
many slow hours in a Test in Australia, he apologised to an Australian
for playing 'like an old spinster defending her honour'.

So much for Jardine as a cricketer. Old acquaintance may perhaps
allow me the liberty of remarking that, if he has sometimes been a
fierce enemy, he has also been a wonderful friend.

Cricket Prints, 1943

*

F. S. Jackson, an Obituary

ANONYMOUS

The passing of Colonel The Honourable Sir Francis Stanley Jackson, PC, GCIE, on March 9, 1947, in his 77th year, came as a shock, not only to all who knew him personally, but also to every lover of cricket who had watched and enjoyed his wonderful prowess on the field of play. From the time that F. S. Jackson at Lord's by his remarkable all-round success helped Harrow gain a victory over Eton by 156 runs in 1888, he went on from strength to strength, until he became one of the finest cricketers ever seen in England. Unfortunately he could not go on any tour to Australia owing to business reasons, and the presence of Lord Hawke in command of Yorkshire until 1910 prevented him from ever being the county captain, though occasionally in charge of the side. He reached the zenith of fame in 1905 when captain of England against Australia. In all five Tests he won the toss; made 492 runs with an average of 70, among his scores being 144 not out at Leeds, 113 at Manchester, 82 not out at Nottingham, 76 and 31 at the Oval; took 13 wickets at 15.46 each, surpassing the efforts of all his colleagues and opponents. Of the five contests, England won that at Nottingham by 213 runs—after declaring with five men out—and that at Manchester by an innings and 80 runs, while they held much the stronger position in each of the three matches left unfinished. By a curious coincidence Stanley Jackson and Joseph Darling, then the Australian captain, were exactly the same age, both having been born on November 21, 1870. That was Darling's third visit as captain and his last tour in England. He died on January 2, 1946, and his obituary in last year's *Wisden* contains some of his experiences in opposition to Jackson.

Regarding his luck in winning the toss in those 1905 Tests and as captain of MCC, for whom he scored 85 in a rain-ruined match at Lord's, Jackson said that at Scarborough, when captain for the seventh time against the Australians: 'I found Darling stripped to the waist. He said, "Now we'll have a proper tossing, and he who gets on top wins the toss." So I said to George Hirst, "Georgie, you come and toss this time." Darling then said, "All right, we'll toss in the old-fashioned way!"' Again winning the toss, Jackson scored 123 and 31 not out, rain preventing a definite result.

Born at Chapel Allerton, near Leeds, Stanley Jackson showed remarkable batting ability when at a preparatory school before he went to Harrow, where he was in the XI for three years, being captain in 1889. He did little on the first occasion, and his father, then the Rt. Hon. W. L. Jackson, a member of the Cabinet in Lord Salisbury's second Government, promised Stanley a sovereign for each wicket he took and a shilling for each run he made. Stanley scored 21 and 59 and took 11 wickets for 68 runs; Harrow won by 156 runs. His father's generosity over cricket ceased with that match. Stanley's only comment was that he was glad he had come off, as it would 'do father so much good'.

Next year, when captain, five wickets fell to him, and his vigorous 68, best score in the match, accounted largely for victory by nine wickets. Proceeding to Cambridge, Jackson gained his Blue as a Freshman, and in 1892 he headed both the batting and bowling averages, and in first-class matches came out third among the amateur bowlers with 80 wickets for less than 19 runs apiece.

Re-elected captain, he led Cambridge to victory by 266 runs in 1893, showing such convincing form that he was given a place in the England team for the first Test at Lord's. He followed a splendid innings of 91 with 103 at the Oval, but when, late in August, the time came for the third Test—at Manchester—he and other Yorkshiremen who might have been included in the side turned out for their county against Sussex at Brighton. He was one of 'Five All-Rounders' given prominence in 1894 *Wisden*.

Describing his first Test innings of 91 in 1893 at Lord's, Sir Stanley smiled and then related that, in the second Test at the Oval, W. G. Grace, the England captain, said, 'With all these batsmen I don't know where to put you.' 'Anywhere will do.' 'Then number seven.' 'Thanks. That's my lucky number; I was the seventh child.' 'And that match brought my first hundred for England. Mold came in last when I was 99. He nearly ran me out, so in desperation I jumped in and drove Giffen high to the seats, reaching 103. Then the bewildered Mold did run me out.'

The Wisden Book of Cricketers' Lives, 1986

✳

A Gentleman's A-Bowling

Dedicated to F. S. Jackson, Lord's 1888

E. E. BOWEN

O Cabby, trot him faster,
 O hurry engine, on!
Come, glory or disaster,
 Before the day be done!
Ten thousand folks are strolling.
 And streaming into view;
A gentleman's a-bowling,
 (More accurately, two.)

With changes and with chances
 The innings come and go,
Alternating advances
 Of ecstasy and woe;
For now, 'tis all condoling,
 And now—for who can tell?
A gentleman's a-bowling—
 It yet may all be well.

Light Blues are nimbly fielding,
 And scarce a bit can pass;
But those the willows wielding
 Have played on Harrow grass!
And there's the ball a-rolling,
 And all the people see
A gentleman's a-bowling,
 And we're a-hitting he!

Ten score to make, or yield her!
 Shall Eton save the match?
Bowl, bowler! go it, fielder!
 Catch, wicket-keeper, catch!
Our vain attempts controlling
 They drive the leather—no!

A gentleman's a-bowling,
And down the wickets go.

Harrow School Songs, 1890

*

Emigrant Boy

DAVID FRITH

Archie Jackson, like Adam Lindsay Gordon, Billy Hughes ('the Little Digger'), Russell Drysdale, Frank Ifield, Patrick White, Charlie Bannerman and a number of other famous Australians, was born on the opposite side of the world. The Jackson family lived at 1 Anderson Place, Rutherglen, south of Glasgow, when Archibald arrived on September 5, 1909. Margaret and Alexander already had two daughters: Lil, aged five, and Peggie, three.

'Sandy' (father Alex) was manager of a brickworks at Belvedere. He had been taken to Australia in a sailing ship with his parents when he was twelve, but returned to Scotland five or six years later. Now, as a 41-year-old working man with responsibilities, he eyed NSW thoughtfully once more. Times were tough in Glasgow.

Thus Sandy struck out again for Australia and paved the way for Mrs Jackson and the children to follow eighteen months later. *Themistocles*, soon to be sunk in the First World War, landed them safely in Sydney on August 1, 1913.

The family set up house in the tilting, rambling old waterside suburb of Balmain: at 14 Ferdinand Street, a small, cosy, iron-roofed, terraced house, built in two storeys of brick, with a laced-iron balcony. It still stands.

After the War the family was completed by the birth of Jeanie, a precious sister for the other girls, and for Archie, whose early disapproval at not getting a baby brother soon evaporated.

'Don't leave her outside in the pram', he often pleaded. 'Someone'll take her away!'

He spoilt Jeanie more with each passing year.

There was never much money about, and Archie had to make do with one pair of pants for the greater part of his boyhood, the sole advantage being that his mother could withhold them whenever he was forbidden from going out.

But the home felt secure and was happy. Sandy worked at Cockatoo Dockyard and gave the rest of his time to his family. He put rubber bars on Archie's worn shoes and they served as soccer boots; he made a bat for him to use in the street games, both by day and under the illumination of the gas lamps—not merely a carved plank, but a real-istically-shaped implement with a *cane handle*. He earned in return a tender adulation.

'Isn't that your boy, Sandy?' said a workmate one afternoon as a row-ing boat floated past the Dock with a small figure lying face-down to avoid recognition. The lad explained that evening that he had only wanted to see his Dad at work. The punishment for truancy was not severe.

The parents were usually good-humoured, too, when he returned with a sackful of apples filched from the orchard up at Mars Field. Other times he amused himself by riding the laundry cart through the narrow Balmain streets.

A well-remembered crisis was when he fought with school-mate Tommy Thompson through four consecutive afternoons before sister Lil felt bound to tell Mum, who went straight down to Birchgrove Park to break it up.

He was no angel. But he was loving, and he was greatly loved.

When Archie's school, Birchgrove, played cricket against Smith Street, he met Bill Hunt and began a lifelong friendship. They became pals during the 1920–21 season, when J. W. H. T. Douglas's MCC team were moving round Australia from one defeat to the next at the mighty hands of Warwick Armstrong, Jack Gregory, Ted McDonald, Charlie Macartney, Herbie Collins, Charlie Kelleway, 'Nip' Pellew, Arthur Mailey—a formidable assembly of skills.

Archie idolised certain cricketers from each side, and he and Bill— when they were not satisfied to play 'numbers cricket' out of the hymn-book in Bible class—had a resourceful manœuvre for getting to the Sydney Cricket Ground. They 'wagged' school at lunchtime, hopped on to a Wood Coffill hearse on its way back to the city, and used their threepence lunch money to get into the ground, where they quenched their thirsts at the bubbler at the base of the Hill, watched the inter-national stars at play—wishing they could be out there too—and went hungry.

After play they usually hitched a ride on the meat wagon back to Balmain, where the mothers strove to fill their bellies.

'They talk about pollution in the 1970s!' said Bill Hunt fifty years later. 'In those days the people of Balmain used to spread coal dust on their bread!'

Archie's special capabilities in the field of sport soon became obvious. He was selected for NSW Schoolboys at both soccer and cricket, travelling to Melbourne under Wendell Bill's captaincy for the summer game and impressing the cricket fraternity there, and distinguishing himself in the inter-state soccer carnival as a slight but highly-skilled centre-forward adept at flicking the ball over the head of a charging opponent and running round him.

He played against South Australia twice, Victoria, and Queensland, scoring thirteen goals.

The Jackson home was hardly a hundred yards from Birchgrove Park, where Balmain District Cricket Club played each Saturday. The captain was whimsical Arthur Mailey, plumber, cartoonist, writer, indefatigable and extravagant spinner of the ball for NSW and Australia.

Soon after little Archie entered the lower grades, playing in short trousers and appearing too fragile for exposure to adult fast bowling, Mailey wrote prophetically of him in the local paper:

Balmain has developed a young batsman who may take a big part in Australian cricket. The club officials must be congratulated upon their success. May other clubs have the same good fortune. It is not often that we see a fifteen-year-old batsman—for he was fifteen two weeks ago—with such a splendid variety of strokes as A. Jackson, the boy cricketer, who scored 71 for Balmain against the juniors last Saturday.

As a rule, in a boy so young, there is that apparent anxiety that affects his cricket, and periods of cramped play occasionally are seen. But Jackson just moves along, flicking this ball past point or through the covers, and turning the next sweetly to leg with the grace of a master. As a second line of defence, his legs are always in a handy position, but it is refreshing to know that he intends to use his bat whenever possible.

I am not going to compare him with the glorious Victor Trumper at this stage, but if a wealth of common sense and ability is an asset, then this boy's future is assured. He played with the Balmain 2nds last season, and should find a place in the first team this year.

As a second string in his bow he has the moral support of twelve juvenile barrackers, whose loyalty and devotion are remarkable. And who would not give something to listen in at some ice cream shop in Balmain while the hero tells of his wonderful experiences of the day's play against the 'big' bowlers?

Young Jackson is going to wreck the averages of some bowlers. Fortunately, I'm in the same team, so it won't be mine.

The grade captains at Balmain were fighting over him by now, and it was felt by the seniors that the cries of 'Too young!' by the lower grades were nothing more than an attempt to keep the budding genius for themselves. When he was blooded in the first team in 1924–25, a season when Australia was in the fervid grip of another MCC tour, Archie, at fifteen years and one month, was thought to be the youngest debutant ever in first-grade cricket.

He had been batting with such style and ease in fourth, third, and second grades that crowds were drawing away from the senior matches to see him—a tiny performer whose pads flapped halfway up his thighs and whose flagging strength as the innings wore on found compensation in pliant wristwork, dancing feet, and uncanny timing and placement. Spectators at Birchgrove, seeing him strain under the weight of a man's bat, once even clubbed together to buy him a Harrow-sized bat.

He lived for cricket. If the silent films at the local were disappointing he would go home before the end and, standing on the dining-room table, practise his footwork against the sideboard mirror—an old C. B. Fry pastime.

One of his problems was sleepwalking—especially, it was noted, during the cricket season. His father found it advisable to tie up the bedroom door handle to save him from falling over the lace ironwork which encased the balcony.

Earlier, before the risk had been realised, he had actually spent the hotter, steamier nights on that balcony, where a bed could be wedged. His somnambulations often led him down to the kitchen late at night: he would slump into the rocking chair while his mother, who knew perfectly well how to handle him, carried on with her ironing. After a few minutes of unreal conversation she would direct him back to bed, and loud snoring soon came as an assurance that the wanderings were at an end for one more night.

Archie ('The Champ') and Bill ('The Count') enjoyed their school-days and made the best of them, for they tended to end early in Balmain. Archie, having passed his Qualifying Certificate at fourteen, had gone to Rozelle School; but a year later he was a schoolboy no more. The family needed his financial help, and he was eager to pay his way.

Joining Jackson (no relation) & McDonald, he worked distractedly in the warehouse until cricket got the better of him. As his career developed and his absences became more frequent he was compelled to leave, and soon found himself working for Alan Kippax in his sports shop in Martin Place. The business had got away to a very sound start in 1926 after the Australian selection had surprisingly overlooked Kippax for the tour of England; now, after inviting the boy to call in, he opened a bank account for him and put him to work.

Kippax was to have a profound influence on Jackson as his mentor and captain in NSW matches. He gave him quiet guidance, encouragement, and, as his employer, generous time to practise and to play during the week.

Kippax played for Waverley, Jackson for Balmain, on the other side of town. But the Fates had brought them together, and Victor Trumper's ghost must have smiled.

Another benefactor had been Herbert Vere Evatt, then a young lawyer living in Balmain, and later to become one of Australia's most distinguished men: Chief Justice of NSW, Leader of the Federal Parliamentary Labor Party, Cabinet Minister, and President of the United Nations Assembly. Dr Evatt and Arthur Mailey saw to it that poverty never prevented a Balmain boy from having cricket equipment and being a paid-up member of the club.

The debt to these men and to sportsmaster John Mitchell was never forgotten by five boys from Rozelle School who all became first-class cricketers: Archie Jackson, Bill Hunt, Syd Hird, Dudley Seddon and Dick Nutt.

In 1923–24 Archie made three centuries for Rozelle, and his average of 69 made no allowance for several retirements. He was also an 'exceedingly fine slip field, and useful change bowler' who claimed on one exhilarating occasion 6 for 1 including a hat-trick.

He and Bill enjoyed their greatest success against Auburn School, whom they dismissed for 7, Jackson 4 for 2, Hunt 6 for 1, with four byes! Syd Hird, who later lived in South Africa, remembered Archie taking 8 for 2: 'yours truly claimed the other two for two runs.' He also recalled a 'tour' up to the Hawkesbury River, when the little Balmain cricketers were greeted almost with disdain. So they batted until almost 500 was on the board, and Archie was one of the centurymakers. They then dismissed the locals for 11 and 13 (or thereabouts).

Every evening the gang played in Birchgrove Park, where a rule had to be introduced to stop Archie batting forever: compulsory retirement at 100. Consequently Archie, upon reaching the nineties, would stonewall. The answer had to be—and was—strategic overthrows to see him to three figures.

At Birchgrove, where Archie had captained the team at the age of twelve, making four centuries and taking 8 for 12 and 7 for 11, another sportsmaster often predicted that he would be playing for Balmain first team at seventeen, NSW at eighteen, and Australia at nineteen. The forecast was bold, yet, as it happened, safe. He was playing for the State at seventeen.

It was the same sportsmaster Byrnes who had felt Archie's absence through illness so severely in a crucial school match that he had authorised the boys to call round and plead with Mrs Jackson to let her son play. He was allowed to bat with a runner, made a few runs, and the Premiership was won.

He could not stay away from the game; his team-mates could never accept his absence with equanimity. This impatience in later years was to hasten his death.

In his first season in Balmain 1sts, following a moderate start and reversion to the 2nds, he was brought up again in an emergency and secured his place for the rest of his years.

He was showing a solid defence and command of every stroke even if he was able to exert precious little physical power. His highest was a fighting 41 not out in two hours, and he finished second in the averages with 30.75. He was now equally at home on turf pitches.

He had batted fearlessly against the fireballs of Jack Gregory and Jack Scott and the briskness of Sam Everett and Charles Kelleway, and the conclusion was inescapable: the 'babe' had an uncanny instinct for batting. His afferent nerve (eye to brain) and efferent nerve (brain to limb) were abnormally sharp, as they are in all top sportsmen.

Nor did he merely allow his skill to evolve only in match play. He practised at Birchgrove Oval from five o'clock till dusk and was back for more in the clear morning air at half-past-seven before setting off to work.

He was a keen reader, not only of Edgar Wallace and travel tales, famous lives and boy's adventure, but of cricket books—particularly those recording the great England *v*. Australia battles.

Most of his dreams must have been of the 'big cricket' which everyone in the district was now predicting for him, though on one sleepwalk he was climbing up to place files on an hallucinatory shelf, thinking himself to be at the warehouse. His father grabbed him as he was about to topple over the balcony. That would have been that.

As the 1925–26 season opened he was just sixteen. At first he struggled, and there were those who began to wonder if the frail prodigy had been but a momentary deception of Nature. Then the runs came.

Opening against Western Suburbs, he carried his bat doggedly for 58 out of 103 and made 61 in the second innings. His 88 against University was dazzling. And his first century in first-grade cricket was recorded against St George, a club due the following season to enlist a promising colt (D. Bradman) from the country.

After Jackson's beautiful 129 there was a collection among the onlookers for which he shyly expressed his gratitude. There was jubilation in his home town.

At the end of the season he stood impertinently atop the Balmain averages with the considerable aggregate of 670 runs at almost 40. He had taken another step up the ladder in being selected for NSW 2nd XI against Victoria, making a modest 25 and 30 while the senior side in Sydney were piling up 708 (Kippax—overcoming a supposed nervous disposition yet again—making 271 not out).

To top off the summer he escaped the hurly-burly of first-grade cricket at Easter when 20 Balmain players and supporters travelled to Goulburn in *three* cars! Little Jackson extricated himself from the vehicle and made 59 and 74, and stroked 35 against Kenmore.

Home-life continued as full of affection and animation as ever, with the unchangeably Scots parents quietly proud of their budding champion of a son and the sisters contesting his company. Dad, a physical-fitness crank who had an incurable weakness for impromptu chin-ups in the kitchen, was incapable of noisy pride, yet no father was ever more gratified at a son's progress. This was the boy who, at the age of two and a half, had attracted a crowd at a Scottish holiday resort when giving a display of his virtuosity with a football.

'I don't want your money!' the infant had bawled indignantly when his audience showed its appreciation.

The family never ceased using certain peculiarly Scottish expressions even after many years of Balmain life, though Archie, as he grew up, spoke with care and ever-improving expression. Remembering him in the age of television, his sisters 'heard' him whenever English actor Roger Moore ('The Saint' and 'James Bond') uttered his lines.

His love of reading matured into an interest in writing, evidenced firstly in his personal letters and later in his newspaper articles. J. C. Davis, Australia's authoritative cricket journalist, felt he could have become a writer of some distinction, and not necessarily only on cricket, when his playing days were past.

Davis had first seen him batting when his fame was nothing more than local. A friend, having watched schoolboy Archie a few days previously, had urged Davis to cast an eye over a 'young Trumper'. They went to Balmain.

'He looks to be Victor reborn', said the friend.

Davis, mesmerised, was bound to agree.

Yet if Trumper's mantle became an impediment to him, Archie Jackson was never to show it.

Archie Jackson, 1987

*

The Captain England Rejected

RICHARD STREETON

Almost alone in cricket folklore the place held by Percy George Herbert Fender has depended on something he failed to do rather than what he did. 'The best captain never chosen to lead England', has been the verdict passed down to later generations. As an all-rounder his greatest deeds were with Surrey and included the fastest hundred made in a first-class match. That innings remains Fender's main legacy to the record books but hardly explains the multitude of stories and legends that continually surrounded his name. He was what was known in his own day as a card; now it would be said he did not conform, or that he was a rebel. He was descended on his father's side from Scottish border outlaws and a number of Fenders ended their days being hanged for stealing English sheep. His mother's forebears were Huguenot refugees from France, who settled and prospered in Gloucestershire. Hereditary instincts were always apparent in Fender's cricket: he batted and bowled more like a buccaneer than a conscript and his captaincy had an astuteness then rare in the county game.

Fender's contemporaries were unanimous in the 1920s that he manipulated the thin Surrey bowling resources with an almost miraculous flair. There were differences in cricket leadership in that era, of course, even if the emphasis was seldom as fixedly on attack as some writers have claimed. Wickets were more palpably sought, with containment and run-saving fields spurned as routine tactics. A greater use of spin bowling brought the chance to vary the tactical thinking and, most significantly of all, to maintain a respectable over rate. Fender's gifts as a captain, though, would have marked him out in any period of the game, irrespective of tactical trends or bowling cults. He had a deep knowledge of cricket, its history, laws and technique, and the judgement to interpret pitches and match situations. He kept dossiers on players and had a knack for recalling a batsman's weaknesses in matters of bowling and strokes and, equally important, his preferences. Fender had the insight to utilize these things at the right moment, and harnessed to this were the craft and knowing instincts of a successful gambler. His ability was all slightly tinged, too, with gamesmanship, though always within the laws.

As a player Fender had the ability to scale peaks reached by few, though, like Constantine's, his talent was erratic. The full potential was only fulfilled intermittently and not often reflected in the scorebook. A rapid-fire fifty, three or four opportune wickets, or a couple of brilliant catches: Fender's cricket tended to be explosive and relevant. It brought disquiet to opponents and excitement to spectators. 'The type who would win a match but would rarely be at the top of the averages,' was how the Australian critic A. G. Moyes summed up Fender in *A Century of Cricketers* (Harrap, 1950). It seems incredible that Fender failed to win more than thirteen caps even in a period when numerous all-rounders flourished and fewer Test matches were played. Above all there has remained the long unfathomed mystery of why Fender— accepted as the supreme tactician of his age—was not chosen as England captain. 'I wish he could have captained England; for surely he earned it,' was R. C. Robertson-Glasgow's view in *More Cricket Prints* (T. Werner Laurie, 1948). Throughout the twenties the leading cricket writers were astonished by England's rejection of Fender: it was a door that stayed permanently closed, locked and heavily bolted in his face.

Fender has disposed of several myths about the subject that were first suggested at the time or have become accepted since. One was that he failed to get the captaincy because it was thought he was Jewish; second because he was not a university man; and third because his business as a wine merchant came close to being considered 'trade' in the class-riddled society of those times. To modern readers these may seem distasteful and unnecessary things to raise, but sixty years ago, sadly, they were meaningful. Fender denied he was Jewish and in any event he did not believe it would have told against him if he had been. In the second case he pointed out, correctly, that England had already chosen several captains who were not Oxford or Cambridge men and that they were to do so again. Finally, to sell wine for a living was a perfectly acceptable occupation by the 1920s.

To find the real reasons why Fender was never England captain it is necessary to enter a delicate labyrinth of personalities and prejudices. Time eased the hurt a little and Fender in old age agreed there had been occasions when he was too sharp, or too outspoken, for his own good. The English have always had reservations—a positive distrust, in fact—about clever people, as numerous politicians who failed to disguise their cleverness have found to their cost. The cricket Establishment in Fender's day was no more hidebound than that found elsewhere in public life. They would have been suspicious of Fender's shrewdness in cricket and would have resented the instances when he acted contrary to normal practice. Not to do the 'done' thing was the biggest sin of all in those days in every sphere and Fender always had an approach and a mind of his own. Like many such men, too, he could be brash and tactless, however justified were his motives. To use a homespun phrase, Fender's face often failed to fit in the circles that mattered.

Fender was already aware by 1923 that senior officialdom regarded him with only qualified approval. He had been vice-captain of the MCC team to South Africa in 1922–23 but was not asked to lead either team in the two Test trials held in 1923. His own form and his leadership of Surrey had been outstanding and not for the first time, nor the last, Fender's case was lobbied in print at great length. The newspapers continued to ignore the pointers and they made Fender and Arthur Gilligan the front runners for the England captaincy in 1924. F. T. Mann and G. E. C. Wood were lesser candidates mentioned by the press for the job of leading England against South Africa, in what was the first home Test series for three years, and then to Australia the following winter. The cricket writers were extremely critical by the standards of those times when Gilligan was chosen to lead the England XI in the Test trial and was then confirmed in office for the first Test match.

Cardus in the *Manchester Guardian* spoke of Lord's having reasons 'not apparent to the man in the street'. H. J. Henley in the *Daily Mail* said 'the best captain in England has again been passed over', and G. A. Faulkner in the *Westminster Gazette* described it as 'one of those incidents that cause a jar the more one thinks about it'. The *Daily Express* noted: 'Happily there is still time for reflection and reconsideration. The selection committee have not finally committed themselves. Let them beware lest a blunder be committed which will put into the shade all the blunders—and they have been many—which have distracted our post-war cricket.' Fender was naturally disappointed but, deep down, Gilligan's appointment did not surprise him. The two men were close friends and the day before Gilligan left for Australia in September he was a guest at Fender's wedding. By then Fender was out of the England side and an episode had occurred which effectively finished his Test-match career for good. Certainly Fender remained convinced that it cost him any lingering hopes he still held of captaining England.

The incident which finally made Fender *persona non grata* came in 1924 when he was rash enough to cross swords, woundingly, with Lord Harris, arguably the most influential figure English cricket has ever had. Lord Harris, President of MCC in 1875, was in his seventies and still held the powerful office of MCC treasurer. He was an autocratic figure at Lord's, serving cricket and cricketers faithfully by the dictums of his time, and a man of rigid principles throughout his long life. Fender remembered him as 'a fair but formidable man'. The first link in the chain of circumstances that led to Fender's incurring the baronial wrath was the dreadfully wet start to the 1924 season. The South Africans, needing more practice than most visiting sides as they adjusted to turf wickets, were badly hampered in their opening matches against Leicestershire and Derbyshire. At both games the captains agreed to cover the wickets and 'Plum' Warner in the *Morning Post* on 6 May, like other journalists present, wrote that this covering was contrary to the regulations. Warner added that the MCC committee might have something to say, 'though the practice has before now obtained at cricket festivals such as Scarborough without any notice being taken of it by MCC . . .'

MCC's response came in a statement which was carried by the newspapers without comment on 22 May. They reminded everyone that covering was in contravention of the appropriate law and went on to claim no knowledge of what had happened in the past at Scarborough in the following terms: 'They now, *for the first time* [author's italics] are informed that it has been for a long time a regular practice to cover the whole of the pitch at Scarborough and possibly at other matches. . . .' This seems to have been extraordinarily naïve of MCC in view of the stature of the Scarborough Festival, with which most of the leading players and officials were usually involved. They escaped any adverse criticism in the national press on this aspect, however, but it was touched upon by Fender in a letter on the whole subject of covering which was published soon afterwards.

Fender was ill-advised enough to recall an occasion at Scarborough a year or two earlier when Lord Harris himself had sought Fender's advice on how covering facilities there could be improved. They had walked across the Scarborough ground together during a stoppage for rain, and when Lord Harris raised the matter Fender had recommended more tarpaulins rather than the type of covering in use. Lord Harris had agreed and said that he would have inquiries made. In other words, Lord Harris, of all people, must have been fully aware of Scarborough's use of covering in the past. Few things could have been more calculated to embarrass Lord Harris and MCC than Fender's disclosure, though in itself it made no impact on either the media or the public. A reader's letter in the *Cricketer* in October 1924 was the only other instance where MCC's two-faced approach to the matter was mentioned in print. A Mr W. F. Curtis of Leicester noted that the pitch had once again been covered for the Yorkshire *v.* MCC match the previous month at Scarborough—in the presence of the festival's patron, Lord Hawke. Mr Curtis recalled MCC's strictures on the subject the previous May and, with tongue in cheek presumably, he wondered if MCC had now changed its mind. This letter provoked no further correspondence or, if it did, the letters were not published.

Whatever the rights and wrongs, Fender had obviously behaved extremely tactlessly and it need hardly be stressed that he never regretted anything as much in his life. The next time Fender was at Lord's, one of the pavilion attendants told him: 'His Lordship would like to see you, sir, in the committee-room.' Fender had already had one 'wigging', as he put it, from Lord Harris, who had remonstrated with him about his habit of leading amateurs and professionals on to the field through the same gate. 'We do not want that sort of thing at Lord's, Fender,' was a summary of that first occasion—guidance given kindly but firmly, and above all explicitly, as Fender recalled. This time Fender's memory was of Lord Harris's extreme anger. He was told something along the lines: 'Don't you ever write anything about me, my views or MCC in print again, young man.' Fender was left in no doubt that he had blotted his copybook badly and that the affair would not be forgotten.

Lord Harris died in 1932 and it has proved impossible to trace any reference by him to what went on that day in the committee-room between himself and Fender. MCC confirmed for the author that Fender's name did not appear in any minutes that dealt with wicket covering in 1924 and the present Lord Harris was unable to help either. He knew his father had several disagreements with Fender, but the family had no record of them. Even when Lord Harris's initial anger passed, the matter must have rankled at Lord's for a long time. It probably brought the breaking-point in what had seldom been an uncensorious view of Fender, who was adamant it was not entirely coincidental that his Test career virtually ended at this time. Nor was he ever asked to tour abroad with MCC again. Fender had been involved in every Test rubber played by England since the First World War. He won his first three caps in the final games of the 1920–21 series in Australia and he played in the last two Tests of 1921 in England. On tour in South Africa Fender played all five Tests of the 1922–23 series and he was picked for the first two Tests in June 1924. After that he was dropped—the man hailed in the press as the best all-round cricketer in England.

It was an unhappy time for Fender in other ways as well. During the second Test at Lord's he had to contend with unsought publicity when his engagement was leaked to some newspapers. The resultant fuss in the middle of a Lord's Test was a further contributory cause of disfavour with the Establishment. Nor had there been any let up at that time to the unsavoury campaign in some newspapers about the captaincy. They continued to dwell on possible reasons for Gilligan's selection ahead of Fender and this speculation was embarrassing to everyone. An outburst in a Sunday newspaper by Parkin, the Lancashire bowler, who criticized Gilligan's handling of England's attack helped to close the official ranks even more firmly behind Gilligan. In addition, Fender lost all bowling form for several weeks and there were also unfounded rumours that he was not available for Australia.

Fender finally knew for certain that he was out of the selectors' reckoning when Gilligan was injured in the Gentlemen *v.* Players match at The Oval in July. Gilligan was hit over the heart by a ball from Howell and, though he hit a hundred the next day, it was an injury which affected Gilligan's own fast bowling for the rest of his career. Gilligan stood down from the fourth Test at Manchester and J. W. H. T. Douglas, approaching forty-two, was hastily recalled as England's captain and added as vice-captain to the early list of tour choices. There were many unexpected selectorial decisions by England in the twenties, not least for the 1924–25 tour, but to many people this was turning back the clock with a vengeance. Fender did actually play in one more Test match. He began the 1929 season in remarkable form and was picked for the first Test against South Africa at Birmingham under J. C. White. Fender in old age did not even remember this late recall by England. In his own mind his Test career ended in 1924. The newspapers, incidentally, never did face the facts and continued their advocacy of Fender for several more years.

In the closing years of his life Fender confessed he had tilted un-
wisely with authority for as long as he could remember, though he also
believed his unconventionality was frequently only ahead of its time.
The first brush with those in high places that he could recall came when
he was about eleven and at St George's College, Weybridge. Fender
headed the winning goal from a corner in a house match and was later
reprimanded by his housemaster, whom he had expected to be pleased.
'That sort of goal is a professional's trick, Fender; no proper footballer
scores a goal with his head.' Later, a century he made for St Paul's
School against Bedford was not mentioned when he irritated his cricket
master by bowling lobs in the same match. A draw had looked certain
and the fact that Fender snatched several wickets with his lobs and took
St Paul's close to victory was considered unimportant. In county
cricket the Lord's officials were not the only ground authority he upset
by leading all his team through the same gate. Fender actually went
further at The Oval and tried to get the Surrey amateurs and professionals to use the same dressing-room. He was dissuaded after talking
with Hobbs and Strudwick. 'With respect, Mr Fender, we like to talk
about you and laugh at what you might do next,' was the gist of what
Hobbs told him, and Fender had the perception to let the matter drop.

Fender was the first man in English press boxes to use a typewriter,
thus disturbing with metallic clatter traditional havens of quiet in which
everyone wrote copy by hand. Fender had to ride out several storms
of protest from colleagues and once at Leeds from a persistent woman
spectator sitting nearby. Fender in his most charming manner offered
to type the threatened letter of complaint to the club secretary for her.

He enlisted the aid of clothing manufacturers to provide lighter cot-
ton vests and underpants for cricketers; he helped design a different-
shaped Surrey cap with a larger peak that shielded the eyes more
effectively. One spring, a leading baseball coach on a visit to London
was invited to The Oval to help improve throwing techniques at fielding practice. All things, possibly, of small import, but they confirmed
Fender as an innovator.

Like many quick-witted men Fender could be impatient with those
lacking his ability to see ahead and he could be downright prickly with
those he felt to be wrong or out of place. He was definitely intolerant
of authority or tradition if he felt it to be out of step with the prevailing circumstances. In his thinking he was thrustful and never hesit-
ated to cut corners, attributes he brought not only to cricket but also

to his business life and to the bridge he played at the highest level. At the same time Fender was a stickler for things to be done properly and never allowed himself or others to desert the high standards of behaviour and commitment he set. If he was a man who tended to be respected rather than revered, his own professionals admired him enormously as a person and player. He was looked upon with the utmost suspicion, undoubtedly, by those who knew him least.

Andy Sandham played throughout the time Fender led Surrey and summarized a theme consistently reiterated among his age group: 'Mr Fender always knew too much for the others—committee men, groundsmen, the other team or their captain. It did not make him popular, but he was too clever for them.'

P. G. H. Fender, 1981

*

Saturday Cricket

GERALD BULLETT

Flowing together by devious channels
From farm and brickyard, forest and dene,
Thirteen men in glittering flannels
Move to their stations out on the green.

Long-limbed Waggoner, stern, unbudging,
Stands like a rock behind the bails.
Dairyman umpire, gravely judging,
Spares no thought for his milking-pails.

Bricklayer bowls, a perfect length.
Grocery snicks and sneaks a run.
Law, swiping with all his strength,
Is caught by Chemist at mid-on.

Two to the boundary, a four and a six,
Put the spectators in fear of their lives:
Shepherd the slogger is up to his tricks,
Blithely unwary of weans and wives.

> Lord of the manor makes thirty-four.
> Parson contributes, smooth and trim,
> A cautious twelve to the mounting score:
> Leg-before-wicket disposes of him.
>
> Patient, dramatic, serious, genial,
> From over to over the game goes on,
> Weaving a pattern of hardy perennial
> Civilization under the sun.

News from the Village, 1952

*

Tom Graveney

FRANK KEATING

I seldom have nightmares. Say a couple a year. But enough to re-establish my stark fear of heights. Extremely scary. I always wake only a split second before I hit the deck—splat! There's a still fevered moment or two for a shaking hand to fumble for the light switch and a smoke. Then, with relief and realization dawning that I'm both in the land of the living and my pungent pit, I will inhale deeply, smile to myself and, content again, think of . . . Clem Attlee, a former Prime Minister, and George Emmett, a former Gloucestershire bat. And thoughts of George soon turn to recollections of Tom. Ah, Tom. Dear Tom. *Our* Tom.

You need an explanation: in 1946, at the age of eight, I was unaccountably sent the thirty miles from Stonehouse in Gloucestershire to a boarding prep school near Hereford. Now, in spite of his aberration on private education, in all other matters my father, bless him, was as trenchant a socialist as you could ever meet. And you didn't meet many in that true-blue neck of the Randwick Woods unless you bumped into Bert Cole, Ben Parkin, Bill Maddocks or my Uncle John planning the revolution in the Woolpack Inn. Anyway, it so came to pass that, between them, they had won the seat for Labour in the 1945 landslide election. Word of this stunning reverse of the established order seeped even over the county border at about the very same time that I had turned up in Hereford as the most midget, meek and miserable mother's boy even such as Dotheboys had seen. The bigger boys bullied and we namby newts cowered and cringed by day and, at nights, wept and then wet the bed.

Many and varying were the forms of torture. You had done well if you survived a day with only an ear twisted off in the boot room, or a bottom blackened with a scrubbing brush and Cherry Blossom. Most horrendous was 'The Tower', so awful that even the leading sadists only summoned the courage once or twice a year. I heard the dreaded, awful, conspiracy, 'Keating for The Tower tonight; pass it round', whispered through the school on three occasions. The school's church tower was more squat Saxon than tall and fluted Norman. But it was high enough to be absolutely petrifying when you were dangling over its edge held, only by the ankles, by two other boys. The rest of the school would watch the fun from below. I'm still surprised no child ever fell to his death. I am certain it is the reason for my recurring nightmares and my fear of heights. (I can never look out of an aeroplane till it is in the clouds.)

On two occasions I was 'towered' for 'family connections'—that is, every other short-trousered prig in the place was, of course, a Conservative, so when I boasted about my father's and uncle's political affiliations, I did so with my heart in my mouth. I cannot remember exactly why, but I was possibly sent to The Tower when the Labour Party nationalized steel and when they 'sold out' the Indian Empire to 'the wogs'. I was hung as a martyr for Clem Attlee's great radicalism.

The third time was altogether different. In the midsummer of 1948, the triumphant march of Bradman's Australian cricketers had the English selectors in all sorts of panic. For the third Test match at Old Trafford, out of the blue, they selected two Gloucestershire players. I would have got away with it had the only selection been Jack Crapp, our doughty left-hander who had scored a century against the tourists in the county fixture at Bristol. But the wee sprog, George Emmett, was another matter altogether, for he was chosen to replace Len Hutton, revered both in the school and the land as a national institution. So my one-man Gloucester gloat at Emmett's selection had its come-uppance at once. In a seething fury the word went round, 'Keating for The Tower tonight.' I was hung as a martyr for Georgie Emmett. (When he failed in both innings there were threats that I should be 'done' again.)

Here is the point of these rambling recollections: if George Emmett had not been picked for that one solitary Test match, it is quite possible that the world would never have seen Tom Graveney bat. After

Bristol Grammar School and National Service in the Army, young Graveney had seemed to have fluffed his apprenticeship as a Gloucestershire cricketer. At the time of that Manchester Test match, which began on 8 July 1948, his 'career' seemed to have ended before it began. On his first-class debut he had made a duck, and followed that with just over 200 runs in 20-odd innings. He was seriously thinking of re-signing for the Army, which he had enjoyed, and taking a PT instructor's course. Certainly he had been demoted to the Gloucestershire Second XI, and looked unlikely for re-engagement.

Then Crapp and Emmett were selected for England. Graveney was hastily dispatched to Bournemouth for the First XI fixture with Hampshire. He made a precocious and calm 47 against the spinners, Knott and Bailey, on a spiteful wicket. In the following match against Somerset at Bristol he scored an undefeated 81. By the time I got home for the holidays, my Stonehouse chums, Peter Beard and Robin Bassett, were filling me in with details of his maiden century, against the Combined Services at Gloucester Wagon Works. It had, they said, been amazingly wizard-prang.

The Cheltenham Festival—nine full days of cricket—couldn't come quick enough. Sometimes we'd catch that chippy little chuffer, the 'Railcar', and change at Gloucester. Other mornings would have us in front of the queue outside Woolworth's in Stroud for the Western National double-decker, over the top past Painswick's yews, and the Prinknash Pottery. We had our greaseproofed-paper sandwiches, a shilling extra for a bottle of Tizer and a pound of plums, a bat and tennis ball for tea-time, and our autograph books. The first time I saw him, Tom made a silky half-century—all coltish, gangly, upright youthfulness, with a high, twirly, backlift and a stirring, bold, flourishing signature in the follow-through—and he came back to the 'gym', blushing at the applause, and signed my book before he went in to lunch. 'T. W. Graveney', neat, joined-up, surprisingly adult.

Next Easter term, I began to feel less of an outsider at school when Dad sent me a present of my first *Wisden*. Even the bully boys asked, nicely, to borrow it. I would show them the Gloucestershire Notes, and the last sentence about the batting—'A pleasant feature of the season was the form of a newcomer, T. W. Graveney, a product of Bristol club cricket, who showed graceful right-handed stroke play.'

By Cheltenham that August, the young man was actually leading our parade. That in itself was a triumph. Schoolboy romantics do not readily forsake their first heroes. And there had been lots of them about in

'Glorse'. True, Charlie Barnett had gone, off to the Lancashire League; and, sure, we missed the Chalford autocrat's hook of nose and stroke; he smacked bumpers, thwack! as if he was smacking down plaice on the wet slabs outside his fishmongers in 'Zoiren' or 'Chelt'. Then there was the aforementioned Jack and Georgie. Crapp was the calm and watchful leftie; we were never in real trouble till he was out. Unperturbable, he would push his ones and twos to keep the numbers rolling in gentle rhythms, but then, of a sudden, he would break out and hit the thing with a clean, wicked ferocity, then lean placid on his sword, the handle supporting his buttocks like a shooting stick, and he would cross his arms and legs and wait, serene, while the ball was retrieved from miles away. 'Good ol' Jack! Give 'em another one, Jack!' we shouted. But he seldom did it twice in succession. Or even twice in a session.

Emmett was in direct contrast. A tiny man with a nutbrown face and whipcord wrists. He had the twinkling feet of an Astaire, and the same sort of hairstyle. His on-drive singed every blade of grass between the bowler and mid-wicket. His cap was a very faded blue because he wore it everywhere—even in bed I bet, we giggled—and there was always a groan of real sadness when he got himself out. Emmett, and especially Crapp, I learned many years later, were the wise and generous mentors and mother-hens to the young chick Graveney.

In Tom's earliest days, Billy Neale also nursed him in the middle orders. He was a farmer, from Grace country, down Thornbury way. He had gone to school, at Cirencester Grammar, with the county's previous emperor and champion, Wally Hammond, and had always been, they said, the one to understand the moods and melancholy of that great, smouldering genius. They would walk together for hours in the orchards of Neale's Breadstone Farm, talking of this and that; after which Wally was refreshed again. Tom's first captain must have been an influence as well: B. O. Allen was Clifton and Cambridge and once got a double century against Hampshire; he looked as fierce as our Latin master and we never dared ask him for an autograph. He went forth to toss for innings in a brown trilby, like they said Hammond used to do, and he blew his nose with a whopping, red-spotted snuff hankie. And like Charlie Barnett, he used to ride to hounds in winter.

There were other tyros, too, with Tom: Milton was to become a dear favourite; the *Yearbook* started calling him 'Clement' and then 'Charlie' before settling, by public demand, on Arthur. He had the soccer player's bow legs—he remains the last 'double' international—and was the most versatile and thrilling fieldsman I ever saw. And Martin

Young, suave and smarmy-haired and always beautifully turned out; his bat always looked pine-fresh new. Arrogant, he had South African connections.

Our bowlers would take up another book: we all tried to copy George Lambert's action—he was faster than Lindwall, for sure. His new ball mucker was Colin Scott, who used to work at the Co-op and had great ten-to-two Underwood feet, and occasionally specialized in sixers. There was Sam Cook (whom the *Yearbook* called 'Cecil' *always*), who was left-arm and reliable and the much-loved apprentice to the very sorcerer himself, our wizard of tweak, Tom Goddard, whose 2,979 career bag of wickets has only been bettered by four others in the whole history of the game. Stumper was Andy Wilson, a tiny tot with massive appeal in every way. He once took ten catches in a match. After all his years keeping to Goddard and Cook, he took bets that he would be the only batsman in the whole land to read Ramadhin's wrong 'un when the West Indies came to Cheltenham in 1950. Both innings Andy shouldered arms to let the little long-sleeved mesmerist's first ball go by outside the off-stump. Both times he was clean bowled. Gloucester were routed that day. Only Graveney made double figures, all blushing uncertainty and middle-of-the-bat, and a man next to me said, 'Our Tom'll be servin' England this side o' twelvemonth.'

And he was. When Denis Compton was injured, Freddie Brown blooded him against the South Africans at Old Trafford in 1951, and on a real sticky he made 15 against Athol Rowan—'every run full of cultured promise', said John Arlott on the wireless. Tom served England for the next ten years. When George was still King he was taking 175 from the Indians at Bombay; when Lindwall and Miller were still lethal he matched Hutton, stroke for stroke, in a partnership of 168 at Lord's; and a couple of years later he collected a century at Sydney with three successive boundaries; onwards a summer or two, and his massively flamboyant 258 nailed down for ever the wispy mystique of Ramadhin and Valentine, after May and Cowdrey had done the tedious, pad-prod spadework earlier in the month.

Yet while these, and even the shortest innings, were a delight, word was going about that he lacked the cruel competitive edge to take a game and an attack by the throat; he was getting out when the very critical need was just to stay in. He was, horror! playing Festival cricket instead of Test match cricket. Never the twain must meet, and he was dropped for, as someone said, 'being happy only to present his ability, but not to enforce it ruthlessly'.

He had moved from Gloucestershire now. But so had we. And wherever I was in the world, I daresay I wasn't the only Gloucester man to sneak a look first at the Worcester scores to see how Tom had done. For it was soon apparent that there, under the old Norman shadow that matched the mellow architecture of his strokes, his batsmanship had actually become even better. It was still joyous and free of care, but now it was more stable, more serene, more *certain*. The England selectors, of course, seemed oblivious to the fact, and though century followed century and Championship followed Championship, not even the wildest betting man would have wagered on a recall by England. But at last they had to. After his four years in the pleasant backwaters of the shires came an almost tangible rumbling of public demand for Graveney's Test match place to be restored, following another woeful England start to the West Indian series of 1966. They turned to Tom, now in his fortieth year.

And at Lord's too! The full-house standing ovation started as he made his way through the Long Room once again. Hall and Griffith and Sobers and Gibbs . . . he returned to grandstand applause after a magnificent 96. 'It's like a dream come true,' he said as he went back up the stairs, eyes moist with tears. In the next match, at Trent Bridge, England were 13 for 3, Hall's Larry Holmes and Griffith's Joe Frazier both murderously, cruelly, hostile. Graveney and Cowdrey alone had the technique and fearlessness to stand unflinchingly firm. Tom finished with 109, and many still shake their heads in wonder and insist it must have been his very best innings.

But there were still more gems in the old man's kitty. A superlative 165 followed at the Oval; then, next summer, a charming 151 against India at Lord's. A few months later he produced a comprehensive retrospective—118 runs against the West Indies. 'Any art gallery in the world would have bought that innings,' wrote Henry Blofeld, who was there. He overflowed with fluent strokes and quite outplayed the 1968 Australians, as he did the Pakistanis in the winter, when Karachi saw his last Test match century. When the West Indies rejoined battle next summer he scored 75 in the first Test then, on the free Sunday of the match, played in his own benefit game at Luton. It was against the rules and Lord's banned him for three Tests—in effect, for ever. But Our Tom of Gloucester had become Worcester's Tom, then England's, then the world's.

As this book is a cricket writers' book, it would be nice to quote the retirement panegyric offered to Graveney after his final Test. It can do more justice than I can to a fine cricketer and a fine man. It was written by one of the very best of writers, J. M. Kilburn, who was for forty diligent and creative years the correspondent of the *Yorkshire Post*: 'Graveney may have disappointed some cricketers by playing in Graveney's way, but he has adorned cricket. In an age preoccupied with accountancy he has given the game warmth and colour and inspiration beyond the tally of the score-book. He has been of the orchard rather than the forest, blossom susceptible to frost but breathing in the sunshine . . . Taking enjoyment as it came, he has given enjoyment that will warm the winters of memory.'

Yet it might never have happened had George Emmett not been picked for his solitary Test match in the midsummer of 1948. The very same day that Tom was dispatched to Bournemouth and I was dangled, head first, from the top of a church tower in Hereford.

Cricket Heroes, 1984

*

Test Match at Lord's

ALAN ROSS

Bailey bowling, McLean cuts him late for one.
I walk from the Long Room into slanting sun.
Two ancients halt as Statham starts his run.
Then, elbows linked, but straight as sailors
On a tilting deck, they move. One, square-shouldered as
    a tailor's
Model, leans over, whispering in the other's ear:
'Go easy. Steps here. This end bowling.'
Turning, I watch Barnes guide Rhodes into fresher air,
As if to continue an innings, though Rhodes may only
    play by ear.

The Cricketer's Companion, 1960

*

Alan Davidson

RICHIE BENAUD

They called him 'Al Pal', or the 'Mayor of Gosford', and he was one of the finest all-round cricketers the world has seen. Few bowlers could match his late swing and awkward movement off the pitch and there weren't many better fieldsmen in any position in the world. As a batsman he more often than not turned the tide for Australia after the early batsmen had failed.

I first struck him in 1945 when he was playing for Gosford High School and represented Northern High Schools against Combined Metropolitan High Schools in a match at the end of the schools season. In those days he was a hard hitting left-hand batsman and, as always, a brilliant fieldsman, but he bowled left arm unorthodox over the wicket deliveries rather than the ones that later made him famous. We went on our first tour together to England in 1953 and thereafter Davidson never missed a match other than through injury, nor an overseas tour. I played against him for a couple of years in this Combined School cricket and then suddenly he came from Gosford to play with Northern Districts and was an immediate success. So much so that he played his first Sheffield Shield match in 1949, only three years after leaving school cricket.

There are great cricketers in every era and Davidson was one of the greatest Australia has produced, particularly in the period from 1957 to 1963. This was after Miller and Lindwall had left the scene—Lindwall temporarily—thus allowing Davidson full scope with the new ball rather than condemning him to come on when the shine had all but disappeared.

He was injury prone—sometimes real, sometimes imaginary—but he never left the field or stopped bowling for any other than a very real reason. I caught Johnny Waite off him one day in Cape Town in one of those dismissals where fieldsmen and captain work on a certain plan and it happens to come off. Alan had been limping back to bowl and then boring in at the batsmen and moving the ball late, either into or away from them. Then he would limp back and Craig would ask him if he were all right—he would say 'no' and get a sympathetic pat on the shoulder and then bore in again and yet another magnificent delivery.

The Cape Town pitch was very slow and I asked Craig if I could come up three yards at gully for the one that flew off the thick edge and wouldn't normally carry. Davo limped back for the next ball and Waite square drove it like a bullet. I caught the red blur, body parallel to the ground, and was just rolling over for the second time when Davo arrived alongside me, saying excitedly, 'It was the old trap, you know. The old trap.' It had taken him just two seconds to get down and the boys thought it was the quickest he had moved all day.

This was the match where, so much was he on the massage table, that we had a copper plaque engraved and nailed on to the massage table and inscribed 'The A. K. Davidson Autograph Massage Table'.

I saw Waite in South Africa some time later and he recalled this particular incident in the context of Davidson's Test performances and bowling skill. Waite contended that Alan was at his best when not feeling 100 per cent fit. He said the real danger time was when you could see him limping back or looking sorry for himself.

I have never played with or against a more penetrative opening bowler, possibly because of the particular angle in which he came at the batsman, bowling from wide of the return crease to a point just outside the off stump and then swinging late to round about middle stump or middle and leg. He wasn't a big swinger of the ball but he certainly moved it as late as anyone I have seen, and this was one of the prime reasons that he was so successful. He only needed to hold the ball across the seam for variety and deliver it with the same action as for the in-swinger and I will defy any batsman in the world to pick the fact that the ball will continue straight on instead of swinging in.

He used to do this sometimes and at other times he would cut the ball away from the right-hander in a fashion that made him the joy of wicket-keeper Wally Grout and his slip fieldsmen. He and Grout used to refer jocularly to the fact that they had 'made' one another, each pointing out that the other would never have done as well without the benefit of either the bowling or wicket-keeping of the other. There was a lot in this for Grout took some magnificent catches off Davidson, both on the off and leg side, and developed a great understanding with him, as well as the ability to pick the way the ball was going to slant.

Willow Patterns, 1969

❊

J. M. Parks at Tunbridge Wells

ALAN ROSS

Parks takes ten off two successive balls from Wright,
A cut to the rhododendrons and a hook for six.
And memory begins suddenly to play its tricks:
I see his father batting, as, if here, he might.

Now Tunbridge Wells, 1951; the hair far lighter,
The body boyish, flesh strung across thin bone,
And arms sinewy as the wrists are thrown
At the spinning ball, the stance much straighter.

Now it is June full of heaped petals
The day steamy, tropical; rain glistens
On the pavilion, shining on corrugated metal.
The closeness has an air that listens.

Then it was Eastbourne, 1935; a date
Phrased like a vintage, sea-fret on the windscreen.
And Parks, rubicund and squat, busily sedate,
Pushing Verity square, moving his score to nineteen.

Images of Then, so neatly parcelled and tied
By ribbons of war—but now through a chance
Resemblance re-opened; a son's stance
At the wicket opens the closed years wide.

And it is no good resisting the interior
Assessment, the fusion of memory and hope
That comes flooding to impose on inferior
Attainment—yesterday, today, twisted like a rope.

Parks drives Wright under dripping green trees,
The images compare and a father waves away
Applause, pale sea like a rug over the knees,
Covering him, the son burying his day

With charmed strokes. And abstractedly watching,
Drowning, I struggle to shake off the Past
Whose arms clasp like a mother, catching
Up with me, summer at half-mast.

The silent inquisitors subside. The crowd,
Curiously unreal in this regency spa, clap,
A confectionery line under bushes heavily bowed
In the damp. Then Parks pierces Wright's leg-trap.

And we come through, back to the present.
Sussex 300 for 2. Moss roses on the hill.
A dry taste in the mouth, but the moment
Sufficient, being what we are, ourselves still.

The Cricketer's Companion, 1959

*

Richie Benaud

CHRISTOPHER MARTIN-JENKINS

The television commentator, whose face and voice are known to millions in Australia and many millions more in Britain, is *really* known to a very few; perhaps only to his wife, Daphne, who became known to Richie through being the most efficient secretary that the formidable E. W. Swanton ever had.

Richie is pretty formidable too, in his own quiet way. He keeps his own counsel. He does a high-pressure job at a savage pace all the year round literally without blinking an eyelid. Never was a more impassive face, a glassier, more unyielding countenance displayed before a camera. But from lips which barely seem to move, in accents and phrases all his own, come, year after year, match after match, words of pungent authority. His knowledge and his impartiality stand out as strongly as his determination to present cricket and its players in the best possible light. Whatever he may have taken out of the game, he has undoubtedly been good for it. No one else has found such favour with the vast majority of cricket viewers at both ends of the world for so long.

That cool exterior is no mask. Behind it lies a calculating brain and a sharp wit. His organization and self-discipline are as immaculate as his attire. Never a crooked tie; never a hair out of place; never hurried; never late; never ruffled. At the end of a day's commentary he introduces the highlights. The editing of these may sometimes be well, sometimes badly balanced. But the man who introduces them is seldom anything other than shrewd in his appraisal of the events of the day or the position of the match. Not that the highlights mark the end of his day. He still has his column to attend to, and often more stories than just one to write. He drives himself extraordinarily hard.

He was the same as a player, and especially as a captain. Such fastidiousness might have made him a rather dull, utilitarian cricketer. He was actually a bold, attacking one; a daring, handsome batsman; an athletic fielder who at Lord's in 1956 held a catch from the blade of Cowdrey's bat in the gully which knocked him over and took the breath away from everyone who saw it; and a leg-break bowler with a perfect action. It gained him more Test wickets than any other leg-spinner in history.

But it was for his captaincy that he became most honoured. How could England have failed to beat Australia in 1958–59 with a side which included May, Cowdrey, Bailey, Dexter, Evans, Graveney, Laker, Lock, Loader, Tyson, Statham and Trueman? Well, one of many reasons, by all accounts, was that Benaud out-captained May. He was quick to see a gap and to go for it; shrewd in finding the right bowlers for the conditions; adept at intimidating the opposition with hustling fields and aggressive bowling. He had been on losing sides against England in 1954–55 and 1956, and he had every motivation for revenge.

In 1961, with Ted Dexter now his adversary, he famously stole a match which Dexter seemed to have won for England by a marvellous attacking innings. Knowing it was hit or miss, Benaud began bowling round the wicket into the rough and, making light of a damaged right shoulder, he spun England to an embarrassing defeat.

Benaud the opportunist and the competitor. He has shown the same quick-witted eye for the main chance in his working life and maintained an admirable standard. He relaxes by playing golf, approaching the game with the same meticulous care he applies to everything else. His clubs are the best you can find; his swing has a professional's arc and strength. He likes to win, and usually does.

Cricket Characters, 1987

*

Club Match

GEORGE MOOR

Across green taffeta the bowler runs
With circling arm. The red ball magnified
Down to the clicking bat. The balls seem suns
Whose planets are the watchers' turning eyes!
The lazy lie with sweet grass in their lips;
The ladies twirl their Japanese sunshades.
All day the ball leaps down, the scratched bat clips;
All day the soft oppressive sun persuades.

The evening offers up the scent of grass
Scorched sweet; the light is little but dies long.
From the pavilion a man will sometimes pass,
Between his lips a drowsy butt of song.
As the moon rises, a great orange glass,
Crickets play on, with clicking sweet and strong.

Beauty and Richness, 1951

*

John Arlott, an Obituary

ANONYMOUS

'After a few comments from Trevor Bailey, it will be Christopher Martin-Jenkins.' With these words, at the end of the Centenary Test against Australia at Lord's in 1980, the distinctive voice of John Arlott ceased to be heard on BBC Radio's ball-by-ball cricket commentaries. Thus ended the career of a broadcaster who extended his presence beyond the bounds of the sport he described with such consummate style. With his rich Hampshire burr, rare gift of description and original turn of phrase, John Arlott delighted, for 35 seasons, not only cricket-lovers but others, including many housewives, who had neither a love nor knowledge of the game. The Arlott accent became one of the most familiar—and most mimicked—in Britain, evoking the essence of both cricket and those qualities of Englishness that surround it—sunny days on village greens and at country pubs and nostalgia for days gone by.

From 1946 until his retirement at the end of the 1980 season Arlott was a member of the BBC ball-by-ball commentary team, covering in that time more than 160 Test matches. In the summer of 1948 his meticulously accurate and colourful descriptions captured the excitement of the matches played in England by Don Bradman's all-conquering Australians and brought huge audiences to the day-long programmes on the BBC Light Programme. He developed a fine sense of timing with which to pace his commentaries. Arlott's broadcasting expertise, knowledge of the game and his audio-charisma were such that he was able to hold the attention of his audience for hours at a time, even when rain stopped play for lengthy periods.

If the rich Arlott accent became synonymous with cricket, Englishness and the BBC, it was not immediately so. In the early post-war days, when Oxbridge English reigned supreme in Broadcasting House, there were those in the organisation who regarded his voice as not quite right for 'the wireless'. Said one BBC executive: 'You have an interesting mind, but a vulgar voice.' Arlott was apparently deterred, fortunately, from attempting to modify his burr by the actor Valentine Dyall who threatened: 'If you change it, I shall personally cut out your tongue.'

John Arlott was also the author of many books, the majority of them on cricket, and from 1968 until 1980 he was cricket correspondent of *The Guardian*.

If this conveys that cricket was Arlott's whole life, that was by no means so. He was a man of many interests and encyclopaedic knowledge. He lived through cricket, and loved it deeply; but the variety of subjects on which he was well-informed often amazed his companions, and he collected, with singular sagacity, aquatints (most of them published between 1775 and 1830) and engraved glass, as well as, inevitably, a well-informed assortment of cricketana. When, before moving to Alderney, which he did within a month of his retirement, he auctioned his wine at Christie's, it was reckoned to be among the best private collections in the country.

Leslie Thomas John Arlott was educated at Queen Mary's School, Basingstoke. His father was assistant registrar and keeper of the town cemetery, where the family lived in the lodge. On leaving school at 16, he became a clerk in a local mental hospital before, in 1934, joining the police force. By 1945, when he resigned from the police as a sergeant, he had spent more time as a detective than on the beat, and his affection for cricket had taken root. By the beginning of the war, through occasional duty at the Hampshire grounds, he had struck up his early friendships with the first-class players of the day.

Arlott entered the BBC in 1945, as a poetry producer, someone having told John Betjeman, who passed on the information, that the police had a poet in their ranks. From the following year, when he began to specialise in cricket (he was never much of a practitioner himself) until his retirement there was hardly a single county cricketer or member of a touring side to England with whom Arlott was not on christian name terms. As president of the Cricketers' Association from 1968, an office which he valued greatly and continued to hold after moving to the Channel Islands, he had a considerable influence on the way in which the first-class game developed.

Arlott was very much closer to the aspirations and thoughts of the 'average' player than to the game's administrators. He had a horror of being looked upon as an 'establishment figure' and never was. He vehemently opposed apartheid and made clear that he would not commentate on the proposed 1970 South Africa Test series in England which subsequently was called off. But during the bitter split caused by the intrusion of Kerry Packer, the Australian entrepreneur, and the creation of World Series Cricket, Arlott's voice was one of moderation. If it had not been for his influence, the 200 or so first-class cricketers over whom he presided might well have acted belligerently enough to have made a settlement between the two sides even more difficult than it was.

The wisdom of his decision to emigrate to Alderney was doubted by many of his friends. He had lived most of his life in Hampshire, the 19 years before his retirement in an old pub in Alresford, and had never been happier than at his oak dining table, surrounded by an untiring audience and numerous bottles of wine. He had a remarkable capacity for work and was a fast worker. His four hymns were written in a single evening: one of them, *God Whose Farm Is All Creation*, is quite widely used. *Fred: A Portrait Of A Fast Bowler*, his book on Trueman, he wrote in a fortnight, during the postal strike of 1971.

Arlott travelled frequently to France, writing several books on wine and being for some years wine correspondent of *The Guardian*. It was more reluctantly that he undertook overseas cricket tours, the only two he made being to South Africa for the BBC in 1948–49 and to Australia as a contributor to the London *Evening News* in 1954–55. Until becoming disenchanted with football, he preferred to stay at home and write about that and to do his monthly article, on all kinds of subjects, for the *Hampshire Magazine*, of which he was a director.

The black tie which Arlott wore from the day the eldest of his three sons was killed in a motor accident in 1968 was the mark of his emotionalism. After his last Test broadcast, the England and Australian players turned and saluted him, a unique tribute which moved him greatly. Soon afterwards, when he was made an honorary life member of MCC (to go with the OBE he was awarded in 1970) he was unsure whether to laugh or cry.

Urged by many friends for many years to write his autobiography he embarked on it without real enthusiasm, writing it in the third person and publishing the first volume, *Basingstoke Boy*, in 1990.

By his first marriage to Dawn Rees, which was dissolved, he had two sons; by the second to Valerie France, who died in 1976, he had one. He married Patricia Hoare a year later.

The Times, December 1991

✳

Hymn on Tomkins' Action

A. A. MILNE

Come sing, my Muse, the Saturday supreme
   (Nor tarry for another's invitation),
When that Great Man, the Captain of our Team—
   Either to hurry up the declaration,
Or since he was a humorist at soul—
Put Tomkins on to bowl.

No breath of wind disturbs the balmy air.
   Our captain, calling 'Woman' indiscreetly,
Padded and gloved leads out his side, and there
   Disposes of the first man rather neatly.
No other catches coming right to hand,
Follows a lengthy stand.

The batsman hits the bowler where he likes,
   To 'off' to 'on'—until at last the Great One,

Not realising that indifferent spikes
    Alone defer the inevitable straight one,
Looks round the field, and sighs, and holloas 'Hi!
Tomkins, *you* have a try.'

Mark how his exultation, ill-concealed,
    Shines in his eyes as he removes his sweater,
And has 'a few balls down' what time the field
    Arrange themselves where they can watch him better:
Five in the deep, and three square-leg, and one
Long stop, out of the sun.

Doubtfully, just at first, he trots around—
    As circles, when disturbed, the anxious plover;
Soon with long strides he glides across the ground,
    Bending his head, as one who makes for cover;
Then, as we wonder if he'll bowl at all,
Stops, and lets fly the ball.

Ah me! a ball too great for little men!
    Deceitfully delivered, full of 'devil',
It rose, and swerved a foot, and 'hung', and then
    For reasons of its own resumed the level,
Bounced much while there, and, bending in from leg,
Removed the middle peg.

For the Luncheon Interval, 1925

*

The Away Game

LOUIS DUFFUS

'Nummy' Deane swore in the slips. A short, vehement oath, more lament than profanity.

'You poor miserable young man,' he might have said in polite company, 'your hopes are doomed.'

And doomed they were, for with that muttered malediction there toppled down in silent dissolution from their dreamy cloud-heights, the airy architecture of years of youthful imagining. As a gale disperses sea spume, so were swept away into Durban's summer air the vision of the green fields of England, the hedgerows, hamlets, half-timbered houses, the song of skylarks, London, Lord's, the glistening snowy slopes of Switzerland, the skyline of Manhattan, the beach of Waikiki— the hundred-and-one fanciful pictures built up around foreign lands.

At that moment, when a contrary kick of the ball turned it away from gloves with the batsman a foot from the crease, any doubts (and there were many) that I would start from this trial game to satisfy the gnawing lust for travel as a cricketer were comprehensively confirmed. Fortunately time was to show that efficiency in flannels was not the only passport to this glamorous dreamland.

We were a school of restless youths—six of us—stimulated to intoxication by assumed delights of what we believed were the romantic places of the earth. Probably no group of individuals swallowed more ravenously than we did the rosy, enticing propaganda of tourist agencies. A bioscope film of ski-ing in the Alps was enough to cause mental ache for weeks. A shop-window scene of the view from the hotel at Banff was a drug the effect of which lasted for days.

If there had existed public houses, where, instead of liquor on shelves, were displayed the poster-artist's invitations to 'Come to Monte Carlo', 'See Holland in Tulip Time' and all the other brands of heady allure, we should have pushed through the side-doors to drink their contents pop-eyed with the irresistible craving of addicts, and no doubt gone home groggy via the gutter.

As it was, we had to be content with smaller, and often self-concocted doses of our own peculiar nectar. All around us was a country richer in colour, vaster in natural splendour, stocked more plenteously with wild life, filled with fascinating native lore, blessed more fabulously with sunshine and with gold and diamonds, than the artificial resorts that disturbed our waking, and often sleeping, hours. Yet we had to yearn, perhaps because they were out of reach, for the tinsel of Paris and the man-made pleasures of Manhattan.

Most of us had camped in the platteland, seen the Victoria Falls, shot at buck, driven within pea-shooter range of lions and giraffes in the Kruger National Park and scaled the Drakensberg, yet we had only scratched the surface of a continent that offered endless exploration. The inconsistent human urge that makes city-bound clerks dream of veld and safaris as they cross the Thames, made us long to sail up London's river. We even came to compiling and exchanging lists of the places which we swore solemnly to see, come fair or frail fortune.

Mine set out the destinations, looked upon as 'musts' by all six—

Switzerland, Paris, New York, the Rockies and Honolulu—and a few like Denmark, Rio de Janeiro and the Vale of Kashmir, which were an individual choice. By common consent Britain was looked upon as a centre for recurrent visit and browsing. Through periodic epidemics we ran high temperatures in a fever of wander-lust. To-day many of the tantalising terminals have been visited, sometimes in disillusionment, but the germ still stirs in fidgety feet.

The imps of imagination worked their hardest on me in the midst of two activities that should have commanded concentrated attention: in the long hours of balancing ledgers, and through sunny Saturdays and Sundays standing on cricket fields. The debits and credits rarely agreed because, although I appeared absorbed in Interest and Amortisation, I was in fact sucking from the pen-holder, as through a hubble-bubble pipe, illicit sensations of distant shores. And when all the world and the skipper thought I was stationed at third man, I was mentally leaning over the rail of a poop deck, meditating on the waterfront of Vancouver.

But let it not be thought that cricket was prostituted to perpetual wool-gathering, a pastime which might have been practised more comfortably on a sunny stoep. While the monotony of accounting drove you to illusory escape, cricket, through the very pleasantness of its associations, inspired the errant mind.

In those days before the authorities, after long pressure, were persuaded that the game should be played on grass, cricket in the Transvaal possessed few of the traditional charms inherent in the fields of England. It was compounded of hardier, cruder character, but none who answered its lure would accept that it was less fascinating, or inferior in feats of skill. Indeed, this was the medium—the matting wicket and the soil outfield—that nurtured the most illustrious of South Africa's cricketers. Faulkner and Vogler, Sinclair, Sherwell, White, Dave Nourse and Herby Taylor.

Its setting had none of England's mellow light. The sun blazed down and burnt into you a two-days' ruddiness. Through the hours you felt the rising warmth of highveld cricket until behind the far-off koppie the sun sank suddenly, like someone pulling down a blind. Then, with a sigh, square-leg would remove his cap.

For the first time throughout the burning summer's day he could see the wicket without frowning through the glare. Another fifteen minutes and the game would be over, for dusk comes hurriedly on the

Witwatersrand. He swept his gaze along the neighbouring range of hills. A brief twilight bathed the lower houses in shadow, but on the ridge-top tiled roofs and golden windows still reflected the day's waning light.

Here through the morning's shimmering heat haze, if cricket had begun with peaceful opening overs and the visiting batsmen were not unduly hasty in wanting to take the shine off the new ball, he might, from his place beside the boundary, have looked beyond the glittering sand of the soil ground to speculate pleasantly upon the movements to be seen in a dozen hillside gardens.

A party of tennis players in white frocks and flannels were walking down the stone steps from a house to the hard court below. One of the players was already on the court waving his racquet. A white-coated servant was coming out of a side door behind them, carrying a tray that gave off a faint glint of glasses and iced drinks.

Next door a native was spraying water from a hose on to a terraced strip of lawn. Beside a thatch-roofed bungalow a girl swung gently in a hammock.

Higher up the hillside he could see figures with bare legs poised in a clearing under a krantz. Every now and then they seemed to fall flat on their faces, leaving behind a faint splash to mark their disappearance.

Or, if visibility were poor, he might just meditate upon the patterns of blue and purple formed by the bloom of jacaranda and bougainvillaea. Another day and the wind would send great woolly clumps of cloud scurrying over the housetops. Artistic pictures they made that tempted the mind away from cricket on midsummer Sunday mornings.

From the ground down in the valley he might see, too, of an afternoon, the great black clouds come creeping from the south-west over the Rand. The symptoms of storm. When the dark curtain was nearly overhead there would be a sudden rush of wind and dust, lightning and thunder, a few large spots of rain falling from the sky—then the downpour and a rush for the pavilion. In a few minutes it would all be over. The sun would be shining again on gleaming wet matting, or else the ground would be flooded and they would all go home.

Now a cloudless day is drawing to a close. The weary bowler sends down a last desperate over. Footsore, sunburnt and blowing with honest fatigue, the cricketers troop off the ground. Their hob-nailed boots clatter over the club-house stoep. It is the hour created by Providence so that men may appreciate showers and long cool drinks.

Congratulations and cheery chaffing echo from the pavilion over the ground. Down in the donga frogs begin a tentative early evening croak. Out in the centre of the oval Sixpence, the ground boy, is methodically rolling up the mat. As he wheels away the pitch he chants a tune of his kraal-land, a low-toned drawling song that his proud ancestors were wont to sing as night fell over the rolling hills of Zululand. From a corner of the plot his wood fire sends over the air its memorable odour of the veld.

Like an incense, its evening scent spread over the sacred ground where cricket was played.

That was one setting for my day-dreams. The other, on a high stool beside a window that looked out over city roof-tops.

One day was like the next except that Mondays, after a week-end of sport—violent in winter and fatiguing in summer—were worst of all. Endless figures to be formed in threes, totted and tidied up, with a month-end search for those that had fallen by the way. Robots we were, or might have been, but for 'Dad', the tall greying Hollander with a beard like General Smuts and internal laughter that shook his massive frame and sent ruddy blushes racing over his mischievous face. How he kept both a sense of humour and cost accounts was as inexplicable to us as his decline to clerkship. For he had been a man of substance in a romantic pre-bomb Europe.

He had travelled to the Argentine to buy horses for the Queen of the Netherlands, hobnobbed in Russia with court officials of the Czar, held high revelry in France, and learned to speak six languages. On warm days after lunch we would find an excuse to consult him and, screened from authority by protecting ledgers, listen enraptured to the exploits of his long departed youth.

On winter days I could edge my stool to a beam of sunlight and watch pigeons on the opposite eaves forever taunting me with their freedom of flight. I looked into the future and saw myself an ageing book-keeper with failing eyesight, rising in dead men's shoes through long years of drudging routine—servile, narrow-minded and spiritless.

The time drew near for the team to leave for England and I could deny the beckonings no longer. It was a career of accounts and security against adventure, uncertainty, perhaps failure, but at least a taste of red-blooded life.

About my only capital was a few years' experience of writing sport in my spare time for a man who had risen the hard way to the sports editorship of the country's largest daily newspaper. I never expect to meet a journalist more tolerant, selfless, or richly endowed with human understanding. I can feel for him now as I recall the embarrassed young man who called on his home on a fateful evening that was to change a whole life, and who suggested that he might send the newspaper some reports of the cricketers' tour in England. Out of pure kindness of heart he committed his company to accept fortnightly mailed articles at the customary, though far from princely, rate of thirty shillings per thousand words.

With that slender contract, the hope of placing similar articles in England, and the cheapest return ticket (except one) that the steamship company provided, I resolved to leave highveld, home and ledgers for whatever kind of wicket St Christopher thought fit to roll out.

The chief of book-keepers took what a later generation would have called a dim view of my irresponsible interruption to a promising future in figures. 'Interruption' was hardly the correct term, for he made it plain that no one would anxiously polish my penholders against my return.

To avoid unnecessarily emphasising the social inequalities existing between the cricketers travelling in luxury suites in the bow, and the would-be 'special correspondent' in the far stern of the ship, and also to give the English Press an opportunity of snapping up, at current rates, advance information about the approaching tourists, I sailed a fortnight before the side.

In the dark of the first morning above the thump and thud of machinery that accompanies a passage in the aftmost regions of a ship, a new harsh, grating sound arose two feet from my bunk pillow. A startled awakening brought forth the complacent explanation from a Lithuanian cabin-mate—'I'm just arranging my mouth.' Every morning, apparently, it was necessary to undertake this gargling adjustment before facing the day. Until it merged into the general symphony of extraneous noises, I used to wonder if perhaps it was a national custom. If someone, such as a milkman, who had occasion to walk through a Lithuanian suburb in the pre-dawn hour might hear echoing down the cobbles a community outburst of mouth arranging.

Otherwise it was an uneventful voyage. The ship's band, somewhere fore, played the popular air of the day, 'Why do I Love You?' and the idle hours were enlivened for me by the presence on board of one of those now dwindling birds of passage—an English professional coach. He was Bert Wensley of Sussex, returning home from Kimberley, and, as an active player of the county, a mine of information on English cricket and cricketers.

As long as modern cricketers can remember, the 'pros' have been coming out to South Africa each Spring. From Yorkshire, Lancashire, Hampshire, Derbyshire, Gloucestershire and other counties they followed the swallows south with the sun. Quaintly-speaking, romantic fellows, they always seemed to young pupils. Adventurers and preachers, bringing a captivating breath of north-country brogue, a vision of tall, smoking chimneys, and the metallic sound of clogs rattling over cobbled streets; or else a suggestion of the sacred air of Lord's and the soft green fields of the south, to the glaring, dusty grounds where cricket used to be played on the African veld.

'Put yer foot across!'

'Keep yer h'elbow up!'

Above the sounds of net practice you would hear their shouts of an evening—Atfield, George Brown, Sam Cadman, Alec Kennedy, Newman, Astill, Lee, Fred Burton, Edwards, Slater, Cox, Bert Wensley, and a dozen more—characters who soon fell to chaffing us with strange attempts to say, 'Hoe gaan dit?' in reply to our Africanised greeting of 'Na lad?'

They were something more than cricket coaches. Recognised as professors of cricket, in their unacademic way, they were just as much teachers of geography, history, humour and dialect. Many a South African youth learnt more of Lancashire's rainfall, the customs of its people and its quaint accents from a professional cricketer on the bench of an iron-roofed cricket pavilion than from a teacher of scholastic distinction in a classroom.

Even if South Africa's young players improve their game under the growing demand for local tuition, something of deep, sentimental attraction will leave the cricket of the land when the last English coach looks back over a boat-rail at the disappearing bulk of Table Mountain.

My closest contact was with Walker Wainwright, the Yorkshire professional, who for ten years came out each season after coaching boys at Winchester.

He would stand behind the net carrying a bat, with which he every now and again played an imaginary stroke, while a young and timid batsman who stood shamefully before scattered stumps, the outcome of a wicked cross-bat shot, listened in awe to the strange language of Sheffield and Leeds.

'Yer all tooked 'oop, Wilfred. If it's up to you, poonch it!'

There would be sounds of bats meeting balls, shouts and laughter from the junior pitches, the dusk giving an air of appealing sadness to the scene, and the voice of the professional correcting those same mistakes that he found in schoolboy cricketers ten years previously and which he continued to find each summer until his last lesson was done.

Sometimes a master would sit on the bench behind the wickets. After thirty years at the school, his days were numbered. He came to drink in once more the evening scene, to revolve memories of thirty summers when Jones Minors failed to get their feet to the pitch of the ball, and from the radiant sunset beyond the koppie, to be soothed into dreaming of Fenner's.

'Watch that 'un', said Wainwright, pointing to a diminutive bowler who, when he crouched to deliver a gigantic spinner, scarcely seemed to come above the top of the bowler's stump. ''E'll be a good bowler some day.'

Generally, however, this crop suffered from inferiority complex when in the 'middle'.

'If I could give 'em each a stiff dose of whisky they'd beat any school team in t' country.

'Reminds me o' Albert Knight, of Leicester', he continued. ''E were a rum fellow, 'e were. Pray 'e would, get down on t' knees and pray each time 'e went in to bat. An' if 'e made nowt, "Well," 'e sez, "it were His wish," and 'e'd let it be. 'E were a gentleman, Albert Knight. 'E'd never call yer Walker, or Tom or 'Arry. Always "Mister Wainwright" it was.'

The sun sank lower. One by one the youngsters trailed off into the gathering gloom. It was just that time of evening when Jack Board, Wainwright's predecessor, wicket-keeper in Lord Hawke's team—he of the twinkling eyes and ruddy complexion—would come up to those youthful enthusiasts whose fervour for cricket encroached upon his dinner hour. 'Ain't yer gotta 'ome?' he would bellow with studiously straight face.

Wainwright came over to the bench with a sly grin. He tilted back his hat, leaned on the bat, and mopped his brow.

'Talkin' of perspirin',' he began, 'I remember Mister Blank at Lord's. 'E always useter pay us sixpence. 'E were a mean 'un. Naturally us "pros" we got to know 'im. Not a "pro" were to be seen when he come lookin' for bowlers. . . . You remember Thompson? Played for Northampton and England. Well, 'e and I were bowling to a gentleman in the nets one day when along comes Jack West to bowl to Mister Blank in t' net next door.

'Jack hadn't bowled to Mister Blank before, so as 'e passed I sez to Jack, "Jack," I sez, "it's only sixpenny tooch." Jack didn't say nowt. First ball 'e bowled 'it t' side o' t' net. Second ball 'it t' other side o' t' net, and t' third ball 'it t' top o' t' net. So then Mister Blank stands up from his crease and glares at Jack. "Look here, West," 'e sez, "I came here to get some practice," 'e sez. "What are you bowling like that for?"

'"Oh, that's on'y t' sixpenny tooch, sir," sez West. "I've got better balls for a shilling." And the gentleman we were bowling to, 'e were a sport, 'e laughed so much I thought we wouldn't have any more practice.'

The native, Jim Fish, was pulling up the last strip of matting before he had finished his tales. Fairy stories they were, of famous players and fields that moved in another, faraway world. Had they no point, they were worth listening to if only for the picturesque Yorkshire dialect employed in their telling.

Fred Geeson, of Leicestershire, had a way of ambling up to the self-same bowler's crease and pulling out the solitary stump with which to demonstrate the pull. 'Put yer h'elbow h'out towards H'Orange Grove', he would say, 'and 'it it 'ard.'

Herby Taylor believes that South African cricketers will inevitably be coached by South African players. There is no reason why they should not make instructors, as good as, if not better than, those who today migrate annually between Cape Town and Southampton in a life of eternal summer.

Yet there are few cricketers who will not feel that with the passing of the English coach something colourful and glamorous will be denied the next age of young South African players.

Cricketers of the Veld, 1946

*

Bodyline and Bradman

RAY ROBINSON

Bodyline shook the nerves of all the Australian batsmen. It intimid-ated Bradman into putting the security of his wicket second to the safety of his body and head; self-preservation remains the first law of nature, even for a Test cricketer. Getting some of his bowling sting into words, Larwood said in his book: 'Whether it is sheer funk or not that makes him draw back I cannot say. But I can say that is the impres-sion which such strokes leave on any critical observer.' That impres-sion was easier to form than to square with Bradman's known temperament.

Don is not a nervy sort. By nature he is calm and self-possessed in everything he does. I once saw him careering at 70 m.p.h. or more along the country highway from Bowral, his home town, in a sports car belonging to 'Wizard' Smith, the racing driver. He coolly took bends at speeds which professional drivers in following cars could not match, despite much swaying, skidding and screeching of tyres. In the first year of the war he enrolled as an air-crew trainee when only two months below the age-limit. Calculating in his decisions, he is immune to stage-fright; he has such a capacity for concentration on the job in hand that the greater the occasion, the tenser the struggle, the bigger the crowd and the louder the noise, the more likely he is to rise to the highest pinnacle of efficiency.

Above all, Bradman is a realist. As such, he recognised instantly that bodyline could not be mastered, that at most it could only be tem-porarily thwarted when conditions handicapped the bowlers. He could see no sense in getting himself knocked about in fruitless martyrdom for a hopeless cause. Any price the enemy had set on his head applied only while he was alive and kicking; he knew that if laid aside by dis-ablement he would not be worth as much as a leg-bye to his team— and might never be the same batsman again.

Midway through the rubber he said he thought it practically impos-sible for even the leading batsmen to make runs against that type of attack without getting at least one or two severe cracks. After the Tests he said that no matter what methods had been adopted he could not conceive that Larwood's attack could possibly have been ineffective. I recall a compassionate comment by Hobbs: 'Bradman would have none of it. He was not going to be hit. He gave it up a little too early, I thought. He has my sympathy.'

The Scar

That stormy season left on Bradman's batsmanship a scar which had not completely faded half a dozen years later.

The Australians' uneasiness about bodyline did not cease when Jardine's team returned home. On their minds was the worry whether it would be unloosed against them again when they visited England in the next year. Bradman wrote an article in August, 1933, urging that the Australian Board of Control should not delay action unduly and said: 'After all, it is the players who have to face the music . . . not the members of the board.'

The members of the board were trying all they knew to obtain an assurance that the same kind of attack would not be used again. After a conversation with the Marylebone Cricket Club's president (Lord Hailsham) the board's representative, Dr Robert Macdonald, a former Queensland cricketer, met a sub-committee of Lord Hawke, Lord Lewisham, Sir Stanley Jackson and Mr W. Findlay, MCC secretary. Macdonald described the talks in what became known as the 'secret letter' because the board decided that members should not disclose its contents even to the State Cricket Association delegates who elected them. The letter said that the MCC sub-committee suggested leaving the matter until the Australian team reached England, when it could be discussed with the captain, manager and any accompanying board members. Macdonald pointed out that the board was entitled to know beforehand whether the English team would use the tactics, because it might be necessary for Australia to include four fast bowlers to maintain the shock attack from both ends in the Test matches.

Lord Hawke: 'Reprisals, by gad!'

Dr Macdonald: 'Not reprisals—reciprocity. Action and reaction on a mutual basis.'

Macdonald's letter added that the friendly relations among the five enabled that to be dismissed laughingly, and the sub-committee agreed that Australia was entitled to know. Its members undertook to give a definite assurance that the tactics would not be used.

In the end, the MCC Committee affirmed that a direct attack by bowler on batsman would be against the spirit of the game but declined to go beyond that by acceding to the board's request for an assurance that the teams could take the field in 1934 with the knowledge that the type of bowling to which exception was taken in Australia would not be repeated.[1] Faced with a deadlock, the Australian board bowed out. Within 48 hours it advised the MCC that it would send a team. The cable was sent before the board chairman (Aubrey Oxlade), who held a telegraphic vote, had received replies from five of the 13 members— Drs A. Robertson and Ramsay Mailer and Messrs. W. L. Kelly (1930 team manager), J. S. Hutcheon and Roger Hartigan (Test century-maker of 1908). In a protest against the board's hurried acceptance Hutcheon and Hartigan said: 'The responsibility of letting Australia down is off our shoulders.'

That was how things stood when the Australians reached England in 1934. Bradman, short of his best in health, handled the situation in a way of his own. In England in 1930 his record-breaking had been combined with a risklessness which crushed bowlers into a state of hopelessness. In the first couple of months of the 1934 tour his batting was far from riskless; he played numbers of adventurous strokes against good balls. He took 10 more innings than in 1930 to reach 1,000. Jardine wrote that Bradman would have considerable difficulty in explaining why he discarded his normal methods in the first three Tests. He said that Bradman almost gave the impression of having made up his mind that a rate of scoring of anything less than eight runs an over was beneath his dignity.

No such vainglorious intent was responsible. Bradman has always been too modest a man and too much a realist for such childishness. I believe his motive was to achieve with cuts and cover-hits something that cables and conversations had not sewn up. He set out to show England's bowlers he was willing to take a chance with strokes against reputable kinds of bowling, that it was not hopeless to try to get him out with length, flight, swerve and spin, that there was no need to resort to bodyline or anything like it.

The effect of some mid-season happenings changed the situation enough to allow Bradman to feel free from the need to continue his self-sacrificing policy of living dangerously. One was that Larwood barred the door of Test cricket against himself by saying he would

[1] Despite the MCC, Voce bowled bodyline against the Australians at Nottingham, in August, 1934, and their protest was supported by the umpires' evidence. It was not until March, 1935, that the MCC instructed umpires to ban a bowler for the remainder of the innings if he persisted with 'direct attack' on batsmen after he had been cautioned.

refuse to play against the Australians and alleging that political influence
had been used with the MCC against Jardine and himself to make the
selection of England's team suitable to the Australians. Another was
the refusal of England's captain, Wyatt, to yield to Bowes' request for
more than four leg-side fieldsmen when the big Yorkshireman was using
bumpers fairly frequently.

In the last two Tests Bradman reverted to his normal method of
playing each ball on its merits. He was again the master but even then
the scar on his batsmanship was visible at times. Early in his great 304
at Leeds he hooked so intemperately at a short one from Bowes that
he hit far above the ball which whizzed a few inches over his stumps.
After a few more bumpers, at the end of an over he walked slowly to
a point more than half-way along the pitch and patted the turf with
studied care, amid a resounding yell from the Yorkshire crowd, who
knew what it was all about. In that great innings he played only 10
false shots in seven hours; nine of them were against Bowes. At the
Oval, where he made 244 in more than five hours without a semblance
of a chance, it was a bumper from Bowes which ended his hopes of
scoring 300 in consecutive Test innings. As the ball climbed near his
cap he tried to hit it to leg with a savage, overhead tennis smash, managed to touch it and was caught by Ames to the leg side of the long-
stop position. In the second innings he was 77 when he drew away
from a ball from Bowes, attempted a hook and lost his leg stump.

So it has been since. Not in every innings or even every match, but
now and again a fast ball rearing at him has apparently caused in
Bradman's mind an unnerving flashback to the days when he was
cricket's hunted stag. Even padding down his left side has not always
given him a feeling of security. Sometimes the bowler was Farnes; at
other times Smith, Allen or Nevell of Middlesex, Clark, Northampton-
shire's fast left-hander, the South African, Crisp, or Perks of Worcestershire, Cowie of New Zealand, or the Victorian, McCormick, who one
November day in 1936 caused Bradman the most cold-sweaty half-hour
he ever endured against an Australian bowler. These incidents have
caused only a momentary flutter in Don's batting. More often than not
they have not cost him his wicket and he has quickly recovered poise.
Mostly they have occurred early on; later in the day he has exacted full
retribution from the bowlers who caused him embarrassment.

After he became Australia's captain Bradman wrote to Gilligan
(England's skipper, 1924–5) before the 1938 tour of Britain a letter which
included: 'Your crying need at present is spin bowling. Australia's attack

for years has been based on length and spin, and what handsome dividends that policy has paid!' If dividends meant matches won, that was a nice point for debate, because in the interval between the times when Australia played two fast bowlers (McDonald–Gregory, 1921, and McCormick–Nash, 1937) Australia had won 12 Tests and England 14, despite the English selectors' weakness for speed. Whether or not Bradman, for once, considered the pen mightier than the bat as an instrument to correct that policy I cannot say, but that passage in his letter prompted Gilligan to say he thought England's policy of banking on fast bowlers needed revision.

To purists the scar is a blemish on Bradman's technique. As it has caused him distressful moments it may seem callous to say so but I wouldn't have him any different. It is one of the things that make him the most interesting, most dramatic batsman modern cricket has known. It adds piquancy to the batting that led Cardus to say Don ought to be given out whenever he misses any sort of ball (even a wide, presumably).

Take an innings when Bradman is ruling the bowlers with a rod of willow and apparently nothing short of an earthquake in mid-wicket can interrupt his progress toward his second or third hundred. The knowledge that the scar is there, and might cause an exciting flurry any time, saves you from being lulled into inattention and perhaps missing the full flavour of his play. Otherwise his very proficiency would sometimes tend to make you sit back and wait until he had scored enough— if ever he feels that way.

Counting everything in, Bradman is the greatest batsman I ever saw. I am grateful for him as he is, scar and all, and would never wish him to be a cricketing counterpart of Superman or some such indestructible character from an adventure strip who overcomes difficulties so easily that he forfeits all claim to credit for his deeds.

Between Wickets, 1948

✻

The Roses Match

Yorkshire v. Lancashire—Old Trafford, 1960

FRED TRUEMAN

The Roses match is a unique cricketing fixture. It would be untrue to say that events at Headingley and Old Trafford during the spring and summer bank holidays have any *direct* link with the troubles of fifteenth century England and yet the indirect ties are there. The county flags, and our blazer badges, are derived from the heraldry which identified the Houses of York and Lancaster, and on the first morning of a modern Roses match it's good to see the actual flowers being worn in the lapels of rival supporters. (While it's easy enough to get the roses in August, I've often wondered about their ready availability during the May game—it must cost a bob or two to go on parade properly dressed at that time of the year.)

Perhaps the oldest story in cricket is about the southerner who ventured into a Roses encounter and his indiscriminating applause finally brought instructions from both his neighbours to 'keep out of this. It's nowt to do with thee.' And that's really the way it is. It is the one fixture a year which means more than any other to the county members and consequently it is not surprising that the legends have grown about it.

Now legends (or at least good legends) have their bases in fact and there is no shortage of fact in the stories which have been handed down. Those who saw the grim, tight-lipped battles of pre-war years will need no convincing about the truth of Emmott Robinson's terse summary of conversation on those occasions, 'We say "How do" in't morning and "Good neet" at t'close and in between we just say, "How's that?"' Emmott was the archetypal Yorkshire professional of the pre-war years and no one who met and talked cricket to him for even thirty seconds would doubt the sheer passion of his involvement in all county matches but the Roses game in particular.

It is said that he made a point of getting to one match earlier than anyone else and, having checked that no one had yet arrived in either dressing room, Emmott took a cushion, went into the showers, removed his trilby hat and knelt to pray: 'Oh Lord, I know that Thou art the great Judge of any cricket match between county or nation. Today

Yorkshire and Lancashire meet in the Roses match. If Yorkshire are the better side, they'll win; if Lancashire are the better side, *they* will win [he must have said that with an utter lack of conviction]. And if there's rain it will probably be a draw. But, Oh Lord, if You will just keep out of it for three days we'll knock Holy Hell out of 'em.'

That sums up as accurately as anything can the feeling of the men who took part in Roses matches of the twenties and thirties. The war changed men and it changed their attitudes. The games of the mid- and late-forties brought together men who had spent long years serving alongside each other and it was difficult to retain the atmosphere of passionate rivalry bordering upon naked hostility.

Nevertheless, the unique atmosphere of the game itself remained. Huge crowds, starved of top-level competitive sport, still crowded into the grounds for the biannual fixtures; gates were closed before eleven o'clock on the Saturday and Monday; and the players, while exchanging a few more elaborate greetings than 'How do' and 'Good neet' were nevertheless locked in mortal combat from the moment the first ball was delivered. Personal rivalries were born and some of them stretched over the years and, in some cases, into different counties.

In the mid-seventies, Leicestershire were playing Yorkshire at Park Avenue, Bradford, and Don Oslear (later to become a Test match umpire) was having his first season of county championship cricket. Roses match blood-letting was something Don had merely read about and certainly he had no reason to expect to encounter it in a game involving Leicestershire. But Leicestershire included in their ranks Ken Higgs—not a native Lancastrian by any stretch of imagination but one who had known the heat and toil of the day in many a Yorkist–Lancastrian skirmish. And he was bowling now to a cordially hated foe, Geoffrey Boycott.

Higgs caused a few playings and missings and suddenly he was transported, no longer was he wearing the leaping fox of the hunting shires but the Red Rose which had seen the slaughter of Towton and Tewkesbury. He denounced Boycott, in the time-honoured prose of fast bowlers, as a 'spawny bastard'. Boycott's reply was not essentially conciliatory. The battle of words grew in intensity to the horrified astonishment of Umpire Oslear. He spoke to the bowler; he spoke to the batsman. Neither took the slightest notice. Finally, he spoke to the Leicestershire captain who happened to be Ray Illingworth, a man not unaccustomed to such exchanges. Illingworth nodded and walked away.

At the end of the over Illingworth strolled over to the other umpire,

Cec. Pepper, and laconically suggested, 'Ask your mate not to interfere in private Roses battles, Pep.'

My earliest memory of a Roses match is one of wonderment. First of all it was only my third first-class game and the other two had been against universities. To be transported into the atmosphere of Old Trafford, 1949, from the tranquil hush of the Parks and Fenner's was like flying to the moon. Sixteen or seventeen international players thronged the dressing rooms, the atmosphere in the ground was tense and highly charged, and the cricket was played with an intensity I was never to find surpassed in any Test. But for the moment it was enough to be there—playing alongside the legendary Len Hutton, every Yorkshire schoolboy's hero.

Rain delayed the start and we batted in the afternoon. At close of play, Leonard was 60 not out and next day he was given some stick in the Sunday papers. (His scoring rate might have seemed like indecent haste in a pre-war game but we now had a new generation of cricket writers who did not appreciate such matters. A not-out 60 on a rain-affected wicket was apparently something to be dismissed with contempt.)

On the Monday morning Len asked me to go out and bowl a few to him in the nets. He returned to the dressing room, changed his shirt, had a cup of tea and then went out and hit the first ball of the day straight back over Bill Roberts' head for six. He went on to make 201 of the most fantastic runs I have ever seen. In the second innings, feeling unwell, he batted lower down the order and was 96 not out when Norman Yardley declared. The man I had revered as I grew up had done his stuff for me, and in the Roses match too. Three years later, when I was called up to play in my first Test I was to breathe my silent gratitude to the Roses match because I had been a bit worried about how I would feel in the atmosphere of international cricket. I need not have worried. The pressures of Test cricket proved to be nothing like those of the game against Lancashire I had played in the previous weekend!

But of all the forty or so of those matches I experienced, the one which always springs immediately to mind is the game at Old Trafford on 30 July, 1 and 2 August 1960. Although we won the championship that year we lost twice to Lancashire, our nearest rivals in the championship, and that caused more despondency than the title brought delight.

'Noddy' Pullar, who often formed a threesome with 'George' Statham, my bowler partner and myself when we were on tour, was no mate in the Roses series. At the time he was in a very good trot which brought him a Roses average of around 70 over four seasons, and in the Whitsuntide game he had hit 121 at Headingley where we were beaten by ten wickets on a spinner's pitch.

In a summer of wretched weather we drew seven matches, won five and lost two before we went to Old Trafford itching to wipe out the memory of that defeat at Headingley. Lancashire were chasing us for the title as well, so the August bank holiday game had even more than the usual Roses significance. Again it was a rain-affected three days and Statham and Higgs bowled us out for 154 in the first innings, getting a lead of 72 largely through the batting of Bob Barber and Alan Wharton. In our second innings we were rolled over for 149, giving Brian Statham 9 for 66 in the match. Lancashire needed only 78 to win and they had all afternoon to get them. It was the sort of situation which would prompt many counties to make a token attempt to get amongst the wickets with their front-line attack and then, as the situation became more hopeless, to introduce the more occasional bowlers to get the job over and out of the way. Not in this case. This was the Roses match.

The Lancashire spinners, Dyson, Higgs and Barber, had all taken wickets in our second innings as well as Statham and it would be alien to all Yorkshire tradition to neglect an opportunity to bowl their spinners. Indeed, I think it was Cardus who recalled meeting George Hirst and Wilfred Rhodes gloomily trudging through Regent's Park one gloriously sunny Sunday morning after a wet Saturday at Lord's. 'Why so solemn,' he asked, 'on such a beautiful morning?'

'It's a grand morning all right,' muttered Rhodes sombrely. 'We were just talking about that "sticky" that's going to waste up t'road.'

So starting with spin was certainly one of the ploys discussed as we planned our campaign in the dressing room. Finally it was discarded as carrying too many risks and we decided on a pace attack, making every possible use of the lift that was in the pitch to give the batsmen as much trouble as possible, with a defensive field setting. We would try to force Lancashire into mistakes while cutting off as many scoring opportunities as possible.

We could not reasonably expect to bowl them out but we could hope to put them under pressure when they got behind the clock. Above all, we wanted to prevent a Lancashire win. Well, don't tell anybody who saw that Tuesday afternoon's play that defensive cricket can never be exciting because I'm pretty sure no one who saw it will ever forget the next two hours.

My partner was Mel Ryan, who had never had a settled place in the side and in fact played only a handful of matches each season. His experience of bowling 'tight', therefore, was limited but he bowled magnificently and although his fifteen overs cost 50 runs that wouldn't be considered particularly expensive in any other context— and he kept chipping in with a wicket as well. At the other end I think I am entitled to count that unchanged spell of sixteen overs as one of the best pieces of bowling in my career.

We set out to put Lancashire under pressure and we didn't half succeed. As wickets went down, with the target of 78 to win getting closer only by painful degrees, hopes began to rise on our side and something close to panic set in on the other. No one left the ground. On the contrary, as the news filtered back to the city centre the offices and shops of Manchester began to empty and the ground to fill. It took a man with no nerves at all, whatever the situation, to swing the pendulum slightly against us—'Chimp' Clayton, the Lancashire wicketkeeper. He had contrived 15 runs which were worth their weight in gold but he was the non-striker when the last ball of the match came to be bowled at a quarter past five. Lancashire were 77 for 8—the scores were level. A wicket would give us a draw; a ball that merely did not yield a run would give us a draw too.

The field was distributed with painstaking care. Everyone chipped in with advice but it was FST who had to bowl that last delivery. The batsman was Jack Dyson, an off-spinning all-rounder who also played football for Manchester City. With all due respect we knew he wasn't especially partial to quick bowling and it was all too clear that he was acutely conscious of the situation. Clayton was pacing about at the other end, wishing like mad he had the strike and giving Dyson all kinds of instructions which I'm sure Jack didn't even hear. I gave him a last lingering look before starting to walk back and I think he expected a bouncer.

That walk back took rather a long time because I was turning over in my mind the problem of what ball to bowl. Finally, I decided on that old standby, usually regarded as the classic delivery for such a situation, the yorker. I concentrated hard, started to run in, my mind filled with a picture of the bottom of the leg-and-middle stump. It was as good a yorker as I have ever bowled but Dyson countered with the only possible effective answer. He shuffled forward, bat and pad close together, and somehow he got an edge. It was an edge just thick enough to deflect the ball wide of Jimmy Binks' outstretched glove and away the ball went to the fine-leg boundary. Coldly the Yorkshire handbook records, 'Yorkshire lost by two wickets at 5.15 p.m. on the third day.' It says nothing of the drama, and the heartbreak, of one single delivery. My figures at the end of a marathon stint read: 16 overs, 4 maidens, 28 runs, 2 wickets. It was as good a spell of bowling as I ever produced in my career but I would have traded one or two more spectacular-looking Test analyses for a runs column which simply read '24' instead of '28'. That was the importance of the Roses match.

Afterwards, as I smoked a reflective pipe in a hushed and disappointed dressing room, my old mate Brian Statham came in and said, 'F.S., one of the best matches I have ever seen; certainly the best Roses match I have ever played in. And after that bowling performance by you and Mel Ryan this afternoon all I can say is, "You were bloody unlucky."'

Unlucky we might have been; gracious, certainly, was that tribute from George. And we still won the championship by 32 points—from Lancashire. But they would count their disappointment in that direction as nothing beside the delight of recording a double over the ancient enemy—as we would have done. Twenty years later I think of the 1960 season not as one when we won the championship but as the time we were beaten twice by Lancashire—and a thick edge off my last ball brought the winning runs. Such wounds are slow to heal . . . .

My Most Memorable Matches, 1982

*

While Roses Blow

THOMAS MOULT

While roses blow the cricket-field is yours.
Measure their season: so your lease endures.
    Match with their fragrance every fruitful sound:
    Tread worthily this sunlit slip of ground.
Soon (ah, too soon!) the autumn's cloud obscures
The sun, and, sunless, never the rose matures,
Or the white-flowering game. What bloom allures
    That's winter-nipped? What bat when football's round?

    While roses blow
Be cricket-hearted. Thus your play ensures
More than a bowler's tricks or many fours.

> It means when summer fades your winter's crowned
> By summer still; great players are most renowned
> For the warm graces that the fame makes yours
> While roses blow.

Willow Patterns, 1969

*

Exit the Amateur

E. W. SWANTON

Brisbane, November 1962. In the context of history the 535th Test match (as I judge it to be), which in a day or two will be making quite a stir in these parts and at home, must seem a small matter compared with the news contained in my breakfast-time cable this morning.

'Amateurs abolished' it announced laconically, and behind the words one saw *finis* written to the oldest of all the traditional rivalries of the cricket field. Not only that, of course. The evolution of the game has been stimulated from its beginnings by the fusion of the two strains, each of which has drawn strength and inspiration from the other. English cricket has been at its best when there has been a reasonably even balance between those who have made the game their livelihood and those who have played it, with whatever degree of application and endeavour, basically for relaxation and enjoyment.

It is easy to wax romantic over the disappearance of the amateur, and I imagine the change will be regretted instinctively by all with any knowledge of the background. On first thought, it is perhaps hard to separate sentiment from practical reality. I can only say, having made the effort, and having regarded the possibility of the decision for some while, that the change strikes me as not only unnecessary but deplorable.

Cricket professionalism has been an honourable estate ever since the first-class game began to take its present form in the middle of the 1890s. But it is, of its nature, dependent, and the essence of leadership is independence. To some extent one must see the change in terms of leadership. This is not to say there have not been some admirable professional captains. Tom Dollery showed the way with Warwickshire, and all know how much the 1962 champions and their runners-up owed respectively to J. V. Wilson and D. Kenyon. Equally, there have been some indifferent amateur captains, and anyone can elaborate this remark according to taste.

Yet other things being roughly equal, there are obvious advantages, especially to the players themselves, in the control of an independent agent with only a season's tenure. The alternative is control by a player from a staff whose members have served their apprenticeship, and graduated, together. A county club have always been able to sack their amateur if he has not given satisfaction, as we have seen. It is by no means so easy to demote a professional captain, as we have also seen.

It has been said, of course, that the word amateur is an anachronism, that to preserve the status is mere humbug. I wonder. As soon as the broken-time principle was sanctioned, and advertising restrictions removed, a distinction was created between the few who cashed in on various perquisites of their fame, and the Simon-Pure amateur. But the latter category was far from extinct. What services in this last decade and more have not D. J. Insole and J. J. Warr rendered respectively to Essex and Middlesex! Each preferred to make a personal sacrifice in order to maintain his independence. It is doubtful whether either would have been elected a county captain when he was, under the new dispensation. It is equally unlikely that my friend, henceforward to be known as Mackenzie (A. C. D. Ingleby-), would have emerged at the age of 24 to captain Hampshire. He would have been lost to the City, or more probably to the Turf, and if half the personal tributes to him are to be believed, Hampshire would never have enthused the cricket world last year by gaining their first Championship. Counties will be inclined to take the safe course when vacancies occur, and appoint the senior man rather than run the risk of jealousies.

With the disappearance in due time of such characters as I have named, will there emerge some system of non-playing managership in order to sustain the captain and help impose discipline? This could happen, and it might even work well. But one is apprehensive of the effect of more control from the committee room.

Again, although I disliked the amateur anomalies as much as the abolitionists, the time when the future structure of the first-class game was precariously in the balance was surely the wrong one to introduce a classless society on the cricket field. If a six-day-a-week Championship is on the way out, might not the future pattern have involved smaller staffs and an inflow of unpaid talent operating mostly at week-ends? The amateur can scarcely be revived now. That section of the history

book is closed tight for ever. When, last summer, a Yorkshire admin-
istrator was advocating what has now come to pass, he was asked the
question: 'If amateur status were to be abolished, would a single
player be brought into the county who could not now be considered?'
He could not say so. That, surely, is an acid question.

Whom will the change include? Whom will it exclude? I only hope that
time proves me a pessimist as well as, patently, a crusted reactionary.

As I Said at the Time, 1983

*

The One-Way Critic

R. C. ROBERTSON-GLASGOW

Upon the groaning bench he took his seat—
    Sunlight and shadow on the dew-blessed grass—
He spread the *Daily Moan* beneath his feet,
    Hitched to his eye an astigmatic glass,
Then, like a corn-crake calling to an owl
    That knows no answer, he began to curse,
Remarking, with an unattractive scowl,
    'The state of cricket goes from bad to worse;
Where are the bowlers of my boyhood's prime?
    Where are the batsmen of the pristine years?
Where are the fieldsmen of the former time?'
    And, as he spoke, my eyelids filled with tears;
For I perhaps alone, knew they were dead,
    Mynn an old myth, and Hambledon a name.
And it occurred to me that I had read
    (In classroom) 'All things always are the same';
So, comfort drawing from this maxim, turned
    To the myopic moaner on the seat;
A flame of rage, not pity, in me burned,
    Yet I replied in accents clear and sweet—
'There *were* no bowlers in your boyhood's prime,
    There *were* no batsmen in the pristine years,
There *were* no fieldsmen in that former time'—
    My voice grew firm, my eyes were dry of tears—

'*Your* fathers cursed the bowlers you adored,
   Your fathers damned the batsmen of your choice,
Your fine, ecstatic rapture they deplored,
   There was the *One-Way Critic*'s ageless voice,
And their immortal curse is yours today,
   The croak which kills all airy Cricket Dryads,
Withers the light on tree and grass and spray,
   The strangling fugue of senile jeremiads.'

I ceas'd; and turn'd to Larwood's bounding run,
And Woolley's rapier flashing in the sun.

                The Brighter Side of Cricket, 1933

*

Packer's Circuit

KIT WRIGHT

Something about this game
eternally fades, to bring
the lost outfielders in,

those whited ruminants
under the layers of green
whom old men at the field-edge

dream, dead name by name,
that played the day with a weeping
willow for ashes, ashes,

till you could believe, by a thin
tide of shadow that washes
play to its close, the ball

swung most sharply in tear-gas,
the rotten grave took spin,
a ghost could make a hundred

with the board of a coffin lid
and Father Time himself
scythe off his balls and sing

for something about this game
eternally fades, to bring
the lost outfielders in.

The Cricketer's Companion, 1960

✳

The Light and the Dark

C. L. R. JAMES

'The Negroid population of the West Indies is composed of a large percentage of actually black people and about fifteen or twenty per cent of
people who are a varying combination of white and black. From the days of
slavery these have always claimed superiority to the ordinary black, and a substantial majority of them still do so (though resenting as bitterly as the black
assumptions of white superiority). With emancipation in 1834 the blacks themselves established a middle class. But between the brown-skinned middle class
and the black there is a continual rivalry, distrust and ill-feeling, which, skilfully played upon by the European peoples, poisons the life of the community. Where so many crosses and colours meet and mingle the shades are
naturally difficult to determine and the resulting confusion is immense. There
are the nearly white hanging on tooth and nail to the fringes of white society, and these, as is easy to understand, hate contact with the darker skin far
more than some of the broader-minded whites. Then there are the browns,
intermediates, who cannot by any stretch of imagination pass as white, but
who will not go one inch towards mixing with people darker than themselves. And so on, and on, and on. Associations are formed of brown
people who will not admit into their number those too much darker than
themselves, and there have been heated arguments in committee as to whether
such and such a person's skin was fair enough to allow him or her to be
admitted without lowering the tone of the institution. Clubs have been known
to accept the daughter who was fair and refuse the father who was black; the
dark-skinned brother in a fair-skinned family is sometimes the subject of jeers
and insults and open intimations that his presence is not required at the family social functions. Fair-skinned girls who marry dark men are often ostra-
cized by their families and given up as lost. There have been cases of fair
women who have been content to live with black men but would not marry
them. Should the darker man, however, have money or position of some

kind, he may aspire, and it is not too much to say that in a West Indian colony the surest sign of a man having arrived is the fact that he keeps company with people lighter in complexion than himself. Remember, finally, that the people most affected by this are people of the middle class who, lacking the hard contact with realities of the masses and unable to attain to the freedoms of a leisured class, are more than all types of people given to trivial divisions and subdivisions of social rank and precedence.'

I had gone to school for years with many of the Maple players. But I was dark. Left to myself I would never have applied for membership to the Maple Club. Some of them wanted me, not all subscribed to the declaration of independence of the Founding Fathers. The Maple cricket captain, concerned only with getting good men for his team, declared that he had no patience with all that foolishness and he was ready to have James in the club; also his brother was married to my mother's sister. He approached me in a roundabout manner: 'Well, I hear you want to join us,' he said with a big smile.

Other faces also wore smiles. When I was scoring heavily W. St Hill had made it his business to come and watch me at the nets. He had told his friends that James could bat and was a coming man. Already whenever he and I met we used to talk. Similarly with Constantine Jnr. Though St Hill and Learie said nothing to me, Shannon wanted me to join them and let me know it. My social and political instincts, nursed on Dickens and Thackeray, were beginning to clarify themselves. As powerful a pull as any was the brilliant cricket Shannon played. Pride also, perhaps, impelled me to join them. In social life I was not bothered by my dark skin and had friends everywhere. It was the principle on which the Maple Club was founded which stuck in my throat.

Interested paragraphs began to appear in the Press that I was joining this one or the other. Finally I decided to do what even then I very rarely did—I decided to ask advice. I spoke to Mr Roach, Clifford Roach's father, a close friend, himself a brown man, but one openly contemptuous of these colour lines. He listened gravely and told me to let him think it over, he would talk to me in a day or two. (Clifford, as tens of thousands of English people know, was as dark as I am, but his hair was not curly and both his parents were brown.)

When Mr Roach was ready he said: 'I understand exactly how you feel about all this God-damned nonsense. But many of the Maple boys are your friends and mine. These are the people whom you are going to meet in life. Join them; it will be better in the end.'

Not altogether convinced, but reassured, I joined Maple and played

cricket and football for them for years. I made fast friends, I became
a member of the committee and vice-captain of the cricket club. The
original colour exclusiveness of the Maple Club has gradually faded
out, but it mattered very much then, in fact it was my first serious personal problem. For that I did not want to be a lawyer and make a lot
of money and be nominated to the Legislative Council by the Governor,
that I preferred to read what I wanted rather than study statics and
dynamics, those were never problems to me. They involved me in
conflict with others. They cost me no inner stress. This did. If Mr
Roach had told me to join Shannon I would have done so without
hesitation. But the social milieu in which I had been brought up was
working on me. I was teaching, I was known as a man cultivated in
literature, I was giving lectures to literary societies on Wordsworth and
Longfellow. Already I was writing. I moved easily in any society in
which I found myself. So it was that I became one of those dark men
whose 'surest sign of . . . having arrived is the fact that he keeps company with people lighter in complexion than himself'.

My decision cost me a great deal. For one thing it prevented me
from ever becoming really intimate with W. St Hill, and kept Learie
Constantine and myself apart for a long time. Faced with the funda-
mental divisions in the island, I had gone to the right and, by cutting
myself off from the popular side, delayed my political development for
years. But no one could see that then, least of all me.

The foregoing makes it easy to misunderstand the atmosphere in which
we played. We never quarrelled. When we played scratch matches or
went to the country on Sundays for a holiday game, Shannon, Maple
and Stingo members mixed easily on the same side. They sent or came
to find me for such games; I went or sent to find them. Where the
antagonisms and differences appeared was in the actual cricket, the
strokes, the length and the catches.

To begin with we all played on the same field. Except for the Queen's
Park Club with its Oval, we all had pitches on the Queen's Park
Savannah, one of the finest open grounds in the world, where thirty
full-size matches can be played without crowding. The grounds of
Maple, Shannon, Stingo and Constabulary were so close that you could
stand on one spot and watch them all at practice. The wickets were
coconut matting on hard clay. They were much the same for all four
innings and on a well-prepared wicket the rise of the ball was fairly
regular. But they took all the spin you put on the ball and there was
always some lift. On the whole, against bowlers who could use it, the

matting was difficult. No visitor ever made a century on it against Trinidad bowlers until 1930. In the Savannah, where the wickets were not so well prepared as at the Oval, there might be a canvas patch just where a good-length ball dropped; a strong breeze blew intermittently from the Dry River. Batting was a problem and fifty runs a triumph. Especially against Shannon, and most especially for a Maple batsman against Shannon. For the Shannon Club played with a spirit and relentlessness, they were supported by the crowd with a jealous enthusiasm which even then showed the social passions which were using cricket as a medium of expression.

Shannon opened their bowling with Constantine and Edwin St Hill, both Test players. In time I opened the Maple batting with Clifford Roach, and I have looked with real envy on English batsmen who opened the England innings against Waite and McCabe of Australia on the monstrous billiard tables of the thirties. First change was Victor Pascall, for long years the best slow left-hander in the West Indies, who had visited England in 1923. Then might follow Cyl St Hill, well over six feet, fast left-hand, his arm as straight as a post. When he dropped the ball on the off-stump it might straighten, to take the outside edge of the bat, or continue to the inside of your ribs. Cyril Fraser, genuine leg-spinner, sound bat and a brilliant field anywhere, would be welcome in most English counties today (though not in the thirties). I exaggerate? I do no such thing.

Take Ben Sealey. Ben made 1,000 runs with three centuries in England in 1933. He was fourth or fifth change for Shannon and took only fifteen wickets in England. On the matting wicket he took three steps, dropped the ball on the leg-wicket at medium pace and could hit the top of the off-stump three times in an over. The English team came in 1930. Ben had Hendren, Haig and Calthorpe in the first match for fifteen runs and, in the second, Sandham, G. T. S. Stevens, Townsend and Astill for thirteen in fifteen overs, nine of which were maidens. In the second innings he bowled nine overs, of which six were maidens, for one wicket. This was at the Queen's Park Oval where the wicket was of a better quality than in the Savannah. I stood next to the sightscreen and enjoyed the sight of these famous batsmen in the same mess as myself with Ben's leg-break. At their best, under their own conditions in the Queen's Park Savannah, the Shannon bowling and fielding would have made a shambles of most English counties then or now. In 1929 the bowling of the Trinidad eleven which won the intercolonial cup consisted of the six Shannon bowlers.

It was not mere skill. They played as if they knew that their club represented the great mass of black people in the island. The crowd did not look at Stingo in the same way. Stingo did not have status enough. Stingo did not show that pride and impersonal ambition which distinguished Shannon. As clearly as if it was written across the sky, their play said: Here, on the cricket field if nowhere else, all men in the island are equal, and we are the best men in the island. They had sting without the venom. No Australian team could teach them anything in relentless concentration. They missed few catches, and looked upon one of their number who committed such a crime as a potential Fifth Columnist. Wilton St Hill chased a ball from slip to third-man as if he were saving the match and not a possible single. Except for the Constantine family, the patriarch, Old Cons, the always genial Learie and his benign uncle, Pascall, Shannon were not given to smiling on the field, and he was an utter nincompoop who was deceived into believing that the Constantine clan was not of the true Shannon toughness. They were not tough with you; they were tough with one another. I have seen Fraser signal for a glove and run to meet Ben Sealey who ran out with one. They met half-way, threw the gloves at ten yards distance, each catching with one hand; and almost before Ben was off the field Fraser was at the wicket ready to bat, while the ground rippled with applause. The crowd expected it from them, and if they lapsed let them know. Queen's Park were the big shots . . . and the great batsmen? They would bowl them out, and show them some batting too. As for Maple, with our insolent rejection of black men, they would show us. They usually did.

Sharp as were the tensions underlying a Maple–Shannon match, their sportsmanship was clean and good fellowship kept breaking in on the field of play. After all, Ben Sealey's family and friends were very close to mine. Sealey, Fraser and I went from sports ground to sports ground competing in athletics. I didn't run as they did, but I used to jump and for years beat them every time—no Shannon superiority there. Clifford Roach was an untalkative but cheerful soul. Whenever he, opening international batsman, and Constantine, opening international bowler, faced each other they had rare fun. I played two high-rising balls from Edwin St Hill down in front of me. At the end of the over, without turning his head, the grim-faced Wilton St Hill murmured as he passed, 'What you think you will get by playing at those!' Next over I dropped my bat out of the way of a similar ball and was weak enough to steal a glance at him. I was met by a stony stare. Later in the week, however, when we met casually, he gave me a long disquisition on the technique of playing such balls, illustrated with reminiscences of Challenor and other players. Challenor might leave one alone. If you bowled him another he got over it and cut through the slips.

Constantine, a privileged person, especially with me, between overs would discuss my play freely. 'You played back to that one?' 'What should I have done?' 'Jumped at it, of course. That's the second time Ben had been on since your are in.' 'Suits you.'

From a fast-rising ball he made one of his incredible back-strokes over mid-on's head. Mid-on, a very tall man, jumped and threw up his hand. The ball touched the very tip of a finger, giving the illusion of a chance. At the end of the over Constantine came over to me in a great wrath. 'That damned Hamid spoilt my stroke,' he complained. 'What did he interfere with it for?'

These were but moments. They were out to beat us, to humble us, to put us in our place. We fought back of course, but in ten years we beat them only once. In another game they had eighty to make, reached 70 for three and won by only one wicket. That day you would have thought they were the last of the Three Hundred at Thermopylae. Constantine had fallen seriously ill after the three-Saturday match had begun. He was looking on and when the eighth wicket fell crawled in to bat in ordinary shoes and clothes. He moved into the wicket to play back, but hadn't the strength to bring his bat down in time and I had him lbw first ball. David, the last man, a slow left-hand bowler, was so frightened that the next ball was in the wicketkeeper's hand before he had finished raising his bat. I have never forgiven myself for not bowling him neck and crop with a plain, straight, pitched-up ball.

Shannon! It is another of their credits that they bore me no ill-will for not joining them. Keen and devoted, they appreciated the same in me. Constantine told me one day, in the only reference he ever made to it: 'If you had joined us we would have made you play cricket.' He meant as an international player. The remark was a tribute to Shannon, not to me. Years afterwards, in a quite insignificant friendly match in Lancashire, I was standing at short-leg when some batsman played an uppish stroke in my direction. Not one county cricketer in three could possibly have got to it, and in any case friendly is friendly. So I thought, until I heard a savage shout from Constantine who had bowled the ball. 'Get to it!' I recognized the note. It was one Shannon player calling to another.

Shannonism symbolized the dynamic forces of the West Indies

yesterday. I ask the question Gibbon first asked and so many historians have followed, and my answer is this: If by some unimaginable catastrophe cricket had been wiped away from the face of the earth the Shannon Club would have preserved cricket's accumulated skills, its historical traditions and its virtues,[1] uncontaminated by any vice and endowed with a sufficient vitality to ensure reconquest of the world. But there was racialism! So what? I am the one to complain. I don't. 'But racialism! In cricket!' Those exquisites remind me of ribaldry about Kant's Categorical Imperative: there was racialism in cricket, there is racialism in cricket, there will always be racialism in cricket. But there ought not to be.

Beyond a Boundary, 1963

*

At Sabina Park

STEWART BROWN

Proudly wearing the rosette
of my skin I strut into Sabina,
England boycotting excitement
bravely, something badly amiss.

Cricket. Not the game they play
at Lord's, the crowd (whoever saw
a crowd at a cricket match?)
are caged, vociferous partisans

quick to take offence. England
sixty eight for none at lunch.
'What sort o battin dat man?
dem caan play cricket again, praps
dem should a borrow Lawrence Rowe!'

---

[1] It is so throughout the West Indies. George Headley who, behind his reserve, is a very human creature, likes a flutter. But as captain of a West Indian Test side, having to toss a coin against G. O. Allen, he found himself in a cold sweat of self-condemnation at spinning a coin on cricket. It took him some time to realize that he was not committing a breach of what had become an integral part of his personality, the ethics of cricket.

And on it goes, the wicket slow
as the batting and the crowd restless.
'Eh white bwoy, ow you brudders dem
does sen we sleep so? Me a pay monies

fe watch dis foolishness? Cho?'
So I try to explain in my Hampshire
drawl about conditions in Kent,
about sticky wickets and muggy days
and the monsoon season in Manchester

but fail to convince even myself.

*

Rites

EDWARD KAMAU BRATHWAITE

Many a time I have seen him savin'
the side (the tailor was saying
as he sat and sewed in his shop).

At de Oval?
Wha' happen las' week at de Oval?

You mean to say that you come
in here wid dat lime-skin cone

that you callin' a hat
pun you head, an' them slip slop shoe strap

on to you foot like a touris';
you sprawl you ass

all over my chair widdout ask-
in' me please leave nor licence,

wastin' muh time when you know very well that uh cahn fine
enough to finish these zoot suits

'fore Christmas' an' on top
o'all this, you could wine up de nerve to stop

me cool cool cool in de middle
o'all me needle

an' t'read; make me prick me hand in me haste;
an' tell me broad an' bole to me face

THAT YOU DOAN REALLY KNOW WHA' HAPPEN
at Kensington Oval?

We was *only* playin' de MCC, man;
M-C-C
who come all de way out from Inglan.

We was battin', you see;
score wasn't too bad; one
hurren an' ninety-

seven fuh three.
The openers out, Tae Worrell out,
Everton Weekes jus' glide two fuh fifty

an' jack is de GIANT to come!
Feller name Wardle
was bowlin'; tossin' it up

sweet sweet slow-medium syrup.
Firs' ball . . .
'No . . . o . . . o . . .'

back down de wicket to Wardle.
Secon' ball . . .
'N . . . o . . . o . . .'

back down de wicket to Wardle.
Third ball comin' up
an' we know wha' goin' happen to syrup:

Clyde back pun he back
foot an' *prax*!
is through extra cover an' four red runs all de way.

'You see dat shot?' the people was shoutin';
'Jesus Chrise, man, wunna see dat shot?'
All over de groun' fellers shakin' hands wid each other

as if was *they* wheelin' de willow
as if was *them* had the power;
one man run out pun de field wid a red fowl cock

goin' quawk quawk quawk in 'e han';
would'a give it to Clyde right then an' right there
if a police hadn't stop 'e!

An' in front o' where I was sittin',
one ball-headed sceptic snatch hat off he head
as if he did crazy

an' pointin' he finger at Wardle,
he jump up an' down
like a sun-shatter daisy an' bawl

out: 'B . . . L . . . O . . . O . . . D, B . . . I . . . G B . . . O . . . Y
bring me he B . . . L . . . O . . . O . . . D'
Who would'a think that for twenty-

five years he was standin' up there
in them Post Office cages, lickin' gloy
pun de Gover'ment stamps.

If uh wasn't there to see fuh meself,
I would'a never believe it,
I would'a never believe it.

But I say it once an' I say it agen:
when things goin' good, you cahn touch
we; but leh murder start an' you cahn fine a man to hole up de side.

Like when Laker come on.
Goin' remember what happenin' then
for the rest o' me life.

This Laker a quiet tall heavy-face fellow
who before he start to do anything ser'ous
is hitch up he pants round he belly.

He bowlin' off-breaks.
Int makin' no fuss
jus' toss up de firs'

one an' *bap!*
Clyde play forward firm
an' de ball hit he pad

an' fly up over de wicket.
Boy, *dis* is cricket!
Laker shift weight

an' toss up de secon';
it pitchin' off-stump an' comin' back sharp
wid de men in de leg trap shinin' like shark.

Clyde stretchin' right out like a man in de dark
an' he kill it.
'N . . . o . . . o . . . o', from de schoolboys, 'hit it, hit it'.

Boy, dis is *cricket*.
Then Laker come down wid he third
one. He wrap up de ball in de palm

o' he han' like a package
AN' MAKE CLYDE WALCOTT LOOK FOOLISH.
Mister man, could'a hear

all de flies that was buzzin' out there
round de bread carts; could'a hear
if de empire fart.

An' then blue murder start:
'Kill one o' dem, Clyde', some wise-
wun was shoutin', 'knock he skull off;

doan let them tangle you up in no leg trap;
use de feet dat God give you!'
Ev'ry blabber mout' talkin',

ev'ry man jack givin' advice;
but we so frighten now at what happenin' there
we could piss we pants if we doan have a care.

'*Swing de bat, man*', one feller was shoutin';
an' Clyde swing de bat but de bat miss
de ball an' de ball hit he pad

an' he pad went *biff*
like you beatin' bed
an' de empire han' stick

in de air
like Francis who dead
an' de bess o' we batsmen out.

The crowd so surprise you int hearin' a shout.
Ev'ry mout' loss.
But I say it once an' I say it agen:

when things goan' good, you cahn touch
we; but leh murder start
an' ol man, you cahn fine a man to hole up de side . . .

                                        The Arrivants, 1973

The Ladies in Play

R. C. ROBERTSON-GLASGOW

'*Ron, ron*, or you will *nevaire* egg-sell at the athletics'—thus was I exhorted, some years ago now, with more zeal than precision, by a Swiss governess who tried to initiate herself and me into the complexities of single-wicket cricket, with croquet hoops as stumps and rooks for spectators. It was my first experience of the Cricketing Lady.

There is evidence that the ladies interested themselves, at least verbally, in the game in the earlier years of George the Third, when Mrs 'Lumpy' Stevens would scream advice not unmingled with abuse at her famous husband of Hambledon CC. There are many instances, ancient and modern, of wives and daughters, and, in the greatest of all cricketing families, of a grandmother, too, who have at the proper moment ceased to 'mind the distaff' and plunged into disputations on the failure of a relative. Indeed, it is on record that a certain great professional batsman was discovered by a companion wandering in a town at night with a wild mien, because, as he said in low and anguished tone: 'I daren't go home. I daren't. The old woman'll tell me exactly why I missed that ball.'

There hangs in the pavilion of the Kent Cricket Club on the St Lawrence ground, Canterbury, an old print, in the Hogarthian manner, of a ladies' cricket match; Married *v.* Single, I believe. It is not a delicate or æsthetic scene. A burlesque and corpulent figure lies sprawling after a fielding failure. Mid-wicket, too, is an object of fun, having, like the mariner's wife of Mr Jacobs, 'lost her good looks and found others'. The gentlemen spectators, scattered in small marquees, are regaling themselves with culpable abandon.

Far otherwise are ladies' cricket matches conducted in these days. Any who saw the Tests and other matches played a few summers ago between England and the visitors from Australia will recall not only the trimness of these athletes and their skill, especially with the bat, which made tough and crochety old male spectators scratch their heads in surprise, but, more than anything, the exactitude of the organisation (making even the LGU seem haphazard!) and the defiance of the weather. The Oval groundsman and his staff must have regarded the next fixture between men as a rest cure!

I was once present, at all material times, at a ladies' County match, to which I must give with a sort of military anonymity the title of Wessex *v.* Loamshire, and to the players themselves, in the manner of Edgar Wallace's heroines and villainesses, spurious names that do not, nevertheless, 'have no reference to any living person'. For this is an unofficial and fragmentary account of the proceedings, and of some of the cricketers I can truthfully say that I did but see her passing by.

First, remembering the inhuman ability at catching and stopping shown by 'Twelve Ladies of the District' in school-days—the much too prehensile fingers and the skirt-protected shins—I remark with fidelity that the fielding of the ladies of Wessex and Loamshire, especially the latter, was faulty in the extreme. Cricketing ladies have often told me, with an admonishing frown, that it is not their wish to be compared with the men. Quite so; but they must admit comparison with each other, and on this occasion, had I been the Loamshire captain, I would have gathered my team at the close of play and said: 'No, Simpson; certainly not; and you, too, Jackson, and you, Micklethwaite; you may not go off to your sherry party; an hour's fielding practice for all of you; the catching was deplorable, and the throwing-in the limit.'

Perhaps it was the heat; yet this alone does not explain the garrulity of the slips, outdoing any post-prandial discussions among men. Nor am I convinced that the conversation turned solely on the artistry or eccentricities of the opposing batsmen, but rather, I fear, on hats and cookery, or other matters of personal adornment and refection.

Wessex scored some 165 for 8 wickets, and left Loamshire two and three-quarter hours to win, which would appear a little generous were it not that the tea interval bisected the Loamshire innings for three-quarters of an hour! Ah, that's the sort of match I have dreamed of playing in!

A lady to whom I award the prosaic name of Johnson scored 90 odd for Wessex, but let the Loamshire fellows bitterly reflect on the five chances that bumped to earth. In the words of a literary colleague, 'Johnson opened very shakily indeed, and cocked up several that were put on the floor before she became at all menacing.' But she made some lovely strokes, with that full sweeping rhythm which seems to desert man in adolescence, and it took a terrific catch at mid-off to dismiss her, expiation nearly enough for the other fumblings. Sixty-eight of her runs came from boundaries, and the next highest score was a desperate 17 by number nine.

For Loamshire, Sanderson, who must have suffered inward agonies from the inequalities of the fielding, bowled 30 overs in a row, except for negligible respite when changing ends. Three for 53 was inadequate reward.

Loamshire began as if their task, even including the tea, were easy; but they were soon forced to change daring for obstinacy, two players being out for very few runs. The second was bowled by one that seemed to go sharply with the arm, but refinements in definition fall flat before another of my friend's diagnoses. 'She was bowled by a perfect length ball that obviously she knew nothing about.' That's the way that men's Test Matches should be described. A simple brutality. The team was saved, as it turned out, by their number four, who was undismissed, though not entirely unbeaten, for 16, made in an hour and forty minutes. 'There was no moving her.' But there was movement around her in plenty; bowlers came and went and came again in bewildering permutation. Then one of the opening batsmen suddenly lost control, and, calling for a run for a stroke straight to close square-leg, was amply run out. The lady who had caught that great catch at mid-off, then arrived to make a hurricane 31 in thirty-five minutes. Still number four remained, majestic amid ruin, 4 more wickets falling with a crash. But number eleven not only averted the hat-trick but stayed for the last over and a half, with fielders perched nearly on her bat, and the stumper twice whipping away the bails more in prophecy than in hope.

A great day; but oh! those slip-fielders! If one should chance to cast her eye on these words, may she blush and amend!

Cricket Prints, 1943

✳

Maurice Read

SIR JOHN SQUIRE

I was half-awake, and blinking to the brilliant sunshine, puzzled by the unfamiliar room and beginning to reconstruct the evening before with a view to discovering where I was, when there was a knock at the door and full enlightenment came. It was Aubrey, cheerful and well-soaped, wearing a very florid red silk dressing-gown and carrying an equally florid blue one which he dropped on the bed. I said I would like some tea, and he called down the stairs: 'Sally, our visitor would like some

Maurice Read 323

tea,' and at once and imperturbably resumed where he had left off with: 'Well, now, of course you're staying over to-night, and will run over and see George this afternoon.'

'I really *can't*, Aubrey,' I said.

'Of course you will,' he repeated, with friendly contempt. 'Would you like breakfast in bed?'

'Certainly not,' I replied hardily. 'I'll stuff some paper in my shoes, soap my blisters, and get on to Winchester as soon as I've had breakfast. You don't seem to understand I'm on a walking tour.'

'Well, you can walk to-morrow, can't you!' he ejaculated. 'Would you like some eggs or will you carry on with the cold bacon?'

'Cold bacon for me.'

'Well, sing out when you're nearly ready and we'll make the coffee.'

When I got down he was ready with another opening.

'You'd much better take a day off to-day,' he said. 'We can see George this afternoon, and it's just occurred to me you'd be sure to like to run over and see the "Tichborne Arms" this morning.'

'Let's talk about it after breakfast,' I said, as I helped myself to coffee, quietly resolved on no account whatever to change my decision to cover a decent distance that day. The last temptation, though, I must admit, was a real one, for the little inn at Tichborne meant a great deal to me.

Suppose, about 1960, a man now in his twenties were suddenly to encounter, in a remote Kentish huddle of cottages, with an ancient church and an ancestral park, a shy inn, thatched, dormered, covered with roses, benches in a little garden in front of it, a great heraldic signboard hanging over it, and written on the lintel: 'Frank Woolley, licensed to sell wines, spirits, beer and tobacco.' His impression would be much the same as that which was made upon men of my generation in the post-war years when they visited the exquisite and secluded village of Tichborne and found Maurice Read in charge both of the inn and of the cricket ground. One of the most polished bats—he was also a wily bowler—who ever played for Surrey, he played for England both here and in Australia, but retired early, in the nineties, when Sir Joseph Tichborne offered him the job of looking after his private ground. There, for more than thirty years, he was a kind of secondary king of the place and, after his old master died, a perfect host both on and off the field. The inn was a minor interest, though, in his quiet way, he loved seeing natives and visitors foregathering in bar and courtyard for beer and laughter in the evenings after matches were over. The ground was his passion; in the early morning and at twilight, whenever he could, he would steal up to it looking for the least blemish in wicket and outfield. And, to the last, he himself played in his peaceful corner, against local sides and men on holiday, a straight bat to the end and, in his late sixties, a beautiful judge of a run and a wary fielder.

On cricketing days and others I had often talked to him, in company and alone. The last time I had seen him was in Winchester Hospital, a few days before he died of a wasting internal disease. There he lay, tired, faintly smiling, uncomplaining. His face—he had a high head, candid blue eyes, a thin aquiline nose, hollow cheeks, fair-grey drooping moustache and brief cropped side-whiskers—a more humane version of the late Lord Lansdowne—was like parchment stretched over bone, and his hands, all knuckles and cords, drooped weakly over the coverlet. An English side was in Australia; he knew every man's form and abilities. 'Incidents' had occurred; he remembered tours of forty years before, and said that they would always occur because of differences in national character.

A nurse brought some minced chicken. He ate a little, then lay back again. He looked the great gentleman he was; there was still in his face the old beauty, modesty, intelligence, dignity, nothing of collapse except extreme leanness; and smiles came into his eyes (for he had never been one, even in health, to laugh aloud except very quietly) as he recalled games long over, and the lusty figures of the past—the bravery of Richardson, the pace of Spofforth, the cunning of 'W.G.', and the sheer impudence of E. M. Grace, 'the Coroner' who, he said, used to insist on a waiter bringing out a large whisky-and-soda as he reached each fifty, and who had once marched out on the field and stayed there in a county match when his name, because he was out of form, had been left out of the XI. We parted at last; he was still talking of 'next season' and playing again. . . .

The Honeysuckle and the Bee, 1937

❋

The Village Pitch

G. D. MARTINEAU

They had no Grand Stand or Marquee,
  Down by the Quarry Farm:
There was a wealth of leafy tree
  Behind the bowler's arm.

There were no score cards to be had,
  Cushions for folk to hire;
Only we saw the butcher's lad
  Bowl out the Village Squire.

Lord's and the Oval truly mean
  Zenith of hard-won fame,
But it was just a village green
  Mothered and made the game.

A Score, a Score and Ten, 1927

*

A Country Cricket Match

MARY RUSSELL MITFORD

I doubt if there be any scene in the world more animating or delightful than a cricket-match—I do not mean a set match at Lord's Ground,
for money, hard money, between a certain number of gentlemen and
players, as they are called—people who make a trade of that noble sport,
and degrade it into an affair of bettings, and hedgings and cheatings,
it may be, like boxing or horse-racing; nor do I mean a pretty fête in a
gentleman's park, where one club of cricketing dandies encounter another such club, and where they show off in graceful costume to a gay
marquee of admiring belles, who condescend so to purchase admiration, and while away a long summer morning in partaking cold colla-
tions, conversing occasionally, and seeming to understand the game—the
whole being conducted according to ball-room etiquette, so as to be

exceedingly elegant and exceedingly dull. No! the cricket that I mean is a real solid old-fashioned match between neighbouring parishes, where each attacks the other for honour and a supper, glory and half-a-crown a man. If there be any gentlemen amongst them, it is well—if not, it is so much the better. Your gentleman cricketer is in general rather an anomalous character. Elderly gentlemen are obviously good for nothing; and your beaux are, for the most part, hampered and trammelled by dress and habit; the stiff cravat, the pinched-in-waist, the dandy-walk—oh, they will never do for cricket! Now, our country lads, accustomed to the flail or the hammer (your blacksmiths are capital hitters) have the free use of their arms; they know how to move their shoulders; and they can move their feet too—they can run; then they are so much better made, so much more athletic, and yet so much lissimer—to use a Hampshire phrase, which deserves at least to be good English. Here and there, indeed, one meets with an old Etonian, who retains his boyish love for that game which formed so considerable a branch of his education; some even preserve their boyish proficiency, but in general it wears away like the Greek, quite as certainly, and almost as fast; a few years of Oxford, or Cambridge, or the Continent, are sufficient to annihilate both the power and the inclination. No! a village match is the thing—where our highest officer—our conductor (to borrow a musical term) is but a little farmer's second son; where a day-labourer is our bowler, and a blacksmith our long-stop; where the spectators consist of the retired cricketers, the veterans of the green, the careful mothers, the girls, and all the boys of two parishes, together with a few amateurs, little above them in rank, and not at all in pretension; where laughing and shouting, and the very ecstasy of merriment and good-humour prevail: such a match, in short, as I attended yesterday, at the expense of getting twice wet through, and as I would attend tomorrow, at the certainty of having that ducking doubled.

For the last three weeks our village has been in a state of great excitement, occasioned by a challenge from our north-western neighbours, the men of B., to contend with us at cricket. Now, we have not been much in the habit of playing matches. Three or four years ago, indeed, we encountered the men of S., our neighbours south-by-east, with a sort of doubtful success, beating them on our own ground, whilst they in the second match returned the compliment on theirs. This discouraged us. Then an unnatural coalition between a high-church curate and an evangelical gentleman-farmer drove our lads from the Sunday-even practice, which, as it did not begin before both services were concluded, and as it tended to keep the young men from the ale-house, our magistrates had winked at if not encouraged. The sport, therefore, had languished until the present season, when under another change of circumstances the spirit began to revive. Half-a-dozen fine active lads, of influence amongst their comrades, grew into men and yearned for cricket; an enterprising publican gave a set of ribands: his rival, mine host of the Rose, and out-doer by profession, gave two; and the clergyman and his lay ally, both well-disposed and good-natured men, gratified by the submission to their authority, and finding, perhaps, that no great good resulted from the substitution of public houses for out-of-doors diversions, relaxed. In short, the practice re-commenced, and the hill was again alive with men and boys, and innocent merriment; but farther than the riband matches amongst ourselves nobody dreamed of going, till this challenge—we were modest, and doubted our own strength. The B. people, on the other hand, must have been braggers born, a whole parish of gasconaders. Never was such boasting! such crowing! such ostentatious display of practice! such mutual compliments from man to man—bowler to batter, batter to bowler! It was a wonder they did not challenge all England. It must be confessed that we were a little astounded; yet we firmly resolved not to decline the combat; and one of the most spirited of the new growth, William Grey by name, took up the glove in a style of manly courtesy, that would have done honour to a knight in the days of chivalry—'We were not professed players,' he said, 'being little better than school-boys, and scarcely older; but, since they have done us the honour to challenge us, we would try our strength. It would be no discredit to be beaten by such a field.'

Having accepted the wager of battle, our champion began forthwith to collect his forces. William Grey is himself one of the finest youths that one shall see—tall, active, slender and yet strong, with a piercing eye full of sagacity, and a smile full of good honour—a farmer's son by station, and used to hard work as farmers' sons are now, liked by everybody, and admitted to be an excellent cricketer. He immediately set forth to muster his men, remembering with great complacency that Samuel Long, a bowler *comme il y en a peu*, the very man who had knocked down nine wickets, had beaten us, bowled us out at the fatal return match some years ago at S., had luckily, in a remove of a quarter of a mile last Ladyday, crossed the boundaries of his old parish, and actually belonged to us. Here was a stroke of good fortune! Our captain applied to him instantly; and he agreed at a word. Indeed,

Samuel Long is a very civilized person. He is a middle-aged man, who looks rather old amongst our young lads, and whose thickness and breadth gave no token of remarkable activity, but he is very active, and so steady a player! so safe! We had half gained the match when we had secured him. He is a man of substance, too, in every way; owns one cow, two donkeys, six pigs, and geese and ducks beyond count— dresses like a farmer, and owes no man a shilling—and all this from pure industry, sheer day-labour. Note that your good cricketer is commonly the most industrious man in the parish; the habits that make him such are precisely those which make a good workman—steadiness, sobriety, and activity—Samuel Long might pass for the beau ideal of the two characters. Happy were we to possess him! Then we had another piece of good luck. James Brown, a journeyman blacksmith and a native, who, being of a rambling disposition, had roamed from place to place for half-a-dozen years, had just returned to settle with his brother at another corner of our village, bringing with him a prodigious reputation in cricket and in gallantry—the gay Lothario of the neighbourhood. He is said to have made more conquests in love and in cricket than any blacksmith in the county. To him also went the indefatigable William Grey, and he also consented to play. No end to our good fortune! Another celebrated batter, called Joseph Hearne, had likewise recently married into the parish. He worked, it is true at the A. mills, but slept at the house of his wife's father in our territories. He also was sought and found by our leader. But he was grand and shy; made an immense favour of the thing; courted courting and then hung back—'Did not know that he could be spared; had partly resolved not to play again—at least not this season; thought it rash to accept the challenge; thought they might do without him—' 'Truly I think so too,' said our spirited champion; 'we will not trouble you, Mr Hearne.'

Having thus secured two powerful auxiliaries and rejected a third, we began to reckon and select the regular native forces. Thus ran our list: William Grey, 1—Samuel Long, 2—James Brown, 3—George and John Simmons, one capital the other so-so—an uncertain hitter, but a good fieldsman, 5—Joel Brent, excellent, 6—Ben Appleton—here was a little pause—Ben's abilities at cricket was not completely ascertained; but then he was so good a fellow, so full of fun and waggery! no doing without Ben. So he figured in the list, 7—George Harris—a short halt there too! Slowish—slow but sure. I think the proverb brought him in, 8—Tom Coper—Oh, beyond the world, Tom Coper! the red-headed gardening lad, whose left-handed strokes send *her* (a cricket-ball, like that other moving thing, a ship, is always of the feminine gender), send her spinning a mile, 9—Harry Willis, another blacksmith, 10.

We had now ten of our eleven, but the choice of the last occasioned some demur. Three young Martins, rich farmers of the neighbourhood, successively presented themselves, and were all rejected by our independent and impartial general for want of merit—cricketal merit. 'Not good enough,' was his pithy answer. Then our worthy neighbour, the half-pay lieutenant, offered his services—he, too, though with some hesitation and modesty, was refused—'Not quite young enough' was his sentence. John Strong, the exceeding long son of our dwarfish mason, was the next candidate—a nice youth—everybody likes John Strong—and a willing, but so tall and so limp, bent in the middle—a threadpaper, six feet high! We were all afraid that, in spite of his name, his strength would never hold out. 'Wait till next year, John,' quoth William Grey, with all the dignified seniority of twenty speaking to eighteen. 'Coper's a year younger,' said John. 'Coper's a foot shorter,' replied William: so John retired: and the eleventh man remained unchosen, almost to the eleventh hour. The eve of the match arrived, and the post was still vacant, when a little boy of fifteen, David Willis, brother to Harry, admitted by accident to the last practice, saw eight of them out, and was voted in by acclamation.

That Sunday evening's practice (for Monday was the important day) was a period of great anxiety, and, to say the truth, of great pleasure. There is something strangely delightful in the innocent spirit of party. To be one of a numerous body, to be authorized to say *we*, to have a rightful interest in triumph or defeat, is gratifying at once to social feeling and to personal pride. There was not a ten-year-old urchin, or a septuagenary woman in the parish who did not feel an additional importance, a reflected consequence, in speaking of 'our side'. An election interests in the same way; but that feeling is less pure. Money is there, and hatred, and politics, and lies. Oh, to be a voter, or a voter's wife, comes nothing near the genuine and hearty sympathy of belonging to a parish, breathing the same air, looking on the same trees, listening to the same nightingales! Talk of a patriotic elector! Give me a parochial patriot, a man who loves his parish. Even we, the female partisans, may partake the common ardour. I am sure I did. I never, though tolerably eager and enthusiastic at all times, remember being in a more delicious state of excitement than on the eve of that battle. Our hopes waxed stronger and stronger. Those of our players who were present were excellent. William Grey got forty notches off his own bat, and that brilliant hitter, Tom Coper, gained eight from two successive balls. As the evening advanced, too, we had encouragement of another sort. A spy, who had been despatched to reconnoitre the enemy's quarters, returned from their practising ground with a most consolatory report. 'Really,' said Charles Grover, our intelligence—a fine old steady judge, one who had played well in his day—'they are no better than so many old women. Any five of ours would beat their eleven.' This sent us to bed in high spirits.

Morning dawned less favourably. The sky promised a series of deluging showers, and kept its word as English skies are wont to do on such occasions; and a lamentable message arrived at the head-quarters from our trusty comrade Joel Brent. His master, a great farmer, had begun the hay-harvest that very morning, and Joel, being as eminent in one field as in another, could not be spared. Imagine Joel's plight! the most ardent of all our eleven! a knight held back from the tourney! a soldier from the battle! The poor swain was inconsolable. At last, one who is always ready to do a good-natured action, great or little, set forth to back his petition; and, by dint of appealing to the public spirit of our worthy neighbour and the state of the barometer, talking alternately of the parish honour and thunder showers, of last matches and sopped hay, he carried his point, and returned triumphantly with the delighted Joel.

In the meantime, we became sensible of another defalcation. On calling over our roll, Brown was missing; and the spy of the preceding night, Charles Grover—the universal scout and messenger of the village, a man who will run half-a-dozen miles for a pint of beer, who does errands for the very love of the trade, who, if he had been a lord, would have been an ambassador—was instantly despatched to summon the truant. His report spread general consternation. Brown had set off at four o'clock in the morning to play in a cricket-match at M., a little town twelve miles off, which had been his last residence. Here was desertion! Here was treachery! Here was treachery against that goodly state, our parish! To send James Brown to Coventry was the immediate resolution; but even that seemed too light a punishment for such delinquency! Then how we cried him down! At ten on Sunday night (for the rascal had actually practised with us, and never said a word of his intended disloyalty) he was our faithful mate, and the best player (take him all in all) of the eleven. At ten in the morning he had run away, and we were well rid of him; he was no batter compared with William Grey or Tom Coper; not fit to wipe the shoes of Samuel

Long, as a bowler; nothing of a scout to John Simmons; the boy David
Willis was worth fifty of him—

> I trust we have within our realm
> Five hundred good as he

was the universal sentiment. So we took tall John Strong, who, with
an incurable hankering after the honour of being admitted had kept
constantly with the players, to take the chance of some such accident—
we took John for our *pis aller*. I never saw anyone prouder than the
good-humoured lad was of this not very flattering piece of preferment.

John Strong was elected, and Brown sent to Coventry; and when I
first heard of his delinquency, I thought the punishment only too mild
for the crime. But I have since learned the secret history of the offence
(if we could know the secret histories of all offences, how much better the world would seem than it does now!) and really my wrath is
much abated. It was a piece of gallantry, of devotion to the sex, or rather
a chivalrous obedience to one chosen fair. I must tell my readers the
story. Mary Allen, the prettiest girl of M., had, it seems, revenged upon
our blacksmith the numberless inconsistencies of which he stood accused.
He was in love over head and ears, but the nymph was cruel. She said
no, and no, and no, and poor Brown, three times rejected, at last
resolved to leave the place, partly in despair, and partly in the hope
which often mingles strangely with a lover's despair, the hope that when
he was gone he should be missed. He came home to his brother's
accordingly, but for five weeks he heard nothing from or of the inex-
orable Mary, and was glad to beguile his own 'vexing thoughts' by
endeavouring to create in his mind an artificial and factitious interest
in our cricket-match—all unimportant as such a trifle must have seemed
to a man in love. Poor James, however, is a social and warm-hearted
person, not likely to resist a contagious sympathy. As the time for the
play advanced, the interest which he had at first affected became genuine and sincere: and he was really, when he left the ground on Sunday
night, almost as enthusiastically absorbed in the event of the next day,
as Joel Brent himself. He little foresaw the new and delightful interest
which awaited him at home, where, on the moment of his arrival, his
sister-in-law and confidante presented him with a billet from the lady
of his heart. It had, with the usual delay of letters sent by private hands
in that rank of life, loitered on the road, in a degree inconceivable to
those who are accustomed to the punctual speed of the post, and had
taken ten days for its twelve miles' journey. Have my readers any wish

to see this *billet-doux*? I can show them (but in strict confidence) a lit-
eral copy. It was addressed,

For mistur jem browne
'blaxmith by
'S'.

The inside ran thus:

Mistur browne this is to Inform you that oure parish plays bramley men
next monty is a week, i think we shall lose without yew, from your humbell
servant to command

Mary Allen.

Was there ever a prettier relenting? a summons more flattering, more
delicate, more irresistible? The precious epistle was undated; but, having ascertained who brought it, and found, by cross-examining the messenger, that the Monday in question was the very next day, we were
not surprised to find that Mistur browne forgot his engagement to us,
forgot all but Mary and Mary's letter, and set off at four o'clock the
next morning to walk twelve miles, and to play for her parish, and in
her sight. Really we must not send James Brown to Coventry—must
we? Though if, as his sister-in-law tells our damsel Harriet he hopes
to do, he should bring the fair Mary home as his bride, he will not
greatly care how little we say to him. But he must not be sent to
Coventry—True-love forbid!

At last we were all assembled, and marched down to H. common,
the appointed ground, which, though in our dominions according to
the maps, was the constant practising place of our opponents, and *terra
incognita* to us. We found our adversaries on the ground as we expected,
for our various delays had hindered us from taking the field so early
as we wished; and as soon as we had settled all preliminaries, the match
began.

But, alas! I have been so long settling my preliminaries, that I have
left myself no room for the detail of our victory, and must squeeze the
account of our grand achievements into as little compass as Cowley,
when he crammed the names of eleven of his mistresses into the narrow space of four eight-syllable lines. *They* began the warfare—those
boastful men of B. And what think you, gentle reader, was the amount
of their innings? These challengers—the famous eleven—how many did
they get? Think! imagine! guess!—You cannot?—Well!—they got twenty-
two, or rather, they got twenty; for two of theirs were short notches,

and would never have been allowed, only that, seeing what they were made of, we and our umpires were not particular—They should have had twenty more if they had chosen to claim them. Oh, how well we fielded! and how well we bowled! our good play had quite as much to do with their miserable failure as their bad. Samuel Long is a slow bowler, George Simmons a fast one, and the change from Long's lobbing to Simmons's fast balls posed them completely. Poor simpletons! they were always wrong, expecting the slow for the quick, and the quick for the slow. Well, we went in. And what were our innings? Guess again!—guess! A hundred and sixty-nine! in spite of soaking showers, and wretched ground, where the ball would not run a yard, we headed them by a hundred and forty-seven; and then they gave in, as well they might. William Grey pressed them much to try another innings. 'There was so much chance', as he courteously observed, 'in cricket, that advantageous as our position seemed, we might, very possibly, be overtaken. The B. men had better try.' But they were beaten sulky and would not move—to my great disappointment; I wanted to prolong the pleasure of success. What a glorious sensation it is to be for five hours together—winning—winning! always feeling what a whist-player feels when he takes up four honours, seven trumps! Who would think that a little bit of leather and two pieces of wood, had such a delightful and delighting power!

The only drawback on my enjoyment was the failure of the pretty boy, David Willis, who, injudiciously put in first, and playing for the first time in a match amongst men and strangers, who talked to him, and stared at him, was seized with such a fit of shamefaced shyness, that he could scarcely hold his bat, and was bowled out without a stroke, from actual nervousness. 'He will come off that,' Tom Coper says—I am afraid he will. I wonder whether Tom had ever any modesty to lose. Our other modest lad, John Strong, did very well; his length told in fielding and he got good fame. He ran out his mate, Samuel Long; who, I do believe, but for the excess of Joel's eagerness, would have stayed in till this time, by which exploit he got into sad disgrace; and then he himself got thirty-seven runs, which redeemed his reputation. William Grey made a hit which actually lost the cricket-ball. We think she lodged in a hedge, a quarter of a mile off, but nobody could find her. And George Simmons had nearly lost his shoe, which he tossed away in a passion, for having been caught out, owing to the ball glancing against it. These, together with a very complete somerset of Ben Appleton, our long-stop, who floundered about in the mud, making faces and attitudes as laughable as Grimaldi, none could tell whether by accident or design, were the chief incidents of the scene of action. Amongst the spectators nothing remarkable occurred, beyond the general calamity of two or three drenchings, except that a form, placed by the side of a hedge, under a very insufficient shelter, was knocked into the ditch in a sudden rush of the cricketers to escape a pelting shower, by which means all parties shared the fate of Ben Appleton, some on land and some by water; and that, amidst the scramble, a saucy gipsy of a girl contrived to steal from the knee of the demure and well-apparelled Samuel Long, a smart handkerchief which his careful dame had tied round it to preserve his new (what is the mincing feminine word?)—his new—inexpressibles, thus reversing the story of Desdemona, and causing the new Othello to call aloud for his handkerchief, to the great diversion of the company. And so we parted; the players retired to their supper, and we to our homes; all wet through, all good-humoured and happy—except the losers.

Our Village, 1832

*

Lament of the Village Groundsman

R. D. D. THOMAS

Zerpose oi must out wi' the mowin' machine
An' water the grass for ter mëake of it green,
  Vor today they be playin' at cricket:
An' chop down they nettles as grow by yon wall
Or they'll waste 'alf o' match a-zeeking the ball
  When its gorn away off o' the wicket.

Come, give oi a 'and with yon roller, my zon,
Though oi reckon it robs the wold gëame ov its vun
  To smooth out they bumps on the wicket.
Now, when oi were a youngster oi used vor to learn
Which 'ummock to 'it vor to mëake the ball turn
  To sharp for 'em even to flick it.

An' zo oi wanted the ball vor to shoot
Oi just let 'un pitch on a dandy-lion root,
   And skim thro' the grass to the wicket,
An' oi knew every patch as 'ould make it to rise
So's to give anybody a clump twixt the eyes
   As failed to duck quick or snick it.

Yet many a vellow got down on 'is knees
And swiped thic ball over the tops o' thëase trees,
   Never 'eeding them bumps on the wicket.
An' it took all the wiles as a man could devize
To get such like stumped or run out by zurprize,
   An' that, zon's the way to play cricket.

Note Book of a Lieutenant in the Italian Campaign, 1944

✻

Our Village

NEVILLE CARDUS

On Saturdays at high noon in a certain village of the Cotswolds, a little cricket field stands silent in the sun. Over the grass walks an old horse, pulling a roller and led by an old man. There is to be a match this afternoon, and though everywhere is quiet, the preparations are going forward. Organization is in the air. The click of a latch on the ground's wooden gate is suddenly heard. Mrs Renshaw and her daughter walk along the path carrying a tea-urn. They keep carefully to the path, for, not being themselves cricketers, they would not dream of putting foot on the grass. Yet Mrs Renshaw, her daughter, and the tea-urn are week by week, summer after summer, indispensable parts in the whole of Ludbury's cricket team. That fact is never overlooked by the XI itself and those who lead the XI to victory and defeat. At every annual meeting of the Ludbury cricket team, held in the schoolroom on a dark February evening, the Rev. W. G. Soames, after he has performed the distribution of medals for good batting, bowling, and fielding, will conclude his remarks by an allusion to Mrs and Miss Renshaw. And invariably he will add, with a display of the jocular, 'Where, indeed, would the Ludbury cricket team be without the ladies?' One year this question was most suddenly and startlingly answered from the back of the hall by George, the club's ancient umpire, who cried out in a loud voice, 'Why, zur, we'd be having to make our own cups of tea, we'd be!' Having accomplished this interruption, George appeared all at once to see something funny in his words; he burst into a great guffaw, and set the whole meeting guffawing too, which was not good for the Rev. Soames's speech.

George is the 'official' umpire of Ludbury CC. That is how he himself puts it. I do not think George is a good umpire; to say the truth he is not impartial. At the finish of every season the Ludbury XI is photographed in flannels; George, clad in his white coat, appears in every group, and invariably he is to be seen standing with his arms folded and his legs stuck out and his face set aggressively—as though determined to merge himself into the general air of combativeness assumed by everybody else in the portrait. But if I say George is not an impartial umpire, it must not be thought he is wickedly unscrupulous. His prejudices are frank and unconcealed; he is partial in his decisions for exactly the same reason that David Smith bowls so fast for Ludbury that his back hurts him all through the following Sunday. George wants Ludbury to win always. Moreover it is my private conviction that George has never correctly read the wording of Rule 3 of the Laws of Cricket as revised by the Marylebone Cricket Club. That rule runs as follows:—'Before the commencement of the match two umpires shall be appointed; one for each end.' Old George, I am certain, when first he read the laws of cricket as a small boy, glanced hastily over the third rule and understood it to signify . . . 'two umpires shall be appointed; one for each side'. It would be of no use attempting to alter George's view of the rule at this time of day; I am afraid he will carry his error to the grave. In Cotswold cricket, of course, each eleven travels with its own umpire. One of these umpires, during a match against Ludbury, once gently remonstrated with George about a strange decision of George's. And George with calm and dignity replied, 'Yew luke after yewr bus'ness and I'll luke after mine.' The implication clearly was that different points of view tend to lead to different judgments.

It is not hard to become a playing member of the Ludbury CC. Neither birth nor residential qualification is necessary. Any afternoon, if you should happen to be strolling round the ground just before the beginning of a match, the chances are that the Ludbury captain—none other than the Rev. W. G. Soames—will approach you and say, 'Would you care for a game, sir?' If your reply should be, 'I'd be delighted, but the fact is I don't play cricket'—well, the Rev. W. G. Soames is certain to say, 'Oh, that doesn't matter at all; you'll soon pick it up. We've a spare suit of flannels in the pavilion. George! Take this gentleman into the dressing-room and give him Mr Robinson's trousers. He's not with us to-day, and this gentleman has kindly agreed to play in his place.' If, on the other hand, you should be in a position to accept the Rev. W. G. Soames's invitation with some confidence, mentioning as you do so the fact that you bowl a pretty off-break and that your batting average is 17.18, the information will be gratefully received and deemed not altogether superfluous. The Rev. W. G. Soames opens Ludbury's batting in company with his gardener, Joseph Huggins. The moment the Rev. Soames breaks his duck he begins to hit; he is an ardent supporter of the movement to 'brighten' cricket and has occasionally written letters to the newspapers on the subject. His favourite stroke is a huge on-drive from, or rather against, a good-length ball on the middle stump. More often than not he is severely bowled, whereupon Joseph Huggins, at the other end of the pitch, turns to the umpire—probably it is George, who as the stumps are sent flying wishes he could retrospectively announce a no-ball—and says, 'George, 'e do be no more patient than you or me.'

Mrs Renshaw leaves her work with the tea-urn and looks through the little window of her room and watches the cricket whenever the Rev. Soames is batting. And at the fall of his wicket she will go back again to the tea-urn saying, 'It's a great shame they never let him have a nice ball.' The Rev. W. G. Soames contributed last year to the controversy upon Cricket Reform. He wrote a long letter to the newspapers, and in it he delivered himself of this statement: 'As to four stumps, perhaps the opinion of a village club cricketer of thirty years' standing will not be without point. County cricket, sir, is not the whole of the game, and the MCC cannot legislate as though only county cricket existed. In our class of cricket there is no demand at all for four stumps. It not infrequently happens, indeed, that we club cricketers find even three stumps to be one too many. I enclose my card and sign myself, sir, Yours truly, A Country Parson.'

Joseph Huggins does not believe in recklessness; he is something of a stonewaller, even though he does spit on his hands a good deal while he is at the wicket. Huggins is every year at the top of the Ludbury batting, just as David Smith every year is top of the bowling. These two strong men are the team's backbone; the other members, save the captain, vary in skill and identity match by match. 'Birds of passage', so George rhetorically calls them. The Rev. Soames does his best to bind together his fortuitous material. Now and again he is not successful. In a match the other day a ball was skied in the middle of the pitch by one of Ludbury's opponents. Three Ludbury fieldsmen moved forward, all eager to take an easy catch. With great presence of mind, the Rev. Soames grappled with the dangerous situation. He 'named' the fieldsman most likely to get to the ball. 'Thompson,' he cried out, commandingly, masterfully, 'Leave it to Thompson.' Each of the three fieldsmen retired backwards with exemplary obedience, and the ball fell to earth between them. Then the Rev. W. G. Soames bethought himself; there was no Thompson playing for Ludbury this week.

Summer after summer the game goes on down in the Cotswolds. David Smith thunders over the earth and bowls his yorker. A ripple of clapping announces that the fifty is up—for seven wickets—and the boy by the score-board sorts out his tins and looks for a Nought and a Seven. In the silences that come over the game you can hear lovely summer-time noises, the low hum of a hot June day as it goes towards evening. When the shadows are lengthening and in the slanting light soft sheen falls on everybody's flannels, the match is finished; the cricketers come walking home to the pavilion, David Smith with his sweater hanging about his great shoulders, and last of all old George, wearing his white coat and in his arms all the six stumps gathered together. Very soon the little field is vacant. Footsteps on the wooden front of the pavilion make gentle echoes. A bird runs quickly over the grass, stops quite still for a moment, then runs on again. In the high trees the rooks are going to their nests. There is the click of the gate's latch at the corner of the field. Mrs Renshaw and Miss Renshaw pass through carrying the urn. The Rev. Soames holds open the gate and follows after. But before he departs on his own way home he says: 'Good evening, Mrs Renshaw; good evening, Miss Renshaw. Thank you so very much. A very enjoyable day, I'm sure, very enjoyable indeed.' Dear cricket of the Cotswolds, would that I were playing you every day—if only to be given the benefit of the doubt by George. 'Not Hout!' he would be sure to say when the bowler hit me on the leg. 'Not quite hout, but nearly.'

The Summer Game, 1928

*

The Dream

NORMAN GALE

One night the Three Selectors
Came and stood beside my bed.
I found it hard to credit
Their belief in what they said.
They begged of me to captain
The Team prepared to go
Across the sea to Bradman,
And I countered them with No!
Immediately the spokesman
Of the Three began to shout
Confoundedly, and scatter
Certain adjectives about.

On hearing that Old England
Was determined (this was odd)
To elect me for a season
As a sort of Cricket god,
I began in turn to colour
Like a beetroot, and to shout
Consumedly, and sprinkle
Other adjectives about.

I told them I was busy
With an Epic in the West.
Instanter those Selectors
Were a mass upon my chest.
Surrendering, I bolted
To the Liner with a bat
And drove for four along the deck
The Steward's yellow cat.

When flannelled in Australia,
How I bruised the willow-wood!
How I punished Clarence Grimmett
As an English Captain should!

The total score of Bradman
When our enterprise was done—
The Ashes in my kitbag—
Was an egg denoting None.

What luck! The heart of England
Would be more than peacock-proud.
My fancy heard the cheering
Of the Homeland, long and loud,
And tried to count the faces
Of the thousands come to roar
In volume, that the welkin might
Oblige, as heretofore.
Her demi-gods had silvered
Afresh the rusted shield,
Had shaken hands with Glory,
Had thunderously appealed.

Close of Play, 1936

*

The Greatest Test Match

NEVILLE CARDUS

On a bright day in the spring of 1921 I went to Lord's, hoping to see the first practice of the Australians. But the place was deserted, save for the man at the gates. He told me Armstrong's men were being entertained that afternoon somewhere in the City, and that they wouldn't be in the nets till after tea. Still, he added, with a touch of human nature not too common at Lord's, if I liked I could enter the ground and sit and enjoy myself in the sun till they came.

I sat on a bench with my feet spread out so that they touched the soft grass. A great calm was over the field. The trees beyond the Nursery were delicate with fresh green, and the fine old pavilion seemed to nod in the sunshine. It was an occasion for a reverie, and I fell to affectionate thoughts upon the great days of cricket, of the history that had been made on the field which stretched before me. I thought of Grace, of Spofforth, of Hornby, of A. G. Steel. . . . Maybe I dozed for a while. Then I was conscious of a voice. 'Would you mind moving up a little? This seat is rather congested.' I looked around and saw sitting by my side a man in a tight black coat which buttoned high on his chest. He had sidewhiskers and wore a low turned-down collar and a high bowler hat. A handkerchief was showing from a breast pocket in his jacket. Not quite awake yet, I moved up. 'Thank you,' he said. 'I'm sorry I disturbed you. A nap carries one comfortably through a long wait at these matches. What a crowd there is!' I looked round. I was in the middle of a big crowd indeed. In front of me sat a parson. He was reading *The Times*. I glanced over his shoulder and saw the headline: 'Egyptian Campaign: Sir G. Wolseley's Despatch'. The man at my side said, 'Were you here yesterday, sir?' and before I could reply he added, 'It was a considerable day's cricket, and the *Post* has an excellent account. Perhaps you've seen it?' He handed me a copy of the *Morning Post*, and, thanking him, I took it. The paper was dated August 29, 1882. In a column headed 'England *v.* Australia' I read that, on the day before, Australia had been dismissed for 63 by Barlow and Peate, and that England, captained by A. N. Hornby, had made in reply 101. Then I understood my situation. And what is more I now understood it without the slightest astonishment. Even the aspect of the ground, which told me it was Kennington Oval and not Lord's, did not embarrass me. It was enough that I was one of the crowd that was to witness the second day's cricket in the ninth Test match—the most famous Test match of all.

I gave the *Post* back to my companion in silence. 'A considerable day's cricket indeed, sir,' said the Parson. 'But England ought to have made more runs. Our batting was distinctly mediocre—almost as bad as the Australians'.' A loud cheer disturbed his argument. Down the pavilion steps walked the England Eleven in single file, led by Hornby. With him was 'W.G.', and he passed along the field with an ambling motion, and the wind got into his great black beard. He spoke to Hornby in a high-pitched voice and laughed. Then he threw the ball to a tall, graceful player just behind him and cried, 'Catch her, Bunny.' Following Grace and Hornby were Lucas, C. T. Studd, J. M. Read, the Hon. A. Lyttelton, Ulyett, Barlow, W. Barnes, A. G. Steel, and Peate. The crowd quietened, awaiting the advent of Australia's first two batsmen, and I again heard the Parson's voice '. . . The English total was distressingly poor. Rarely have I seen poorer batting from an All England Eleven. The fact is, sir, that for some little time now English cricket has been deteriorating. Our batsmen don't hit the ball as hard as they used to do, and even our bowling . . .' Another cheer drowned his discourse. 'Bannerman and Massie,' said my companion. 'I should imagine Bannerman's the youngest man in the match.' The Parson was prompt with his correction. 'I believe S. P. Jones, who was twenty-one on the 1st of the month, is the junior member of the two teams. Studd is, I fancy, eleven months older than Jones. Bannerman is twenty-three at least, and Giffen is six days younger than Bannerman.' My companion was silenced, but I ventured a question. 'How old is Spofforth?' Pat came the answer, 'Twenty-seven on the ninth of next month.'

The crowd, including even the Parson, went as quiet as a mouse as Barlow began the English bowling to Bannerman. Lyttelton, behind the wicket, crouched low. It was exactly a quarter past twelve. The next half-hour was a tumultuous prelude to the day. Bannerman was all vigilance, while Massie played one of the great innings of Test cricket. He hurled his bat at every ball the slightest loose, and his hits crashed ponderously to the boundary. He was the living image of defiance as he faced the Englishmen, glaring round the field his challenge. At one huge drive from Barlow's bowling my companion murmured, 'I've never seen a bigger hit than that at the Oval.' But the Parson over-heard him. 'When the Australians were here in '78,' he said, 'W. H. Game, playing for Surrey, hit a ball from Spofforth to square-leg right out of the ground.' Still, he admitted that this Massie fellow hit them quite hard enough. In half an hour England's advantage of 38 was gone. Hornby called up bowler after bowler, Studd for Barlow, Barnes for Studd. Steel tried his hand at 56—the sixth bowler in less than three-quarters of an hour. When Australia's score was 47 Massie lifted a ball to long-on. 'Lucas is there,' said the Parson; 'he'll get it all r——. Good Lord!' For Lucas dropped the ball and blushed red as the crowd groaned out of its soul.

'Sixty-six for none,' murmured the man at my side; 'they're 28 on with all their wickets intact. If Massie prevails—ah, bravo, sir; well bowled, well bowled!' A ball from Steel had tempted Massie, and just as he jumped out it broke back and wrecked the wicket. Massie walked to the pavilion, roared home by an admiring but much relieved crowd. His innings was worth 55 to Australia, made out of 66 in less than an hour.

Bonnor came next, and the English out-fields dropped deep and had apprehensive thoughts. Would not Massie's example make this bearded giant a very Jehu? But Hornby has an inspiration. He asks Ulyett to bowl instead of Steel. And Ulyett moves to the wicket like a man ploughing against a breaker, puts the last ounce of his Yorkshire strength into a thunderbolt of a ball that sends Bonnor's middle stump flying. The crowd is only just getting back the breath lost in approval of this feat when Bannerman is caught by Studd at extra mid-off. Bannerman has batted seventy minutes for 13. 'Quick work for him!' says the Parson. And with the broad bat of Bannerman out of the way the English bowlers begin to see daylight. Peate's slow left-hand deliveries spin beautifully, as though controlled by a string. The Australians now, save Murdoch, are just guessing. The fourth wicket falls at 75, the fifth at 79. Australia are all out 122. 'Only 85 to win,' says the Parson. 'It's our game after all, though Lucas did his best to lose it.'

It was a true autumn afternoon going to its fall in grey light when 'W.G.' and Hornby went to the wicket to face Spofforth and Garratt. The crowd filled the ground, but so silent was it as Grace took his guard that one could hear the tink-tink of a hansom cab coming closer and closer along the Vauxhall Road. Spofforth's first over was fast— he let the ball go with a quick leap, dropping his arm at the moment of release. Blackham 'stood back' when Grace was batting, but crept up for Hornby. 'Beautiful wicket-keeping,' murmured my companion. 'Pinder was not less gifted,' said the Parson. And he added, 'I have not seen Spofforth bowl as fast as this for some time. He has latterly cultivated medium-pace variations.' Both Hornby and Grace began confidently, and at once the tension lifted. Hornby made a lovely cut from Spofforth and a dainty leg stroke for a couple.

Spofforth uprooted Hornby's off stump with England's score 15, and with his next ball clean bowled Barlow. The crowd gave out a suspicion of a shiver, but the advent of bluff George Ulyett was reassuring, especially as Grace welcomed him with a fine leg hit from Garratt for three and a beautiful on drive to the boundary from Spofforth. 'Thirty up,' said my companion; 'only 55 to get.' England was still 30 for two when Spofforth crossed over to the pavilion end. Now I was behind his arm; I could see his superb break-back. And he bowled mainly medium pace this time. With each off-break I could see his right hand, at the end of the swing over, finish near the left side, 'cutting' under the ball. Sometimes his arm went straight over and continued straight down in the follow-through—and then the batsman had to tackle fierce top spin. There was the sense of the inimical in his aspect now. He seemed taller than he was a half-hour ago, the right arm of him more sinuous. There was no excitement in him; he was, the Parson said, cold-blooded. Still Ulyett faced him bravely while Grace, at the other end, time after time moved from his crease with a solid left leg and pushed the ball away usefully. 'Fifty up', said my companion, 'for two wickets. It's all over—we want only 34 now.' And at 51 Spofforth bowled a very fast one to Ulyett, who barely snicked it. It served though; Blackham snapped the catch, and his 'Hzat!' was hoarse and aggressive. Lucas came in, and with two runs more 'W.G.' was caught at mid-off. 'What a stroke!' said the Parson. 'I'm afraid he's not the Grace he was.' Four for 53, and Lyttelton and Lucas in. Lyttelton hits out big-heartedly, but the field is like a net tightly drawn. It is suddenly understood by every man of us that the game is in the balance. 'The wicket must be bad,' says somebody.

Lucas stonewalls, with a bat as straight as a die. Spofforth bowls a maiden; Boyle bowls a maiden; Spofforth bowls another maiden. The air is growing thick. 'Get runs or get out, for the Lord's sake,' says somebody. The field creeps closer and closer to the wicket. Spofforth and Boyle are like uncanny automatons, bowling, bowling, bowling. . . . Six successive maidens. 'This,' says the Parson, 'this is intolerable.' One's heart is aching for an honest boundary hit. . . . And the human bowling machines send down six more successive maidens. Think of it; twelve successive maidens, and the game in that state, the crowd in that purgatory. 'When Grace was a boy of eighteen I saw him make 50 on this very ground and he played every ball he got.' It was the Parson again, but now he sounded a little strained, a little unhappy. At the end of the twelfth successive maiden, a hit was purposely misfielded that Spofforth might have a 'go' at Lyttelton. The batsmen fell into the snare. Four more maidens, and spinning is Lyttelton's wicket. 'Anyhow, that's over and done with!' thankfully breathes the crowd. Better all be dead than dying! England five for 66—19 needed. Steel comes next and Lucas hits a boundary. Roars the crowd 'Bravo!' then catches breath. Steel caught and bowled Spofforth none—Maurice Read clean bowled second ball. England seven for 70. 'Incredible!' say 20,000 people in dismal unison. Barnes, the next man, hits a two. Thirteen to win. Heaven bless us, Blackham has blundered! He allows three byes. Run Barnes, run Lucas! Spofforth is inscrutable as the crowd makes its noises. His next ball is too fast for eyes at the boundary's edge to see. Lucas comes down on it, though—hard, determined. And the ball rolls ever so gently on to the wicket and disturbs the bail. Poor Lucas bows his head and departs, and blasphemy is riot throughout the crowd and is communicated by stages to the outer darkness of Kennington Road.

The stars are set against England—our cricketers are for the first time on English soil face to face with a victorious Australian XI. With ten to struggle for, Blackham catches Barnes off his glove, and the last man is here—poor Peate, who is the best slow bowler in England and not a bit more of a cricketer than that, and what good are his mysteries of spin now? Studd is there yet, though; only ten runs and it is our game. Perhaps *he*—Peate has hit a two. It was audacious, but maybe the ball was a safe one to tackle. A bad ball's a bad ball at any time. Peate has nerve (so we are telling ourselves, desperately): he's the right man: he'll play the steady game to good stuff and leave the job to Studd. . . . The stark truth is that Peate hit out wildly yet again at a slow from Boyle, missed it, and was bowled. There was a hollow laugh somewhere as the wicket went back, but whether it came from this world or the next I couldn't say. Studd did not get a ball. 'Why, man, did you try to hit: why couldn't you just stop them?' they asked Peate. 'Well,' he replied, 'I couldn't trust Maister Studd!'

As Peate's wicket was broken, ten thousand people rushed the rails and hid the green field. Spofforth was carried shoulder-high to the pavilion, and there the mob praised a famous man. I, too, wanted to get up and shout, but somehow I was rooted to my seat. I was probably the only man in that multitude on the pavilion not standing up, and as I sat there I had a strange sense of making a lonely hole in a solid black mass. The Parson was standing on the seat beside me. His boots were not more than two feet from my eyes and I could see the fine ribbed work on the upper edge of the soles. The cheering came downwards to me, sounding remote. I lost grip on events. It seemed that I sat there till the ground was almost deserted, till over the field came a faint mist, and with it the vague melancholy of twilight in a great city. Time to go home, I thought . . . a great match . . . great days . . . great men . . . all gone . . . far away . . . departed glory. . . . A hand of someone touched my shoulder and I heard him say: 'The Orsetralians are on the way, and they'll be in the nets at four o'clock. Nice in the sun, isn't it?'

Days in the Sun, 1924

*

The Flower Show Match

SIEGFRIED SASSOON

My window was wide open when I went to bed, and I had left the curtains half-drawn. I woke out of my deep and dreamless sleep to a gradual recognition that I was at home and not in the cubicled dormitory at Ballboro'. Drowsily grateful for this, I lay and listened. A cock was crowing from a neighbouring farm; his shrill challenge was faintly echoed by another cock a long way off.

I loved the early morning; it was luxurious to lie there, half-awake, and half-aware that there was a pleasantly eventful day in front of me. . . . Presently I would get up and lean on the window-ledge to see what was happening in the world outside. . . . There was a starling's nest under the window where the jasmine grew thickest, and all of a sudden I heard one of the birds dart away with a soft flurry of wings. Hearing it go, I imagined how it would fly boldly across the garden: soon I was up and staring at the treetops which loomed motionless against a flushed and brightening sky. Slipping into some clothes I opened my door very quietly and tiptoed along the passage and down the stairs. There was no sound except the first chirping of the sparrows in the ivy. I felt as if I had changed since the Easter holidays. The drawing-room door creaked as I went softly in and crept across the beeswaxed parquet floor. Last night's half-consumed candles and the cat's half-empty bowl of milk under the gate-legged table seemed to belong neither here nor there, and my own silent face looked queerly at me out of the mirror. And there was the familiar photograph of 'Love and Death', by Watts, with its secret meaning which I could never quite formulate in a thought, though it often touched me with a vague emotion of pathos. When I unlocked the door into the garden the early morning air met me with its cold purity; on the stone step were the bowls of roses and delphiniums and sweet peas which Aunt Evelyn had carried out there before she went to bed; the scarlet disc of the sun had climbed an inch above the hills. Thrushes and blackbirds hopped and pecked busily on the dew-soaked lawn, and a pigeon was cooing monotonously from the belt of woodland which sloped from the garden toward the Weald. Down there in the belt of river-mist a goods train whistled as it puffed steadily away from the station with a distinctly heard clanking of buffers. How little I knew of the enormous world beyond that valley and those low green hills.

From over the fields and orchards Butley Church struck five in mellow tones. Then the clock indoors whizzed and confirmed it with a less resonant tongue. The Flower Show Match was hours away yet—more than six hours in fact. Suppose I'd better go back to bed again, I thought, or I'll be feeling tired out before the match begins. Soon the maids would be stirring overhead, padding about the floor and talking in muffled voices. Meanwhile I stole down to the pantry to cut myself a piece of cake. What a stuffy smelling place it was, with the taps dripping into the sink and a bluebottle fly buzzing sleepily on the ceiling. I inspected the village grocer's calendar which was hanging from a nail. On it there was a picture of 'The Relief of Ladysmith' . . . Old Kruger and the Boers. I never could make up my mind what it was all about, that Boer War, and it seemed such a long way off. . . . Yawning and munching I went creaking up to my room. It was broad daylight out of doors, but I was soon asleep again.

II

After breakfast there was no time to be wasted. First of all I had to rummage about for the tin of 'Blanco', which was nowhere to be found. Probably the parlour-maid had bagged it; why on earth couldn't they leave things alone? I knew exactly where I'd left the tin at the end of last holidays—on the shelf in the schoolroom, standing on an old case of beetles (of which, for a short time, I had been a collector). And now, unless I could find the tin quickly, there'd never be time for me to 'Blanco' my pads, for they took ever so long to dry in the sun, even on a blazing hot day like this one. . . .

'Really, it's a bit thick, Aunt Evelyn; someone's taken my tin of "Blanco",' I grumbled. But she was already rather fussed, and was at that moment preoccupied in a serious discussion with Mabb, the gardener, about the transportation of the crockery which she was lending for the Cricket Tea.

In a hasty parenthesis she confessed that she had given the tin to Dixon only a week or two ago, so I transferred myself and my grimy pads to the harness room, where I discovered Dixon putting the finishing touches to his white cricket boots; he had already cleaned mine, and he apologized for not having done my pads, as he had been unable to find them. While I busied myself with dabbing and smearing the pads we had a nice chat about county cricket; he also told me how he had taken a 'highly commended' at the Crystal Palace Dog Show with one of the smooth-haired collies which he had recently begun breeding. There had been a lull in his horse-buying activities after I went to school; since then I had given up my riding, as my aunt could not afford to keep a cob specially for me to ride in the holidays. So Dixon had consoled himself with his collies and village cricket: and the saddles were only used when he was exercising the sedate horse which now shared the carriage work with the smart little pony Rocket.

Leaving my pads to dry in the sun, I sauntered contentedly back to the house to have a squint at the morning paper, which never arrived until after breakfast. I had a private reason for wanting to look at the *Morning Post*. I was a firm believer in predestination, and I used to improvise superstitions of my own in connection with the cricket matches I played in. Aunt Evelyn was rustling the newspaper in the drawing-room, where she was having a short spell of inactivity before setting forth to judge the vegetables and sweet peas. Evidently she was reading about politics (she was a staunch Tory).

'I can't understand what that miserable Campbell-Bannerman is up to: but thank heaven the Radicals will never get in again,' she exclaimed, handing me the sheet with the cricket news on it.

Carrying this into the garden I set about consulting the omens for my success in the match. I searched assiduously through the first-class scores, picking out the amateurs whose names, like my own, began with S, and whose initial was G. There were only two that day: the result was most unsatisfactory. *G. Shaw run out*, 1: *G. Smith, c. Lilley, b. Field*, 0. According to that I should score half a run. So I called in professional assistance, and was rewarded with: *Shrewsbury, not out*, 127. This left me in a very awkward position. The average now worked out at 64. The highest score I had ever made was 51, and that was only in a practice game at Ballboro'. Besides, 51 from 64 left 13, an unlucky number. It was absurd even to dally with the idea of my making sixty-four in the Butley Flower Show Match. Anything between twenty and thirty would have been encouraging. But Aunt Evelyn's voice from the drawing-room window informed me that she would be starting in less than ten minutes, so I ran upstairs to change into my flannels. And, anyhow, the weather couldn't have been better. . . . While we were walking across the fields Aunt Evelyn paused on the top of a stile to remark that she felt sure Mr Balfour would be a splendid Prime Minister. But I was meditating about Shrewsbury's innings. How I wished I could bat like him, if only for one day!

The village of Butley contained, as one of its chief characters, a portly and prosperous saddler named William Dodd. It was Dodd who now greeted us at the field-gate and ushered Aunt Evelyn into the large, tropical-temperatured tent where the judges had already begun their expert scrutiny of the competing vegetables.

In the minds of most of the inhabitants of Butley William Dodd was an immemorial institution, and no village affairs could properly be transacted without his sanction and assistance. As a churchwarden on Sundays his impressive demeanour led us to suppose that, if he was not yet on hat-raising terms with the Almighty, he at any moment expected to be. During a Parliamentary Election he was equally indispensable, as he supervised the balloting in the village schoolroom; and the sanguine solemnity with which he welcomed the Conservative candidate left no doubt at all as to his own political opinions. He was a man much respected by the local gentry, and was on free and easy terms with the farmers of the neighbourhood. In fact, he was a sort of unofficial mayor of the village, and would have worn his robes, had they existed, with dignity and decorum. Though nearer fifty than forty, he was still one of the most vigorous run-getters in the Butley eleven, and his crafty underarm bowling worked havoc with the tail-end of many an opposing team. On Flower Show day he was in all his glory as captain of the cricket team and secretary and treasurer of the Horticultural Society, and his manner of receiving my aunt and myself was an epitome of his urbane and appreciative attitude toward the universe with which the parish of Butley was discreetly associated. Waggish persons in the village had given him the nickname 'Did-I-say-Myself'. Anyone who wanted to discover the origin of this witticism could do so by stopping outside the saddler's shop on a summer morning for a few minutes of gentle gossip. Laying aside whatever implement of his craft he happened to be using, he would get up and come to the door in his protuberant apron, and when interrogated about 'the team for to-morrow', 'Let me see,' he would reply in a gravely complacent voice, 'Let me see, there's Mr Richard Puttridge; and Myself; my brother Alfred; Tom Dixon; Mr Jack Barchard; young Bob Ellis—and did I say Myself?'—and so on, counting the names on his stubby fingers, and sometimes inserting 'and I think I said Myself' again toward the end of the recital. But his sense of his own importance was justified when he had a bat in his hand. No one could gainsay that.

Having, so to speak, received the freedom of the Flower Show from this worthy man, there was nothing more for me to do until the rest of the players had arrived. At present there wasn't a cricketer to be seen on the small but well-kept ground, and it seemed unlikely that the match would start before noon. It was now a little after eleven and a cloudless day. Sitting in the shadow of a chestnut tree I watched the exertions of a muscular man with a mallet. He was putting up a 'coconut shy' in the adjoining meadow, where a steam roundabout, some boat-swings, a shooting gallery, and other recreative facilities were in readiness for the afternoon. On the opposite side of the cricket field had been erected a Tea Tent, which would contain such spectators as were prevented, by their social status, from shying at coconuts or turning almost upside-down in a boat-swing. The ground sloped from the Tea Tent to the side where I was sitting (twenty-five summers ago), so that the genteel onlookers were enabled to feel themselves perceptibly above the rest of the proceedings.

Behind the Tent was a thick thorn hedge; beyond the hedge ran the dusty high road to the village. In the later afternoon of a cricket match there would be several dilatory vehicles drawn up on the other side of the hedge, and the drivers would watch the game in Olympian detachment. There would be the carrier's van, and the brewer's dray, and the baker's cart, and the doctor's gig, and sometimes even a wagon-load of hay. None of them ever seemed to be pressed for time, and once they were there they were likely to stay till the end of the innings. Rooks would be cawing in the vicarage elms, and Butley, with its huddle of red roofs and square church tower, was a contented-looking place.

In my retrospect the players are now beginning to appear in ones and twos. Some skim easily across the greensward on bicycles; others arrive philosophically on foot, pausing to inspect the wicket, which has a nasty habit of causing fast bowling to 'bump' after a spell of dry weather.

Dixon and I were having a little practice up against the fence when Aunt Evelyn emerged from the Flower Show Tent with a bevy of head-gardeners. She signalled to me, so I clambered over the palings and went up to her. She only wanted to tell me that she would be back again after lunch and did so hope she wouldn't miss my innings.

Climbing over the fence again I became aware of the arrival of the Rotherden eleven in a two-horse brake. It was close on twelve o'clock, but they'd had a fourteen-mile drive and the road was up and down hill all the way. How enormous they looked as they sauntered across the ground—several of them carrying cricket bags. I should be lucky if I made any runs at all against such men as they were!

Butley Church clock was tolling twelve while our opponents were bearing down on us from the other side of the field, with William Dodd already half-way across to meet them. But the Rotherden men appeared to be in no great hurry to begin the game as they stopped to have a look at the wicket. Meanwhile Butley bells chimed sedately to the close of the mellow extra celebration which Providence allowed them every three hours without fail. . . .

'I suppose they've got their best team?' I faltered to Dixon, whose keen gaze was identifying the still distant stalwarts.

'You bet they have!' he replied with a grim smile.

Two of the tallest men had detached themselves from the others and were now pacing importantly down the pitch with Dodd between them. Dixon indicated this group. 'They've got Crump and Bishop, anyhow,' he remarked. . . . Crump and Bishop! The names had a profound significance for me. For many years I had heard Dixon speak of them, and I had even watched them playing in a few Flower Show Matches. Heavily built men in dark blue caps, with large drooping moustaches, one of them bowling vindictively at each end and Butley wickets falling fast; or else one of them batting at each end and Butley bowling being scored off with masterful severity.

But they had also produced a less localized effect on me. Rotherden was on the 'unhunted' side of our district; it was in a part of the county which I somehow associated with cherry-blossom and black-and-white timbered cottages. Also it had the charm of remoteness, and whenever I thought of Crump and Bishop, I comprehensively visualized the whole fourteen miles of more or less unfamiliar landscape which lay between Butley and Rotherden. For me the names meant certain lovely glimpses of the Weald, and the smell of mown hayfields, and the noise of a shallow river flowing under a bridge. Yet Crump was an ordinary auctioneer who sold sheep and cattle on market days, and Bishop kept the 'Rose and Crown' at Rotherden.

III

Butley had lost the toss. As we went on to the field I tightened the black and yellow scarf which I wore round my waist; the scarf proved that I had won a place in my House Eleven at school, and it was my sole credential as a cricketer. But to-day was more exciting and important than any House Match, and my sense of my own inferiority did not prevent me from observing every detail of the proceedings which I am now able to visualize so clearly across the intervening years.

The umpires in their long white coats have placed the bails on the stumps, each at his own end, and they are still satisfying themselves that the stumps are in the requisite state of exact uprightness. Tom Seamark, the Rotherden umpire, is a red-faced sporting publican who bulks as large as a lighthouse. As an umpire he has certain emphatic mannerisms. When appealed to he expresses a negative decision with a severe and stentorian 'NOT OOUT': but when adjudicating that the batsman is out, he silently shoots his right arm toward the sky—an impressive and irrevocable gesture which effectively quells all adverse criticism. He is, of course, a tremendous judge of the game, and when not absorbed by his grave responsibilities he is one of the most jovial men you could meet with.

Bill Sutler, our umpire, is totally different. To begin with, he has a wooden leg. Nobody knows how he lost his leg; he does not deny the local tradition that he was once a soldier, but even in his cups he has never been heard to claim that he gave the limb for Queen and Country. It is, however, quite certain that he is now a cobbler (with a heavily waxed moustache) and Butley has ceased to deny that he is a grossly partisan umpire. In direct contrast to Tom Seamark he invariably signifies 'not out' by a sour shake of the head: when the answer is an affirmative one he bawls 'Hout' as if he'd been stung by a wasp. It is reputed that (after giving the enemy's last man out leg-before in a closely-fought finish) he was once heard to add, in an exultant undertone: 'and I've won my five bob.' He has also been accused of making holes in the pitch with his wooden leg in order to facilitate the efforts of the Butley bowlers.

The umpires are in their places. But it is in the sunshine of my own clarified retrospection that they are wearing their white coats. While I was describing them I had forgotten that they have both of them been dead for many years. Nevertheless, their voices are distinctly audible to me. 'Same boundaries as usual, Bill?' shouts Seamark, as loudly as if he were talking to a deaf customer in his tap-room. 'Same *as* usual, Muster Seamark; three all round and four over the fence. Draw at six-thirty, and seven if there's anything in it,' says Sutler. And so, with an intensified detachment, I look around me at the Butley players, who are now safely distributed in the positions which an omniscient Dodd has decreed for them.

I see myself, an awkward overgrown boy, fielding anxiously at mid-on. And there's Ned Noakes, the whiskered and one-eyed wicket-keeper, alert and active, though he's forty-five if he's a day. With his one eye (and a glass one) he sees more than most of us do, and his enthusiasm for the game is apparent in every attitude. Alongside of him lounges big Will Picksett, a taciturn good-natured young yokel; though over-deliberate in his movements, Will is a tower of strength in the team, and he sweeps half-volleys to the boundary with his enormous brown arms as though he were scything a hayfield. But there is no more time to describe the fielders, for Dodd has thrown a bright red ball to Frank Peckham, who is to begin the bowling from the top end. While Crump and Bishop are still on their way to the wickets I cannot help wondering whether, to modern eyes, the Butley team would not seem just a little unorthodox. William Dodd, for example, comfortably dressed in a pale pink shirt and grey trousers; and Peter Baitup, the ground-man (whose face is framed in a 'Newgate fringe') wearing dingy white trousers with thin green stripes, and carrying his cap in his belt while he bowls his tempting left-hand slows. But things were different in those days.

In the meantime Bill Crump has taken his guard and is waiting with watchful ease to subjugate the first ball of the match, while Peckham, a stalwart fierce-browed farmer, takes a final look round the field. Peckham is a fast bowler with an eccentric style. Like most fast bowlers, he starts about fifteen paces from the wicket, but instead of *running* he *walks* the whole way to the crease, very much on his heels, breaking his aggressive stride with a couple of systematic hops when about half-way to his destination. Now he is ready. Seamark pronounces the word 'Play!' And off he goes, walking for all he is worth, gripping the ball ferociously, and eyeing the batsman as if he intended to murder him if he can't bowl him neck and crop. On the ultimate stride his arm swings over, and a short-pitched ball pops up and whizzes alarmingly near Crump's magnificent moustache. Ned Noakes receives it rapturously with an adroit snap of his gauntlets. Unperturbed, and with immense deliberation, Crump strolls up the pitch and prods with his bat the spot where he has made up his mind that the ball hit the ground on its way toward his head. The ground-man scratches his nose apologetically. 'Don't drop 'em too short, Frank,' says Dodd mildly, with an expostulatory shake of his bristly grey cranium. Thus the match proceeds until, twenty-five years ago, it is lunch time, and Rotherden has made seventy runs with three wickets down. And since both Crump and Bishop have been got rid of, Butley thinks it hasn't done badly.

The Luncheon Tent stood on that part of the field where the Flower Show ended and the swings and roundabouts began. Although the meal was an informal affair, there was shy solemnity in the faces of most of the players as they filtered out of the bright sunshine into the sultry, half-lit interior, where the perspiring landlord of the 'Chequers' and his buxom wife were bustling about at the climax of their preparations. While the cricketers were shuffling themselves awkwardly into their places, the brawny barman (who seemed to take catering less seriously than his employers) sharpened the carving-knife on a steel prong with a rasping sound that set one's teeth on edge while predicting satisfactory slices of lamb and beef, to say nothing of veal and ham pie and a nice bit of gammon of bacon.

As soon as all were seated Dodd created silence by rapping the table; he then put on his churchwarden face and looked toward Parson Yalden, who was in readiness to take his cue. He enunciated the grace in slightly unparsonic tones, which implied that he was not only Rector of Rotherden, but also a full member of the MCC and first cousin once removed to Lord Chatwynd. Parson Yalden's parishioners occasionally complained that he paid more attention to cricket and pheasant shooting than was fit and proper. But as long as he could afford to keep a hard-working curate he rightly considered it his own affair if he chose to spend three days a week playing in club and country-house matches all over the county. His demeanour when keeping wicket for his own parish was both jaunty and magisterial, and he was renowned for the strident and obstreperous bellow to which he gave vent when he was trying to bluff a village umpire into giving a batsman out 'caught behind'. He was also known for his habit of genially engaging the batsman in conversation while the bowler was intent on getting him out, and I have heard of at least one occasion when he tried this little trick on the wrong man. The pestered batsman rounded on the rather foxy-faced clergyman with, 'I bin playing cricket nigh on thirty years, and parson or no parson, I take the liberty of telling you to hold your blasted gab.'

But I hurriedly dismissed this almost unthinkable anecdote when he turned his greenish eyes in my direction and hoped, in hearty and ingratiating tones, that I was 'going to show them a little crisp Ballboro' batting'.

The brisk clatter of knives and forks is now well started, and the barman is busy at his barrel. Conversation, however, is scanty, until Tom Seamark, who is always glad of a chance to favour the company with a sentiment, clears his throat impressively, elevates his tankard, fixes Jack Barchard with his gregarious regard, and remarks, 'I should like to say, sir, how very pleased and proud we all are to see you safe 'ome again in our midst.' Jack Barchard has recently returned from the Boer War where he served with the Yeomanry. The 'sentiment' is echoed from all parts of the table, and glasses are raised to him with a gruff 'Good 'ealth, sir,' or 'Right glad to see you back, Mr Barchard.' The returned warrior receives their congratulations with the utmost embarrassment. Taking a shy sip at my ginger-beer, I think how extraordinary it is to be sitting next to a man who has really been 'out in South Africa'. Barchard is a fair-haired young gentleman farmer. When the parson suggests that 'it must have been pretty tough work out there', he replies that he is thundering glad to be back among his fruit trees again, and this, apparently, is about all he has to say about the Boer War.

But when the meal was drawing to an end and I had finished my helping of cold cherry-tart, and the barman began to circulate with a wooden platter for collecting the half-crowns, I became agonizingly aware that I had come to the match without any money. I was getting into a panic while the plate came clinking along the table, but quiet Jack Barchard unconsciously saved the situation by putting down five shillings and saying, 'All right, old chap, I'll stump up for both.' Mumbling, 'Oh, that's jolly decent of you,' I wished I could have followed him up a hill in a 'forlorn hope'. . . . He told me, later on, that he never set eyes on a Boer the whole time he was in South Africa.

The clock struck three, and the Reverend Yalden's leg-stump had just been knocked out of the ground by a vicious yorker from Frank Peckham. 'Hundred and seventeen. Five. Nought,' shouted the Butley scorer, popping his head out of the little flat-roofed shanty which was known as 'the pavilion'. The battered tin number-plates were rattled on to their nails on the scoring-board by a zealous young hobbledehoy who had undertaken the job for the day.

'*Wodger* say last man made?' he bawled, though the scorer was only a few feet away from him.

'Last man, *Blob*.'

The parson was unbuckling his pads on a bench near by, and I was close enough to observe the unevangelical expression on his face as he looked up from under the brim of his panama hat with the MCC ribbon round it. Mr Yalden was not a popular character on the Butley ground, and the hobbledehoy had made the most of a heaven-sent opportunity.

From an undersized platform in front of the Horticultural Tent the

Butley brass band now struck up 'The Soldiers of the Queen'. It's quite like playing in a county match, I thought, as I scanned the spectators, who were lining the fence on two sides of the field. Several easily recognizable figures from among the local gentry were already sauntering toward the Tea Tent, after a gossiping inspection of the Flower Show. I could see slow-moving Major Carmine, the best dressed man in Butley, with his white spats and a carnation in his buttonhole; and the enthusiastic curate, known as 'Hard Luck' on account of his habit of exclaiming, 'Oh, hard luck!' when watching or taking part in games of cricket, lawn tennis, or hockey. He was escorting the Miss Pattons, two elderly sisters who always dressed alike. And there was Aunt Evelyn, with her red sunshade up, walking between rosy-faced old Captain Huxtable and his clucking, oddly dressed wife. It was quite a brilliant scene which the Butley Band was doing its utmost to sustain with experimental and unconvincing tootles and drum-beatings.

Soon afterwards, however, the Soldiers of the Queen were overwhelmed by the steam-organ which, after a warning hoot, began to accompany the revolving wooden horses of the gilded roundabout with a strident and blaring fanfaronade. For a minute or two the contest of cacophonies continued. But in spite of a tempestuous effort the band was completely outplayed by its automatic and unexhaustible adversary. The discord becoming intolerable, it seemed possible that the batsmen would 'appeal against the music' in the same way that they sometimes 'appeal against the light' when they consider it inadequate. But William Dodd was equal to the emergency; with an ample gesture he conveyed himself across the ground and prohibited the activity of the steam-organ until the match was finished. The flitting steeds now revolved and undulated noiselessly beneath their gilded canopy, while the Butley Band palavered peacefully onward into the unclouded jollity of the afternoon.

The clock struck four. Rotherden were all out for 183 and Tom Dixon had finished the innings with a confident catch on the boundary off one of Dodd's artfully innocent lobs. No catches had come my way, so my part in the game had been an unobtrusive one. When Dodd and Picksett went out to open our innings it was a matter of general opinion in the Beer Tent that the home team had a sporting chance to make the runs by seven o'clock, although there were some misgivings about the wicket and it was anticipated that Crump and Bishop would make the ball fly about a bit when they got to work.

Having ascertained that I was last but one on the list in the score-book, I made my way slowly round the field to have a look at the Flower Show. As I went along the boundary in front of the spectators who were leaning their elbows on the fence I felt quite an important public character. And as I shouldn't have to go in for a long while yet, there was no need to feel nervous. The batsmen, too, were shaping confidently, and there was a shout of 'Good ole Bill! That's the way to keep 'em on the carpet!' when Dodd brought off one of his cele-brated square-cuts to the hedge off Bishop's easy-actioned fast bowl-ing. Picksett followed this up with an audacious pull which sent a straight one from Crump skimming first bounce into the Tea Tent, where it missed the short-sighted doctor's new straw hat by half an inch and caused quite a flutter among the tea-sipping ladies.

'Twenty up,' announced the scorer, and the attendant hobbledehoy nearly fell over himself in his eagerness to get the numbers up on the board. A stupendous appeal for a catch at the wicket by the Reverend Yalden was countered by Sutler with his surliest shake of the head, and the peg-supported umpire was the most popular man on the field as he ferried himself to his square-leg location at the end of the over. Forty went up; then Dodd was clean bowled by Crump.

''Ow's *that*?' bawled a ribald Rotherden partisan from a cart in the road, as the rotund batsman retreated; warm but majestic, he acknow-ledged the applause of the onlookers by a slight lifting of his close-fitting little cap. Everybody was delighted that he had done so well, and it was agreed that he was (in the Beer Tent) 'a regular chronic old sport' and (in the Tea Tent) 'a wonderful man for his age'. Modest Jack Barchard then made his appearance and received a Boer War ovation.

Leaving the game in this prosperous condition, I plunged into the odoriferous twilight of the Horticultural Tent. I had no intention of staying there long, but I felt that I owed it to Aunt Evelyn to have a look at the sweet peas and vegetables at any rate. When I emerged the home team had lost two more wickets and the condition of the game was causing grave anxiety. Reluctantly I drifted toward the Tea Tent for a period of social victimization.

The Tea Tent was overcrowded and I found Aunt Evelyn sitting a little way outside it in comparative seclusion. She was in earnest com-munication with Miss Clara Maskall, a remarkable old lady who had been born in the year of the Battle of Waterloo and had been stone-deaf for more than sixty years.

My aunt was one of the few people in the neighbourhood who enjoyed meeting Miss Maskall. For the old lady had a way of forgetting that the rest of the world could hear better than she could, and her quavering comments on some of the local gentlefolk, made in their presence, were often too caustic to be easily forgotten. She was reputed to have been kissed by King George the Fourth. She was wearing a bunched-up black silk dress, and her delicately withered face was framed in a black poke-bonnet, tied under the chin with a white lace scarf. With her piercingly alert eyes and beaky nose she looked like some ancient and intelligent bird. Altogether she was an old person of great distinction, and I approached her with an awful timidity. She had old-fashioned ideas about education, and she usually inquired of me, in creaking tones, whether I had recently been flogged by my schoolmaster. . . . Miss Maskall had made the game seem rather remote. She cared nothing for cricket, and had only come there for an afternoon spree. But she was taciturn during her tour of the Flower Show: when we tucked her into her shabby old victoria she leant back and closed her eyes. Years ago she must have had a lovely face. While we watched her carriage turn the corner I wondered what it felt like to be eighty-seven; but I did not connect such antiquity with my own future. Long before I was born she had seen gentlemen playing cricket in queer whiskers and tall hats.

Next moment I was safely back in the present, and craning my neck for a glimpse of the score-board as I hustled Aunt Evelyn along to the Tea Tent. There had been a Tea Interval during our absence, so we hadn't missed so very much. Five wickets were down for ninety and the shadows of the cricketers were growing longer in the warm glare which slanted down the field. A sense of my own share in the game invaded me and it was uncomfortable to imagine that I might soon be walking out into the middle to be bowled at by Crump and Bishop, who now seemed gigantic and forbidding. And then impetuous Ned Noakes must needs call Frank Peckham for an impossibly short run, and his partner retreated with a wrathful shake of his head. Everything now depended on Dixon who was always as cool as a cucumber in a crisis.

'Give 'em a bit of the long handle, Tom!' bawled someone in the Beer Tent, while he marched serenely toward the wicket, pausing for a confidential word with Noakes who was still looking a bit crestfallen after the recent catastrophe. Dixon was a stylish left-hander and never worried much about playing himself in. Bishop was well aware of this, and he at once arranged an extra man in the outfield for him. Sure enough, the second ball he received was lifted straight into the long-off's hands. But the sun was in the fielder's eyes and he misjudged the flight of the catch. The Beer Tent exulted vociferously. Dixon then set about the bowling and the score mounted merrily. He was energetically supported by Ned Noakes. But when their partnership had added over fifty, and they looked like knocking off the runs, Noakes was caught in the slips off a bumping ball and the situation instantly became serious again.

Realizing that I was next in but one, I went off in a fluster to put my pads on, disregarding Aunt Evelyn's tremulous 'I do so hope you'll do well, dear'. By the time I had arrived on the other side of the ground, Amos Hickmott, the wheelwright's son, had already caused acute anxiety. After surviving a tigerish appeal for 'leg-before', he had as near as a toucher run Dixon out in a half-witted endeavour to escape from the bowling. My palsied fingers were still busy with straps and buckles when what sounded to me like a deafening crash warned me that it was all over with Hickmott. We still wanted seven runs to win when I wandered weakly in the direction of the wicket. But it was the end of an over, and Dixon had the bowling. When I arrived the Reverend Yalden was dawdling up the pitch in his usual duck-footed progress when crossing from one wicket to the other.

'Well, young man, you've got to look lively this time,' he observed with intimidating jocosity. But there seemed to be a twinkle of encouragement in Seamark's light blue eye as I established myself in his shadow.

Dixon played the first three balls carefully. The fourth he smote clean out of the ground. The hit was worth six, but 'three all round and four over' was an immemorial rule at Butley. Unfortunately, he tried to repeat the stroke, and the fifth ball shattered his stumps. In those days there were only five balls to an over.

Peter Baitup now rolled up with a wide grin on his fringed face, but it was no grinning moment for me at the bottom end when Sutler gave me 'middle-and-leg' and I confronted impending disaster from Crump with the sun in my eyes. The first ball (which I lost sight of) missed my wicket by 'a coat of varnish' and travelled swiftly to the boundary for two byes, leaving Mr Yalden with his huge gauntlets above his head in an attitude of aggrieved astonishment. The game was now a tie. Through some obscure psychological process my whole being now became clarified. I remembered Shrewsbury's century and became as bold as brass. There was the enormous auctioneer with the ball in his hand. And there I, calmly resolved to look lively and defeat his destructive aim. The ball hit my bat and trickled slowly up the pitch. 'Come on!' I shouted, and Peter came gallantly on. Crump was so taken by surprise that we were safe home before he'd picked up the ball. And that was the end of the Flower Show Match.

Memoirs of a Fox Hunting Man, 1928

*

The Field

FRANCIS COLGATE BENSON

Can you imagine this whole earth could yield
A spot more beautiful than our old cricket field?
Ring'd 'round with immemorial elms it lies
A fair green lawn,
Where at the break of dawn
Grey squirrels play
And robin redbreasts herald the coming day.

Blue sky and sunshine, white sheets unfurled and wickets set,
Now come a flannel'd host to battle, yet
On this fair field
Shall blows be bloodless and the stronger yield.
Our grand old game is like that older game of life,
The youth, a junior at the nets,
Impatient of instruction, frets,
For wider fields of strife,
Self-confident, would play the faster balls—
And so, misjudging, down his wicket falls.

School days are over, now with bat in hand he goes to take his
        knock in life's great game.
Will he be stumpt or bowl'd or caught, or gain renown like
        those immortals who are known to fame?

We cannot all be kings of pace
As in his day our own great 'Bart' was king,
Or, like that bearded giant Grace,
Record a boundary with each mighty swing.
But should our strength be not enough to score a single run,
Yet should we be well satisfied to know our best was done.

And when the grim bowler with his deathly pace
Begins that last 'over' which we all must face
Be of good cheer;
If you have ever done your best nor tried to run your partner
     out, then though the whole world shouts 'How's that?',
     still have no fear.
The answer may be 'you are out', but you will hear
A gentle voice exclaim
'Well played, sir; you've been chosen for a higher game

The shadows fall, the day is done,
The battle o'er and the victory won.
Dawn . . . Day . . . and Gloam.
See there the evening star,
Set like a beacon light afar,
To guide the traveller home.
This mortal game must end. The old scarred bats be laid
     away.
We heed no more the friendly battle call, and those we leave
     behind will say
'They're resting here awhile, that's all, until they pass, as
     through an open door
To meet their Captain who has gone before'.

For we are sure that He Who even marks the sparrow's fall
Will not refuse to us another cricket ball.
Great Captain, in that many mansioned home, we humbly
     pray Thee, yield
Some little space,
Where we may place
Again our cricket field.

'Mid pastures green, by waters still
We'll meet again, I know we will,
And praise the Name of Him Who gave the Field and rules
the Game.

Songs of the Cricket Field, 1932

❊

The First Cup-Match

JOHN FINNEMORE

On the next Thursday afternoon there was rather a heavy muster of spectators on Big Ground. Many came to see what sort of fight Teddy Lester would put up with his weak team against the powerful School House Eleven. They knew that Teddy always did his best when his back was to the wall, and they fancied that his batting would be worth watching, no matter how poorly his men might figure against the excellent School House bowling.

This array of spectators was reinforced by the whole of the Upper Third. Word had been passed round that one of their members had been chosen to play in the first game for Jayne's, an honour which had never fallen to a member of the Upper Third within the memory of man; and all his form-comrades from many Houses had gathered to see what young Sandys would do.

There was some rather sharp criticism of Teddy for including such a child—as Frank appeared—in the Eleven. Many said that Teddy had been influenced entirely by the boy's name, and that Frank would be outclassed in a House Eleven, and let his captain down. Some of the sharpest criticism was uttered in Jayne's itself, and the loudest voice among the carpers was that of Huntley.

'Of all the howling asses in the world, that fool Lester just about takes the cake!' said Huntley when he saw that the name of the youngster he had tried to whop was on the same list as his own. 'To think of his shoving in a cheeky little scug like that whelp, and all because the wretched little beast is the brother of an old friend of his!'

'I don't know,' said Chettle with a grin; 'it won't be half bad fun to see the little swot upset by the School House bowling. It will make Lester look such a fool. All Slapton will be laughing at him.'

'That's all very well,' replied Huntley virtuously; 'but we must think of the House. Just see how Lester is chucking the House chances away! Why didn't he put in Barnes here? Old Barnes can run and throw no end well. He'd be jolly useful in the field, and the man who saves a run is as good as the man who makes one.'

Barnes, who had been dreadfully disgruntled at being left out of the House Eleven, snuffled assent, and tried to look like a martyr. So it was with great hopes of Frank's downfall that these three came down after dinner to Big Ground.

The captains met to toss. Rooke of the School House, fast bowler of the First Eleven, and a good bat, spun up a shilling. Teddy said, 'Heads!' Heads it wasn't. 'We'll take first knock,' said Rooke, and Teddy nodded, as if to say, 'And well you may on such a wicket.'

The wicket was capital, fast and easy; and Teddy muttered to Ito, 'Hard lines I lost the toss. We're in for a dose of leather-hunting!' But he led his men out at once, and placed his field very carefully for the Bat, who was to open the bowling.

Rooke brought another First Eleven man in with him to bat, and there was deep attention given to the game all round the ring when the umpire called, 'Play!'

The Bat's first over was superb. He was in great form for bowling a very fast ball that went with the arm. Two of the balls were good enough for a wicket anywhere, and it was only by sheer luck that Rooke stopped them. Both were on his blind spot; but in each case he followed the safe old trick of playing straight in front of the wicket, and so turned aside the threatened danger. At the end of the over Rooke, good bat though he was, could not repress a sigh of relief upon finding his end of the wicket still held up, and he stood aside to see how his partner would fare with Teddy's slows.

The first ball was a trimmer, for it broke beautifully; not a big break, but that little artful turn of the ball which often is thrice as fatal as the big break right across the wicket. Burnett of the School House played at it and missed it. He was lucky in not getting it on the edge of his bat, whence it would have gone spinning into the padded hands which now seized it so safely. The hands were those of Ito, who had developed into a first-rate wicket-keeper. The Japanese boy made up for his lack of inches and want of reach by a remarkable quickness, by a sure holding of the ball when it came within his grasp, and by an unfailing judgment of its flight. Burnett pulled himself together and played the rest of Teddy's over very carefully. The last ball he placed for a single, and thus had to face the Bat when he resumed bowling. Now the Bat knew very well that Burnett, though a capital bat, had a great dislike for a 'yorker', and the wily Bat laid himself out to take advantage of this weakness in his opponent. Darting up to the wicket, his eyes rolling wildly behind his big spectacles, the Bat lammed one of his best down the pitch. It was a clipper. The length was perfect, the speed terrific. It caught Burnett in a hopeless complication of ideas, and he was forced to pay the penalty, for no one can trifle with a dead-straight 'yorker'. In the first place, Burnett half stepped forward, thinking to try that safe dodge of coming out and making the ball into a simple full pitch, when he changed his mind and decided to play back; and while he was thus halting between two decisions the ball shot under his bat, and there was a rattle behind him. The wickets were broken, all three of them. The ball had taken the middle and leg, and glanced outside to the off. It was a real 'spread-eagle'.

Out went Burnett, while Jayne's cheered heartily. One wicket, one run—that was all right so far. But now there came in Darton, a genuine old-fashioned 'stonewaller', and at him the Bat cannoned in vain. He rarely raised his bat three inches from his block-hole, and it was always dropped like a shutter over his wickets. If the ball was not on the wicket it was allowed to pass. Nothing would tempt him to hit, not even the most enticing of long hops, and he was a regular heartbreaker for a bowler.

At the other end, Rooke played himself in very cautiously, and did not offer to punish anything until he had got the pace of the ground and tasted the quality of the bowling. Then he began to hit a little, and the School House score began to rise quietly and steadily by ones and twos.

Suddenly the School House partisans round the ring burst into a loud cheer, and there was a clapping of hands. The fifty had gone up— fifty for one wicket! That was pretty healthy, and there was another round of cheers for Rooke, who was now beginning to pick up runs very freely.

'Lester will change his bowling now,' said the knowing ones, and that was just what Teddy did. He did not take the Bat off, as Jimmy was bowling in his lion-hearted style, sending them down with tremendous speed and dead on the wicket. In almost every over there was a ball that was worth a wicket, but Jayne's bowling was up against two very good men, one a scorer and the other a sticker. As for Darton, he had not yet broken his duck. The score-sheet stood at fifty, with Rooke forty-six, Burnett one, extras three, Darton nought. But it was a very useful nought, and every one knew it; and there were cries of 'Well played, Darton! Keep your sticks up, old man!'

Teddy had two change bowlers, Huntley and Storr, and neither was up to much. But sometimes any change is better than none, and he pondered which to try. Huntley bowled medium over-arm, while Storr sent up lobs. 'Storr's lobs are no good against Rooke,' thought Teddy; 'he'll lift 'em over the elms. I'll try Huntley for a couple of overs. If he isn't on it, I'll see what little Sandys can do.'

He tossed the ball to Huntley, and the big Fifth Form youth caught it with a satisfied grin. He fancied his bowling tremendously, and he had for some time been wondering why Lester hadn't the sense to make a change and set him on.

Huntley stood for some moments at the wicket from which he was to bowl, ordering the field about with all the authority of a second Kaiser Bill. He waved his hand for third man to move a little farther out; he beckoned to the long-stop to come closer in; he moved this man and that man until the field was exactly to his mind.

But alas for all these manœuvrings! The only chance for him would have been to put the field outside the ropes, for that was where Rooke landed his first ball. It was a slowish long hop, and the captain of the School House had now thoroughly got his eye in. He made one jump at it, picked it up as clean as a whistle, and sent it soaring like a bird right over the heads of the spectators. The School House shouted rapturously at the first six of the day. A moment later they shouted louder still for the second six.

'I'll put a man well out in the country,' thought Huntley, 'and bag Rooke that way. I'll tempt him with another one, and he won't get it so far.' So he sent the man in the deep right out to the boundary, and pitched another 'ticer to Rooke.

Rooke rose to the bait, and the ball rose in the air; but, unluckily for Huntley's plans, the ball went at least ten yards farther than the last, and up jumped the figures again. Now Huntley tried the off theory, in hopes that Rooke would nick the ball in among the slips. But Rooke smote the leather with a fierce late cut, which sent the ball whizzing to the boundary in double-quick time. Four. Another round of cheers from the School House. Huntley's next ball was a savage full toss. He had meant it for a three-quarter length, but he was too flurried by this ferocious punishment to judge his length properly. The merciless batsman lifted it promptly over the ropes. Six. The School House bellowed afresh; and when the two remaining balls were driven to the boundary—one to off, and one to leg, for four apiece—they abandoned themselves to a frenzy of delight, and were not finished yelling when the field was changed over, and the Bat was ready to sling 'em down from his end.

Teddy's face had never moved a muscle while this awful punishment was being delivered. Thirty runs from a single over! It spelt destruction to Jayne's. Not that his hopes had ever been high for a single moment; but to see the match chucked away like this—it was frightful. 'I shall have to go back myself,' thought Teddy, 'if little Sandys is no good. But I'll try him for an over first. It's no use in the world to put Storr on. His lobs would be simply pie for old Rooke.'

Jimmy West bowled a capital over; but by this time Darton, too, had got his eye in, and every ball was blocked in the methodical fashion of that master at sticking in. Every one was wondering whether Huntley would get another over, and there was a murmur of disappointment among the School House crowd when they saw the ball tossed to another member of Jayne's Eleven. But the murmur rose to one of wonder, and laughter rang out also, when they saw to whom the ball was entrusted.

'Who's that dame-school kid going on to bowl at Rooke?' was the general query, and every eye was fixed on the diminutive figure of Frank Sandys, as that player picked up the ball and walked quietly toward the bowling-crease.

'I say,' was the general comment, 'what does that infant suppose he can do against a bat like Rooke? What can Lester be thinking of to let a young pup like that have a shot in a cup-game? Rooke will lift him out of the meadow.'

But that was still to be seen. It is the great glory of cricket that it is a contest of pure skill. If the dwarf can bowl a ball good enough to hit the giant's wicket, the giant cannot make use of his strength to go down the pitch and fetch the dwarf one for luck. No; he must trudge back to the pavilion looking as pleasant as he can manage. And if the dwarf can handle a bat well enough to hit the giant to the boundary, the giant must see the fours pile up, and only try to bowl harder and better.

The situation now was very interesting. Not that the School House felt in the smallest degree uneasy. They simply watched with the deepest attention to see the contest between these two boys, one near the bottom of the school, the other near the top; one little more than a child, the other of the size and strength of a grown man.

'Which side of the wicket, sir?' asked the umpire of Frank, helping him off with his sweater.

'Right hand, over the wicket,' replied the boy.

The umpire gave Rooke guard, and then stood back. Frank took his place ready to bowl. He had made no attempt to chuck a few down to the wicket-keeper, as many bowlers do in order to loosen the arm, because that would have given his style away, and he wished to retain the advantage of the surprise which his style would cause to the batsman.

The surprise was great and genuine. Rooke had taken guard in rather a careless fashion, and in his own mind was saying severe things of Teddy Lester's cheek in turning a child loose upon an old seasoned batsman, when the ball came down the pitch. He had been intending to hit it a good smack to the boundary without particularly troubling to treat it with respect; but in a second he was bustling himself to keep it out of his wicket. The flight was very peculiar. The delivery was purely that of a bowler who intends an off break; but, to the astonishment of Rooke, the ball curled away to leg, and then broke back, a most puzzling ball. The surprise of the batsman was shared by the spectators. They were immensely astonished to see Rooke, that most correct of batsmen, leap in and save his wickets with his pads. He had played at the ball with his bat and missed it; nothing but his legs saved him from being clean bowled first ball by this little googly demon.

'Jerusha!' breathed the School House; 'that was a jolly stiff googly. Where did that kid learn the trick? Old Rooke was as near as nothing pipped that time.'

The ball was tossed back to Frank, and he prepared once more to take his neat little run up to the wicket. He was now watched with closest attention. Every eye was fixed on the short, broad figure, as he shot up to the crease and delivered the ball. This ball was pitched a little shorter, and broke rather more squarely. As it crossed in front of him, Rooke lashed out at it and caught it fairly, a low skimming drive almost straight. But with a couple of cat-like bounds Frank placed himself on its line, shot up a hand to its fullest reach, and secured the ball with a most brilliant one-handed catch.

Caught and bowled! With his first ball he had put the School House captain in difficulties, and with his second he had dismissed him.

There was a great shout of applause all round the ring. The dwarf had beaten the giant!

Teddy strolled over to the bowler. 'Young un,' he remarked, 'can you do that often?'

'Oh yes, Lester,' replied the cherub, beaming, 'I can keep the googlies going all day. But I'm afraid it's the only ball I've got, bar a straight fast one, which I mix up with 'em now and again, but not too often.'

'Ha, ha!' chuckled Teddy; 'I spy the hand of Thomas in this. Your strategy, my son, is beyond your years.'

'Tom has given a lot of attention to my cricket,' said Frank. 'He isn't half a bad chap for a brother, is old Tom.'

'I fancy not,' laughed Teddy. 'I rather fancy not. So you've got a straight one, have you? How fast?'

'I'll show you when I begin again,' replied Frank.

'All right,' said Teddy. 'But, look here, my infant phenomenon; I know these chaps, and you don't. Bowl your little artful googlies, and keep your eye on me between the balls. When you see me rub my left ear so'—and Teddy performed the action—'then you slap in that fast one as hard as you can pelt. I'll pick the man for you to practise on.'

'Right, Lester. Here comes the new batsman. What is he like?'

'Rayner! Just the fellow to try it on. Puzzle him with a googly or two, then give him a stinger.'

'All right! You give me the tip.'

Teddy went back to his place, and Frank picked up the ball, which was now thrown back to him after it had been shied round the fieldsmen.

Rayner was a Second Eleven man, a very careful bat, but rather stiff and deliberate in his movements. Now, Rayner had pondered carefully on his captain's downfall, and had made up his mind on a plan to meet these cunning devices. 'I'll put my pads in front of 'em,' said Rayner to himself. 'All these googly chaps break 'em, and you can't be given leg-before. Then, when I'm well in front of the wicket, I can slam at 'em and take my chance of getting a few runs.'

He put his plan into practice at once. Frank pitched down a ball, and Rayner missed it; but it hit Rayner's pads instead of the wickets, and rolled aside. Frank pitched down another ball, and this time Rayner was in luck, and caught it a mighty smack. It would have meant four if any other fielder than the Bat had been in the way; but Jimmy West made no mistake, and Rayner, who had begun to run, had to go back quickly.

Now Frank pitched down a ball so slow that Rayner waited for it like a cat waiting to pounce on a mouse. Its length was too good for driving, unless Rayner had come boldly to meet it, and he wished to play himself in before he tried any hitting. At last Rayner pounced upon it, but missed, just as he had missed the first ball he had received, and the ball gently rapped on his pads and turned aside.

'By Jove!' muttered Rayner to himself, 'that's a no end good plan of mine. The pads are the things to play this little artful beggar with! I'll stick to that dodge.'

So he did, for exactly one more ball; but this time his dodge didn't work. The little googly demon had seen Teddy's signal, so he ran up to the wicket at just the same pace, delivered the ball with just the same action, and it wasn't a googly at all—it was a ripping good, fast, straight ball. When Rayner hopped in front of his wickets and missed it with his bat, it rapped on his pads as usual, but the result was not as usual. The umpire held up his finger. 'Out!' he said.

'What's the matter?' gasped Rayner.

'Leg before,' said the umpire.

Jayne's crowd rocked with laughter at seeing Rayner so neatly tricked; and when they saw Frank leaving the wicket on the conclusion of his over, they gave him a rousing cheer. He had taken two good wickets in his first over for no runs.

'Young man,' said his captain, as they passed in the moving across between overs, 'if you keep on like this you may happen to get your House-cap before this season's over. Just think of that glory!'

Frank chuckled to show that he appreciated Teddy's little joke, and the Bat set to work once more. It is an odd thing, but when wickets once begin to go down they seem to set others tumbling; and, to the joy of Jayne's, the Bat got that sticker Darton with his fourth ball of this over. The Bat sent down a real trimmer, and there was such a spin on it that it deceived even such a steady old bird as Darton, and found the edge of his bat. It was the merest brush of a touch, not nearly enough to send the ball into the slips, but there was a splendid pair of hands waiting for it, and the Bat roared 'Howzat!' as Ito snapped the ball.

'Out!' said the umpire, and Darton went back to the pavilion, having played a most useful innings without scoring a single run.

In his next over Frank secured another victim; and then came a big hitter, who had a positive delight in leaping out and slashing at the pitch of anything that was sent down at him. This redoubtable slogger, whose name was Poole, caught hold of half-a-dozen balls, and was well over twenty when he lifted a cunning googly high to long-off. Huntley was there, and the catch, though lofty, was plain and easy. He dropped it; the crowd sang out, 'Butter fingers!' and Huntley went red with rage.

Frank tried Poole with another of the same brand, and again he got hold of it and sent it whizzing into the air. Frank ran back like the wind for the catch, and Huntley ran in also. It happened that Frank won the race by a few yards and took the ball beautifully right under Huntley's nose. Frank had not the smallest notion that Huntley had run in, and was so near; but Huntley thought that the little bowler had purposely snatched the catch from him in derision of the catch he had dropped, and he was furious.

By this time the best men of the School House had been disposed of, and among the rabbits who formed the tail of the Eleven the Bat raged like fury. His fast balls mowed their wickets down like grass; and Frank helped himself to one, so that when the innings was over his analysis read uncommonly well—four wickets for eleven runs, and three of the wickets among the best of the School House. But the School House were not dissatisfied. They had put together one hundred and seventeen for the innings; and, considering the weakness of Jayne's batting, they thought it sufficient.

As it happened, there was no more play that afternoon. During the interval a loud peal of thunder was heard, and a storm rolled swiftly up. Down came a tremendous torrent of rain. The spectators fled for shelter; the players crowded into the pavilion. They waited an hour; but the downpour was so unrelenting that the captains decided that further play that afternoon was impossible, and on every hand a break was made for the Houses and tea, the match being left to be finished the next afternoon.

All through first school it rained steadily. During second school it eased off, and stopped; and before dinner the two captains, Rooke and Teddy Lester, strolled down to Big Ground and looked at the pitch. They decided that the match could go on, and after dinner there was a steady stream of spectators heading for Big Ground. School House was jubilant. 'We shall knock out Jayne's twice easily enough inside the figure our men have put up, and it will be our game,' they said. 'Just fancy Rooke and Jamieson let loose against Jayne's lot on a tricky wicket! They might just as well throw up the match.' And, to tell the truth, the general opinion of the school broadly agreed with that of these keen partisans.

The School House had two very fine bowlers and two or three useful changers. Rooke and Jamieson, the principal bowlers, both belonged to the First Eleven. Rooke was a tip-top fast bowler, who could send real snorters down the pitch by the hour together, never seeming to tire, and very rarely losing his length, as some fast bowlers will when they get bottled up by a good bat. Jamieson was a medium-pace leg-break man, a terror to any batsman on a greasy or sticky wicket. As a rule, a wet wicket suited him top-hole, and the School House crew wore smiles a foot across as they sauntered down to Big Ground.

Teddy had written out the batting list in his study, and when he fastened it up in the pavilion there was a small crowd of interested readers around it at once. His own was the first name on the list. Every one expected that. He was the finest man to open an innings, not merely in Jayne's, but in all Slapton. That was not a surprise. What fellows wanted to know was the name of the man whom Teddy would take in with him. Sandys! There was a murmur of surprise. Teddy was going to open the innings with that little new kid in the Third, who could bowl jolly well, but seemed quite out of place to start the batting with the finest batsman in the school. Sandys's place, to all appearance, should have been among the rabbits, anywhere at nine, ten, or last wicket.

And when he and Teddy left the pavilion, marching together for the wickets, there was a huge guffaw all round the ring.

'I say,' said one wit, 'Lester's taking his fag in with him. What can a little kid like that do against Rooke and Jamieson? Whichever of them gets first ball at him will bowl his young head off!'

As they went, Teddy was talking to Frank.

'Young man,' said Teddy, 'I shouldn't wonder if we *don't* get a quite easy wicket to start with. If we do, I'm going to lump 'em and knock a few up before the evil day comes when Jamieson's ball will get up and look at you, and then come in like one o'clock and send your bails flying.'

Frank nodded. He was looking a little grave. He knew this was a big trial, and he was making up his mind to bring off his level best, if he had just a streak of luck and could get the pace of the ground.

'How does this wicket work, Lester?' he asked.

'While it's very wet it works OK,' replied Teddy. 'But as soon as it begins to dry on top, then you may look out for fireworks.'

'I see,' replied Frank with a little nod.

'Go down to the far end,' said the captain. 'I'll take the first over. You'll soon see the run of the ground; and, in any case, keep 'em down. The School House are jolly good fielders. Old Rooke drills them at stopping and catching hard and often.'

The batsmen took their places, and Rooke turned the new ball in his hands and got a firm grip of the seam. He did not need a long run to get up his great speed, and his action was so easy that a batsman who did not know him found the ball much faster than might be expected. This clever touch of deception had gained Rooke many and many a wicket.

But Teddy had played against Rooke very often, and was quite ready for the ball, which came like a shot from a gun. It was coming across the wicket, going with the arm to leg, for Rooke was a left-handed bowler. Very cleverly Teddy caught it and shaped its course rather than hit it. The ball slid away to leg with all its original power behind it, and the spectators saw a red streak across the green level of the ground as the leather flew to the boundary. There was a general cheer for a good start. Teddy had sent the first ball away for four. The second ball was altogether too good a length for any but the most respectful treatment, and Teddy played it back along the ground to the bowler. The third ball was a tempting long hop; Teddy cut it to the boundary, amid cheers. The fourth ball he put between the slips; but it was splendidly fielded, and was only worth a single. Now Frank had to face the mighty fast bowler.

Every eye was fixed on the pair who now opposed each other. Little Sandys was so small that the contrast was simply ludicrous between him and Rooke, who stood with the height and strength of a man, ready to run up to the wicket and bowl at him. But many of those who laughed quite failed to notice that, though his inches were few, Frank's short form was very sturdy and compact, and might well be stored with much strength. Next moment they became convinced of this fact when they saw how Frank handled Rooke's first ball at him.

Rooke himself was rather 'waxy' at having to bowl at this little boy.

'Hang it all!' muttered the great School House bowler to himself, 'I can't put steam on to bowl at this impudent infant. What on earth does Lester mean by dragging such a kid into the team? It's simply making a fool of me to have to bowl at a child from the bottom end of the school. I'll try him with a straight one of moderate pace. That ought to be enough for the little beggar!'

So Rooke went rather carelessly up to the wicket, to show every one that he considered he ought not to be bothered with bowling at a little boy, and pitched up a perfectly straight ball. But, lacking his usual speed, the ball also lacked his usual length, and was a half-volley pure and simple.

And Frank promptly gave it the treatment that every half-volley deserves. Timing his drive perfectly, he jumped boldly forward and

caught the ball with a smack which was heard all over the ground, and
sent it whizzing high above Rooke's head. So admirable was the timing—which, after all, is the main thing in a big drive—that every ounce
of the little batsman's strength was put to its utmost use, and the ball
dropped clean over the ropes for six. This wonderful hit was greeted
with a roar of surprise and delight, and Rooke flushed red as fire. His
next ball was much faster and rather more to the off. Frank got well
over it, and made a brilliant square out of it. The ground was so dead
that the ball was easily fielded before it reached the boundary; but the
batsmen ran two for the hit, and Frank drew a fresh cheer from the
ring of onlookers.

Now the first over had passed, and Jayne's could draw breath and
discuss the chances of their batsmen. One tremendous question had
been settled—that of the condition of the wicket. It was certainly neither tricky nor treacherous. It might become so as it dried, but there
was nothing wrong with it now but slowness. It was so wet that it
was quite dead and easy.

This was seen even more plainly when Teddy took his stand against
Jamieson. Had the wicket given Jamieson's leg-breaks any help they
would have been deadly; but now they turned so slowly that Teddy's
wonderful eye enabled him to lay hold of them with ease. He carted
the first and third to the boundary, turned the fourth to leg for two,
and contented himself with keeping the others out of his wickets.

In this over Frank had no share; the batting all fell to Teddy. But
the younger batsman took careful note of Jamieson's style of delivery,
and fancied he could see what to do himself when his time came to
face Jamieson's bowling.

It was now Rooke's turn to take the ball, and he stepped the full
length for a real smashing delivery. Gone to the winds were his ideas
of treating this mysterious youth tenderly; gone were his plans for getting him to hit up an easy long hop or something of that sort; for he
saw that such plans were of no use against an opponent who, though
looking a mere infant, was yet up to every move in the game. Spinning
up to the wicket, he let fly a real snorter, dead on the middle stump,
perfectly straight, and terribly fast. Out came Frank, with foot well forward and bat well down, and smothered it neatly as it pitched, and
sent it back to Rooke's feet.

'Played, sir! Played!' the cry went up in many quarters. From Jayne's
corner it rang like a trumpet, and the smaller boys shrieked like seamews
in a storm. Each youngster felt it like a personal added glory that it

was a member of the Third who was standing up to the mighty Rooke like a veteran, and playing steadily at deliveries before which ordinary batsmen trembled and gave themselves up for lost.

Every ball of this over was of Rooke's best, real smashers every one. And to every one Frank stood up like a master. The last ball he managed, by a neat piece of wrist-work, to turn for two, so that the over was not a maiden.

'Who's that little beggar you've got up at the other end, Lester?' said Rooke to Teddy, as the fieldsmen crossed over.

'Young Sandys there?' said Teddy. 'New chap in our House. Brother of Tom Sandys. You remember noble old Tom?'

'Rather!' exclaimed Rooke. 'Wonderfully good man was Tom Sandys. His brother, eh? But where did the youngster pick up his cricket? He plays like a fellow years and years older than he can be.'

'Well, he's not such a chicken, after all,' replied Teddy. 'He's a regular deceiver in his looks. But he plays well. Tom has given his cricket a good deal of attention, and reckons him a promising bat.'

'Bit more than promising, I should say,' returned Rooke dryly. 'Why, hang the little beggar! that last over I sent down was a jolly good one, though I say it myself. I know I couldn't have tried harder if I'd been bowling at the MCC.'

'It was a nailing good over, Rooke,' agreed Teddy—'good enough for nine men out of ten. The young un's going to be a useful man.'

A Record First-Wicket Score

By this time Jamieson had taken the ball and was stepping his distance. Teddy went back to his crease, and Rooke strolled into the slips. Teddy placed the first ball to third man, and the batsmen ran a single. Every one looked to see how the little wonder would shape against the puzzling leg-breaks of Jamieson, balls which would upset anybody if the bowler could only find a spot.

But, on this wet, easy pitch, Frank found no difficulty at all with them. He hit every one he received, and hit it hard and kept it low. But so keen was the fielding of the School House that it was impossible to start for a run until the last ball of the over, which he got away finely to leg for two.

The bowlers now redoubled their efforts, and for several overs the two batsmen had to be very careful. But both, while exceedingly watchful in defence, kept a shrewd eye open to pick out the right ball to hit, and when it came along that ball had punishment dealt out to it very faithfully.

Suddenly Jayne's sent up a rapturous cheer. Fifty was up. It seemed impossible that the two steady players had put such a number together; but there it was on the board, and the School House people began to look uneasy, and openly to express their desire for the fall of a wicket.

Rooke now determined on heroic measures, and went in for a double change, in hopes that the move would lead to the downfall of the younger batsman. He had not much hope now of shifting Teddy. That wonderful cricketer had got his eye in, had got the pace of the wicket, and was batting now with his usual coolness and judgment. 'Not much chance of getting Lester,' reflected Rooke to himself; 'but I should be uncommonly glad to see the back of that youngster. He plays like a real sticker.'

The words were true. There was a quiet decision about Frank's style which looked almost comic in conjunction with his air of extreme youth. His forward play was clean and sharp; his hitting was prompt and brisk. Never once did he wait for the ball to meet the bat. The bat was brought upon the ball with a promptitude and force which meant that the ball had got to go somewhere, and that somewhere, as a rule, was precisely between two fieldsmen, the leather moving at a lively pace.

The two new bowlers were Fane and Leigh. Fane was a Second Eleven man, famous for bowling a very slow ball, which could be very dangerous if the wicket suited it. He had a queer high pitch with it, so that the ball seemed to hang in the air for a long time before it fell and came along to the wicket.

Teddy had played against him many a time, and knew that the simple-looking ball called for a great deal of watching, and accordingly he watched the first two balls of the over carefully. But the dead-easy wicket had no work in it at all, and the ball was, for the moment at any rate, a mild donkey-drop.

As such Teddy treated them without mercy. He missed one, but sent the other three to the boundary. Leigh was a House bowler, a man of no school distinction, but a medium fast bowler, who was often deadly if he had a bit of luck to start with. This time he certainly ran short of the bit of luck.

Frank felt pretty sure of the wicket, and had begun to hit a little before the first-choice bowlers went off. Now he saw his chance, as Leigh began to pitch up long hops, and Frank went out to drive them. He hit every ball of the over, and the uproar from Jayne's House grew and grew with every ball he hit. He sent the first two to the boundary, the third was stopped, the fourth went for two, the fifth for four, and the sixth was lifted over the ropes.

That over knocked the unlucky Leigh all to pieces, and Rooke did not put him on again. It had been a costly experiment. The terrible little batsman had helped himself to twenty runs for that single over. Teddy had taken twelve off Fane, and the score had leaped at a bound to eighty-two.

Fane was given an over again, and Teddy hit him all over the place, and fetched up the hundred. Rooke thought for a moment, and pitched the ball to his last change bowler, a fellow named Dickenson, who bowled artful lobs.

Rooke's hope was that Dickenson might tempt the smaller batsman to hit up one; but Frank smote the first square to leg, and they ran three. Now Teddy got the bowling; and he loved lobs, and hit Dickenson's balls hard and often, so that the score sailed swiftly up. He whacked one to the boundary, and there was a perfect yell from Jayne's and resounding cheers from other parts of the field. The hundred and twenty had been hoisted, the School House score had been passed, and the two batsmen were still unparted.

In the interval between the overs Teddy strolled down the pitch. Frank came to meet him, and the captain murmured in his ear, 'We'll clout 'em now for all we're worth, Sandys. This pitch is going, so we'll use the last half-hour for what we can get. Never mind if you lose your wicket. Hit 'em now, and hit 'em hard. I'm going to.'

The next half-hour saw pandemonium reign around the ropes. Every spectator made noise enough for a dozen; he shouted, yelled, laughed, or cheered in turn, and sometimes tried to do these things all at once. The School House partisans did most of the yelling, while the others did most of the laughing; for the two batsmen took any and every risk to pile up runs. They hit at everything, stole short runs, risked another run on a bigger hit, whacked the ball here, whacked it there, and kept the pot boiling in the wildest and merriest fashion.

At length the laughter and the yelling rose to a tempest of uproar. For the first time since this fury of mad hitting began, Frank made a mis-hit. The ball went straight to the hands of Rooke himself, a first-class man of the First Eleven, and—he dropped it.

The noise was beyond description. Immense roars of laughter from the general mass of spectators; howls of fury and denunciation from the School House, howls directed against their own chief.

There was another ball to the over. Nothing daunted, Frank went for it like a little fury, and smote it hard and low past third man. They ran three amid a fresh outburst of cheers.

'Over!' called the umpire, and Teddy turned to study the telegraph. It presented the most remarkable sight ever seen on Big Ground at Slapton. Total, two hundred and twenty-seven. No. 1—that was Teddy himself—one hundred and twenty-four; No. 2—young Frank Sandys—ninety-five; extras, eight, a splendid testimony to the keenness of the School House fielding.

'I'll give the young 'un a chance for his century,' thought Teddy. 'He's got the batting, but I'll only wait for one over again in any case.'

In the great excitement of this tap-and-run business, the bowlers were getting as wild as any one. The first ball sent down was a clear wide. But Frank ran at it and gave it a crack which fetched two. The next ball went whizzing down, and he missed it; it smashed his wickets in every direction. The crowd roared in huge disappointment that he had not reached his hundred, then burst into a great shout of relief and laughter when they noticed the umpire signalling 'No ball!' and saw Frank turning back to bat.

The most extraordinary things seemed to be happening in this extra-ordinary game; and when he leapt like a little tiger at the next ball and sent it humming to the boundary there was an immense outburst of relief and delight, and he was cheered to the very echo. For the rest of the over the batsmen went quietly, and at its close Teddy walked up to Rooke. 'I declare!' he said, and Rooke nodded.

When the batsmen and the Eleven were seen to be leaving the field there was renewed excitement among the spectators, and upon learning that Teddy had declared, all felt that a new interest had come into the match. The School House figure had been exactly doubled. The pair of wonderful champions who had come out for Jayne's were returning unbeaten at a total score of two hundred and thirty-four. Could the School House equal their first score on a wicket already bad, and rapidly becoming worse?

Teddy Lester, Captain of Cricket, 1920

✳

Boy at a Cricket Match

HUGO WILLIAMS

Holding his hands like strange ivy,
He twines them round his mother's broad shadow;
She is his tree, only with her he grows.
For him she keeps her leaves, her first love,
All the year round. He does not know.

(The sun coming through branches, green,
And leaves, like warm water unseen.)

Turning horizon-smiling eyes around,
He sees the sky aghast with light
Between the trees, oppressive boughs, and sees
The bowler flex his arms like wings
And knows a real need for flight.

The Cricketer's Companion, 1959

*

Tom Brown

THOMAS HUGHES

Another two years have passed, and it is again the end of the summer half-year at Rugby; in fact, the School has broken up. The fifth-form examinations were over last week, and upon them have followed the Speeches, and the sixth-form examinations for exhibitions; and they too are over now. The boys have gone to all the winds of heaven, except the town boys and the eleven, and a few enthusiasts besides who have asked leave to stay in their houses to see the result of the cricket matches. For this year the Wellesburn return match and the Marylebone match are played at Rugby, to the great delight of the town and neighbourhood, and the sorrow of those aspiring young cricketers who have been reckoning for the last three months on showing off at Lord's ground.

The Doctor started for the Lakes yesterday morning, after an interview with the Captain of the eleven, in the presence of Thomas, at which he arranged in what school the cricket dinners were to be, and all other matters necessary for the satisfactory carrying out of the festivities; and warned them as to keeping all spirituous liquors out of the close, and having the gates closed by nine o'clock.

The Wellesburn match was played out with great success yesterday, the School winning by three wickets; and to-day the great event of the cricketing year, the Marylebone match, is being played. What a match it has been! The London eleven came down by an afternoon train yesterday, in time to see the end of the Wellesburn match; and as soon as it was over, their leading men and umpire inspected the ground, criticising it rather unmercifully. The Captain of the School eleven, and one or two others, who had played the Lord's match before, and knew old Mr Aislabie and several of the Lord's men, accompanied them: while the rest of the eleven looked on from under the Three Trees with admiring eyes, and asked one another the names of the illustrious strangers, and recounted how many runs each of them had made in the late matches in *Bell's Life*. They looked such hard-bitten, wiry, whiskered fellows, that their young adversaries felt rather desponding as to the result of the morrow's match. The ground was at last chosen, and two men set to work upon it to water and roll; and then, there being yet some half-hour of daylight, some one had suggested a dance on the turf. The close was half full of citizens and their families, and the idea was hailed with enthusiasm. The cornopean-player was still on the ground; in five minutes the eleven and half a dozen of Wellesburn and Marylebone men got partners somehow or another, and a merry country-dance was going on, to which everyone flocked, and new couples joined in every minute, till there were a hundred of them going down the middle and up again—and the long line of School buildings looked gravely down on them, every window glowing with the last rays of the western sun, and the rooks clanged about in the tops of the old elms, greatly excited, and resolved on having their country-dance too, and the great flag flapped lazily in the gentle western breeze. Altogether it was a sight which would have made glad the heart of our brave old founder, Lawrence Sheriff, if he were half as good a fellow as I take him to have been. It was a cheerful sight to see; but what made it so valuable in the sight of the Captain of the School eleven was, that he there saw his young hands shaking off their shyness and awe of the Lord's men, as they crossed hands and capered about on the grass together; for the strangers entered into it all, and threw away their cigars, and danced and shouted like boys; while old Mr Aislabie stood by looking on in his white hat, leaning on a bat, in benevolent enjoyment. 'This hop will be worth thirty runs to us to-morrow, and will be the making of Raggles and Johnson,' thinks the young leader, as he revolves many things in his mind, standing by the side of Mr Aislabie, whom he will not leave for a minute, for he feels that the character of the School for courtesy is resting on his shoulders.

But when a quarter to nine struck, and he saw old Thomas beginning to fidget about with the keys in his hand, he thought of the Doctor's parting monition, and stopped the the cornopean at once, notwithstanding the loud-voiced remonstrances from all sides; and the crowd scattered away from the close, the eleven all going into the School-house, where supper and beds were provided for them by the Doctor's orders.

Deep had been the consultations at supper as to the order of going in, who should bowl the first over, whether it would be best to play steady or freely; and the youngest hands declared that they shouldn't be a bit nervous, and praised their opponents as the jolliest fellows in the world, except perhaps their old friends the Wellesburn men. How far a little good-nature from their elders will go with the right sort of boys!

The morning had dawned bright and warm, to the intense relief of many an anxious youngster, up betimes to mark the signs of the weather. The eleven went down in a body before breakfast, for a plunge in the cold bath in the corner of the close. The ground was in splendid order, and soon after ten o'clock, before spectators had arrived, all was ready, and two of the Lord's men took their places at the wicket, the School, with the usual liberality of young hands, having put their adversaries in first. Old Bailey stepped up to the wicket, and called play, and the match has begun.

'Oh, well bowled! well bowled, Johnson!' cried the Captain, catching up the ball and sending it high above the rook trees, while the third Marylebone man walks away from the wicket, and old Bailey gravely sets up the middle stump again and puts the bails on.

'How many runs?' Away scamper three boys to the scoring-table, and are back again in a minute amongst the rest of the eleven, who are collected together in a knot between wicket. 'Only eighteen runs and three wickets down!' 'Huzza, for old Rugby!' sings out Jack Raggles the long-stop, toughest and burliest of boys, commonly called 'Swiper

Jack'; and forthwith stands on his head, and brandishes his legs in the air in triumph, till the next boy catches hold of his heels, and throws him over on to his back.

'Steady there, don't be such an ass, Jack,' says the Captain; 'we haven't got the best wicket yet. Ah, look out now at cover-point,' adds he, as he sees a long-armed, bare-headed, slashing-looking player coming to the wicket. 'And, Jack, mind your hits; he steals more runs than any man in England.'

And they all find that they have got their work to do now; the new-comer's off-hitting is tremendous, and his running like a flash of light-ning. He is never in his ground, except when his wicket is down. Nothing in the whole game so trying to boys; he has stolen three byes in the first ten minutes, and Jack Raggles is furious, and begins throw-ing over savagely to the further wicket, until he is sternly stopped by the Captain. It is all that young gentleman can do to keep his team steady, but he knows that everything depends on it, and faces his work bravely. The score creeps up to fifty, the boys begin to look blank, and the spectators, who are now mustering strong, are very silent. The ball flies off his bat to all parts of the field, and he gives no rest and no catches to any one. But cricket is full of glorious chances, and the god-dess who presides over it loves to bring down the most skilful players. Johnson, the young bowler, is getting wild, and bowls a ball almost wide to the off; the batter steps out and cuts it beautifully to where cover-point is standing very deep, in fact almost off the ground. The ball comes skimming and twisting along about three feet from the ground; he rushes at it, and it sticks somehow or other in the fingers of his left hand, to the utter astonishment of himself and the whole field. Such a catch hasn't been made in the close for years, and the cheering is maddening. 'Pretty cricket,' says the Captain, throwing him-self on the ground by the deserted wicket with a long breath; he feels that a crisis is passed.

I wish I had space to describe the whole match; how the Captain stumped the next man off a leg-shooter, and bowled slow lobs to old Mr Aislabie, who came in for the last wicket. How the Lord's men were out by half-past twelve o'clock for ninety-eight runs. How the Captain of the School eleven went in first to give his men pluck, and scored twenty-five in beautiful style; how Rugby was only four behind in the first innings. What a glorious dinner they had in the fourth-form School, and how the cover-point hitter sang the most topping comic songs, and old Mr Aislabie made the best speeches that ever were heard, afterwards. But I haven't space, that's the fact, and so you must fancy it all, and carry yourselves on to half-past seven o'clock, when the School are again in, with five wickets down and only thirty-two runs to make to win. The Marylebone men played carelessly in their second innings, but they are working like horses now to save the match.

There is much healthy, hearty, happy life scattered up and down the close; but the group to which I beg to call your special attention is there, on the slope of the island which looks towards the cricket-ground. It consists of three figures; two are seated on a bench, and one on the ground at their feet. The first, a tall, slight, and rather gaunt man, with a bushy eyebrow, and a dry humorous smile, is evidently a clergyman. He is carelessly dressed, and looks rather used up, which isn't much to be wondered at, seeing that he has just finished six weeks of examination work; but there he basks, and spreads himself out in the evening sun, bent on enjoying life, though he doesn't quite know what to do with his arms and legs.

And by his side, in white flannel shirt and trousers, straw hat, the Captain's belt, and the untanned yellow cricket shoes which all the eleven wear, sits a strapping figure, near six feet high, with ruddy tanned face, and whiskers, curly brown hair, and a laughing, dancing eye. He is leaning forward with his elbows resting on his knees, and dandling, in his strong brown hands, his favourite bat with which he has made thirty or forty runs to-day. It is Tom Brown, grown into a young man nineteen years old, a præpostor and Captain of the eleven, spending his last day as a Rugby boy.

And at their feet on the warm dry ground, similarly dressed sits Arthur, Turkish fashion, with his bat across his knees. He too is no longer a boy, less of a boy in fact than Tom, if one may judge from the thoughtfulness of his face, which is somewhat paler, too, than one could wish; but his figure, though slight, is well knit and active, and all his old timidity has disappeared, and is replaced by silent quaint fun, with which his face twinkles all over, as he listens to the broken talk between the other two in which he joins every now and then.

All three are watching the game eagerly, and joining in the cheering which follows every good hit. It is pleasing to see the easy, friendly footing which the pupils are on with their master, perfectly respectful, yet with no reserve and nothing forced in their intercourse. Tom has clearly abandoned the old theory of 'natural enemies' in this case at any rate.

But it is time to listen to what they are saying, and see what we can gather out of it.

'I don't object to your theory,' says the master, 'and I allow you have made a fair case for yourself. But now, in such books as Aristophanes for instance, you've been reading a play this half with the Doctor, haven't you?'

'Yes, the Knights,' answered Tom.

'Well, I'm sure you would have enjoyed the wonderful humour of it twice as much if you had taken more pains with your scholarship.'

'Well, sir, I don't believe any boy in the form enjoyed the sets-to between Cleon and the Sausage-seller more than I did—eh, Arthur?' said Tom, giving him a stir with his foot.

'Yes, I must say he did,' said Arthur. 'I think, sir, you've hit upon the wrong book there.'

'Not a bit of it,' said the master. 'Why, in those very passages of arms, how can you thoroughly appreciate them unless you are master of the weapons? and the weapons are the language which you, Brown, have never half worked at; and so, as I say, you must have lost all the delicate shades of meaning which make the best part of the fun.'

'Oh! well played—bravo, Johnson!' shouted Arthur, dropping his bat and clapping furiously, and Tom joined in with a 'Bravo, Johnson!' which might have been heard at the chapel.

'Eh! what was it? I didn't see,' inquired the master; 'they only got one run, I thought?'

'No, but such a ball, three-quarters length and coming straight for his leg bail. Nothing but that turn of the wrist could have saved him, and he drew it away to leg for a safe one. Bravo, Johnson!'

'How well they are bowling, though,' said Arthur; 'they don't mean to be beat, I can see!'

'There, now,' struck in the master; 'you see that's just what I have been preaching this half-hour. The delicate play is the true thing. I don't understand cricket, so I don't enjoy those fine draws which you tell me are the best play, though when you or Raggles hit a ball hard away for six I am as delighted as anyone. Don't you see the analogy?'

'Yes, sir,' answered Tom, looking up roguishly, 'I see; only the question remains whether I should have got most good by understanding Greek particles or cricket thoroughly. I'm such a thick, I never should have had time for both.'

'I see you are incorrigible,' said the master with a chuckle; 'but I refute you by an example. Arthur there has taken in Greek and cricket too.'

'Yes, but no thanks to him; Greek came natural to him. Why, when he first came I remember he used to read Herodotus for pleasure as I did Don Quixote, and couldn't have made a false concord if he'd tried ever so hard—and then I looked after his cricket.'

'Out! Bailey has given him out—do you see, Tom?' cries Arthur. 'How foolish of them to run so hard.'

'Well, it can't be helped; he has played very well. Whose turn is it to go in?'

'I don't know; they've got your list in the tent.'

'Let's go and see,' said Tom, rising; but at this moment Jack Raggles and two or three more came running to the island moat.

'Oh, Brown, mayn't I go in next?' shouts the Swiper.

'Whose name is next on the list?' says the Captain.

'Winter's, and then Arthur's,' answers the boy who carries it; 'but there are only twenty-six runs to get, and no time to lose. I heard Mr Aislabie say that the stumps must be drawn at a quarter past eight exactly.'

'Oh, do let the Swiper go in,' chorus the boys; so Tom yields against his better judgment.

'I dare say now I've lost the match by this nonsense,' he says, as he sits down again; 'they'll be sure to get Jack's wicket in three or four minutes; however, you'll have the chance, sir, of seeing a hard hit or two,' adds he, smiling, and turning to the master.

'Come, none of your irony, Brown,' answers the master. 'I'm beginning to understand the game scientifically. What a noble game it is too!'

'Isn't it? But it's more than a game. It's an institution,' said Tom.

'Yes,' said Arthur, 'the birthright of British boys, old and young, as *habeas corpus* and trial by jury are of British men.'

'The discipline and reliance on one another which it teaches is so valuable, I think,' went on the master; 'it ought to be such an unselfish game. It merges the individual in the eleven; he doesn't play that he may win, but that his side may.'

'That's very true,' said Tom; 'and that's why football and cricket, now one comes to think of it, are such much better games than fives or hare-and-hounds, or any others, where the object is to come in first or to win for oneself, and not that one's side may win.'

'And then the Captain of the eleven!' said the master; 'what a post is his in our school world! almost as hard as the Doctor's; requiring skill and gentleness and firmness, and I know not what other rare qualities.'

'Which don't he may wish he may get?' said Tom, laughing; 'at any rate he hasn't got them yet, or he wouldn't have been such a flat to-night as to let Jack Raggles go in out of his turn.'

'Ah! the Doctor never would have done that,' said Arthur, demurely. 'Tom, you've a great deal to learn yet in the art of ruling.'

'Well, I wish you'd tell the Doctor so, then, and get him to let me stop till I'm twenty. I don't want to leave, I'm sure.'

'What a sight it is,' broke in the master, 'the Doctor as a ruler. Perhaps ours is the only little corner of the British Empire which is thoroughly, wisely, and strongly ruled just now. I'm more and more thankful every day of my life that I came here to be under him.'

'So am I, I'm sure,' said Tom; 'and more and more sorry that I've got to leave.'

'Every place and thing one sees here reminds one of some wise act of his,' went on the master. 'This island now—you remember the time, Brown, when it was laid out in small gardens, and cultivated by frost-bitten fags in February and March?'

'Of course I do,' said Tom; 'didn't I hate spending two hours in the afternoons grubbing in the tough dirt with the stump of a fives bat? But turf-cart was good fun enough.'

'I dare say it was, but it was always leading to fights with the towns-people; and then the stealing flowers out of all the gardens in Rugby for the Easter show was abominable.'

'Well, so it was,' said Tom, looking down; 'but we fags couldn't help ourselves. But what has that to do with the Doctor's ruling?'

'A great deal, I think,' said the master; 'what brought island-fagging to an end?'

'Why, the Easter speeches were put off till Midsummer,' said Tom, 'and the sixth had the gymnastic poles put up here.'

'Well, and who changed the time of the speeches, and put the idea of gymnastic poles into the heads of their worships the sixth form?' said the master.

'The Doctor, I suppose,' said Tom. 'I never thought of that.'

'Of course you didn't,' said the master, 'or else, fag as you were, you would have shouted with the whole school against putting down old customs. And that's the way that all the Doctor's reforms have been carried out when he has been left to himself—quietly and naturally, putting a good thing in the place of a bad, and letting the bad die out; no wavering and no hurry—the best thing that could be done for the time being, and patience for the rest.'

'Just Tom's own way,' chimed in Arthur, nudging Tom with his elbow, 'driving a nail where it will go'; to which allusion Tom answered by a sly kick.

'Exactly so,' said the master, innocent of the allusion and bye-play.

Meantime Jack Raggles, with his sleeves tucked up above his great brown elbows, scorning pads and gloves, has presented himself at the wicket; and having run one for a forward drive of Johnson's, is about to receive his first ball. There are only twenty-four runs to make, and four wickets to go down; a winning match if they play decently steady. The ball is a very swift one, and rises fast, catching Jack on the outside of the thigh, and bounding away as if from india-rubber, while they run two for a leg-bye amidst great applause, and shouts from Jack's many admirers. The next ball is a beautifully pitched ball for the outer stump, which the reckless and unfeeling Jack catches hold of, and hits right round to leg for five, while the applause becomes deafening: only seventeen runs to get with four wickets—the game is all but ours!

It is over now, and Jack walks swaggering about his wicket, with the bat over his shoulder, while Mr Aislabie holds a short parley with his men. Then the cover-point hitter, that cunning man, goes on to bowl slow twisters. Jack waves his hand triumphantly towards the tent, as much as to say, 'See if I don't finish it all off now in three hits.'

Alas, my son Jack! the enemy is too old for thee! The first ball of the over Jack steps out and meets, swiping with all his force. If he had only allowed for the twist! but he hasn't, and so the ball goes spinning up straight into the air, as if it would never come down again. Away runs Jack, shouting and trusting to the chapter of accidents, but the bowler runs steadily under it, judging every spin, and calling out 'I have it,' catches it, and playfully pitches it on to the back of the stalwart Jack, who is departing with a rueful countenance.

'I knew how it would be,' says Tom, rising. 'Come along, the game's getting very serious.'

So they leave the island and go to the tent, and after deep consultation, Arthur is sent in, and goes off to the wicket with a last exhortation from Tom to play steady and keep his bat straight. To the suggestions that Winter is the best bat left Tom only replies, 'Arthur is the steadiest, and Johnson will make the runs if the wicket is only kept up.'

'I am surprised to see Arthur in the eleven,' said the master, as they stood together in front of the dense crowd which was now closing in round the ground.

'Well, I'm not quite sure that he ought to be in for his play,' said Tom, 'but I couldn't help putting him in. It will do him so much good, and you can't think what I owe him.'

The master smiled. The clock strikes eight, and the whole field becomes fevered with excitement. Arthur after two narrow escapes, scores one; and Johnson gets the ball. The bowling and fielding are superb, and Johnson's batting worthy the occasion. He makes here a two, and there a one, managing to keep the ball to himself, and Arthur backs up and runs perfectly: only eleven runs to make now, and the crowd scarcely breathe. At last Arthur gets the ball again, and actually drives it forward for two, and feels prouder than when he got the three best prizes at hearing Tom's shout of joy, 'Well played, well played, young 'un!'

But the next ball is too much for a young hand, and his bails fly different ways. Nine runs to make and two wickets to go down—it is too much for human nerves.

Before Winter can get in, the omnibus which is to take the Lord's men to the train pulls up at the side of the close, and Mr Aislabie and Tom consult, and give out that the stumps will be drawn after the next over. And so ends the great match. Winter and Johnson carry out their bats, and, it being a one day's match, the Lord's men are declared the winners, they having scored the most in the first innings.

But such a defeat is a victory; so think Tom and all the School eleven, as they accompany their conquerors to the omnibus, and send them off with three ringing cheers, after Mr Aislabie has shaken hands all round, saying to Tom, 'I must compliment you, sir, on your eleven, and I hope we shall have you for a member if you come up to town.'

Tom Brown's School Days, 1857

✳

The One-Way Boy

R. C. ROBERTSON-GLASGOW

When coaching boys the other day,
Recalling legs that legward stray,
Wearily pleading that it mars
The style, if bats are scimitars;
Persuading bowlers that their length
And rectitude are more than strength,

However jovially applied
If all it ends in is—a wide.
The father of some cricketer,
A heavy man, approach'd, said, 'Sir,
My boy is *always* caught at slip;
It gives me one gigantic pip:
Now can you give me any reason
Why this should happen *all* the season,
Instead of intermittently,
As it occurs with you or me?'
'Show me the boy,' quoth I, 'sir, please.'
Whereat, scorbutic, ill-at-ease,
Stole from behind his ample father
A boy, obscured till now, or rather
What might have passed for boy, by chance,
But for his cow-like countenance:
Never in any town or rank
Saw I a face so *wholly* blank:
No freckle, twinkle; nothing dimply;
It was a facial Sahara, simply.
'Put on those pads' his father said
As if conversing with the dead,
'And show the gentleman the stroke,
Concerning which I lately spoke.'
He donned them filially resign'd.
I gave him guard, to leg inclined,
I bowled him long-hops free from guile,
Full-pitchers you could hit a mile,
Half-volleys straight, half-volleys wide,
Swervers, delicious for the glide;
He never swerved, nor lost his grip,
But snicked the ruddy lot to slip.
Strange wonders have there been in Cricket—
Once, in a match, I took a wicket,
Shod in a heel-less evening shoe
(A confidence 'twixt me and you),
Jones bowled a ball through Grace's beard,
And Ranji only Lockwood feared,
But never, since the game began,
Since old men stood while young men ran,

Was such consummate batsmanship
As to hole out, each ball, at slip.
'Take off those pads,' his father said
(Resuming converse with the dead)
'You've shown the gentleman the stroke
By which my heart and mother's broke;
Good-day, sir!' and with footsteps slow
He took his tragedy in tow,
The parent first, the portent after,
Leaving me deep in awe and laughter.

The Brighter Side of Cricket, 1933

❊

Mixed Emotions

L. P. HARTLEY

I still have the scoring cards but whereas I can remember our innings
in detail, theirs, although the figures are before me, remains a blur,
until the middle. Partly, no doubt, because our batsmen were all known
to me personally, and theirs, with one exception, were not. Also because
it looked such an easy win for us—as the scores, all in single figures,
of the first five batsmen testify—that I withdrew some of my attention:
one cannot concentrate on a walk-over. The excitement of our innings
seemed far away and almost wasted—as if we had put out all our
strength to lift a pin. I remember feeling rather sorry for the villagers,
as one after another their men went back, looking so much smaller
than when they had walked to the wicket. And as the game receded
from my mind the landscape filled in. There were two bows: the arch
of the trees beyond the cricket field, and the arch of the sky above
them; and each repeated the other's curve. This delighted my sense of
symmetry; what disturbed it was the spire of the church. The church
itself was almost invisible among the trees, which grew over the mound
it stood on in the shape of a protractor, an almost perfect semi-circle.
But the spire, instead of dividing the protractor into two equal seg-
ments, raised its pencil-point to the left of the centre—about eight
degrees, I calculated. Why could not the church conform to Nature's
plan? There must be a place, I thought, where the spire would be seen
as a continuation of the protractor's axis, producing the perpendicular

indefinitely into the sky, with two majestic right angles at its base, like flying buttresses, holding it up. Perhaps some of the spectators enjoyed this view. I wished I could go in search of it, while our team was skittling out the village side.

But soon my eye, following the distressful spire into the heavens, rested on the enormous cloud that hung there, and tried to penetrate its depths. A creation of the heat, it was like no cloud I had ever seen. It was pure white on top, rounded and thick and lustrous as a snow-drift; below, the white was flushed with pink, and still further below, in the very heart of the cloud, the pink deepened to purple. Was there a menace in this purple tract, a hint of thunder? I did not think so. The cloud seemed absolutely motionless; scan it as I would, I could not detect the smallest alteration in its outline. And yet it *was* moving—moving towards the sun, and getting brighter and brighter as it approached it. A few more degrees, and then—

As I was visualizing the lines of the protractor printed on the sky I heard a rattle and a clatter. It was Ted Burgess going out to bat; he was whistling, no doubt to keep his spirits up.

He was carrying his bat under his arm, rather unorthodox. How did I feel about him? Did I want him, for instance, to come out first ball? Did I want to see him hit a six and then come out? I was puzzled, for until now my feelings had been quite clear: I wanted everyone on our side to make runs, and everyone on their side not to.

The first ball narrowly shaved his wicket and then I knew: I did not want him to get out. The knowledge made me feel guilty of disloyalty, but I consoled myself by thinking that it was sporting, and therefore meritorious, to want the enemy to put up a fight; besides, they were so far behind! And in this state of uneasy neutrality I remained for several overs while Ted, who got most of the bowling, made several mis-hits including one skier, which the pantry-boy might have caught had not the sun been in his eyes.

Then he hit one four, and then another; the ball whistled across the boundary, scattering the spectators. They laughed and applauded, though no one felt, I think, that it was a serious contribution to the match. More mis-hits followed and then a really glorious six which sailed over the pavilion and dropped among the trees at the back.

A scatter of small boys darted off to look for it and while they were hunting the fieldsmen lay down on the grass; only Ted and his part-ner and the two umpires remaining standing, looking like victors on a stricken field. All the impulse seemed to go out of the game: it was a moment of complete relaxation. And even when the finder had triumphantly tossed the ball down into the field, and play began again, it still had a knockabout, light-hearted character. 'Good old Ted!' someone shouted when he hit his next boundary.

With the score card in front of me I still can't remember at what point I began to wonder whether Ted's displayful innings might not influence the match. I think it was when he had made his fifty that I began to see the red light and my heart started pounding in my chest.

It was a very different half-century from Mr Maudsley's, a triumph of luck, not of cunning, for the will, and even the wish to win seemed absent from it. Dimly I felt that the contrast represented something more than the conflict between Hall and village. It was that, but it was also the struggle between order and lawlessness, between obedience to tradition and defiance of it, between social stability and revolution, between one attitude to life and another. I knew which side I was on; yet the traitor within my gates felt the issue differently, he backed the individual against the side, even my own side, and wanted to see Ted Burgess pull it off. But I could not voice such thoughts to the hosts of Midian prowling around me under the shade of the pavilion veranda. Their looks had cleared marvellously and they were now taking bets about the outcome not without sly looks at me; so spying a vacant seat beside Marian I edged my way down to her and whispered:

'Isn't it exciting?' I felt this was not too much betrayal of our side.

When she did not answer I repeated the question. She turned to me and nodded, and I saw that the reason she didn't answer was because she couldn't trust herself to speak. Her eyes were bright, her cheeks were flushed, and her lips trembled. I was a child and lived in the society of children and I knew the signs. At the time I didn't ask myself what they meant, but the sight of a grown-up person so visibly affected greatly increased my emotional response to the game, and I could hardly sit still, for I always wriggled when excited. The conflict in my feelings deepened: I could not bear to face the fact, which was becoming more apparent to me every moment, that I wanted the other side to win.

Another wicket fell and then another; there were two more to go and the village needed twenty-one runs to pass our total. The spectators were absolutely silent as the new batsman walked out. I heard their captain say 'Let him have the bowling, Charlie,' but I doubted whether Ted would fall in with this; he had shown no sign of wishing to 'bag' the bowling. It was the last ball of the over; the new batsman survived it, and Ted, facing us, also faced the attack.

Lord Trimingham had two men in the deep field, and long-on was standing somewhat to our right. Ted hit the first ball straight at us. I thought it was going to be a six but soon its trajectory flattened. As it came to earth it seemed to gather speed. The fieldsman ran and got his hand to it, but it cannoned off and hurtled threateningly towards us. Mrs Maudsley jumped up with a little cry; Marian put her hands in front of her face; I held my breath; there was a moment of confusion and anxious inquiry before it was discovered that neither of them had been touched. Both ladies laughed at their narrow escape and tried to pass it off. The ball lay at Mrs Maudsley's feet looking strangely small and harmless. I threw it to long-on, who, I now saw, was one of our gardeners. But he ignored it. His face twisted with pain he was nursing his left hand in his right and gingerly rubbing it.

Lord Trimingham and some of the other fielders came towards him and he went out to meet them; I saw him showing them his injured hand. They conferred; they seemed to come to a decision; then the group dispersed, the handful of players returned to the wicket, and Lord Trimingham and the gardener returned to the pavilion.

Confusion reigned in my mind: I thought all sorts of things at the same time: that the match was over, that the gardener would be maimed for life, that Ted would be sent to prison. Then I heard Lord Trimingham say: 'We've had a casualty. Pollin has sprained his thumb, and I'm afraid we shall have to call on our twelfth man.' Even then I did not know he meant me.

My knees quaking I walked back with him to the pitch. 'We've got to get him out,' he said. 'We've got to get him out. Let's hope this interruption will have unsettled him. Now, Leo, I'm going to put you at square leg. You won't have much to do because he makes most of his runs in front of the wicket. But sometimes he hooks one, and that's where you can help us.' Something like that: but I scarcely heard, my nervous system was so busy trying to adjust itself to my new role. From spectator to performer, what a change!

Miserably nervous, I followed the movements of the bowler's hand, signalling me to my place. At last I came to rest in a fairy ring, and this absurdly gave me confidence, I felt that it might be a magic circle and would protect me. Two balls were bowled from which no runs were scored. Gradually my nervousness wore off and a sense of elation took possession of me. I felt at one with my surroundings and upheld by the long tradition of cricket. Awareness such as I had never known sharpened my senses; and when Ted drove the next ball for four, and got another four from the last ball in the over, I had to restrain an impulse to join in the enemy's applause. Yet when I saw, out of the tail of my eye, a new figure going up on the score-board, I dare not look at it, for I knew it was the last whole ten we had in hand.

The next over was uneventful but increasingly tense; the new bats-man stamped and blocked and managed to smother the straight ones; the lower half of his body was more active than the upper. But he got a single off the last ball and faced the bowling again.

It was not the same bowling, however, that had given Ted Burgess his boundaries in the preceding over. As I crossed the pitch I saw that a change was pending. Lord Trimingham had the ball, and was throw-ing it gently from one hand to the other; he made some alterations in the field, and for a moment I feared he was going to move me out of my magic circle; but he did not.

He took a long run with a skip in the middle but the ball was not very fast; it seemed to drop rather suddenly. The batsman hit out at it and it soared into the air. He ran, Ted ran, but before they reached their opposite creases it was safe in Lord Trimingham's hands. It was evidence of our captain's popularity that, even at this critical juncture, the catch was generously applauded. The clapping soon subsided, how-ever, as the boy who kept the telegraph moved towards the score-board. The figures came with maddening slowness. But what was this? Total score 9, wickets 1, last man 135. Laughter broke out among the spectators. The board boy came back and peered at his handiwork. Then to the accompaniment of more laughter, he slowly changed the figures round.

But funny though it seemed, the mistake didn't really relieve the ten-sion, it added to it by suggesting that even mathematics were subject to nervous upset. And only eight runs—two boundaries—stood between us and defeat.

As the outgoing met the incoming batsman and exchanged a word with him, at which each man nodded, I tried for the last time to sort my feelings out. But they gathered round me like a mist, whose shape can be seen as it advances but not when it is on you, and in the thick, whirling vapours my mind soon lost its way. Yet I kept my sense of the general drama of the match and it was sharpened by an awareness, which I couldn't explain to myself, of a particular drama between the bowler and the batsman. Tenant and landlord, commoner and peer, village and hall—these were elements in it. But there was something else, something to do with Marian, sitting on the pavilion steps watch-ing us.

It was a prideful and sustaining thought that whereas the spectators could throw themselves about and yell themselves hoarse, we, the players could not, must not, show the slightest sign of emotion. Certainly the bowler, digging his heel into the ground, a trick he had before starting his run, and Ted facing him his shirt clinging to his back, did not.

Lord Trimingham sent down his deceptively dipping ball but Ted did not wait for it to drop, he ran out and hit it past cover point to the boundary. It was a glorious drive and the elation of it ran through me like an electric current. The spectators yelled and cheered, and suddenly the balance of my feelings went right over: it was their victory that I wanted now, not ours. I did not think of it in terms of the three runs that were needed; I seemed to hear it coming like a wind.

I could not tell whether the next ball was on the wicket or not, but it was pitched much further up and suddenly I saw Ted's face and body swinging round, and the ball, travelling towards me on a rising straight line like a cable stretched between us. Ted started to run and then stopped and stood watching me, wonder in his eyes and a wild disbelief.

I threw my hand above my head and the ball stuck there, but the impact knocked me over. When I scrambled up, still clutching the ball to me, as though it was a pain that had started in my heart, I heard the sweet sound of applause and saw the field breaking up and Lord Trimingham coming towards me. I can't remember what he said—my emotions were too overwhelming—but I remember that his congratulations were the more precious because they were reserved and understated, they might, in fact, have been addressed to a *man*; and it was as a man, and not by any means the least of men, that I joined the group who were making their way back to the pavilion. We went together in a ragged cluster, the defeated and the surviving batsmen with us, all enmity laid aside, amid a more than generous measure of applause from the spectators. I could not tell how I felt; in my high mood of elation the usual landmarks by which I judged such things were lost to view. I was still in the air, though the scaffolding of events which had lifted me had crumbled. But I was still aware of one separate element that had not quite fused in the general concourse of passions; the pang of regret, sharp as a sword-thrust, that had accompanied the catch. Far from diminishing my exultation, it had somehow raised it to a higher power, like the drop of bitter in the fount of happiness; but I felt that I should be still happier—that it would add another cubit to my stature—if I told Ted of it. Something warned me that such an avowal would be unorthodox; the personal feelings of cricketers were concealed behind their stiff upper lips. But I was almost literally above myself; I knew that the fate of the match had turned on me, and I felt I could afford to defy convention. Yet how would he take it? What were his feelings? Was he still elated by his innings or was he bitterly disappointed by its untimely close? Did he still regard me as a friend, or as an enemy who had brought about his downfall? I did not greatly care; and seeing that he was walking alone (most of the players had exhausted their stock of conversation) I sidled up to him and said, 'I'm sorry, Ted. I didn't really mean to catch you out.' He stopped and smiled at me. 'Well, that's very handsome of you,' he said. 'It was a damned good catch, anyway. I never thought you'd hold it. To tell you the truth I'd forgotten all about you being at square leg, and then I looked round and there you were, by God. And then I thought, "It'll go right over his head," but you stretched up like a concertina. I'd thought of a dozen ways I might get out, but never thought I'd be caught out by our postman.' 'I didn't mean to,' I repeated, not to be cheated of my apology. At that moment the clapping grew louder and some enthusiasts coupled Ted's name with it. Though we were all heroes, he was evidently the crowd's favourite; and I dropped back so that he might walk in alone. His fellow-batsmen in the pavilion were making a great demonstration; even the ladies of our party, sitting in front, showed themselves mildly interested as Ted came by. All except one. Marian, I noticed, didn't look up.

As soon as we were back at the Hall I said to Marcus, 'Lend me your scoring-card, old man.'

'Why, didn't you keep one, pudding-face?' he asked me.

'How could I, you dolt, when I was fielding?'

'Did you field, you measly microbe? Are you quite sure?'

When I had punished him for this, and extracted his score-card from him, I copied on to mine the items that were missing.

'E. Burgess c. sub. b. Ld Trimingham 81,' I read. 'Why, you might have put my name in, you filthy scoundrel.'

' "C. sub." is correct,' he said. 'Besides, I want to keep this card clean, and it wouldn't be if your name was on it.'

The Go-Between, 1953

*

Authors, Artists, Actors, and Lord's

ALBERT KINROSS

The most delightful of my London (or near-London) matches were those I played in for the Authors. The late E. W. Hornung, of 'Raffles' fame, arranged them and they were mostly played at Esher.

I had seen a paragraph in the paper saying that Hornung was getting up a side of Authors to play against a side of Artists, so I wrote and asked whether he had room for me. I did not know him, but cricket is cricket. He replied at once in the most friendly spirit and I was able to get him down to Brondesbury for some net-practice, which he needed. Like so many men who are hardly average players, he was an out-and-out enthusiast. There were to be three days of it, he told me, the first against the Artists, the second against Esher, the third at Elstree, against the Elstree Masters, a very hot side. But we were pretty useful ourselves.

Conan Doyle was our captain, and in some ways he reminded me of 'W.G.' He hadn't the beard, but he was much the same make of a man, solid, four-square, and an 'all rounder'. He could bowl as well as bat and was untiring. Hesketh-Prichard, who that year was bowling for the 'Gents' as well as for Hampshire, was our star bowler, and J. C. Snaith, who I believe has played for Notts, was little behind him and an excellent bat. E. V. Lucas, a pretty bat and a good field, Shan Bullock and Horace Bleackley, both good bats, young Graves, Hornung, myself, and a brace of celebrities made up our side. The celebrities may have been A. E. W. Mason and J. M. Barrie, neither of whom appeared to take the game very seriously, though I have been told that Barrie, in his day, was quite a cunning slow bowler. He certainly sported a most businesslike cap and blazer done in colours of his own invention. He and Mason, however, were balanced by Edwin Abbey, RA, and one or two other artists who, presumably, were better painters than cricketers.

This side, with certain variations, met at Esher every year. P. G. Wodehouse, I remember, joined us, an old Dulwich boy and still rather the schoolboy. He, as Lucas before him, was doing comic stuff for the *Globe*. Esher, then something like a village, put us up and fed us; its ladies turned out for tea with us on the field; and in the evening there were dinner-parties.

I had the luck to make top score, 46 not out, in our first game; Lucas made 22; the stars, I think, failed us. The Artists, led by Hilliard Swinstead, beat us. They included Harold Speed, Adrian Stokes, Chevalier Taylor, and other well-known men; and later came Gerard Chowne, whom I was glad to meet again in Salonica before he fell. A delightful companion was Gerard Chowne; I know we were both happy to find one another in that arid place and lunch and talk together. I believe, had he lived, he would have made a wider name for himself, something like that made by Fantin-Latour. Cyril Foley, another old cricketer, who had played for Middlesex, was also to be found out there.

Edwin Abbey was rather a pet with us. He was an American who had taken enthusiastically to the game and perhaps to England. He was painting the great series of mural decorations which now adorn the Boston Public Library and which illustrate 'The Quest and Achievement of the Holy Grail'. They are ruined by being set in a room with a bad light, but perhaps some day Boston will know better. We all liked Abbey and did our best *not* to get him out, and the Artists, I think, had much the same feeling towards Barrie.

The leading family at Esher, that of old Mr Martineau, put many of us up, and I was young enough then to feel a little alarmed at the thought that I was housed under the same roof as the great Conan Doyle. One morning, waking early, I heard what I took to be the note of a typewriting machine. 'He's at it already!' I thought. The chirping went on. I jumped out of bed and found a robin on my window-sill, rattling away at a hundred words a minute. These matches were long since over, when, in April, 1915, I was in hospital at Torquay, recovering from a broken head which I had acquired in France. A visitor came in. It was Conan Doyle, in search of certain facts which he needed for a War History he was writing. He asked men who had been in the thick of it questions. A curious and unexpected encounter.

We beat the Elstree Masters, then a great side, including numerous old blues. Snaith did most of the damage, outbowling even Hesketh-Prichard. It was his day; length and everything came right and he seemed to find the 'blind spot' with a devastating regularity. Every one of those ten wickets fell to him. He was a fastish medium bowler who spun them, while Hesketh-Prichard had great height as well as great pace.

At Esher we were beaten, the side including S. A. P. Kitcat, who played for Gloucestershire, and several Martineaus, one of whom wore Cambridge blue, and good men like the Peacheys and Gillespie. Yet the finest player I every saw at Esher was a parson of the name of Meyrick-Jones. Like the great Studd, he had given to missionary work what might have gone into first-class cricket. He hadn't held a bat that season, yet he took a century with an ease and variety which weren't far short of genius.

I have often paused over men who could, but don't, and men who could but don't get the chance; for cricket, like literature, has its 'mute, inglorious' Miltons. The first-class professional cricketer is often the child of hazard, and I sometimes wonder what would have become of Hobbs had he been born in Rutlandshire and not come under the notice of Tom Hayward. At Dymchurch in Romney Marsh I once saw a young bus-conductor of the name of Swan make as pretty a century as I have ever seen, quite unaware that he was doing anything out of the ordinary. A born cricketer, he promised to be good enough for any county, but he had no one to speak up for him in the right quarter. Fielder, the Kentish and All England fast bowler, was a farm labourer employed by my friend, Cecil Golding, who went out of his way to bring the young man's gifts to the attention of the proper authorities. As with authorship, there's a good deal of luck in it, and some men are born to miss things, while others will make the most of opportunity.

In addition to our games at Esher we sometimes went to Lord's and did battle with teams of Actors and Publishers. Needless to say, St John's Wood was not blocked with traffic on these occasions, though the Actors proved something of an attraction. Far more so than we poor Authors, who were so misprized that one charitable firm of bat-makers arrived with the offer of a guinea weapon to the one of us who should make top score. Neither Doyle, nor Hornung, nor any of us leapt at it, exactly.

The Actors were captained by Aubrey Smith, the same 'round-the-corner Smith' who had bowled for Sussex, and Oscar Asche, Rutland Barrington, Gerald du Maurier, Haydn Coffin, young Warner (the brother of Grace and son of Charles), and one of the famous Fosters all turned out and gave us a very good game. We were mostly the same old crowd which had tackled the Artists, with the addition of Lacon Watson, of Cecil Headlam, a real good wicket-keeper, and Leo and Philip Trevor, who not only writes excellently about cricket but could play it. An exceptional judge of a run and fond of running them short, he gave me credit for the same capacity, and I remember once that I was rather glad than otherwise to see the last of him after we had, time and again, taken our lives in our hands and put on a rapid forty, mostly in singles. He was tubby and short, yet a magnificent sprinter. Doyle himself, besides being an inspiring captain, was the hero of these games. There was nothing showy about him, but in his unostentatious way, he usually delivered the goods, made runs, took wickets, and held catches. I had the bad luck to drop one when I was fielding on the boundary and the audience let me know exactly what they thought about it. I realised then, as never before, what the first-class cricketer, with an immensely larger audience behind the ropes, is 'up against' when he does ditto. Small boys, especially, seemed very candid.

The Publishers were not so good a side and we beat them easily, though in S. S. Pawling of Heinemann's they had one uncommon bowler who could send down a fast in-swinger with an authentic fizz— a brute of a ball to start on and bad enough at any time. I speak with feeling, for it was one of these that laid me low.

I had never hoped to see Lord's again after the war, save as a very middle-aged spectator, yet a few enthusiasts at the Authors' Club, led by H. M. Walbrook, the writer on the theatre, and J. C. Squire, got up a side and challenged the Actors of to-day. I was the only survivor of our pre-war side who played that day, and while we were willing but hardly competent, those accursed Actors seemed to have gathered new strength. They had batting, bowling, and fielding. Young Alec Waugh did his best, and Clifford Bax hit some big hits for us, and Powell-Jones collected a really high-class fifty, and Reginald Berkeley bowled and bowled well, but what with the Brothers O'Gorman of Surrey and Desmond Roberts, to go no further, we hadn't a chance.

An Unconventional Cricketer, 1930

*

How Plaxtol Beat Roughway

ALBERT KINROSS

It's a long time ago, and I'm old, sir,
And my mem'ry is not very clear;
But if I am to tell you that story,
Then it's you 'as to pay fer the beer.

I am old, I jest said, an' all tottery,
But my hair it has allus been grey;

An' that come about on the day, sir,
When Plaxtol fust walloped Roughway.

Kinross is my name; I was captain—
I was captain o' Plaxtol . . . Good 'ealth!
I was captain o' Plaxtol, I was, sir—
The cricket club's captain . . . Good 'ealth!

Then we played in the Park, side o' Fairlawne,
Where was bullocks all fattin' an' wild,
An' Ted Bennett 'e was our groundsman,
'Oo rolled an' 'oo mowed till 'e biled.

But it's not o' the Park nor Ted Bennett
My story's about—it's the day
That the match o' the season was played, sir,
When Plaxtol fust walloped Roughway.

Now Roughway's nex' village to our'n, sir;
You passed it, you says?—that may be:
There's some as backs Roughway 'gin us, sir,
But Plaxtol's the village fer me!

The challenge was sent by Fred Taylor,
Our sec'tary, beamin' an' slick;
An' 'e wrote wot I told un to write, sir
An' soined it an' give it a lick.

'E wrote off ter Roughway, 'e did, sir,
'E challenged 'em fairly an' square,
An' we played 'em that day in the Park, sir—
Ah, don't yer jest wish you'd been there!

An' Parkin's the name o' the man, sir,
'Oo answered 'im fixin' the day
When Plaxtol, the village we're in, sir,
Fust walloped the lads o' Roughway.

Well, sir, since you asked, I'll name it—
Another quart ale . . . Good 'ealth!
I was captain o' Plaxtol, I was, sir,
The cricket club's captain . . . Good 'ealth!

I was captain, a tall, fine, young feller;
I could bowl, I could bat, all the day,
When we played that great match in the Park, sir
An' walloped, an' walloped, Roughway.

Ted Bennett 'e'd rolled out a pitch, sir,
As green an' as flat as your 'and;
An' there we stood, ten fine young fellers,
Not countin' o' me in command.

We could bowl, we could bat, we could field, sir;
We could throw, we could catch, we could run;
But o' all o' them chaps as turned out, sir,
I think it was me took the bun!

There was Toller 'oo farmed side the mill, sir,
A lad made o' muscle an' brawn—
It was 'e 'oo'd said loud 'e'd make Roughway
A-wish it 'ad never been born.

Kep' wicket 'e did—'e was allus
A-shoutin' an' 'ollerin', ' 'Ow is it?'
Afore e'd got 'old o' the ball, sir—
An' then 'e was sorry 'e sez it!

There was Gunner 'oo rode with the letters
An' Gunner 'oo served in the shop—
That there grocer's—they fielded close in, sir—
There was nothing that they couldn't stop!

Them Gunners could field like two cats, sir,
They was wiry an' lean as a gun,
An' they'd sworn there'd be nor't left o' Roughway
When they 'ad concluded an' done.

There was Coomber, red'eaded an' ging'ry—
'E 'ad ginger inside 'im as well—
And 'e'd said 'e would settle ole Roughway,
An' send it a-flyin' to—Happledore.

There was Martin, the butcher, a bowler
'Oo allus a-bowled wi' 'is 'ead,
An' 'e'd said 'e would make pore ole Roughway
A-wish it was buried an' dead.

Jo Allcorn, a stout lad as ever
Went up to the wicket was there;
An', speakin' o' Roughway, 'e'd said, sir,
'Termorrer we combs their 'air!'

Well, sir, since you asked, I'll name it—
Another quart ale . . . Good 'ealth!
I was captain o' Plaxtol, I was, sir,
The cricket club's captain . . . Good 'ealth!

Tom Jenner was there. 'E could bowl, sir!
'E could bowl all day an' all night;
An' 'e'd said 'e'd make o' them Roughways
A-die in their pads o' fright!

Will Fielder, a slow 'un an' steady,
'E'd turned out for 'is side;
An' 'e'd said no word 'ad Will, sir—
'E'd kep' 'is thoughts inside.

An' 'arry, 'is son, 'ad come with 'im,
A lad still in 'is teens,
Who'd said, 'What-'o them Roughways
An' won't we give 'em beans!'

Jack Naylor, 'e was the last, sir,
An' ready for 'ard knocks;
For 'e'd gone an' tucked 'is trousers
Right deep down in his socks!

An' our umpire was ole 'Awkins,
It was 'e 'oo stood in white;
An' we knew that when we asked 'im
'E'd give 'em 'Out' all right!

An' 'Awkins' son was scorer;
'E sat in the tent an' scored
An' when 'e wasn't asleep, sir,
'E 'ollered, 'Ten up on the board!'

So now you know the side, sir,
That turned out on that day,
When I was captain o' Plaxtol,
An' we fair walloped Roughway.

Well, sir, since you asked, I'll name it—
Same's before . . . Good 'ealth!
I was captain o' Plaxtol I was, sir,
The cricket club's captain . . . Good 'ealth!

That's a gallon o' beer I've 'ad, sir,
An' it's risin' into my 'ead,
An' thankin' you fer the treat, sir,
I'd best be off ter my bed.

Oh, my story, the story I promised yer,
If that's what I 'eard yer say,
About Plaxtol winnin' the game, sir,
An' playin' ole Nick wi' Roughway?

There ain't no story to speak of;
It rained that 'ole clock round—
'Twas the Plaxtol weather beat Roughway
An' drove 'em off the ground!

(Quick exit.)

An Unconventional Cricketer, 1930

✻

Tribulations of a Captain

A. A. MILNE

I. The Choosing of the Day

As soon as I had promised to take an eleven down to Chartleigh I knew that I was in for trouble; but I did not realise how great it would be until I consulted Henry Barton. Henry is a first-class cricketer, and it was my idea that he should do all the batting for us, and such of the bowling as the laws allowed. I had also another idea, and this I explained to Henry.

'As you are aware,' I said, 'the ideal side contains five good bats, four good bowlers, a wicket-keeper, and Henry Barton.'

'Quite so,' agreed Henry.

'That is the principle on which one selects an eleven. Now, I intend to strike out a line of my own. My team shall consist of three authors or journalists, two solicitors, four barristers, a couple from the Stock Exchange, some civil servants and an artist or two. How many is that?'

'Nineteen.'

'Well, that's the idea, anyhow.'

'It's a rotten idea.'

'No, it's a splendid idea. I wonder nobody has thought of it before. I send a solicitor and a journalist in first. The journalist uses the long handle, while the solicitor plays for keeps.'

'And where does the artist come in?'

'The artist comes in last, and plays for a draw. You are very slow to-day, Henry.'

Henry, the man of leisure, thought a moment.

'Yes, that's all very well for you working men,' he said at last, 'but what do I go as? Or am I one of the barristers?'

'You go as "with Barton". Yes. If you're very good you shall have an "H" in brackets after you. "With Barton (H)".'

The method of choosing my team being settled, the next thing was the day. 'Any day in the first week in July,' the Chartleigh captain had said. Now at first sight there appear to be seven days in the week, but it is not really so. For instance, Saturday. Now there's a good day! What could one object to in a Saturday?

But do you imagine Henry Barton would let it pass?

'I don't think you'll get eleven people for the Saturday,' he said. 'People are always playing cricket on Saturday.'

'Precisely,' I said. 'Healthy exercise for the London toiler. That's why I'm asking 'em.'

'But I mean they'll have arranged to play already with their own teams. Or else they'll be going away for week-ends.'

'One can spend a very pretty week-end at Chartleigh.'

'H'm, let me think. Any day in the week, isn't it?'

'Except, apparently, Saturday,' I said huffily.

'Let's see now, what days are there?'

I mentioned two or three of the better-known ones.

'Yes. Of course, some of those are impossible, though. We'd better go through the week and see which is best.'

I don't know who Barton is that he should take it upon himself to make invidious distinctions between the days of the week.

'Very well, then,' I said. 'Sunday.'

'Ass.'

That seemed to settle Sunday, so we passed on to Monday.

'You won't get your stockbroker on Monday,' said Henry. 'It's Contanger day or something with them every Monday.'

'Stocktaking, don't you mean?'

'I dare say. Anyhow, no one in the House can get away on a Monday.'

'I must have my stockbrokers. Tuesday.'

Tuesday, it seemed, was hopeless. I was a fool to have thought of Tuesday. Why, everybody knew that Tuesday was an impossible day for——

I forget what spoilt Tuesday's chance. I fancy it was a busy day for Civil Servants. No one in the Home Civil can get away on a Tuesday. I know that sounds absurd, but Henry was being absurd just then. Or was it barristers? Briefs get given out on a Tuesday, I was made to understand. That brought us to Wednesday. I hoped much from Wednesday.

'Yes,' said Henry. 'Wednesday might do. Of course most of the weeklies go to press on Wednesday. Rather an awkward day for journalists. What about Thursday?'

I began to get annoyed.

'Thursday my flannel trousers go to the press,' I said—'that is to say, they come back from the wash then.'

'Look here, why try to be funny?'

'Hang it, who started it? Talking about Contanger-days. Contanger— it sounds like a new kind of guano.'

'Well, if you don't believe me——'

'Henry, I do. Thursday be it, then.'

'Yes, I suppose that's all right,' said Henry doubtfully.

'Why not? Don't say it's sending-in day with artists,' I implored. 'Not *every* Thursday?'

'No. Only there's Friday, and——'

'Friday is *my* busy day,' I pleaded—'my one ewe lamb. Do not rob me of it.'

'It's a very good day, Friday. I think you'd find that most people could get off then.'

'But why throw over Thursday like this? A good, honest day, Henry. Many people get born on a Thursday, Henry. And it's a marrying day, Henry. A nice, clean, sober day, and you——'

'The fact is,' said Henry, 'I've suddenly remembered I'm engaged myself on Thursday.'

This was too much.

'Henry,' I said coldly, 'you forget yourself—you forget yourself strangely, my lad. Just because I was weak enough to promise you an "H" after your name. You seem to have forgotten that the "H" was to be in brackets.'

'Yes, but I'm afraid I really am engaged.'

'Are you really? Look here—I'll leave out the "with" and you shall be one of us. There! Baby, see the pretty gentlemen!'

Henry smiled and shook his head.

'Oh, well,' I said, 'we must have you. So if you say Friday, Friday it is. You're quite sure Friday is all right for solicitors? Very well, then.'

So the day was settled for Friday. It was rather a pity, because, as I said, in the ordinary way Friday is the day I put aside for work.

II. The Selection Committee

The committee consisted of Henry and myself. Originally it was myself alone, but as soon as I had selected Henry I proceeded to co-opt him, reserving to myself, however, the right of a casting vote in case of any difference of opinion. One arose, almost immediately, over Higgins. Henry said:

    (a) That Higgins had once made ninety-seven.

    (b) That he had been asked to play for his county.

    (c) That he was an artist, and we had arranged to have an artist in the team.

In reply I pointed out:

(*a*) That ninety-seven was an extremely unlikely number for anyone to have made.

(*b*) That if he had been asked he evidently hadn't accepted, which showed the sort of man he was: besides which, what was his county?

(*c*) That, assuming for the moment he had made ninety-seven, was it likely he would consent to go in last and play for a draw, which was why we wanted the artist? And that, anyhow, he was a jolly bad artist.

(*d*) That hadn't we better put it to the vote?

This was accordingly done, and an exciting division ended in a tie.

> Those in favour of Higgins . . 1
> Those against Higgins . . . 1

The Speaker gave his casting vote against Higgins.

Prior to this, however, I had laid before the House the letter of invitation. It was as follows (and, I flatter myself, combined tact with a certain dignity):—

'DEAR ——, I am taking a team into the country on Friday week to play against the village eleven. The ground and the lunch are good. Do you think you could manage to come down? I know you are very busy just now with

> Contangers,
> Briefs,
> Clients,
> Your Christmas Number,
> Varnishing Day,
> (*Strike out all but one of these*)

but a day in the country would do you good. I hear from all sides that you are in great form this season. I will give you all particulars about trains later on. Good-bye. Remember me to ——. How is ——? Ever yours.

'*P.S.*—Old Henry is playing for us. He has strained himself a little and probably won't bowl much, so I expect we shall all have a turn with the ball.'

Or, 'I don't think you have ever met Henry Barton, the cricketer. He is very keen on meeting you. Apparently he has seen you play somewhere. He will be turning out for us on Friday.

'*P.P.S.*—We might manage to have some bridge in the train.'

'That,' I said to Henry, 'is what I call a clever letter.'

'What makes you think that?'

'It is all clever,' I said modestly. 'But the cleverest part is a sentence at the end. "I will give you all particulars about trains later on." You see, I have been looking them up, and we leave Victoria at seven-thirty A.M. and get back to London Bridge at eleven-forty-five P.M.'

The answers began to come in the next day. One of the first was from Bolton, the solicitor, and it upset us altogether. For, after accepting the invitation, he went on: 'I am afraid I don't play bridge. As you may remember, I used to play chess at Cambridge, and I still keep it up.'

'Chess,' said Henry. 'That's where White plays and mates in two moves. And there's a Black too. He does something.'

'We shall have to get a Black. This is awful.'

'Perhaps Bolton would like to do problems by himself all the time.'

'That would be rather bad luck on him. No, look here. Here's Carey. Glad to come, but doesn't play bridge. He's the man.'

Accordingly we wired to Carey: 'Do you play chess? Reply at once.' He answered, 'No. Why?'

'Carey will have to play that game with glass balls. Solitaire. Yes. We must remember to bring a board with us.'

'But what about the chess gentleman?' asked Henry.

'I must go and find one. We've had one refusal.'

There is an editor I know slightly, so I called upon him at his office. I found him writing verses.

'Be brief,' he said, 'I'm frightfully busy.'

'I have just three questions to ask you,' I replied.

'What rhymes with "yorker"?'

'That wasn't one of them.'

'Yorker—corker—por——'

'Better make it a full pitch,' I suggested. 'Step out and make it a full pitch. Then there are such lots of rhymes.'

'Thanks, I will. Well?'

'One. Do you play bridge?'

'No.'

'Two. Do you play chess?'

'I can.'

'Three. Do you play cricket? Not that it matters.'

'Yes, I do sometimes. Good-bye. Send me a proof, will you? By the way, what paper is this for?'

'*The Sportsman*, if you'll play. On Friday week. Do.'

'Anything, if you'll go.'

'May I have that in writing?'

He handed me a rejection form.

'There you are. And I'll do anything you like on Friday.'

I went back to Henry and told him the good news.

'I wonder if he'll mind being black,' said Henry. 'That's the chap that always gets mated so quickly.'

'I expect they'll arrange it among themselves. Anyhow, we've done our best for them.'

'It's an awful business, getting up a team,' said Henry thoughtfully. 'Well, we shall have two decent sets of bridge, anyway. But you ought to have arranged for twelve aside, and then we could have left out the chess professors and had three sets.'

'It's all the fault of the rules. Some day somebody will realise that four doesn't go into eleven, and then we shall have a new rule.'

'No, I don't think so,' said Henry. 'I don't fancy "Wanderer" would allow it.'

III. In the Train

If there is one thing I cannot stand, it is ingratitude. Take the case of Carey. Carey, you may remember, professed himself unable to play either bridge or chess; and as we had a three-hour journey before us it did not look as though he were going to have much of a time. However, Henry and I, thinking entirely of Carey's personal comfort, went to the trouble of buying him a solitaire board, with glass balls complete. The balls were all in different colours.

I laid this before Carey as soon as we settled in the train.

'Whatever's that?'

'The new game,' I said. 'It's all the rage now, the man tells me. The Smart Set play it every Sunday. Young girls are inveigled into lonely country houses and robbed of incredible sums.'

Carey laughed scornfully.

'So it is alleged,' I added. 'The inventor claims for it that in some respects it has advantages which even cricket cannot claim. As, for instance, it can be played in any weather: nay, even upon the sick bed.'

'And how exactly is it played?'

'Thus. You take one away and all the rest jump over each other. At each jump you remove the jumpee, and the object is to clear the board. Hence the name—solitaire.'

'I see. It seems a pretty rotten game.'

That made me angry.

'All right. Then don't play. Have a game of marbles on the rack instead.'

Meanwhile Henry was introducing Bolton and the editor to each other.

'Two such famous people,' he began.

'Everyone', said Bolton, with a bow, 'knows the editor of——'

'Oh yes, there's that. But I meant two such famous chess players. Bolton', he explained to the editor, 'was twelfth man against Oxford some years ago. Something went wrong with his heart, or he'd have got in. On his day, and if the board was at all sticky, he used to turn a good deal from QB4.'

'Do you really play?' asked Bolton eagerly. 'I have a board here.'

'Does he play! Do you mean to say you have never heard of the Trocadero Defence?'

'The Sicilian Defence——'

'The Trocadero Defence. It's where you palm the other man's queen when he's not looking. Most effective opening.'

They both seemed keen on beginning, so Henry got out the cards for the rest of us.

I drew the younger journalist, against Henry and the senior stock-broker. Out of compliment to the journalist we arranged to play half-a-crown a hundred, that being about the price they pay him. I dealt, and a problem arose immediately. Here it is.

'A deals and leaves it to his partner B, who goes No Trumps. Y leads a small heart. B's hand consists of king and three small diamonds, king and one other heart, king and three small clubs, and three small spades. A plays the king from Dummy, and Z puts on the ace. What should A do?'

Answer. Ring communication-cord and ask guard to remove B.

'Very well,' I said to Dummy. 'One thing's pretty clear. You don't bowl to-day. Long-leg both ends is about your mark. Somewhere where there's plenty of throwing to do.'

Later on, when I was Dummy, I strolled over to the chess players.

'What's the ground like?' said the editor, as he finessed a knight.

'Sporting. Distinctly sporting.'

'Long grass all round, I suppose?'

'Oh, lord, no. The cows eat up all that.'

'Do you mean to say the cows are allowed on the pitch?'

'Well, they don't put it that way, quite. The pitch is allowed on the cows' pasture land.'

'I suppose if we make a hundred we shall do well?' asked somebody.

'If we make fifty we shall declare,' I said. 'By Jove, Bolton, that's a pretty smart move.'

I may not know all the technical terms, but I do understand the idea of chess. The editor was a pawn up and three to play, and had just advanced his queen against Bolton's king, putting on a lot of check side as it seemed to me. Of course, I expected Bolton would have to retire his king; but not he! He laid a stymie with his bishop, and it was the editor's queen that had to withdraw. Yet Bolton was only spare man at Cambridge!

'I am not at all sure', I said, 'that chess is not a finer game even than solitaire.'

'It's a finer game than cricket,' said Bolton, putting his bishop back in the slips again.

'No,' said the editor. 'Cricket is the finest game in the world. For why? I will tell you.'

'Thanks to the glorious uncertainty of our national pastime', began the journalist, from his next Monday's article.

'No, thanks to the fact that it is a game in which one can produce the maximum of effect with the minimum of skill. Take my own case. I am not a batsman, I shall never make ten runs in an innings, yet how few people realise that! I go in first wicket down, wearing my MCC cap. Having taken guard with the help of a bail, I adopt Palairet's stance at the wicket. Then the bowler delivers: either to the off, to leg, or straight. If it is to the off, I shoulder my bat and sneer at it. If it is to leg, I swing at it. I have a beautiful swing, which is alone worth the money. Probably I miss, but the bowler fully understands that it is because I have not yet got the pace of the wicket. Sooner or later he sends down a straight one, whereupon I proceed to glide it to leg. You will see the stroke in Beldam's book. Of course, I miss the ball, and am given out l.b.w. Then the look of astonishment that passes over my face, the bewildered inquiry of the wicket-keeper, and finally the shrug of good-humoured resignation as I walk from the crease! Nine times out of ten square-leg asks the umpire what county I play for. That is cricket.'

'Quite so,' I said, when he had finished. 'There's only one flaw in it. That is that quite possibly you may have to go in last to-day. You'll have to think of some other plan. Also on this wicket the ball always goes well over your head. You couldn't be l.b.w. if you tried.'

'Oh, but I do try.'

'Yes. Well, you'll find it difficult.'

The editor sighed.

'Then I shall have to retire hurt,' he said.

Bolton chuckled to himself.

'One never retires hurt at chess,' he said, as he huffed the editor's king. 'Though once', he added proudly, 'I sprained my hand, and had to make all my moves with the left one. Check.'

The editor yawned, and looked out of the window.

'Are we nearly there?' he asked.

IV. In the Field

It is, I consider, the duty of a captain to consult the wishes of his team now and then, particularly when he is in command of such a heterogeneous collection of the professions as I was. I was watching a match at the Oval once, and at the end of an over Lees went up to Dalmeny, and had a few words with him. Probably, I thought, he is telling him a good story that he heard at lunch; or, maybe, he is asking for the latest gossip from the Lobby. My neighbour, however, held other views.

'There,' he said, 'there's ole Walter Lees asking to be took off.'

'Surely not,' I answered. 'Dalmeny had a telegram just now, and Lees is asking if it's the three-thirty winner.'

Lees then began to bowl again.

'There you are,' I said triumphantly, but my neighbour wouldn't hear of it.

'Ole Lees asked to be took off, and ole Dalmeny' (I forget how he pronounced it, but I know it was one of the wrong ways)—'ole Dalmeny told him he'd have to stick on a bit.'

Now that made a great impression on me, and I agreed with my friend that Dalmeny was in the wrong.

'When I am captaining a team,' I said, 'and one of the bowlers wants to come off, I am always ready to meet him half-way, more than half-way. Better than that, if I have resolved upon any course of action, I always let my team know beforehand; and I listen to their objections in a fair-minded spirit.'

It was in accordance with this rule of mine that I said casually, as we were changing, 'If we win the toss I shall put them in.'

There was a chorus of protest.

'That's right, go it,' I said. 'Henry objects because, as a first-class cricketer, he is afraid of what *The Sportsman* will say if we lose. The editor naturally objects—it ruins his chance of being mistaken for a county player if he has to field first. Bolton objects because heavy exercise on a hot day spoils his lunch. Thompson objects because that's the way he earns his living at the Bar. His objection is merely technical, and is reserved as a point of law for the Court of Crown Cases Reserved. Markham is a socialist and objects to authority. Also he knows he's got to field long-leg both ends. Gerald——'

'But why?' said Henry.

'Because I want you all to see the wicket first. Then you can't say you weren't warned.' Whereupon I went out and lost the toss.

As we walked into the field the editor told me a very funny story. I cannot repeat it here for various reasons. First, it has nothing to do with cricket; and, secondly, it is, I understand, coming out in his next number, and I should probably get into trouble. Also it is highly technical, and depends largely for its success upon adequate facial expression. But it amused me a good deal. Just as he got to the exciting part, Thompson came up.

'Do you mind if I go cover?' he asked.

'Do,' I said abstractedly. 'And what did the vicar say?'

The editor chuckled. 'Well, you see, the vicar, knowing, of course, that——'

'Cover, I suppose,' said Gerald, as he caught us up.

'What? Oh yes, please. The vicar did know, did he?'

'Oh, the vicar *knew*. That's really the whole point.'

I shouted with laughter.

'Good, isn't it?' said the editor. 'Well, then——'

'Have you got a cover?' came Markham's voice from behind us.

I turned round.

'Oh, Markham,' I said, 'I shall want you cover, if you don't mind. Sorry—I must tell these men where to go—well, then, you were saying——'

The editor continued the story. We were interrupted once or twice, but he finished it just as their first two men came out. I particularly liked that bit about the——

'Jove,' I said suddenly, 'we haven't got a wicket-keeper. That's always the way. Can you keep?' I asked the editor.

'Isn't there anyone else?'

'I'm afraid they're all fielding cover,' I said, remembering suddenly. 'But, look here, it's the chance of a lifetime for you. You can tell 'em all that——'

But he was trotting off to the pavilion.

'Can anybody lend me some gloves?' he asked. 'They want me to keep wicket. Thing I've never done in my life. Of course I always field cover in the ordinary way. Thanks awfully. Sure you don't mind? Don't suppose I shall stop a ball though.'

'Henry,' I called, 'you're starting that end. Arrange the field, will you? I'll go cover. You're sure to want one.'

Their first batsman was an old weather-beaten villager called George. We knew his name was George because the second ball struck him in the stomach and his partner said, 'Stay there, George,' which seemed to be George's idea too. We learnt at lunch that once, in the eighties or so, he had gone in first with Lord Hawke (which put him on a level with that player), and that he had taken first ball (which put him just above the Yorkshireman).

There the story ended, so far as George was concerned; and indeed it was enough. Why seek to inquire if George took any other balls besides the first?

In our match, however, he took the second in the place that I mentioned, the third on the back of the neck, the fourth on the elbow, and the fifth in the original place; while the sixth, being off the wicket, was left there. Nearly every batsman had some pet stroke, and we soon saw that George's stroke was the leg-bye. His bat was the second line of defence, and was kept well in the block. If the ball escaped the earthwork in front, there was always a chance that it would be brought up by the bat. Once, indeed, a splendid ball of Henry's which came with his arm and missed George's legs, snicked the bat, and went straight into the wicket-keeper's hands. The editor, however, presented his compliments, and regretted that he was unable to accept the enclosed, which he accordingly returned with many thanks.

There was an unwritten law that George could not be l.b.w. I cannot say how it arose—possibly from a natural coyness on George's part about the exact significance of the 'l.' Henry, after appealing for the best part of three overs, gave it up, and bowled what he called 'googlies' at him. This looked more hopeful, because a googly seems in no way to be restricted as to the number of its bounces, and at each bounce it had a chance of doing something. Unfortunately it never did George. Lunch came and the score was thirty-seven—George having compiled in two hours a masterly nineteen; eighteen off the person, but none the less directly due to him.

'We must think of a plan of campaign at lunch,' said Henry. 'It's hopeless to go on like this.'

'Does George drink?' I asked anxiously. It seemed the only chance.

But George didn't. And the score was thirty-seven for five, which is a good score for the wicket.

V. At the Wickets

At lunch I said: 'I have just had a wire from the Surrey committee to say that I may put myself on to bowl.'

'That is good hearing,' said Henry.

'Did they hear?' asked Gerald anxiously, looking over at the Chartleigh team.

'You may think you're very funny, but I'll bet you a—a—anything you like that I get George out.'

'All right,' said Gerald. 'I'll play you for second wicket down, the loser to go in last.'

'Done,' I said, 'and what about passing the salad now?'

After lunch the editor took me on one side and said: 'I don't like it. I don't like it at all.'

'Then why did you have so much?' I asked.

'I mean the wicket. It's dangerous. I am not thinking of myself so much as of——'

'As of the reading public?'

'Quite so.'

'You think you—you would be missed in Fleet Street—just at first?'

'You are not putting the facts too strongly. I was about to suggest that I should be a "did not bat".'

'Oh! I see. Perhaps I ought to tell you that I was talking just now to the sister of their captain.'

The editor looked interested.

'About the pad of the gardener?' he said.

'About you. She said—I give you her own words—"Who is the tall, handsome man keeping wicket in a MCC cap?" So I said you were a well-known county player, as she would see when you went in to bat.'

The editor shook my hand impressively.

'Thank you very much,' he said. 'I shall not fail her. What county did you say?'

'Part of Flint. You know the little bit that's got into the wrong county by mistake? That part. She had never heard of it; but I assured her it had a little bit of yellow all to itself on the map. Have you a pretty good eleven?'

The editor swore twice—once for me and once for Flint. Then we went out into the field.

My first ball did for George. I followed the tactics of William the First at the Battle of Hastings, 1066. You remember how he ordered his archers to shoot into the air, and how one arrow fell and pierced the eye of Harold, whereupon confusion and disaster arose. So with George. I hurled one perpendicularly into the sky, and it dropped (after a long time) straight upon the batsman. George followed it with a slightly contemptuous eye . . . all the way. . . .

All the way. Of course, I was sorry. We were all much distressed. They told us afterwards he had never been hit in the eye before. . . . One gets new experiences.

George retired hurt. Not so much hurt as piqued, I fancy. He told the umpire it wasn't bowling. Possibly. Neither was it batting. It was just superior tactics.

The innings soon closed, and we had sixty-one to win, and, what seemed more likely, fifty-nine and various other numbers to lose. Sixty-one is a very unlucky number with me—oddly enough I have never yet made sixty-one; like W. G. Grace, who had never made ninety-three. My average this season is five, which is a respectable number. As Bolton pointed out—if we each got five to-day, and there were six extras, we should win. I suppose if one plays chess a good deal one thinks of these things.

Harold, I mean George, refused to field, so I nobly put myself in last and substituted for him. This was owing to an argument as to the exact wording of my bet with Gerald.

'You said you'd get him out,' said Gerald.

'I mean "out of the way", "out of the field", "out of——"'

'I meant "out" according to the laws of cricket. There are nine ways. Which was yours, I should like to know?'

'Obstructing the ball.'

'There you are.'

I shifted my ground.

'I didn't say I'd get him out,' I explained. 'I said I'd get him. Those were my very words. "I will get George." Can you deny that I got him?'

'Even if you said that, which you didn't, the common construction that one puts upon the phrase is——'

'If you are going to use long words like that,' I said, 'I must refer you to my solicitor Bolton.'

Whereupon Bolton took counsel's opinion, and reported that he could not advise me to proceed in the matter. So Gerald took second wicket, and I fielded.

However, one advantage of fielding was that I saw the editor's innings from start to finish at the closest quarters. He came in at the end of the first over, and took guard for 'left hand round the wicket'.

'Would you give it me?' he said to Bolton. 'These country umpires. . . . Thanks. And what's that over the wicket? Thanks.'

He marked two places with the bail.

'How about having it from here?' I suggested at mid-on. 'It's quite a good place and we're in a straight line with the church.'

The editor returned the bail, and held up his bat again.

'That "one-leg" all right? Thanks.'

He was proceeding to look round the field when a gentle voice from behind him said: 'If you wouldn't mind moving a bit, sir, I could bowl.'

'Oh, is it over?' said the editor airily, trying to hide his confusion. 'I beg your pardon, I beg your pardon.'

Still he had certainly impressed the sister of their captain, and it was dreadful to think of the disillusionment that might follow at any moment. However, as it happened, he had yet another trick up his sleeve. Bolton hit a ball to cover, and the editor, in the words of the local paper, 'most sportingly sacrificed his wicket when he saw that his partner had not time to get back. It was a question, however, whether there was ever a run possible.'

Which shows that the reporter did not know of the existence of their captain's sister.

When I came in, the score was fifty-one for nine, and Henry was still in. I had only one ball to play, so I feel that I should describe it in full. I have four good scoring strokes—the cut, the drive, the hook and the glance. As the bowler ran up to the crease I decided to cut the ball to the ropes. Directly, however, it left his hand, I saw that it was a ball to hook, and accordingly I changed my attitude to the one usually adopted for that stroke. But the ball came up farther than I expected, so at the last moment I drove it hard past the bowler. That at least was the idea. Actually, it turned out to be a beautiful glance shot to the leg boundary. Seldom, if ever, has Beldam had such an opportunity for four action photographs on one plate.

Henry took a sixer next ball, and so we won. And the rest of the story of my team, is it not written in the journals of *The Sportsman* and *The Chartleigh Watchman*, and in the hearts of all who were privileged to compose it? But how the editor took two jokes I told him in the train, and put them in his paper (as his own), and how Carey challenged the engine-driver to an eighteen-hole solitaire match, and how . . . these things indeed shall never be divulged.

The Day's Play, 1910

*

The Dream of Glory

ALAN MILLER

Apart from his wife—whom he loved very dearly—Septimus Jones lived for two things; his work and cricket.

He was a parson, so his job in life wasn't an easy one. In fact, even in a small country parish where homely folk dwelt, it was difficult. But he slogged away at it; christening the babies, trying to make the children behave themselves, marrying the serious lovers, appeasing the quarrelsome, visiting the sick, and burying the dead.

It was wearying and often disappointing labour; but to it he brought the courage, the optimism, the friendliness, and the unselfishness of an old cricketer. And remember! Cricketers are the salt of the earth!

The Great Game—with all it used to be, still is, and ever should be—meant a tremendous lot to this plump little priest with the round red face, the bald head, the boyish smile, and the enormous hands with long fingers.

Ah, those hands! Forty years ago and more, what wizardry had they not performed with a cricket-ball! The break both ways, the flight in the air, the deceptive delivery, the ball that unexpectedly kept low, the top-spinner, the cleverly-disguised faster one, the immaculate length of them all, *and* his speciality, the 'popper': that innocent-looking slow ball which rose sharply—and from any kind of wicket—with off or leg break! He was very proud of it; though he couldn't have told you exactly how he did it.

You played forward quite correctly, the ball jumped up almost straight from the pitch, its break took it to the edge of your bat—and out you went, to a catch that a child could have held, at fine leg or in the slips! It was no good looking angrily for a spot on the wicket. Septimus didn't rely on that!

Yes, those huge hands with the long fingers had done wonderful things in the past. His style was in the best tradition. He attacked a batsman's skill; not his nerves or body. His bowling was as academically cultured as his batting and fielding were pathetic.

But nothing happened as a result of this exceptional ability. No distinction, no Blue, no County Cap came his way, because his parents, though gentlefolk, were poor. Some quite good club cricket—that was as far as he ever went; for there was much study to be done and many examinations to be passed before ordination. Then came a curacy in a slum-parish, and much harder work. Life grew very serious, and he loved his calling.

Before he was thirty, the strain of his endeavours found a weakness. A valve of his heart went wrong. The trouble had a long and ominous medical name. He was told to 'go slow'—to take things more easily. A grim injunction indeed at his age! Needless to say, it went unheeded.

Physical cricket ended; but *mental* cricket lived on, more strongly each year; till now, in 1948, the slum-work reluctantly given up a decade ago, and a cure of souls in the West Country his lot, he was very worried. Very worried indeed!

It was those Australians again! The beggars worked at cricket—we played at it! Well, it was our casual way, and he wouldn't change it. But things were serious! Here they were—young, well-fed, disciplined, medically passed for the tour, and trained up to concert-pitch. In his opinion, it was the strongest batting side ever sent over; and, though some of it wasn't of a vintage that appealed to *him*, the bowling was more than good enough to deal with the Old Country—now, alas, weaker than she had ever been!

It was very sad. It was tragic. Sometimes he couldn't sleep for thinking about it. What had we? *Honestly*, what had we? It was a distressing fact that we possessed no bowlers who were really up to Test standard—nobody like Richardson, Rhodes, Blythe, Tate, Farnes Barnes, Verity, and many others, now elderly men grimly watching the sorry state of things, or else young again and presumably disporting themselves in the Elysian Fields, where Septimus imagined the turf must always be in very fine condition.

A wicket-keeper? Well, of course, that was a different matter. England without a brilliant wicket-keeper would be too awful to contemplate! Yes, the cheery Evans was a worthy successor to the great ones—Ames, Strudwick & Co. *But*, even here there was a slight snag! Evans was perfect at his job; but Ames used to do more than keep wicket! He was good for a century against the finest bowling. Dash it, even now—

his keeping-days over—he was knocking up the runs as gaily as ever for his county. Ah, that Canterbury Festival!

But our batting! *Eheu fugaces!* In the whole of this still fair land, we had just four reliable Test batsmen worthy of the name—and they were hampered in their methods by the knowledge that there was no-one to back them up if their wickets fell unexpectedly. The dour and stolid Hutton and Washbrook—so typical of their counties—and the Middlesex Twins! Ah, those Twins! How they loved and lived the game for the game's sake! Why couldn't they be dour too—restraining their knightly daring—and resist touching or 'having a go' at the ball which, by all the rubrics of skill, never deserved to get a wicket?

Yes, things were in a bad way with a vengeance! Like all sportsmen worthy of the name, he could take a licking; but to be so weak that Australia's victories could give her little genuine satisfaction, was damnable! Yes, *damnable*—a strong word of course, but justified.

He had thought it all out very thoroughly; and it was getting on his nerves. His wife knew that; and so did his doctor. It was no good telling him not to worry. Not the slightest! Cricket was in his very being. He even preached about it, and had done for years.

'The Christian Life! What is it?' he would ask, almost fiercely, from the pulpit. Then—with a beaming smile of happy conviction—he would tell them that the Christian Life was courage, unselfishness, patience, love of one's fellows, a struggle against odds on a bad wicket, sometimes in poor light, against venomous bowling if the Devil was in the field, and against powerful and merciless batting if he was at the wicket. The Toss was the luck of one's birth—the type of bedroom you were born in. The Game was Life. The Close of Play was Death. The Reward? 'Ah, the Reward, my friends!' he would say—his little eyes moist and his lips trembling. '*That* passeth all understanding!'

Yes, when Septimus Jones brought cricket into a sermon—well, it got you!

Once in the dim past—1905, to be exact—there had been a game he would never forget. His club was enjoying a very good season; so good that, after a little influential wire-pulling, the MCC consented to send an extra strong side down. But more than this! Oh yes, *much* more! With them came one of the great ones—indeed, one of the greatest! He was at the prime of his career; one of the finest batsmen of all time. Let us call him Ulysses. Did he, Septimus wondered, remember the day when a certain young club-cricketer—very near his ordination—tied him up for an over and a half, and then, with the unexpected faster one, went clean through him; with the result that the bails flew joyfully heavenward and the welkin rang?

Yes, even now he probably remembered it; because that evening, after stumps were drawn, and the shadows of the elms were lengthening across the ground—surely the most serene shadows of all!—Ulysses had taken this young man to the nets and made him bowl at him for twenty minutes. Then he had slapped him on the back and advised him to take up the game seriously. Indeed, he had said more! What never-fading joy those words had given!

'Don't let it go to your head, my boy; but I'll tell you this. On your bowling *today*, I've never faced anything better!'

But alas, nothing came of it! That autumn he was ordained, and went to the slum-parish. The stipend was small—very small—*and* there was a very sweet and winsome young lady on his horizon. The years slipped by—matrimony, work, more and more work, less and less cricket—and then that heart-valve began to give trouble. Perhaps he was not the only potentially world-famous bowler denied the chance of proving his worth in big cricket. It is a sad fact that, unless you make the game your doubtful and modest livelihood, you must be comfortably off to play for your county.

And so we come to 1948. Septimus and his wife—childless, to their sorrow, both in their sixties, and tired after much good work—are in their country vicarage. He is very worried as a result of listening to almost every moment of the Test broadcasts; and she is anxious about the way in which the depressing news seems to be getting on his mind.

After the Fourth Test—when his dwindling hopes were dashed yet again—he became so restless that she persuaded him to take a sleeping-tablet with his nightcap. He had developed a dread of England being put out for the lowest total ever. The fear of this seemed to haunt him—so much so that she felt sure he was not well.

She asked the doctor to have a look at him. He was a benevolent old country GP, but not over-observant. He was far more expert at bringing people into the world than postponing their departure from it. As a result of his rapid, though very friendly, examination, he gave Mrs Jones the astounding information that Septimus wasn't as young as he used to be, and told her to keep on with the sleeping-tablets.

'Once this Test-Match business is over, he'll be better,' he assured her. 'The country's cricket-mad! As if there weren't far more important things to think about!'

But he wouldn't have dared say that to her husband!

On the Sunday before the last Test, Septimus was very tired. At evensong, the congregation noticed a blueness in his florid complexion, an unusual weariness in his voice, and an absence of the customary sparkle in his eyes. Over more than one supper-table in the village, anxiety was expressed about the health of the well-loved vicar.

In bed that night, he read a little, as usual. The 1948 Wisden had only arrived at the vicarage a few days previously; and, though fatigued and not feeling very well, he studied in intently and critically till he found difficulty in focusing his eyes on the print.

Then, after putting it back noiselessly—his wife was already asleep— among the other cricket-books at his bedside, he turned out the light.

What sort of night would he have, he wondered? There was a queer pain in his chest—there had been all day. Perhaps it was a touch of indigestion. He had been eating rather quickly lately: he always did when he was worried. Those tablets had been a help, though. Trust Jean to know what was good for him! What a grand little wife she had been all through the years! God had indeed blessed him.

After a few minutes, he thought he heard the telephone ringing. He listened carefully. Yes, it was!

Very quietly he got up, and in the dark—for fear that turning on the light again might wake her—he found the door, opened it carefully and went downstairs. The bell was ringing—as it sometimes does— in a way that suggested urgency. He picked up the receiver.

'Hello!' he said.

'Is that Duncombe 83?' asked the operator.

'Yes, it is.'

'Hold on, please. Long-distance call.'

Long distance! Curious at this time of night! Whoever could it be? Perhaps there was some mistake. The connection was soon made.

'Is that the Reverend Septimus Jones?' asked a man's voice.

'Yes. Who's speaking?'

'Splendid! We looked you up in *Crockford*. This is Robins.'

'*Who*?' asked Septimus mystified.

'Robins. R. W. V. Middlesex.'

'You don't mean the cricketer!' he exclaimed with boyish excitement.

'That's me. Do you remember Ulysses?'

'Do I not! But good gracious, that's over forty years ago!'

'I know it is. But he remembers you all right! Oh yes, he's never forgotten you and your bowling!'

'Well I'm blessed!' said Septimus; and his voice was trembling a little. This was wonderful! 'That's very kind of him—very kind indeed!'

'The old boy's like that. Besides, apparently you gave him something to remember! I'm speaking for him now. He wants you to come up tomorrow and stay with him for a fortnight. All homely—nothing formal. Can you manage it?'

'Tomorrow! For a fortnight! *Me*!'

'That's the idea. It's important too. You'll know why later. I've looked up the trains. Can you catch the Riviera at Plymouth?'

'Well, yes—I suppose I *could*.'

'Good man! We'll meet you at Paddington.'

'But you know, this is all very sudden and unexpected,' began Septimus.

'Of course it is! And all the better for that! You'll see! Bring your flannels and boots.'

'*Flannels*! At *my* age!'

'Yes, rather! You've still got them, haven't you?'

'Oh yes. I wear them in the garden sometimes. It reminds me of the old days!'

'That's the spirit! Ulysses does too—and he can give you a few years! But don't get too nostalgic about the *old* days!'

'You know, I can't quite understand all this,' said Septimus, bewildered.

'Of course you can't! You're not meant to—at least, not yet. Well, that's that! See you on the Riviera at Paddington tomorrow. *Tomorrow*— Monday, as ever is!'

'Well, yes, I suppose so.'

'Make it a cert! Ulysses is relying on you. We can't let *him* down, you know!'

'All right. Yes, I'll be there.'

'That's great! Till then! By-bye' And he rang off.

What a metamorphosis this phone-call brought about in Septimus! He felt—and even looked—younger; much younger. His worries departed, and so did the pain in his chest. His wife was astounded, as well she might be. Arrangements were quickly made. The flannels—now seemingly afflicted with jaundice—and the boots were packed; also the very faded blazer. A retired and aged colleague—who liked being a guinea-pig, and whose sermons, almost as well-worn as their author, were, to say the least of it, pedestrian—promised to hold the fort while Septimus was away.

He got off safely, enjoyed the journey immensely, and in due course arrived at Paddington, where Ulysses—white-haired now, but alert and handsome as ever—and Robins met him. He was whirled away in a large car.

Very soon he knew why he had been summoned. The Selection Committee were very worried about the Fifth Test. Among their troubles was the fact that Watkins, on whom they placed great hopes, had been compelled to cry off, owing to an injury involving his bowling-arm. They asked Ulysses whom they should choose in his place. He said that if they wanted a bowler who could get even this Australian team out and send the Oval crowd right off its head—as he felt quite sure they did—Septimus was the man, if still on his feet and traceable. As proof of this, he had told them of that day long ago.

They ventured to point out that by now Septimus must be well over sixty; but Ulysses retorted that if they picked him for England, the exhilaration of being chosen would certainly rejuvenate him. He also reminded them that a slow bowler doesn't tire himself out, but can go on for hours if necessary; especially if you let him field in a position which enables him to be more or less somnolent between overs.

And so—provided he shaped satisfactorily in a very secret try-out at the Lords nets on the morrow—he would be in the team; though, for their own personal safety, they were not going to announce the name of the player replacing Watkins till just before the match began. With no little justification, they dreaded the attitude of the Press if it knew that a man not so far off the allotted span, who had never played for a county, and who indeed had not played at all for over thirty years, had been selected to turn out in the last Test-Match!

As they talked things over that evening, Ulysses—comfortable with his whisky and cigar, and looking magnificent—seemed absolutely convinced of the wisdom of his advice and confident that a bombshell was going to be dropped into the cricket world. Later on, Robins and Septimus listened—almost like enthusiastic schoolboys—as he told them of incidents in great games of long ago, and of the prowess and idiosyncrasies of those whose names will live for ever where English is spoken and the magic sound of willow thwacking leather is heard.

The try-out at Lord's went off splendidly. Ulysses superintended it. Hobbs and Hammond, who had been let into the secret, turned out and Septimus bowled several overs to each of them. They were astounded —and inwardly rejoiced that he had been out of the game while they were making their records. Robins also tried to keep his wicket intact and to avoid putting up catches off the 'popper', but without success. Never had they seen the ball do such extraordinary things off a lifeless pitch which would have broken the average bowler's heart. They shuddered to think what this plump little parson could make it do on a 'sticky dog'! Beyond all doubt, the fellow was a wizard. They told him so!

The time passed very pleasantly and remarkably quickly. Ulysses sent for his own tailor, who measured Septimus and fixed him up with snow-white new flannels, the yellow ones being ruled out of the question for such a special occasion. Probably very wisely, he firmly refused to have fresh boots.

Each afternoon, these two old cricketers—the one nearly eighty and the other sixty-five—practised on a wicket set on the tennis-court. Septimus experimented and polished up his technique. Ulysses batted and was very proud of his protégé.

At Lord's on the Friday, Septimus met the rest of the English team, solemnly sworn to secrecy by Ulysses. At first they were inclined to be amused and thought the old 'un was having them on a piece of toast. However, when Hutton and the Twins had tried some of the newcomer's bowling, their amusement quickly changed to amazement— even to somewhat humiliating embarrassment! Hobbs and Hammond —who had had some—stood watching and chuckling.

Then came the great day—or rather the first day of the match. The really great day was not yet. It had been arranged that Septimus should field almost on the boundary at long fine leg, where, with luck, he would not have much to do between his overs. He was also assured that, whatever the score, England would declare at nine wickets, so as to save him from possibly getting laid out by a bumper. While the Old Country was at the wicket, he was to sit in the pavilion with Ulysses. Thus he would have privacy, since none but the great ones would venture to speak to him when he was in such august company. On the way out from the pavilion, and on the return to it, two big 'uns—the skipper and Bedser—were to be his escort, so that he would be spared the attentions of the inquisitive *and*—Ulysses correctly foretold—the madly enthusiastic. In short, everything was to be homely and comfortable for him.

But his introduction to the match was gradual. Yardley won the toss and decided to bat. Thus, for the whole of Saturday and some of Monday, Septimus spent his time in the company of Ulysses, watching the game with great interest. In fact, he had no need to change, since Hutton and Dewes managed to survive the initial onslaught and did pretty well. The Twins, though not at their best, since their style was

cramped by the fear of what those who followed them might get up—
or down—to, knocked up a slow 102 between them, and the innings
proceeded at somewhat funereal pace with no serious casualties.

He was introduced to Bradman & Co. At first, when they were told
that this elderly parson was in the team and that he was the mysterious 'S. Jones' on the score-card, they naturally thought it was a leg-
pull. But Ulysses—whose word even *they* dared not question—told
them that it was so far from a joke that their laughter might prove to
be one of their own extra special boomerangs!

Five minutes after lunch on the Monday—somewhat to the surprise
of the huge crowd—Yardley declared at the fall of the ninth wicket,
the total being 318.

After a firm handshake and a confident smile from Ulysses, Septimus—
closely behind his captain, and with Bedser at his side—went out with
the rest of the team. When the welcoming applause had subsided, he
heard the buzz that went round the ground as the spectators became
aware of his plump little figure and bald head. But he didn't mind—
not a bit! He *knew* somehow that he wasn't going to let Ulysses and
the Old Country down.

Very soon Morris and Barnes were at the wicket. They looked determined and formidable. He expected them to. After all, they were great
batsmen with wonderful records! He trotted down to his place in the
field. The buzz was louder here, since he was only a few yards from
the boundary. But he had worked for years in a London slum; he knew
these kindly Cockneys. *They* wouldn't make fun of him! And if he did
well, how they would take him to their hearts—as indeed they had
done, for other reasons, years ago. No, he could hear no jeering. One
wag shouted 'Good luck to you, Daddy!' But he liked that! He knew
it was meant sincerely. He was tempted to turn and smile his thanks;
but the game was about to begin.

Bedser bowled the first over—hefty, energetic stuff. It was a maiden;
and the batsman left three tempting outswingers alone.

Then came the great moment! He walked up to the wicket, and
Yardley, smiling, *handed* him the ball. 'Good luck, old man!' he said—
and, dash it, the great big chap seemed a bit upset!

He gave his sweater to the umpire—a contemporary! He grinned.
Did he sense what was coming? The buzzing in the crowd sank almost
to silence. Doubtless the 'know-alls' were wondering how a man of his
age could bowl fast—for there had been but one over with the new
ball. The side knew where to field for him: they had been carefully

instructed. Barnes, looking very aggressive, took his guard. He surveyed the scene and then prepared to face this new England bowler who, for some reason, had been exhumed from the past.

Septimus took but four or five short steps in his run-up. Over went his arm, and the wizardry of those long fingers began. His first ball— a very slow one—was on its way! Barnes watched it carefully: he was taking no chances. It was well pitched up to him on the line of the off stump. He played forward, but misjudged its length. It was a leg-break—a tremendous break too! When the ball was caught at second slip, the crowd went mad; but the bat had gone nowhere near it. Barnes looked at the pitch and prodded it with his bat. Yardley, at mid-off, smiled broadly. The next ball was of a different length and a shade faster. Barnes was in two minds about it, but decided to step back and play a push-shot. He was just in time. The ball kept very low. He managed to stop it with the bottom of his bat. It travelled about a foot. Evans popped round and, grinning, tossed it back to Septimus. By now the crowd was impressed. This old boy certainly knew something! But then they had a shock. Septimus sent down a simple full-toss which Barnes promptly hit for six. Yardley looked inquiringly at the bowler. He got a wink in reply. The next was also a full-toss, but of a different kind. *This* one wasn't ground-bait! Barnes went for it, but the ball did something curious in the air. It seemed to swing a lot, and it changed its expected trajectory towards the end of its flight. Barnes 'failed to connect'—failed by quite a great deal! It fell about eighteen inches from the wicket, broke in smartly, and the leg stump went back. The crowd yelled—loudly and long—and Barnes, not looking very pleased, departed.

Septimus had said that if he had any luck, he didn't want a fuss; so Yardley and the rest restrained their delight and appeared to consider the event quite in the natural order of things.

Then came the Don, appearing in his last Test-Match! His reception was of course deservedly terrific. Yardley greeted him personally and the team cheered. When calm was restored, the game proceeded.

Septimus earned yet more respect with his first ball to the Master. It was a weird one—a kind of Chinaman; in fact quite a mandarin! It beat the bat, but missed the stumps. The next also was not hit, but it brought about a loud appeal—*dis*allowed—from Evans and Compton for l.b.w. Thus ended the first over of Septimus. His analysis so far was 1 for 6—and the crowd let him have it! In fact, the ovation he received from that portion of it near him at long fine leg was embarrassing.

Then Bedser had his second over—a very expensive one. His length was erratic and Morris twice drove him firmly to the boundary and square-cut him for a couple.

Back came Septimus to renew his attack on the Don. The first two balls were ably smothered before they could get up to any devilry. *Then it happened*! The third—his first 'popper'—had him nicely taken in the slips. The crowd rose and yelled hysterically. 'S. Jones' had done it! As the Don walked away he turned, smiled generously, and playfully shook his fist at Septimus. But Septimus wasn't smiling! What *had* he done! Getting Bradman out for a duck in his last Test-Match—wasn't that a bit unkind? He asked Yardley about it; but the skipper slapped him on the back and shook with speechless laughter.

Hassett arrived and skilfully managed to play out the rest of the over. The cheers broke out again for a wicket-maiden—and what a wicket!

Again Morris dealt severely with Bedser—two more boundaries. Septimus returned to mystify Hassett with the first three balls and to flick the bails off prettily with the fourth.

Miller came in. There was a gleam in his eyes which meant slaughter if possible for Septimus. He knew very little about the first ball he received, but he cracked the next one to the boundary with a 'neck-or-nothing' drive.

Edrich now came on, hurling himself and the ball about with his customary vigour. It was an unsuccessful but eventful over. Morris took two fours and a single off it, and Septimus had his first essay at fielding; trying to stop a very fast one—almost a wide—which eluded Evans and went for four byes. In his endeavour to prevent this, Septimus overbalanced and sat down rather heavily. The crowd enjoyed this and cheered him loyally. The team nearly laughed their heads off.

Septimus—undamaged thanks to his adiposity, but with the seat of his new flannels bearing witness to his tumble—returned to attack the indomitable Morris. He gave him four 'poppers' in succession—each flighted differently and of slightly varying length and direction. The fourth had him neatly caught by Hutton at fine leg. Morris looked at the pitch before departing.

Then came Harvey. 'Ah!' thought Septimus. 'The baby of the side! No duck for this boy if *I* can help it!' He gave him a couple of guileless deliveries, purposely pitched a bit short. Harvey drove the first to the on boundary and square-cut the second for two. Septimus was pleased.

Then Edrich attacked Miller—and Miller returned the compliment!

A huge six, a smashing four, and a quickly-run single made the over costly. At its conclusion, Edrich put on his sweater.

So back came Septimus to tackle Miller. It was a duel the crowd watched in almost silent tension—a gem of an over! It began with a very deceptive full-toss, which did *not* go out of the ground! In fact, Miller was very nearly stumped. Then came the unexpected faster one, which resulted in a hard chance of caught and bowled, but Septimus only managed to divert it along the ground to Yardley. The third ball— a 'popper'—fell into Miller's pad. The fourth, intended by the batsman for an on-drive, went to the off boundary. The fifth missed the bails by about half-an-inch, and the sixth—a wicked off-break which kept very low—flattened the middle stump! So wild was the applause that the famous gasometers must have trembled!

Loxton came in, and Hollies replaced Edrich. By now, Septimus— his analysis 5 for 20—felt he was being selfish. For the rest of the innings, which closed at 104, he just kept the batsmen quiet and bowled maidens, while Hollies and Young—who had learnt a lot by watching him—got a couple apiece and Lindwall was run out. Young Harvey carried his bat for 15.

At the end of the innings, pandemonium broke out and the police were very busy restraining would-be invaders. When the last wicket fell, for safety Septimus trotted quickly to the middle of the field. Then, surrounded by the team and with the skipper and Bedser on either side of him, he began his embarrassing journey to the pavilion. Yardley— bellowing in his ear to make himself heard above the din—said 'Shall we risk the follow-on? Can you do it again?' In reply Septimus shouted 'Yes, I think so; but *please* give the others a chance first!'

Through the narrow lane of cheering spectators they went, and at last the pavilion steps were reached. At the top of them, waiting to greet him, stood his host—tall, erect, and immaculate in his beautifully-cut Glen-check—with his hand outstretched. For a second or two he said nothing. Beneath the smartly-trimmed white moustache the lips were trembling, and Septimus noticed that the steel-blue eyes were very moist. Then Ulysses coughed and said 'Come and have one!'

The second innings provided less thrills for the crowd. As Septimus had desired, Yardley kept him more or less in reserve, not calling on him till the score was 63 for 1—Barnes having gone early, l.b.w. to Bedser, and Morris and the Don obviously settling down.

At first, the crowd were restive because Septimus was remaining at long fine leg and long-field, which meant staying more or less in the same position; but at last they came to the conclusion that his age must be the reason, and that he was having a rest. They gave him a great ovation when he was put on to break the partnership; which he quickly did, getting Bradman again—and a handshake from him for it —clean bowled for 38, and, in the next over, Hassett l.b.w. for 2. Then he went off. At 110 for 4—Hollies having got Miller stumped for 12— Yardley brought him back to deal with Morris, who was proving obstinate as usual. This he achieved in his second over with another of his crafty full-tosses. Then he was again relieved by Young. By now, the crowd felt sure it knew what was going on. Yardley was scheming for an innings victory, but bearing in mind that Septimus was an elderly man who must be a little weary. He was not called on again.

At 6.15 the board showed 188 for 9. Septimus seemed to have infected the others with his skill. They were *bowling*—not merely achieving maidens and keeping the rate of scoring down! They were *attacking* in a 'You're for it, my lad!' spirit. It was good to watch. Finger-tips were at work, the ball was whipping off the pitch—and brains were being used! Hollies was magnificent, and Young's variation of length and flight a joy to behold.

There was but one wicket to fall—and *at last* an England victory was imminent. Loxton was still unbeaten with a sturdy 30 to his credit. Young tossed him a tantalizing one. He went for it with all he had— the game was lost anyway! He hit it very hard to leg—a terrific clout, but skied. Up and up it went; surely a grand six? Septimus watched it fascinated. Then suddenly he realized that it might not carry the distance. By Jove, it might be a catch! Je*hosh*aphat! He'd show 'em he could do more than bowl! He set off—at full speed—along the boundary, cheered frantically by the friendly crowd; madly cheered, as if he were a potential Derby-winner. But alas, it seemed that he would never get there in time! It looked like coming down about a yard from the fence. At roughly six feet from where he judged it must fall, he made a violent effort. He might *just* manage it! He dived forward at full length, his arms outstretched, his hands ready to grasp the ball—and fell flat on his face.

But as he fell, everything suddenly changed. No longer could he hear the wild encouraging yells of the Oval crowd. In fact, he could neither hear nor see anything at all.

Whatever had happened to him? He seemed to have plunged into utter darkness and silence as he lay there—physically and mentally inert.

Yet, in some mysterious way, he knew full well that there was noth-ing to worry about—nothing at all!

Then, after a little while, he heard something. Something beautiful; so *very* beautiful! It was music, soft and melodious. But what a melody! He loved music and knew a great deal about it; but he had never heard anything as wonderful as this. Where could it be coming from?

Soon it gradually rose—in a magnificent crescendo—from its entran-cing gentleness to something tremendous!

He would never have believed that there could be such a volume of pleasing sound. He felt the vibrations of it, but they didn't hurt—they invigorated! But what *was* it? Ah! *Now* he knew! Yes, of course! It was the majestic tumult of many trumpets!

In it were blended the joyous freedom of bird-song and the solemn grandeur of mighty organs. Its triumphant theme—how could he describe it? It was impossible; beyond his power of thought—far beyond it!

But why wasn't he frightened? He was all alone, sightless, not know-ing where he was, and conscious of nothing but this stupendous har-mony—but he wasn't frightened! Oh no! he was glad of it! he had never been so glad before! Uncomprehending, yet he seemed to under-stand. *Trumpets?* Surely the word reminded him of something—some-thing he had heard or read a long time ago? But what did it matter?

Soon the power of movement came back to him; and quickly too! He got to his feet—but with what agility! He felt young, virile, active, and eager. In happy bewilderment, he stood quite still, surrounded by the music.

Then gradually the darkness departed; and in the gathering light were the scents of summer and the breezes of spring.

He was standing on grass—the most emerald grass he had ever seen! It gleamed and scintillated. He moved his feet on it—it was like thick velvet!

Around him was a mist—a glistening mist, the colour of the wild-rose. Above him was a sky such as he would never have believed pos-sible. Its blue was that of the cornflower, and in it were many stars—some smaller than others, but all larger than any he had ever seen. They flashed, sparkled, and twinkled; seemingly according to their size.

Then the mist began to dissolve, and suddenly he was aware that, through it, figures were approaching him. They were hurrying, as if anxious to reach him quickly. When they were nearer, he could hear their rich laughter and see their hands waving in welcome. There were many of them, and they were all men; clad—as Septimus loved to be—

in flannels! Among these smiling faces there were some he had seen in the field, and others only in pictures. Yes, without doubt, *these were the giants of the Past*!

Now they had started running, as if very eager to get to him. Leading them came a big and almost lumbering One who, curiously enough, easily kept ahead of the others, in spite of his bulk! His great beard— now golden—was luminous; and in his eyes was the innocent merriment of a child.

He put out his strong right hand. Septimus grasped it gladly! The others crowded round—how marvellous it was to see these Immortals so near to him! Nearest of all—almost touching his shoulder—was an England and Yorkshire player; a bowler after his own heart. He had been a soldier too.

Then the big man spoke; and his voice was high-pitched for one of such size.

'Well played, young 'un!' he said. 'Well played!' And all the others waved their caps and shouted 'Well played!' too!

Young 'un! *Young* 'un! YOUNG!

What a glorious word!

When Mrs Jones woke up on the Monday morning, she suddenly realized that the room was unusually quiet. Septimus always breathed heavily in his sleep, and he sometimes snored; but she couldn't hear him now. She looked across at his bed and saw that it was empty, with the clothes half-flung aside.

Feeling a little anxious, she got up, put on her dressing-gown, and went towards the door. Just before she reached it, she nearly stumbled over his body. He was lying full-length on his face, with his arms stretched out. The hands were nearly touching, and their fingers were bent—just as if he had died in an attempt to grasp something!

Later on that mournful day, when she had recovered from the first shock of her husband's death, the doctor called again to see how she was.

Whatever he remembered—or did not remember—about medicine, he certainly knew how to talk to the bereaved; and very early in her widowhood, she found comfort in the old man's quietly-spoken and consoling words. They came from a kind heart that had known a similar sorrow. A quarter of a century ago, the Pale Herald had summoned a beautiful young wife, and nothing could be done to save her. Oh yes, he understood!

As he was leaving, she told him something she had been thinking all day.

'If only he could have lived a little longer!' she said wistfully. 'Just another fortnight! I know it worried him in a way; it's sad to think he missed the last Test-Match.'

'Never mind!' said the doctor, patting her gently on the shoulder. 'It'll all come right again someday, when the sun shines on both sides of the hedge. We know that, thank God! Goodbye. I'll be in again in the morning.'

And he went out into the Devon twilight, leaving her to her solitude and her memories.

'Missed the last Test-Match?' Set your heart at rest, dear lady! *He* didn't miss the last Test-Match!

He won it!

Close of Play, 1949

*

The Extra Inch

SIEGFRIED SASSOON

O Batsman, rise and go and stop the rot,
And go and stop the rot.
(It was indeed a rot,
Six down for twenty-three.)
The batsman thought how wretched was his lot,
And all alone went he.

The bowler bared his mighty, cunning arm,
His vengeance-wreaking arm,
His large yet wily arm,
With fearful powers endowed.
The batsman took his guard. (A deadly calm
Had fallen on the crowd.)

O is it a half-volley or long-hop,
A seventh-bounce long-hop,

A fast and fierce long-hop,
That the bowler letteth fly?
The ball was straight and bowled him neck and crop
He knew not how nor why.

Full sad and slow pavilionwards he walked.
The careless critics talked;
Some said that he was yorked;
A half-volley at a pinch.
The batsman murmured as he inward stalked,
'It was the extra inch.'

Cricket, 1903

*

Rise and Fall

BRUCE HAMILTON

Cecil's father had little sympathy with the aspirations of his son's friend. He was not sure that playing games for money was not a species of harlotry, and he had a lurking fear that Cecil might go the same way. But he was touched by the look of misery on the boy's face when he returned, and reported the failure of his mission. 'S'pose I'll have to go back to Burrington,' Teddy muttered, very near tears. 'Cousin Phil won't half laugh.'

'I fail to see the necessity for discouragement at present,' said Mr French in his pedantic way. 'I believe that this Mr Jordan is a person of no particular consequence. I understand that he is only acting in a temporary capacity.'

'What do you think I should do then, sir?' asked Teddy, not very hopefully.

'Assuming that practice has already commenced, I would recommend you to go to the cricket ground tomorrow, and endeavour to see Mr Meadows.'

'I say, Dad!' Cecil exclaimed. 'That's an idea!'

It was, of course, the obvious idea, and should have occurred to one or both of the boys before. Teddy's mind had been running on rails. He had, for years, fixed on the secretary as the proper channel for negotiations, and in his discomfiture at Mr Gilbert's absence had looked no further than his successor.

Of course, Arthur Meadows was the man! He had captained the County for only two years before Albert's death, but had already endeared himself to the crowd and players alike. Albert had always spoken of him with affectionate respect. He was a man able to exact loyalty and obedience without effort, and although he was not a great player, his enthusiasm for the game, in all its phases, was inexhaustible. Sometimes, in the old days, he would stroll across to where Somerset House was practising during the morning break, and take a boy's bat to demonstrate a stroke, or give a word of advice or praise without a hint of patronage.

Teddy was in a high state of nerves next morning. He had two main worries. First, if Mr Jordan was on the ground and saw him, would he turn him off? He could only keep his eyes open and hope for the best. Second, what should he wear? To come in full flannels would seem to take too much for granted. He decided on a compromise. He would wear a cricket shirt and a blazer, but the trousers of his dark grey suit, secured by a belt.

Knowing the habits of the players, he did not go down to the ground till eleven. The nets were up, and practice was in full swing. It was a cold, windy morning, with the sun coming and going behind low clouds. Teddy recognised most of the players, Arthur Meadows among them, but the only one to pay any attention to him was Shelly, now one of the leading batsmen of the side, who looked at him curiously once or twice. There were three or four younger fellows whom he did not know, mostly, he supposed, members of the ground staff taken on since he had left Midhampton. They hardly seemed older than himself, and he did not think their bowling looked so good as his own. Perhaps they were batsmen.

After standing behind the nets for a few minutes, Teddy went out on to the field, took off his blazer, and stationed himself where he could stop drives. There were three nets going, and he was kept fairly busy at his self-imposed task, which he shared with two other boys rather younger than himself. He fielded cleanly enough. Once he ran a dozen yards to take a very good catch from a hit by Lemon. Tanner was the bowler, and he called out, 'Well held, young 'un,' as Teddy self-consciously returned the ball.

At half past twelve Mr Meadows, who had just finished batting, came across the ground to go to the pavilion. His way took him within a few yards of Teddy, who was suddenly overcome by a sort of paralysis. He made half a movement towards the captain, but his tongue seemed to stick in his mouth. Mr Meadows caught his eye, smiled, and walked on; but he had not gone three paces before he stopped and turned back.

'Aren't you Baa-Lamb's boy?' he asked.

Teddy was still incapable of speech. He nodded.

'I thought your face was familiar.' Mr Meadows looked at him kindly. He had fair hair, very clear blue eyes, and a large curved nose, giving him the look of an agreeable, rather ridiculous bird.

'Still keen on cricket?' he asked. 'I remember seeing you when you were at your prep school. You had quite an idea about bowling.'

'I'm awfully keen, sir. I wondered if—'

Mr Meadows rubbed his nose—a characteristic gesture, suggesting he was conscious of its excessive size, which he thought to reduce by attrition.

'You'd like to have a try, I suppose. Well, why not? No time like the present.'

He led the way back to the nets, Teddy following almost incredulously. Mr Meadows spoke to Lemon, who was about to bowl.

'George, let this young man have your ball for a bit, will you? It's Baa-Lamb's son.'

Teddy wished he had not said that. It set a standard of expectation that was not fair to him. It was one thing to be an unknown youngster given a bowl, a youngster who might surprise listless onlookers. It was quite another to be measured by his father's standard. He was aware of eyes turned on him in an interest much too keen for his comfort. The ball felt large and heavy in his hand.

He bowled his first much too fast—sheer nervousness. It was a long hop. Shelly played a merciful stroke, pushing the ball gently into the on-side net. Lemon spoke as he walked back to take his run for the second, 'Take it easy. Work up to your natural pace.'

Teddy managed to grin, but the words had not reached his brain. He felt his control slipping. Another bad ball would have shattered him. Fortunately he bowled a good one, more by chance than design; a slowish yorker, looking as if it was going to pitch half-volley length, but coming right up. Shelly spotted it only just in time, nearly playing on as he came down hard at the last moment.

'Good one!' Arthur Meadows called out.

All at once Teddy's nerve came back. He was doing something he had done hundreds of times before. He had three familiar stumps to bowl at, and in his hand a ball, which he knew perfectly well what to do with. He had been practising for nearly a month; and there was nothing in it. He set himself to attack Shelly's off-stump with length balls of just above medium pace, turning in an inch or two, but varied by an occasional one which went with the arm. There was no occasion for any more mercy. Shelly was twice beaten without being bowled, and once put up an easy return to a well-disguised slower ball. Only rarely was he able to get his cover-drive to work on one that was a little over-pitched. There was nothing spectacular about Teddy's bowling; what was significant was its normality, that it looked hardly distinguishable in class and certainty from that of the professionals bowling with him.

When Shelly was replaced by Mr Pearson-Phillips, the star of last year's Grammar School eleven, Teddy had his reward. He found the edge of the bat several times, and finally lowered the leg stump with a ball that came back five or six inches. 'That'll do, old man,' said Mr Meadows presently. 'Quite enough for a start.'

Teddy put on his blazer. Evidently he was not to be given an innings to-day—perhaps it was just as well, for he knew his batting was nothing like so good as his bowling.

'You did very well,' said Mr Meadows, and then asked him a few questions about himself. 'I'd like you to keep on coming up in the mornings for a bit,' he said at the end. 'I take it you're free?'

'I'm free all right, sir.'

'Good. Make it ten-thirty to-morrow, then.'

Teddy could hardly wait for Cecil to come home that night. He met him outside Mercer's, earlier than in the old days, and broke the news. Together they examined the implications of Mr Meadows' invitation to keep on coming up in the mornings. They decided he wouldn't have said that unless he was seriously thinking of taking Teddy on. Obviously, he couldn't have offered an engagement straight away—it was absurd. There were other people to consult, and besides, as far as Mr Meadows knew, to-day's performance might have been a flash in the pan.

'But I think I bowled well,' said Teddy, with guarded optimism. 'And some of them were sending down awful piffle. Old Joe Tanner kept on bowling full tosses and half-volleys—I could have swiped them myself.'

Cecil was more cautious. 'Joe Tanner was always a rotten bowler. Besides, you've been practising; they've only just started.' But his caution was in the nature of an insurance premium paid to destiny. He did not believe in tempting providence. In his heart he was almost as exultant as his friend.

Actually, Teddy was kept in suspense just over a week. In that time he got on familiar terms with the players, who called him Ted, and were liberal with encouragement and advice. At this stage, indeed, he felt it would be hard to imagine a more delightful set of fellows. Most of them had known and loved the father, and they vied with each other in showing the son new tricks, until Joe Tanner, the senior professional, protested, 'Can't you let the boy alone? Filling his head with all that stuff. You'll make him too big for his boots.'

He continued to bowl well, until he became entirely untroubled by any question as to what impression he was making, concentrating on the problem with which each batsman confronted him. He learned something he had not realised before—that a batsman is an individual, not just a member of the opposing side. Thus a good length to little Plant might be a gift four to Lemon with his long reach; Willis could cut anything the least suspicion short on the off, but was weak in playing a well-pitched up ball on the leg stump, which Joe Tanner (who hardly ever cut) could turn as he liked; Arthur Meadows hated having to play back; and Pearson-Phillips would nearly always mistime a flighted ball.

His own batting disappointed him. He was able to play some nice-looking strokes off the medium-paced bowlers, though he seldom saw runs in them, but Lemon's speed was a little bit too much for him, and he never seemed able to position his feet right for Plant's leg-spinner. He was wise enough not to worry over-much, knowing that everything depended on his bowling.

Now and then he was conscious that people were watching him—old players and big-wigs of the club, like Colonel Thornborough, and Mr 'Batty' Drakes, famous amateur wicket-keeper of a dozen years ago. He sensed that he was being discussed, but the circumstance no longer bothered him—indeed it was rather a stimulus. Once Mr Jordan appeared, and actually came and spoke to him quite pleasantly; from the way he talked you would have thought Teddy was his own discovery.

On the Saturday week a trial match was played. Teddy was put on Mr Stokes' side, which batted first, and showing rather scratchy early-season form, were out for 129. Teddy's contribution, at Number Ten, was 5. Then Joe Tanner, after being dropped in the slips, got going. Mr Stokes and his bowlers toiled away, Teddy (third change) among them, but at the close Mr Meadows' side had made 237 for 6. Teddy's seven overs had yielded 26 runs without a success, although Buckley was dropped at the wicket off him; and he felt he had little cause for self-congratulation.

But as he was getting his things together, Mr Meadows came up to him and said:

'Well, Ted, the Committee have decided to take you on, if you want the job. Not much in it at the present, of course—twenty-five bob a week, and maybe some tips. Of course, in a year or two, if you get in the eleven, it'll be more. Are you game?'

Teddy could only say, 'Thanks, Mr Meadows, thanks ever so much.'

And so a hero was on his way. But the career of a cricketer is short. In not much more than a decade the body fails and, sadly, so does the applause . . .

He finished the season fairly well, with an average of 36, the highest in his career. But towards the end he found himself getting very tired, and almost anxious to get out as soon as he had made 50 or so. Long days in the field too—and there were many of these for Midhampton in these lean years—took their toll of him. The eternal up and down, in the slips, hour after hour, left him nearly prostrate when the reaction came at the end of the day's play. The end of the last match in August was a blessed release. He had never felt like that before.

Early in the New Year he had an attack of acute lumbago. He made a slow and painful recovery, and was not properly fit when practice started. He failed badly in the first two matches, played in bitterly cold weather. Presently, when the sun came out, he began to loosen up, and did better. But two or three good innings in June were followed by a bad patch, from which he seemed unable to recover. He was not seeing the ball so quickly, and frequently mistimed through hurrying his strokes. Luck went against him; if there was an accident, a run-out or a play-on—or if a particularly unplayable ball was bowled, or a superlative catch was made, he was the victim. His best score in July was 35, made with perversely effortless skill at a moment when runs were of no value whatever.

What was worse, his fielding began to deteriorate. His reactions were slower, his eye and muscles less responsive to the exacting demands made of slip fielders, and he began to put them on the ground once or twice too often. Late in July Le Mesurier moved him to mid-on—an ominous change. He had more time in his new position, and did well enough in getting to balls which went reasonably near him. But of course he was called on to do a certain amount of running, and he had lost his pace.

One day at Leyton he was sent three times in an over to chase forcing shots on the on side. On the last occasion, running towards the boundary, he heard a voice from the crowd—'Pick 'em up, daddy!' followed by a general guffaw. He concealed his mortification, but he was profoundly shocked.

Of course, he was no longer a young man. He had been saying that to himself for quite a few years now, but had never before felt it as being true. Yet he was not really old for a cricketer—not long past forty. He should be good for another half dozen years at least. If only he didn't get so tired. He recalled what Dr Littlehampton had told him, years ago, that he had not the sort of constitution he could afford to take liberties with. He would submit himself to a severe regime of training during the coming off-season—be careful what he ate, knock off those extra drinks he had been taking of late, in fact give up drink altogether. Careful living would give him reserves of strength to draw on.

One morning a week later, back in Midhampton, he came down to his breakfast in good spirits. He was feeling better than he had for some time, and the day before he had taken a really good 57 off the Lancashire bowlers. He read a laudatory account of his innings in the *Courier*, and then picked up a letter, which he had previously glanced at and taken for a bill. But the envelope was stamped with the name of the County Club, and his heart suddenly misgave him. He hastily opened the letter.

Dear Lamb,

At a meeting of the Committee held to-day, it was decided that certain players would not be re-engaged next season. I am sorry to say your name is on the list. I hasten to notify you, so that you will have plenty of time to make your arrangements.

The Committee desires me to convey to you their appreciation of your many years of splendid service, and to wish you all success and good luck in the future. May I also add my personal good wishes?

Sincerely yours,
EDWARD T. GAUL (*Secretary*)

He went early to the ground, and found the secretary in his office. He greeted Teddy a little self-consciously.

'You mustn't be upset, Ewe-Lamb,' he said. 'You've had a good run—been one of the great figures in the county. And you're not finished with the game—some way or another I don't mind betting you'll be in it for twenty or twenty-five years more. But time catches up with us all in the end.'

Teddy achieved a forced calm.

'Look here, Mr Gaul,' he said. 'I know there's no sentiment about the business side of county cricket. If you can't keep up you drop out. But I'm not really through. Remember I was ill last winter, and I never really recovered until just lately. I'm all right now; I did all right yesterday, didn't I? Can't you persuade them to give me another year?— then if they feel the same way I won't have any grouse. They won't regret it. I swear they won't.'

Mr Gaul shrugged his shoulders.

'There's nothing I can do,' he said. 'I'm only the mouth-piece. Of course, if you were to approach the members of the Committee personally you might do something. But it wouldn't be fair of me to give you too much hope.'

'But it's such short notice.'

'I don't know about that. In lots of counties a professional doesn't hear his agreement's not being renewed till half way through the winter. You've got over eight months to get fixed up for next season—and I haven't the slightest doubt you will.'

Teddy went the rounds of the Committee. He found a tendency in each individual to shift the responsibility on to other shoulders. He was given little encouragement to believe that the decision was likely to be reversed, but Gerald Stokes, who seemed more open to argument than the others, promised to raise the subject again if Teddy's form for the remainder of the season seemed to justify it.

His last interview was with Le Mesurier, whom he recognised as the main agent of his dismissal.

'I know we haven't always hit it off, skipper. I'm sure you don't bear me a grudge for old differences. I know you can get me another year to prove I'm not finished. I'd be grateful if you would—more grateful than I can say.'

Le Mesurier looked at him steadily.

'I'm sure you're not suggesting I'd let any personal considerations affect my judgment.'

Teddy stammered: 'No, skipper, of course not.'

'That's all right, then. We all have to think of the interests of the County. I'll be frank with you, Lamb. If it was only a question of your batting, we might carry you a few years longer. But the trouble is, you're dead weight in the field. We've got to get younger blood in the side.'

'It's only because I've been in poor health. I can get back my fielding. If I go in strict training.'

'You must pardon me for thinking you're over-optimistic.'

The painful truth was that Teddy was in far better health than at any time since the beginning of the year. In the next few matches things went his way—runs came fairly freely, the catches stuck in his hands. He reminded Gerald Stokes of his promise, and was told the matter would be brought up when the Committee met, on the second day of the last match of the season.

When the day's play was over he was told by Mr Gaul that the Committee had reviewed his case, but was unable to alter its decision.

At five o'clock on the following afternoon, Teddy came out to bat for the last time for Midhampton. The match was with Sussex—the county against which he had made his début. Thus was the cycle completed. Of the men who had played at Hove, in that match long ago, not one was left in the Sussex side—though Fender still played for Surrey, and Robert Relf for a minor county. Of the Midhampton side, Lumley and Teddy alone remained. Jim Revill was still getting hundreds for Middlesex, and Shelly had only dropped out the year before.

There was no hope of Midhampton winning the game, only of playing out time. The public announcement that Teddy would not be playing next summer had been made, and it was generally known that this was his last match. As he came out to bat—at Number Seven now—someone in the pavilion started a cheer—'Good old Ted'; and it was taken up and accompanied him all the way to the wicket, where Duleepsinhji came up and smiled and patted him on the back. 'Good old Ted'—it was a bitter-sweet moment. It had been young Ted, or Ewe-Lamb, not so long ago.

He faced the bowling, calmly resolved to take special care, to finish if he could with a gesture. Quite soon he realised that the Sussex bowlers were making not the slightest effort to get him out. They had been overtaken by that chivalrous camaraderie, amounting almost to sentimentality, which comes over all good cricketers at certain junctures. There was nothing much at stake in this last match of the season; and old Ted was to be given a run for his money. But at the other end there was no relaxation, and at twenty-past six the ninth wicket fell.

Even then Teddy could feel no hostility about the attack. It didn't really matter to Sussex about winning the match, what did matter was that he should get his fifty. And off the last ball of the day, an obliging long hop from James Parks, he got it, with a good clean hook to the pavilion rails. The exigencies of the little drama had been fulfilled—he had 'saved the match'.

'Well, that's the end of that,' he said, as he ran out of the applause and reached the dressing-room. The other players clustered round him, congratulating and making much of him; curiously moved, for it was a moment which must come to them all. Teddy took it quietly, smiling and chaffing back. It was good to have appearances to keep up; it helped him out. He wasn't going to shed tears all over the dressing-room.

From the moment when he first heard his fate it was clear to Teddy that there was only one course open to him. Being thrown on the labour market in early middle age with no qualifications whatever except his skill at and knowledge of cricket, he was restricted even with regard to the very limited number of occupations connected with the game. He could not hope for a contract with a northern League club since he had lost his bowling, and the same disability reduced the likelihood of his getting a permanent coaching job at a school to vanishing point. It had then to be umpiring, and he immediately sent in his application to be considered for next year's list.

He had nearly three months to wait before the meetings of the First and Second class captains who made the selections; and they were anxious months. He had a little over fifty pounds saved, just enough to carry him through the winter if he used the utmost care. But it was not pleasant to think about what was to happen afterwards, if he failed to get work. In anticipation of the worst he left his lodgings and went to board in a very poor quarter of the town, near the Railway Station.

It was now November—a bad time for finding employment. He did, however, manage to get a job at a public house in a poor quarter of the town—what in an earlier age would have been called a potman's job. The place was sordid, the wage was poor, and he had to sleep out. Also there were no tips, but the landlord took a generous view of his assistant's requirements in the matter of beer. In this environment Teddy coarsened rapidly. He felt the need of compensation, and his normal taciturnity became varied by bursts of boastful loquacity, and sometimes of quarrelsomeness. He became involved in one or two silly, rather unreal fights, and then one which, while perhaps silly, was by no means unreal. Through this, in which he lost a tooth and got a badly split lip, he became enmeshed in an affair with the barmaid. This was a maid hardly younger than himself, unclean and unattractive, but shrewish and fiercely possessive. The wear and tear wrought on his system by his passages with this harridan was the chief cause of his decision to leave Warfield in the spring.

His idea was to go on the tramp for a few weeks. His lumbago had been very bad during the winter, and he believed that plenty of exercise now the weather was warmer would put him on his feet again. He would sleep at the Unions, doing what work was required of him, and get what other work he could, or take what food might be offered him, from the people from whom he solicited work; then return to Midhampton and look for a regular job when he felt better.

It seemed a sensible plan. But he had, perhaps, over-estimated his stamina, and his luck was poor. On the second stage of his journey, walking from Cawston to Midhampton, where he intended spending no more time than was required for admission to the Union, he was overtaken by a heavy rain on top of the Common. There was no shelter among the gorse, and by the time he got into the town and reached the workhouse he was badly chilled. The next day he could not get up, and was transferred to the Infirmary. It was pneumonia, and he lay in bed for a month. When, at the end of six weeks, he was discharged he had not got much strength back.

He took a room in the street in which he had lived the winter after his retirement. It was a cheaper one than at that time though—a small top room with no furniture but a verminous bed and two chairs. On the landing outside was a gas ring and oven, uncertainly responsive to pennies. At this he was permitted to do his own cooking, when he could afford to buy anything to cook.

He had—and it was a small satisfaction—succeeded in achieving anonymity. Nobody at all at the workhouse had recognised him, and in his slum he was just 'Mr Lamb'—'old Mr Lamb' he was often called, when spoken of in the third person. This loss of identity he had, however, to abandon when after a week of unsuccessful attempts to find work, he went before the Public Assistance Committee.

His application for relief was turned down. He was unqualified for unemployment benefit, and he was not aged or disabled. The workhouse was indicated as a possible resource for him. But one of the members of the Committee remembered him, and a day or two later

Teddy was given a job—the delivery of newspapers, morning and evening, in one of the better sections of the town. The wage was a boy's wage—just sufficient to find him something to eat when his very small room rent had been paid. But it only took up about three hours of the day, as much as he felt fit for at the time. And his extreme poverty did have the beneficial effect of keeping him off drink.

The greater part of each day he spent in the newspaper and reference room of the Public Library. But one warm day late in June he found himself feeling better than he had for a long time. There was a home match at the County Ground, and he experienced a sudden nostalgia for the old place. More from a sense of shame than any other cause, he had deliberately cut himself off from everyone and everything to do with the ground. He had had his life there, with all of its setbacks a very successful one, and there above all he felt unwilling to exhibit his distress. But this morning it struck him forcibly that his attitude had been surly and over-sensitive. The county owed him a debt, when all was said; it could hardly let him sink to the extreme of poverty, and he had no reason to feel shame in accepting whatever might be offered him from that source.

It was, however, almost as much a sudden desire to see some cricket that sent him, after a brief internal debate, to the ground. He could not, of course, afford a shilling. The gate-keeper at the turnstile at the North entrance was unfamiliar to him. He nodded uncertainly and made to push his way in.

'Morning,' he said, 'You know me, I suppose.'

The gate-man looked at him and replied, with more candour than courtesy, 'No, my lad. I don't.'

'I'm Ted Lamb—Ewe-Lamb they used to call me here.'

'Is that so?' retorted the man. 'Pleased to meet you.'

It was not clear to Teddy whether the gate-keeper did not believe him, or simply had never heard of him.

'Aren't you going to let me in?' he asked.

'I'll let you in,' he answered. 'It's a bob, you know.'

'But, good lord!' Teddy expostulated. 'I tell you I'm Ted Lamb. Do you mean to say that after serving the county for twenty odd years I've got to pay to see a day's cricket?'

'Sorry, I've no instructions. You'd better get a note from the Secretary.'

'Well, let me go and see the Secretary.'

'I can't let you in without paying. You write a letter to the Secretary. If you get a note from him it will be all right.'

'Listen,' said Teddy. 'Have you ever heard of me?'

'I ain't been here long. I kind of remember the name, though. But how do I know you're who you say you are?'

Teddy lost his temper.

'You silly sod. How the bloody hell did you ever get the job?'

'None of that language—or I'll get a policeman to talk to you. You run along home.'

'Let me in!' shouted Teddy. 'You let me get the other side, or I'll show you some language.'

Very few people were coming in at this entrance, and the scene so far had not been a public one. But at this moment an elderly gentleman approached the gate.

'Come, Fraser, what's all this trouble about?' he demanded, not without self-importance.

Teddy turned and recognised him at once. 'Mr Gladman, you know me, don't you? Seems to me people in Midhampton have short memories. This man won't let me in, and as good as called me a liar when I told him who I was.'

The old gentleman scrutinised Teddy.

'Your face *is* familiar,' he said. 'But I can't quite place it—why, hang it, you're Ewe-Lamb!'

Teddy answered humbly. 'Yes, sir. I know I've altered quite a bit.'

'My dear fellow,' Mr Gladman exclaimed, warmly apologetic, and he took his arm. 'I'm shocked that this should have happened. Come along in.'

He turned to the gate-keeper. 'Lamb was one of our stalwarts for more years than I like to remember. You take a good look at him and let him in whenever he wants to come. Mr Gaul would not be very pleased to hear about this.'

Teddy followed the buffer into the ground, and accompanied him at a slow pace towards the pavilion. Mr Gladman's affable but by no means stupid glance rested on him more than once. Eventually he took him into the pavilion, and deposited him in the professionals' enclosure. 'You'll find some old friends here,' he announced at large. 'Boys, I expect most of you remember Ewe-Lamb.'

Teddy passed an uncomfortable hour. There were several new faces— had he ever been so beefy as these young men, he wondered—and of those remaining from his later days none had been particular cronies of his. Men like Heath, and Beal, and Farrar said a few words to him, but it was clear that his shabbiness and seediness was an affront to them. Lumley had retired—the last link with his early days. It was a relief when Levison, who had been playing a good innings, got out at last. He recognised Teddy with unaffected pleasure, and sat talking to him till lunch time, finally carrying him off to eat with the rest of the players.

In the late afternoon, when the Midhampton side was in the field, Mr Gaul came up to him.

'You're not looking too well, Lamb,' he said, after a few minutes small talk. 'I hope you're doing all right.'

'Not too well, sir,' Teddy replied. 'I'm finding it hard to make do. You see, I never had any other trade.'

Mr Gaul nodded. 'I know. You had a lot of bad luck when you were playing, too. Are you looking for a job?'

'I'd take anything I could get.'

'I was talking about you to Mr Gladman this morning. You see, Lamb, we recognise we owe you something. But the county simply can't *make* jobs. Everyone knows what our finances are like. It's only the generosity of a few people that enables us to carry on at all. And we can't bank on that for ever.'

'It'd be a bad day for Midhampton if the county had to close down, sir.'

'We're all hoping it won't come to that. But you see the difficulty— if we were flourishing we could offer you something decent. As it is, the only possible opening—I don't suppose you'd care about it.'

'What is it, sir?'

'Well; selling score cards. The usual thing, what you get depending on sales. It's a pretty wretched living but it is a living as long as the season lasts. And perhaps later, if we strike better times, or when any-one leaves, we could find you something better.'

Teddy swallowed his pride.

'I'd be very glad of it, sir. I do need the money.'

Into the sunshine, round the arena, the melting asphalt verge burning his feet—'Card! Last wicket down—Card! Last Wicket down—Card!' Back to the dark little printing office and the clatter of the ancient machine, belching out more pasteboard slips or adding an afterthought, at the fall of each wicket, to the unsold cards returned. Sometimes the bookstall would give him some 'Cricketers' to take round, or a sou-venir of the All India tour, or postcards—'Portrait of the Midhampton and All-Indian teams, twopence'. He was diffident at first, but quickly became inured, and raucous. A small hunched figure, without dignity. Very rarely he was recognised, and sometimes a kindly person told him not to worry about the change. Once he got half a crown that way. It was easy come, easy go, what there was of it. He still worked on his newspaper job, and, on match days, when he had earned enough to buy himself a decent supper, he spent the rest at one of the bars on the ground. He did not get paid till the end of the day, but he always knew how he stood, and the people at the bars found they could trust him. A good day was a day when he got tight. On August Bank Holiday he could hardly sell his cards quickly enough, but he managed to find time to slip in a drink every half hour or so. At five o'clock he was almost incapable, and the crowd laughed at him as he lurched around. 'Good old Ted,' someone said. 'Another little one won't do you any harm.'

Pro: An English Tragedy, 1946.

*

Millom

NORMAN NICHOLSON

The soft mouths of summer bite at the eyes,
Toothless as a rose and red as the ragged robin;
 Mouths on lip
 Rouse to sleep
And the green of the field reflected in the skies.

The elder-flower curls inward to a dream,
And memories swarm as a halo of midges;
 Children on the grass,
 Wicket-high, pass,
In blue sailor jackets and jerseys brown and cream.

Among the champion, legendary men
I see my childhood roll like a cricket-ball.
 To watch that boy
 Is now my joy—
That he could watch me not was *his* joy then.

Rockface, 1948

*

Old Man at a Cricket Match

NORMAN NICHOLSON

'It's mending worse,' he said,
    Turning west his head,
Strands of anxiety ravelled like old rope,
    Skitter of rain on the scorer's shed
        His only hope.

    Seven down for forty-five,
    Catches like stings from a hive,
And every man on the boundary appealing—
    An evening when it's bad to be alive,
        And the swifts squealing.

    Yet without boo or curse
    He waits leg-break or hearse,
Obedient in each to lease and letter—
    Life and the weather mending worse,
        Or worsening better.

Rockface, 1948

✻

By Char-à-banc to the Country

A. G. MACDONELL

'Don't forget Saturday morning Charing Cross Underground Station,'
ran the telegram which arrived at Royal Avenue during the week, 'at
ten fifteen sharp whatever you do don't be late Hodge.'

Saturday morning was bright and sunny, and at ten minutes past 10
Donald arrived at the Embankment entrance of Charing Cross Underground Station, carrying a small suitcase full of clothes suitable for out-
door sports and pastimes. He was glad that he had arrived too early,
for it would have been a dreadful thing for a stranger and a foreigner
to have kept such a distinguished man, and his presumably distinguished

colleagues, even for an instant from their national game. Laying his bag down on the pavement and putting one foot upon it carefully—for Donald had heard stories of the surpassing dexterity of metropolitan thieves—he waited eagerly for the hands of a neighbouring clock to mark the quarter-past. At twenty minutes to 11 an effeminate-looking young man, carrying a cricketing bag and wearing a pale-blue silk jumper up to his ears, sauntered up, remarked casually, 'You playing?' and, on receiving an answer in the affirmative, dumped his bag at Donald's feet and said, 'Keep an eye on that like a good fellow, I'm going to get a shave,' and sauntered off round the corner.

At five minutes to 11 there was a respectable muster, six of the team having assembled. But at five minutes past, a disintegrating element was introduced by the arrival of Mr Harcourt with the news, which he announced with the air of a shipwrecked mariner who has, after twenty-five years of vigilance, seen a sail, that in the neighbourhood of Charing Cross the pubs opened at 11. So that when Mr Hodge himself turned up at twenty-five minutes past 11, resplendent in flannels, a red-and-white football shirt with a lace-up collar, and a blazer of purple-and-yellow stripes, each stripe being at least two inches across, and surmounted by a purple-and-yellow cap that made him somehow reminiscent of one of the Michelin twins, if not both, he was justly indignant at the slackness of his team.

'They've no sense of time,' he told Donald repeatedly. 'We're late as it is. The match is due to begin at half-past 11, and it's fifty miles from here. I should have been here myself two hours ago but I had my Sunday article to do. It really is too bad.'

When the team, now numbering nine men, had been extricated from the tavern and had been marshalled on the pavement, counted, recounted, and the missing pair identified, it was pointed out by the casual youth who had returned, shining and pomaded from the barber, that the char-à-banc had not yet arrived.

Mr Hodge's indignation became positively alarming and he covered the twenty yards to the public telephone box almost as quickly as Mr Harcourt covered the forty yards back to the door of the pub. Donald remained on the pavement to guard the heap of suitcases, cricket-bags, and stray equipment—one player had arrived with a pair of flannels rolled in a tight ball under his arm and a left-hand batting glove, while another had contributed a cardboard box which he had bought at Hamley's on the way down, and which contained six composite cricket-balls, boys' size, and a pair of bails. It was just as well that Donald did remain on guard, partly because no one else seemed to care whether the luggage was stolen or not, partly because Mr Hodge emerged in a perfect frenzy a minute or two later from the telephone box to borrow two pennies to put in the slot, and partly because by the time the telephone call was at last in full swing and Mr Hodge's command over the byways of British invective was enjoying complete freedom of action, the char-à-banc rolled up beside the kerb.

At 12.30 it was decided not to wait for the missing pair, and the nine cricketers started off. At 2.30, after halts at Catford, the White Hart at Sevenoaks, the Angel at Tunbridge Wells, and three smaller inns at tiny villages, the char-à-banc drew up triumphantly beside the cricket ground of the Kentish village of Fordenden.

Donald was enchanted at his first sight of rural England. And rural England is the real England, unspoilt by factories and financiers and tourists and hustle. He sprang out of the char-à-banc, in which he had been tightly wedged between a very stout publisher who had laughed all the way down and had quivered at each laugh like the needle of a seismograph during one of Japan's larger earthquakes, and a youngish and extremely learned professor of ballistics, and gazed eagerly round. The sight was worth an eager gaze or two. It was a hot summer's afternoon. There was no wind, and the smoke from the red-roofed cottages curled slowly up into the golden haze. The clock on the flint tower of the church struck the half-hour, and the vibrations spread slowly across the shimmering hedgerows, spangled with white blossom of the convolvulus, and lost themselves tremulously among the orchards. Bees lazily drifted. White butterflies flapped their aimless way among the gardens. Delphiniums, larkspur, tiger-lilies, evening-primrose, monkshood, sweet-peas, swaggered brilliantly above the box hedges, the wooden palings, and the rickety gates. The cricket field itself was a mass of daisies and buttercups and dandelions, tall grasses and purple vetches and thistle-down, and great clumps of dark-red sorrel, except, of course, for the oblong patch in the centre—mown, rolled, watered —a smooth, shining emerald of grass, the Pride of Fordenden, the Wicket.

The entire scene was perfect to the last detail. It was as if Mr Cochran had, with his spectacular genius, brought Ye Olde Englyshe Village straight down by special train from the London Pavilion, complete with synthetic cobwebs (from the Wigan factory), hand-made socks for ye gaffers (called in the cabaret scenes and the North-West Mounted Police scenes, the Gentlemen of the Singing Ensemble), and aluminium Eezi-

Milk stools for the dairymaids (or Ladies of the Dancing Ensemble). For there stood the Vicar, beaming absent-mindedly at everyone. There was the forge, with the blacksmith, his hammer discarded, tightening his snake-buckled belt for the fray and loosening his braces to enable his terrific bowling-arm to swing freely in its socket. There on a long bench outside the Three Horseshoes sat a row of elderly men, facing a row of pint tankards, and wearing either long beards or clean-shaven chins and long whiskers. Near them, holding pint tankards in their hands, was another group of men, clustered together and talking with intense animation. Donald thought that one or two of them seemed familiar, but it was not until he turned back to the char-à-banc to ask if he could help with the luggage that he realized that they were Mr Hodge and his team already sampling the proprietor's wares. (A notice above the door of the inn stated that the proprietor's name was A. Bason and that he was licensed to sell wines, spirits, beers, and tobacco.)

All round the cricket field small parties of villagers were patiently waiting for the great match to begin—a match against gentlemen from London is an event in a village—and some of them looked as if they had been waiting for a good long time. But they were not impatient. Village folk are very seldom impatient. Those whose lives are occupied in combating the eccentricities of God regard as very small beer the eccentricities of Man.

Blue-and-green dragonflies played at hide-and-seek among the thistle-down and a pair of swans flew overhead. An ancient man leaned upon a scythe, his sharpening-stone sticking out of a pocket in his velveteen waistcoat. A magpie flapped lazily across the meadows. The parson shook hands with the squire. Doves cooed. The haze flickered. The world stood still.

At twenty minutes to 3, Mr Hodge had completed his rather tricky negotiations with the Fordenden captain, and had arranged that two substitutes should be lent by Fordenden in order that the visitors should field eleven men, and that nine men on each side should bat. But just as the two men on the Fordenden side, who had been detailed for the unpleasant duty of fielding for both sides and batting for neither, had gone off home in high dudgeon, a motor-car arrived containing not only Mr Hodge's two defaulters but a third gentleman in flannels as well, who swore stoutly that he had been invited by Mr Hodge to play and affirmed that he was jolly well going to play. Whoever stood down, it wasn't going to be him. Negotiations therefore had to be reopened, the pair of local Achilles had to be recalled, and at ten minutes to 3 the match began upon a twelve-a-side basis.

Mr Hodge, having won the toss by a system of his own founded upon the differential calculus and the Copernican theory, sent in his opening pair to bat. One was James Livingstone, a very sound club cricketer, and the other one was called, simply, Boone. Boone was a huge, awe-inspiring colossus of a man, weighing at least eighteen stone and wearing all the majestic trappings of a Cambridge Blue. Donald felt that it was hardly fair to loose such cracks upon a humble English village until he fortunately remembered that he, of all people, a foreigner, admitted by courtesy to the National Game, ought not to set himself up to be a judge of what is, and what is not, cricket.

The Fordenden team ranged themselves at the bidding of their captain, the Fordenden baker, in various spots of vantage amid the daisies, buttercups, dandelions, vetches, thistle-down, and clumps of dark-red sorrel; and the blacksmith having taken in, just for luck as it were, yet another reef in his snake-buckle belt, prepared to open the attack. It so happened that, at the end at which he was to bowl, the ground behind the wicket was level for a few yards and then sloped away rather abruptly, so that it was only during the last three or four intensive, galvanic yards of his run that the blacksmith, who took a long run, was visible to the batsman or indeed to anyone on the field of play except the man stationed in the deep field behind him. This man saw nothing of the game except the blacksmith walking back dourly and the blacksmith running up ferociously, and occasionally a ball driven smartly over the brow of the hill in his direction.

The sound club player having taken guard, having twiddled his bat round several times in a nonchalant manner, and having stared arrogantly at each fieldsman in turn, was somewhat surprised to find that, although the field was ready, no bowler was visible. His doubts, however, were resolved a second or two later, when the blacksmith came up, breasting the slope superbly like a mettlesome combination of Vulcan and Venus Anadyomene. The first ball which he delivered was a high full-pitch to leg, of appalling velocity. It must have lighted upon a bare patch among the long grass near long-leg, for it rocketed, first bounce, into the hedge and four byes were reluctantly signalled by the village umpire. The row of gaffers on the rustic bench shook their heads, agreed that it was many years since four byes had been signalled on that ground, and called for more pints of old-and-mild. The other members of Mr Hodge's team blanched visibly and called for more pints of bitter. The youngish professor of ballistics, who was in next, muttered something about muzzle velocities and started to do a sum on the back of an envelope.

The second ball went full-pitch into the wicket-keeper's stomach and there was a delay while the deputy wicket-keeper was invested with the pads and gloves of office. The third ball, making a noise like a partridge, would have hummed past Mr Livingstone's left ear had he not dexterously struck it out of the ground for six, and the fourth took his leg bail with a bullet-like full-pitch. Ten runs for one wicket, last man six. The professor got the fifth ball on the left ear and went back to the Three Horseshoes, while Mr Harcourt had the singular misfortune to hit his wicket before the sixth ball was even delivered. Ten runs for two wickets and one man retired hurt. A slow left-hand bowler was on at the other end, the local rate-collector, a man whose whole life was one of infinite patience and guile. Off his first ball the massive Cambridge Blue was easily stumped, having executed a movement that aroused the professional admiration of the Ancient who was leaning upon his scythe. Donald was puzzled that so famous a player should play so execrable a stroke until it transpired, later on, that a wrong impression had been created and that the portentous Boone had gained his Blue at Cambridge for rowing and not for cricket. Ten runs for three wickets and one man hurt.

The next player was a singular young man. He was small and quiet, and he wore perfectly creased white flannels, white silk socks, a pale-pink silk shirt, and a white cap. On the way down in the char-à-banc he had taken little part in the conversation and even less in the beer-drinking. There was a retiring modesty about him that made him conspicuous in that cricket eleven, and there was a gentleness, an almost finicky gentleness about his movements which hardly seemed virile and athletic. He looked as if a fast ball would knock the bat out of his hands. Donald asked someone what his name was, and was astonished to learn that he was the famous novelist, Robert Southcott himself.

Just as this celebrity, holding his bat as delicately as if it was a flute or a fan, was picking his way through the daisies and thistle-down towards the wicket, Mr Hodge rushed anxiously, tankard in hand, from the Three Horseshoes and bellowed in a most unpoetical voice: 'Play carefully, Bobby. Keep your end up. Runs don't matter.'

'Very well, Bill,' replied Mr Southcott sedately. Donald was interested by this little exchange. It was the Team Spirit at work—the captain instructing his man to play a type of game that was demanded by the state of the team's fortunes, and the individual loyally suppressing his instincts to play a different type of game.

Mr Southcott took guard modestly, glanced furtively round the field as if it was an impertinence to suggest that he would survive long enough to make a study of the fieldsmen's positions worth while, and hit the rate-collector's first ball over the Three Horseshoes into a hay-field. The ball was retrieved by a mob of screaming urchins, handed back to the rate-collector, who scratched his head and then bowled his fast yorker, which Mr Southcott hit into the saloon bar of the Shoes, giving Mr Harcourt such a fright that he required several pints before he fully recovered his nerve. The next ball was very slow and crafty, endowed as it was with every iota of fingerspin and brain-power which a long-service rate-collector could muster. In addition, it was delivered at the extreme end of the crease so as to secure a background of dark laurels instead of a dazzling white screen, and it swung a little in the air; a few moments later the urchins, by this time delirious with ecstasy, were fishing it out of the squire's trout stream with a bamboo pole and an old bucket.

The rate-collector was bewildered. He had never known such a travesty of the game. It was not cricket. It was slogging; it was wild, unscientific bashing; and furthermore, his reputation was in grave danger. The instalments would be harder than ever to collect, and Heaven knew they were hard enough to collect as it was, what with bad times and all. His three famous deliveries had been treated with contempt—the leg-break, the fast yorker, and the slow, swinging off-break out of the laurel bushes. What on earth was he to try now? Another six and he would be laughed out of the parish. Fortunately the village umpire came out of a trance of consternation to the rescue. Thirty-eight years of umpiring for the Fordenden Cricket Club had taught him a thing or two and he called 'Over' firmly and marched off to square-leg. The rate-collector was glad to give way to a Free Forester, who had been specially imported for this match. He was only a moderate bowler, but it was felt that it was worth while giving him a trial, if only for the sake of the scarf round his waist and his cap. At the other end the fast bowler pounded away grimly until an unfortunate accident occurred. Mr Southcott had been treating with apologetic contempt those of his deliveries which came within reach, and the blacksmith's temper had been rising for some time. An urchin had shouted, 'Take him orf!' and the other urchins, for whom Mr Southcott was by now a firmly established deity, had screamed with delight. The captain had held one or two ominous consultations with the wicket-keeper and other advisers, and the blacksmith knew that his dismissal was at hand unless he produced a supreme effort.

It was the last ball of the over. He halted at the wicket before going back for his run, glared at Mr Harcourt, who had been driven out to umpire by his colleagues—greatly to the regret of Mr Bason, the landlord of the Shoes—glared at Mr Southcott, took another reef in his belt, shook out another inch in his braces, spat on his hand, swung his arm three or four times in a meditative sort of way, grasped the ball tightly in his colossal palm, and then turned smartly about and marched off like a Pomeranian grenadier and vanished over the brow of the hill. Mr Southcott, during these proceedings, leant elegantly upon his bat and admired the view. At last, after a long stillness, the ground shook, the grasses waved violently, small birds arose with shrill clamours, a loud puffing sound alarmed the butterflies, and the blacksmith, looking more like Venus Anadyomene than ever, came thundering over the crest. The world held its breath. Among the spectators, conversation was suddenly hushed. Even the urchins, understanding somehow that they were assisting at a crisis in affairs, were silent for a moment as the mighty figure swept up to the crease. It was the charge of Von Bredow's Dragoons at Gravelotte over again.

But alas for human ambitions! Mr Harcourt, swaying slightly from leg to leg, had understood the menacing glare of the bowler, had marked the preparation for a titanic effort, and—for he was not a poet for nothing—knew exactly what was going on. And Mr Harcourt sober had a very pleasant sense of humour, but Mr Harcourt rather drunk was a perfect demon of impishness. Sober, he occasionally resisted a temptation to try to be funny. Rather drunk, never. As the giant whirlwind of vulcanic energy rushed past him to the crease, Mr Harcourt, quivering with excitement and internal laughter, and wobbling uncertainly upon his pins, took a deep breath and bellowed, 'No ball!'

It was too late for the unfortunate bowler to stop himself. The ball flew out of his hand like a bullet and hit third-slip, who was not looking, full pitch on the knee-cap. With a yell of agony third-slip began hopping about like a stork until he tripped over a tussock of grass and fell on his face in a bed of nettles, from which he sprang up again with another drum-splitting yell. The blacksmith himself was flung forward by his own irresistible momentum, startled out of his wits by Mr Harcourt's bellow in his ear, and thrown off his balance by his desperate effort to prevent himself from delivering the ball, and the result

was that his gigantic feet got mixed up among each other and he fell
heavily in the centre of the wicket, knocking up a cloud of dust and
dandelion-seed and twisting his ankle. Rooks by hundreds arose in
protest from the vicarage cedars. The urchins howled like intoxicated
banshees. The gaffers gaped. Mr Southcott gazed modestly at the ground.
Mr Harcourt gazed at the heavens. Mr Harcourt did not think the
world had ever been, or could ever be again, quite such a capital
place, even though he had laughed internally so much that he had got
hiccups.

Mr Hodge, emerging at that moment from the Three Horseshoes,
surveyed the scene and then the scoreboard with an imperial air. Then
he roared in the same rustic voice as before:

'You needn't play safe any more, Bob. Play your own game.'

'Thank you, Bill,' replied Mr Southcott as sedately as ever, and, on
the resumption of the game, he fell into a kind of cricketing trance,
defending his wicket skilfully from straight balls, ignoring crooked ones,
and scoring one more run in a quarter of an hour before he inadver-
tently allowed, for the first time during his innings, a ball to strike his
person.

'Out!' shrieked the venerable umpire before anyone had time to
appeal.

The score at this point was sixty-nine for six, last man fifty-two.

The only other incident in the innings was provided by an American
journalist, by name Shakespeare Pollock—an intensely active, alert, on-
the-spot young man. Mr Pollock had been roped in at the last moment
to make up the eleven, and Mr Hodge and Mr Harcourt had spent
quite a lot of time on the way down trying to teach him the funda-
mental principles of the game. Donald had listened attentively and had
been surprised that they made no reference to the Team Spirit. He
decided in the end that the reason must have been simply that everyone
knows all about it already, and that it is therefore taken for granted.

Mr Pollock stepped up to the wicket in the lively manner of his
native mustang, refused to take guard, on the ground that he wouldn't
know what to do with it when he had got it, and, striking the first ball
he received towards square leg, threw down his bat, and himself set
off at a great rate in the direction of coverpoint. There was a paralysed
silence. The rustics on the bench rubbed their eyes. On the field no
one moved. Mr Pollock stopped suddenly, looked round, and broke
into a genial laugh.

'Darn me—' he began, and then he pulled himself up and went on in refined English, 'Well, well! I thought I was playing baseball.' He smiled disarmingly round.

'Baseball is a kind of rounders, isn't it, sir?' said cover-point sympathetically.

Donald thought he had never seen an expression change so suddenly as Mr Pollock's did at this harmless, and true, statement. A look of concentrated, ferocious venom obliterated the disarming smile. Cover-point, simple soul, noticed nothing, however, and Mr Pollock walked back to the wicket in silence and was out next ball.

The next two batsmen, Major Hawker, the team's fast bowler, and Mr Hodge himself, did not score, and the innings closed at sixty-nine, Donald not-out nought. Opinion on the gaffers' bench, which corresponded in years and connoisseurship very closely with the Pavilion at Lord's, was sharply divided on the question whether sixty-nine was, or was not, a winning score.

After a suitable interval for refreshment, Mr Hodge led his men, except Mr Harcourt who was missing, out into the field and placed them at suitable positions in the hay.

The batsmen came in. The redoubtable Major Hawker, the fast bowler, thrust out his chin and prepared to bowl. In a quarter of an hour he had terrified seven batsmen, clean bowled six of them, and broken a stump. Eleven runs, six wickets, last man two.

After the fall of the sixth wicket there was a slight delay. The new batsman, the local rate-collector, had arrived at the crease and was ready. But nothing happened. Suddenly the large publisher, who was acting as wicket-keeper, called out, 'Hi! Where's Hawker?'

The words galvanized Mr Hodge into portentous activity.

'Quick!' he shouted. 'Hurry, run, for God's sake! Bob, George, Percy, to the Shoes!' and he set off at a sort of gallop towards the inn, followed at intervals by the rest of the side except the pretty youth in the blue jumper, who lay down; the wicket-keeper, who did not move; and Mr Shakespeare Pollock, who had shot off the mark and was well ahead of the field.

But they were all too late, even Mr Pollock. The gallant Major, admitted by Mr Bason through the back door, had already lowered a quart and a half of mild-and-bitter, and his subsequent bowling was perfectly innocuous, consisting, as it did, mainly of slow, gentle full-pitches to leg which the village baker and even, occasionally, the rate-collector hit hard and high into the long grass. The score mounted steadily.

Disaster followed disaster. Mr Pollock, presented with an easy chance of a run-out, instead of lobbing the ball back to the wicket-keeper, had another reversion to his college days and flung it with appalling velocity at the unfortunate rate-collector and hit him in the small of the back, shouting triumphantly as he did so, 'Rah, rah, rah!' Mr Livingstone, good club player, missed two easy catches off successive balls. Mr Hodge allowed another easy catch to fall at his feet without attempting to catch it, and explained afterwards that he had been all the time admiring a particularly fine specimen of oak in the squire's garden. He seemed to think that this was a complete justification of his failure to attempt, let alone bring off, the catch. A black spot happened to cross the eye of the ancient umpire just as the baker put all his feet and legs and pads in front of a perfectly straight ball, and, as he plaintively remarked over and over again, he had to give the batsman the benefit of the doubt, hadn't he? It wasn't as if it was his fault that a black spot had crossed his eye just at that moment. And the stout publisher seemed to be suffering from the delusion that the way to make a catch at the wicket was to raise both hands high in the air, utter a piercing yell, and trust to an immense pair of pads to secure the ball. Repeated experiments proved that he was wrong.

The baker lashed away vigorously and the rate-collector dabbed the ball hither and thither until the score—having once been eleven runs for six wickets—was marked up on the board at fifty runs for six wickets. Things were desperate. Twenty to win and five wickets—assuming that the blacksmith's ankle and third-slip's knee-cap would stand the strain—to fall. If the lines on Mr Hodge's face were deep, the lines on the faces of his team when he put himself on to bowl were like plasticine models of the Colorado Canyon. Mr Southcott, without any orders from his captain, discarded his silk sweater from the Rue de la Paix, and went away into the deep field, about a hundred and twenty yards from the wicket. His beautifully brushed head was hardly visible above the daisies. The professor of ballistics sighed deeply. Major Hawker grinned a colossal grin, right across his jolly red face, and edged off in the direction of the Shoes. Livingstone, loyal to his captain, crouched alertly. Mr Shakespeare Pollock rushed about enthusiastically. The remainder of the team drooped.

But the remainder of the team was wrong. For a wicket, a crucial wicket, was secured off Mr Hodge's very first ball. It happened like this. Mr Hodge was a poet, and therefore a theorist, and an idealist. If he was to win a victory at anything, he preferred to win by brains

and not by muscle. He would far sooner have his best leg-spinner miss
the wicket by an eighth of an inch than dismiss a batsman with a fast,
clumsy full-toss. Every ball that he bowled had brain behind it, if not
exactness of pitch. And it so happened that he had recently watched a
county cricket match between Lancashire, a county that he detested in
theory, and Worcestershire, a county that he adored in fact. On the
one side were factories and the late Mr Jimmy White; on the other,
English apples and Mr Stanley Baldwin. And at this particular match,
a Worcestershire bowler, by name Root, a deliciously agricultural name,
had outed the tough nuts of the County Palatine by placing all his
fieldsmen on the leg-side and bowling what are technically known as
'in-swingers'.

Mr Hodge, at heart an agrarian, for all his book-learning and his
cadences, was determined to do the same. The first part of the performance was easy. He placed all his men upon the leg-side. The second
part—the bowling of the 'in-swingers'—was more complicated, and
Mr Hodge's first ball was a slow long-hop on the off-side. The rate-
collector, metaphorically rubbing his eyes, felt that this was too good
to be true, and he struck the ball sharply into the untenanted off-side
and ambled down the wicket with as near an approach to gaiety as a
man can achieve who is cut off by the very nature of his profession
from the companionship and goodwill of his fellows. He had hardly
gone a yard or two when he was paralysed by a hideous yell from the
long grass into which the ball had vanished, and still more by the sight
of Mr Harcourt, who, aroused from a deep slumber amid a comfortable couch of grasses and daisies, sprang to his feet and, pulling himself together with miraculous rapidity after a lightning if somewhat
bleary glance round the field, seized the ball and unerringly threw down
the wicket. Fifty for seven, last man twenty-two. Twenty to win: four
wickets to fall.

Mr Hodge's next ball was his top-spinner, and it would have, or
might have, come very quickly off the ground had it ever hit the ground:
as it was, one of the short-legs caught it dexterously and threw it back
while the umpire signalled a wide. Mr Hodge then tried some more
of Mr Root's stuff and was promptly hit for two sixes and a single.
This brought the redoubtable baker to the batting end. Six runs to win
and four wickets to fall.

Mr Hodge's fifth ball was not a good one, due mainly to the fact
that it slipped out of his hand before he was ready, and it went up and
came down in a slow, lazy parabola, about seven feet wide of the

wicket on the leg-side. The baker had plenty of time to make up his mind. He could either leave it alone and let it count one run as a wide; or he could spring upon it like a panther and, with a terrific six, finish the match sensationally. He could play the part either of a Quintus Fabius Maximus Cunctator, or of a sort of Tarzan. The baker concealed beneath a modest and floury exterior a mounting ambition. Here was his chance to show the village. He chose the sort of Tarzan, sprang like a panther, whirled his bat cyclonically, and missed the ball by about a foot and a half. The wicket-keeping publisher had also had time in which to think and to move, and he also had covered the seven feet. True, his movements were less like the spring of a panther than the sideways waddle of an aldermanic penguin. But nevertheless he got there, and when the ball had passed the flashing blade of the baker, he launched a mighty kick at it—stooping to grab it was out of the question—and by an amazing fluke kicked it on to the wicket. Even the ancient umpire had to give the baker out, for the baker was still lying flat on his face outside the crease.

'I was bowling for that,' observed Mr Hodge modestly, strolling up the pitch.

'I had plenty of time to use my hands,' remarked the wicket-keeper to the world at large, 'but I preferred to kick it.'

Donald was impressed by the extraordinary subtlety of the game.

Six to win and three wickets to fall.

The next batsman was a schoolboy of about sixteen, an ingenuous youth with pink cheeks and a nervous smile, who quickly fell a victim to Mr Harcourt, now wideawake and beaming upon everyone. For Mr Harcourt, poet that he was, understood exactly what the poor, pink child was feeling, and he knew that if he played the ancient dodge and pretended to lose the ball in the long grass, it was a hundred to one that the lad would lose his head. The batsman at the other end played the fourth ball of Mr Livingstone's next over hard in the direction of Mr Harcourt. Mr Harcourt rushed towards the spot where it had vanished in the jungle. He groped wildly for it, shouting as he did so, 'Come and help. It's lost.' The pink child scuttered nimbly down the pitch. Six runs to win and two wickets to fall. Mr Harcourt smiled demoniacally.

The crisis was now desperate. The fieldsmen drew nearer and nearer to the batsmen, excepting the youth in the blue jumper. Livingstone balanced himself on his toes. Mr Shakespeare Pollock hopped about almost on top of the batsmen, and breathed excitedly and audibly. Even the imperturbable Mr Southcott discarded the piece of grass which he had been chewing so steadily. Mr Hodge took himself off and put on the Major, who had by now somewhat lived down the quart and a half.

The batsmen crouched down upon their bats and defended stubbornly. A snick through the slips brought a single. A ball which eluded the publisher's gigantic pads brought a bye. A desperate sweep at a straight half-volley sent the ball off the edge of the bat over third-man's head and in normal circumstances would have certainly scored one, and possibly two. But Mr Harcourt was on guard at third-man, and the batsmen, by nature cautious men, one being old and the sexton, the other the postman and therefore a Government official, were taking no risks. Then came another single off a miss-hit, and then an interminable period in which no wicket fell and no run was scored. It was broken at last disastrously, for the postman struck the ball sharply at Mr Pollock, and Mr Pollock picked it up and, in an ecstasy of zeal, flung it madly at the wicket. Two overthrows resulted.

The scores were level and there were two wickets to fall. Silence fell. The gaffers, victims simultaneously of excitement and senility, could hardly raise their pint pots—for it was past 6 o'clock, and the front door of the Three Horseshoes was now as wide open officially as the back door had been unofficially all afternoon.

The Major, his face redder than ever and his chin sticking out almost as far as the Napoleonic Mr Ogilvy's, bowled a fast half-volley on the leg-stump. The sexton, a man of iron muscle from much digging, hit it fair and square in the middle of the bat, and it flashed like a thunderbolt, waist-high, straight at the youth in the blue jumper. With a shrill scream the youth sprang backwards out of its way and fell over on his back. Immediately behind him, so close were the fieldsmen clustered, stood the mighty Boone. There was no chance of escape for him. Even if he had possessed the figure and the agility to perform backsomersaults, he would have lacked the time. He had been unsighted by the youth in the jumper. The thunderbolt struck him in the midriff like a red-hot cannon-ball upon a Spanish galleon, and with the sound of a drumstick upon an insufficiently stretched drum. With a fearful oath, Boone clapped his hands to his outraged stomach and found that the ball was in the way. He looked at it for a moment in astonishment and then threw it down angrily and started to massage the injured spot while the field rang with applause at the brilliance of the catch.

Donald walked up and shyly added his congratulations. Boone scowled at him.

'I didn't want to catch the bloody thing,' he said sourly, massaging away like mad.

'But it may save the side,' ventured Donald.

'Blast the bloody side,' said Boone.

Donald went back to his place.

The scores were level and there was one wicket to fall. The last man in was the blacksmith, leaning heavily upon the shoulder of the baker, who was going to run for him, and limping as if in great pain. He took guard and looked round savagely. He was clearly still in a great rage.

The first ball he received he lashed at wildly and hit straight up in the air to an enormous height. It went up and up, until it became difficult to focus it properly against the deep, cloudless blue of the sky, and it carried with it the hopes and fears of an English village. Up and up it went and then at the top it seemed to hang motionless in the air, poised like a hawk, fighting, as it were, a heroic but forlorn battle against the chief invention of Sir Isaac Newton, and then it began its slow descent.

In the meanwhile things were happening below, on the terrestrial sphere. Indeed, the situation was rapidly becoming what the French call *mouvementé*. In the first place, the blacksmith forgot his sprained ankle and set out at a capital rate for the other end, roaring in a great voice as he went, 'Come on, Joe!' The baker, who was running on behalf of the invalid, also set out, and he also roared 'Come on, Joe!' and side by side, like a pair of high-stepping hackneys, the pair cantered along. From the other end Joe set out on his mission, and he roared 'Come on Bill!' So all three came on. And everything would have been all right, so far as the running was concerned, had it not been for the fact that Joe, very naturally, ran with his head thrown back and his eyes goggling at the hawk-like cricket-ball. And this in itself would not have mattered if it had not been for the fact that the blacksmith and the baker, also very naturally, ran with their heads turned not only upwards but also backwards as well, so that they too gazed at the ball, with an alarming sort of squint and a truly terrific kink in their necks. Half-way down the pitch the three met with a magnificent clang, reminiscent of early, happy days in the tournament-ring at Ashby-de-la-Zouche, and the hopes of the village fell with the resounding fall of their three champions.

But what of the fielding side? Things were not so well with them. If there was doubt and confusion among the warriors of Fordenden, there was also uncertainty and disorganization among the ranks of the invaders. Their main trouble was the excessive concentration of their forces in the neighbourhood of the wicket. Napoleon laid it down that it was impossible to have too many men upon a battlefield, and he used to do everything in his power to call up every available man for a battle. Mr Hodge, after a swift glance at the ascending ball and a swift glance at the disposition of his troops, disagreed profoundly with the Emperor's dictum. He had too many men, far too many. And all except the youth in the blue silk jumper, and the mighty Boone, were moving towards strategical positions underneath the ball, and not one of them appeared to be aware that any of the others existed. Boone had not moved because he was more or less in the right place, but then Boone was not likely to bring off the catch, especially after the episode of the last ball. Major Hawker, shouting 'Mine, mine!' in a magnificently self-confident voice, was coming up from the bowler's end like a battle-cruiser. Mr Harcourt had obviously lost sight of the ball altogether, if indeed he had ever seen it, for he was running round and round Boone and giggling foolishly. Livingstone and Southcott, the two cracks, were approaching competently. Either of them would catch it easily. Mr Hodge had only to choose between them and, coming to a swift decision, he yelled above the din, 'Yours, Livingstone!' Southcott, disciplined cricketer, stopped dead. Then Mr Hodge made a fatal mistake. He remembered Livingstone's two missed sitters, and he reversed his decision and roared 'Yours Bobby!' Mr Southcott obediently started again, while Livingstone, who had not heard the second order, went straight on. Captain Hodge had restored the *status quo*.

In the meantime the professor of ballistics had made a lightning calculation of angles, velocities, density of the air, barometer-readings and temperatures, and had arrived at the conclusion that the critical point, the spot which ought to be marked in the photographs with an X, was one yard to the north-east of Boone, and he proceeded to take up station there, colliding on the way with Donald and knocking him over. A moment later Bobby Southcott came racing up and tripped over the recumbent Donald and was shot head first into the Abraham-like bosom of Boone. Boone stepped back a yard under the impact and came down with his spiked boot, surmounted by a good eighteen stone of flesh and blood, upon the professor's toe. Almost simultaneously, the portly wicket-keeper, whose movements were a positive triumph of the spirit over the body, bumped the professor from behind. The learned man was thus neatly sandwiched between Tweedledum and Tweedledee, and the sandwich was instantly converted into a ragout by Livingstone, who made up for his lack of extra weight—for he was always in perfect training—by his extra momentum. And all the time Mr Shakespeare Pollock hovered alertly upon the outskirts like a Rugby scrum-half, screaming American University cries in a piercingly high tenor voice.

At last the ball came down. To Mr Hodge it seemed a long time before the invention of Sir Isaac Newton finally triumphed. And it was a striking testimony to the mathematical and ballistical skill of the professor that the ball landed with a sharp report upon the top of his head. Thence it leapt up into the air a foot or so, cannoned on to Boone's head, and then trickled slowly down the colossal expanse of the wicket-keeper's back, bouncing slightly as it reached the massive lower portions. It was only a foot from the ground when Mr Shakespeare Pollock sprang into the vortex with a last ear-splitting howl of victory and grabbed it off the seat of the wicket-keeper's trousers. The match was a tie. And hardly anyone on the field knew it except Mr Hodge, the youth in the blue jumper, and Mr Pollock himself. For the two batsmen and the runner, undaunted to the last, had picked themselves up and were bent on completing the single that was to give Fordenden the crown of victory. Unfortunately, dazed with their falls, with excitement, and with the noise, they all three ran for the same wicket, simultaneously realized their error, and all three turned and ran for the other—the blacksmith, ankle and all, in the centre and leading by a yard, so that they looked like pictures of the Russian *troika*. But their effort was in vain, for Mr Pollock had grabbed the ball and the match was a tie.

And both teams spent the evening at the Three Horseshoes, and Mr Harcourt made a speech in Italian about the glories of England and afterwards fell asleep in a corner, and Donald got home to Royal Avenue at 1 o'clock in the morning, feeling that he had not learnt very much about the English from his experience of their national game.

England, Their England, 1933

❋

An Englishman's Crease

HUBERT PHILLIPS

I've been standin' 'ere at this wicket since yesterday, just
  arter tea;
My tally to date is eleven and the total's an 'undred an' three;
The crowd 'as been booin' an' bawlin'; it's booed and it's
  bawled itself 'oarse,
But barrackin', bawlin' an' booin' I takes as a matter of
  course.
'Oo am I to be put off my stroke, Mum, becos a few 'ooligans
  boos?
An Englishman's crease is 'is castle: I shall stay 'ere as long as
  I choose.

It's not when the wicket's plumb easy that a feller can give of
  'is best;
It's not 'ittin' out like a blacksmith that wins any sort of a
  Test.
The crowd, they knows nuthink about it; they wants us to
  swipe at the ball;
But the feller 'oo does what the crowd wants, I reckon 'e's
  no use at all.
'Oo am I to be put off my stroke, Mum, becos a few 'ooligans
  boos?
An Englishman's crease is 'is castle, I shall stay 'ere as long as
  I choose.

News Chronicle, 1951

*

Some Players Awaken

HUGH DE SELINCOURT

I

On Saturday morning, August 4, 1921, at a quarter past five, Horace Cairie woke up and heard the rustle of wind in the trees outside his bedroom window. Or was it a gentle, steady rain pattering on the leaves? Oh, no, it couldn't be! That would be too rotten. Red sky at night shepherd's delight. And the sky last night had been red as a great rose and redder, simply crimson. 'Now mind, if you over-excite yourself and don't get proper sleep, you won't be able to enjoy the match or anything!' his mother had said, and Horace knew that what she said was true. Still, what was a fellow to do? Turn over and go to sleep? If it rained, it rained, and there was an end of it: his getting up to see whether the pattery, rustly sound was the wind or rain would not alter the weather. For a chap of fifteen and a few months he feared that he was an awful kid.

He got out of bed deliberately as any man and walked to the window. He leaned out as far as he could lean and surveyed the morning sky with the solemnity of an expert.

Not a cloud was to be seen anywhere; only a breath of wind sufficient to rustle a few dried ivy leaves against the window-sill. A delicate haze spread over the country to the hills.

What a day it would be to watch a cricket match, and suppose Joe Furze couldn't turn out and he were asked to play! And suppose, when he went in to bat five runs were wanted and he got a full toss to leg and hit it plumb right for a four and then with a little luck . . . or supposing Tillingford had batted first and the others wanted six runs and he had a great high catch and held it or a real fast one and jumped out and it stuck in his fingers. Oh, goodness, what a clinking game cricket was! Splendid even to watch. And old Francis always let him mark off the tens and put the figures up on the scoring board.

Meanwhile it was still three good hours to breakfast, and if he curled up in bed and went to sleep the time would pass more quickly, and if he were wanted to play he would be in better form than if he mooched about the garden on an empty stomach.

What a morning! What a morning! What luck!

'Now then, darling, you'll be late for breakfast.'

Horace leaped out of bed at his mother's voice.

'Is old Francis here yet?'

'Been here an hour or more.'

'Has he brought any message?'

'Not that I know of.'

'Oh, curse! Of course I shan't be wanted to play.'

'A very good thing, too, dear. I don't like your playing with men.'

'Oh, rot, mum! What complete piffle! I'm not a kid.'

He kissed her first on one cheek then on the other.

'You will never understand about cricket, will you?'

He began to wash himself with more speed than care, and after a hurried wipe with a towel, climbed into shirt and shorts, slapped his head with two hair brushes while he trod into laceless sand shoes, stooped to tug each over the refractory heel, and fell downstairs, struggling into an ancient blazer.

'Half a sec.!' he shouted in at the open dining-room door and rushed out into the garden to find old Francis. He ran hard towards the potting shed, but seeing Francis sweeping the leaves up on the drive he stopped his swift run, and carefully adjusting his coat collar, strolled up towards him. Old Francis had watched him come tearing out of the house, watched him slow up, knew what he was mad to know: so he went on sweeping with the briefest possible edition of greeting, of which 'orn' was alone audible. After a little he said drily:

'Looks like rain, don't it?'

'Oh, I dunno! No, do you think so?'

'Ah! Uncommon like rain. Smell it everywhere.'

He leaned on his broom and sniffed the air up dubiously. Then he went on sweeping.

'I say!' said the boy. 'Would it be all right if you let me mark off the ones again, do you think? And shove up the numbers.'

'Shouldn't wonder. But there won't be no cricket; not this afternoon.'

'Why not? The rotters haven't scratched, have they?'

'Scratched, not that I knows on. Much sensibler if *we 'ad*, seeing the team as we've had to rake up. Be getting they old chaps from the Union before we're done. Ah! And some on 'em wouldn't be half bad, I lay; not too slippy on their feet.'

He referred thereby to a never-to-be-forgotten occasion (by others, it seemed, at any rate) when Horace in his eagerness to dash in and save one had fallen at full length and the batsman had secured two

runs: a blackish day for Horace and a blackish day for his flannels, for
the ground was not dry and he had chosen a bare patch on which to
lie extended. He let the reference pass with a blush and persisted:

'Why, you don't mean Dick Fanshawe isn't playing?'

'Oh, no, he's all right.'

'Or Teddie White or Sid Smith?'

Old Francis grudgingly asserted that they were certain to turn out.

'Tom Hunter, can't he play?'

'He's game, bless you! Tom not play!'

'Well, who isn't?'

'It ain't so much who isn't as who is!'

He continued sweeping with easy, rhythmical strokes, his dark eyes
watching Horace from under thick eyebrows. The rhythmical motion
of the broom fascinated the boy, who shifted his feet, thrust his hands
into his pockets, began to whistle, half-guessed, yet dared not ask the
blunt question which he ached to put.

'You might fetch that barrer down if you like.'

'Well, I said I'd only be half a sec.!'

'Don't then if you don't like.'

Horace ran off for the wheelbarrow, which he set down with a bang,
so that the boards for lifting the leaves fell off. 'That's it! Upset the
blummin' lot,' said old Francis, flicking stray leaves up on to the near
heap.

Slowly stooping with the boards he carefully raised a pile of mould
and twigs and leaves, which he deposited and pressed down into the
barrow; as he leaned on the boards he said slowly:

'As I was saying, it's who is!'

'What do you mean—who is?'

'Playing! They'll be raisin' a team from the infants next. And Raveley
arn't a blind school.'

'Oh, chuck it, Francis, tell us.'

'Tell us! Tell us what? And how about your half sec. or whatever it
was, and your porridge getting cold? Never knew such a chap. No, I'm
dashed if I did. Still there it is. Mr McLeod said to me last night: "Do
you think that young Cairie would play to-morrow?" "Play?" I said.
"But surely to goodness you don't want . . ."'

'I say, you don't mean it?' asked Horace, tremulous with excitement.

'Yes, I do,' said Francis, changing his manner. 'They were saying
how Joe Furze couldn't leave his wife with the moving, and who should
they get, and I said why not you; you're mad to play, and arn't too

bad in the field, and as likely to make a run or two as any of the rest, so there you are.'

'Oh! I say, you are an old ripper!'

'Bit of a show up, I expect, but never mind!'

'I say, you weren't serious about the rain?'

'Rain!' scoffed old Francis. 'Rain! Why, it couldn't rain, not if it tried ever so. Not to-day. It'll be a fair scorcher and no mistake!'

Horace stretched himself in sheer glee, then made a sudden dive at the ribs of old Francis, on which he landed a friendly punch. Francis raised the broom on high, threatening. 'Now then!' he growled.

The boy collared him round the waist, was undone, raised and used as a weight to press the leaves down in the barrow, tickled meanwhile to helpless laughter.

'I'll learn yer,' declared old Francis. 'And just you slip off to break-fast now, or there'll be trouble. That's right. Scatter them leaves everywhere.'

II

Six o'clock!

Automatically Mrs Smith slipped her feet out of bed and twisted up her long hair, sitting on the edge of the bed in which Sid Smith lay asleep by the side of a baby, also sleeping. She kept yawning.

She dressed without hurry or delay, watched by two little boys of three and four, at whom she made, from time to time, expressive ges-tures suggesting what would happen if they broke the silence. It was clear that another baby was well on the way.

Sid snored and stirred, moving against the baby, who opened his eyes. Mrs Smith looked at both with annoyance. Not that she was one to stand any nonsense from either.

Fastening her skirt she stepped across the room (a little smaller than young Horace Cairie's room) and leaning her face forward she said in a fierce whisper to the two little boys, who continued their impassive stare:

'You lay there, the two of you, mind.'

And she thrust an inquiring hand under the clothes.

'Tst! Filthy!' she muttered with a look of disgust. 'Wash! Wash! Wash! No end to it!'

In spite of her tousled, unkempt condition, it was still quite pos-sible to recognise the prim parlourmaid of six years before, celebrated for the way she kept her glass, for her fine needlework, and for her immaculate manner and appearance. There was still pride in the poise of her head.

She was no sooner out of the room than Jackie, the eldest boy, leaped out of bed, climbed over the baby, and snuggled up against the sleeping man, who opened his eyes and said gruffly:

'Hullo, matey!'—yawning. Then, ''Ere, this ain't Sunday.'

'I say, give us a penny, dad!'

The baby awoke, crying. Sid craned his neck round to inspect him. Then heaved himself round in bed to lift him up. He drew his hand back, scowling.

''Struth, all over the bed-clothes!' Jackie looked unhappy, conscious that he had hit on a wrong morning for a penny.

''Ere!' said his father, 'get out of it!'

Jackie, infant as he was, realised that it would be wiser not to climb across his father, but to make a slight detour by the bottom of the bed. In squeezing out between the end of the bed and the wall, however, he unfortunately dragged down his father's flannel trousers, which were hanging on the rail, a small rent having been stitched up in them on the Friday evening. Making his way on all fours, in a praiseworthy effort to conceal his existence, he, without knowing it, dragged the trousers after him across the room, and just by his own bed, being pleasantly inconspicuous, he sat up, and was seated with damp nightshirt on the trousers, which were not in consequence improved. His little brother, who had watched his progress across the floor, leaning over to see what Jackie was doing, fell out of bed and howled.

'Now then!' shouted Sid, 'you ain't hurt yerself.'

'Just you stop that noise!' came Mrs Smith's voice from the kitchen beneath.

'The little blighter's pitched hisself out of bed!' shouted Sid.

'Ain't hurt, is he?'

'No,' shouted Sid. 'A bit scared!'

'I'll scare him! Young monkey.'

Sid Smith was by no means a brute. But it was an understood thing that, except on Sunday mornings, he did no work of any kind in the house before going to his own work. Fortunately for him, he was able to bear without too much compunction the loud woes of children, unless his head was thick after an exceptionally good time.

Mrs Smith appeared carrying a tin bowl full of water, which she set on a soap box, a convenient washstand:

'Didn't I tell you not to budge from yer bed?' she said angrily to

Jackie, who, not managing to avoid the slap aimed at his ear, howled lustily. Her reaching out for the baby was the sign for Sid to rise, which he did with much yawning and stretching and scratching of his head.

'Stop that blinkin' row,' he announced to the room in general, as he picked a Woodbine out of its paper on the mantelpiece, lighted it, and put on his trousers, pants and socks under his long nightshirt.

'A nice mess,' he announced, blowing out a long puff of smoke, and watching his wife undo the baby's napkins.

'Faugh!' said his wife, pitching the dirty napkin on to the floor. 'Wash! Wash! Wash!'

The napkin fell on the trousers, which were now a little way under the small boys' bed. Sid put on his vest and shirt and buckled his belt, and went downstairs in his socks to put on his working boots in the scullery.

The baby was held seated in the bowl crying bravely while Mrs Smith dexterously wiped it over with a rubber sponge.

'When's this blasted kettle goin' to boil?' came a shout from the kitchen.

'How can I tell?' was the prompt retort.

'Choked up with these great lumps o' coal!'

'Why can't you have set the oil lamp to rights then?' she shouted back, adding softly to herself, 'Great booby! Can't set his hand to nothing!'

'Now then, you two!' she cried to the little boys, as she dried the baby with nimble fingers.

Jackie and his brother climbed out of bed and pulled off their night-shirts, coming very slowly nearer to their mother, who rolled the baby in a blanket and set it, without getting up, on the bed, seizing Jackie's arm on the return swing. Rapidly she topped and tailed each small boy with the same rubber sponge and dried them on a dish-clout. While she was putting on their shirts, Sid appeared in the doorway, whitening one of his cricket boots, the sight of which always infuriated his wife.

'I'll just put them trousers away,' he said, making towards the bed. 'Where in hell are them trousers?' he cried.

'How should I know where you put 'em? They were mended last night, that's all I know.'

'I laid 'em on the bed-rail, folded.' He was peering behind the bed, under the thrown-back bed-clothes.

'Blinkin' swarm o' kids,' he muttered. 'Home—I don't think. All right for a man, this is.'

'All right, my man. I've got ears in me head.'

'Ah! And look out you don't get a thick ear, my gal, afore you're much older.' He was groping angrily on the floor now—smoke in his eyes from the cigarette end between his lips.

'Blast it!' he cried. 'What's this? Look here.'

And rising slowly he lifted the forlorn, soiled trousers. Dismay extinguished anger on his face. It was only on the cricket field that Sid Smith, a bowler famed for many miles around, was able to feel a man's self-respect.

'I say, Liz, wash 'em through for me, old gal.'

'*H'm!* A likely thing on a Saturday morning too; and you being back for your dinner 'fore I've hardly swept out the bedroom. Cricket! Playing the fine gentleman in your white trousers and your white boots. Fat lot of games a woman gets, don't she?'

'Clean 'em up and run the iron over 'em, Liz,' he pleaded in dejection.

'And who was talkin' of thick ears a moment gone?'

'Go on! You know I don't mean half what I say.'

'Good thing for you you don't. Don't come messin' me about now just because you wants a thing done. Oh, yes, I'll see to 'em.'

'That's a mummy!' cried Sid, hoisting Jackie up, who, thinking the moment favourable, clung round his father's neck whispering hoarsely: 'Give us a penny, dad.' His mind was fixed on a certain brightly-coloured sweet he had seen in Straker's window.

'Not half a sharp kid, is he?' smiled Sid.

'Oh, go on, do, and have your breakfast. You're nothing but a pair of kids the two of you.'

'Want penny too,' began Jackie's small brother, and persisted in his request until both children were let out with a hunk of bread each and strict injunctions on no account to get into mischief or to come bothering back round mum, who was specially busy that morning.

Meanwhile Sid disposed of two large slices of bread and dripping at the corner of the kitchen table, and drank two mugs of tea, after which he set out on the three-mile walk to his work, cad to a bricklayer. He called back to his wife: 'If you're havin' a walk round after tea you might have a look in on the field. We're playin' Raveley, and we could walk home together.'

'Oh, well, I'll see how things go. I may and I mayn't.'

III

'It's eight o'clock, sir,' said the neat housemaid, as she set the morning tea-tray on the bed-table by the side of Edgar Trine.

'Oh, thanks, Kate, thanks,' said Trine, turning sleepily over.

Kate went noiselessly on the thick carpet, pulling back one heavy curtain after another.

She emptied the water from the basin, wiped it out with a special cloth, set a bright brass can full of boiling water in the shining basin, and wrapped the can in a clean face-towel to keep it warm.

'I say, pour me out a cup of tea, Kate,' came a nice voice from the bed.

'Sugar and milk. Yes, I do hate pouring out tea. I'd almost rather not drink it than pour it out for myself.'

Spoilt young devil! Kate should have thought, no doubt; but she didn't. She liked to pour out young Mr Edgar's tea. He was always the perfect gentleman.

'Thanks, most awfully. I say, do you mind? In that dinner-jacket pocket, my cigarette case. One left, I'll swear. Thanks. Oh, and matches. Yes; thanks most awfully.'

Kate folded up the dinner-jacket and trousers, to be taken downstairs for brushing; inspected his white shirt, which she considered clean enough to wear for dinner once more; rejected the collar, however, which she put silently into the basket.

'First-rate cup of tea, this, Kate.'

'I'm glad, sir.'

'Pour me out another, there's a dear, good girl.'

She did so.

'You're riding this morning, sir. Miss Emily asked me to remind you.'

'Confound it, so I am. Yes, and playing for the village this afternoon. A heavy day, Kate. What sort of weather is it?'

'Beautiful, sir,' answered Kate, laying out his breeches and underclothing.

'You might ask James to bring the two-seater round about a quarter past two, will you? And I say, do look and see if I've a decent pair of white trousers. Perhaps you wouldn't mind fetching them out of the drawer and letting me have a look.'

Kate brought five pairs and laid them on the bed.

'How all this muck accumulates, I don't know!' he grumbled. 'Not a decent pair among the lot. Such foul flannel, too, since the war. Pick out the best for me, and see my cricket boots are done, do you mind? And tell that young ass to wipe the white off the edge of the soles and the heels. I say, Kate, is Sid Smith playing to-day?'

'Yes, sir; I expect so.'

'Do you know, if he'd had coaching he'd be a class bowler.'

'He's always been a keen cricketer, sir.'

'Rather. He used to bowl at me, do you remember, when I was a nipper at school? Didn't he marry your sister, Kate?'

'Yes, sir.'

'Got a jolly little family, too, hasn't he?'

'Yes, sir.'

'Lucky beggar!'

Kate hated to cadge, and she could not bring out what was on the tip of her tongue to ask. Her sister had often told her she was a silly to keep herself back; but there! She couldn't ask for things, though it did seem a shame they should be lying where they weren't wanted, and young Mr Edgar would be only too pleased, if she did ask; he was always so kind and thoughtful.

'Who's the match against—Raveley?'

'Yes, sir, I believe so.' Her chance had gone.

'Best cricket going, village cricket,' said Edgar judicially. 'Real keenness. Oh, I'm all for village cricket. If I were down here more, I wouldn't mind running the show. Breakfast nine, I suppose? All right. Thanks.'

He lounged out of bed as Kate closed the door, into the bathroom, which opened out of his bedroom, and turned on the taps for a tepid bath, into which he poured verbena water.

At three minutes to nine, his toilet complete, he strolled down, fresh and clean, in his riding things to the dining-room, where a large breakfast was brought in at nine punctually. He topped up with three slices of the best ham, he told the mater, he had tasted for many a long day.

'We may be coming to see the match, dear, this afternoon,' his mother said as she left the dining-room. 'I am so delighted you're playing for the village. With all this discontent that's about nowadays, it is so good for them all. I am sure we ought all to mix with the people far more than we do.'

'Go on, Mater,' laughed her son. 'You're becoming a regular Bolshie, we all know that. I only play because I like playing for the village better than playing for the Martlets, say. It may not be such good cricket, but I swear it's a better game.'

IV

Mr John McLeod, Secretary and Treasurer of the Tillingfold Cricket Club, lifted his round bald head with extreme care not to waken the old lady who lay motionless by his side, and turned it slowly in her direction. Through the curtains filtered dim light, by which he saw that her eyes were closed; but as he began to screw his legs out of bed the eyes opened, twinkling.

He lay back laughing. 'Done again, by the Lord, done again! Oh, you, Maria!'

She laughed, too, a pleasant chuckle.

'Don't I know you're like a boy with his stocking on a Christmas morning any day of a cricket match? Just you lay still now, please.'

There they lay—round, stoutish, smiling, rubicund; two tumps, two ducks.

'Ah! I must give up cricket, Maria.'

'Nonsense, John. And you enjoying it so!'

'Ah, yes! Maria, before it gives up me. Give the young 'uns a chance, too. I'm slow between the wickets now, Maria.'

'Don't talk so silly, John, please.'

'Bless the woman, if she's not lighted the spirit-lamp and the kettle's on the boil, and me thinkin' I'd surprise her with a nice hot cup of tea as soon as her blessed eyes opened.'

'Got took in this time, didn't you, John?' said Maria, quietly wetting the tea in the pot.

'Not the first time either, by the Lord! Not the first time either!' he cried, enjoying the joke hugely. Maria was pulling up the blind. 'I knew it! A perfect day.' His thoughts ran on. 'And the trouble there is sometimes to get a team together. By the Lord, you'd think you was wantin' 'em to go to the dentist. It's that war's upset us all. And no wonder. Grumble, grumble, grouse, grouse! If it's not one thing, it's another. What a delicious cup of tea, Maria! Dee-licious! Ah! things won't never be the same again. Still, what's it matter? We have glorious, nice games, and if they must grouse, let 'em. Dee-licious cup o' tea, Maria. I'll have another!'

It was poured out for him.

'My goodness! If only Mr Gauvinier had a little tact! He's a good captain, a first-rate captain. He knows the game in his bones and nothing's too much trouble. But he's 'asty. He can't help himself, he's 'asty. "*Always try a catch, Mr Skinney!*" he sings out.' The memory tickled him. He repeated the the words with a singular relish: '"*Always try a catch, Mr Skinney!*" Well, Walter Skinney thought it wiser to take a step back. Don't blame him, the ball was travelling, and him nicely in the deep, a stinger, cruel; and Wally he swears it wasn't no catch, and won't be shouted at before everybody, not he, at his time of life, as though he were a bloomin' nipper who didn't know the difference between a long hop and a catch. And of course, catch or no catch, there wasn't no *use* in shoutin'. And there's plenty say he's conceited. Well, he may be. Anyhow, he knows his own mind, and the deuce of it is he's so often right. But out it always comes; plump and square. No tact, I say, no tact. Still, there it is. I like the beggar. Lord, Maria, I'd do anything for that feller!'

'The club wouldn't be much without you, John. That's all I know.'

'Oh, I help, yes, I help. Bless my soul! I've always had the luck, Maria. Here we are. Nice little house in a beautiful village. Comfortable; son doing well; daughter married. Just the job I love, arranging the matches, smoothing things down, name on card; oh, capital; gives you a little niche in the life of the place. And at the bottom they're as good-hearted a lot of chaps as you could find. All of them; or nearly all of them. And they haven't all of 'em had our luck, Maria.'

'You've deserved your luck, John,' said his wife earnestly.

At that he became very grave.

'You can't say that, Maria. You can't say that, my dear. There's a many I've met in life as have deserved far more than I have, and met nothing but trouble, trouble, trouble; one trouble after another. Terrible. And they've stuck it and carried on, when I'd 'ave been smashed up and broken, Maria; stuck it too and carried on without a one like you always there to help. Oh! there are good men in this world; good, brave men.'

'Yes, and some mean, bad ones, too, John.'

'Ah! well, that's true; and I sometimes wonder there ain't more. That's a fact, I do. But bless my soul, Maria, I wish they'd get together a bit more. We could make that ground the prettiest little ground in England. It's getting better, of course. But what can you do, when the football starts in September, playing over the square; when any turf needs a good dressing and a rest? It is fair heart-breaking!'

'Oo-ah! that's a nasty twinge. I'll have to get you to give me back a rub, Maria, my dear. This'll have to be my last season, I fear. Give the young 'uns a chance! Of course I'm all right at point—no running to do, and if a smartish one comes I can get to it pretty quick, and I don't say it's not as likely to stick in my hand as not: but a sudden stoop! That's where the bother of it is; a sudden stoop! Well, I can't, and I'm not as fast as I was between the wickets, Maria, though being a judge of a run and backing up properly I'm not so slow as some. But that sudden stoop, Maria. Ah, well, can't be done, and there's an end of it, can't—be—done! Just look at it! What a perfect day! Just look at it, now, I ask you.'

'Yes, but a nasty cold breeze comes creeping up so often; and I do hope you'll be sensible and wear your nice, warm undervest, John. It holds closer to the skin; and if you wear a nice bow tie on your cricket shirt, the collar'll not flap open and no one won't see as you're wearing a undervest.'

'I'm not vain, Maria, as you know, my dear. But I do hate to appear ridic'lous; and I heard one of the toffs say of someone else: "My God! Look, he's wearin' an underfug." That was the word he used. "Underfug." There's etiquette, you know, Maria, and there's a deal more than comfort to be thought of in clothes.'

'I never heard such nonsense, John. Toff or no toff, I think it a most vulgar expression.'

'One's very sensitive about these little things, Maria. I don't know why one should be. Always at the beginning, you know, when one walks on to the field first; you don't know how shy I always feel. I believe other fellows do, too, somehow; but one can't mention it. Of course it passes off as soon as the game begins. I don't believe wild horses, now, could drag me on to the field in one of them little blazer things, *you know*—it would seem so unsuitable.'

'Well, I never, John, and men talk of women being vain.'

'Ah, it's not quite vain. It's sensitive, Maria; sensitive to the eyes of others.'

Meanwhile, Mrs McLeod was dressed, and helping John into an old woolly jacket. She set a large board on his knee and a book; for John had been a sign-writer, and his hobby other than secretarial duties of the Tillingfold Cricket Club was the making of manuscript books. Many who were not interested in cricket would stop to admire the calligraphy of the club notices, the list of teams, and so forth, exhibited in the Post Office window.

'The height of luxury! Did anyone see the like of this, now?' John McLeod commented as these arrangements were being made. 'Waited on like a lord. Breakfast in bed! Well, I never. No man ever had such a wife!'

'Ah!' she laughed. 'I know you well enough by this time, my boy. If I didn't keep you safe in bed, you'd be running round all over the place wearin' yourself out, and by the time the day was done, what with you and your cricket, I should be having a sick man on my hands.'

She left him happily at work, the two pillows behind his back, the bolster on end, the board of his own making leaning on his doubled-up knees. He hummed while he worked—tunes of a melancholy grandeur, which was in odd contrast with his rubicund, cheery face; a blended tune which for the most part opened with 'Sun of my Soul, thou Saviour dear,' and somehow got lost in the heaving sorrow of 'the long, long way to go'. Perhaps the melancholy drone was useful in damping his good spirits down to the accurate precision required in the performance of his work. It was years since he had made a blot.

Breakfast was at length brought in. Coffee, toast (in rounds) two boiled eggs, some hot rashers of bacon: the board was removed, a large napkin tied round his neck, in case of any little accidents, dear, as she said, and he had nothing to do but tuck in, as he said.

'Oh, Maria, Maria! You spoil me, my dear. No wonder I've got a girth when you bring up such a breakfast, knowing well as I can never resist a good breakfast, never. But would you say now, as how, generally speaking, I did eat particular 'earty? Yet here I am, round as a barrel, and getting rounder, whereas old Silas Ragg, he's thin as a lath, and tough as wire, and he won't never see six-and-fifty again, and can bowl all afternoon easy as an old machine and never turn a hair. It 'ud kill me to bowl three overs.'

'You must have plenty of nourishing food in you, fat or no fat, when you're going to take all that exercise. Wringing wet with perspiration you gets: and your system must be kep' up somehow. But this little parcel come from the stores.'

She produced a large envelope stuffed with something soft, which John pinched thoughtfully: 'No, it can't be them!' he ruminated.

'Never knew Mr Boyle before his word. "This week ain't possible, Mr McLeod," he said, "not if I stretches a point ever so." By the Lord, it is them, though!' he cried, eagerly pulling out a dozen sky-blue cricket caps.

'Now, please,' said his wife, 'finish your breakfast while the coffee's hot.'

'Here we are, seven and three-quarters,' said John, after some fumbling among the caps, too engrossed to hear any plea for delay. 'Just hold that mirror up, my love,' he went on, fitting the cap on his bald head. 'How's that now? Something like, eh? How's it suit me? A bit more over the forehead, don't you think? So. They're cunning little chaps and no mistake; work out at three bob a-piece too with the monogram.'

'Fine!' said Mrs McLeod. 'I'm sure it's a mere boy you look in that little hat. But you must finish your breakfast now, or I shall get vexed with you.'

She had been trying her best not to laugh; the sight of her husband's gleeful old countenance under the little cricket cap as he sat up in bed proved too much for her, and she shook with laughter as she leaned forward to pat his face so that his feelings, always a little touchy on the score of appearance, might not be hurt.

John laughed, too, but not quite so whole-heartedly.

'You was always one to laugh,' he said. 'Bless you! But, Maria, my dear, I don't look ridic'lous now, do I?' he added, on such a note of anxiety that she forced control for a moment to answer:

'Ridic'lous—not you!'

But his earnest look promptly overcame her.

'Perhaps I had better keep to my old cloth cap,' he spoke regretfully. 'I'm used to it. And so are the others.'

She moved her hands in strenuous denial and shook her head from side to side. At length she managed to say:

'Oh, I'm not laughing *at* you, like: no indeed; I wouldn't do such a thing, but, oh! you are such an old dear.'

'Magnificent idea! These little caps, you know.' Mrs McLeod was carefully wiping her eyes with her pocket handkerchief, relapsing into good-humoured laughter from time to time. 'Ted Bannister's idea. Makes all the difference to the look of a team.'

'Oh, dear!' crooned Mrs McLeod. 'Will Mr Bannister be wearing one too, then?'

'Of course he will, my dear,' said John, becoming a little severe.

'What time will the match begin?'

'The usual time. Wickets pitched at 2.30,' he quoted the official list which hung in the Post Office window, as though to assert his dignity. But he could not withstand the infection of his wife's merriment as she faltered: 'Oh! I'll be there—with Mrs Bannister.'

So John began to chuckle:

'Ah! There won't half be some leg-pulling, I lay a sovereign. You should have heard 'em on at each other at the meeting. Old Teddie White, he swore as he'd never wear one. Obstinate devil, and I don't believe he will. Won't make himself a figure of fun. Old-fashioned, that's what they are. Sticks to their 'abits like their skins, and a sight closer some on 'em. Old Henry, he's always sore about the gentry havin' more chances and all that humbug. If we all wears 'em, Lord bless my soul, it'll fair put the wind up those Raveley chaps. We'll have 'em beat before the coin's tossed.'

'Oh, dear!' said Maria feebly, 'it'll be good as a play to see you all.'

'Yes,' said John meditatively. 'I think I'll just stroll round and give 'em out this morning like. More chance to get the chaps to wear 'em p'raps.'

'Oh, no, you don't!' said Maria, with an amazing access of resolution. 'Not you, my boy! You don't stir from that bed now, please, till eleven o'clock. They may want warning' (here laughter took her) 'to be prepared, but you really mustn't move, John, and get tiring yourself out.'

He was turning the cap on his fist, studying the cut and the monogram.

'Try it on once more, dear,' she begged.

He obeyed. She was enchanted.

'I mustn't forget to pull him well down over the forehead,' he said with great gravity.

'No,' she agreed. 'Not on any account.'

'You won't get laughing too much on the cricket field now, will you?' he said, rather shyly.

'Oh, no!' she answered very demurely. 'I hope I know by this time what's proper.'

She removed the breakfast things and left him with his board upon his knees. But no tune of even the most melancholy grandeur could keep his thoughts from wandering on towards all the incomprehensibly unnecessary unhappiness which he knew existed in the beautiful village: the crossness, the unkindness, the gossip. 'Ah, they've not all had your luck, my boy,' he said to himself to appease his anger. 'Suppose you had to shovel rubble all day like Sid Smith, where'd your temper be of an evening; or to do any work you couldn't fancy, with another chap bossing you all the time. Who's really happy now in this village? Oh dear! Oh dear! Oh dear! If it's not one thing, it's another!'

He leaned back gazing forlornly at his board, to which he suddenly gave a severe blow.

'Driftin' into the miserables,' he said to himself. 'Driftin' into the miserables! What use is there in that now—on a perfect morning, with a glorious game of cricket waiting for me this afternoon. By the Lord Harry! It's best not to think of some things.'

'Maria!' he called very loud. 'Maria!'

She was on the landing and opened the door almost immediately.

'Yes, John, what's the matter?'

'Ah, well, now you mustn't be cross, my dear; but I can't lie on here. Really I can't. What with the match and the caps coming and all, I'm too excited. I can't keep quiet and do me writing. My thoughts go rushing about all over the place to where they've no business at all, no business at all.'

'You're a wilful man, John,' she said, smiling. 'Most wilful. But you must promise me to wear your undervest, now, won't you?'

'All right, my dear,' he agreed a little ruefully. 'I promise, if it'll make your mind easier.'

'Oh, far easier, John, far easier,' she answered him.

The Cricket Match, 1924

*

Pride of the Village

EDMUND BLUNDEN

A new grave meets the hastiest passer's eye,
It's reared so high, it lacks not some white wreath;
Old ones are not so noticed; low they lie
And lower till the equal grass forgets
The bones beneath.

His now, a modest hillock it must be,
The wooden cross scarce tells such as pass by
The painted name; beneath the chestnut tree
Sleep centuries of such glories and regrets.
But I can tell you, boys who that way run
With bat and ball down to the calm smooth leas,
Your village story's somewhere bright with one
To whom all looked with an approving joy
In hours like these.
Cricket to us, like you, was more than play,
It was a worship in the summer sun,
And when Tom Fletcher in the month of May
Went to the field, the feet of many a boy
Scarce pressed the buttercups; then we stood there

Rapt, as he took the bat and lit day's close,
Gliding and glancing, guiding fine or square
The subtlest bowls, and smoothing, as wave-wise
Rough-hurled they rose,
With a sweet sureness; his especial ease
Did what huge sinews could not; to a hair
His grey eye measured, and from the far trees
Old watchers lobbed the ball with merry cries.

And when the whitened creases marked the match,
Though shaking hands and pipes gone out revealed
The hour's impress and burden, and the catch
Or stumps askew meant it was Tom's turn next,
He walked a field
Modest, and small, and seldom failed to raise
Our score and spirits, great delight to watch;
And where old souls broke chuckling forth in praise
Round the ale booth, Tom's cricket was the text.

Summers slipt out of sight; next summer—hush!
The winter came between, and Tom was ill,
And worse, and with the spring's sweet rosy flush,
His face was flushed with perilous rose; he stayed
Indoors, and still
We hoped; but elders said, 'Tom's going home.'
The brake took cricketers by inn and bush,
But Tom not there! What team could leave out Tom?
He took his last short walk, a trembling shade.
And 'short and sweet', he said, for his tombstone
Would be the word; but paint and wood decay,
And since he died the wind of war has blown
His old companions far beyond the green
Where many a day
He made his poems out of bat and ball.
Some few may yet be left who all alone
Can tell you, boys who run at cricket's call,
What a low hillock by your path may mean.

Poems 1914–1930, 1940

*

The Native Heath

EDMUND BLUNDEN

Beside that small round pond which is almost kept a secret by the massed spears of reeds rank upon rank, and beside the casual thistle-topped track which leads to an outpost farm in a kind of Netherlandish country of dikes and pollards and people working on stilts, nobody would expect to see a game of cricket played. Perhaps none ever is now. The house hard by with roofs like cliffs is in the possession of strangers, and the woods which once grew primroses enough for all the children for miles to gather and then no lack, scarcely know the flower. But in the thistly field by the pond I can remember more than one game of cricket—I speak of almost forty years ago—as an annual event which has remained in my mind much as though I had been present at some Elizabethan feast of sheep-shearers or haymakers. These old-fashioned games, which nothing of Elizabethan colour or music befriended, happened once a year, well before the general season of cricket began, and without any selection committees or posted notices. The word would go round among the boys that, however marvellous it sounded while spring was still doubtfully contesting 'unmatured green vallies cold', the match in the meadow by the pond would be played on the approaching holiday.

So on the day we went. 'Way up, Noble.' 'What cheer, Goog.' There was no question of choosing the players, or eleven a side. Those who came, played. They were of all sizes, little chaps and big; in all costumes, some in loose black leggings, some with trousers tied below the knee with coconut twine; and no particular sides were picked up. So long as someone was bowling, someone batting, the rest fielding out (with varying enthusiasm), and everybody umpiring, the match was always a success. It faded away without the strife of aggregates. The players were chiefly unfamiliar faces to me, for this field lay at the end of our sprawling parish, and the sportsmen came together from secluded cottages far down lanes bordering the orchards and shaws and hop-gardens thereabouts. What continued to keep me thinking was by no means the performance with bat and ball, a whiskery old ball, but the odd spontaneity of the whole assembly, once a year; and I observed that the young men, and one or two watch-chained elders, who then appeared as cricketers, did not for the most part make another appearance in this line of business when summer offered full chances. Indeed, even to my childish eye, they cut rather awkward figures in such appearances. What made them risk it, this once a year? What old tradition of crowded games and dances had dwindled into this pathetic little outing?

The thing might have stayed in my thoughts just as an isolated antiquarian trifle; yet, when time had carried me beyond that extreme boundary of my old home, making things once habitual claim the right of the peculiar and significant, I was more and more impressed by the depth of the cricket tradition in that part of England. It arose like a ghost out of the ground, haunting this or that stretch of short grass or pathway side, luring us to it without question or anything but willing hearts. On occasion (in the true ghost way) the spirit was absent, and though the fine evening would seem the most gloriously suitable for the game, nobody turned up. Probably garden or farm jobs prevailed. These intervals did no harm to the next occasions when once more plenty of us came along to the unmarked place of play, and kept up an eager contest till the livelong daylight had failed and there was only glimmer enough for jests and pranks. I could draw a map of the several cricket pitches which nature and custom got ready for us, between the immemorial ring of trees by the weir where the past had seen celebrated cricketers flourish, and the mill-pool two miles east, by the banks of which pleasant-voiced Mrs Bellamy used to bowl a brilliantly varnished bouncing ball with pictures on it at her young family and their friends. It would be a map of something more than a child's play, if there is much more in human life than that.

Digressions may multiply in these pages, and this point may be almost too early for one; but as I think of those games, coming and going like wild flowers, a short speech from one of my first companions is distinct in my hearing. It will be a clearer comment than anything of my own. The cottage gardeners' flower-show of every summer was regularly the occasion for a game among the boys of the National School, who pitched their brass-topped stumps excitedly in the corner of the flaring meadow—the roundabouts would do later in the day, *and* the coconuts. My father joined in, and accordingly the cricket gained dignity and, for an hour or so, was as monotonous to us as a Test Match. There he stood at the wicket on one afternoon never to be forgotten— a batsman of some calibre, a grown-up, a large batsman. Behind the other wicket Will Bellamy, who was a sturdy boy, with a mighty serious expression, clutching the ball in one hand and clenching the other, prepared to bowl at the giant. The first or second time he tried the ball sailed over an oak tree in the next meadow, aromatic with swathes of new-mown hay. Once or twice more the ball flew afar as the magician smote. But then, not quite losing hope, Will whirled his arm over again, the bat flashed and the wicket fell! I am not sure that the game was allowed to continue after this climax; but I recollect (when time had travelled on) walking past the empty field under the starry arch of a December night with Will, who, being about twelve years of age, crowned a solemn conversation with the following pronouncement: 'I think that was the Best Ball I ever Bowled *in my life.*'

The tradition of the game in our valley of the orchards maintaining its easy succession year upon year, suddenly grew clearer to me a long time afterwards on an evening when, sitting at a window overlooking the green and listening to the shouts of 'Throw in' caused by the slashing batsmanship of a black-haired girl there, I glanced into the newly bought volume of letters of an eighteenth-century poet. The popular author of *The Minstrel* (as I then discovered) stayed now and then in a mood of Arcadian fondness and the picturesque, in the village adjoining ours. He was a Scot, but was not unkind to our southern manners, and he did not disdain to record in his reports to the philosophers at home a cricket match of yearly consequence played, with lots of beer and cheerfulness, in a field opposite the village church. There amid the long grass matches were still being played until the first World War, and may yet be after the second, though Sports Clubs perhaps do not quite pass as direct heirs of the sons of the village, in sight of their friend and enemy the 'stubborn glebe', taking off their jackets as if to assail it once again—but this time for a diversion.

Long live diversion! Among all the charming things that I have had the luck to meet with in town and country, the unofficial, undeveloped game and play will not swiftly lose my love, even though I may not now or ever delve out my reason for loving it. Yet many others besides must feel a lightening of all that was a burden when all of a sudden the children, punctual as the swallow or the bluebell, and inquiring no more than those into the theory of their revivals, come out with the sport of the season. Wanton wits inform me that these seasons of games are directed by nothing more mysterious than business ingenuity; but I cannot see that at the present hour when the little boys are lashing far from new tops, and not less fascinated than in better times, when new tops were so numerous. Marbles, tops of various shape and various function—the window-breaker never was so bad as his name, the peg-top always looked more sinister to me—had-you-last, tipcat or nip-cat, rounders, skipping, hopscotch, high-cockalorum, wagon and horses, show-your-light, hide-ee-up, hoops, sheep and wolf and a host of other sports besides cricket with a rag ball, come kindly out of the past at childhood's call. When it is decided that the new one must come, the old goes away in a twinkling into the strange country where it sleeps. Some of these games, you may tell me, are under suspicion of having gone for ever,—

'Where's Troy, and where's the Maypole in the Strand?'

Modernity does not refrain from the toys of children: games in the end must die like parts of Homer and Shakespeare, or be modified as much as the cricket bat of to-day, spliced and complex-handled, is altered from the curved cudgel of the same name in the days of George the Third. Modification is a deity worth a canto of some new poet's imagining. When we reflect that, as a masterly philologer was remind-ing me lately, 'a newt' and 'an eft' are the same word, we may con-clude that the unusual appearance of a thing does not constitute a new thing. Because we did not lately see a game we knew, a toy we smiled at in the village street or in Mariners' Court, we need not at once turn to composing elegies for its being at last irrecoverably sent away from the world. The game may, like baseball, subject to this modification, rise afresh in a shape of rapid tremendous power, conquering con-tinents. Or it may steal in among its old company very much as it was, a *revenant* which frightens nobody and in action is as courteous and acceptable as the weather around its glittering eyes and clapping hands.

I sometimes hear it proposed that cricket, the ever changeful, change-less game which some even among the English view as the prime English eccentricity, is a something to which, for thorough appreciation, a man must have been bred from the cradle[1] or about there. If this is the truth, I qualify; for in our village and our county the game was so native, so constant, so beloved without fuss that it came to me as the air I breathed and the morning and evening. Time has altered me, though some who know me will not admit it in this connection; but there were many of us whose childhood was moulded in the same way. Some boys of course did not enjoy cricket, and we wondered at them, and thought them

[1] The old story is not so well known now as to be withheld: A member of a noted cricketing family was asked what he thought of the promise of a younger brother. He answered, 'Not much; but he's had no chance, poor fellow, he was too delicate to begin till he was SIX years old.'

unsocial. Some of the older people reproved the zealous as 'cricket-mad', but we heard that for all their growlings they were once players —indeed it came out that Mr J. who frowned and even cast impreca-tions on the noise of our playground game, was a collector of books on cricket. Others never took a seat on the boundary of the village ground, who all the same did not miss a football match. Still, it may be held that cricket lay much as Wordsworth's heaven about boys like me in our infancy, in act and word colouring our minds—and who was I to quarrel with the world into which I had come? There per-petually you had the cherry orchard, there the grammar school, there the dairy farm, the brewery, the wharf, the church, the cricket field— and I was convinced, if convincing was required, that God had been doing his best in all these arrangements.

Those were the days of clergymen cricketers. Our own vicar was the greatest example of these whom I ever saw. I have certainly encoun-tered others whose careers were longer—one, for example, who deliv-ered at me the most agitating underhand bowling at the age of seventy, and duly added me to his monotonous list of victims. But the impres-sion this ancient lobster made was in every way narrower. It astonished me to watch the vicar on Sundays in summer, when morning and evening for a few hours he became the priest and bore the sway and dignity, imparted the light and consolation of a sound divine. I secretly marvelled that this should be the same man who yesterday kept wicket and slaughtered the over-pitched ball with such absolute, single devo-tion. It was a similar though a lowlier Sabbath mystery in the case of some of the choirmen, who had divested themselves, it seemed, not only of their cricket boots and pads but also of their principal object in life—for that one day of the week. But I had my suspicions. In the vestry, during the crowded expectant moments before we marched forth singing our hymn, or 'Lead me, Lord' to our choir seats, I observed that the vicar with a rich smile would sometimes hold a whispered con-versation apart with one or two of his cricketers. It might have been, of course, enlightenment on a theological nicety, or a thought on church music, but I did get the impression that the Sunday paper had not been safely received at the Vicarage before the vicar left, and that some such inquiry as 'How many did Kent make altogether?' or 'Did the Australians put us in, then?' was made and answered. (News in those days did not come before its time.) Or it might be something nearer home: 'That fellow you ran out seemed pretty miserable about some-thing, Judd.'—'Yes, sir, he told the scorer that you had told him to go—"safe run there, my boy."' 'Well,—did I?' stroking a smooth chin as if in a deep consideration.[1]

The epitaph of the vicar now glimmers upon the nave of the church which he, so many years, served with ability, affection and religion. It is a just tribute to his worth as a parish priest, though no short inscription could intimate that handsome presence (yielding a touch of the Falstaffian peculiarly blended with the aristocratic) or renew the strong and stirring notes of that voice. 'When the wicked man turneth away from his wickedness. . . .' 'Let your light so shine before men' (how welcome he made the very offertory!)—monitions like these echo on for me still in his intonation, and even as a child I determined that, as *he* had drawn my attention to them, I ought to do something about them. He, if any one in the land, had authority. The tablet to his memory cannot re-create the light of his countenance, though it gives his dates; and in the opinion of some who knew him it lacks something else, which was not beyond its powers or its proper nature. The centuries will read it (if the bombs go on missing it, as a scattering of them did one startling summer night) never guessing that the subject was for many summers the pattern of cricket enthusiasm, the incumbent of the village ground. And in that era that was something.

Biographical information on any man's gravestone has been growing sparser lately than I could wish. I have a passion for it. I love to be allowed a little more to see of the men and women who once enjoyed life, or experienced it at least, than bare names and chronology allow. It may be nothing to them, as Thomas Hardy felt when he wrote the wonderful elegiac song, 'Friends Beyond', but it is something to us who can still consider 'the moral and the mystery of man'. Somewhere I read the last letter of a man who was about to be hanged for a murder, and as I remember it, it bore a postscript, 'No more cricket, George.' If that were added to any inscription which indicated the other part of the story, it might be a voice from the tomb which would not require the old preamble, 'Stop, passer-by'.

Our cordial parson, to come back to the upper side of the daisies, was well known in many a cricket field besides our own, and in higher company than our local matches attracted; sometimes, it may be, he put over an old sermon because the week's demands on him and his

---

[1] 'Id, quod fieri non debet, factum valet,' but I don't think the vicar had any legal training.

cricket bag had given no time for writing a new one. ('How did you like my sermon?' 'I like it better every time I hear it.') I only know of one cricketer who could combine the most able attention to a terrific match with the writing of something as remote from it as the works of Sir Thomas Browne. It was not our old friend. He put on his white sun-hat with a single purpose, a first great Cause. The vicar was a wicket-keeper of heavy build but a light and menacing rapidity in action. As has been hinted, he did not spare the foolish, and they say he played some tricks on his slower-thinking adversaries. I saw him once stump a batsman with such utter speed and indolence mixed as Ames of Kent in later days could show when Freeman lured the striker out of his ground—but the vicar's chance on the occasion I noted was the briefest imaginable. When his turn came to swing the bat he attacked the ball with a vengeance other than the Lord's, but possibly a theologian could explicate a relationship and justify the vicar's own Article. A slovenly bad ball, 'a godly and wholesome doctrine' of driving it and all such out of the earth.

As he grew old, and fell lame, the world underwent changes which he did not find easy—who did? There was a local change which must often have grieved him when he looked forth from the fine vicarage windows southward, into that lustrous light which is so often found over the valley there. The cricket ground, scene of so many of his deeds and quips and social interchanges, had been ploughed up during the first World War, and was no longer used except by fat sheep cleaning up kale. The velvety greensward, the music of the bat well used, the laugh at the unfortunate 'leather-hunter' on a hot chase, the bearded mower going to and from behind the horse in his leather shoes, the old men commending or disrelishing play from the bench by the oak, the call from the pavilion that sent the tins hustling up on the score-board, the players arriving with their radiant caps and blazers, or strolling out to the pitch with bare heads catching the sunlight, the deck chairs, the teacups, the gentle ladies who presided over them—none there any more. Just stripped, untidy stems of kale.

Yet the old man would have himself driven down to the new ground, though it was not the rendezvous for all the old schools and all the lions of polite cricket that the old one had been. Sitting forward in the pavilion (*that* structure at least had survived and had made itself at home in a new situation) he scanned the match with a quiet eye, and he seemed to approve of what he saw. At last he fell talking very gently (we had heard him in other voice) of things long past, and he did not lack a hearer or two who could travel back over that road with him, a little surprised to find it so. He talked, as old people are said to do so much, of small matters that had chanced long before and might have been supposed to have left no mark as they flitted by; but we see that it is the great ones which may pass more utterly. His memories arose in multitude as he sat composedly there, cricket coincidence, humours, personal touches among them but not only those; for he had discerned that the game itself, if it is found in its natural bearings, is only the agreeable wicket-gate to a landscape of human joys and sorrows, and is greatest where it fades away most imperceptibly into their wider horizon. Glance from your post in the long field, young cricketer (the next batsman is taking his full two minutes to come in) away to those farms and woods, spires and hills about you; rest your high spirits a moment on the composure of that young mother with her sleeping baby, on the old white horse as still as if he was carved in chalk on the down. One day you will seek in your mind for the scores of the match which are now so important and definite, and they will not be there—only, in place of them, the assurance of an eternal summer, a grace that homes within the minds and hearts of your kindred, and around all their works and days.

We knew more than one young cricketer for whom the favourite game darkened into a premature sunless season. No one was ever spoken of more kindly by everybody, nor perhaps with higher or oftener repeated hopes, so far as a village view extends. Freddie, or Froggie, was a born athlete, and upon a scene where most plodded on with mere rustic sturdiness he arrived with the economy and roguery of the artist. He was a little fellow, and a shapely one, like the poet Keats; and he had a face eloquent of strength and intention like the poet Keats, as I may say now that I have become familiar with that occasional cricketer's portraits. A good style of speech and selection of knowledge distinguished him, he could play a bugle and he could sing, he did all with a charming attentiveness to the instructor; but his country fame was drawn from football and even more from cricket. When it was my honour, and immense it was that day, to play in a match for the first time, I was sent creeping in to bat at the end of an innings, and the other batsman was Fred, who had been in possession of the wicket for an hour or more. His score was sixty so far, and he had been breaking all the rules of academic batsmanship to everybody's satisfaction. By the kindness of all concerned I was not prevented from holding up one end until, with ever increasing glorious freedom, he had achieved what was then almost a mythical feat—his hundred runs.

To me, on whom reflected glory beamed for a minute, when that day was becoming distant, the hero still appeared almost literally 'apparelled in celestial light'. He went on his way, in the cricket of the region, on our own ground or on others (the torment of missing him!) and all the way his brilliance grew. Clubs flourishing in places miles off tempted him to play for them, and not just for the runs he brought them. I still remember a discussion among my elders of some enchanting innings by him which brought quite a modest total in runs.

One day I saw him at the church steps, with a flushed face, a bright colouring of which I was not old enough to understand the omen until someone told me. He was going to die. Still I hoped, and the next time I saw him, languid in a wheeled chair, I asked him when he would have another last-wicket partnership with me. He could smile at that; but his cricket had already gone dim while, as I heard in scraps of talk, he religiously contemplated the world to which he was going. 'Going home', the farm labourers called it. How quietly he was going! In the vast and bewildering music of the world I have known, to this hour his song is clear, now so quick and lyrical, and then so slow and petitioning. Perhaps it amounts to that ancient one after all, 'Whom the Gods love, die young.'

The village is not small, in extent or population, and in the old vicar's reign it had a first and a second cricket team; so far as I could judge such matters these were divided quite firmly by the barrier of class. It was only now and then that one of the villagers proper, such as my beloved Froggie, through sheer accomplishment or upon an unforeseen vacancy, was seen among the grand folks composing the first team. The demands of the workman's week, after all, conflicted with the ample time-table of that polished cricket and that lovely lunch, which was not neglected on account of any state of the game, and yet lovelier tea, from which the ladies soon distributed lots of cream horns and slabs of Madeira cake among the delighted if slightly awestricken little boys round the scoreboard. So the first team was in a sort a minor Marylebone Cricket Club and its players were assembled from near and far. Among these visitants I had more than one hero, not, of course, so dear to my heart as Froggie; but still my heart leapt up at a noonday sight of them on the path to the ground in its best array, like a billiard table but better. Who could have dreamed that the golden-headed, rosy-cheeked young man, the Etonian of the Victorian novelist, whose slow bowling to watch was like a classical deity's physical exercises, should have had almost as brief a career as my young friend? As I trotted with consciousness of my daring beside his long stride, he presently noticed that

I was there, and he talked to me—an honour which still retains its flash of sunshine. But he was intent on his cricket, and rescuing his bag from me and giving me a whole sixpence he was soon being slapped on the back in the pavilion, where it was not for me to follow him even if I had had time from school. This tall landowner, and fine, thinking bowler in the Kentish school of slow bowling, measured to an inch of length and almost of break, never came back from the War of 1914–1918 which even he in his higher sphere had been no better able than we to see gathering its fire-hearted tempest over our southern hills.

To follow the fortunes of the first team even when the match was played at home was too difficult for us unless a holiday coincided, and matches played away were only items in the news and appeared in the *Messenger*; or perhaps my father had been summoned (by the vicar, very secret and urgent) from coloured chalks, desk and harmonium to fill the place of the slow bowler. In that case, the day was long; I would fidget about into the last light of evening for his return and report. He had to be coaxed, even then; he was a miserly, disappointing reporter. Had I been looking on, I believe I could have said more by way of description. But he was a cricketer of a devoted nature. I fear he used to bowl with a tense, total mind, and would not then have perceived that the game was leaving him a memory of other things. He did not even, at that date, mention the sublime pies which used to crown one particular cricket lunch table. He does now, *regnante Woolton*; it is worth coupons hearing him!

Altogether, the second eleven was the one for me. For one thing, the players were almost entirely our own, the same men as I saw spraying apple-trees or graining inn parlour doors or fixing taps; among whom even the clerk from the railway station, which was a little out of the way from the village street, was something of a guest. For another, the games were half-day games and played on Saturdays mostly, and even if they were played 'away', the enemy ground was usually not beyond walking distance. Or one might be given a ride in the horse brake, and that meant 'good talk' and temporary intimacy with the heroes. They would treat us, could you believe it! as cricketers, too. 'Where's that damned scorebook you boys keep?' grunted Jack Clarke to me—Jack was a figure almost as famous as his friend Froggie—as the wheels clattered over the road to some village beyond the hill. I had it in my pocket, as certainly as a soldier has his paybook, and Jack put on a solemn expression and imaginary spectacles as he looked at the pages, carefully filled. 'Who's this that made 90?' he asked. This

happened to be my score, but I had to confess that so imposing a figure
was reached by adding up a number of very small ones, several weeks'
work, I fear. 'Well,' he said, closing the book and eyeing the country,
'I'm disappointed,' but he had done his good deed; that little black
book had been transformed into more than our private record.

The words of older people, which are little or nothing to them, in
the uttering, are often curiously cherished by children. My sisters used
to dog the footsteps of the Builder and Contractor, good solid unhur-
rying steps they were, until he would *say* something. It was sure to be
something really good-humoured, and might be followed by the bestow-
ing of a penny, but the conversation was the main adventure, not the
cash. These older people knew things. They had a bigger map of possibilities in their minds. They could so nonchalantly open gates and
doors, real or thinking ones, which without them would have been
locked to us. And they took an interest in *us*—'what standard' we were
in, had we spilt the milkcan again since last time, who had the prettiest curls, did we like holidays or the Band of Hope, where was master Gilbert and the rest. The words used by these fathers of mankind
were not infrequently attractive in themselves. 'How will you do it?
Elbow-grease. What's that? You go and try.' 'Bless me, lost another
ball? You want the dibs—the spondulicks—the wherewithal, that's all
you want.' 'He's a *comical* young beggar,'—how right, how unfore-
known that adjective was; the problem settled. 'I'd say June-eatings was
the nicest apple,' 'Now you ask your good mother to give you some
camomile tea next time'—these things were such discoveries. I am sorry
'camomile' in our place was not 'cow-mumble' as in some, but 'mush-
a-rooms' was usual. And one day Mr Ladder would be giving us a
wonderful red-handkerchief-full of those.

Cricket Country, 1944

✳

Brighter Cricket

IVOR BROWN

A dozen overs, every ball a dolly:
    The artful Podger watches them for spin,
Then gently pats each succulent half-volley:
    There's talent money and the points to win.

He's going to get his benefit next summer;
   His average is better than last year.
The Glumshire bowlers go from glum to glummer,
   He'll get his thirty e'er the night is here.
Sing hey for Glumshire, that's the teak to stick it!
   Sing ho for Starkshire, who can stick still more!
Sing hey for all the purple hours of cricket!
   What's that? Hurst Park, Fast Flapper. Nine to four.
Who'd mock the game or libel British lads,
While Podger's playing time out with his pads?

Masques and Phases, 1921

*

The Crooked Bat

ARTHUR MARSHALL

Crooked meaning not straight: not crooked meaning dishonest. It always seemed to me, as a schoolboy reluctantly playing cricket in the 1920s, that a straight bat, so highly prized by the experts, was in my case mere foolishness, sending the ball, when I managed to make contact with it, feebly back whence it had come. With a crooked bat there was at least a chance of deflecting the offensive weapon either to right or left and scoring a 'run'. To attempt to score anything at all may savour of self-advertisement but that was never my aim. My sights were not set on a ribboned coat or a captain's hand on my shoulder smote. The sole purpose of a run was to remove me, however briefly, from the end where the action was.

Cricket was a manly game. Manly masters spoke of 'the discipline of the hard ball'. Schools preferred manly games. Games were only manly if it was possible while playing them to be killed or drowned or, at the very least, badly maimed. Cricket could be splendidly dangerous. Tennis was not manly, and if a boy had asked permission to spend the afternoon playing croquet he would have been instantly punished for his 'general attitude'. Athletics were admitted into the charmed lethal circle as a boy could, with a little ingenuity, get impaled during the pole-vault or be decapitated by a discus and die a manly death. Fives were thought to be rather tame until one boy ran his head into a stone buttress and got concussion and another fainted dead away from heat and fatigue. Then everybody cheered up about fives. The things to aim at in games were fright and total exhaustion. It was felt that these, coupled with a diet that was only modestly calorie-laden, would keep our thoughts running along the brightest and most wholesome lines. As a plan, this was a failure.

For cricket matches against other schools, the school pavilion was much in evidence. At my preparatory school, Stirling Court on the Hampshire coast, the pavilion smelt strongly of linseed oil and disinfectant and for its construction reliance had been largely placed on corrugated iron. Within could be found cricket nets and spiders and dirty pads and spiders and old team photographs and old spiders. There was also a bat signed by Hobbs which we proudly displayed to opposing players in an unconscious spirit of gamesmanship. But despite this trophy, a sad air of failure and decay pervaded the building. From its windows innumerable cricketing disasters had been witnessed: for example, our defeat by Dumbleton Park when our total score had been eight, three of which were byes. There had been, too, the shaming afternoon when our captain, out first ball, had burst into a torrent of hysterical tears.

But cricket did have one supreme advantage over football. It could be stopped by rain. Every morning at prayers, devout cricket-haters put up a plea for a downpour. As we were in England, our prayers were quite frequently answered, but nothing, nothing but the death of the headmaster could stop football. We could hardly pray for the headmaster, a nice man, to die. In rain, sleet, hail and lightning, shivering and shuddering and soaked to the skin, we battled on. Even in dense fog we kept at it, a shining example to Dartmoor working parties. But cricket was another matter, cricket was a more sensitive affair altogether, and if, as I fear, there is cricket in heaven, there will also, please God, be rain.

When the dread moment arrived and our side went in, I found myself, low down on the list, actually at the wicket and taking guard ('Leg stump, please'), and positively holding a bat. But held straight or crooked, sooner or later there would come the musical sound of skittling pegs and flying bails and I could remove myself and my pad and sit down. And once safely installed on a rug by the hedge and more or less out of sight, day-dreams took over.

At most schools in the 'twenties there was never any question of being let off cricket. The thought of asking not to play it never entered anybody's head. If it had, the consequences, at a public school any-how, were clearly foreseeable. Suppose, let us say, a poetically-minded boy had announced that he wished to spend the afternoon writing an ode, he would have been immediately beaten (four strokes) by the Head of the House. Poetry was unhealthy stuff. Look at Byron. If the poet had been more specific and had said that he wanted to write an Ode to the Matron ('Oh Matron, when with grizzled head half bent with care, sweet ministrant of salve and unguent, breasting thy way defiant bust worn high . . .'), he would have been beaten (six strokes) by the Housemaster, and the poor (certainly) innocent (probably) Matron would have found herself writing to the scholastic agents, Chitty and Gale, for a new situation ('. . . said to have pleasant personality . . . pre-pared take sole charge . . . excellent "mixer" . . .'). If the embryo Shelley had said that he wished to write an Ode to the Captain of Cricket ('Oh Dennis, when with auburn head half bent with care . . .'), expulsion would have been considered, this extreme measure being subsequently watered down, after an infinity of scowls and threats, to a beating (eight strokes) by the Headmaster. These ceremonies used to take place at 9 p.m., the Headmaster sporting a dinner-jacket and being freshly vitamin-charged. The beatings were done, as usual, in the spirit of this hurts me more than you, which was said to be plenty.

At cricket there was never any thought of excusing those unfortu-nate enough to wear glasses. It was pre-contact lens days and short-sighted boys left their spectacles in their blazers in the pavilion. They stood, when batting, blinded by the sun and enfeebled by cruel Nature, peering uncertainly up the pitch in a hopeless attempt to see whence Nemesis was coming. They had to rely heavily on their other senses. Their sense of hearing supplied the thud and thunder of the bowler's cricketing boots, the wicket-keeper's heavy breathing (now coming from a lower angle as he crouched down in readiness) and the disagreeable whistling sound of the ball itself which indicated that it had been released and was on its way. Their sense of smell supplied the wind-borne unpleasantnesses of hot flannel, hot sock, hot boy, all of minimal value as directional guides. And their sense of touch told them, sharply and painfully, that the ball had arrived.

And here there was an unfairness. The boys in the First and Second XIs, fully sighted and well able to protect themselves, were provided with a contraption called a 'box', a snug and reinforced padded leather compartment worn about the crutch and into which they tucked, I assume, whatever came most easily to hand. It would have been considered a gross impertinence for any lesser player to plead for this protection. In the lower echelons, our genitals were expendable.

Girls Will Be Girls, 1974

*

Ninth Wicket

A. P. HERBERT

The bowling looks exceptionally sound,
    The wicket seems unusually worn,
The balls fly up or run along the ground;
    I rather wish that I had not been born.
I have been sitting here since two o'clock;
    My pads are both inelegant and hot;
I do not want what people call my 'knock',
    And this pavilion is a sultry spot.
I shall not win one clap or word of praise,
    I know that I shall bat like a baboon;
And I can think of many better ways
    In which to spend a summer afternoon.
I might be swimming in a crystal pool;
    I might be wooing some delicious dame;
I might be drinking something long and cool—
    I can't imagine why I play this game.

Why is the wicket seven miles away,
    And why have I to walk it all alone?
I hope that Bottle's bat will drive today—
    I ought to buy a weapon of my own.
I wonder if this walk will ever cease;
    They should provide a motor-car or crane
To drop the batsman on the popping-crease
    And, when he's out, convey him back again.
Is it a dream? Can this be truly me,
    Alone and friendless in a waste of grass?
The fielding side are sniggering, I see,
    And long-leg sort of shudders as I pass.

How very small and funny I must look!
  I only hope that no one knows my name.
I might be in a hammock with a book—
  I can't imagine why I play this game.

Well, here we are. We feel a little ill.
  What is this pedant of an umpire at?
Middle and off, or centre—what you will;
  It cannot matter where I park the bat.
I look around me in a knowing way
  To show that I am not to be cajoled;
I shall play forward gracefully and pray. . . .
  I have played forward and I am not bowled.
I do not like the wicket-keeper's face,
  And why are all these fielders crowding round?
The bowler makes an imbecile grimace,
  And mid-off makes a silly whistling sound.
These innuendoes I could do without;
  They mean to say the ball defied the bat.
They indicate that I was nearly out;
  Well, darn their impudence! I know all that.
Why I am standing in this comic pose,
  Hemmed in by men that I should like to maim?
I might be lying in a punt with Rose—
  I can't imagine why I play this game.

And there are people sitting over there
  Who fondly hope that I shall make a run;
They cannot guess how blinding is the glare;
  They do not know the ball is like a bun.
But, courage, heart! We have survived a ball;
  I pat the pitch to show that it is bad;
We are not such a rabbit, after all;
  Now we shall show them what is what, my lad!
The second ball is very, very swift;
  It breaks and stands up steeply in the air;
It looks at me, and I could swear it sniffed;
  I gesture at it, but it is not there.
Ah, what a ball! Mind you, I do not say
  That Bradman, Hobbs, and Ranji in his prime,

Rolled into one, and that one on his day,
   Might not have got a bat to it in time. . . .
But long-stop's looking for my middle-stump,
   And I am walking in a world of shame;
My captain has addressed me as a chump—
   I can't imagine why I play this game.

Mild and Bitter, 1936

*

'A Sticky Wicket, Sir'

P. G. WODEHOUSE

London brooded under a grey sky. There had been rain in the night, and the trees were still dripping. Presently, however, there appeared in the leaden haze a watery patch of blue; and through this crevice in the clouds the sun, diffidently at first but with gradually increasing confidence, peeped down on the fashionable and exclusive turf of Grosvenor Square. Stealing across the square its rays reached the massive stone walls of Drexdale House, until recently the London residence of the earl of that name; then, passing through the window of the breakfast room, played lightly on the partially bald head of Mr Bingley Crocker, late of New York, in the United States of America, as he bent over his morning paper. Mrs Bingley Crocker, busy across the table reading her mail, the rays did not touch. Had they done so she would have rung for Bayliss, the butler, to come and lower the shade, for she endured liberties neither from man nor from Nature.

'Bingley, you aren't listening! What is that you are reading?'

Mr Crocker tore himself from the paper.

'This? Oh, I was looking at a report of that cricket game you made me go and see yesterday.'

'Oh, I am glad you have begun to take an interest in cricket. It is simply a social necessity in England. Why you ever made such a fuss about taking it up I can't think. You used to be so fond of watching baseball, and cricket is just the same thing.'

A close observer would have marked a deepening of the look of pain on Mr Crocker's face. Women say this sort of thing carelessly, with no wish to wound; but that makes it nonetheless hard to bear.

From the hall outside came faintly the sound of the telephone, then the measured tones of Bayliss answering it. Mr Crocker returned to his paper. Bayliss entered.

'Lady Corstorphine desires to speak to you on the telephone, madam.'

Half-way to the door Mrs Crocker paused, as if recalling something that had slipped her memory.

'Is Mr James getting up, Bayliss?'

'I believe not, madam. I am informed by one of the house-maids who passed his door a short time back that there were no sounds.'

Mrs Crocker left the room. Bayliss, preparing to follow her example, was arrested by an exclamation from the table.

'Say!' His master's voice. 'Say, Bayliss, come here a minute. Want to ask you something.'

The butler approached the table. It seemed to him that his employer was not looking quite himself this morning. There was something a trifle wild, a little haggard, about his expression. He had remarked on it earlier in the morning in the servants' hall.

As a matter of fact, Mr Crocker's ailment was a perfectly simple one. He was suffering from one of those acute spasms of homesickness which invariably racked him in the earlier summer months. Ever since his marriage, five years previously, and his simultaneous removal from his native land, he had been a chronic victim to the complaint. The symptoms grew less acute in winter and spring, but from May onward he suffered severely.

Poets have dealt feelingly with the emotions of practically every variety except one. They have sung of Ruth, of Israel in bondage, of slaves pining for their native Africa, and of the miner's dream of home. But the sorrows of the baseball enthusiast, compelled by fate to live three thousand miles away from the Polo Grounds, have been neglected in song. Bingley Crocker was such a one, and in summer his agonies were awful. He pined away in a country where they said 'Well played, sir!' when they meant 'At-a-boy!'

'Bayliss, do you play cricket?'

'I am a little past the age, sir. In my younger days—'

'Do you understand it?'

'Yes, sir. I frequently spend an afternoon at Lord's or the Oval when there is a good match.'

Many who enjoyed a merely casual acquaintance with the butler would have looked on this as an astonishingly unexpected revelation of humanity in Bayliss, but Mr Crocker was not surprised. To him, from the very beginning, Bayliss had been a man and a brother, who was always willing to suspend his duties in order to answer questions dealing with the thousand and one problems which the social life of England presented. Mr Crocker's mind had adjusted itself with difficulty to the niceties of class distinction, and though he had cured himself of his early tendency to address the butler as 'Bill', he never failed to consult him as man to man in his moments of perplexity. Bayliss was always eager to be of assistance. He liked Mr Crocker. True, his manner might have struck a more sensitive man than his employer as a shade too closely resembling that of an indulgent father toward a son who was not quite right in the head; but it had genuine affection in it.

Mr Crocker picked up his paper and folded it back at the sporting page, pointing with a stubby forefinger.

'Well, what does all this mean? I've kept out of watching cricket since I landed in England, but yesterday they got the poison needle to work and took me off to see Surrey play Kent at that place, the Oval, where you say you go sometimes.'

'I was there yesterday, sir. A very exciting game.'

'Exciting? How do you make that out? I sat in the bleachers all afternoon, waiting for something to break loose. Doesn't anything ever happen at cricket?'

The butler winced a little, but managed to smile a tolerant smile. This man, he reflected, was but an American, and as much more to be pitied than censured. He endeavoured to explain.

'It was a sticky wicket yesterday, sir, owing to the rain.'

'Eh?'

'The wicket was sticky, sir.'

'Come again.'

'I mean that the reason why the game yesterday struck you as slow was that the wicket—I should say the turf—was sticky—that is to say, wet. Sticky is the technical term, sir. When the wicket is sticky the batsmen are obliged to exercise a great deal of caution, as the stickiness of the wicket enables the bowlers to make the ball turn more sharply in either direction as it strikes the turf than when the wicket is not stickly.'

'That's it, is it?'

'Yes, sir.'

'Thanks for telling me.'

'Not at all, sir.'

Mr Crocker pointed to the paper.

'Well, now, this seems to be the boxscore of the game we saw yesterday. If you can make sense out of that, go to it.'

The passage on which his finger rested was headed Final Score, and ran as follows:

SURREY

FIRST INNINGS

Hayward, c. Woolley b. Carr	67
Hobbs, run out	0
Hayes, st. Huish b. Fielder	12
Ducat, b. Fielder	33
Harrison, not out	11
Sandham, not out	6
Extras	10
Total (for four wickets)	139

Bayliss inspected the cipher gravely.

'What is it you wish me to explain, sir?'

'Why, the whole thing. What's it all about?'

'It's perfectly simple, sir. Surrey won the toss and took first knock. Hayward and Hobbs were the opening pair. Hayward called Hobbs for a short run, but the latter was unable to get across and was thrown out by mid-on. Hayes was the next man in. He went out of his ground and was stumped. Ducat and Hayward made a capital stand considering the stickiness of the wicket, until Ducat was bowled by a good length off-break and Hayward caught at second slip off a googly. Then Harrison and Sandham played out time.'

Mr Crocker breathed heavily through his nose.

'Yes!' he said. 'Yes! I had an idea that was it. But I think I'd like to have it once again slowly. Start with these figures. What does that sixty-seven mean, opposite Hayward's name?'

'He made sixty-seven runs, sir.'

'Sixty-seven! In one game?'

'Yes, sir.'

'Why, Home-Run Baker couldn't do it!'

'I am not familiar with Mr Baker, sir.'

'I suppose you've never seen a ball game?'

'Ball game, sir?'

'A baseball game?'

'Never, sir.'

'Then, Bill,' said Mr Crocker, reverting in his emotion to the bad habit of his early London days, 'you haven't lived. See here!'

Whatever vestige of respect for class distinctions Mr Crocker had managed to preserve during the opening stages of the interview now definitely disappeared. His eyes shone wildly and he snorted like a warhorse. He clutched the butler by the sleeve and drew him closer to the table, then began to move forks, spoons, cups, and even the contents of his plate, about the cloth with an energy little short of feverish.

'Bayliss?'

'Sir?'

'Watch!' said Mr Crocker, with the air of an excitable high priest about to initiate a novice into the mysteries.

He removed a roll from the basket.

'You see this roll? That's the home plate. This spoon is first base. Where I'm butting this cup is second. This piece of bacon is third. There's your diamond for you. Very well then. These lumps of sugar are the infielders and the outfielders. Now we're ready. Batter up! He stands here. Catcher behind him. Umps behind catcher.'

'Umps, I take it, sir, is what you would call the umpire?'

'Call him anything you like. It's part of the game. Now here's the box, where I've put this dab of marmalade, and here's the pitcher winding up.'

'The pitcher would be equivalent to our bowler?'

'I guess so, though why you should call him a bowler gets past me.'

'The box, then, is the bowler's wicket?'

'Have it your own way. Now pay attention. Play ball! Pitcher's winding up. Put it over, Mike, put it over! Some speed, kid! Here it comes right in the groove. Bing! Batter slams it and streaks for first. Outfielder— this lump of sugar—boots it. Bonehead! Batter touches second. Third? No! Get back! Can't be done. Play it safe. Stick round the sack, old pal. Second batter up. Pitcher getting something on the ball now beside the cover. Whiffs him. Back to the bench, Cyril! Third batter up. See him rub his hands in the dirt. Watch this kid. He's good! Let's two alone, then slams the next right on the nose. Whizzes round to second. First guy, the one we left on second, comes home for one run. That's a game! Take it from me, Bill, that's a game!'

Somewhat overcome with the energy with which he had flung himself into his lecture, Mr Crocker sat down and refreshed himself with cold coffee.

'Quite an interesting game,' said Bayliss. 'But I find, now that you have explained it, sir, that it is familiar to me, though I have always known it under another name. It is played a great deal in this country.'

Mr Crocker started to his feet.

'Is it? And I've been five years without finding it out! When's the next game scheduled?'

'It is known in England as rounders, sir. Children play it with a soft ball and a racket, and derive considerable enjoyment from it. I have never heard of it before as a pastime for adults.'

Two shocked eyes stared into the butler's face.

'Children?' The word came in a whisper. 'A racket?'

'Yes, sir.'

'You—you didn't say a soft ball?'

'Yes, sir.'

A sort of spasm seemed to convulse Mr Crocker. He had lived five years in England, but not till this moment had he realized to the full how utterly alone he was in an alien land.

Piccadilly Jim, 1917

*

Cricket Master
(*An Incident*)

JOHN BETJEMAN

My undergraduate eyes beholding,
    As I climbed your slope, Cat Hill:
Emerald chestnut fans unfolding,
    Symbols of my hope, Cat Hill.
What cared I for past disaster,
Applicant for cricket master,
Nothing much of cricket knowing,
Conscious but of money owing?
    Somehow I would cope, Cat Hill.

'The sort of man we want must be prepared
To take our first eleven. Many boys
From last year's team are with us. You will find
Their bowling's pretty good and they are keen.'

'And so am I, Sir, very keen indeed.'
Oh where's mid-on? And what is silly point?
Do six balls make an over? Help me, God!
'Of course you'll get some first-class cricket too;
The MCC send down an A team here.'
My bluff had worked. I sought the common-room,
Of last term's pipe-smoke faintly redolent.
It waited empty with its worn arm-chairs
For senior bums to mine, when in there came
A fierce old eagle in whose piercing eye
I saw that instant-registered dislike
Of all unhealthy aesthetes such as me.
'I'm Winters—you're our other new recruit
And here's another new man—Barnstaple.'
He introduced a thick Devonian.
'Let's go and have some practice in the nets.
You'd better go in first.' With but one pad,
No gloves, and knees that knocked in utter fright,
Vainly I tried to fend the hail of balls
Hurled at my head by brutal Barnstaple
And at my shins by Winters. Nasty quiet
Followed my poor performance. When the sun
Had sunk behind the fringe of Hadley Wood
And Barnstaple and I were left alone
Among the ash-trays of the common-room,
He murmured in his soft West-Country tones:
'D'you know what Winters told me, Betjeman?
He didn't think you'd ever held a bat.'
     The trusting boys returned. 'We're jolly glad
You're on our side, Sir, in the trial match.'
'But I'm no good at all.' 'Oh yes, you are.'
When I was out first ball, they said 'Bad luck!
You hadn't got your eye in.' Still I see
Barnstaple's smile of undisguised contempt,
Still feel the sting of Winters' silent sneer.
Disgraced, demoted to the seventh game,
Even the boys had lost their faith in me.
God guards his aesthetes. If by chance these lines
Are read by one who in some common-room
Has had his bluff called, let him now take heart:
In every school there is a sacred place

More holy than the chapel. Ours was yours:
I mean, of course, the first-eleven pitch.
Here in the welcome break from morning work,
The heavier boys, of milk and biscuits full,
Sat on the roller while we others pushed
Its weighty cargo slowly up and down.
We searched the grass for weeds, caressed the turf,
Lay on our stomachs squinting down its length
To see that all was absolutely smooth.

 The prize-day neared. And, on the eve before,
We masters hung our college blazers out
In readiness for tomorrow. Matron made
A final survey of the boys' best clothes—
Clean shirts. Clean collars. 'Rice, your jacket's torn.
Bring it to me this instant!' Supper done,
Barnstaple drove his round-nosed Morris out
And he and I and Vera Spencer-Clarke,
Our strong gymnasium mistress, squashed ourselves
Into the front and rattled to The Cock.

 Sweet bean-fields then were scenting Middlesex;
Narrow lanes led between the dairy farms
To ponds reflecting weather-boarded inns.
There on the wooden bench outside The Cock
Sat Barnstaple, Miss Spencer-Clarke and I,
At last forgetful of tomorrow's dread
And gazing into sky-blue Hertfordshire.
Three pints for Barnstaple, three halves for me,
Sherry of course for Vera Spencer-Clarke.

 Pre-prize-day nerves? Or too much bitter beer?
What had that evening done to Barnstaple?
I only know that singing we returned;
The more we sang, the faster Barnstaple
Drove his old Morris, swerving down the drive
And in and out the rhododendron clumps,
Over the very playing-field itself,
And then—oh horror!—right across the pitch
Not once, but twice or thrice. The mark of tyres
Next day was noticed at the Parents' Match.

Summoned by Bells, 1960

*

Dissertation on Cricket

DUDLEY CAREW

Dr Johnson remarked that if he had no reference to posterity he would spend his life driving briskly in a post-chaise with a pretty woman, and, never minding the company of pretty women, there are few more enjoyable ways of spending the English summer in peace-time than riding briskly about the country in trains and cars from one cricket ground to another. To be sure an object beyond the mere watching of cricket is necessary lest eternal contemplation lead to surfeit, to spiritual malaise and dissatisfaction, but when it is duty which prompts the journey from Sheffield to Bournemouth, when there is added to the delights of a day in the sun the satisfaction of sending off at 6.30 by telegraph messenger an 800 word or so account of the day's play, then indeed does life seem a pleasant and gracious thing and there is little more to be asked of the gods. The work has been done and, while it is far harder work than the envious unfortunates who get their cricket through the stop-press columns of the evening papers would allow, it is work performed in the most perfect of settings and is as harmless and innocent as any way of making money in this world can be. Occasionally, in the days when Test-matches crowded other news out of the head-lines, 'stories' were published which generated bad feeling and brought the name of cricket, which lived before Test-matches and will survive them, into disrepute, but generally the worst a conscientious correspondent has to reproach himself with is the crime of accusing first-slip of dropping a catch when actually the ball pitched a yard in front of him. The question of perspective is one which troubles all who have to write about the game, for what appears to be a possible chance eighty yards away and at an angle of 75 degrees from the wicket, bears a very different aspect to the men actually fielding in the slips. Field-glasses are all very well, but the best possible aid to vision is an imagination which can put the spectator 'in the middle' and enable him to follow the game from the point of view of those actually batting, bowling and fielding. In spite of Dr Johnson and his remark about sheep being judges of mutton, it is true that no one can so write a perfect account of a first-class cricket match who has not himself been a first-class cricketer, and that no one who has not played any kind of cricket can write an account of any value at all. The perfect account. That is an account which demands not only the experience of a first-class cricketer, but of a mind which can interpret what the eye is seeing and a style, a mode of expression, which can, in its turn, interpret the mind. It is not surprising that ideal accounts are rare, for all too often the prose of the man who can appreciate why fine-leg has been shifted a yard, why Jones, who has just taken two wickets in one over, has been taken off; why Smith, after starting off with three 4's, has relapsed into defence, is too feeble to give that knowledge any adequate representation. The most interesting, and the least obvious, details of the day's play are submerged in a flood of figures which are available to anyone who can look over the scorer's shoulder or keep the analysis. There are, of course, brilliant exceptions, but it remains true that far too many of the hundreds of thousands of words which have been written on the game by men who have made their names in it might have been the product of any spectator in the mound who has his score-card and his wits about him, who clocks the batsmen in, makes a note of the bowling changes and counts the fours. And now for *any* form of cricket. That means an under-sixteen house-team, the most primitive village cricket, the kind of club cricket which does not get its scores into the newspapers; it means any cricket which gives a man a sense of the feel of the ball, of what it is like to stand under a high catch, of the look of the popping crease and the places worn by the bowler's footsteps have to a batsman preparing to take his first ball. It means allowance for nerves, for a loose nail in a cricket-boot, for indigestion, for worrying about a telegram, for thinking of the *envoi* of a *ballade* in the intervals of walking from third-man to mid-on, for private and practical jokes, for being in love, for being mad nor' nor' west, and it remembers that it is sometimes difficult to distinguish between a half-volley and a yorker.... Given that capacity to imagine, to put oneself in the position of the man who is batting, bowling or fielding, the game takes on a new interest and meaning, and even those maiden-overs, or rather, above all, those maiden overs which drive the uninitiated into taverns or arguments about the superiority of football, take their place in the pattern the game is making. For a game of cricket is at work from the first ball to the last in shaping an outline and design for itself; sometimes the design degenerates into dullness and incompetence and a man may waste his time in looking for subtlety in the motive that prompts a batsman to pat a half-volley carefully to mid-off, but design there always is and there is interest even in the tracing of the course and impulse of its failure. In every game there is a moment of destiny, a moment when fortune hesitates which way she will incline, when the genius of the match is poised and is ready to follow the side which has the courage and intelligence to take charge of her. The moment may proclaim itself in a bold and obvious onslaught or a successful attack by a number 7 batsman; it may hide in twenty minutes of stern defensive play while a bad wicket is slowly recovering and the score-board stands static to mock those who believe that its convulsions alone can measure excitement; it may flash out in an inspired piece of fielding, in an astute move of captaincy, in the heart a bowler finds to continue for one more over; it may come in the first hour or in the last, but it is present in every match, even in those which end in the most obvious of draws or of victories by an innings. A man who has had experience of cricket can never quite take anything for granted. Arthur Richardson, in that great Test match at the Oval in 1926 which regained the Ashes for England, bowled eight consecutive overs at Hobbs and it is certain that from the ring Hobbs made the bowling look difficult to play, but Richardson, on a pitch that was wickedness itself when he first took the ball at the Vauxhall end, but which was bound to grow easier as time went on, bowled round the wicket to a cluster of short-legs. It was a form of attack George Macaulay, one of the greatest of all bowlers in the period between the two wars, found extremely profitable when ever the pitch was inclined to help him, but it is never the most deadly form of attack on a turning pitch—the ball which spins the other way is that—and Richardson, as a bowler, was not in the same class as Macaulay. Whether Hobbs was deliberately bluffing—as M. A. Noble is inclined to think he was—or whether he truly found the ball impossible to get away is a secret Hobbs has kept to himself, but, whatever the truth of that historic duel the man who saw the possibility that all might not be as it seemed got a great deal more out of watching than the man who did not think of looking beyond the obvious. The truth is that cricket is an extremely complex game, and any effort to simplify it is bound to defeat its own ends. During the war one-day matches were the rule at Lord's, and because they sometimes resulted in exciting finishes—on September 7th, 1940, the crowd after watching the German bombers sail back across the evening sky after they had raided the docks had the felicity of seeing Gray take four wickets in seven balls—they led to a most ill-informed clamour for one-day matches in peace-time. One-day matches, however, exciting though they may be, are no more than a childish variation of real cricket, and compare with it as a game of beggar-my-neighbour to contract bridge. First-class cricket is an affair of tactics and timing; there is the clock as well as the opposing side to be taken into consideration; brains and nerves matter as well as brawn and, a point the advocates of brighter cricket always forget, there can be virtue, beauty and intelligence in bowling. Bowling can be directed at keeping down runs as well as taking wickets, but those who wish to see the game simplified to a matter of 6's would presumably only require of the bowler that he should trundle up the requisite numbers of half-volleys and long-hops. There is nothing more splendid than the sight of a hitter taking a hostile and well-planned attack by the throat and subduing it, and conversely, nothing more dreary can be imagined than a succession of boundaries against a lifeless bowler well aware that he only exists to keep up a rate of scoring which it is fondly and vainly hoped will satisfy a crowd with dirt-track and greyhound stadium notions of speed.

Cricket has got to have the courage of its own aristocracy. Few things before the war were more insidiously dangerous than the cult of the 'little man' and the courage, and greatness, of what the apostles of that cult are pleased to fancy were representative of the 'little man' in the war will greatly help to strengthen a legend which has little basis in reality. 'And when the critic of politics and literature, feeling that this war is after all heroic, looks around him to find the hero, he can point to nothing but a mob,' wrote G. K. Chesterton of an earlier conflict, and he meant the word 'mob' to carry the sense of surge and valour. The men who made themselves in 1914 into one 'of the iron armies of the world', and in this war became the Eighth Army were everything which the 'little man' in his essence is not. He, the 'little man', stood for a fatuous complacency, a morbid self-satisfaction, an entire and monstrous unwillingness to concern himself with anything that did not immediately touch his hire-purchase comfort. Anything to save himself the trouble of thinking, anything which made no demand upon his spirit, his brain, or his stunted sense of loveliness—quick results and flashy action were his motto. There is a danger that, in the name of democracy, he will demand the heads of many institutions that have proved their worth in the rich history of English life, and, a little but not insignificant member among them, cricket. Cricket, if it is to survive, must resist, for cricket can live only by its own conscious exclusiveness. Not the exclusiveness of the 'old school tie' and the Long Room at Lord's, but the exclusiveness of a secret society, the passwords of which are as often heard in the bars of the pubs of the back streets of

Leeds as in the committee rooms of the county clubs. To turn cricket into a cross between rounders and tip-and-run is as much an insult to the boy who bowls to a wicket chalked against a brick wall as it is to the man who has his initials printed in front of his name on the score-card—and the sooner those who profess to care for the game at the same time as they put forward plans which would turn it into a cari-cature of itself realize that simple fact the better. In the period between the two wars the game indeed suffered grievously at the hands of those who would exploit it under the cover of a clamorous regard for its interest. Lord Hawke once made a remark to the effect that he hoped England would never be captained by a professional and the howl that went up was shrill, deafening, and proof of an invincible ignorance and prejudice. Had those who so abused Lord Hawke said in conversation to a party of Yorkshire professionals a quarter of the nonsense that per-colated into print, they would hardly have lived to tell the tale, but the immense services Lord Hawke has rendered to professional cricketers as a class did not interest, and were probably unknown to them. Lord Hawke's remark made snappy headlines and that was enough—there was little evidence that any effort was made to try to understand what Lord Hawke meant although any Gentlemen *v.* Players match would have afforded a clue. The truth is that professionals as a rule do not make good captains—their relationship to other players adds to the nat-ural difficulties of their position—and, what is even more important, they do not care for the job. In the same way the fuss which was made about (*a*) professionals walking out of a different gate at Lord's and (*b*) the iniquity of members of the England team not spending their nights during Test-matches at the same hotel rose from a failure to under-stand the professional's point of view. Cricket, in spite of the fact that one of the most important of the season's games is called Gentlemen *v.* Players, in spite of those gates at Lord's, is the most truly democratic game there is because it is free of that class-consciousness, that in-verted snobbery, with which its 'reformers' are so anxious to saddle it. The professional does not worry himself into a fit of inferiority com-plex over the separate gate, for the simple reason that he seldom thinks of it, and the fact that a professional may like to choose his own hotel or stay with his own friends never seems to occur to those who are so keen to champion his cause. The relationship between the amateurs and professionals of an ordinary county side is regulated by the kind of unwritten and well-regulated laws which operate in most of our national institutions which are worth preserving, and, when friction does occur in a side, it usually arises not from antagonism between paid and unpaid, but between two parties of professionals at logger-heads with one another.

Cricket, to return to the argument, must have the courage of its own integrity and convictions, for once it yields either to some outcry about 'democracy' or, more important, consents to tamper with its laws and introduce time-limit innings or some other foolery, it alienates those who love it and will fail to please those whom it approaches cap in hand. No one who cares for the excitements of the dirt-track and the greyhound stadium is going to be impressed even by six 6's in an over, and those who really love the game, the knowledgeable men with cloth caps who throng the grounds at Bramall Lane and Old Trafford, the slow-speaking men who watch at Canterbury and Maidstone and play out in the evenings at the local pub the events of the day's play—these men will be disgusted and sick at heart and the game will live for them only in their memories.

To the Wicket, 1946

*

The Pitch at Night

G. D. MARTINEAU

The sunset brings the twilight chill
    That steals, all noiseless, on the air.
The wind-freed world is standing still,
    The smoothed, worn ground looks strangely bare.

The bowler's run has blurred the crease,
    Which glints, a dim and spectral white,
Half sad, half comforting, this peace
    That settled o'er the ground at night.

Steps give a faintly eerie hiss
    On less tried turf towards the rough
(Was I too hard on Jones's miss,
    Or was I not quite hard enough?)

Here is an ancient, useless pad.
The score-board stares, a square of ink.
Some of this outfield's rather bad. . . .
It's colder now; to bed, I think.

The Cricketer, 1940

*

Epitaph

GEORGE McWILLIAM

As in life so in death lies a bat of renown,
Slain by a lorry (three ton);
His innings is over, his bat is laid down:
To the end a poor judge of a run.

The Book of Cricket Verse, 1953

Acknowledgements

The editor and publishers are grateful for permission to reproduce the following copyright material:

Cyril Alington, 'Lord's 1928' from *Eton Faces*, 1933. Extract from *Edward Lyttelton: An Appreciation* (John Murray (Publishers) Ltd., 1943), reprinted by permission of the publishers.

H. S. Altham and E. W. Swanton, from *A History of Cricket* (George Allen & Unwin). Reprinted by permission of HarperCollins Publishers Ltd.

John Arlott, 'To John Berry Hobbs on his Seventieth Birthday' from *John Arlott's Book of Cricketers* (Lutterworth, 1979); 'Garfield Sobers' from *The Cricketer*, reprinted by permission of the Estate of John Arlott.

F. S. Ashley-Cooper, from *Cricket Highways and Byways* (George Allen & Unwin Ltd., 1927).

Richie Benaud, from *Willow Patterns* (Hodder & Stoughton, 1969). Copyright © Richie Benaud, 1969. Reprinted by permission of Curtis Brown Ltd., London on behalf of Richie Benaud.

John Betjeman, from *Summoned by Bells* (John Murray (Publishers) Ltd.). Reprinted by permission of the publishers.

Edmund Blunden, 'Pride of the Village', 'The Season Opens' and extract from *Cricket Country*. Reprinted by permission of the Peters Fraser & Dunlop Group Ltd.

Edward Kamau Brathwaite, from *The Arrivants* (Oxford University Press), © OUP 1969. Reprinted by permission of the publishers.

Christopher Brookes, from *English Cricket* (Weidenfeld & Nicolson, 1978). Reprinted by permission of the publishers.

Gerald Bullett, from *News from the Village* (Cambridge University Press, 1952).

Neville Cardus, from *Days in the Sun* (Rupert Hart-Davis, 1924, 1949) and from *The Summer Game* (Rupert Hart-Davis). Reprinted by permission of Margaret Hughes.

Dudley Carew, from *To the Wicket* (Chapman & Hall, 1946).

Alfred Cochrane, 'The Catch' from *Collected Verse*, 1903.

W. E. W. Collins, from *Leaves from an Old Country Cricketer's Diary* (William Blackwood & Sons, 1908).

Bernard Darwin, from *W. G. Grace* (Gerald Duckworth & Co. Ltd.). Reprinted by permission of the publishers.

'Andrew Ducat, an Obituary' from *The Wisden Book of Cricketers' Lives*, 1986 (Macdonald, 1986).

John Finnemore, from *Teddy Lester: Captain of Cricket* (W & R Chambers Ltd., 1920).

David Foot, from *Cricket's Unholy Trinity* (Stanley Paul, 1985). Reprinted by permission of Random House UK Ltd.

David Frith, from *The Golden Age of Cricket 1890–1914* (Lutterworth Press, 1978); from *Archie Jackson, the Keats of Cricket* (Pavilion, 1987), reprinted by permission of the publishers.

Bruce Hamilton, from *Pro: An English Tragedy* (The Cresset Press, 1946).

L. P. Hartley, from *The Go-Between* (Hamish Hamilton, 1953). Copyright © the Estate of L. P. Hartley, 1953. Reprinted by permission of Hamish Hamilton Ltd.

A. P. Herbert, 'Ninth Wicket' from *Mild and Bitter*. Reprinted by permission of A. P. Watt Ltd. on behalf of Crystal Hale and Jocelyn Herbert.

Jack Hobbs, from *Playing for England! My Test-Cricket Story* (Victor Gollancz Ltd., 1931). Reprinted by permission of the publishers.

C. L. R. James, from *Beyond a Boundary* (Hutchinson, 1963). Reprinted by permission of Random House UK Ltd.

Frank Keating, from *Gents and Players* (Robson Books, 1987), and from *Cricket Heroes*. Reprinted by permission of Lennard Associates Ltd.

Albert Kinross, from *An Unconventional Cricketer* (Harold Shaylor, 1930).

A. G. Macdonell, from *England, Their England* (Macmillan, 1933).

George McWilliam, from *The Book of Cricket Verse* (Rupert Hart-Davis, 1953).

Arthur Marshall, from *Girls Will Be Girls* (Hamish Hamilton, 1974). Reprinted by permission of April Young Ltd.

Christopher Martin-Jenkins, from *Cricket Characters*, 1987. Reprinted by permisison of Lennard Associates Ltd.

G. D. Martineau, 'The Village Pitch' from *A Score, A Score and Ten* (Methuen, 1927). 'The Pitch at Night' from *The Cricketer*, 1940, reprinted by permission of The Cricketer Ltd. Extract from *The Valiant Stumper: A History of Wicket-Keeping* (Stanley Paul, 1957), reprinted by permission of Random House UK Ltd.

Anthony Meredith, from *The Demon and the Lobster: Charles Kortright and Digby Jephson, Remarkable Bowlers in the Golden Age* (William Heinemann Ltd.). Reprinted by permission of Reed Consumer Books Ltd.

Alan Miller, from *Close of Play* (St Hughes Press, 1949).

A. A. Milne, from *The Day's Play* (Methuen, 1910), copyright © A. A. Milne, 1910. 'Hymn on Tomkins' Action' from *For the Luncheon Interval: Cricket and Other Verses* (Methuen, 1925), copyright © A. A. Milne, 1925. Reprinted by permission of Curtis Brown Ltd., London.

George Moor, from *Beauty and Richness* (W. Maclellan, 1951).

Thomas Moult, from *Willow Patterns* (Hodder & Stoughton, 1969).

Norman Nicholson, from *Collected Poems* (Faber & Faber). Reprinted by permission of David Higham Associates Ltd.

Ian Peebles, from *Denis Compton: The Generous Cricketer* (Macmillan, 1971).

Hubert Phillips, from *News Chronicle*, 1951 (London and Continental Communications).

R. C. Robertson-Glasgow, 'The One-Way Critic' from *The Brighter Side of Cricket*, 1933, and extract from *Cricket Prints: Some Batsmen and Bowlers 1920–1940* (Bodley Head).

Ray Robinson, from *Between Wickets* (Collins, 1948). Reprinted by permission of the executor.

Alan Ross, 'Test Match at Lord's' and 'J. M. Parks at Tunbridge Wells'. Reprinted by permission of the author.

Siegfried Sassoon, 'The Extra Inch', 'The Blues At Lord's' and from *Memoirs of a Foxhunting Man* (Faber & Faber, 1928). Reprinted by permission of George Sassoon.

Vernon Scannell, 'Wicket Maiden' from *The Cricketer's Companion*, ed. Alan Ross (Penguin Books). Reprinted by permission of the author.

Hugh de Selincourt, from *The Cricket Match* (Rupert Hart-Davis, 1949). Reprinted by permission of HarperCollins Publishers Ltd.

Sir John Squire, from *The Honeysuckle and the Bee* (William Heinemann, 1937). Reprinted by permission of the Peters Fraser & Dunlop Group Ltd.

Richard Streeton, from *P. G. H. Fender: A Biography* (Faber & Faber). Reprinted by permission of the publishers.

E. W. Swanton, from *The Daily Telegraph*; extract from *As I Said at the Time* (Willow Books, 1983), copyright © E. W. Swanton 1983. Reprinted by permission of Curtis Brown Ltd., London on behalf of E. W. Swanton.

Times Newspapers Ltd., *John Arlott Obituary*. Copyright © Times Newspapers Ltd., 1991. Used with permission.

S. M. Toyne, from *History Today* (History Today Ltd., 1955). Reprinted by permission of the publishers.

G. M. Trevelyan, from *English Social History: A Survey of Six Centuries, Chaucer to Queen Victoria* (Longmans, 1944). Reprinted by permission of the publishers.

Fred Trueman with Don Mosey, from *My Most Memorable Matches* (Stanley Paul, 1982). Reprinted by permission of Random House UK Ltd.

Roland Wild, from *The Biography of Ranjitsinhji* (The Griffon Press, 1934).

Hugo Williams, from *The Cricketer's Companion*, ed. Alan Ross (Penguin Books). Reprinted by permission of the author.

P. G. Wodehouse, 'Missed!' and extract from *Piccadilly Jim* (Penguin Books).

Ralph Wotherspoon, 'The Band at Play' from *The Cricketer*, 1940. Reprinted by kind permission of The Cricketer Ltd.

Kit Wright, from *The Cricketer's Companion*, ed. Alan Ross (Penguin Books).

While every effort has been made to secure permission, we may have failed in a few cases to trace the copyright holder. We apologize for any apparent negligence.

Index of Authors

General Index